NTC's AMERICAN IDIOMS Dictionary

Second Edition

Richard A. Spears, Ph.D.

Associate Editor, First Edition
Linda Schinke-Llano

National Textbook Company
NTC a division of *NTC Publishing Group* • Lincolnwood, Illinois USA

ACKNOWLEDGMENTS

We are grateful to Sylvia Aruffo for her efforts in systematically gathering idiomatic phrases from the students in her English classes. In addition, we wish to thank the students who brought in long lists of expressions they did not understand, and who tested a pilot version of this dictionary.

We also gratefully acknowledge the contributions to the entry list made by Betty Kirkpatrick.

CONTENTS

TO THE USER

All languages have phrases or sentences that cannot be understood literally. Even if you know all the words in a phrase and understand all the grammar of the phrase completely, the meaning may still be confusing. A phrase or sentence of this type is said to be idiomatic. Many proverbs, informal phrases, and common sayings offer this kind of problem. This dictionary is a collection of the idiomatic phrases and sentences that occur frequently in American English. The second edition contains over 1,000 idiomatic expressions not listed in the first edition and a number of new features that provide additional convenience and simplicity.

How to Use This Dictionary

1. First, try looking up the complete phrase that you are seeking in the dictionary. Each expression is alphabetized under the first word of the phrase. For example, **in so many words** will be found in the section dealing with the letter "i." Entry phrases are never inverted or reordered like **so many words, in; words, in so many;** or **many words, in so.** Initial articles — *a, an, the* — are not part of the entry except in the case of proverbs or other complete sentences, where the choice of article is invariant. In the entry heads, the words *someone* or *one* stand for persons, and *something* stands for things.

2. If you do not find the phrase you want or if you cannot decide exactly what the phrase is, look up any major word in the phrase in the *Phrase-Finder Index,* which begins on page 402. There you will find all the phrases that contain the key word you have looked up. Pick out the phrase you want and find it in the dictionary. Instructions on how to use the *Phrase-Finder Index* can be found on page 401.

3. An entry head may have one or more alternate forms. The entry head and its alternates are printed in **boldface type,** and the alternate forms are preceded by "AND." Two or more alternate forms are separated by a semicolon. For example:

bear a grudge (against someone)
AND **have a grudge against someone; hold a grudge (against someone)** to have an old resentment for someone; to have continual anger for someone. □ *She bears a grudge against the judge who sentenced her.* □ *I have a grudge against my landlord for overcharging me.* □ *How long can a person hold a grudge? Let's be friends.*

4. Many of the entry phrases have more than one major sense or meaning. These senses or meanings are numbered with boldface numerals. For example:

stand for something 1. to endure something. □ *The teacher won't stand for any whispering in class.* □ *We just can't stand for that kind of behavior.* **2.** to signify something. □ *In a traffic signal, the red light stands for "stop."* □ *The abbreviation* Dr. *stands for "doctor."* **3.** to endorse or support an ideal. □ *The mayor claims to stand for honesty in government and jobs for everyone.* □ *Every candidate for public office stands for all the good things in life.*

5. Individual numbered senses may have additional forms that appear in boldface type, in which case the AND and the additional form(s) follow the numeral. For example:

balance the accounts 1. AND **balance the books** to determine through accounting that accounts are in balance, that all money is accounted for. □ *Jane was up all night balancing the accounts.* □ *The cashier was not allowed to leave the bank until the manager balanced the books.* **2.** to get even [with someone]. □ *Tom hit Bob.*

Bob balanced the accounts by breaking Tom's toy car. □ *Once we have balanced the accounts, we can shake hands and be friends again.*

6. The boldface entry head (together with any alternate forms) is usually followed by a definition or an explanation. Alternate definitions are separated by a semicolon (;). These additional definitions are usually given to show slight differences in meaning or interpretation. Sometimes an alternate definition is given when the vocabulary of the first definition is difficult. For example:

dead on one's or its feet exhausted; worn out; no longer effective or successful. □ *Ann is so tired. She's really dead on her feet.* □ *He can't teach effectively anymore. He's dead on his feet.* □ *This inefficient company is dead on its feet.*

7. Some entries are followed by instructions to look up some other phrase. For example:

scarcer than hen's teeth See *(as) scarce as hen's teeth.*

8. A definition may be followed by comments in parentheses. These comments tell about some of the variations of the phrase, explain what the phrase alludes to, give other useful information, or indicate cross-referencing. For example:

desert a sinking ship AND **leave a sinking ship** to leave a place, a person, or a situation when things become difficult or unpleasant. (Rats are said to be the first to leave a ship that is sinking.) □ *I hate to be the one to desert a sinking ship, but I can't stand it around here anymore.* □ *There goes Tom. Wouldn't you know he'd leave a sinking ship rather than stay around and try to help?*

9. When the comments apply to all the numbered senses of an entry, the comments are found before the first numbered sense. For example:

> **slow on the draw** (Slang. Compare with *quick on the draw.*) **1.** slow in drawing a gun. (Cowboy and gangster talk.) □ *Bill got shot because he's so slow on the draw.* □ *The gunslinger said, "I have to be fast. If I'm slow on the draw, I'm dead."* **2.** AND **slow on the uptake** slow to figure something out; slow-thinking. □ *Sally didn't get the joke because she's sort of slow on the draw.* □ *Bill—who's slow on the uptake—didn't get the joke until it was explained to him.*

10. Some definitions are preceded by additional information in square brackets. This information makes the definition clearer by supplying information about the typical grammatical context in which the phrase is found. For example:

> **serve someone right** [for an act or event] to punish someone fairly. [for doing something] □ *John copied off my test paper. It would serve him right if he fails the test.* □ *It'd serve John right if he got arrested.*

11. Some entries are cross-referenced to similar idiomatic phrases that are related in form or meaning. For example:

> **in the black** not in debt; in a financially profitable condition. (Compare with *in the red. In* can be replaced with *into.* See the explanation at *in a bind* and the examples.) □ *I wish my accounts were in the black.* □ *Sally moved the company into the black.*

12. Sometimes the numbered senses refer only to people or things, but not both, even though the entry head indicates both *someone or something.* In such cases, the numeral is followed by "[with *someone*]" or "[with *something*]." For example:

> **blow someone or something away 1.**
> to kill or destroy someone or
> something. (Slang. Also literal.) □
> *He drew his gun and blew the thief*
> *away.* ⊤ *His bad attitude blew*
> *away the whole deal.* **2.** [with *someone*] to overcome someone emotionally. □ *The bad news really*
> *blew me away.* □ *Your news just*
> *blew me away! How exciting!*

13. Examples are introduced by a □ or a ⊤ and are in *italic type*. The ⊤ introduces an example containing two elements that have been transposed, such as a particle and the object of a verb. This is typically found with phrasal verbs. For example:

> **gloss something over** to cover up or
> conceal an error; to make something appear right by minimizing
> or concealing the flaws. □ *When I*
> *asked him not to gloss the flaws*
> *over, he got angry.* ⊤ *When Mr.*
> *Brown was selling me the car, he*
> *tried to gloss over its defects.*

14. An entry head appears in *slanted type* whenever the phrase is referred to in a definition or cross-reference.

15. Some entry heads stand for two or more idiomatic expressions. Parentheses are used to show which parts of the phrase may or may not be there. For example: **(all) set to do something** stands for **all set to do something** and **set to do something**.

TERMS AND SYMBOLS

☐ (a box) marks the beginning of an example.

⊤ (a box containing a "T") marks the beginning of an example in which two elements of the phrase, usually a particle and an object, are transposed.

AND indicates that an entry head has variant forms that are the same or similar in meaning as the entry head. One or more variant forms are preceded by AND.

Also literal. indicates that the idiomatic expression also has a common, literal interpretation.

entry block is the body of an entry starting with a bold face word or phrase and running to the next bold face word or phrase. *Entry blocks* are separated by white space.

entry head is the first phrase or word, in boldface type, of an *entry block;* the phrase or word that the definition explains.

Fixed order. indicates that a group of two or more words always appears in the same order, such as "fast and furious," but not "furious and fast."

formal indicates an expression that is literary in origin or usually reserved for writing.

informal refers to a very casual expression that is most likely to be spoken and not written.

jocular describes an expression that is intended to be humorous.

see means to turn to the *entry head* indicated.

see also means to consult the *entry head* indicated for additional information or to find expressions similar in form or meaning to the *entry head* containing the *see also* instruction.

see under means to turn to the *entry head* indicated and look for the phrase you are seeking *within* the entry indicated, usually after AND.

ABOUT THIS DICTIONARY

NTC's American Idioms Dictionary is designed for easy use by life-long speakers of English, as well as the new-to-English speaker or learner. The dictionary uses over 12,000 examples to illustrate the meanings of approximately 8,500 idiomatic forms in over 6,000 entry blocks. An appendix includes 500 irreversible binomial and trinomial phrases. The dictionary contains a unique Phrase-Finder Index that allows the user to identify and look up any expression in the dictionary from a single key word.

This is a dictionary of form and meaning. It focuses on the user's need to know the meaning, usage, and appropriate contexts for each idiomatic phrase. The definitions and examples provide sufficient information to allow a person trained in English grammar to parse the idiomatic expressions. Persons who do not understand English grammar or English grammar terminology and who cannot themselves parse the idiomatic expressions or example sentences do not derive much benefit from grammatical explanations. The dictionary relies on clarity, simplicity, and carefully written examples to lead the user to the meaning and appropriate usage of each idiomatic expression.

The special features that make this book useful for learners do not detract from or interfere with its usefulness for the life-long English speaker, and should, in fact, add to its usefulness. Specialized knowledge of English lexical and sentential semantics and English grammar is not used in indexing, defining, or explaining the idiomatic expressions.

Idioms or idiomatic expressions are often defined as "set phrases" or "fixed phrases." The number of idiomatic expressions that are totally invariant is really quite small, however, even when the English proverbs are included in this category. Most such phrases can vary the choice of noun or pronoun and most select from a wide variety of verb tense and aspect patterns. Adjectives and some adverbs can be added at will to idiomatic phrases. Furthermore, the new-to-English user is faced with the difficulty of isolating an idiomatic expression from the rest of the sentence and determining where to find it in a dictionary of idioms. If the user fails to extract the essential idiomatic expression, the likelihood of finding it in *any* dictionary is reduced considerably.

In dictionaries that list each idiomatic expression under a "key word," there may be some difficulty in deciding what the "key word" is. In phrases such as **on the button** or **in the cards**, the key word, the only noun in the phrase, is easy to determine if one has correctly isolated the phrase from the sentence in which it was found. In phrases that have more than one noun, such as **all hours of the day and night** or **A bird in the hand is worth two in the bush**, deciding on a "key word" may be more difficult. It is even more difficult when the only noun in the phrase is one of the variable words, such as with **go around with her old friends, go around with Jim, go around with no one at all,** which are examples of **go around with someone.**

This dictionary uses the *Phrase-Finder Index* to get around the problems users face with trying to isolate the complete idiom and trying to predict its location in the dictionary. Simply look up *any* major word — noun, verb, adjective, or adverb — in the Phrase-Finder Index, and you will find the form of the entry head that contains the definition you seek.

For instance, in trying to unravel the sentence "This one is head and shoulders above the others," the idiomatic expression **head and shoulders above someone or something** will be listed in the index under *HEAD, SHOULDERS,* and *ABOVE.* The *Phrase-Finder Index* allows the user to determine which portion of the sentence is the idiom as well as the form of the idiom chosen to be an entry head.

Another important feature for the learner is the use of object placeholders indicating human and nonhuman. Typical dictionary entries for idiomatic phrases — especially for phrasal verbs, prepositional verbs, and phrasal prepositional verbs — omit direct objects, as in **put on hold, bail out,** or **see through**. This dictionary uses the stand-in pronouns *someone* and *something* to indicate whether the verb in the phrase calls for an object, where the object should go in the sentence, whether the object can be human or nonhuman, and if there are different meanings dependent on whether the object is human or nonhuman. All of that information is vital to learners of English, although it seems to come perfectly naturally to life-long English speakers. For example, there is a big difference between **put someone on hold** and **put something on hold**, or between **bail someone out** and **bail something out**. There is also a great difference between **see something through** and **see through something**. These differences may never be revealed if the entry heads are just **put on hold, bail out,** and **see through,** with no object indicated.

Many idioms have optional parts. In fact, a phrase may seem opaque simply because it is really just an ellipsis of a longer, less opaque phrase. This dictionary shows as full a form of an idiom as possible with the frequently omitted parts in parentheses. For example: **back down (from someone or something)** and **be all eyes (and ears).**

The dictionary includes numerous irreversible binomials and trinomials—sequences of two or three words that are in a fixed order, such as *fast and furious*, but not *furious and fast*. These sequences are listed in the Appendix, beginning on page 525, and those that require explanation are cross-referenced to entries in the dictionary.

A

A bird in the hand is worth two in the bush. a proverb meaning that something you already have is better than something you might get. □ *Bill has offered to buy my car for $4,000. Someone else might pay more, but a bird in the hand is worth two in the bush.* □ *I might be able to find a better price, but a bird in the hand is worth two in the bush.*

A fool and his money are soon parted. a proverb meaning that a person who acts unwisely with money soon loses it. (Often said about a person who has just lost a sum of money because of poor judgment.) □ *When Bill lost a $400 bet on a horse race, Mary said, "A fool and his money are soon parted."* □ *When John bought a cheap used car that fell apart the next day, he said, "Oh, well, a fool and his money are soon parted."*

A friend in need is a friend indeed. a proverb meaning that a true friend is a person who will help you when you really need someone. (Compare with *fair-weather friend.*) □ *When Bill helped me with geometry, I really learned the meaning of "A friend in need is a friend indeed."* □ *"A friend in need is a friend indeed" sounds silly until you need someone very badly.*

A little bird told me. learned from a mysterious or secret source. (Often given as an evasive answer to someone who asks how you learned something. Rude in some circumstances.) □ *"All right," said Mary, "where did you get that information?" John replied, "A little bird told me."* □ *A little bird told me where I might find you.*

A little knowledge is a dangerous thing. a proverb meaning that incomplete knowledge can embarrass or harm someone or something. □ *The doctor said, "Just because you've had a course in first aid, you shouldn't have treated your own illness. A little knowledge is a dangerous thing."* □ *John thought he knew how to take care of the garden, but he killed all the flowers. A little knowledge is a dangerous thing.*

A penny saved is a penny earned. a proverb meaning that money saved through thrift is the same as money earned by employment. (Sometimes used to explain stinginess.) □ *"I didn't want to pay that much for the book," said Mary. "After all, a penny saved is a penny earned."* □ *Bob put his money in a new bank that pays more interest than his old bank, saying, "A penny saved is a penny earned."*

A rolling stone gathers no moss. a proverb that describes a person who keeps changing jobs or residences and, therefore, accumulates no possessions or responsibilities. □ *"John just can't seem to stay in one place," said Sally. "Oh, well, a rolling stone gathers no moss."* □ *Bill has no furniture to bother with because he keeps on the move. He keeps saying that a rolling stone gathers no moss.*

abide by something to follow the rules of something; to obey someone's orders. □ *John felt that he had to abide by his father's wishes.* □ *All drivers are expected to abide by the rules of the road.*

able to breathe (easily) again AND **able to breathe (freely) again** able to relax and recover from a busy or stressful time; able to catch one's breath. (*Able to* can be replaced with *can*.) □ *Now that the lion has been caught, we'll be able to breathe freely again.* □ *Now that the annual sale is over, the sales staff will be able to breathe again.* □ *Final exams are over, so I can breathe easily again.*

able to breathe (freely) again See the previous entry.

able to do something blindfolded AND **able to do something standing on one's head** able to do something easily and quickly, possibly without even looking. (Informal. Rarely literal. *Able to* can be replaced with *can*.) □ *Bill boasted that he could pass his driver's test blindfolded.* □ *Mary is very good with computers. She can program blindfolded.* □ *Dr. Jones is a great surgeon. He can take out an appendix standing on his head.*

able to do something standing on one's head See the previous entry.

able to make something able to attend an event. (Informal. Also literal. *Able to* can be replaced with *can*.) □ *I don't think I'll be able to make your party, but thanks for asking me.* □ *We are having another one next month. We hope you can make it then.*

able to take a joke to be able to accept ridicule good-naturedly; to be the object or butt of a joke willingly. (*Able to* can be replaced with *can*.) □ *Let's play a trick on Bill and see if he's able to take a joke.* □ *Better not tease Ann. She can't take a joke.*

able to take just so much able to endure only a limited amount of discomfort. (*Able to* can be replaced with *can*.) □ *Please stop hurting my feelings. I'm able to take just so much.* □ *I can take just so much.*

able to take something able to endure something; able to endure abuse. (Often in the negative. *Able to* can be replaced with *can*. See also the previous entry.) □ *Stop yelling like that.*

I'm not able to take it anymore. □ *Go ahead, hit me again. I can take it.*

above and beyond (something) more than is required. (Fixed order.) □ *Her efforts were above and beyond. We appreciate her time.* □ *All this extra time is above and beyond her regular hours.*

(above and) beyond the call of duty in addition to what is required; more than is required in one's job. □ *We didn't expect the police officer to drive us home. That was above and beyond the call of duty.* □ *The English teacher helped students after school every day, even though it was beyond the call of duty.*

above suspicion to be honest enough that no one would suspect you; to be in a position where you could not be suspected. □ *The general is a fine old man, completely above suspicion.* □ *Mary was at work at the time of the accident, so she's above suspicion.*

aboveboard AND **honest and aboveboard; open and aboveboard** in the open; visible to the public; honest. (Especially with *keep*, as in the examples. Fixed order.) □ *Don't keep it a secret. Let's make sure that everything is aboveboard.* □ *You can do whatever you wish, as long as you keep it honest and aboveboard.* □ *The inspector had to make sure that everything was open and aboveboard.*

absent without leave AND **AWOL** absent from a military unit without permission; absent from anything without permission. (**AWOL** is an abbreviation. This is a serious offense in the military.) □ *The soldier was taken away by the military police because he was absent without leave.* □ *John was AWOL from school and got into a lot of trouble with his parents.*

according to all accounts AND **by all accounts** from all the reports; everyone is saying. □ *According to all accounts, the police were on the scene immediately.* □ *According to all accounts, the meeting broke up over a very* *minor matter.* □ *By all accounts, it was a very poor performance.*

according to Hoyle according to the rules; in keeping with the way it is normally done. (Refers to the rules for playing games. Edmond Hoyle wrote a book about games. This expression is usually used for something other than games.) □ *That's wrong. According to Hoyle, this is the way to do it.* □ *The carpenter said, "This is the way to drive a nail, according to Hoyle."*

according to one's own lights according to the way one believes; according to the way one's conscience or inclinations lead one. (Rarely used informally.) □ *People must act on this matter according to their own lights.* □ *John may have been wrong, but he did what he did according to his own lights.*

according to someone or something as said or indicated by someone or something. □ *According to the weather forecast, this should be a beautiful day.* □ *According to my father, this is a very good car to buy.* □ *It's too cold to go for a walk, according to the thermometer.*

accustomed to someone or something to be used to or comfortable with someone or something; to accept someone or something as common and usual. □ *We are accustomed to wearing shoes.* □ *They aren't accustomed to paying a visit without bringing a gift.* □ *I'll never become accustomed to you.*

ace in the hole something or someone held (secretly) in reserve; anything that can help in an emergency. (Slang. Refers to an ace dealt facedown in poker.) □ *The hostages served as the terrorists' ace in the hole for getting what they wanted.* □ *The twenty-dollar bill in my shoe is my ace in the hole.*

acid test a test whose findings are beyond doubt or dispute. □ *Her new husband seems generous, but the acid test will be if he lets her mother stay with them.* □ *The senator isn't very popular just now, but the acid test will be if he gets reelected.*

acknowledge receipt (of something) to inform the sender that what was sent was received. (Commonly used in business correspondence.) □ *In a letter to a shoe company, Mary wrote, "I'm happy to acknowledge receipt of four dozen pairs of shoes."* □ *John acknowledged receipt of the bill.* □ *The package hasn't arrived, so I'm unable to acknowledge receipt.*

acknowledge someone to be right to admit or state that someone is correct about something. □ *Mary acknowledged Bill to be right about the name of the store.* □ *Bill said that the car was useless, and the mechanic acknowledged him to be right.*

acquire a taste for something to develop a liking for food, drink, or something else; to learn to like something. □ *One acquires a taste for fine wines.* □ *Many people are not able to acquire a taste for foreign food.* □ *Mary acquired a taste for art when she was very young.*

across the board equally for everyone or everything. □ *The school board raised the pay of all the teachers across the board.* □ *Congress cut the budget by reducing the money for each department ten percent across the board.*

act as someone to perform in the capacity of someone, temporarily or permanently. □ *I'll act as your supervisor until Mrs. Brown returns from vacation.* □ *This is Mr. Smith. He'll act as manager from now on.*

act high-and-mighty to act proud and powerful. (Informal. Fixed order.) □ *Why does the doctor always have to act so high-and-mighty?* □ *If Sally wouldn't act so high-and-mighty, she'd have more friends.*

act of faith an act or deed demonstrating religious faith; an act or deed showing trust in someone or something. □ *He lit candles in church as an act of faith.* □ *For him to trust you with his safety was a real act of faith.*

act of God an occurrence (usually an accident) for which no human is responsible; an act of nature such as a storm, an earthquake, or a windstorm. □ *My insurance company wouldn't pay for the damage because it was an act of God.* □ *The thief tried to convince the judge that the diamonds were in his pocket due to an act of God.*

act of war an international act of violence for which war is considered a suitable response; (figuratively) any hostile act between two people. □ *To bomb a ship is an act of war.* □ *Can spying be considered an act of war?* □ *"You just broke my stereo," yelled John. "That's an act of war!"*

act one's age to behave more maturely; to act as grown-up as one really is. (This is frequently said to a child.) □ *Come on, John, act your age. Stop throwing rocks.* □ *Mary! Stop picking on your little brother. Act your age!*

act something out to perform an imaginary event as if one were in a play. □ *Bill always acted his anger out by shouting and pounding his fists.* Ⓣ *The psychiatrist asked Bill to act out the way he felt about getting fired.*

act up to misbehave; to run or act badly. □ *John, why do you always have to act up when your father and I take you out to eat?* □ *My arthritis is acting up. It really hurts.* □ *My car is acting up. I could hardly get it started this morning.*

Actions speak louder than words. a proverb meaning that it is better to do something about a problem than just talk about it. □ *Mary kept promising to get a job. John finally looked her in the eye and said, "Actions speak louder than words!"* □ *After listening to the senator promising to cut federal spending, Ann wrote a simple note saying, "Actions speak louder than words."*

add fuel to the fire AND **add fuel to the flame** to make a problem worse; to say or do something that makes a bad situation worse; to make an angry person get even more angry. □ *To spank a crying child just adds fuel to the fire.* □ *Bill was shouting angrily, and Bob tried to get him to stop by laughing at*

him. *Of course, that was just adding fuel to the flame.*

add fuel to the flame See the previous entry.

add insult to injury to make a bad situation worse; to hurt the feelings of a person who has already been hurt. □ *First, the basement flooded, and then, to add insult to injury, a pipe burst in the kitchen.* □ *My car barely started this morning, and to add insult to injury, I got a flat tire in the driveway.*

add up (to something) 1. to total up to a particular amount. □ *The bill added up to $200.* □ *These groceries will add up to almost sixty dollars.* □ *These numbers just won't add up.* **2.** to mean something; to signify or represent something; to result in something. □ *All this adds up to trouble!* □ *I don't understand. What does all this add up to?* □ *If you think about it carefully, these facts add up perfectly.*

address someone as something 1. to talk to or write to a person, using a particular title. □ *They addressed Abraham Lincoln as "Mr. President."* □ *A physician is usually addressed as "Doctor."* **2.** to treat a person you are talking with in a particular manner. □ *You should address him as your equal.* □ *Do not address me as your superior.*

advanced in years See *up in years.*

afraid of one's own shadow easily frightened; always frightened, timid, or suspicious. (Never used literally.) □ *After Tom was robbed, he was even afraid of his own shadow.* □ *Jane has always been a shy child. She has been afraid of her own shadow since she was three.*

after a fashion in a manner that is just barely adequate; poorly. □ *He thanked me—after a fashion—for my help.* □ *Oh, yes, I can swim, after a fashion.*

after all 1. anyway; in spite of what had been decided. (Often refers to a change in plans or a reversal of plans.) □ *Mary had planned to go to the bank first, but she came here after all.* □ *It* *looks like Tom will go to law school after all.* **2.** remember; consider the fact that. □ *Don't punish Tommy! After all, he's only three years old!* □ *After all, we really didn't hurt anyone!*

after all is said and done when everything is settled or concluded; finally. (See also *when all is said and done.* Fixed order.) □ *After all was said and done, it was a lovely party.* □ *After all is said and done, it will turn out just as I said.*

after hours after the regular closing time; after any normal or regular time, such as one's bedtime. □ *John was arrested in a bar after hours.* □ *The soldier was caught sneaking into the barracks after hours.* □ *John got a job sweeping floors in the bank after hours.*

after the fact after something has happened; after something, especially a crime, has taken place. (Primarily a legal phrase.) □ *John is always making excuses after the fact.* □ *Remember to lock your car whenever you leave it. If it's stolen, there is nothing you can do after the fact.*

after the fashion of someone or something in the manner or style of someone or something. (See also *after a fashion.*) □ *She walks down the street after the fashion of a grand lady.* □ *The church was built after the fashion of an English cathedral.*

against someone's will without a person's consent or agreement. □ *You cannot force me to come with you against my will!* □ *Against their will, the men were made to stand up against the wall and be searched.*

against the clock in a race with time; in a great hurry to get something done before a particular time. (See also *race against time.*) □ *Bill set a new track record, running against the clock. He lost the actual race, however.* □ *In a race against the clock, they rushed the special medicine to the hospital.*

ahead of one's time having ideas or attitudes that are too advanced to be acceptable to or appreciated by the so-ciety in which one is living. □ *People buy that artist's work now, but his paintings were laughed at when he was alive. He was ahead of his time.* □ *Mary's grandmother was ahead of her time in wanting to study medicine.*

ahead of the game being early; having an advantage over a situation; having done more than necessary. (Informal or slang. Also literal.) □ *Whenever we go to a movie, we show up ahead of the game and have to wait.* □ *Bill has to study math very hard to keep ahead of the game.* □ *Bob does extra work so he's always ahead of the game.*

ahead of time beforehand; before the announced time. □ *If you show up ahead of time, you will have to wait.* □ *Be there ahead of time if you want to get a good seat.*

aid and abet someone to help someone; to incite someone to do something that is wrong. (Fixed order.) □ *He was scolded for aiding and abetting the boys who were fighting.* □ *It's illegal to aid and abet a thief.*

aim to do something to mean to do something; to intend to do something in the future. (Folksy.) □ *I aim to paint the house as soon as I can find a brush.* □ *He aims to take a few days off and go fishing.*

air one's grievances to complain; to make a public complaint. □ *I know how you feel, John, but it isn't necessary to air your grievances over and over.* □ *I know you're busy, sir, but I must air my grievances. This matter is very serious.*

air one's dirty linen in public AND **wash one's dirty linen in public** to discuss private or embarrassing matters in public, especially when quarreling. (This *linen* refers to sheets and table-cloths or other soiled cloth.) □ *John's mother had asked him repeatedly not to air the family's dirty linen in public.* □ *Mr. and Mrs. Johnson are arguing again. Why must they always air their dirty linen in public?* □ *Jean will talk to anyone about her financial problems.*

Why does she wash her dirty linen in public?

air something out to freshen up something by placing it in the open air; to freshen a room by letting air move through it. □ *It's so stale in here. Mary, please open a window and air this place out.* □ *Please take this pillow outside and air it out.* ⊤ *I'll have to air out the car. Someone has been smoking in it.*

alive and kicking AND **alive and well** well and healthy. (Informal. Fixed order.) □ JANE: *How is Bill?* MARY: *Oh, he's alive and kicking.* □ *The last time I saw Tom, he was alive and well.*

alive and well See the previous entry.

alive with someone or something covered with, filled with, or active with people or things. □ *Look! Ants everywhere. The floor is alive with ants!* □ *When we got to the ballroom, the place was alive with dancing.* □ *The campground was alive with campers from all over the country.*

all and sundry everyone; one and all. (Folksy. Fixed order.) □ *Cold drinks were served to all and sundry.* □ *All and sundry came to the village fair.*

all around Robin Hood's barn going somewhere not by a direct route; going way out of the way [to get somewhere]; by a long and circuitous route. □ *We had to go all around Robin Hood's barn to get to the little town.* □ *She walked all around Robin Hood's barn looking for a shop that sold Finnish glassware.*

all at once 1. suddenly. □ *All at once the chair broke, and Bob fell to the floor.* □ *All at once she tripped on a stone.* **2.** all at the same time. □ *The entire group spoke all at once.* □ *They were trying to cook dinner, clean house, and paint the closet all at once.*

(all) at sea (about something) confused; lost and bewildered. □ *Mary is all at sea about getting married.* □ *When it comes to higher math, John is totally at sea.*

(all) balled up troubled; confused; in a mess. (Slang.) □ *Look at you! You're really all balled up!* □ *John is all balled up because his car was stolen.* □ *Of course this typewriter won't work. It's all balled up.*

(all) beer and skittles all fun and pleasure; easy and pleasant. (Skittles is the game of ninepins, a game similar to bowling. Fixed order.) □ *Life isn't all beer and skittles, you know!* □ *For Sam, college was beer and skittles. He wasted a lot of time and money.*

all better now improved; cured. (Folksy or juvenile.) □ *My leg was sore, but it's all better now.* □ *I fell off my tricycle and bumped my knee. Mommy kissed it, and it's all better now.*

all day long throughout the day; during the entire day. □ *We waited for you at the station all day long.* □ *I can't keep smiling all day long.*

(all) dressed up dressed in one's best clothes; dressed formally. □ *We're all dressed up to go out to dinner.* □ *I really hate to get all dressed up just to go somewhere to eat.*

all for something very much in favor of something. (*For* is usually emphasized.) □ *Bill is all for stopping off to get ice cream.* □ *Mary suggested that they sell their house. They weren't all for it, but they did it anyway.*

(all) for the best good in spite of the way it seems; better than you think. (Often said when someone dies after a serious illness.) □ *I'm very sorry to hear of the death of your aunt. Perhaps it's for the best.* □ *I didn't get into the college I wanted, but I couldn't afford it anyway. It's probably all for the best.*

all gone used up; finished; over with. □ *Oh, the strawberry jelly is all gone.* □ *We used to have wonderful parties, but those days are all gone.*

(all) Greek to me unintelligible to me. (Usually with some form of *be*.) □ *I can't understand it. It's Greek to me.* □ *It's all Greek to me. Maybe Sally knows what it means.*

6

all hours (of the day and night) very late in the night or very early in the morning. □ *Why do you always stay out until all hours of the day and night?* □ *I like to stay out till all hours.*

all in tired; exhausted; *all tuckered out.* □ *I just walked all the way from town. I'm all in.* □ *"What a day!" said Sally. "I'm all in."*

all in a day's work part of what is expected; typical or normal. □ *I don't particularly like to cook, but it's all in a day's work.* □ *Putting up with rude customers isn't pleasant, but it's all in a day's work.* □ *Cleaning up after other people is all in a day's work for a chambermaid.*

all in all considering everything that has happened; in summary and in spite of any unpleasantness. □ *All in all, it was a very good party.* □ *All in all, I'm glad that I visited New York City.*

all in good time at some future time; *in good time;* soon. (This phrase is used to encourage people to be patient and wait quietly.) □ *When will the baby be born? All in good time.* □ MARY: *I'm starved! When will Bill get here with the pizza?* TOM: *All in good time, Mary, all in good time.*

(all) in one breath spoken very rapidly, usually while one is very excited. □ *Ann said all in one breath, "Hurry, quick! The parade is coming!"* □ *Jane was in a play, and she was so excited that she said her whole speech in one breath.* □ *Tom can say the alphabet all in one breath.*

all in one piece safely; without damage. (Informal.) □ *Her son come home from school all in one piece, even though he had been in a fight.* □ *The package was handled carelessly, but the vase inside arrived all in one piece.*

(all) in the family restricted to one's own family, as with private or embarrassing information. (Especially with keep.) □ *Don't tell anyone else. Please keep it all in the family.* □ *He only told his brother because he wanted it to remain in the family.*

(all) joking aside AND **(all) kidding aside** being serious for a moment; in all seriousness. □ *I know I laugh at him but, joking aside, he's a very clever scientist.* □ *I know I threatened to leave and go round the world, but, joking aside, I need a vacation.*

(all) kidding aside See the previous entry.

all kinds of someone or something a great number of people or things; a great amount of something, especially money. (Informal. Also literal = all types.) □ *There were all kinds of people there, probably thousands.* □ *The Smith family has all kinds of money.*

all manner of someone or something all types of people or things. □ *We saw all manner of people there. They came from every country in the world.* □ *They were selling all manner of things in the country store.*

all night long throughout the whole night. □ *I couldn't sleep all night long.* □ *John was sick all night long.*

all of a sudden suddenly. □ *All of a sudden lightning struck the tree we were sitting under.* □ *I felt a sharp pain in my side all of a sudden.*

all or nothing (Fixed order.) **1.** everything or nothing at all. □ *Sally would not accept only part of the money. She wanted all or nothing.* □ *I can't bargain over trifles. I will have to have all or nothing.* **2.** time to choose to do something or not to do it. □ *It was all or nothing. Tim had to jump off the truck or risk drowning when the truck went into the water.* □ *Jane stood at the door of the airplane and checked her parachute. It was all or nothing now. She had to jump or be looked upon as a coward.*

all-out effort a very good and thorough effort. (See also *make an all-out effort.*) □ *We need an all-out effort to get this job done on time.* □ *The* government began an all-out effort to reduce the federal budget.

all-out war total war, as opposed to small, warlike acts or threats of war. □ *We are now concerned about all-out war in the Middle East.* □ *Threats of all-out war caused many tourists to leave the country immediately.*

all over 1. finished; dead. (Compare with *all over with.*) □ *Dinner is all over. I'm sorry you didn't get any.* □ *It's all over. He's dead now.* **2.** everywhere. (See also *all over the earth.*) □ *Oh, I just itch all over.* □ *She's spreading the rumor all over.*

all over but the shouting decided and concluded; finished except for a celebration. (An elaboration of *all over*, which means "finished.") □ *The last goal was made just as the final whistle sounded. Tom said, "Well, it's all over but the shouting."* □ *Tom worked hard in college and graduated last month. When he got his diploma, he said, "It's all over but the shouting."*

all over the earth AND **all over the world** everywhere. □ *Grass grows all over the earth.* □ *It's the same way all over the world.*

all over the place everywhere; in all parts of a particular location. □ *Tom, stop leaving your dirty clothes all over the place.* □ *We keep finding this kind of problem all over the place.*

all over the world See *all over the earth.*

all over town 1. everywhere in town. □ *Our dog got loose and ran all over town.* □ *Jane looked all over town for a dress to wear to the party.* **2.** known to everyone in town. □ *Now keep this a secret. I don't want it all over town.* □ *In a short time the secret was known all over town.*

(all) over with finished. (See also *all over.*) □ *His problems are all over with now.* □ *After dinner is all over with, we can play cards.*

all right 1. well, good, or okay, but not excellent. (Informal. This phrase has all the uses that *okay* has.) □ *I was a little sick, but now I'm all right.* □ *His work is all right, but nothing to brag about.* □ *All right, it's time to go.* **2.** beyond a doubt; as the evidence shows. □ *The dog's dead all right. It hasn't moved at all.* □ *The train's late all right. It hasn't been late in months.* **3.** hooray. (An exclamation of encouragement.) □ *The Bears won! All right!* □ *All right! That's the way to do it!*

All right for you! That's it for you!; That's the last chance for you! (Juvenile and informal. Usually said by a child who is angry with a playmate.) □ *All right for you, John. See if I ever play with you again.* □ *All right for you! I'm telling your mother what you did.*

all right with someone agreeable to someone. □ *If you want to ruin your life and marry Tom, it's all right with me.* □ *I'll see if it's all right with my father.*

all set ready to begin; okay. □ TOM: *Is everything all right?* JANE: *Yes, we are all set.* □ *We are ready to leave now. Are you all set?*

(all) set to do something prepared or ready to do something. □ *Are you set to cook the steaks?* □ *Yes, the fire is ready, and I'm all set to start.*

(all) shot to hell totally ruined. (Informal. Use *hell* with caution.) □ *My car is all shot to hell and can't be depended on.* □ *This knife is shot to hell. I need a sharper one.*

(all) skin and bones See *nothing but skin and bones.*

all sweetness and light very sweet, innocent, and helpful. (Perhaps insincerely so. Fixed order.) □ *She was mad at first, but after a while, she was all sweetness and light.* □ *At the reception, the whole family was all sweetness and light, but they argued and fought after the guests left.*

all systems (are) go everything is ready. (Informal. Originally said when preparing to launch a rocket.) □ *The* *rocket is ready to blast off—all systems are go.* □ TOM: *Are you guys ready to start playing?* BILL: *Sure, Tom, all systems go.*

all talk (and no action) talking about doing something, but never actually doing it. □ *The car needs washing, but Bill is all talk and no action on this matter.* □ *Bill keeps saying he'll get a job soon, but he's all talk and no action.* □ *Bill won't do it. He's just all talk.*

All that glitters is not gold. a proverb meaning that many attractive and alluring things have no value. □ *The used car looked fine but didn't run well at all. "Ah, yes," thought Bill, "all that glitters is not gold."* □ *When Mary was disappointed about losing Tom, Jane reminded her, "All that glitters is not gold."*

all the livelong day throughout the whole day. (Folksy.) □ *They kept at their work all the livelong day.* □ *Bob just sat by the creek fishing, all the livelong day.*

all the rage in current fashion. □ *A new dance called the "floppy disc" is all the rage.* □ *Wearing a rope instead of a belt is all the rage these days.*

all the same AND **just the same** **1.** nevertheless; anyhow. (Also literal.) □ *They were told not to bring presents, but they brought them all the same.* □ *His parents said no, but John went out just the same.* **2.** See the following entry.

all the same (to someone) AND **just the same (to someone)** of no consequence to someone; immaterial to someone. □ *It's all the same to me whether we win or lose.* □ *If it's just the same to you, I'd rather walk than ride.* □ *If it's all the same, I'd rather you didn't smoke.*

all the time **1.** throughout a specific period of time. □ *Bill was stealing money for the last two years, and Tom knew it all the time.* □ *Throughout December and January, Jane had two jobs all the time.* **2.** at all times; con-

tinuously. □ *Your blood keeps flowing all the time.* □ *That electric motor runs all the time.* **3.** repeatedly; habitually. □ *She keeps a handkerchief in her hand all the time.* □ *She hums softly all the time.*

all the way from the beginning to the end; the entire distance, from start to finish. (See also *go all the way (with someone)*.) □ *The ladder reaches all the way to the top of the house.* □ *I walked all the way home.*

all thumbs very awkward and clumsy, especially with one's hands. □ *Poor Bob can't play the piano at all. He's all thumbs.* □ *Mary is all thumbs when it comes to gardening.*

all to the good for the best; for one's benefit. □ *He missed the train, but it was all to the good because the train had a wreck.* □ *It was all to the good that he died without suffering.*

all told totaled up; including all parts. □ *All told, he earned about $700 last week.* □ *All told, he has many fine characteristics.*

(all) tuckered out tired out; worn out. (Folksy.) □ *Poor John worked so hard that he's all tuckered out.* □ *Look at that little baby sleeping. She's really tuckered out.*

all walks of life all social, economic, and ethnic groups. □ *We saw people there from all walks of life.* □ *The people who came to the art exhibit represented all walks of life.*

(all) well and good good; desirable. (Fixed order.) □ *It's well and good that you're here on time. I was afraid you'd be late again.* □ *It's all well and good that you're passing English, but what about math and science?*

all wet mistaken; wrongheaded; on the wrong track. (Also literal.) □ *It's not that way, John. You're all wet.* □ *If you think that prices will come down, you're all wet.*

all wool and a yard wide genuinely warmhearted and friendly. (Informal and folksy. Refers to woolen cloth that is 100% wool and exactly one yard wide.) □ *Old Bob is a true gentleman —all wool and a yard wide.* □ *The banker, hardly all wool and a yard wide, wouldn't give us a loan.*

All work and no play makes Jack a dull boy. a proverb meaning that one should have recreation as well as work. (*Jack* does not refer to anyone in particular, and the phrase can be used for persons of either sex. Fixed order.) □ *Stop reading that book and go out and play! All work and no play makes Jack a dull boy.* □ *The doctor told Mr. Jones to stop working on weekends and start playing golf, because all work and no play makes Jack a dull boy.*

all worked up (about something) See the following entry.

all worked up (over something) AND **all worked up (about something)** excited and agitated about something. (See also *get worked up (over something).*) □ *Tom is all worked up over the threat of a new war.* □ *Don't get all worked up about something that you can't do anything about.* □ *Bill is all worked up again. It's bad for his health.*

all year round throughout all the seasons of the year; during the entire year. □ *The public swimming pool is enclosed so that it can be used all year round.* □ *In the South they can grow flowers all year round.*

allow for someone or something 1. to plan on having enough of something (such as food, space, etc.) for someone. □ *Mary is bringing Bill on the picnic, so be sure to allow for him when buying the food.* □ *Allow for an extra person when setting the table tonight.* **2.** to plan on the possibility of something. □ *Allow for a few rainy days on your vacation.* □ *Be sure to allow for future growth when you plant the rosebushes.*

All's well that ends well. a proverb meaning that an event that has a good ending is good even if some things went wrong along the way. (This is the name of a play by Shakespeare.) □ *I'm glad you finally got here, even*

though your car had a flat tire on the way. Oh, well. All's well that ends well. □ *The groom was late for the wedding, but everything worked out all right. All's well that ends well.*

along in years See *up in years.*

alongside (of) someone or something as compared to a person or a thing. (Informal. Also literal. The things being compared need not be beside one another.) □ *Our car looks quite small alongside of theirs.* □ *My power of concentration is quite limited alongside of yours.*

alpha and omega both the beginning and the end; the essentials, from the beginning to the end; everything, from the beginning to the end. (Fixed order.) □ *He was forced to learn the alpha and omega of corporate law in order to even talk to the lawyers.* □ *He loved her deeply; she was his alpha and omega.*

amount to something [for someone or something] to be or to become valuable or successful. □ *Most parents hope that their children will amount to something.* □ *I put $200 in the bank, and I hope it will amount to something in twenty years.* □ *I'm glad to see that Bill Jones finally amounts to something.*

amount to the same thing AND **come to the same thing** to be the same as something. □ *Borrowing can be the same as stealing. If the owner does not know what you have borrowed, it amounts to the same thing.* □ *Beer, wine. They come to the same thing if you drink and drive.*

An ounce of prevention is worth a pound of cure. a proverb meaning that it is easier and better to prevent something bad than to deal with the results. □ *When you ride in a car, buckle your seat belt. An ounce of prevention is worth a pound of cure.* □ *Every child should be vaccinated against polio. An ounce of prevention is worth a pound of cure.*

and change [some number of dollars] plus between 1 and 99 cents more.

□ *The book cost $12.49. That's twelve dollars and change.* □ *Subway fare is now one dollar and change.*

and something to spare AND **with something to spare** with extra left over; with more than is needed. (*Something* can be used literally.) □ *I had as much flour as I needed with something to spare.* □ *Fred said he should have enough cash to last the week—with money to spare.*

and the like and other similar things. (Informal.) □ *Whenever we go on a picnic, we take potato chips, hot dogs, soda pop, and the like.* □ *I'm very tired of being yelled at, pushed around, and the like.*

and then some and even more; more than has been mentioned. (Folksy.) □ *John is going to have to run like a deer and then some to win this race.* □ *The cook put the amount of salt called for into the soup and then some.*

and what have you and so on; and other similar things. □ *Their garage is full of bikes, sleds, old boots, and what have you.* □ *The merchant sells writing paper, pens, string, and what have you.*

another country heard from a catch phrase said when someone makes a comment or interrupts. □ *Jane and Bill were discussing business when Bob interrupted to offer an opinion. "Another country heard from," said Jane.* □ *In the middle of the discussion, the baby started crying. "Another country heard from," said Tom.*

(another) nail in someone's or something's coffin something that will harm or destroy someone or something. □ *Every word of criticism that Bob said about the boss was a nail in his coffin.* □ *Losing the export order was the final nail in the company's coffin.*

answer for someone or something 1. [with *something*] to assume responsibility for something. □ *John had to answer for the theft of the bicycle since it was found at his house.* □ *Someday*

we'll all have to answer for our wrongdoings. **2.** [with *someone*] to vouch for someone; to tell of the goodness of someone's character. □ *Mr. Jones, who had known the girl all her life, answered for her. He knew she was innocent.* □ *I will answer for Ted. He could not hurt a flea.*

answer someone's purpose AND **serve someone's purpose** to fit or suit someone's purpose. □ *This piece of wood will answer my purpose quite nicely.* □ *The new car serves our purpose perfectly.*

answer to someone to explain to someone; to justify one's actions to someone. (Usually with *have to.*) □ *If John cannot behave properly, he'll have to answer to me.* □ *The car thief will have to answer to the judge.*

any number of someone or something a large number; a sufficiently large number. (Used when the exact number is not important.) □ *Any number of people can vouch for my honesty.* □ *I can give you any number of reasons why I should join the army.* □ *I ate there any number of times and never became ill.*

any port in a storm a phrase indicating that when one is in difficulties one must accept any way out, whether one likes the solution or not. □ *I don't want to live with my parents, but it's a case of any port in a storm. I can't find an apartment.* □ *He hates his job, but he can't get another. Any port in a storm, you know.*

appear as something to act a certain part in a play, opera, etc. □ *Madame Smith-Franklin appeared as Carmen at the City Opera last season.* □ *The actor refused to appear as a villain in the play.*

appear out of nowhere to appear suddenly, without warning. (Almost the same as *come out of nowhere.*) □ *A huge bear appeared out of nowhere and roared and threatened us.* □ *A butler appeared out of nowhere and took our coats.*

apple of someone's eye someone's favorite person or thing; a boyfriend or a girlfriend. □ *Tom is the apple of Mary's eye. She thinks he's great.* □ *John's new stereo is the apple of his eye.*

apples and oranges a pair of words representing two entities that are not similar. (Fixed order.) □ *You can't talk about Fred and Ted in the same breath! They're apples and oranges.* □ *Talking about her current book and her previous best-seller is like comparing apples and oranges.*

arm in arm linked or hooked together by the arms. □ *The two lovers walked arm in arm down the street.* □ *Arm in arm, the line of dancers kicked high, and the audience roared its approval.*

armed and dangerous pertaining to someone who is suspected of a crime and has not been captured. (This is a warning to police officers who might try to capture this suspect. Fixed order.) □ *Max is at large, presumed to be armed and dangerous.* □ *The suspect has killed once and is armed and dangerous.*

armed to the teeth heavily armed with deadly weapons. □ *The bank robber was armed to the teeth when he was caught.* □ *There are too many guns around. The entire country is armed to the teeth.*

(a)round the clock continuously for twenty-four hours at a time. □ *The priceless jewels were guarded around the clock.* □ *Grandfather was so sick that he had to have nurses round the clock.*

(a)round-the-clock constant; day and night. (Adjective.) □ *Grandfather required around-the-clock care.* □ *I tuned into the around-the-clock news station.*

arrange something with someone 1. AND **arrange to do something with someone** to plan an event to include another person or persons. □ *Jane arranged a meeting with Ann.* □ *Bill arranged to go to the station with Tom and Mary.* **2.** to get someone's consent for something. □ *Mary arranged the* entire affair with her employer. □ *The new mother arranged the christening with the pastor.*

arrange to do something with someone See under *arrange something with someone.*

arrive in a body See *come in a body.*

arrive on the scene See *come on the scene.*

as a duck takes to water easily and naturally. (Informal.) □ *She took to singing just as a duck takes to water.* □ *The baby adapted to bottle-feeding as a duck takes to water.*

as a (general) rule usually; almost always. □ *He can be found in his office as a general rule.* □ *As a general rule, Jane plays golf on Wednesdays.* □ *As a rule, things tend to get less busy after supper time.*

as a last resort as the last choice; if everything else fails. □ *Call the doctor at home only as a last resort.* □ *As a last resort, she will perform surgery.*

as a matter of course normally; as a normal procedure. □ *The nurse always takes your temperature as a matter of course.* □ *You are expected to make your own bed as a matter of course.*

as a matter of fact actually; in addition to what has been said; in reference to what has been said. (See also *matter-of-fact.*) □ *As a matter of fact, John came into the room while you were talking about him.* □ *I'm not a poor worker. As a matter of fact, I'm very efficient.*

as a result of something because of something that has happened. □ *As a result of the accident, Tom couldn't walk for six months.* □ *We couldn't afford to borrow money for a house as a result of the rise in interest rates.*

as a token (of something) symbolic of something, especially of gratitude; as a memento of something. □ *He gave me a rose as a token of the time we spent together.* □ *Here, take this $100 as a token of my appreciation.* □ *I* *can't thank you enough. Please accept this money as a token.*

as an aside as a comment; as a comment that is not supposed to be heard by everyone. □ *At the wedding, Tom said as an aside, "The bride doesn't look well." □ At the ballet, Billy said as an aside to his mother, "I hope the dancers fall off the stage!"*

as bad as all that as bad as reported; as bad as it seems. (Usually expressed in the negative.) □ *Come on! Nothing could be as bad as all that. □ Stop crying. It can't be as bad as all that.*

(as) big as all outdoors very big, usually referring to a space of some kind. (Folksy.) □ *You should see Bob's living room. It's as big as all outdoors. □ The new movie theater is as big as all outdoors.*

(as) big as life AND **(as) big as life and twice as ugly** an exaggerated way of saying that a person or a thing appeared in a particular place. (Folksy. The second phrase is slang.) □ *The little child just stood there as big as life and laughed very hard. □ I opened the door, and there was Tom as big as life. □ I came home and found this cat in my chair, as big as life and twice as ugly.*

(as) big as life and twice as ugly See the previous entry.

(as) black as one is painted as evil as described. (Usually negative.) □ *The landlord is not as black as he is painted. □ Young people are rarely black as they are painted in the media.*

(as) black as pitch very black; very dark. □ *The night was as black as pitch. □ The rocks seemed black as pitch against the silver sand.*

(as) blind as a bat with imperfect sight; blind. □ *My grandmother is as blind as a bat. □ I'm getting blind as a bat. I can hardly read this page.*

(as) busy as a beaver AND **(as) busy as a bee** very busy. □ *I don't have time to talk to you. I'm as busy as a beaver. □ You don't look busy as a beaver to*

me. □ Whenever there is a holiday, we are all as busy as bees.

(as) busy as a bee See the previous entry.

(as) busy as Grand Central Station very busy; crowded with customers or other people. (This refers to Grand Central Station in New York City.) □ *This house is as busy as Grand Central Station. □ When the tourist season starts, this store is busy as Grand Central Station.*

(as) clean as a whistle very clean. □ *The wound isn't infected. It's clean as a whistle. □ I thought the car would be filthy, but it was as clean as a whistle.*

(as) clear as crystal 1. very clear; transparent. □ *The stream was as clear as crystal. □ She cleaned the windowpane until it was clear as crystal.* **2.** very clear; easy to understand. □ *The explanation was as clear as crystal. □ Her lecture was not clear as crystal, but at least it was not dull.*

(as) clear as mud not understandable. (Informal.) □ *Your explanation is as clear as mud. □ This doesn't make sense. It's clear as mud.*

(as) comfortable as an old shoe very comfortable; very comforting and familiar. □ *This old house is fine. It's as comfortable as an old shoe. □ That's a great tradition—comfortable as an old shoe.*

(as) cool as a cucumber calm and not agitated; with one's wits about one. (Informal.) □ *The captain remained as cool as a cucumber as the passengers boarded the lifeboats. □ During the fire the homeowner was cool as a cucumber.*

(as) crazy as a loon very silly; completely insane. (Folksy.) □ *If you think you can get away with that, you're as crazy as a loon. □ Poor old John is crazy as a loon.*

(as) dead as a dodo dead; no longer in existence. (Informal.) □ *Yes, Adolf Hitler is really dead—as dead as* *a dodo.* □ *That silly old idea is dead as a dodo.*

(as) dead as a doornail dead. (Informal.) □ *This fish is as dead as a doornail.* □ *John kept twisting the chicken's neck even though it was dead as a doornail.*

(as) different as night and day completely different. □ *Although Bobby and Billy are twins, they are as different as night and day.* □ *Birds and bats appear to be similar, but they are different as night and day.*

(as) dry as dust 1. very dry. □ *The bread is as dry as dust.* □ *When the leaves are dry as dust, they break into powder easily.* **2.** very dull; very boring. □ *This book is as dry as dust. I am going to stop reading it.* □ *Her lecture was dry as dust — just like her subject.*

(as) dull as dishwater AND **(as) dull as ditchwater** very uninteresting. □ *I'm not surprised that he can't find a partner. He's as dull as dishwater.* □ *Mr. Black's speech was as dull as dishwater.*

(as) dull as ditchwater See the previous entry.

(as) easy as (apple) pie very easy. (Informal.) □ *Mountain climbing is as easy as pie.* □ *Making a simple dress out of cotton cloth is easy as pie.*

(as) easy as duck soup very easy; requiring no effort. (Informal. When a duck is cooked, it releases a lot of fat and juices, making a "soup" without effort.) □ *Finding your way to the shopping center is easy as duck soup.* □ *Getting Bob to eat fried chicken is as easy as duck soup.*

(as) easy as falling off a log AND **(as) easy as rolling off a log** very easy. (Folksy.) □ *Passing that exam was as easy as falling off a log.* □ *Getting out of jail was easy as rolling off a log.*

(as) easy as rolling off a log See the previous entry.

(as) far as anyone knows AND **so far as anyone knows** to the limits of anyone's knowledge. (Informal. The *anyone* can be replaced with a more specific noun or pronoun.) □ *As far as anyone knows, this is the last of the great herds of buffalo.* □ *Far as I know, this is the best one.* □ *These are the only keys to the house so far as anyone knows.*

as far as it goes as much as something does, covers, or accomplishes. (Usually said of something that is inadequate.) □ *Your plan is fine as far as it goes. It doesn't seem to take care of everything, though.* □ *As far as it goes, this law is a good one. It should require stiffer penalties, however.*

as far as possible AND **so far as possible** as much as possible; to whatever degree is possible. □ *We must try, as far as possible, to get people to stop smoking in buses.* □ *As far as possible, the police will issue tickets to all speeding drivers.* □ *I'll follow your instructions so far as possible.*

(as) far as someone or something is concerned AND **so far as someone or something is concerned 1.** [with *someone*] for all that someone cares; if someone is to make the decision. □ *You can take your old dog and leave as far as I'm concerned.* □ *Far as I'm concerned, you can get out and never come back.* □ *So far as I'm concerned, you're okay.* **2.** [with *something*] having to do with something; pertaining to something; as for something. □ *This bill? As far as that's concerned, the committee will have to take care of it.* □ *As far as the roof's concerned, it will just have to last another year.*

(as) fit as a fiddle healthy and physically fit. □ *Mary is as fit as a fiddle.* □ *Tom used to be fit as a fiddle. Look at him now!*

(as) flat as a pancake very flat. (Informal.) □ *The punctured tire was as flat as a pancake.* □ *Bobby squashed the ant flat as a pancake.*

as for someone or something 1. AND **as to someone or something** regarding someone or something. □ *As for the mayor, he can pay for his own dinner.* □ *As for you, Bobby, there will be no dessert tonight.* □ *As for this chair,* *there is nothing to do but throw it away.* □ *As to your idea about building a new house, forget it.* **2.** [with *someone*] quoting someone; speaking for someone. □ *As for me, I prefer vegetables to meat.* □ *As for Tom, he refuses to attend the concert.*

(as) free as a bird carefree; completely free. □ *Jane is always happy and free as a bird.* □ *The convict escaped from jail and was as free as a bird for two days.* □ *In the summer I feel free as a bird.*

(as) fresh as a daisy very fresh; fresh and alert. □ *The morning dew was as fresh as a daisy.* □ *Sally was fresh as a daisy and cheerful as could be.*

(as) full as a tick AND **(as) tight as a tick** very full of food or drink. (Informal. Refers to a tick that has filled itself full of blood.) □ *Little Billy ate and ate until he was as tight as a tick.* □ *Our cat drank the cream until he became full as a tick.*

(as) funny as a barrel of monkeys AND **more fun than a barrel of monkeys** very funny. (Almost the same as *as much fun as a barrel of monkeys.*) □ *Todd was as funny as a barrel of monkeys.* □ *The entire evening was funny as a barrel of monkeys.* □ *The party was more fun than a barrel of monkeys.*

(as) funny as a crutch not funny at all. □ *Your trick is about as funny as a crutch. Nobody thought it was funny.* □ *The well-dressed lady slipped and fell in the gutter, which was funny as a crutch.*

(as) good as done the same as being done; almost done. (Many different past participles can replace *done* in this phrase: *cooked, dead, finished, painted, typed,* etc.) □ *This job is as good as done. It'll just take another second.* □ *Yes, sir, if you hire me to paint your house, it's as good as painted.* □ *When I hand my secretary a letter to be typed, I know that it's as good as typed right then and there.*

(as) good as gold genuine; authentic. □ *Mary's promise is as good as gold.*

□ *Yes, this diamond is genuine — good as gold.*

as good as one's word obedient to one's promise; dependable in keeping one's promises. □ *He was as good as his word. He lent me the books as promised.* □ *She said she would baby-sit and she was as good as her word.*

(as) happy as a clam happy and content. (Note the variations in the examples.) □ *Tom sat there smiling, as happy as a clam.* □ *There they all sat, eating corn on the cob and looking happy as clams.*

(as) happy as a lark visibly happy and cheerful. (Note the variations in the examples.) □ *Sally walked along whistling, as happy as a lark.* □ *The children danced and sang, happy as larks.*

(as) hard as nails very hard; cold and cruel. (Refers to the nails that are used with a hammer.) □ *The old loaf of bread was dried out and became as hard as nails.* □ *Ann was unpleasant and hard as nails.*

(as) high as a kite AND **(as) high as the sky 1.** very high. □ *The tree grew as high as a kite.* □ *Our pet bird got outside and flew up high as the sky.* **2.** drunk or drugged. □ *Bill drank beer until he got as high as a kite.* □ *The thieves were high as the sky on drugs.*

(as) high as the sky See the previous entry.

(as) hot as hell very hot. (Informal. Use *hell* with caution.) □ *It's as hot as hell outside. It must be near 100 degrees.* □ *I hate to get into a car that has been parked in the sun. It's hot as hell.*

(as) hungry as a bear very hungry. (Informal.) □ *I'm as hungry as a bear. I could eat anything!* □ *Whenever I jog, I get hungry as a bear.*

(as) innocent as a lamb guiltless; naive. □ *"Hey! You can't throw me in jail,"* cried the robber. *"I'm innocent as a lamb."* □ *Look at the baby, as innocent as a lamb.*

as it were as one might say. (Sometimes used to qualify an assertion that may not sound reasonable.) □ *He carefully constructed, as it were, a huge sandwich.* □ *The Franklins live in a small, as it were, exquisite house.*

(as) large as life in person; actually, and sometimes surprisingly, present at a place. □ *I thought Jack was away, but there he was as large as life.* □ *Jean was not expected to appear, but she turned up large as life.*

(as) light as a feather of little weight. □ *Sally dieted until she was as light as a feather.* □ *Of course I can lift the box. It's light as a feather.*

(as) likely as not probably; with an even chance either way. □ *He will as likely as not arrive without warning.* □ *Likely as not, the game will be canceled.*

as long as 1. AND **so long as** since; because. □ *As long as you're going to the bakery, please buy some fresh bread.* □ *So long as you're here, please stay for dinner.* **2.** AND **so long as** if; only if. □ *You may have dessert so long as you eat all your vegetables.* □ *You can go out this evening as long as you promise to be home by midnight.* **3.** for a specified length of time. □ *You may stay out as long as you like.* □ *I didn't go to school as long as Bill did.*

as luck would have it by good or bad luck; as it turned out; by chance. □ *As luck would have it, we had a flat tire.* □ *As luck would have it, the check came in the mail today.*

(as) mad as a hatter 1. crazy. (From the crazy character called the Hatter in Lewis Carroll's *Alice's Adventures in Wonderland.*) □ *Poor old John is as mad as a hatter.* □ *All these screaming children are driving me mad as a hatter.* **2.** angry. (This is a misunderstanding of *mad* in the first sense. Folksy. The first *as* can be omitted.) □ *You make me so angry! I'm as mad as a hatter.* □ *John can't control his temper. He's always mad as a hatter.*

(as) mad as a hornet angry. □ *You make me so angry. I'm as mad as a hornet.* □ *Jane can get mad as a hornet when somebody criticizes her.*

(as) mad as a March hare crazy. (From the name of a character in Lewis Carroll's *Alice's Adventures in Wonderland.*) □ *Sally is getting as mad as a March hare.* □ *My Uncle Bill is mad as a March hare.*

(as) mad as a wet hen angry. (Folksy.) □ *Bob was screaming and shouting— as mad as a wet hen.* □ *What you said made Mary mad as a wet hen.*

(as) mad as hell very angry. (Informal. Use *hell* with caution.) □ *He made his wife as mad as hell.* □ *Those terrorists make me mad as hell.*

as much fun as a barrel of monkeys a great deal of fun. (Almost the same as *(as) funny as a barrel of monkeys.*) □ *Roger is as much fun as a barrel of monkeys.* □ *The circus was as much fun as a barrel of monkeys.*

(as) naked as a jaybird naked. □ *"Billy," called Mrs. Franklin, "get back in the house and get some clothes on. You're as naked as a jaybird."* □ *Tom had to get naked as a jaybird for the doctor to examine him.*

(as) nutty as a fruitcake silly; crazy. (Slang. A fruitcake usually has lots of nuts in it.) □ *Whenever John goes to a party, he gets as nutty as a fruitcake.* □ *Sally has been acting as nutty as a fruitcake lately.*

(as) old as the hills very old. □ *The children think their mother's as old as the hills, but she's only forty.* □ *That song's not new. It's old as the hills.*

as one as if a group were one person. (Especially with *act*, *move*, or *speak*.) □ *All the dancers moved as one.* □ *The chorus spoke as one.*

(as) plain as day (Informal.) **1.** very plain and simple. □ *Although his face was as plain as day, his smile made him look interesting and friendly.* □ *Our house is plain as day, but it's comfortable.* **2.** clear and understandable. □ *The lecture was as plain as day. No one* *had to ask questions.* □ *His statement was plain as day.*

(as) plain as the nose on one's face obvious; clearly evident. (Informal.) □ *What do you mean you don't understand? It's as plain as the nose on your face.* □ *Your guilt is plain as the nose on your face.*

(as) pleased as punch very pleased; very pleased with oneself. (Refers to the character Punch in [English] Punch and Judy shows. *Punch* is sometimes capitalized.) □ *Wally was as pleased as punch when he won the prize.* □ *She seems pleased as punch, but she knows she doesn't deserve the award.*

(as) poor as a church mouse very poor. □ *My aunt is as poor as a church mouse.* □ *The Browns are poor as church mice.*

(as) pretty as a picture very pretty. □ *Sweet little Mary is as pretty as a picture.* □ *Their new house is pretty as a picture.*

(as) proud as a peacock very proud; haughty. □ *John is so arrogant. He's as proud as a peacock.* □ *The new father was proud as a peacock.*

(as) quick as a flash See the following entry.

(as) quick as a wink AND **(as) quick as a flash** very quickly. □ *As quick as a wink, the thief took the lady's purse.* □ *I'll finish this work quick as a wink.* □ *The dog grabbed the meat as quick as a flash.* □ *The summer days went by quick as a flash.*

(as) quick as greased lightning very quickly; very fast. (Folksy. See also *like greased lightning.*) □ *Jane can really run. She's as quick as greased lightning.* □ *Quick as greased lightning, the thief stole my wallet.*

(as) quiet as a mouse very quiet; shy and silent. (Informal. Often used with children.) □ *Don't yell; whisper. Be as quiet as a mouse.* □ *Mary hardly ever says anything. She's quiet as a mouse.*

(as) quiet as the grave very quiet; silent. □ *The house is as quiet as the grave when the children are at school.* □ *This town is quiet as the grave now that the offices have closed.*

(as) regular as clockwork dependably regular. (Informal.) □ *She comes into this store every day, as regular as clockwork.* □ *Our tulips come up every year, regular as clockwork.*

(as) right as rain correct; genuine. (Folksy.) □ *Your answer is as right as rain.* □ *John is very dependable. He's right as rain.*

(as) scarce as hens' teeth AND **scarcer than hens' teeth** very scarce or nonexistent. (Chickens don't have teeth.) □ *I've never seen one of those. They're as scarce as hens' teeth.* □ *I was told that the part needed for my car is scarcer than hens' teeth, and it would take a long time to find one.*

(as) sharp as a razor 1. very sharp. □ *The penknife is sharp as a razor.* □ *The carving knife will have to be as sharp as a razor to cut through this meat.* **2.** very sharp-witted or intelligent. □ *The old man's senile, but his wife is as sharp as a razor.* □ *Don't say too much in front of the child. She's as sharp as a razor.*

(as) sick as a dog very sick; sick and vomiting. □ *We've never been so ill. The whole family was sick as dogs.* □ *Sally was as sick as a dog and couldn't go to the party.*

(as) slick as a whistle quickly and cleanly; quickly and skillfully. □ *Tom took a broom and a mop and cleaned the place up as slick as a whistle.* □ *Slick as a whistle, Sally pulled off the bandage.*

(as) slippery as an eel devious; undependable. □ *Tom can't be trusted. He's as slippery as an eel.* □ *It's hard to catch Joe in his office because he's slippery as an eel.*

(as) sly as a fox smart and clever. □ *My nephew is as sly as a fox.* □ *You have to be sly as a fox to outwit me.*

(as) snug as a bug in a rug cozy and snug. (Informal. The kind of thing said when putting a child to bed.) □ *Let's pull up the covers. There you are, Bobby, as snug as a bug in a rug.* □ *What a lovely little house! I know I'll be snug as a bug in a rug.*

(as) sober as a judge **1.** very formal, somber, or stuffy. □ *You certainly look gloomy, Bill. You're sober as a judge.* □ *Tom's as sober as a judge. I think he's angry.* **2.** not drunk; alert and completely sober. □ *John's drunk? No, he's as sober as a judge.* □ *You should be sober as a judge when you drive a car.*

(as) soft as a baby's bottom very soft and smooth to the touch. □ *This cloth is as soft as a baby's bottom.* □ *No, Bob doesn't shave yet. His cheeks are soft as a baby's bottom.*

(as) soon as possible at the earliest time. □ *I'm leaving now. I'll be there as soon as possible.* □ *Please pay me as soon as possible.*

(as) sound as a dollar **1.** very secure and dependable. □ *This investment is as sound as a dollar.* □ *I wouldn't put my money in a bank that isn't sound as a dollar.* **2.** sturdy and well-constructed. (An extension of sense 1.) □ *This house is as sound as a dollar.* □ *The garage is still sound as a dollar. Why tear it down?*

(as) steady as a rock very steady and unmovable; very stable. □ *His hand was steady as a rock as he pulled the trigger of the revolver.* □ *You must remain as steady as a rock when you are arguing with your supervisor.*

(as) strong as an ox very strong. □ *Tom lifts weights and is as strong as an ox.* □ *Now that Ann has recovered from her illness, she's strong as an ox.*

(as) stubborn as a mule very stubborn. □ *My husband is as stubborn as a mule.* □ *Our cat is stubborn as a mule.*

as the crow flies straight across the land, as opposed to distances measured on a road, river, etc. (Folksy.) □ *It's twenty miles to town on the highway, but only ten miles as the crow flies.* □ *Our house is only a few miles from the lake as the crow flies.*

(as) thick as pea soup very thick. (Informal. Usually used in reference to fog.) □ *This fog is as thick as pea soup.* □ *Wow, this coffee is strong! It's thick as pea soup.*

(as) thick as thieves very close-knit; friendly; allied. □ *Mary, Tom, and Sally are as thick as thieves. They go everywhere together.* □ *Those two families are thick as thieves.*

(as) tight as a tick See *(as) full as a tick.*

(as) tight as Dick's hatband very tight. □ *I've got to lose some weight. My belt is as tight as Dick's hatband.* □ *This window is stuck tight as Dick's hatband.*

as to someone or something See under *as for someone or something.*

(as) tough as old boots **1.** very tough. □ *This meat is tough as old boots.* □ *Bob couldn't eat the steak. It was as tough as old boots.* **2.** very strong; not easily moved by feelings such as pity. □ *Margaret is never off work. She's as tough as old boots.* □ *Don't expect sympathy from the boss. She's tough as old boots.*

(as) ugly as sin very ugly. □ *The new building is as ugly as sin.* □ *The old woman is ugly as sin, but she dresses beautifully.*

(as) warm as toast very warm and cozy. □ *The baby will be warm as toast in that blanket.* □ *We were as warm as toast by the side of the fire.*

(as) weak as a kitten weak; weak and sickly. □ *John is as weak as a kitten because he doesn't eat well.* □ *Oh! Suddenly I feel weak as a kitten.*

(as) white as a sheet very pale. □ *Jane was white as a sheet for weeks after her illness.* □ *Mary went as white as a sheet when she heard the news.*

(as) white as the driven snow very white. □ *I like my bed sheets to be as white as the driven snow.* □ *We have a* *new kitten whose fur is white as the driven snow.*

(as) wise as an owl very wise. □ *Grandfather is as wise as an owl.* □ *My goal is to be wise as an owl.*

aside from someone or something not including someone or something. □ *Aside from a small bank account, I have no money at all.* □ *Aside from Mary, I have no friends.*

ask for something to do something that will cause trouble. (Also literal.) □ *Don't talk to me that way! You're really asking for it.* □ *Anyone who acts like that is just asking for a good talking to.*

ask for the moon to ask for too much; to make great demands. □ *When you're trying to get a job, it's unwise to ask for the moon.* □ *Please lend me the money. I'm not asking for the moon!*

ask for trouble AND **look for trouble** to seem to be trying to get into trouble; to do something that would cause trouble; to do or say something that will cause trouble. □ *Stop talking to me that way, John. You're just asking for trouble.* □ *The guard asked me to leave unless I was looking for trouble.* □ *Anybody who threatens a police officer is just asking for trouble.* □ *You're looking for trouble if you ask the boss for a raise.*

ask someone out to ask a person for a date. □ *Mary hopes that John will ask her out.* ⊤ *John doesn't want to ask out his best friend's girl.*

asleep at the switch not attending to one's job; failing to do one's duty at the proper time. □ *The guard was asleep at the switch when the robber broke in.* □ *If I hadn't been asleep at the switch, I'd have seen the stolen car.*

assault and battery a violent attack [upon someone] followed by a beating. (A criminal charge. Fixed order.) □ *Max was charged with two counts of assault and battery.* □ *Dave does not go out at night because he does not want to be a victim of assault and battery.*

at a loss (for words) unable to speak; speechless; befuddled. □ *I was so sur-prised that I was at a loss for words.* □ *Tom was terribly confused—really at a loss.*

at a premium at a high price; priced high because of something special. □ *Sally bought the shoes at a premium because they were of very high quality.* □ *This model of car is selling at a premium because so many people want to buy it.*

at a set time at a particular time; at an assigned time. □ *Each person has to show up at a set time.* □ *Do I have to be there at a set time, or can I come whenever I want?*

at a sitting at one time; during one period. (Usually refers to an activity that takes place while a person is seated.) □ *The restaurant could feed only sixty people at a sitting.* □ *I can read about 300 pages at a sitting.*

at a snail's pace very slowly. □ *When you watch a clock, time seems to move at a snail's pace.* □ *You always eat at a snail's pace. I'm tired of waiting for you.*

at a stretch continuously; without stopping. □ *We all had to do eight hours of duty at a stretch.* □ *The baby doesn't sleep for more than three hours at a stretch.*

at all without distinguishing; without qualification. (See the examples for word order variations.) □ *It really wasn't very cold at all.* □ *It really wasn't at all cold.* □ *Tom will eat anything at all.* □ *Jane isn't at all hungry.* □ *Grandma was always ready to go anywhere at all.*

at all costs AND **at any cost** regardless of the difficulty or cost; no matter what. □ *I intend to have that car at all costs.* □ *I'll get there by six o'clock at all costs.* □ *Mary was going to get that job at any cost.*

at all times constantly; continuously. □ *You must keep your passport handy at all times when you are traveling in a foreign country.* □ *When you're in a crowd, you must watch your child at all times.*

at an early date soon; some day soon. □ *The note said, "Please call me at an early date."* □ *You're expected to return the form to the office at an early date.*

at any cost See *at all costs.*

at any rate anyway. (Informal. Frequently used as an introduction to a conclusion or a final statement. Also literal.) □ *At any rate, we had a nice time at your party. We are grateful that you asked us.* □ *It's not much, at any rate, but it's the best we can do.*

at best AND **at most** in the best view; in the most positive judgment; as the best one can say. □ *I believe her to be totally negligent. Her actions were careless at best.* □ *At best we found their visit pleasantly short.* □ *The dinner was not at all pleasant. At best the food was not burned.* □ *At most she was careless, but not criminal.* □ *We found their visit pleasingly short at most.*

at close range very near; in close proximity. (Usually used in regard to shooting.) □ *The hunter fired at the deer at close range.* □ *The powder burns tell us that the gun was fired at close range.*

at cross-purposes with opposing purposes; with goals that interfere with each other. □ *We are arguing at cross-purposes. We aren't even discussing the same thing.* □ *Bill and Tom are working at cross-purposes. They'll never get the job done right.*

at death's door near death. (Euphemistic.) □ *I was so ill that I was at death's door.* □ *The family dog was at death's door for three days, and then it finally died.*

at ease relaxed and comfortable. □ *I don't feel at ease driving when there is a lot of traffic.* □ *Mary is most at ease when she's near the sea.*

at every turn everywhere; everywhere one looks. □ *There is a new problem at every turn.* □ *Life holds new adventures at every turn.*

at face value from outward appearance; from what something first appears to be. (From the value printed on the "face" of a coin or bank note.) □ *Don't just accept her offer at face value. Think of the implications.* □ *Joan tends to take people at face value and so she is always getting hurt.*

at first initially; at the beginning. □ *He was shy at first. Then he became more friendly.* □ *At first we chose the red one. Later we switched to the blue one.*

at first blush See the following entry.

at first glance AND **at first blush** when first examined; at an early stage. □ *At first glance, the problem appeared quite simple. Later we learned just how complex it really was.* □ *He appeared quite healthy at first glance.* □ *At first blush, she appeared to be quite old.*

(at) full blast using full power; as loudly as possible. □ *The neighbors had their televisions on at full blast.* □ *The car radio was on full blast. We couldn't hear what the driver was saying.*

at full speed AND **at full tilt** as fast as possible. □ *The motor was running at full speed.* □ *John finished his running at full speed.* □ *Things are now operating at full tilt.*

at full tilt See the previous entry.

at half-mast halfway up or down. (Primarily referring to flags. Can be used for things other than flags as a joke.) □ *The flag was flying at half-mast because the general had died.* □ *Americans fly flags at half-mast on Memorial Day.* □ *The little boy ran out of the house with his pants at half-mast.*

at hand close by. (Used with both time and distance. See also *close at hand; near at hand.*) □ *I don't happen to have your application at hand at the moment.* □ *With the holiday season at hand, everyone is very excited.*

at home at or in one's dwelling. □ *Is Mary at home, or is she still at work?* □ *What time will she be at home?*

at home with someone or something comfortable with someone or something; comfortable doing something. (See also *feel at home.*) □ *Tom is very much at home with my parents.* □ *Sally seems to be very much at home with her car.* □ *Mary seems to be at home with her job.*

at it again doing something again. (Informal.) □ *I asked Tom to stop playing his trumpet, but he's at it again.* □ *They are at it again. Why are they always fighting?*

at large **1.** free; uncaptured. (Usually said of criminals running loose.) □ *At noon the day after the robbery, the thieves were still at large.* □ *There is a murderer at large in the city.* **2.** in general; according to a general sample. □ *Truck drivers at large don't like the new law.* □ *Students at large felt that the rule was too strict.* **3.** representing the whole group rather than its subsections. (Always refers to a special kind of elective office.) □ *He ran for representative at large.* □ *She represented shareholders at large on the governing board.*

at least **1.** no less than; no fewer than. □ *There were at least four people there that I knew.* □ *I want to spend at least three weeks in Mexico.* **2.** anyway; in spite of difficulties. □ *At least we had a good evening, even though the afternoon was rainy.* □ *At least we came away with some of our money left.*

at leisure **1.** resting; not working. □ *What do you usually do when you are at leisure?* □ *During the summer when you are at leisure, you ought to play golf.* **2.** AND **at one's leisure** at one's convenience. □ *Choose one or the other at your leisure.* □ *Please drop by at your leisure.*

at length **1.** after some time; finally. □ *At length, the roses bloomed, and the tomatoes ripened.* □ *And at length, the wizard spoke.* **2.** AND **at some length** for quite a long time. □ *He spoke on and on at some length.* □ *He described the history of his village at length.*

at liberty free; unrestrained. □ *The criminal was set at liberty by the judge.* □ *You're at liberty to go anywhere you wish.* □ *I'm not at liberty to discuss the matter.*

at loggerheads (with someone) in opposition; at an impasse; in a quarrel. □ *Mr. and Mrs. Franklin have been at loggerheads for years.* □ *The two political parties were at loggerheads during the entire legislative session.* □ *She was at loggerheads with him for years.*

at (long) last after a long wait; finally. □ *At last the hostages were released.* □ *Sally earned her diploma at long last.*

at loose ends restless and unsettled; unemployed. □ *Just before school starts, all the children are at loose ends.* □ *When Tom is home on the weekends, he's always at loose ends.* □ *Jane has been at loose ends ever since she lost her job.*

at most See *at best.*

at odds (with someone) in opposition to someone; *at loggerheads (with someone).* □ *Mary is always at odds with her father about how late she can stay out.* □ *John and his father are always at odds too.*

at once immediately; at this very moment. □ *John, come here at once!* □ *Bring me my coffee at once!* □ *Shall I do it at once or wait until morning?*

at one fell swoop AND **in one fell swoop** in a single incident; as a single event. (This phrase preserves the old word *fell,* meaning "terrible" or "deadly.") □ *The party guests ate up all the snacks at one fell swoop.* □ *When the stock market crashed, many large fortunes were wiped out in one fell swoop.*

at one's best in the best of health; displaying the most civilized behavior. (Often in the negative.) □ *I'm not at my best when I'm angry.* □ *He's at his best after a good nap.*

at one's leisure See under *at leisure.*

at one's wit's end at the limits of one's mental resources. □ *I'm at my wit's* *end with this problem. I cannot figure it out.* □ *Tom could do no more. He was at his wit's end.*

at present now; at this point in time. □ *We are not able to do any more at present.* □ *We may be able to lend you money next week, but not at present.*

at random without sequence or order. □ *Sally picked four names at random from the telephone book.* □ *The gunman walked into the crowded restaurant and fired at random.* □ *Jane will read almost anything. She selects four novels at random at the library each week and reads them all.*

at sea (about something) See *(all) at sea (about something).*

at sixes and sevens disorderly; lost and bewildered; *at loose ends.* (Fixed order.) □ *Mrs. Smith is at sixes and sevens since the death of her husband.* □ *Bill is always at sixes and sevens when he's home by himself.*

at some length See under *at length.*

at someone's beck and call ready to obey someone. (Fixed order.) □ *What makes you think I wait around here at your beck and call? I live here too, you know!* □ *It was a fine hotel. There were dozens of maids and waiters at our beck and call.*

at someone's doorstep AND **on someone's doorstep** in someone's care; as someone's responsibility. □ *Why do you always have to lay your problems at my doorstep?* □ *I shall put this issue on someone else's doorstep.* □ *I don't want it on my doorstep.*

at someone's earliest convenience as soon as it is easy or convenient for someone. (This is also a polite way of saying *immediately.*) □ *Please stop by my office at your earliest convenience.* □ *Bill, please have the oil changed at your earliest convenience.*

at someone's mercy See *at the mercy of someone.*

at someone's request due to someone's request; on being asked by someone. □ *At his mother's request, Tom stopped*

playing the saxophone. □ *At the request of the police officer, Bill pulled his car over to the side of the road.*

at sometime sharp exactly at a named time. □ *You must be here at noon sharp.* □ *The plane is expected to arrive at seven forty-five sharp.*

at stake to be won or lost; at risk; hanging in the balance. □ *That's a very risky investment. How much money is at stake?* □ *I have everything at stake on this wager.*

at that rate in that manner; at that speed. (See also *at this rate.*) □ *If things keep progressing at that rate, we'll be rich by next year.* □ *At that rate we'll never get the money that is owed us.*

at the appointed time at the announced or assigned time. □ *The cab pulled up in the driveway at the appointed time.* □ *We all met at the hotel at the appointed time.*

at the bottom of the hour on the half hour; the opposite of *at the top of the hour.* (Typically heard on television or the radio.) □ *Hear the news on WNAG at the bottom of the hour.* □ *We will have an interview with Harry Kravitz at the bottom of the hour.*

at the bottom of the ladder at the lowest level of pay and status. □ *Most people start work at the bottom of the ladder.* □ *When Ann got fired, she had to start all over again at the bottom of the ladder.*

at the break of dawn See the following entry.

at the crack of dawn AND **at the break of dawn** at the earliest light of the day. □ *Jane was always up at the crack of dawn.* □ *The birds start singing at the break of dawn.*

at the drop of a hat immediately and without urging. □ *John was always ready to go fishing at the drop of a hat.* □ *If you need help, just call on me. I can come at the drop of a hat.*

at the eleventh hour at the last possible moment. (See also *eleventh-hour* decision.) □ *She always turned her term papers in at the eleventh hour.* □ *We don't worry about death until the eleventh hour.*

at the end of nowhere at a remote place; at some distance from civilization. □ *They live way out in the country at the end of nowhere.* □ *The police will never find us here at the end of nowhere.*

at the end of one's rope AND **at the end of one's tether** at the limits of one's endurance. □ *I'm at the end of my rope! I just can't go on this way!* □ *These kids are driving me out of my mind. I'm at the end of my tether.*

at the end of one's tether See the previous entry.

at the end of the day when everything else has been taken into consideration. (Also literal.) □ *At the end of the day you will have to decide where you want to live.* □ *The committee interviewed many applicants for the post, but at the end of the day made no appointment.*

at the expense of someone or something to the detriment of someone or something; to the harm of someone or something. □ *He had a good laugh at the expense of his brother.* □ *He took a job in a better place at the expense of a larger income.*

at the last gasp at the very last; at the last chance; at the last minute. (Refers to someone's last breath before death.) □ *She finally showed up at the last gasp, bringing the papers that were needed.* □ *We got there at the last gasp, just before our names were called.*

at the last minute at the last possible chance. (Compare with *at the eleventh hour.*) □ *Please don't make reservations at the last minute.* □ *Why do you ask all your questions at the last minute?*

at the latest no later than. □ *Please pay this bill in ten days at the latest.* □ *I'll be home by midnight at the latest.*

at the mercy of someone AND **at someone's mercy** under the control of someone; without defense against someone. □ *We were left at the mercy of the arresting officer.* □ *Mrs. Franklin wanted Mr. Franklin at her mercy.*

at the outset at the beginning. (See also *from the outset.*) □ *It seemed like a very simple problem at the outset.* □ *At the outset, they were very happy. Then they had money problems.*

at the point of doing something See *on the point of doing something.*

at the present time AND **at this point (in time)** now; *at present.* (Used often as a wordy replacement for *now.*) □ *We don't know the location of the stolen car at the present time.* □ *The tomatoes are doing nicely at the present time.* □ *At this point in time, we feel very sad about his death.* □ *Yes, it's sad, but there is nothing we can do at this point.*

at the same time nevertheless; however. (Also literal.) □ *Bill was able to make the car payment. At the same time, he was very angry about the bill.* □ *We agree to your demands. At the same time, we object strongly to your methods.*

at the top of one's lungs See the following entry.

at the top of one's voice AND **at the top of one's lungs** with a very loud voice. □ *Bill called to Mary at the top of his voice.* □ *How can I work when you're all talking at the top of your lungs?*

at the top of the hour at the exact beginning of the hour. (Typically heard on television or the radio. See also *at the bottom of the hour.*) □ *Every class in my school starts at the top of the hour.* □ *Our next newscast will be at the top of the hour.*

at the (very) outside at the very most. □ *The car repairs will cost $300 at the outside.* □ *I'll be there in three weeks at the outside.*

at (the) worst in the worst view; in the most negative judgment; as the worst one can say about something. □ *At worst, Tom can be seen as greedy.* □

Ann will receive a ticket for careless driving, at the worst.

at this juncture at this point; at this pause. □ *There is little more that I can say at this juncture.* □ *We can, if you wish, at this juncture, request a change in venue.*

at this point (in time) See *at the present time.*

at this rate at this speed. (Compare with *at any rate* and *at that rate*.) □ *Hurry up! We'll never get there at this rate.* □ *At this rate, all the food will be gone before we get there.*

at this stage See the following entry.

at this stage of the game AND **at this stage** at the current point in some event; currently. (The first phrase is informal.) □ *We'll have to wait and see. There isn't much we can do at this stage of the game.* □ *At this stage, we are better off not calling the doctor.*

at times sometimes; occasionally. □ *I feel quite sad at times.* □ *At times, I wish I had never come here.*

at will whenever one wants; freely. (Compare with *at liberty*.) □ *You're free to come and go at will.* □ *The soldiers were told to fire their guns at will.* □ *You can eat anything you want at will.*

at work 1. working (at something); busy (with something). □ *Tom is at work on his project. He'll be finished in a minute.* □ *Don't disturb me when I'm busy at work.* **2.** at one's place of work. □ *I'm sorry to call you at work, but this is important.* □ *She's at work now. She'll be home at supper time.*

attract someone's attention to cause someone to take notice; to get someone's attention. □ *I called and waved to attract Ann's attention.* □ *A small yellow flower attracted my attention.*

augur well for someone or something to indicate or predict good things for someone or something. (Usually in the negative.) □ *This latest message does not augur well for the hostages.* □ *I am afraid that this does not augur well for the outcome of the election.*

avoid someone or something like the plague to avoid someone or something totally. (Informal.) □ *What's wrong with Bob? Everyone avoids him like the plague.* □ *I don't like opera. I avoid it like the plague.*

away from one's desk not available for a telephone conversation; not available to be seen. (Sometimes said by the person who answers a telephone in an office. It means that the person whom the caller wants is not immediately available due to personal or business reasons.) □ *I'm sorry, but Ann is away from her desk just now. Can you come back later?* □ *Tom is away from his desk, but if you leave your number, he will call you right back.*

AWOL See *absent without leave.*

B

babe in the woods a naive or innocent person; an inexperienced person. □ *Bill is a babe in the woods when it comes to dealing with plumbers.* □ *As a painter, Mary is fine, but she's a babe in the woods as a musician.*

back and fill to act indecisively; to change one's direction repeatedly; to reverse one's course. (Originally nautical, referring to alternately filling the sails with wind and releasing the wind. Fixed order.) □ *The president spent most of his speech backing and filling on the question of taxation.* □ *The other candidate was backing and filling on every issue, depending on whom she was addressing.*

back and forth backwards and forwards; first one way and then another way. (Compare with *to and fro*. Fixed order.) □ *The young man was pacing back and forth in the hospital waiting room.* □ *The pendulum on the clock swung back and forth.*

back down (from someone or something) AND **back off (from someone or something)** to yield to a person or a thing; to fail to carry through on a threat. □ *Jane backed down from her position on the budget.* □ *It's probably better to back down from someone than to have an argument.* □ *John agreed that it was probably better to back down than to risk getting shot.* □ *Bill doesn't like to back off from a fight.* □ *Sometimes it's better to back off than to get hurt.*

back East to or from the eastern United States, often the northeastern or New England states. (See also *down South*, *out West*, and *up North*. This is used even by people who have never been in the East.) □ *Sally felt that she had to get back East for a few days.* □ *Tom went to school back East, but his brother attended college in the Midwest.*

back in circulation **1.** [for a thing to be] available to the public again. (Said especially of things that are said to circulate, such as money, library books, and magazines.) □ *I've heard that gold coins are back in circulation in Europe.* □ *I would like to read* War and Peace. *Is it back in circulation, or is it still checked out?* **2.** [for a person to be] socially active again; dating again after a divorce or breakup with one's lover. (Informal.) □ *Now that Bill is a free man, he's back in circulation.* □ *Tom was in the hospital for a month, but now he's back in circulation.*

back of the beyond the most remote place; somewhere very remote. (Informal.) □ *John hardly ever comes to the city. He lives at the back of the beyond.* □ *Mary likes lively entertainment, but her husband likes to vacation in the back of the beyond.*

back off (from someone or something) See *back down (from someone or something)*.

back order something [for a merchant] to order something that is not in stock and then make delivery to the customer when the goods become available. (The merchant may hold your money until the order is filled.) □ *The store didn't have the replacement part for my vacuum cleaner, so the manager back ordered it for me.* □ *The* shop had to back order some of the items on my list.

back out (of something) to withdraw from something you have agreed to do; to break an agreement. (Also literal.) □ *The buyer tried to back out of the sale, but the seller wouldn't permit it.* □ *Please don't back out of our date.* □ *Mary backed out at the last minute.*

back someone or something up to support someone or something; to concur with someone. (Also literal.) □ *Please back me up in this argument.* ⊤ *I would like you to back up John in this discussion.*

back the wrong horse to support someone or something that cannot win or succeed. (Also literal, as in horse racing.) □ *I don't want to back the wrong horse, but it seems to me that Jed is the better candidate.* □ *Fred backed the wrong horse in the budget hearings.*

back-to-back 1. adjacent and touching backs. □ *They started the duel by standing back-to-back.* □ *Two people who stand back-to-back can manage to see in all directions.* **2.** following immediately. (Said of things or events.) □ *The doctor had appointments set up back-to-back all day long.* □ *I have three lecture courses back-to-back every day of the week.*

back to square one back to the beginning. (As with a board game. See also the following entry.) □ *Negotiations have broken down, and it's back to square one.* □ *We lost the appeal of the court case, so it's back to square one.*

back to the drawing board time to start over again; it is time to plan something over again. (Note the variations shown in the examples.) □ *It didn't work. Back to the drawing board.* □ *I flunked English this semester. Well, back to the old drawing board.*

back to the salt mines time to return to work, school, or something else that might be unpleasant. (The phrase implies that the speaker is a slave who works in the salt mines.) □ *It's eight o'clock. Time to go to work! Back to the* salt mines. □ *School starts in the fall, and then it's back to the salt mines again.*

bad blood (between people) unpleasant feelings or animosity between people. □ *There is bad blood between Fred and Jim. They cannot be civil to one another.* □ *There is no bad blood between us. I don't know why we should quarrel.*

bad-mouth someone or something to say bad things about someone or something; to libel someone. (Slang.) □ *Mr. Smith was always bad-mouthing Mrs. Smith. They didn't get along.* □ *John bad-mouths his car constantly because it doesn't run.*

bag and baggage AND **part and parcel** with one's luggage; with all one's possessions. (Informal. Fixed order. See also *part and parcel (of something)*.) □ *Sally showed up at our door bag and baggage one Sunday morning.* □ *All right, if you won't pay the rent, out with you, bag and baggage!* □ *Get all your stuff—part and parcel—out of here!*

bag of tricks a collection of special techniques or methods. □ *What have you got in your bag of tricks that could help me with this problem?* □ *Here comes Mother with her bag of tricks. I'm sure she can help us.*

bail out (of something) 1. to jump out of an airplane (with a parachute). □ *John still remembers the first time he bailed out of a plane.* □ *When we get to 8,000 feet, we'll all bail out and drift down together. We'll open our parachutes at 2,000 feet.* **2.** to abandon a situation; to get out of something. (Informal.) □ *John got tired of school, so he just bailed out.* □ *Please stay, Bill. You've been with us too long to bail out now.*

bail someone or something out 1. [with *someone*] to deposit a sum of money that allows someone to get out of jail while waiting for a trial. □ *John was in jail. I had to go down to the police station to bail him out.* ⊤ *You kids are always getting into trouble. Do you* *really expect me to bail out the whole gang of you every time you have a problem?* **2.** [with *something*] to remove water from the bottom of a boat by dipping or scooping. □ *Tom has to bail the boat out before we get in.* ⊤ *You should always bail out a boat before using it.* **3.** to rescue someone or something from trouble or difficulty. □ *The proposed law was in trouble, but Todd bailed it out at the last minute.* □ *I was going to be late with my report, but my roommate lent a hand and bailed me out at the last minute.*

bait and switch a deceptive merchandising practice where one product is advertised to get people's attention [the bait], but pressure is applied to get the customer to purchase a more expensive item. (Fixed order.) □ *Walter described the appliance store as bait and switch, since they never seemed to have in stock the bargains that they advertised.* □ *Max accused the merchant of bait and switch and stalked out of the store.*

balance the accounts 1. AND **balance the books** to determine through accounting that accounts are in balance, that all money is accounted for. □ *Jane was up all night balancing the accounts.* □ *The cashier was not allowed to leave the bank until the manager balanced the books.* **2.** to get even [with someone]. □ *Tom hit Bob. Bob balanced the accounts by breaking Tom's toy car.* □ *Once we have balanced the accounts, we can shake hands and be friends again.*

balance the books See under *balance the accounts.*

ball and chain a person's special burden; a job. (Usually considered slang. Fixed order. Prisoners are sometimes fettered with a chain attached to a leg on one end and a heavy metal ball on the other.) □ *Tom wanted to quit his job. He said he was tired of that old ball and chain.* □ *Mr. Franklin always referred to his wife as his ball and chain.*

ball of fire a very active and energetic person who always succeeds. (Usually considered slang.) □ *Sally is a real ball of fire — she works late every night.* □ *Ann is no ball of fire, but she does get the job done.*

balled up See *(all) balled up.*

bang one's head against a brick wall See *beat one's head against the wall.*

bank on something to count on something; to rely on something. □ *The weather service said it wouldn't rain, but I wouldn't bank on it.* □ *My word is to be trusted. You can bank on it.*

baptism of fire a first experience of something, usually something difficult or unpleasant. □ *My son's just had his first visit to the dentist. He stood up to the baptism of fire very well.* □ *Mary's had her baptism of fire as a teacher. She was assigned to the worst class in the school.*

bargain for something AND **bargain on something** to plan for something; to expect something. (Informal. Also literal.) □ *We knew it would be difficult, but we didn't bargain for this kind of trouble.* □ *I bargained on an easier time of it than this.*

bargain on something See the previous entry.

barge in (on someone or something) to break in on someone or something; to interrupt someone or something. □ *Oh! I'm sorry. I didn't mean to barge in on you.* □ *They barged in on the church service and caused a commotion.* □ *You can't just barge in like that!*

bark up the wrong tree to make the wrong choice; to ask the wrong person; to follow the wrong course. □ *If you think I'm the guilty person, you're barking up the wrong tree.* □ *The baseball players blamed their bad record on the pitcher, but they were barking up the wrong tree.*

base one's opinion on something to make a judgment or form an opinion from something. □ *You must not base your opinion on one bad experience.* □ *I base my opinion on many years of studying the problem.*

batten down the hatches to prepare for difficult times. (A nautical expression, meaning, literally, to seal the hatches against the arrival of a storm.) □ *Here comes that contentious Mrs. Jones. Batten down the hatches!* □ *Batten down the hatches, Congress is in session again.*

battle something out to argue something to a conclusion; to fight something to a conclusion. □ *The Senate and the House disagree on the bill, so they will have to battle a compromise out.* T *The two young toughs went into the alley to battle out their disagreement.*

bawl someone out to scold someone in a loud voice. □ *The teacher bawled the student out for arriving late.* T *Teachers don't usually bawl out students.*

be a cold fish to be a person who is distant and unfeeling. (Informal or slang.) □ *Bob is so dull—a real cold fish.* □ *She hardly ever speaks to anyone. She's a cold fish.*

be a copycat to be a person who copies or mimics what someone else does. (Usually juvenile.) □ *Sally wore a pink dress just like Mary's. Mary called Sally a copycat.* □ *Bill is such a copycat. He bought a coat just like mine.*

be a credit to someone or something to be of value or benefit to someone or something; to be of enough value or worth as to enhance someone or something. □ *I always want to be a credit to my school.* □ *John is not what you would call a credit to his family.*

be a drag (on someone) to be a burden to someone; to bore someone. (Slang.) □ *Mr. Franklin is a drag on Mrs. Franklin.* □ *Yes, I'd expect him to be a drag.*

be a fan of someone to be a follower of someone; to idolize someone. □ *My mother is still a fan of the Beatles.* □ *I'm a great fan of the mayor of the town.*

be a goner to be dead or finished; to be as good as dead or nearly dead. (In-

formal.) □ *The boy brought the sick fish back to the pet store to get his money back. "This one is a goner," he said.* □ *John thought he was a goner when his parachute didn't open.*

be a must to be something that you must do. (Informal.) □ *When you're in San Francisco, see the Golden Gate Bridge. It's a must.* □ *It's a must that you brush your teeth after every meal.*

be a past master at something to have been proven extremely good or skillful at an activity. □ *Mary is a past master at cooking omeletes.* □ *Pam is a past master at the art of complaining.*

be a sitting duck to be vulnerable to attack, physical or verbal. □ *You are a sitting duck out there. Get in here where the enemy cannot fire at you.* □ *The senator was a sitting duck because of his position on school reform.*

be a thorn in someone's side to be a constant bother or annoyance to someone. □ *This problem is a thorn in my side. I wish I had a solution to it.* □ *John was a thorn in my side for years before I finally got rid of him.*

be about something to get busy doing something, especially doing one's business. □ *It's eight o'clock, and it's time I was about my homework.* □ *Goodbye, Jane. I must be about my business.*

be-all and (the) end-all See *(the) be-all and (the) end-all.*

be all ears to be listening eagerly and carefully. (See also the following entry.) □ *Well, hurry up and tell me. I'm all ears.* □ *Be careful what you say. The children are all ears.*

be all eyes (and ears) to be alert for something to happen; to wait eagerly for something to happen or for someone or something to appear. (See also the previous entry.) □ *There they were, sitting at the table, all eyes. The birthday cake was soon to be served.* □ *Nothing can escape my notice. I'm all eyes and ears.*

be all things to all men AND **be all things to all people** [for someone or something] to be liked or used by all people; [for someone or something] to be everything that is wanted by all people. □ *You simply can't be all things to all people.* □ *The candidate set out to be all things to all men and came off looking very wishy-washy.*

be all things to all people See the previous entry.

be an unknown quantity to be a person or thing about which no one is certain. □ *John is an unknown quantity. We don't know how he's going to act.* □ *The new clerk is an unknown quantity. Things may not turn out all right.*

be at someone's service to be ready to help someone in any way. (Rarely literal. It probably indicates an offer of minimal help, except when said by a servant.) □ *The count greeted me warmly and said, "Welcome to my home. Just let me know what you need. I'm at your service."* □ *The desk clerk said, "Good morning, madam. I'm at your service."*

be behind in something AND **be behind on something** to have failed to do enough. □ *I'm behind in my car payments.* □ *She's behind on her work.*

be behind on something See the previous entry.

be beside oneself (with something) to be in an extreme state of some emotion. □ *I was beside myself with joy.* □ *Sarah could not speak. She was beside herself with anger.* □ *I laughed so hard I was beside myself.*

be curtains for someone or something to be the death, end, or ruin of someone or something. (Informal. From the lowering or closing of the curtains at the end of a stage performance.) □ *If the car hadn't swerved, it would have been curtains for the pedestrians.* □ *If they can't get into the export market, it's curtains for the whole company.*

be death on something to be very harmful to something. (Informal or slang.) □ *The salt they put on the roads in the winter is death on cars.* □ *That teacher is death on slow learners.*

be even steven to be even (with someone or something). (Informal or slang.) □ *Bill hit Tom; then Tom hit Bill. Now they are even steven.* □ *Mary paid Ann the $100 she owed her. Ann said, "Good, we are even steven."*

be flying high 1. to be very successful in one's ambitions; to obtain an important or powerful position. (Often with the implication that this will not last very long.) □ *The government is flying high just now, but wait until the budget is announced.* □ *He's flying high these days, but he comes from a very poor family.* **2.** to be in a state of euphoria. (From good news, success, or drugs.) □ *Wow! Todd is really flying high. Did he discover a gold mine?* □ *Sally is flying high. What's she on?*

be friends with someone to be a friend of someone. □ *Sally is friends with Bill.* □ *Mary and Bill are friends with one another.*

be from Missouri to require proof; to have to be shown (something). (From the nickname for the state of Missouri, the Show Me State.) □ *You'll have to prove it to me. I'm from Missouri.* □ *She's from Missouri and has to be shown.*

be into something to be interested in something; to be involved in something. (Slang.) □ *Did you hear? Tom is into skydiving!* □ *Too many people are into drugs.*

be (like) an open book to be someone or something that is easy to understand. □ *Jane's an open book. I always know what she is going to do next.* □ *The committee's intentions are an open book. They want to save money.*

be of age to be old enough to marry or to sign legal agreements. (See also *come of age.*) □ *Now that Mary is of age, she can buy her own car.* □ *When I'm of age, I'm going to get married and move to the city.*

be of service (to someone) to help someone; to serve someone. (A phrase often used by salesclerks. See also *be at someone's service.*) □

Good morning, madam. May I be of service to you? □ *Welcome to the Warwick Hotel. May I be of service?*

be off 1. to be spoiled; to be running incorrectly, as with a mechanical device. □ *Oh! I'm afraid that this meat is off. Don't eat it.* □ *I don't have the exact time. My watch is off.* 2. to leave; to depart. □ *Well, I must be off. Good-bye.* □ *The train leaves in an hour, so I must be off.*

be off on the wrong foot AND **be off to a bad start** to have started something with negative factors. (See also *get off on the wrong foot; get off to a bad start; start off on the wrong foot.*) □ *I'm sorry we are off to a bad start. I tried to be friendly.* □ *I hope that we won't be off to a bad start after our little argument.*

be off to a bad start See the previous entry.

be old hat to be old-fashioned; to be outmoded. (Informal.) □ *That's a silly idea. It's old hat.* □ *Nobody does that anymore. That's just old hat.*

be one's brother's keeper to be responsible for someone else. □ *I can't force these kids to go to school and get an education so they can get jobs. I am not my brother's keeper.* □ *You can't expect me to be my brother's keeper. Each of us should be responsible!*

be oneself again to be healthy again; to be calm again; to be restored. □ *After such a long illness, it's good to be myself again.* □ *I'm sorry that I lost my temper. I think I'm myself again now.*

be poles apart to be very different; to be far from coming to an agreement. □ *Mr. and Mrs. Jones don't get along well. They are poles apart.* □ *They'll never sign the contract because they are poles apart.*

be sick to vomit. (Euphemistic. Also with *get,* as in the examples. Also literal.) □ *Mommy, Billy just got sick on the floor.* □ *Oh, excuse me! I think I'm going to be sick.* □ *Bob was sick all over the carpet.*

be so See *be too.*

be that as it may even if what you say is true. □ *I am sorry to hear that, but, be that as it may, you still must carry out your responsibilities.* □ *Be that as it may, I still cannot help you.*

be the last person to be the most unlikely person of whom one could think in a particular situation; to be the most unlikely person to do something. □ *Bob was the last person for Tom to insult. He's so hot-tempered.* □ *Mary was the last person to ask to chair the meeting—she's so shy.*

be the spit and image of someone AND **be the spitting image of someone** to look very much like someone; to resemble someone very closely. (Folksy. The first version has fixed order. The second version is a frequent error.) □ *John is the spit and image of his father.* □ *I'm not the spit and image of anyone.* □ *At first, I thought you were saying spitting image.*

be the spitting image of someone See the previous entry.

be the teacher's pet to be the teacher's favorite student. □ *Sally is the teacher's pet. She always gets special treatment.* □ *The other students don't like the teacher's pet.*

be too AND **be so** to be something (despite anything to the contrary). (An emphatic form of *is, am, are, was, were.* See also *do too, have too.*) □ MOTHER: *Billy, you aren't old enough to be up this late.* BILLY: *I am too!* □ *I was so! I was there exactly when I said I would be!*

be well-disposed toward someone or something to feel positively toward someone or something; to feel favorable toward someone or something. □ *I do not think I will get a raise since the boss is not well-disposed toward me.* □ *The senators are well-disposed toward giving themselves a raise.*

be with someone to be on someone's side; to be allied with someone. (Also literal.) □ *Keep on trying, John. We* are all with you. □ *I'm with you in your efforts to win reelection.*

bear a grudge (against someone) AND **have a grudge (against someone); hold a grudge (against someone)** to have an old resentment for someone; to have continual anger for someone. (See also *nurse a grudge (against someone).*) □ *She bears a grudge against the judge who sentenced her.* □ *I have a grudge against my landlord for overcharging me.* □ *How long can a person hold a grudge? Let's be friends.*

bear fruit to yield results; to give (literal or figurative) fruit. □ *Our apple tree didn't bear fruit this year.* □ *I hope your new plan bears fruit.* □ *We've had many good ideas, but none of them has borne fruit.*

bear one's cross AND **carry one's cross** to carry or bear one's burden; to endure one's difficulties. (This is a biblical theme. It is always used figuratively except in the biblical context.) □ *It's a very bad disease, but I'll bear my cross.* □ *I can't help you with it. You'll just have to carry your cross.*

bear someone or something in mind See *keep someone or something in mind.*

bear something out to demonstrate or prove that something is right. □ *I hope that the facts will bear your story out.* ⊤ *I'm sure that the facts will bear out my story.*

bear the brunt (of something) to withstand the worst part or the strongest part of something, such as an attack. □ *I had to bear the brunt of her screaming and yelling.* □ *Why don't you talk with her the next time? I'm tired of bearing the brunt.*

bear watching to need watching; to deserve observation or monitoring. □ *This problem will bear watching.* □ *This is a very serious disease, and it will bear watching for further developments.*

bear with someone or something to be patient with someone or something; to endure someone or something. □ *Please bear with me while I fill out this*

form. □ *Please bear with my old car. It'll get us there sooner or later.*

beard the lion in his den to face an adversary on the adversary's home ground. □ *I went to the tax collector's office to beard the lion in his den.* □ *He said he hadn't wanted to come to my home, but it was better to beard the lion in his den.*

beat a dead horse to continue fighting a battle that has been won; to continue to argue a point that is settled. (A dead horse will not run no matter how hard it is beaten.) □ *Stop arguing! You have won your point. You are just beating a dead horse.* □ *Oh, be quiet. Stop beating a dead horse.*

beat a (hasty) retreat to retreat or withdraw very quickly. □ *We went out into the cold weather, but beat a retreat to the warmth of our fire.* □ *The dog beat a hasty retreat to its own yard.*

beat a path to someone's door [for people] to come to someone in great numbers. (So many people will wish to come and see you that they will wear down a pathway to your door.) □ *I have a product so good that everyone is beating a path to my door.* □ *If you really become famous, people will beat a path to your door.*

beat about the bush See the following entry.

beat around the bush AND **beat about the bush** to avoid answering a question; to stall; to waste time. □ *Stop beating around the bush and answer my question.* □ *Let's stop beating about the bush and discuss this matter.*

beat one's brains out (to do something) to work very hard (to do something). (Also literal. Informal or slang.) □ *I beat my brains out to solve the problem.* □ *That's the last time I'll beat my brains out trying to cook a nice dinner for you.*

beat one's head against the wall AND **bang one's head against a brick wall** to waste one's time trying to accomplish something that is completely hopeless. □ *You're wasting your time* *trying to fix up this house. You're just beating your head against the wall.* □ *You're banging your head against a brick wall trying to get that dog to behave properly.*

beat someone down (to size) AND **knock someone down (to size)** to make a person more humble, possibly by beating. (See also *cut someone down (to size)*.) □ *If you keep acting so arrogant, someone is going to beat you down to size.* □ *It's time someone knocked you down to size.* □ *I'll try to be more thoughtful. I don't want anyone to beat me down.*

beat someone to the draw See the following entry.

beat someone to the punch AND **beat someone to the draw** to do something before someone else does it. □ *I wanted to have the first new car, but Sally beat me to the punch.* □ *I planned to write a book about computers, but someone else beat me to the draw.*

beat someone up to harm or subdue a person by beating and striking. □ *The robber beat me up and took my money.* ⊤ *I really want to beat up that robber.*

beat something into someone's head to force someone to learn something, possibly through violence. (This can be a threat of violence and should not be used casually.) □ *I studied for hours. I have never beat so much stuff into my head in such a short time.* □ *You're going to learn this math if I have to beat it into your head.*

beat the band very much; very fast. (Folksy. This has no literal meaning.) □ *The carpenter sawed and hammered to beat the band.* □ *They baked cookies and pies to beat the band.*

beat the clock to do something before a deadline; to finish before the time is up. □ *Sam beat the clock, arriving a few minutes before the doors were locked.* □ *They were afraid they would be late and hurried in order to beat the clock.*

beat the gun to manage to do something before the ending signal. (Orig-inally from sports, referring to making a goal in the last seconds of a game. See also *jump the gun*.) □ *The ball beat the gun and dropped through the hoop just in time.* □ *Tom tried to beat the gun, but he was one second too slow.*

beat the living daylights out of someone AND **beat the stuffing out of someone; beat the tar out of someone; whale the tar out of someone** to beat or spank someone, probably a child. (Folksy. These are all threats to do violence and should not be used casually.) □ *If you do that again, I'll beat the living daylights out of you.* □ *The last time Bobby put the cat in the refrigerator, his mother beat the living daylights out of him.* □ *If you continue to act that way, I'll beat the tar out of you.* □ *He wouldn't stop, so I beat the stuffing out of him.* □ *He threatened to whale the tar out of each of them.*

beat the pants off someone 1. to beat someone severely. (Informal. Refers to physical violence, not the removal of someone's pants.) □ *The thugs beat the pants off their victim.* □ *If you do that again, I'll beat the pants off you.* **2.** to win out over someone. (Informal. This has nothing to do with violence or removing pants.) □ *In the footrace, Sally beat the pants off Jane.* □ *Tom beats the pants off Bob when it comes to writing poetry.*

beat the rap to escape conviction and punishment (for a crime). (Slang, especially criminal slang.) □ *He was charged with drunk driving, but he beat the rap.* □ *The police hauled Tom in and charged him with a crime. His lawyer helped him beat the rap.*

beat the stuffing out of someone See *beat the living daylights out of someone.*

beat the tar out of someone See *beat the living daylights out of someone.*

Beauty is only skin-deep. a proverb meaning that looks are only superficial. □ BOB: *Isn't Jane lovely?* TOM: *Yes, but beauty is only skin-deep.* □ *I* know that she looks like a million dollars, but beauty is only skin-deep.

becoming to someone complimentary to someone; enhancing one's good looks. (Usually refers to clothing, hair, and other personal ornaments.) □ *That hairstyle is very becoming to you.* □ *Your new fur coat is becoming to you.*

bed-and-breakfast a type of sleeping arrangement for travelers or tourists where people are accommodated with a place to sleep and breakfast the next morning in a small inn or private home. (Fixed order.) □ *We visited every European country and stayed in a bed-and-breakfast every night.* □ *I had to take a bed-and-breakfast because the hotels in the city were much too expensive.*

bed of roses a situation or way of life that is always happy and comfortable. □ *Living with Pat can't be a bed of roses, but her husband is always smiling.* □ *Being the boss isn't exactly a bed of roses. There are so many problems to take care of.*

beef something up to make something stronger; to supplement something. (Informal or slang.) □ *The government decided to beef the army up by buying hundreds of new tanks.* Ⓣ *Okay, let's beef up the opening song. Please, everyone, sing louder!*

been had been mistreated; been cheated or dealt with badly. (Informal or slang.) □ *They were cheated out of a thousand dollars. They've really been had.* □ *Look what they did to my car. Boy, have I been had.*

been through the mill been badly treated; exhausted. (Informal.) □ *This has been a rough day. I've really been through the mill.* □ *This old car is banged up, and it hardly runs. It's been through the mill.*

beer and skittles See *(all) beer and skittles.*

before long soon. □ *Billy will be grown-up before long.* □ *Before long, we'll be without any money if we keep spending so much.*

before you can say Jack Robinson almost immediately. (Often found in children's stories.) □ *And before you could say Jack Robinson, the bird flew away.* □ *I'll catch a plane and be there before you can say Jack Robinson.*

before you know it almost immediately. □ *I'll be there before you know it.* □ *If you keep spending money like that, you'll be broke before you know it.*

beg off (on something) to ask to be released from something; to refuse an invitation. □ *I'm sorry. I'll have to beg off on your invitation.* □ *I have an important meeting, so I'll have to beg off.*

beg the question to evade the issue; to carry on a false argument where one assumes as proved the very point that is being argued. □ *Stop arguing in circles. You're begging the question.* □ *It's hopeless to argue with Sally. She always begs the question.*

beg to differ (with someone) to disagree with someone; to state one's disagreement with someone in a polite way. (Usually used in a statement made to the person being disagreed with. Fixed order.) □ *I beg to differ with you, but you have stated everything exactly backwards.* □ *If I may beg to differ, you have not expressed things as well as you seem to think.*

beggar description to defy description; to be unable to be described □ *The house was a mess. The place beggared description.* □ *Our reaction to the proposal beggars description. We were deeply disturbed for days.*

Beggars can't be choosers. a proverb meaning that one should not criticize something one gets for free. □ *I don't like the old hat that you gave me, but beggars can't be choosers.* □ *It doesn't matter whether people like the free food or not. Beggars can't be choosers.*

begin to see daylight to begin to see the end of a long task. (See also *see the light (at the end of the tunnel).*) □ *I've been working on my thesis for two years, and at last I'm beginning to see* *daylight.* □ *I've been so busy. Only in the last week have I begun to see daylight.*

begin to see the light to begin to understand (something). □ *My algebra class is hard for me, but I'm beginning to see the light.* □ *I was totally confused, but I began to see the light after your explanation.*

beginning of the end the start of the termination of something or of someone's death. □ *When he stopped coughing and remained still, I knew it was the beginning of the end.* □ *The enormous federal deficit marked the beginning of the end as far as our standard of living is concerned.*

behind closed doors in secret; away from observers, reporters, or intruders. (Also literal.) □ *They held the meeting behind closed doors, as the law allowed.* □ *Every important issue was decided behind closed doors.*

behind someone's back in secret; without someone's knowledge. □ *Please don't talk about me behind my back.* □ *She sold the car behind his back.*

behind the eight ball in a difficult or awkward position. (Informal.) □ *Bob broke his wife's crystal vase and is really behind the eight ball.* □ *I ran over the neighbor's lawn with my car, so I'm really behind the eight ball.*

behind the scenes privately; out of public view. □ *The people who worked behind the scenes are the real heroes of this project.* □ *I worked behind the scenes in the play.* □ *We don't usually thank the people who are behind the scenes.*

behind the times old-fashioned. □ *Sarah is a bit behind the times. Her clothes are quite old-fashioned.* □ *Our legislature is a bit behind the times.*

belabor the point to spend too much time on a point of discussion. □ *I don't want to belabor the point, but the sooner we get these things settled, the better.* □ *If the speaker would agree not to belabor the point further, I will place it on the agenda for the next meeting.*

believe it or not to choose to believe something or not. □ *Believe it or not, I just got home from work.* □ *I'm over fifty years old, believe it or not.*

bell, book, and candle symbols of witchcraft. (Fixed order.) □ *Look, I can't work miracles! Do you expect me to show up at your house with bell, book, and candle, and make everything right? You have to take charge of your own destiny!* □ *On the top shelf of the tiny used-book store, Jim saw a bell, book, and candle sitting in a row, and he knew he was going to find some very interesting reading material.*

belt something out to sing or play a song loudly and with spirit. □ *When she's playing the piano, she really belts the music out.* Ⓣ *She really knows how to belt out a song.*

bend over backwards (to do something) See *fall over backwards (to do something).*

bend someone's ear to talk to someone, perhaps annoyingly. □ *Tom is over there, bending Jane's ear about something.* □ *I'm sorry. I didn't mean to bend your ear for an hour.*

bent on doing something determined to do something. □ *Jane was bent on having her own apartment.* □ *Her mother was bent on keeping her at home.*

beside oneself (with something) excited; disturbed; emotionally uncontrolled. □ *He was beside himself with grief.* □ *She laughed and laughed until she was beside herself.*

beside the point AND **beside the question** irrelevant; of no importance. □ *That's very interesting, but beside the point.* □ *That's beside the point. You're evading the issue.* □ *Your observation is beside the question.*

beside the question See the previous entry.

best bib and tucker one's best clothing. (Folksy. Fixed order.) □ *I always put on my best bib and tucker on Sundays.*

□ *Put on your best bib and tucker, and let's go to the city.*

best-laid plans of mice and men AND **best-laid schemes of mice and men** the best thought-out plans of anyone. (*Mice and men* is fixed order.) □ *If a little rain can ruin the best-laid plans of mice and men, think what an earthquake might do!* □ *The best-laid schemes of mice and men are often disturbed by any small matter.*

best-laid schemes of mice and men See the previous entry.

best part of something almost all of something; a large part of something; the major part of something. □ *The discussion took the best part of an hour.* □ *The best part of the meeting was taken up by budgetary matters.*

bet one's bottom dollar AND **bet one's life** to be quite certain (about something). (Both are informal and folksy. A *bottom dollar* is the last dollar.) □ *I'll be there. You bet your bottom dollar.* □ *I bet my bottom dollar you can't swim across the pool.* □ *You bet your life I can't swim that far.* □ *I bet my life on it.*

bet one's life See the previous entry.

better late than never better to do something late than not at all. □ *I wish you had come here sooner, but better late than never.* □ *She bought a house when she was quite old. Better late than never.*

better off (doing something) AND **better off (if something were done)** in a better position if something were done. □ *She'd be better off selling her house.* □ *They are better off flying to Detroit.* □ *They would be better off if they flew to Detroit.* □ *I'm better off now.*

better off (if one were somewhere else) See *better off (somewhere).*

better off (if something were done) See *better off (doing something).*

better off (somewhere) AND **better off (if one were somewhere else)** in a better position somewhere else. □ *They would be better off in Florida.* □ *We'd*

all be better off if we were in Florida. □ *I know I'd be better off.*

between a rock and a hard place AND **between the devil and the deep blue sea** in a very difficult position; facing a hard decision. (Informal.) □ *I couldn't make up my mind. I was caught between a rock and a hard place.* □ *He had a dilemma on his hands. He was clearly between the devil and the deep blue sea.*

between life and death in a position where living or dying is an even possibility. (Especially with *caught* or *hovering*.) □ *And there I was on the operating table, hovering between life and death.* □ *The mountain climber hung by his rope, caught between life and death.*

between the devil and the deep blue sea See *between a rock and a hard place.*

between you, me, and the lamppost secretively, just between you and me. (Fixed order.) □ *Just between you, me, and the lamppost, Fred is leaving school.* □ *Now don't tell anyone else. This is just between you, me, and the lamppost.*

betwixt and between (Fixed order.) **1.** between (people or things). □ *I liked the soup and the dessert and all that came betwixt and between.* □ *I sat betwixt and between all the actors who weren't on stage.* **2.** undecided. □ *I wish she would choose. She has been betwixt and between for three weeks.* □ *Tom is so betwixt and between about getting married. I don't think he's ready.*

beyond a reasonable doubt almost without any doubt. (A legal phrase.) □ *The jury decided beyond a reasonable doubt that she had committed the crime.* □ *She was also found guilty beyond a reasonable doubt.*

beyond measure more than can be measured; in a very large amount. □ *They brought in hams, turkeys, and roasts, and then they brought vegetables and salads beyond measure.* □ *They thanked all of us beyond measure.*

beyond one's depth **1.** in water that is too deep. (See also *in over one's head.*) □ *Sally swam out until she was beyond her depth.* □ *Jane swam out to get her even though it was beyond her depth, too.* **2.** beyond one's understanding or capabilities. □ *I'm beyond my depth in algebra class.* □ *Poor John was involved in a problem that was really beyond his depth.*

beyond one's means more than one can afford. (See also *live beyond one's means.*) □ *I'm sorry, but this house is beyond our means. Please show us a cheaper one.* □ *They felt that a Caribbean cruise is beyond their means.*

beyond the call of duty See *(above and) beyond the call of duty.*

beyond the pale unacceptable; outlawed. □ *Your behavior is simply beyond the pale.* □ *Because of Tom's rudeness, he's considered beyond the pale and is never asked to parties anymore.*

beyond the shadow of a doubt completely without doubt. (Said of a fact, not a person. See also *beyond a reasonable doubt.*) □ *We accepted her story as true beyond the shadow of a doubt.* □ *Please assure us that you are certain of the facts beyond the shadow of a doubt.*

beyond words more than one can say. (Especially with *grateful, shocked,* and *thankful.*) □ *Sally was thankful beyond words.* □ *I don't know how to thank you. I'm grateful beyond words.*

bid adieu to someone or something AND **bid someone or something adieu** to say good-bye to someone or something. (This *adieu* is French for *good-bye* and should not be confused with *ado.*) □ *Now it's time to bid adieu to all of you gathered here.* □ *He silently bid adieu to his favorite hat as the wind carried it down the street.*

bid someone or something adieu See the previous entry.

bide one's time to wait patiently. □ *I've been biding my time for years, just waiting for a chance like this.* □ *He's*

not the type just to sit there and bide his time. He wants some action.

big and bold large and capable of getting attention. (Usually refers to things, not people. Fixed order.) □ *The lettering on the book's cover was big and bold, and it got lots of attention, but the price was too high.* □ *She wore a brightly colored dress. The pattern was big and bold and the skirt was very full.*

big as all outdoors See *(as) big as all outdoors.*

big as life and twice as ugly See *(as) big as life and twice as ugly.*

big frog in a small pond to be an important person in the midst of less important people. □ *I'd rather be a big frog in a small pond than the opposite.* □ *The trouble with Tom is that he's a big frog in a small pond. He needs more competition.*

big of someone generous of someone; kind or forgiving of someone. (Sometimes sarcastic.) □ *He gave me some of his apple. That was very big of him.* □ *It was big of Sally to come over and apologize like that.*

binge and purge to overeat and vomit, alternatively and repeatedly. (A symptom of the condition called anorexia. Fixed order.) □ *She had binged and purged a number of times before she finally sought help from a doctor.* □ *Terry had been binging and purging for a number of years and was very, very thin.*

birds and the bees human reproduction. (A euphemistic way of referring to human sex and reproduction. Fixed order.) □ *My father tried to teach me about the birds and the bees.* □ *He's twenty years old and doesn't understand about the birds and the bees.*

bird's-eye view **1.** a view seen from high above. (Refers to the height of a flying bird.) □ *We got a bird's-eye view of Cleveland as the plane began its descent.* □ *From the top of the tower you get a splendid bird's-eye view of the village.* **2.** a brief survey of something; a hasty look at something. (Refers to the smallness of a bird's eye.) □ *The course provides a bird's-eye view of the works of Mozart, but it doesn't deal with them in enough detail for your purpose.* □ *All you need is a bird's-eye view of the events of World War II to pass the test.*

Birds of a feather flock together. a proverb meaning that people of the same type seem to gather together. □ *Bob and Tom are just alike. They like each other's company because birds of a feather flock together.* □ *When Mary joined a club for redheaded people, she said, "Birds of a feather flock together."*

bite off more than one can chew to take (on) more than one can deal with; to be overconfident. (This is used literally for food and figuratively for other things, especially difficult projects.) □ *Billy, stop biting off more than you can chew. You're going to choke on your food someday.* □ *Ann is exhausted again. She's always biting off more than she can chew.*

bite one's nails to be nervous or anxious; to bite one's nails from nervousness or anxiety. (Used both literally and figuratively.) □ *I spent all afternoon biting my nails, worrying about you.* □ *We've all been biting our nails from worry.*

bite one's tongue to struggle not to say something that you really want to say. (Used literally only to refer to an accidental biting of one's tongue.) □ *I had to bite my tongue to keep from telling her what I really thought.* □ *I sat through that whole conversation biting my tongue.*

bite someone's head off to speak sharply and angrily to someone. (Also literal.) □ *There was no need to bite Mary's head off just because she was five minutes late.* □ *The boss has been biting everybody's head off since his accident.*

bite the bullet to put up with or endure (something). (Informal or slang.) □ *I didn't want to go to the doctor, but I bit the bullet and went.* □ *John, you just*

have to bite the bullet and do what you're told.

bite the dust to fall to defeat; to die. (Typically heard in movies about the old western frontier.) □ *A bullet hit the sheriff in the chest, and he bit the dust.* □ *Poor old Bill bit the dust while mowing the lawn. They buried him yesterday.*

bite the hand that feeds one to do harm to someone who does good things for you. (Not literal.) □ *I'm your mother! How can you bite the hand that feeds you?* □ *She can hardly expect much when she bites the hand that feeds her.*

bitter pill to swallow an unpleasant fact that has to be accepted. □ *It was a bitter pill for her brother to swallow when she married his enemy.* □ *We found his deception a bitter pill to swallow.*

black-and-blue bruised; showing signs of having been physically harmed. (Fixed order.) □ *The child was black-and-blue after having been struck.* □ *She was black-and-blue all over after falling out of the tree.*

black as one is painted See *(as) black as one is painted.*

black as pitch See *(as) black as pitch.*

black out to faint or pass out. □ *Sally blacked out just before the crash.* □ *I was so frightened that I blacked out for a minute.*

black sheep of the family the worst member of the family. □ *Mary is the black sheep of the family. She's always in trouble with the police.* □ *He keeps making a nuisance of himself. What do you expect from the black sheep of the family?*

blast off [for a rocket] to shoot into the sky. □ *What time does the rocket blast off?* □ *It won't blast off today. It has been canceled.*

blaze a trail to make and mark a trail. (Either literally or figuratively.) □ *The scout blazed a trail through the* forest. □ *Professor Williams blazed a trail in the study of physics.*

bleep something out to replace a word or phrase in a radio or television broadcast with some sort of musical tone. (This is sometimes done to prevent a bad word or other information from being broadcast.) □ *He tried to say the word on television, but they bleeped it out.* ⊤ *They tried to bleep out the whole sentence.*

blessing in disguise something that turns out to be fortunate and advantageous after seeming to be the opposite at first. □ *Our missing the train was a blessing in disguise. It was involved in a crash.* □ *It was a blessing in disguise that I didn't get the job. I was offered a better one the next day.*

blind as a bat See *(as) blind as a bat.*

blind leading the blind having to do with a situation where people who don't know how to do something try to explain it to other people. □ *Tom doesn't know anything about cars, but he's trying to teach Sally how to change the oil. It's a case of the blind leading the blind.* □ *When I tried to show Mary how to use a computer, it was the blind leading the blind.*

blood, sweat, and tears the signs of great personal effort. (Fixed order.) □ *There will be much blood, sweat, and tears before we have completed this project.* □ *After years of blood, sweat, and tears, Timmy finally earned a college degree.*

bloody but unbowed [one's head] showing signs of a struggle, but not bowed in defeat. (Fixed order.) □ *Liz emerged from the struggle, her head bloody but unbowed.* □ *We are bloody but unbowed and will fight to the last.*

blow a fuse See the following entry.

blow a gasket AND **blow a fuse; blow one's cork; blow one's top; blow one's stack** to become very angry; to lose one's temper. (Slang.) □ *I was so mad I almost blew a gasket.* □ *I've never heard such a thing. I'm going to blow a fuse.* □ *I blew my cork when he*

hit me. □ *I was so mad I could have blown my top.* □ *I makes me so mad I could blow my stack.*

blow-by-blow account AND **blow-by-blow description** a detailed description (of an event) given as the event takes place. (This referred originally to boxing.) □ *I want to listen to a blow-by-blow account of the prizefight.* □ *The lawyer got the witness to give a blow-by-blow description of the argument.*

blow-by-blow description See the previous entry.

blow hot and cold to be changeable or uncertain (about something). (*Hot and cold* also has its literal meaning. Fixed order.) □ *He keeps blowing hot and cold on the question of moving to the country.* □ *He blows hot and cold about this. I wish he'd make up his mind.*

blow off steam See *let off steam.*

blow one's cookies See *blow one's lunch.*

blow one's cool See *lose one's cool.*

blow one's cork See *blow a gasket.*

blow one's lines See *fluff one's lines.*

blow one's lunch AND **blow one's cookies** to vomit. (Slang.) □ *The accident was so horrible I almost blew my lunch.* □ *Don't run so hard, or you'll blow your cookies.*

blow one's own horn See *toot one's own horn.*

blow one's stack See *blow a gasket.*

blow one's top See *blow a gasket.*

blow over to go away without causing harm. □ *If we are lucky, the storm will blow over.* □ *Given time, all this controversy will blow over.*

blow someone or something away **1.** to kill or destroy someone or something. (Slang. Also literal.) □ *He drew his gun and blew the thief away.* ⊤ *His bad attitude blew away the whole deal.* **2.** [with *someone*] to overcome someone emotionally. □ *The bad news really blew me away.* □ *Your news just blew me away! How exciting!*

blow someone or something off 1. [with *something*] to neglect or bumble something. (Slang.) □ *He would do better in school if he didn't blow his math class off.* Ⓣ *He blew off his homework.* **2.** [with *someone*] to deceive or cheat someone. (Slang.) □ *She really blew me off on the question of grades. She was really failing all the time.* Ⓣ *She blew off the teacher by cheating on the test.*

blow someone or something to smithereens to explode someone or something into tiny pieces. □ *The bomb blew the ancient church to smithereens.* □ *The mortar blew the entire squad to smithereens.*

blow someone's cover to reveal someone's true identity or purpose. □ *The spy was very careful not to blow her cover.* □ *I tried to disguise myself, but my dog recognized me and blew my cover.*

blow someone's mind (Slang.) **1.** to destroy the function of one's brain. □ *It was a terrible experience. It nearly blew my mind.* □ *She blew her mind on drugs.* **2.** to overwhelm someone; to excite someone. □ *It was so beautiful, it nearly blew my mind.* □ *The music was so wild. It blew my mind.*

blow something to ruin or waste something. □ *I had a chance to do it, but I blew it.* □ *He blew the whole five dollars on candy.*

blow something out of all proportion to cause something to be unrealistically proportioned relative to something else. (The *all* can be left out.) □ *The press has blown this issue out of all proportion.* □ *Let's be reasonable. Don't blow this thing out of proportion.*

blow the lid off (something) to reveal something, especially wrongdoing; to make wrongdoing public. □ *The police blew the lid off the smuggling ring.* □ *The government is glad that they blew the lid off.*

blow the whistle (on someone) to report someone's wrongdoing to someone (such as the police) who can stop the wrongdoing. □ *The citizens' group blew the whistle on the street gangs by calling the police.* □ *The gangs were getting very bad. It was definitely time to blow the whistle.*

blow up to fall apart or get ruined. (Also literal.) □ *The whole project blew up. It will have to be canceled.* □ *All my planning was blown up this afternoon.*

blow up (at someone) to get angry at someone; to lose one's temper and yell at someone. □ *I'm sorry. I didn't mean to blow up.* □ *You'd blow up, too, if you'd had a day like mine.*

blow up in someone's face 1. to blow up or explode suddenly. □ *The bomb blew up in the robber's face.* □ *The firecracker blew up in his face and injured him.* **2.** [for something] to get ruined while someone is working on it. □ *All my plans blew up in my face.* □ *It is terrible for your life to get ruined and blow up in your face.*

blue around the gills See *pale around the gills.*

bog down to slow down; to become stuck. □ *The project bogged down because of so much red tape.* □ *We bog down every year at this time because many of our workers go on vacation.*

boggle someone's mind to confuse someone; to overwhelm someone; to blow someone's mind. □ *The size of the house boggles my mind.* □ *She said that his arrogance boggled her mind.*

boil down to something to reduce to something; to come down to something; to be essentially something. (Also literal.) □ *It all boils down to whether you wish to buy a car.* □ *It boils down to a question of good health.*

boil something down to summarize something; to make information more concise. (Also literal in reference to liquids.) □ *I don't have time to listen to the whole story. Please boil it down for me.* Ⓣ *Please boil down the report so I can read it on the plane.*

bone of contention the subject or point of an argument; an unsettled point of disagreement. □ *We've fought for so long that we've forgotten what the bone of contention is.* □ *The question of a fence between the houses has become quite a bone of contention.*

bone up (on something) to study something thoroughly; to review the facts about something. □ *I have to bone up on the state driving laws because I have to take my driving test tomorrow.* □ *I take mine next month, so I'll have to bone up, too.*

boot someone or something out See *kick someone or something out.*

bore someone stiff AND **bore someone to death** to bore someone very much. (*Stiff* is an old slang word meaning "dead.") □ *The play bored me stiff.* □ *The lecture bored everyone to death.*

bore someone to death See the previous entry.

bored stiff very bored. □ *We were all bored stiff.* □ *During the first half of the opera, Bill was bored stiff. He slept during the second half.*

bored to death very bored. □ *The children were bored to death.* □ *I've never been so bored to death in my life.*

born and bred See the following entry.

born and raised AND **born and bred** born and nurtured through childhood, usually in a specific place. (Fixed order.) □ *She was born and raised in a small town in western Montana.* □ *Freddy was born and bred on a farm and had no love for city life.*

born out of wedlock born to an unmarried mother. □ *The child was born out of wedlock.* □ *In the city many children are born out of wedlock.*

born with a silver spoon in one's mouth born with many advantages; born to a wealthy family. □ *Sally was born with a silver spoon in her mouth.* □ *I'm glad I was not born with a silver spoon in my mouth.*

borrow trouble to worry needlessly; to make trouble for oneself. □ *Worrying too much about death is just borrowing trouble.* □ *Do not get involved with politics. That's borrowing trouble.*

boss someone around to give orders to someone; to keep telling someone what to do. □ *Stop bossing me around. I'm not your employee.* ⊤ *Captain Smith bosses around the whole crew. That's his job.*

bottle something up 1. to constrict something as if it were put in a bottle. □ *The patrol boats bottled the other boats up at the locks on the river.* ⊤ *The police bottled up the traffic while they searched the cars for the thieves.* **2.** to hold one's feelings within; to keep from saying something that one feels strongly about. □ *Let's talk about it, John. You shouldn't bottle it up.* ⊤ *Don't bottle up your problems. It's better to talk them out.*

bottom out to reach the lowest point. □ *The price of wheat bottomed out last week. Now it's rising again.* □ *My interest in school bottomed out in my junior year, so I quit and got a job.*

bound and determined determined. (Fixed order.) □ *We were bound and determined to get there on time.* □ *I'm bound and determined that this won't happen again.*

bound for somewhere on the way to somewhere; planning to go to somewhere. □ *I'm bound for Mexico. In fact, I'm leaving this afternoon.* □ *I'm bound for the bank. Do you want to go, too?*

bound hand and foot with hands and feet tied up. (Fixed order.) □ *The robbers left us bound hand and foot.* □ *We remained bound hand and foot until the maid found us and untied us.*

bound to (do something) to be certain to do something. □ *They are bound to come home soon. They always come home early.* □ *Oh, yes. They are bound to.*

bow and scrape to be very humble and subservient. □ *Please don't bow and scrape. We are all equal here.* □ *The* *salesclerk came in, bowing and scraping, and asked if he could help us.*

bow out to quit and depart; to resign; to retire. □ *I've done all that I can do. Now is the time to bow out.* □ *Most workers bow out at the normal retirement age.*

bowl someone over to surprise or overwhelm someone. (Also literal.) □ *The news bowled me over.* □ *The details of the proposed project bowled everyone over.*

brain someone to strike a person on the skull as if to knock out the person's brains. □ *I thought he was going to brain me, but he only hit me on the shoulder.* □ *If you don't do it, I'll brain you.*

bread and butter [a person's] livelihood or income. (Also literal, referring to food. Fixed order.) □ *Selling cars is a lot of hard work, but it's my bread and butter.* □ *It was hard to give up my bread and butter, but I felt it was time to retire.*

bread-and-butter letter a letter or note written to follow up on a visit; a thank-you note. (Fixed order.) □ *When I got back from the sales meeting, I took two days to write bread-and-butter letters to the people I met.* □ *I got sort of a bread-and-butter letter from my nephew, who wants to visit me next summer.*

bread and water the most minimal meal possible; a prison meal. (Usually used in reference to being in prison or jail. Fixed order.) □ *Max knew that if he got in trouble again it would be at least a year on bread and water.* □ *This dinner is terrible again. I would rather have bread and water! Why don't we ever have pizza?*

Break a leg! good luck. (Theatrical slang. This is said to actors before a performance instead of *Good luck.* Also literal.) □ *Before the play, John said to Mary, "Break a leg!"* □ *Saying "Break a leg!" before a performance is an old theatrical tradition.*

break camp to close down a campsite; to pack up and move on. □ *Early this morning we broke camp and moved on northward.* □ *Okay, everyone. It's time to break camp. Take those tents down and fold them neatly.*

break down 1. [for something] to fall apart; [for something] to stop operating. (See also *break someone or something down.*) □ *The air-conditioning broke down, and we got very warm.* □ *The car broke down in the parking lot.* 2. [for one] to lose control of one's emotions; [for one] to have a nervous collapse. □ *He couldn't keep going. He finally broke down and wept.* □ *I was afraid I'd break down.*

break even for income to equal expenses. (This implies that money was not earned or lost.) □ *Unfortunately my business just managed to break even last year.* □ *I made a bad investment, but I broke even.*

break ground (for something) to start digging the foundation for a building. □ *The president of the company came to break ground for the new building.* □ *This was the third building this year for which this company has broken ground.* □ *When will they break ground?*

Break it up! Stop fighting!; Stop it! (Said to two or more people causing a disturbance.) □ *All right! Break it up, you guys!* □ *Stop your talking! Break it up and get back to work.*

break loose (from someone or something) to get away from a person or a thing that is holding one. (Compare with *cut loose (from someone or something).*) □ *The criminal broke loose from the police officer.* □ *It's hard to break loose from home.* □ *I was twenty years old before I could break loose.*

break new ground to begin to do something that no one else has done; to pioneer (in an enterprise). (See also *break ground (for something).*) □ *Dr. Anderson was breaking new ground in cancer research.* □ *They were breaking new ground in consumer electronics.*

break off (with someone) to end a friendship with someone, especially a boyfriend or a girlfriend. □ *Tom has finally broken off with Mary.* □ *I knew it couldn't last. He was bound to break off.*

break one's back (to do something) See the following entry.

break one's neck (to do something) AND **break one's back (to do something)** to work very hard to do something. (Never used in its literal sense.) □ *I broke my neck to get here on time.* □ *That's the last time I'll break my neck to help you.* □ *There is no point in breaking your back. Take your time.*

break one's word not to do what one said one would do; not to keep one's promise. (The opposite of *keep one's word.*) □ *Don't say you'll visit your grandmother if you can't go. She hates people to break their word.* □ *If you break your word, she won't trust you again.*

break out 1. to burst forth suddenly, as with a fire, a riot, giggling, shouting, etc. □ *A fire broke out in the belfry.* □ *A round of giggling broke out when the teacher tripped.* □ *A riot almost broke out when the police came.* **2.** [for one's face] to erupt in pimples. □ *Bob's face has started breaking out badly.* □ *My face breaks out when I eat a lot of chocolate.*

break out (in something) to erupt with something such as a rash, a cold sweat, or pimples. □ *After being in the woods, I broke out in a rash. I think it's poison ivy.* □ *I hate to break out like that.* □ *When I eat chocolate, I break out in pimples.* □ *I was so frightened I broke out in a cold sweat.* □ *The patient broke out in a cold sweat.*

break (out) in(to) tears to start crying suddenly. □ *I was so sad that I broke out into tears.* □ *I always break into tears at a funeral.* □ *It's hard not to break out in tears under those circumstances.*

break out (of something) to escape from something, often by destructive means. (Especially from prison, but also in figurative senses.) □ *The con-*

victs plotted to break out of prison. □ *You don't have the guts to break out of jail!* □ *Don finally broke out of the depression that had held him captive for so long.* □ *The lion broke out of its cage.*

break someone or something down 1. [with *someone*] to force someone to give up and tell secrets or agree to do something. □ *After threats of torture, they broke the spy down.* Ⓣ *They broke down the agent by threatening violence.* **2.** [with *something*] to tear something down; to destroy something. □ *They used an ax to break the door down.* Ⓣ *We broke down the wall with big hammers.*

break someone or something in 1. [with *someone*] to train someone to do a job; to supervise a new person learning a new job. □ *It takes time to break a new worker in.* Ⓣ *Are they hard to break in?* Ⓣ *I have to break in a new worker.* **2.** [with *something*] to make something fit by wearing or using it. Ⓣ *I'll be glad when I've finished breaking in these shoes.* □ *Yes, it takes time to break them in.* Ⓣ *They are easy to break in, though.* □ *The car will run better after I break it in.*

break someone or something up 1. [with *someone*] to cause a person to laugh, perhaps at an inappropriate time. (Informal.) □ *John told a joke that really broke Mary up.* Ⓣ *The comedian's job was to break up the audience by telling jokes.* **2.** [with *something*] to destroy something. □ *The storm broke the docks up on the lake.* Ⓣ *The police broke up the gambling ring.* **3.** [with *something*] to put an end to something. □ *The police broke the fight up.* Ⓣ *Walter's parents broke up the party at three in the morning.*

break someone's fall to cushion a falling person; to lessen the impact of a falling person. □ *When the little boy fell out of the window, the bushes broke his fall.* □ *The old lady slipped on the ice, but a snowbank broke her fall.*

break someone's heart to cause someone emotional pain. □ *It just broke* my heart when Tom ran away from home. □ Sally broke John's heart when she refused to marry him.

break something down (for someone) to explain something to someone in simple terms or in an orderly fashion. □ She doesn't understand. You will have to break it down for her. □ I can help. This is a confusing question. Let me break it down for you.

break something down (into something) to divide something into smaller parts; to divide something into its component parts. □ Please break this paragraph down into sentences. T The chemist broke down the compound into a number of elements. □ Walter broke the project down into five tasks and assigned them to various people.

break something to pieces to shatter something. (Informal.) □ I broke my crystal vase to pieces. □ I dropped a glass and broke it to pieces.

break the back of something to end the domination of something; to reduce the power of something. □ The government has worked for years to break the back of organized crime. □ This new medicine should break the back of the epidemic.

break the bank to use up all one's money. (As in casino gambling where a gambler wins more money than the house has on hand.) □ It will hardly break the bank if we go out to dinner just once. □ Buying a new dress at that price won't break the bank.

break the ice to initiate social interchanges and conversation; to get something started. (The ice sometimes refers to social coldness. Also literal.) □ Tom is so outgoing. He's always the first one to break the ice at parties. □ It's hard to break the ice at formal events. □ Sally broke the ice by bidding $20,000 for the painting.

break the news (to someone) to tell someone some important news, usually bad news. □ The doctor had to break the news to Jane about her hus-

band's cancer. □ I hope that the doctor broke the news gently.

break through (something) to break something and pass through; to overcome something. (Either literal or figurative.) □ Tom was able to break through racial barriers. □ They are hard to break through in some places. □ The scientists broke through the mystery surrounding the disease and found the cause.

break up (with someone) to end a love affair or a romance. □ Tom finally broke up with Mary. □ I thought they would break up. He has been so moody lately.

breaking and entering the crime of forcing one's way into a place. (A criminal charge. Fixed order.) □ Max was charged with four counts of breaking and entering. □ It was not an act of breaking and entering. The thief just opened the door and walked right in.

breath of fresh air 1. air that is not stale or smelly. (This is the literal sense.) □ I feel faint. I think I need a breath of fresh air. □ You look ill, John. What you need is a breath of fresh air. 2. air that is not (figuratively) contaminated with unpleasant people or situations. (This is a sarcastic version of sense 1.) □ You people are disgusting. I have to get out of here and get a breath of fresh air. □ I believe I'll go get a breath of fresh air. The intellectual atmosphere in here is stifling. 3. a new, fresh, and imaginative approach (to something). (Usually with like.) □ Sally, with all her wonderful ideas, is a breath of fresh air. □ New furniture in this room is like a breath of fresh air.

breathe down someone's neck 1. to keep close watch on someone; to watch someone's activities. (Refers to standing very close behind a person.) □ I can't work with you breathing down my neck all the time. Go away. □ I will get through my life without your help. Stop breathing down my neck. 2. to try to hurry someone along; to make someone get something done on time. (The subject does not have to be a person. See the second example.) □ *I have to finish my taxes today. The tax collector is breathing down my neck.* □ *I have a deadline breathing down my neck.*

breathe easy to assume a relaxed state after a stressful period. □ *After all this is over, I'll be able to breathe easy again.* □ *He won't be able to breathe easy until he pays off his debts.*

breathe one's last to die; to breathe one's last breath. □ *Mrs. Smith breathed her last this morning.* □ *I'll keep running every day until I breathe my last.*

bricks and mortar buildings; the expenditure of money on buildings rather than something else. (The buildings referred to can be constructed out of anything. Fixed order.) □ *The new president of the college preferred to invest in new faculty members rather than bricks and mortar.* □ *Sometimes people are happy to donate millions of dollars for bricks and mortar, but they never think of the additional cost of annual maintenance.*

bright and early very early. (Fixed order.) □ *Yes, I'll be there bright and early.* □ *I want to see you here on time tomorrow, bright and early, or you're fired!*

bright-eyed and bushy-tailed very cheerful and eager. (Refers to the twinkling eyes and quick, energetic movements of a squirrel. Fixed order.) □ *She appeared at the top of the stairs, bright-eyed and bushy-tailed, ready to start the day.* □ *I am awake, but I am hardly bright-eyed and bushy-tailed.*

bring down the curtain (on something) See *ring down the curtain (on something).*

bring home the bacon to earn a salary. (Folksy.) □ *I've got to get to work if I'm going to bring home the bacon.* □ *Go out and get a job so you can bring home the bacon.*

bring someone around **1.** to bring someone for a visit; to bring someone for someone (else) to meet. □ *Please bring your wife around sometime. I'd love to meet her.* □ *You've just got to bring the doctor around for dinner.* **2.** to bring someone to consciousness. □ *The doctor brought Tom around with smelling salts.* □ *The boxer was knocked out, but the doctor brought him around.* **3.** to persuade someone (to accept something); to manage to get someone to agree (to something). □ *The last debate brought a lot of voters around to our candidate.* □ *I knew I could bring her around if I just had enough time to talk to her.*

bring someone or something out in droves to lure or draw out someone or some creature in great number. □ *The availability of free drinks brought people out in droves.* □ *The fresh grass sprouts brought the deer out in droves.*

bring someone or something up **1.** to mention a person or a thing. □ *I'm sorry. I won't bring him up again.* ⊤ *Please don't bring up that matter again.* ⊤ *Please don't bring up John Jones's name again.* **2.** to raise a child or an animal. □ *Her uncle brought her up.* ⊤ *It's difficult to bring up a pet monkey.*

bring someone or something up to date to make someone or something more modern. (See also *bring someone up to date (on someone or something).*) □ *Let's buy some new furniture and bring this room up to date.* □ *John tried to bring himself up to date by changing his hairstyle. He still looked like the same old John.*

bring someone to to bring someone to consciousness; to wake someone up. (See also *bring someone around; come to.*) □ *The nurse brought the patient to.* □ *She's hurt! Come on, help me bring her to.*

bring someone up to date (on someone or something) to tell someone the news about something. □ *Please bring me up to date on the Middle East situation.* □ *Please bring me up to date on John. I want to hear all the news.* □ *And bring me up to date, too.*

bring something about to make something happen. □ *Is she clever enough to bring it about?* ⊤ *Oh, yes, she can bring about anything she wants.*

bring something crashing down (around one) to destroy something that one has built; to destroy something that one has a special interest in. □ *She brought her whole life crashing down around her.* □ *Bob's low grade in English brought everything crashing down.*

bring something home to someone to cause someone to realize the truth of something. □ *Seeing the starving refugees on television really brings home the tragedy of their situation.* □ *It wasn't until she failed her test that the importance of studying was brought home to her.*

bring something into question to question something; to express suspicion about something. □ *It was necessary to bring your part in this matter into question.* □ *The city council brought the building project into question.*

bring something off to make something happen; to produce a great event. □ *She managed to bring the party off with no difficulty.* ⊤ *She brought off a similar party last season.*

bring something to a head to cause something to come to the point when a decision has to be made or an action taken. □ *The latest disagreement between management and the union has brought matters to a head. There will be an all-out strike now.* □ *It's a relief that things have been brought to a head. The disputes have been going on for months.*

bring something to light to make something known; to discover something. □ *The scientists brought their findings to light.* □ *We must bring this new evidence to light.*

bring the house down to excite a theatrical audience to laughter or applause or both. □ *This is a great joke. The last time I told it, it brought the*

house down. ⊤ *It didn't bring down the house; it emptied it.*

bring up the rear to move along behind everyone else; to be at the end of the line. (Originally referred to marching soldiers.) □ *Here comes John, bringing up the rear.* □ *Hurry up, Tom! Why are you always bringing up the rear?*

broad in the beam with wide hips or large buttocks. (From a nautical expression for a wide ship.) □ *I am getting a little broad in the beam. It's time to go on a diet.* □ *John is just naturally broad in the beam.*

brush up (on something) to learn something; to review something. □ *I think I should brush up on my Spanish before I go to Mexico.* □ *I've heard you speak Spanish. You need to do more than brush up.*

buck for something to aim, try, or strike for a goal. (Originally referred to trying to get a higher military rank.) □ *Bill acts that way because he's bucking for corporal.* □ *Tom is bucking for a larger office.*

buck up cheer up. □ *Buck up, old friend! Things can't be all that bad.* □ *I know I have to buck up. Life must go on.*

buckle down (to something) to settle down to something; to begin to work seriously at something. □ *If you don't buckle down to your job, you'll be fired.* □ *You had better buckle down and get busy.*

bug out to leave; to pack up and get out. (Slang.) □ *It's time to bug out. Let's get out of here.* □ *I just got a call from headquarters. They say to bug out immediately.*

bug someone to irritate someone; to bother someone. (Slang.) □ *Go away! Stop bugging me!* □ *Leave me alone. Go bug someone else.*

build a fire under someone to do something to make someone start doing something. (Informal. Also literal.) □ *The teacher built a fire under the students, and they really started working.*

□ *Somebody built a fire under Bill, so he finally went out and got a job.*

build castles in Spain See the following entry.

build castles in the air AND **build castles in Spain** to daydream; to make plans that can never come true. (Not literal.) □ *Ann spends most of her time building castles in Spain.* □ *I really like to sit on the porch in the evening, just building castles in the air.*

build (someone or something) up **1.** to make someone or something bigger or stronger. □ *Tom is eating lots of fresh fruits and vegetables to build himself up for basketball.* □ *Tom needs to build up.* □ *Tom needs to build himself up.* Ⓣ *The farmer built up his stone fences where they had weakened.* **2.** to advertise, praise, or promote someone or something. Ⓣ *Theatrical agents work very hard to build up their clients.* Ⓣ *An advertising agency can build up a product so much that everyone will want it.*

build something to order to build something especially for someone. (See also *make something to order*.) □ *Our new car was built to order just for us.* □ *My company builds computers to order. No two are alike.*

build up to something to lead up to something; to work up to something. □ *You could tell by the way she was talking that she was building up to something.* □ *The sky was building up to a storm.*

bull in a china shop a very clumsy person around breakable things; a thoughtless or tactless person. (China is fine crockery.) □ *Look at Bill, as awkward as a bull in a china shop.* □ *Get that big dog out of my garden. It's like a bull in a china shop.* □ *Bob is so rude, a regular bull in a china shop.*

bump into someone AND **run into someone** to chance on someone; to meet someone by chance. (Also literal.) □ *Guess who I bumped into downtown today?* □ *I ran into Bob Jones yesterday.*

bump someone off AND **knock someone off** to kill someone. (Slang, especially criminal slang.) □ *They tried to bump her off, but she was too clever and got away.* Ⓣ *The crooks bumped off the witness to the crime.* □ *They tried to knock them all off.*

bundle of nerves someone who is very nervous and anxious. □ *Mary was a bundle of nerves until she heard that she passed the test.* □ *You always seem to be such a bundle of nerves.*

burn one's bridges (behind one) **1.** to make decisions that cannot be changed in the future. □ *If you drop out of school now, you'll be burning your bridges behind you.* □ *You're too young to burn your bridges that way.* **2.** to be unpleasant in a situation that you are leaving, ensuring that you'll never be welcome to return. □ *If you get mad and quit your job, you'll be burning your bridges behind you.* □ *No sense burning your bridges. Be polite and leave quietly.* **3.** to cut off the way back to where you came from, making it impossible to retreat. □ *The army, which had burned its bridges behind it, couldn't go back.* □ *By blowing up the road, the spies had burned their bridges behind them.*

burn one's bridges in front of one to create future problems for oneself. (A play on *burn one's bridges (behind one)*.) □ *I made a mistake again. I always seem to burn my bridges in front of me.* □ *I accidently insulted a math teacher whom I will have to take a course from next semester. I am burning my bridges in front of me.*

burn (oneself) out to do something so long and so intensely that one gets sick and tired of doing it. □ *I burned myself out as an opera singer. I just cannot do it anymore.* □ *Tom burned himself out playing golf. He can't stand it anymore.* □ *Tom burned out too young.*

burn out [for electrical or mechanical devices] to break down and become useless. □ *I hope the light bulb in the* *ceiling doesn't burn out. I can't reach it.* ⊤ *The motor burned out.*

burn someone at the stake 1. to set fire to a person tied to a post (as a form of execution). □ *They used to burn witches at the stake.* □ *Look, officer, I only ran a stop sign. What are you going to do, burn me at the stake?* **2.** to chastise or denounce someone severely, but without violence. □ *Stop yelling. I made a simple mistake, and you're burning me at the stake for it.* □ *Sally only spilled her milk. There is no need to shout. Don't burn her at the stake for it.*

burn someone in effigy to burn a dummy or other figure that represents a hated person. (See also *hang someone in effigy*.) □ *For the third day in a row, they burned the king in effigy.* □ *Until they have burned you in effigy, you can't really be considered a famous leader.*

burn someone or something to a crisp to burn someone or something totally or very badly. □ *The flames burned him to a crisp.* □ *The cook burned the meat to a crisp.*

burn someone up to make someone very angry. (Informal. Also literal.) □ *People like that just burn me up!* □ *It burns me up to hear you talk that way.* ⊤ *His answers really burned up the committee members.*

burn the candle at both ends to work very hard and stay up very late at night. □ *No wonder Mary is ill. She has been burning the candle at both ends for a long time.* □ *You can't keep on burning the candle at both ends.*

burn the midnight oil to stay up working, especially studying, late at night. (Refers to working by the light of an oil lamp.) □ *I have to go home and burn the midnight oil tonight.* □ *If you burn the midnight oil night after night, you'll probably become ill.*

burn with a low blue flame to be very angry. (Refers to the imaginary heat caused by extreme anger.) □ *By the time she showed up three hours late, I*

was burning with a low blue flame. □ *Whenever Ann gets mad, she just presses her lips together and burns with a low blue flame.*

burned to a cinder burned very badly. (Not necessarily literal.) □ *I stayed out in the sun too long, and I am burned to a cinder.* □ *This toast is burnt to a cinder.*

burned up very angry. □ *I've never been so burned up in my life.* □ *I'm really burned up at Bob.*

burst at the seams [for someone] to explode (figuratively) with pride or laughter. (Also literal.) □ *Tom nearly burst at the seams with pride.* □ *We laughed so hard we just about burst at the seams.*

burst in on someone or something to enter a room, interrupting someone or some activity. (Often without knocking or seeking permission to enter.) □ *Tom burst in on his sister and her boyfriend while they were kissing.* □ *I must ask you not to burst in on a board meeting again. Whatever it is can wait.*

burst into flames to catch fire suddenly; to ignite all at once. □ *Suddenly, the car burst into flames.* □ *It was so hot in the forest fire that a few trees literally burst into flames.*

burst into tears AND **burst out crying** to begin to cry suddenly. (See also *break (out) in(to) tears*.) □ *After the last notes of her song, the audience burst into tears, such was its beauty and tenderness.* □ *The brother and sister burst into tears on hearing of the death of their dog.* □ *Some people find themselves bursting out crying for no reason at all.*

burst out crying See the previous entry.

burst out laughing to begin to laugh suddenly. □ *The entire audience burst out laughing at exactly the wrong time, and so did the actors.* □ *Every time I think of you sitting there with a lap full of noodle soup, I burst out laughing.*

burst with joy to be full to the bursting point with happiness. (See also *burst* at the seams.) □ *When I got my grades, I could have burst with joy.* □ *Joe was not exactly bursting with joy when he got the news.*

burst with pride to be full to the bursting point with pride. (See also *burst at the seams*.) □ *My parents were bursting with pride when I graduated from college.* □ *I almost burst with pride when I was chosen to go up in the space shuttle.*

bury one's head in the sand AND **hide one's head in the sand** to ignore or hide from obvious signs of danger. (Refers to an ostrich, which we picture with its head stuck into the sand or the ground.) □ *Stop burying your head in the sand. Look at the statistics on smoking and cancer.* □ *And stop hiding* your *head in the sand. All of us will die somehow, whether we smoke or not.*

bury the hatchet to stop fighting or arguing; to end old resentments. □ *All right, you two. Calm down and bury the hatchet.* □ *I wish Mr. and Mrs. Franklin would bury the hatchet. They argue all the time.*

business as usual having things go along as usual. □ *Right after the flood, it was business as usual in all the stores.* □ *Please, everyone, business as usual. Let's get back to work.*

business end of something the part or end of something that actually does the work or carries out the procedure. □ *Keep away from the business end of the electric drill to avoid getting hurt.* □ *Don't point the business end of that gun at anyone. It might go off.*

busman's holiday leisure time spent doing something similar to what one does at work. □ *Tutoring students in the evening is too much of a busman's holiday for our English teacher.* □ *It's a bit of a busman's holiday to ask her to be wardrobe mistress for our amateur production in the summer. She's a professional dressmaker.*

bust a gut (to do something) to work very hard; to strain oneself to do

something. (Slang. The word *gut* is considered impolite in some circumstances. *Bust* is an informal form of *burst*.) □ *I don't intend to bust a gut to get there on time.* □ *I busted a gut to get there the last time, and I was the first one there.*

busy as a bee See *(as) busy as a bee*.

busy as Grand Central Station See *(as) busy as Grand Central Station*.

but for someone or something if it were not for someone or something. □ *But for the railing, I'd have fallen down the stairs.* □ *But for the children, Mrs. Smith would have left her husband years ago.*

butt in (on someone or something) to interrupt someone or something. □ *Pardon me for butting in on your conversation, but this is important.* □ *John butted in on Tom and Jane to tell them that the mail had come.* □ *That's a strange reason to butt in. What was in the mail?*

butter someone up to flatter someone. □ *I believe my landlady prefers for me to butter her up rather than getting the rent on time.* Ⓣ *If I butter up the landlady, she allows me to be a few days late.*

button one's lip to get quiet and stay quiet. (Often used with children.) □ *All right now, let's button our lips and listen to the story.* □ *Button your lip, Tom! I'll tell you when you can talk.*

buy a pig in a poke to purchase or accept something without having seen or examined it. (*Poke* means "bag." Compare with *buy something sight unseen*.) □ *Buying a car without test-driving it is like buying a pig in a poke.* □ *He bought a pig in a poke when he ordered a diamond ring by mail.*

buy someone off to bribe someone; to win someone over by gifts or favors. □ *It's not hard to buy politicians off.* Ⓣ *They bought off the whole city council with campaign contributions.*

buy something to believe someone; to accept something to be a fact.

Informal. Also literal.) □ *It may be true, but I don't buy it.* □ *I just don't buy the idea that you can swim that far.*

buy something for a song to buy something cheaply. □ *No one else wanted it, so I bought it for a song.* □ *I could buy this house for a song, because it's so ugly.*

buy something on credit to purchase something now and pay for it later (plus interest). (See also *sell something on credit.*) □ *Almost everyone who buys a house buys it on credit.* □ *I didn't have any cash with me, so I used my credit card and bought a new coat on credit.*

buy something sight unseen to buy something without seeing it first. (Compare with *buy a pig in a poke.*) □ *I bought this land sight unseen. I didn't know it was so rocky.* □ *It isn't usually safe to buy something sight unseen.*

buy something to go AND **get something to go; have something to go; order something to go** to purchase food to take out; to make a purchase of cooked food to be taken elsewhere to be eaten. □ *Let's stop here and buy six hamburgers to go.* □ *I didn't thaw anything for dinner. Let's stop off on the way home and get something to go.* □ *No, I don't want to sit at a table. I'll just have a cup of coffee to go.*

by a hair('s breadth) AND **by a whisker** just barely; by a very small distance. (The *whisker* phrase is folksy.) □ *I just missed getting on the plane by a hair's breadth.* □ *I made it by a hair!* □ *The arrow missed the deer by a whisker.*

by a mile by a great distance. (An exaggeration in this case. Also literal.) □ *You missed the target by a mile.* □ *Your estimate of the budget deficit was off by a mile.*

by a whisker See *by a hair('s breadth).*

by all accounts See *according to all accounts.*

by all appearances apparently; according to what one sees. □ *She is, by all appearances, ready to resume work.* □ *By all appearances, we ought to be approaching the airport.*

by all means certainly; yes; absolutely. (Compare with *by any means.*) □ *I will attempt to get there by all means.* □ BOB: *Can you come to dinner tomorrow?* JANE: *By all means. I'd love to.*

by all means of something using every possible manner of something to do something. □ *People will be arriving by all means of transportation.* □ *The surgeon performed the operation by all means of instruments.*

by and by after a period of time has passed. (Most often seen in children's stories.) □ *By and by the bears returned home, and can you guess what they found?* □ *And by and by the little boy became a tall and handsome prince.*

by and large generally; usually. (Originally a nautical expression. Fixed order.) □ *I find that, by and large, people tend to do what they are told to do.* □ *By and large, rosebushes need lots of care.*

by any means by any way possible. □ *I need to get there soon by any means.* □ *I must win this contest by any means, fair or unfair.* □ *It cannot be done by any means.*

by chance by accident; without cause; randomly. □ *The contestants were chosen by chance.* □ *We met only by chance, and now we are the closest of friends.*

by choice due to conscious choice; on purpose. □ *I do this kind of thing by choice. No one makes me do it.* □ *I didn't go to this college by choice. It was the closest one to home.*

by coincidence by an accidental and strange similarity; by an unplanned pair of similar events or occurrences. □ *We just happened to be in the same place at the same time by coincidence.* □ *By coincidence, the circus was in town when I was there. I'm glad because I love circuses.*

by dint of something because of something; due to the efforts of something.

(*Dint* is an old word meaning "force," and it is never used except in this phrase.) □ *They got the building finished on time by dint of hard work and good organization.* □ *By dint of much studying, John got through college.*

by fits and starts irregularly; unevenly; with much stopping and starting. (Informal. Fixed order.) □ *Somehow, they got the job done by fits and starts.* □ *By fits and starts, the old car finally got us to town.*

by guess and by golly by luck; with the help of God. (Folksy. *Golly* is a disguise of *God.* Fixed order.) □ *They managed to get the shed built by guess and by golly.* □ *I lost my ruler and had to install the new floor tile by guess and by golly.*

by hook or (by) crook by any means, legal or illegal. (Folksy. Fixed order.) □ *I'll get the job done by hook or by crook.* □ *I must have that house. I intend to get it by hook or crook.*

by leaps and bounds rapidly; by large movements forward. (Fixed order.) □ *Our garden is growing by leaps and bounds.* □ *The profits of my company are increasing by leaps and bounds.*

by means of something using something; with the use of something. □ *I opened the bottle by means of a bottle opener.* □ *I was able to afford a car by means of a loan.*

by mistake in error; accidentally. □ *I'm sorry. I came into the wrong room by mistake.* □ *I chose the wrong road by mistake. Now we are lost.*

by no means absolutely not; certainly not. □ *I'm by no means angry with you.* □ BOB: *Did you put this box here?* TOM: *By no means. I didn't do it, I'm sure.*

by return mail by a subsequent mailing (back to the sender). (A phrase indicating that an answer is expected soon, by mail.) □ *Since this bill is overdue, would you kindly send us your check by return mail?* □ *I answered your request by return mail over a year ago. Please check your records.*

by shank's mare by foot. (*Shank* refers to the shank of the leg. Folksy. See also go (somewhere) by shank's mare.) □ *My car isn't working, so I'll have to travel by shank's mare.* □ *I'm sore because I've been getting around by shank's mare.*

by the book See *by the numbers.*

by the day one day at a time. □ *I don't know when I'll have to leave town, so I rent this room by the day.* □ *Sally is in such distress. She manages to live only by the day.*

by the dozen twelve at a time; in a group of twelve. (Almost the same as the following entry.) □ *I purchase socks by the dozen.* □ *Eggs are usually sold by the dozen.* □ *Around here we have problems by the dozen.*

by the dozens many; by some large, indefinite number. (Similar to but less than *hundreds.* Almost the same as the previous entry.) □ *Just then people began showing up by the dozens.* □ *I baked cakes and pies by the dozens.*

by the handful in measurements equal to a handful; lots. □ *Billy is eating candy by the handful.* □ *People began leaving by the handful at midnight.*

by the hour at each hour; after each hour. □ *It kept growing darker by the hour.* □ *I have to take this medicine by the hour.* □ *The illness is getting worse by the hour.*

by the month one month at a time. □ *Not many apartments are rented by the month.* □ *I needed a car for a short while, so I rented one by the month.*

by the nape of the neck by the back of the neck. (Mostly found in real or mock threats.) □ *He grabbed me by the nape of the neck and told me not to turn around if I valued my life. I stood very still.* □ *If you do that again, I'll pick you up by the nape of the neck and throw you out the door.*

by the numbers AND **by the book** according to the rules. (Informal.) □ *He always plays the game by the numbers. He never cheats.* □ *I want all* *my people to go by the numbers. This place is totally honest.* □ *We always go by the book in matters like this.*

by the same token in the same way; reciprocally. □ *Tom must be good when he comes here, and, by the same token, I expect you to behave properly when you go to his house.* □ *The mayor votes for his friend's causes. By the same token, the friend votes for the mayor's causes.*

by the seat of one's pants by sheer luck and very little skill. (Informal. Especially with *to fly.*) □ *I got through school by the seat of my pants.* □ *The jungle pilot spent most of his days flying by the seat of his pants.*

by the skin of one's teeth just barely; by an amount equal to the thickness of the (imaginary) skin on one's teeth. (Informal or slang.) □ *I got through that class by the skin of my teeth.* □ *I got to the airport late and missed the plane by the skin of my teeth.*

by the sweat of one's brow by one's efforts; by one's hard work. □ *Tom raised these vegetables by the sweat of his brow.* □ *Sally polished the car by the sweat of her brow.*

by the way incidentally; in addition; while I think of it. □ *By the way, I'm not going to the bank today.* □ *Oh, by the way, your shoes need polishing.*

by the week one week at a time. □ *I plan my schedules by the week.* □ *Where can I rent a room by the week?*

by the year one year at a time. □ *Most apartments are available by the year.* □ *We budget by the year.*

by virtue of something because of something; due to something. □ *She's permitted to vote by virtue of her age.* □ *They are members of the club by virtue of their great wealth.*

by way of something 1. passing through something; via something. □ *He came home by way of Toledo.* □ *She went to the bank by way of the drugstore.* **2.** in illustration; as an example. □ *By way of illustration, the professor drew a picture on the board.* □ *He read them a passage from Shakespeare by way of example.*

by word of mouth by speaking rather than writing. □ *I learned about it by word of mouth.* □ *I need it in writing. I don't trust things I hear about by word of mouth.*

C

call a meeting to ask that people assemble for a meeting; to request that a meeting be held. □ *The mayor called a meeting to discuss the problem.* □ *I'll be calling a meeting of the town council to discuss the new building project.*

call a spade a spade to call something by its right name; to speak frankly about something, even if it is unpleasant. □ *Well, I believe it's time to call a spade a spade. We are just avoiding the issue.* □ *Let's call a spade a spade. The man is a liar.*

call for someone or something to arrive to collect or pick up a person or a thing. (Used especially when you are to pick someone up and are acting as an escort.) □ *I will call for you about eight this evening.* □ *The messenger will call for your reply in the morning.*

call it a day to quit work and go home; to say that a day's work has been completed. □ *I'm tired. Let's call it a day.* □ *The boss was mad because Tom called it a day at noon and went home.*

call it a night to end what one is doing at night and go [home] to bed. □ *At midnight, I called it a night and went to bed.* □ *Guest after guest called it a night, and at last we were alone.*

call it quits to quit; to resign from something; to announce that one is quitting. (Informal.) □ *Okay! I've had enough! I'm calling it quits.* □ *Time to go home, John. Let's call it quits.*

call of nature the need to go to the lavatory. (Humorous.) □ *Stop the car here! I have to answer the call of nature.*

□ *There was no break in the agenda to take account of the call of nature.*

call someone down to reprimand a person; to *bawl someone out.* □ *The teacher had to call Sally down in front of everybody.* □ *"I wish you wouldn't call me down in public," cried Sally.*

call someone names to call a person unpleasant or insulting names. (Usually viewed as a juvenile act.) □ *Mommy! John is calling me names again!* □ *We'll never get anywhere by calling one another names.*

call someone on the carpet to reprimand a person. (The phrase presents images of a person called into the boss's carpeted office for a reprimand.) □ *One more error like that and the boss will call you on the carpet.* □ *I'm sorry it went wrong. I really hope he doesn't call me on the carpet again.*

call someone or something in to call on the special talents, abilities, or power of someone or something. □ *They had to call a new doctor in.* Ⓣ *Yes, they had to call in a specialist.* Ⓣ *They had to call in a huge tractor to move the boulder.*

call someone or something into question to cause someone or something to be evaluated; to examine or re-examine the qualifications or value of someone or something. □ *Because of her poor record, we were forced to call Dr. Jones into question.* □ *We called Dr. Jones's qualifications into question.* □ *They called the whole project into question.* Ⓣ *I cannot call into question the entire medical profession.*

call someone or something off 1. to call a halt to an attack by someone or something. □ *Please call your dog off. It's trying to bite me!* T *Okay, you can call off the police. I surrender.* T *It's time to call off the manhunt. The criminal has given himself up.* **2.** [with *something*] to cancel an event. □ *It's too late to call the party off. The first guests have already arrived.* T *Because of rain, they called off the baseball game.*

call someone or something up 1. to call a person, business, or office on the telephone. □ *Mary called the company up and ordered a new supply of medicine.* T *The generals called up the regiment near the end of the war.* T *Tom called up Mary.* **2.** [with *something*] to summon information from a computer. T *John used a computer to call up the information.* T *With a few strokes on the computer keyboard, Sally called up the figures she was looking for.*

call someone's bluff to demand that someone prove a claim; to demonstrate that a person is or is not being deceptive. □ *All right, I'll call your bluff. Show me you can do it!* □ *Tom said, "I've got a gun here in my pocket, and I'll shoot if you come any closer!" "Go ahead," said Bill, calling his bluff.*

call the dogs off to stop threatening, chasing, or hounding (a person); (literally) to order dogs away from the chase. (Informal. Note the variations in the examples.) □ *All right, I surrender. You can call your dogs off.* T *Tell the sheriff to call off the dogs. We caught the robber.* T *Please call off your dogs!*

call the meeting to order to start a meeting officially; to announce that the meeting has started. □ *The president called the meeting to order shortly after noon.* □ *We cannot do anything until someone calls the meeting to order.*

call the shots AND **call the tune** to make the decisions; to decide what is to be done. (Informal.) □ *Sally always wants to call the shots, and Mary doesn't like to be bossed around. They don't get along well.* □ *Sally always wants to call the tune.* □ *Look here, friend, I'm calling the shots. You just be quiet.*

call the tune See the previous entry.

cancel something out to destroy the effect of something; to balance something. T *This last payment cancels out my debt.* □ *Yes, your last payment cancels it out.* T *Bob's two good grades canceled out his two failing grades.*

can't See the expressions listed at *not able*, as well as those listed below.

can't carry a tune [to be] unable to sing a simple melody; lacking musical ability. (Almost always negative. Also with *cannot.*) □ *I wish that Tom wouldn't try to sing. He can't carry a tune.* □ *Listen to poor old John. He really cannot carry a tune.*

can't do anything with someone or something not [to be] able to manage or control someone or something. (Also with *cannot.*) □ *Bill is such a problem. I can't do anything with him.* □ *My hair is such a mess. I just can't do anything with it.*

can't help but do something [to be] unable to choose any but one course of action. (Also with *cannot.*) □ *Her parents live nearby, so she can't help but go there on holidays.* □ *Bob is a tennis fan and can't help but travel to Wimbledon each year.*

can't hold a candle to someone not [to be] equal to someone; unable to measure up to someone. (Also with *cannot.*) □ *Mary can't hold a candle to Ann when it comes to auto racing.* □ *As for singing, John can't hold a candle to Jane.*

can't make heads or tails (out) of someone or something [to be] unable to understand someone or something. (Also with *cannot.*) □ *John is so strange. I can't make heads or tails of him.* □ *Do this report again. I can't make heads or tails out of it.*

can't see beyond the end of one's nose [to be] unaware of the things that might happen in the future; not farsighted; self-centered. (Also with *cannot*.) □ *John is a very poor planner. He can't see beyond the end of his nose.* □ *Ann can't see beyond the end of her nose. She is very self-centered.*

can't see one's hand in front of one's face [to be] unable to see very far, usually due to darkness or fog. (Also with *cannot*.) □ *It was so dark that I couldn't see my hand in front of my face.* □ *Bob said that the fog was so thick he couldn't see his hand in front of his face.*

can't stand (the sight of) someone or something AND **can't stomach someone or something** [to be] unable to tolerate someone or something; disliking someone or something extremely. (Also with *cannot*.) □ *I can't stand the sight of cooked carrots.* □ *Mr. Jones can't stand the sight of blood.* □ *None of us can stand this place.* □ *Nobody can stand Tom when he smokes a cigar.* □ *I can't stomach your foul language.* □ *I just can't stomach Mr. Smith.*

can't stomach someone or something See the previous entry.

cap and gown the academic cap or mortarboard and the robe worn in academic ceremonies. (Fixed order.) □ *We all had to rent cap and gown for graduation.* □ *I appeared wearing my cap and gown, but I had shorts on underneath because it gets so hot at that time of year.*

carried away excited or moved to (extreme) action (by someone or something). □ *The crowd got carried away and did a lot of damage to the park.* □ *I know that planning a party is fun, but don't get carried away.*

carry (a lot of) weight (with someone or something) to be very influential with someone or some group of people. □ *Your argument does not carry a lot of weight with me.* □ *The senator's testimony carried a lot of weight with the council.* □ *Her opinion carries weight with most of the members.*

carry a torch (for someone) to be in love with someone who is not in love with you; to brood over a hopeless love affair. (Also with *the*.) □ *John is carrying a torch for Jane.* □ *Is John still carrying a torch?* □ *Yes, he'll carry the torch for months.*

carry coals to Newcastle to do something unnecessary; to do something that is redundant or duplicative. (Newcastle is an English town from which coal was shipped to other parts of England.) □ *Taking food to a farmer is like carrying coals to Newcastle.* □ *Mr. Smith is so rich he doesn't need any more money. To give him money is like carrying coals to Newcastle.*

carry on (about someone or something) to make a great fuss over someone or something; to cry and become out of control about someone or something. (Note the variation in the examples.) □ *Billy, stop carrying on about your tummy ache like that.* □ *Billy, you must stop carrying on so.* □ *The child carried on endlessly about his mother.*

carry on somehow to manage to continue somehow, in spite of problems. □ *Even though we did not have a lot of money, we managed to carry on somehow.* □ *Don't worry about us. We will carry on somehow.*

carry on (with someone or something) 1. [with *something*] to continue with something. □ *Can I please carry on with my work now?* □ *Yes, please carry on.* **2.** [with *someone*] to behave improperly with someone; to be affectionate in public. □ *Look at Jane carrying on with Tom. They ought to be ashamed.* □ *Jane, stop carrying on like that!*

carry on without someone or something to manage to continue without someone or something. □ *I don't know how we will be able to carry on without you.* □ *We can't carry on without a leader!*

carry one's cross See *bear one's cross*.

carry one's (own) weight AND **pull one's (own) weight** to do one's share; to earn one's keep. □ *Tom, you must be more helpful around the house. We all have to carry our own weight.* □ *Bill, I'm afraid that you can't work here anymore. You just haven't been carrying your weight.* □ *If you would just pull your weight, we would finish this by noon.*

carry over to extend into another time period or location. □ *I don't like for bills to carry over into the next month.* □ *Please do not let the paragraph carry over.*

carry something off to make a planned event work out successfully. (Also literal, meaning to take something away.) □ *It was a huge party, but the hostess carried it off beautifully.* T *The magician carried off the trick with great skill.*

carry something out to perform a task; to perform an assignment. (Also literal.) □ *"This is a very important job,"* said Jane. *"Do you think you can carry it out?"* T *The students didn't carry out their assignments.*

carry something over to let something like a bill extend into another period of time; to extend to another location. □ *We'll carry the amount of money due over into the next month.* T *Yes, please carry over the balance.* □ *We'll have to carry this paragraph over to the next page.*

carry the ball 1. to be the player holding the ball, especially in football when a goal is made. (Sports.) □ *It was the fullback carrying the ball.* □ *Yes, Tom always carries the ball.* **2.** to be in charge; to make sure that a job gets done. (See also *drop the ball.*) □ *We need someone who knows how to get the job done. Hey, Sally! Why don't you carry the ball for us?* □ *John can't carry the ball. He isn't organized enough.*

carry the day AND **win the day** to be successful; to win a competition, argument, etc. (Originally meaning to win a battle.) □ *Our team didn't play well at first, but we won the day in the end.*

□ *Hard work won the day and James passed his exams.*

carry the torch 1. to uphold a set of goals; to lead or participate in a (figurative) crusade. □ *The battle was over, but John continued to carry the torch.* □ *If Jane hadn't carried the torch, no one would have followed, and the whole thing would have failed.* **2.** See *carry a torch (for someone).*

carry the torch (for someone) See *carry a torch (for someone).*

carry the weight of the world on one's shoulders to appear to be burdened by all the problems in the whole world. □ *Look at Tom. He appears to be carrying the weight of the world on his shoulders.* □ *Cheer up, Tom! You don't need to carry the weight of the world on your shoulders.*

carry through (on something) See *follow through (on something).*

case in point an example of what one is talking about. □ *Now, as a case in point, let's look at nineteenth-century England.* □ *Fireworks can be dangerous. For a case in point, look what happened to Bob Smith last week.*

cash-and-carry a method of buying and selling goods at the retail level where the buyer pays cash for the goods and carries the goods away. (As opposed to paying on credit or having something delivered. Fixed order.) □ *Sorry, we don't accept credit cards. This is strictly cash-and-carry.* □ *I bought the chair cash-and-carry before I realized that there was no way to get it home.*

cash in (on something) to earn a lot of money at something; to make a profit at something. (See also *cash something in.*) □ *This is a good year for farming, and you can cash in on it if you're smart.* □ *It's too late to cash in on that particular clothing fad.*

cash in one's chips to die. (Slang. From an expression in the card game poker.) □ *Bob cashed in his chips yesterday.* □ *I'm too young to cash in my chips.*

cash on the barrelhead money paid for something when it is purchased; money paid at the time of sale. (Folksy. See also *cash-and-carry*.) □ *I don't extend credit. It's cash on the barrelhead only.* □ *I paid $12,000 for this car — cash on the barrelhead.*

cash or credit [a purchase made] either by paying cash or by putting the charges on a credit account. (Fixed order.) □ *When Fred had all his purchases assembled on the counter, the clerk asked, "Cash or credit?"* □ *That store does not give you a choice of cash or credit. They want cash only.*

cash something in to exchange something with cash value for the amount of money it is worth. □ *I should have cashed my bonds in years ago.* ⊤ *It's time to cash in your U.S. savings bonds.* ⊤ *I need to cash in an insurance policy.*

cast about for someone or something See the following entry.

cast around for someone or something AND **cast about for someone or something** to seek someone or something; to seek a thought or an idea. (Refers to a type of a person rather than a specific person.) □ *John is casting around for a new cook. The old one quit.* □ *Bob is casting about for a new car.* □ *Mary cast about for a way to win the contest.*

cast doubt(s) (on someone or something) to cause someone or something to be doubted. □ *The police cast doubt on my story.* □ *How can they cast doubt? They haven't looked into it yet.* □ *The city council cast doubt on John and his plan.* □ *They are always casting doubts.*

cast in the same mold very similar. □ *The two sisters are cast in the same mold — equally mean.* □ *All the members of the family are cast in the same mold and they all end up in prison.*

cast one's lot in with someone to join in with someone and accept whatever happens. □ *Mary cast her lot with the*

group going to Spain. They had a wonderful time. ⊤ *I decided to cast in my lot with the home team this year.*

cast (one's) pearls before swine to waste something good on someone who doesn't care about it. (From a biblical quotation.) □ *To sing for them is to cast pearls before swine.* □ *To serve them French cuisine is like casting one's pearls before swine.*

cast the first stone to make the first criticism; to be the first to attack. (From a biblical quotation.) □ *Well, I don't want to be the one to cast the first stone, but she sang horribly.* □ *John always casts the first stone. Does he think he's perfect?*

Cat got your tongue? Why do you not speak?; Speak up and answer my question! (Folksy.) □ *Answer me! What's the matter, cat got your tongue?* □ *Why don't you speak up? Cat got your tongue?*

catch-as-catch-can the best one can do with whatever is available. □ *We went hitchhiking for a week and lived catch-as-catch-can.* □ *There were ten children in our family, and every meal was catch-as-catch-can.*

catch cold AND **take cold** to contract a cold (the disease). □ *Please close the window, or we'll all catch cold.* □ *I take cold every year at this time.*

catch forty winks AND **catch some Zs; take forty winks** to take a nap; to get some sleep. (Informal. See *forty winks*.) □ *I'll just catch forty winks before getting ready for the party.* □ *Tom always tries to catch some Zs before going out for a late evening.* □ *I think I'll go to bed and take forty winks. See you in the morning.* □ *Why don't you go take forty winks and call me in about an hour?*

catch hell See *get the devil*.

catch it to get into trouble and receive punishment. (Informal. See also *get the devil*. Also literal.) □ *I know I'm going to catch it when I get home.* □ *Bob hit Billy in the face. He really caught it from the teacher.*

catch (on) fire to ignite and burn with flames. □ *Keep your coat away from the flames, or it will catch fire.* □ *Lightning struck the prairie, and the grass caught on fire.*

catch on (to someone or something) to figure someone or something out; to solve a puzzle; to see through an act of deception. □ *Mary caught on to Bob and his tricks.* □ *Ann caught on to the woman's dishonest plan.* □ *The woman thought that Ann wouldn't catch on.*

catch one off one's guard See *catch someone off guard.*

catch one with one's pants down to catch someone doing something, especially something that ought to be done in secret or in private. (Informal. Use with caution. This probably refers indirectly to having one's pants down in the bathroom.) □ *John couldn't convince them he was innocent. They caught him with his pants down.* □ *Did you hear that John took the camera? The store owner caught him with his pants down.*

catch one's breath to resume one's normal breathing after exertion; to return to normal after being busy or very active. □ *I don't have time to catch my breath.* □ *I ran so fast that it took ten minutes to catch my breath.*

catch one's death (of cold) AND **take one's death of cold** to contract a cold; to catch a serious cold. (See *catch cold.*) □ *If I go out in this weather, I'll catch my death of cold.* □ *Dress up warm or you'll take your death of cold.* □ *Put on your raincoat or you'll catch your death.*

catch sight of someone or something to see someone or something briefly; to get a glimpse of someone or something. □ *I caught sight of the rocket just before it flew out of sight.* □ *Ann caught sight of the robber as he ran out of the bank.*

catch some Zs See *catch forty winks.*

catch someone in the act (of doing something) to catch a person doing something illegal or private. (See also *in the act (of doing something).*) □ *They know who set the fire. They caught someone in the act.* □ *I caught Tom in the act of stealing a car.*

catch someone napping to find someone unprepared. (Informal. Literally, to catch someone asleep.) □ *The enemy soldiers caught our army napping.* □ *The thieves caught the security guard napping.*

catch someone off-balance to catch a person who is not prepared; to surprise someone. (Also literal.) □ *Sorry I acted so flustered. You caught me off-balance.* □ *The robbers caught Ann off-balance and stole her purse.*

catch someone off guard AND **catch one off one's guard** to catch a person at a time of carelessness. (Compare with *catch someone off-balance.*) □ *Tom caught Ann off guard and frightened her.* □ *She caught me off my guard, and I told the location of the jewels.*

catch someone red-handed to catch a person in the act of doing something wrong. (See also *caught red-handed.*) □ *Tom was stealing the car when the police drove by and caught him red-handed.* □ *Mary tried to cash a forged check at the bank, and the teller caught her red-handed.*

catch someone's eye AND **get someone's eye** to establish eye contact with someone; to attract someone's attention. (Also with *have,* as in the example.) □ *The shiny red car caught Mary's eye.* □ *Tom got Mary's eye and waved to her.* □ *When Tom had her eye, he smiled at her.*

catch the devil See *get the devil.*

catch up (to someone or something) AND **catch up (with someone or something)** to move faster in order to reach someone or something who is moving in the same direction. □ *The red car caught up with the blue one.* □ *Bill caught up with Ann, and they walked to the bank together.* □ *He had to run to catch up to her.*

catch up (with someone or something)
See the previous entry.

caught in the act seen doing something illegal or private. □ *Tom was caught in the act.* □ *She's guilty. She was caught in the act.*

caught in the cross fire See the following entry.

caught in the middle AND **caught in the cross fire** caught between two arguing people or groups, making it difficult to remain neutral. (Both are also literal.) □ *The cook and the dishwasher were having an argument, and Tom got caught in the middle. All he wanted was his dinner.* □ *Mr. and Mrs. Smith tried to draw me into their argument. I don't like being caught in the middle.* □ *Bill and Ann were arguing, and poor Bobby, their son, was caught in the cross fire.*

caught red-handed caught in the act of doing something wrong. □ *Tom was caught red-handed.* □ *Many car thieves are caught red-handed.*

caught short to be without something you need, especially money. □ *I needed eggs for my cake, but I was caught short.* □ *Bob had to borrow money from John to pay for the meal. Bob is caught short quite often.*

cause a commotion See the following entry.

cause a stir AND **cause a commotion** to cause people to become agitated; to cause trouble in a group of people; to shock or alarm people. (Notice the example with *quite.*) □ *When Bob appeared without his evening jacket, it caused a stir in the dining room.* □ *The dog ran through the church and caused quite a commotion.*

cause (some) eyebrows to raise to shock people; to surprise and dismay people. (See also *raise some eyebrows.*) □ *John caused eyebrows to raise when he married a poor girl from Toledo.* □ *If you want to cause some eyebrows to raise, just start singing as you walk down the street.*

cause (some) tongues to wag to cause people to gossip; to give people something to gossip about. □ *The way John was looking at Mary will surely cause some tongues to wag.* □ *The way Mary was dressed will also cause tongues to wag.*

cave in (to someone or something) for someone to collapse and give in to someone else or to something. (Also literal in reference to caves, tunnels, ceilings, etc.) □ *Mr. Franklin always caves in to Mrs. Franklin.* □ *It's easier to cave in than to go on fighting.* □ *Tom caved in to the pressure of work.*

cease and desist to stop doing something and stay stopped. (A legal phrase. Fixed order.) □ *The judge ordered the merchant to cease and desist the deceptive practices.* □ *When they were ordered to cease and desist, they finally stopped.*

chalk something up to something to recognize something as the cause of something else. □ *We chalked her bad behavior up to her recent illness.* Ⓣ *I had to chalk up the loss to experience.* Ⓣ *I chalked up my defeat to my impatience.*

champ at the bit to be ready and anxious to do something. (Originally said about horses.) □ *The kids were champing at the bit to get into the swimming pool.* □ *The dogs were champing at the bit to begin the hunt.*

chance something to risk doing something; to try doing something. □ *I don't usually ride horses, but this time I will chance it.* □ *Bob didn't have reservations, but he went to the airport anyway, chancing a cancellation.*

chance (up)on someone or something to find someone or something by chance. □ *I just happened to chance upon this excellent restaurant down by the river. The food is superb.* □ *We were exploring a small Kentucky town when we chanced on an old man who turned out to be my great-uncle.*

change hands [for something] to be sold or passed from owner to owner. □ *How many times has this house* *changed hands in the last ten years?* □ *We built this house in 1920, and it has never changed hands.*

change horses in the middle of the stream to make major changes in an activity that has already begun; to choose someone or something else after it is too late. □ *I'm already baking a cherry pie. I can't bake an apple pie. It's too late to change horses in the middle of the stream.* □ *The house is half-built. It's too late to hire a different architect. You can't change horses in the middle of the stream.*

change someone's mind to cause a person to think differently (about someone or something). □ *Tom thought Mary was unkind, but an evening out with her changed his mind.* □ *I can change my mind if I want to. I don't have to stick with an idea.*

change someone's tune to change the manner of a person, usually from bad to good, or from rude to pleasant. □ *The teller was most unpleasant until she learned that I'm a bank director. Then she changed her tune.* □ *"I will help change your tune by fining you $150," said the judge to the rude defendant.*

change the subject to begin talking about something different. □ *They changed the subject suddenly when the person whom they had been discussing entered the room.* □ *We'll change the subject if we are embarrassing you.*

chapter and verse detailed, in reference to sources of information. (A reference to the method of referring to biblical text. Fixed order.) □ *He gave chapter and verse for his reasons for disputing that Shakespeare had written the play.* □ *The suspect gave chapter and verse of his associate's activities.*

charge someone or something up 1. [with *someone*] to get someone excited and enthusiastic. Ⓣ *The speaker charged up the crowd to go out and raise money.* □ *Mrs. Smith tried to charge her husband up about getting a job.* **2.** [with *something*] to restore a charge to an electrical storage battery. (Also without *up.*) Ⓣ *They charged up the*

battery overnight. □ *My car charges the battery whenever the engine runs.*

charged up 1. [of someone] excited; enthusiastic □ *The crowd was really charged up.* □ *Tom is so tired that he cannot get charged up about anything.* **2.** [of something] full of electrical power. (Also without *up.*) □ *The battery is completely charged up.* □ *If the battery isn't charged, the car won't start.*

charm the pants off (of) someone to use charming behavior to persuade someone to do something. (Use with some caution.) □ *She is so nice. She just charms the pants off of you.* □ *He will try to charm the pants off you, but you can still refuse to take the job if you don't want to do it.*

cheat on someone to commit adultery; to be unfaithful to one's lover. □ *"Have you been cheating on me?" cried Mrs. Franklin.* □ *"No, I haven't been cheating on you," said Mr. Franklin.*

check in (on someone or something) See *look in (on someone or something).*

check into something See *look into something.*

checks and balances a system where power is kept in control and balance between the various branches of government. (Fixed order.) □ *The newspaper editor claimed that the system of checks and balances built into our Constitution has been subverted by party politics.* □ *We depend on checks and balances in government to keep despots from seizing control of the government.*

cheek by jowl side by side; close together. □ *The pedestrians had to walk cheek by jowl along the narrow streets.* □ *The two families lived cheek by jowl in one house.*

cheer someone on to give words or shouts of encouragement to someone who is trying to do something. □ *John was leading in the race, and the whole crowd was cheering him on.* □ *Sally* *was doing so well in her performance that I wanted to cheer her on.*

cheer someone up to make a sad person happy. □ *When Bill was sick, Ann tried to cheer him up by reading to him.* ⊤ *Interest rates went up, and that cheered up all the bankers.*

cheer up to become more happy. □ *Things are bad for you now, but you'll cheer up when they get better.* □ *Cheer up, Tom! Things can't be that bad.*

cheesed off bored; depressed; annoyed. □ *He was cheesed off with his job.* □ *She was cheesed off when she missed the bus.*

chew someone out AND **eat someone out** to scold someone; to bawl someone out thoroughly. (Informal. Used much in the military.) □ *The sergeant chewed the corporal out; then the corporal chewed the private out.* ⊤ *The boss is always chewing out somebody.* ⊤ *The coach ate out the entire football team because of their poor playing.*

chew the fat AND **chew the rag** to have a chat with someone; to talk very informally with one's close friends. (Informal.) □ *Hi, old buddy! Come in and let's chew the fat.* □ *They usually just sat around and chewed the rag. They never did get much done.*

chew the rag See the previous entry.

chicken out (of something) to withdraw from something due to fear or cowardice. (Informal.) □ *Jane was going to go parachuting with us, but she chickened out at the last minute.* □ *I'd never chicken out of parachute jumping, because I'd never agree to do it in the first place!*

child's play something very easy to do. □ *The test was child's play to her.* □ *Finding the right street was child's play with a map.*

chilled to the bone very cold. □ *I was chilled to the bone in that snowstorm.* □ *The children were chilled to the bone in the unheated room.*

chime in (with something) to add one's voice to something; to add something

to the discussion, usually by interrupting. □ *Billy chimed in by reminding us to come to dinner.* □ *Everyone chimed in on the final chorus of the song.*

chink in one's armour a special weakness that provides a means for attacking or impressing someone otherwise invulnerable. □ *His love for his child is the chink in his armour.* □ *Jane's insecurity is the chink in her armour.*

chip in (on something) AND **chip in something on something; chip something in (on something)** to contribute a small amount of money to a fund that will be used to buy something. □ *Would you care to chip in on a gift for the teacher?* □ *Yes, I'd be happy to chip in.* □ *Could you chip in a dollar on the gift, please?*

chip in something on something See the previous entry.

chip off the old block a person (usually a male) who behaves in the same way as his father or resembles his father. (Usually informal.) □ *John looks like his father—a real chip off the old block.* □ *Bill Jones, Jr., is a chip off the old block. He's a banker just like his father.*

chip something in (on something) See *chip in (on something)*.

chips and dip potato chips, or some other kind of crisply fried substance, and a sauce or dressing to dip them into before eating them. (Fixed order.) □ *There were tons of chips and dip and all kinds of cold pop available for everyone.*

choke someone up to make a person become overemotional and speechless; to make a person begin to cry. (Informal.) □ *The sight of all those smiling people choked Bob up, and he couldn't go on speaking.* ⊤ *The funeral procession choked up the whole family.*

choke something off to stifle something; to force something to an end. □ *The car ran over the hose and choked the water off.* ⊤ *The president choked off the debate.*

choose up sides to form into two opposing teams by having a leader or captain take turns choosing players. □ *Let's choose up sides and play baseball.* □ *When I choose up sides, all the best players don't end up on the same team.*

church and state established religion and government. (Usually in reference to the separation of church and state. This refers to eradicating even the slightest evidence of religion in connection with government as well as assuring that the U.S. government does not establish a state religion. Fixed order.) □ *The city council stopped beginning each meeting with a prayer because someone suggested that it violated the principle of the separateness of church and state.* □ *Many countries do not have the separation of church and state.*

clam up to shut up; to refuse to talk; to close one's mouth (as tightly as a clam closes its shell). (Slang.) □ *You talk too much, John. Clam up!* □ *When they tried to question her, she clammed up.*

clamp down (on someone or something) to become strict with someone; to become strict about something. (Also literal.) □ *Because Bob's grades were getting worse, his parents clamped down on him.* □ *The police have clamped down on speeders in this town.* □ *Things have already gone too far. It's too late to clamp down.*

clap eyes on someone or something to see someone or something, perhaps for the first time; to *set eyes on someone or something.* (Informal.) □ *I wish she had never clapped eyes on her fiancé.* □ *I haven't clapped eyes on a red squirrel for years.*

clean as a whistle See *(as) clean as a whistle.*

clean out (of something) See *fresh out (of something).*

clean up to make a great profit. (Informal. Also literal.) □ *John won at the races and really cleaned up.* □ *Ann cleaned up by taking a job selling encyclopedias.*

clean up one's act to reform one's conduct; to improve one's performance. (Informal. Originally referred to polishing one's stage performance.) □ *Since Sally cleaned her act up, she has become very productive.* T *If you don't clean up your act, you'll be sent home.*

clear as crystal See *(as) clear as crystal.*

clear as mud See *(as) clear as mud.*

clear out to get out (of some place); to leave. □ *All right, you people, clear out of here now.* □ *I knew right then that it was time to clear out.*

clear sailing progress made without any difficulty; an easy situation. □ *Once you've passed that exam, it will be clear sailing.* □ *Working there was not all clear sailing. The boss had a very bad temper.*

clear someone's name to prove that someone is not guilty of a crime or misdeed. □ *I was accused of theft, but I cleared my name.* □ *The student was accused of cheating, but her name was cleared.*

clear something up 1. to explain something; to solve a mystery. □ *I think that we can clear this matter up without calling in the police.* T *First we have to clear up the problem of the missing jewels.* **2.** to cure a disease or a medical condition. (Especially facial pimples.) □ *There is no medicine that will clear pimples up.* T *The doctor will give you something to clear up your cold.*

clear the air to get rid of doubts or hard feelings. (Sometimes this is said about an argument or other unpleasantness. The literal meaning is also used.) □ *All right, let's discuss this frankly. It'll be better if we clear the air.* □ *Mr. and Mrs. Brown always seem to have to clear the air with a big argument before they can be sociable.*

clear the decks get out of the way; get out of this area. (From a naval expression, "Clear the decks for action!" urging seaman to prepare for battle or other action.) □ *Clear the decks! Here comes the teacher.* □ *Clear the decks and take your seats.*

clear the table to remove the dishes and other eating utensils from the table after a meal. (The opposite of *set the table.*) □ *Will you please help clear the table? □ After you clear the table, we'll play cards.*

clear up 1. [for a problem] to become solved. □ *This matter won't clear up by itself. □ The confusion cleared up very quickly when I explained.* **2.** [for a disease] to cure itself or run its course. □ *I told you your pimples would clear up without special medicine. □ My rash cleared up in a week.*

climb on the bandwagon to join others in supporting someone or something. □ *Come join us! Climb on the bandwagon and support Senator Smith! □ Look at all those people climbing on the bandwagon! They don't know what they are getting into!*

climb the wall(s) to do something desperate when one is extremely anxious, bored, or excited. (Informal or slang.) □ *I'm so upset I could climb the wall. □ The meeting was so long and the speaker so boring that most of the audience wanted to climb the wall.*

clip someone's wings to restrain someone; to reduce or put an end to a teenager's privileges. (Informal.) □ *You had better learn to get home on time, or I will clip your wings. □ My mother clipped my wings. I can't go out tonight.*

cloak-and-dagger involving secrecy and plotting. (Fixed order.) □ *A great deal of cloak-and-dagger stuff goes on in political circles. □ A lot of cloak-and-dagger activity was involved in the appointment of the director.*

close at hand within reach; handy. (See also *at hand.*) □ *I'm sorry, but your letter isn't close at hand. Please remind me what you said in it. □ When you're cooking, you should keep all the ingredients close at hand.*

close in (on someone or something) to overwhelm or surround someone or something. □ *My problems are closing in on me. □ The wolves closed in on the elk. □ They howled as they closed in.*

close one's eyes to something to ignore something; to pretend that something is not really happening. □ *You can't close your eyes to hunger in the world. □ I just closed my eyes to the problem and pretended that it wasn't there.*

close ranks to move closer together in a military formation. □ *The soldiers closed ranks and marched on the enemy. □ All right! Stop that talking and close ranks.*

close ranks (behind someone or something) to support someone or something; to back someone or something. □ *We will close ranks behind the candidate. □ She needs our help. Let's close ranks behind her and give her the support she needs.*

close ranks (with someone) to join with someone. □ *We can fight this menace only if we close ranks. □ Let's all close ranks with Ann and adopt her suggestions.*

close something down AND **shut something down** to make something stop operating; to put something out of business. □ *The police closed the factory down.* Ⓣ *The manager shut down the factory for the holidays.* Ⓣ *The city council closed down the amusement park.*

close the books (on someone or something) to put an end to a matter that concerns someone or something. (The *books* here refers to financial accounting records.) □ *It's time to close the books on the Franklin case. □ Yes, let's close the books on Mr. Franklin. □ You closed the books too soon. Here is some new information.*

close the door on someone or something See *shut the door on someone or something.*

close to home AND **where one lives** affecting one personally and intimately. (Informal.) □ *Her remarks were a bit too close to home. I was afraid she was discussing me! □ She's got me figured out all right. She knows where I live. □ Every criticism she made of the performance hit a little too close to home for my comfort. I didn't know I was so* *bad!* □ *When you go through an experience like that and see the horror of a hurricane face to face, that sort of gets you where you live!*

close to someone fond of someone; very good friends with someone. □ *Tom is very close to Mary. They may get married.* □ *Mr. Smith isn't exactly close to Mrs. Smith.*

close up shop to quit working, for the day or forever. (Informal.) □ *It's five o'clock. Time to close up shop.* □ *I can't make any money in this town. The time has come to close up shop and move to another town.*

closefisted (with money) See *tightfisted (with money).*

cloud up 1. [for the sky] to get cloudy, as if it were going to rain. □ *All of a sudden it clouded up and began to rain.* □ *It usually clouds up at sunset.* **2.** [for someone] to grow very sad, as if to cry. (See also *turn on the waterworks.*) □ *The baby clouded up and let out a howl.* □ *Whenever Mary got homesick, she'd cloud up. She really wanted to go home.*

clue someone in (on something) to inform someone of something. (Informal.) □ *Please clue me in on what's going on.* □ *Yes, clue her in.*

clutch at straws to continue to seek solutions, ideas, or hopes that are insubstantial. □ *When you talk of inheriting money, you are just clutching at straws.* □ *That is not a real solution to the problem. You are just clutching at straws.*

coast-to-coast from the Atlantic to the Pacific Ocean (in the continental U.S.A.); all the land between the Atlantic and Pacific Oceans. □ *My voice was once heard on a coast-to-coast radio broadcast.* □ *Our car made the coast-to-coast trip in eighty hours.*

coat and tie [for men] a jacket or sports coat and necktie. (A standard of dress between casual and a suit. Fixed order.) □ *My brother was not wearing a coat and tie, and they would not admit him into the restaurant.* □ *I always carry a coat and tie in my car just in case I have to dress up a little for something.*

cock-and-bull story a silly, made-up story; a story that is a lie. (Fixed order.) □ *Don't give me that cock-and-bull story.* □ *I asked for an explanation, and all I got was your ridiculous cock-and-bull story!*

cock of the walk someone who acts more important that others in a group. □ *The deputy manager was cock of the walk until the new manager arrived.* □ *He loved acting cock of the walk and ordering everyone about.*

coffee and Danish a cup of coffee and a Danish sweet roll. (Fixed order.) □ *A few of us like to have coffee and Danish before we start work.* □ *Coffee and Danish is not my idea of a good breakfast!*

coffee-table book a book that is more suitable for display than for reading, typically, an illustrated book left on the coffee-table for visitors to examine. □ *This book is more of a coffee-table book than an art book. I prefer something more scholarly.* □ *We purchased a coffee-table book for Jan's birthday.*

coffee, tea, or milk a choice of beverage. (Originally used by airline personnel when offering something to drink to the passengers. Fixed order.) □ *She asked me if I wanted coffee, tea, or milk, and I chose just plain water.* □ *Would you prefer coffee, tea, or milk to go with your meal?*

cold comfort no comfort or consolation at all. □ *She knows there are others worse off than she is, but that's cold comfort.* □ *It was cold comfort to the student that others had failed as badly as he did.*

cold, hard cash cash, not checks or promises. (Informal.) □ *I want to be paid in cold, hard cash, and I want to be paid now!* □ *Pay me now! Cash on the barrelhead — cold, hard cash.*

come a cropper to have a misfortune; to fail. (Literally, to fall off one's horse.) □ *Bob invested all his money* *in the stock market just before it fell. Boy, did he come a cropper.* □ *Jane was out all night before she took her tests. She really came a cropper.*

come about 1. to happen. □ *How did this come about?* □ *This came about due to the severe weather.* **2.** [for a sailboat] to turn. □ *Look how easily this boat comes about.* □ *Now, practice making the boat come about.*

Come again? Say it again. I did not hear you. (Folksy.) □ TOM: *Hello, Grandfather.* GRANDFATHER: *Come again? You'll have to talk louder.* □ *The farmer looked at me and said, "Come again?"*

Come again. to come back; to return some other time. □ *I'm so glad you enjoyed our party. Please come again sometime.* □ *The store clerk gave me my change and my purchase and said, "Thank you. Come again."*

Come and get it! Dinner is ready. Come and eat it! (Folksy.) □ *A shout was heard from the kitchen, "Come and get it!"* □ *No one says "Come and get it!" at a formal dinner.*

come and gone already arrived and already departed. (Fixed order.) □ *No, Joy is not here. She's come and gone.* □ *Sorry, you are too late for your appointment. The doctor has come and gone.*

come apart at the seams suddenly to lose one's emotional self-control. (Informal. From the literal sense, referring to a garment falling apart. See also *burst at the seams; fall apart at the seams.*) □ *Bill was so upset that he almost came apart at the seams.* □ *I couldn't take anymore. I just came apart at the seams.*

come (a)round 1. finally to agree or consent (to something). □ *I thought he'd never agree, but in the end he came around.* □ *She came round only after we argued for an hour.* **2.** to return to consciousness; to wake up. □ *He came around after we threw cold water in his face.* □ *The boxer was knocked out, but came round in a few seconds.*

come away empty-handed to return without anything. (See also *go away empty-handed.*) □ *All right, go gambling. Don't come away empty-handed, though.* □ *Go to the bank and ask for the loan again. This time don't come away empty-handed.*

come by something 1. to travel by a specific carrier, such as a plane, a boat, or a car. □ *We came by train. It's more relaxing.* □ *Next time, we'll come by plane. It's faster.* **2.** to find or get something. □ *How did you come by that haircut?* □ *Where did you come by that new shirt?*

come by something honestly 1. to get something honestly. □ *Don't worry. I came by this watch honestly.* □ *I have a feeling she didn't come by it honestly.* **2.** to inherit something—a character trait—from one's parents. □ *I know I'm mean. I came by it honestly, though.* □ *She came by her kindness honestly.*

come clean (with someone) to be completely honest with someone; to confess (everything) to someone. □ *The lawyer said, "I can help you only if you come clean with me."* □ *All right, I'll come clean. Here is the whole story.*

come down [for something] to descend (to someone) through inheritance. □ *All my silverware came down to me from my great-grandmother.* □ *The antique furniture came down through my mother's family.*

come down hard on someone or something to attack vigorously; to scold someone severely. □ *Tom's parents really came down hard on him for coming home late.* Ⓣ *Yes, they came down on him hard.*

come down in the world to lose one's social position or financial standing. □ *Mr. Jones has really come down in the world since he lost his job.* □ *If I were unemployed, I'm sure I'd come down in the world, too.*

come down to earth to become realistic; to become alert to what is going on around one. (Informal.) □ *You have very good ideas, John, but you* must come down to earth. We can't possibly afford any of your suggestions. □ Pay attention to what is going on. Come down to earth and join the discussion.

come down to something to be reduced to something; to amount to no more than something. (Informal. Similar to *boil down to something.*) □ *It comes down to whether you want to go to the movies or stay at home and watch television.* □ *It came down to either getting a job or going back to college.*

come down with something to become ill with some disease. □ *I'm afraid I'm coming down with a cold.* □ *I'll probably come down with pneumonia.*

come from far and wide to come from many different places. (Fixed order.) □ *Everyone was there. They came from far and wide.* □ *We have foods that come from far and wide.*

come full circle to return to the original position or state of affairs. □ *The family sold the house generations ago, but things have come full circle and one of their descendants lives there now.* □ *The employer's power was reduced by the unions at one point, but matters have come full circle again.*

come hell or high water no matter what happens. (Informal. Use *hell* with caution. Fixed order.) □ *I'll be there tomorrow, come hell or high water.* □ *Come hell or high water, I intend to have my own home.*

come home (to roost) [for a problem] to return to cause trouble [for someone]. □ *As I feared, all my problems came home to roost.* □ *Yes, problems all come home eventually.*

come home to someone to become apparent to someone; to be realized by someone. □ *The truth of the matter suddenly came home to me.* □ *It all came home to me while I was taking a bath. Suddenly I understood everything.*

come in a body AND **arrive in a body** to arrive as a group. □ *All the guests came in a body.* □ *Things become very busy when everyone arrives in a body.*

come in for something AND **fall in for something** to receive something; to acquire something. □ *Billy came in for a good bawling-out when he arrived home.* □ *Mary came in for a tremendous amount of money when her aunt died.* □ *Sally fell in for a lot of trouble when she bought a used car.*

come in handy to be useful or convenient. (Informal.) □ *A small television set in the bedroom would come in handy.* □ *A good hammer always comes in handy.* □ *A nice cool drink would come in handy about now.*

come in out of the rain to become alert and sensible; to *come down to earth.* (Also literal. See also *not know enough to come in out of the rain.*) □ *Pay attention, Sally! Come in out of the rain!* □ *Bill will fail if he doesn't come in out of the rain and study.*

come into its own See the following entry.

come into one's own AND **come into its own** 1. [for one] to achieve one's proper recognition. □ *Sally finally came into her own.* □ *After years of trying, she finally came into her own.* 2. [for something] to achieve its proper recognition. □ *The idea of an electric car finally came into its own.* □ *Film as an art medium finally came into its own.*

come into something to inherit something. (Also literal. See also *come in for something*, which is very close in meaning.) □ *Jane came into a small fortune when her aunt died.* □ *Mary came into a house and a new car when her rich uncle died.*

come of age to reach an age when one is old enough to own property, get married, and sign legal contracts. □ *When Jane comes of age, she will buy her own car.* □ *Sally, who came of age last month, entered into an agreement to purchase a house.*

come off to happen; to take place. (Informal. Also literal.) □ *What time does this party come off?* □ *How did your speech come off?* □ *It came off very well.*

Come off it! Tell the truth!; Be serious! (Slang.) □ *Come off it, Bill! I don't believe you!* □ *Come on, Jane. Come off it! That can't be true.*

come off second-best to win second place or worse; to lose out to someone else. □ *John came off second-best in the race.* □ *Why do I always come off second-best in an argument with you?*

come on to hurry up; to follow (someone). □ *Come on! I'm in a hurry.* □ *If you don't come on, we'll miss the train.*

come on like gangbusters to approach people in a wild and exciting manner; to seem very active and pushy when approaching people. □ *Why is she so unpolished? She comes on like gangbusters and frightens people away.* □ *The people in this town seem to come on like gangbusters and they seem very rude at first.*

come on somehow to appear somehow to other people. (Informal. Especially with *strong,* which means "intense." See also the previous entry.) □ *Jane comes on like a very unpleasant person.* □ *She really comes on strong.* □ *John doesn't care how he comes on.*

come on the scene AND **arrive on the scene** to appear in a certain area or place. (Used in particular in police reports or dramatizations of police reports.) □ *What time did the picnickers come on the scene?* □ *The witness arrived on the scene at about 7:13 P.M.*

come out 1. to become; to turn out. (Also literal.) □ *We'll just have to wait and see how things come out.* □ *I'm baking a cake. I hope it comes out okay.* **2.** to be presented to the public; to be released to the public. □ *My new book came out last month.* □ *Mary Ann Smith came out last fall at a lovely party.*

come out ahead to end up with a profit; to improve one's situation. (Compare with *break even.*) □ *I hope you come out ahead with your investments.* □ *It took a lot of money to buy the house, but I think I'll come out ahead.*

come out for someone or something to announce one's support for someone or something. □ *I'm coming out for Senator Brown's reelection.* □ *All the employees came out for a longer workweek.*

come out in the wash to work out all right. (Informal. This means that problems or difficulties will go away as dirt goes away in the process of washing.) □ *Don't worry about that problem. It'll all come out in the wash.* □ *This trouble will go away. It'll come out in the wash.*

come out of nowhere to appear suddenly. (Almost the same as *appear out of nowhere.*) □ *Suddenly, a truck came out of nowhere.* □ *Without warning, the storm came out of nowhere.*

come out of one's shell to become more friendly; to be more sociable. □ *Ann, you should come out of your shell and spend more time with your friends.* □ *Come out of your shell, Tom. Go out and make some friends.*

come out of the blue to appear suddenly as if from nowhere. (*The blue* refers to the blue sky.) □ *This idea came out of the blue, and I think it is a good one.* □ *Sally showed up at the party even though no one told her where it was. She just came out of the blue.*

come out of the closet 1. to reveal one's secret interests. □ *Tom Brown came out of the closet and admitted that he likes to knit.* □ *It's time that all of you lovers of chamber music came out of the closet and attended our concerts.* **2.** to reveal that one is a homosexual. □ *Tom surprised his parents when he came out of the closet.* □ *It was difficult for him to come out of the closet.*

come out with something to say something; to announce something. □ *Sometimes Jane comes out with the most interesting comments.* □ *Jane came out with a long string of curse words.*

come over 1. to join this party or side; to change sides or affiliation. □ *Tom was formerly an enemy spy, but last year he came over.* □ *I thought that Bill* *was a Republican. When did he come over? 2.* to come for a visit. □ *See if Ann wants to come over.* □ *I can't come over. I'm busy.*

come someone's way to come to someone. □ *I wish a large sum of money would come my way.* □ *I hope that no bad luck comes my way.*

come through 1. to do what one is expected to do, especially under difficult conditions. □ *You can depend on Jane. She'll always come through.* □ *We thought that there would be no food, but Tom came through at the last minute with everything we needed.* **2.** [for something] to be approved; [for something] to gain approval. □ *Our mortgage loan application finally came through!* □ *Your papers came through, and you can be sure that the matter has been taken care of.*

come through something with flying colors to survive something quite well. (See *with flying colors.*) □ *Todd came through the test with flying colors.* □ *Mr. Franklin came through the operation with flying colors.*

come to to become conscious; to wake up. □ *We threw a little cold water in his face, and he came to immediately.* □ *Come to, John! You act as if you were in a daze.*

come to a bad end to have a disaster, perhaps one that is deserved or expected; to die an unfortunate death. □ *My old car came to a bad end. Its engine burned up.* □ *The evil merchant came to a bad end.*

come to a dead end to come to an absolute stopping point. □ *The building project came to a dead end.* □ *The street came to a dead end.* □ *We were driving along and came to a dead end.*

come to a head to come to a crucial point; to come to a point when a problem must be solved. □ *Remember my problem with my neighbors? Well, last night the whole thing came to a head.* □ *The battle between the two factions of the city council came to a head yesterday.*

come to a pretty pass to develop into a bad, unfortunate, or difficult situation. □ *Things have come to a pretty pass when people have to beg in the streets.* □ *When parents are afraid of their children, things have come to a pretty pass.*

come to a standstill to stop, temporarily or permanently. □ *The building project came to a standstill because the workers went on strike.* □ *The party came to a standstill until the lights were turned on again.*

come to an end to stop; to finish. □ *The party came to an end at midnight.* □ *Her life came to an end late yesterday.*

come to an untimely end to come to an early death. □ *Poor Mr. Jones came to an untimely end in a car accident.* □ *Cancer caused Mrs. Smith to come to an untimely end.*

come to blows (over something) to fight about something, usually by striking blows, or verbally. □ *They got excited about the accident, but they never actually came to blows over it.* □ *Yes, they aren't the kind of people who come to blows.*

come to grief to fail; to have trouble or grief. □ *The artist wept when her canvas came to grief.* □ *The wedding party came to grief when the bride passed out.*

come to grips with something to face something; to comprehend something. □ *He found it difficult to come to grips with his grandmother's death.* □ *Many students have a hard time coming to grips with algebra.*

come to life to become alive or lively. (Usually used in a figurative sense.) □ *The party came to life about midnight.* □ *As the anesthetic wore off, the patient came to life.*

come to light to become known. □ *Some interesting facts about your past have just come to light.* □ *If too many bad things come to light, you may lose your job.*

come to mind [for a thought or idea] to enter into one's consciousness.

(Compare with *cross someone's mind*.) □ *Do I know a good barber? No one comes to mind right now.* □ *Another idea comes to mind. Why not cut your own hair?*

come to naught See the following entry.

come to nothing AND **come to naught** to amount to nothing; to be worthless. □ *So all my hard work comes to nothing.* □ *Yes, the whole project comes to naught.*

come to one's senses to wake up; to become conscious; to start thinking clearly. □ *John, come to your senses. You're being quite stupid.* □ *In the morning I don't come to my senses until I have had two cups of coffee.*

come to pass to happen. (Formal.) □ *When did all of this come to pass?* □ *When will this event come to pass?*

come to rest to stop moving. □ *When the car comes to rest, you can get in.* □ *The leaf fell and came to rest at my feet.*

come to terms (with someone or something) 1. to come to an agreement with someone. □ *I finally came to terms with my lawyer about his fee.* □ *Bob, you have to come to terms with your father.* **2.** to learn to accept someone or something. (See also *come to grips with something*.) □ *She had to come to terms with the loss of her sight.* □ *She couldn't come to terms with her unemployed husband.*

come to the fore to become prominent; to become important. □ *The question of salary has now come to the fore.* □ *Since his great showing in court, my lawyer has really come to the fore in city politics.*

come to the point AND **get to the point** to get to the important part (of something). □ *He has been talking a long time. I wish he would come to the point.* □ *Quit wasting time! Get to the point!* □ *We are talking about money, Bob! Come on, get to the point.*

come to the same thing See *amount to the same thing*.

come to think of it I just remembered. □ *Come to think of it, I know someone who can help.* □ *I have a screwdriver in the trunk of my car, come to think of it.*

come true to become real; for a dream or a wish actually to happen. □ *When I got married, all my dreams came true.* □ *Coming to the big city was like having my wish come true.*

come unglued to lose emotional control; to have a mental breakdown; to break out into tears or laughter. (Slang.) □ *When Sally heard the joke, she almost came unglued.* □ *When the bank took away my car, I came unglued and cried and cried.*

come up to happen unexpectedly. (Also literal.) □ *I'm sorry, I cannot come to your party. Something has come up.* □ *The storm came up so quickly that I almost got blown away.*

come up in the world to improve one's status or situation in life. □ *Since Mary got her new job, she has really come up in the world.* □ *A good education helped my brother come up in the world.*

come up smelling like roses to end up looking good or respectable after being involved in some difficult or notorious affair. □ *It was a nasty political campaign, but both candidates came up smelling like roses.* □ *I was not surprised that my congressional representative came up smelling like roses after his colleagues investigated him.*

come up with someone or something to find or supply someone or something. □ *I came up with a date at the last minute.* □ *My mom is always able to come up with a snack for me in the afternoon.* □ *I don't have the tool you need, but I'll see if I can come up with something.*

come what may no matter what might happen. □ *I'll be home for the holidays, come what may.* □ *Come what may, the mail will get delivered.*

come with the territory to be expected under circumstances like this. (Refers to the details and difficulties attendant to something like the assignment of a specific sales territory to a salesperson. When one accepts the assignment, one accepts the problems.) □ *There is a lot of paperwork in this job. Oh, well, I guess it comes with the territory.* □ *There are problems, but that comes with the territory.*

come within an ace of doing something See the following entry.

come within an inch of doing something AND **come within an ace of doing something** almost to do something; to come very close to doing something. (The reference to distance is usually metaphorical.) □ *I came within an inch of going into the army.* □ *I came within an inch of falling off the roof.* □ *She came within an ace of buying the house.*

comfortable as an old shoe See *(as) comfortable as an old shoe.*

commit something to memory to memorize something. □ *We all committed the Gettysburg Address to memory.* Ⓣ *I committed to memory the whole list of names and numbers.*

confide in someone to tell secrets or personal matters to someone. □ *Sally always confided in her sister Ann.* □ *She didn't feel that she could confide in her mother.*

conk out to pass out; to go to sleep. (Slang.) □ *Bob bumped his head on a tree branch and conked out.* □ *I usually conk out just after the late news at midnight.*

conspicuous by one's absence to have one's absence (from an event) noticed. □ *We missed you last night. You were conspicuous by your absence.* □ *How could the bride's father miss the wedding? He was certainly conspicuous by his absence.*

contradiction in terms a statement containing a seeming contradiction. □ *A wealthy pauper is a contradiction in terms.* □ *A straight-talking politician may seem a contradiction in terms.*

control the purse strings to be in charge of the money in a business or a household. □ *I control the purse strings at our house.* □ *Mr. Williams is the treasurer. He controls the purse strings.*

cook someone's goose to damage or ruin someone. □ *I cooked my own goose by not showing up on time.* □ *Sally cooked Bob's goose for treating her the way he did.*

cook something up to plot something; to improvise something. (Also literal.) □ *Mary cooked an interesting party up at the last minute.* Ⓣ *Let me see if I can cook up a way to get you some money.*

cook the accounts to cheat in bookkeeping; to make the accounts appear to balance when they do not. □ *Jane was sent to jail for cooking the accounts of her mother's store.* □ *It's hard to tell whether she really cooked the accounts or just didn't know how to add.*

cooking with gas doing things the right way. (Informal. From an advertising slogan.) □ *That's great. Now you're cooking with gas.* □ *Things are moving along nicely with the project. The entire staff is really cooking with gas.*

cool as a cucumber See *(as) cool as a cucumber.*

cool down See *cool off.*

Cool it! Calm down!; Take it easy! (Slang.) □ *Don't get mad, Bob. Cool it!* □ *Cool it, you guys! No fighting around here.*

cool off AND **cool down 1.** to lose or reduce heat. □ *I wish my soup would cool off. I'm hungry.* □ *It'll cool down this evening, after dusk.* **2.** to let one's anger die away. □ *I'm sorry I got angry. I'll cool off in a minute.* □ *Cool off, Tom. There is no sense getting so excited.* **3.** to let one's passion or love die away. □ TED: *Is Bob still in love with Jane?* BILL: *No, he's cooled off a lot.* □ TED: *I thought that they were both cooling down.*

cool one's heels to wait (for someone). (Informal.) □ *I spent all afternoon* cooling my heels in the waiting room while the doctor talked on the telephone. □ All right. If you can't behave properly, just sit down here and cool your heels until I call you.

cool someone down AND **cool someone off** 1. to reduce someone's anger. (Also literal.) □ I just stared at him while he was yelling. I knew that would cool him down. □ The coach talked to them for a long time. That cooled them off. 2. to reduce someone's passion or love. □ When she slapped him, that really cooled him down. □ Dating Mary was too intense, so Bill cooled himself off by dating Sally for a while.

cool someone off See the previous entry.

cop a plea to plead guilty to a crime in hopes of receiving a lighter punishment. (Slang, especially criminal slang.) □ The robber copped a plea and got only two years in jail. □ When you cop a plea, it saves the court system a lot of money.

cop out to get out of a difficult situation; to sneak out of a difficult situation. (Slang.) □ At the last minute she copped out on us. □ Things were going badly for Senator Phillips, so he copped out by resigning.

cost a pretty penny to cost a lot of money. □ I'll bet that diamond cost a pretty penny. □ You can be sure that house cost a pretty penny. It has seven bathrooms.

cost an arm and a leg to cost too much. (Fixed order.) □ It cost an arm and a leg, so I didn't buy it. □ Why should a little plastic part cost an arm and a leg?

cough something up to produce something (that someone has requested). (Informal. Also literal.) □ All right, Bill. Cough the stolen diamonds up or else. □ Okay, okay. I'll cough them up. Ⓣ Bill had to cough up forty dollars to pay for the broken window.

could do with someone or something to want or need someone or something; to benefit from someone or something. (Compare with go for someone or something.) □ I could do with a nice cool drink right now. □ I could do with some help on this project. □ This house could do with some cleaning up. □ They said they could do with John to help them finish faster. □ My car could do with a bigger engine.

could(n't) care less unable to care at all. (Informal. **Could care less** is almost slang.) □ John couldn't care less whether he goes to the party or not. □ So she won first place. I couldn't care less. □ I could care less if I live or die.

count noses to count people. □ I'll tell you how many people are here after I count noses. □ Everyone is here. Let's count noses so we can order hamburgers.

count on someone or something to rely on someone or something. □ Can I count on you to be there at noon? □ I want to buy a car I can count on in winter weather.

count one's chickens before they hatch to plan how to utilize good results of something before those results have occurred. (Frequently used in the negative.) □ You're way ahead of yourself. Don't count your chickens before they hatch. □ You may be disappointed if you count your chickens before they hatch.

count someone in (on something) to include someone in something. (Compare with count someone out (for something).) □ If you're looking for a group to go mountain climbing, count me in on it. Ⓣ I would like to count in your entire family, but there isn't enough room. □ Please count me in.

count someone out (for something) to exclude someone from something. (Compare with count someone in (on something).) □ Please count me out for the party next Saturday. I have other plans. □ You should count the whole family out. We are going to the beach for the weekend.

cover a lot of ground 1. to travel over a great distance; to investigate a wide expanse of land. □ *The prospectors covered a lot of ground, looking for gold.* □ *My car can cover a lot of ground in one day.* **2.** to deal with much information and many facts. □ *The history lecture covered a lot of ground today.* □ *Mr. and Mrs. Franklin always cover a lot of ground when they argue.*

cover for someone 1. to make excuses for someone; to conceal someone's errors. □ *If I miss class, please cover for me.* □ *If you're late, I'll cover for you.* **2.** to handle someone else's work. □ *Dr. Johnson's partner agreed to cover for him during his vacation.* □ *I'm on duty this afternoon. Will you please cover for me? I have a doctor's appointment.*

cover someone's tracks (up) to conceal one's trail; to conceal one's past activities. □ *She was able to cover her tracks up so that they couldn't find her.* Ⓣ *It's easy to cover up your tracks if you aren't well known.* □ *The robber failed to cover his tracks.*

cover something up to conceal something. (Also literal.) Ⓣ *They covered up the truth about the crime.* □ *We'll cover this little matter up and make up a story for the press.*

cover the territory See the following entry.

cover the waterfront AND **cover the territory** to deal with many things, much space, or much information from many points of view. (Informal.) □ *That lecture really covered the waterfront. I could hardly follow it.* □ *Why can't she stick to the point? She has to cover the territory every time she talks.*

cozy up (to someone) to be extra friendly with someone, perhaps in hope of special favors in return. (Informal or slang.) □ *Look at that lawyer cozying up to the judge!* □ *Lawyers who cozy up like that usually get into big trouble.*

crack a book to open a book to study. (Slang. Almost always in the negative.) □ *I passed that test with an A, and I didn't even crack a book.* □ *If you*

think you can get through college without cracking a book, you're wrong.*

crack a joke to tell a joke. (Informal.) □ *She's never serious. She's always cracking jokes.* □ *As long as she's cracking jokes, she's okay.*

crack a smile to smile a little, perhaps reluctantly. (Informal.) □ *She cracked a smile, so I knew she was kidding.* □ *The soldier cracked a smile at the wrong time and had to march for an hour as punishment.*

crack down (on someone or something) to be hard on someone or something; to enforce a rule or law more strenuously. □ *They are cracking down on speeding around here.* □ *It's about time they cracked down.*

crack open a bottle to open a bottle; to remove the cork or seal from a bottle, usually a bottle of an alcoholic drink. □ *They cracked open a bottle to celebrate her arrival.* □ *Let's crack open a bottle of champagne and celebrate.*

crack someone or something up 1. [with *something*] to crash something; to destroy something (in an accident). (Also literal.) □ *The driver cracked the car up in an accident.* Ⓣ *The pilot cracked up the plane.* **2.** [with *someone*] to make someone laugh. □ *She told a joke that really cracked us up.* Ⓣ *I cracked up my history class with a silly remark.*

crack something wide open 1. to crack or split something. □ *The earthquake cracked the field wide open.* □ *They used dynamite to crack the boulder wide open.* **2.** to expose and reveal some great wrongdoing. □ *The police cracked the drug ring wide open.* □ *The newspaper story cracked the trouble at city hall wide open.*

crack up 1. [for a plane, boat, car, etc.] to crash. □ *The plane cracked up in the storm.* □ *The boat cracked up on the rocks.* **2.** [for someone] to break out in laughter. □ *The audience really cracked up during the second act.* □ *The class cracked up when I told my joke, but the teacher didn't like it.* **3.** to go crazy. (Slang.) □ *The mayor cracked up after only a year in office.* □ *I was afraid the mayor would crack up because of too much work.*

cramp someone's style to limit someone in some way. □ *I hope this doesn't cramp your style, but could you please not hum while you work?* □ *To ask him to keep regular hours would really be cramping his style.*

crank something out to produce something; to make something in a casual and mechanical way. (Slang.) □ *John can crank a lot of work out in a single day.* Ⓣ *That factory keeps cranking out cars even though no one buys them.*

crash and burn to fail spectacularly. (Also literal, as with a car or a plane. Fixed order.) □ *Poor Chuck really crashed and burned when he made his presentation at the sales meeting.* □ *Mary just knew that the whole project would crash and burn if she didn't keep a close watch on it.*

crazy about someone or something AND **mad about someone or something; nuts about someone or something** very fond of someone or something. (Slang.) □ *Ann is crazy about John.* □ *He's crazy about her, too.* □ *I'm mad about their new song.* □ *Our whole family is nuts about homemade ice cream.*

crazy as a loon See *(as) crazy as a loon.*

cream of the crop the best of all. □ *This particular car is the cream of the crop.* □ *The kids are very bright. They are the cream of the crop.*

create a scene See *make a scene.*

create a stink (about something) AND **make a stink (about something); raise a stink (about something)** to make a major issue out of something; to make much over something; to make a lot of complaints and criticisms about something. (Slang. Compare with *make a federal case out of something.*) □ *Tom created a stink about Bob's remarks.* □ *Why did he make a stink about that?* □ *Tom is always trying to raise a stink.*

create an uproar AND **make an uproar** to cause an outburst or sensation. (Especially with *such.*) □ *The dog got into church and made an uproar.* □ *Her poodle created an uproar in the restaurant.* □ *Why did you make such an uproar?*

creature comforts things that make people comfortable. □ *The hotel room was sparse, but all the creature comforts were there.* □ *The entire country of Adonia seemed to lack the expected creature comforts.*

cross a bridge before one comes to it to worry excessively about something before it happens. (Note the variations in the examples.) □ *There is no sense in crossing that bridge before you come to it.* □ *She's always crossing bridges before coming to them. She needs to learn to relax.*

cross a bridge when one comes to it to deal with a problem only when one is faced with the problem. (Note the variations in the examples.) □ *Please wait and cross that bridge when you come to it.* □ *He shouldn't worry about it now. He can cross that bridge when he comes to it.*

cross-examine someone to ask someone questions in great detail; to question a suspect or a witness at great length. □ *The police cross-examined the suspect for three hours.* □ *The lawyer plans to cross-examine the witness tomorrow morning.*

cross one's fingers See *keep one's fingers crossed (for someone or something).*

cross one's heart (and hope to die) to pledge or vow that the truth is being told. □ *It's true, cross my heart and hope to die.* □ *It's really true — cross my heart.*

cross someone up to give someone trouble; to defy or betray someone. (Also without *up.*) □ *You really crossed me up when you told Tom what I said.* □ *Please don't cross me up again.*

cross someone's mind See *pass through someone's mind.*

cross someone's palm with silver to pay money to someone in payment for a service. (A fortune-teller might ask for a potential customer to cross her palm with silver. Used in that sense or jocularly for something like tipping a porter.) □ *I crossed his palm with silver, but he still stood there.* □ *You will find that things happen much faster in hotels if you cross the staff's palms with silver fairly often.*

cross swords (with someone) (on something) to enter into an argument with someone. □ *I don't want to cross swords with Tom on this matter.* □ *The last time we crossed swords, we had a terrible time.*

cross the Rubicon to do something that inevitably commits one to following a certain course of action. (The crossing of the River Rubicon by Julius Caesar inevitably involved him in a war with the senate in B.C. 49.) □ *Jane crossed the Rubicon by signing the contract.* □ *Find another job before you cross the Rubicon and resign from this one.*

crushed by something demoralized; with hurt feelings. (Also literal.) □ *The whole family was completely crushed by the news.* □ *I was just crushed by your attitude. I thought we were friends.*

crux of the matter the central issue of the matter. (*Crux* is an old word meaning "cross.") □ *All right, this is the crux of the matter.* □ *It's about time that we looked at the crux of the matter.*

cry before one is hurt to cry or complain before one is injured. □ *Bill always cries before he's hurt.* □ *There is no point in crying before one is hurt.*

cry bloody murder to scream as if something very serious has happened. (See also *scream bloody murder*.) □ *Now that Bill is really hurt, he's crying bloody murder.* □ *There is no point in crying bloody murder about the bill if you aren't going to pay it.*

cry crocodile tears See *shed crocodile tears.*

cry one's eyes out to cry very hard. □ *When we heard the news, we cried our eyes out with joy.* □ *She cried her eyes out after his death.*

cry over spilled milk to be unhappy about something that cannot be undone. □ *I'm sorry that you broke your bicycle, Tom. But there is nothing that can be done now. Don't cry over spilled milk.* □ *Ann is always crying over spilled milk.*

cry wolf to cry or complain about something when nothing is really wrong. □ *Pay no attention. She's just crying wolf again.* □ *Don't cry wolf too often. No one will come.*

crying need for someone or something a definite or desperate need for someone or something. □ *There is a crying need for someone to come in and straighten things out.* □ *All the people in that area have a crying need for better housing.*

crying shame a very unfortunate situation; a real shame. □ *It's a crying shame that people cannot afford adequate housing.* □ *That everyone could not attend the concert was a crying shame.*

cue someone in 1. to give someone a cue; to indicate to someone that the time has come. □ *Now, cue the orchestra director in.* Ⓣ *All right, cue in the announcer.* **2.** to tell someone what is going on. (Informal. Almost the same as *clue someone in (on something)*.) □ *I want to know what's going on. Cue me in.* Ⓣ *Cue in the general about the troop movement.*

Curiosity killed the cat. a proverb meaning that it is dangerous to be curious. □ *Don't ask so many questions, Billy. Curiosity killed the cat.* □ *Curiosity killed the cat. Mind your own business.*

curl someone's hair AND **make someone's hair curl** to frighten or alarm someone; to shock someone with sight, sound, or taste. (Also literal.) □ *Don't ever sneak up on me like that* *again. You really curled my hair.* □ *The horror film made my hair curl.*

curl up and die to retreat and die. □ *When I heard you say that, I could have curled up and died.* □ *No, it wasn't an illness. She just curled up and died.*

curry favor (with someone) to try to win favor from someone. □ *The lawyer tried to curry favor with the judge.* □ *It's silly to curry favor. Just act yourself.*

cut a big swath See *cut a wide swath.*

cut a fine figure to look good; to look elegant. (Formal. Usually said of a male.) □ *Tom really cuts a fine figure on the dance floor.* □ *Bill cuts a fine figure since he bought some new clothes.*

cut a wide swath AND **cut a big swath** to seem important; to attract a lot of attention. □ *In social matters, Mrs. Smith cuts a wide swath.* □ *Bob cuts a big swath whenever he appears in his military uniform.*

cut above someone or something a measure or degree better than someone or something else. (Especially with *average,* as in the examples.) □ *Your shirt is beautiful, but mine is a cut above yours.* □ *John isn't the best mechanic in town, but he's a cut above average.*

cut across something to reach beyond something; to embrace a wide variety; to slice across a figurative boundary or barrier. (Also literal.) □ *His teaching cut across all human cultures and races.* □ *This rule cuts across all social barriers.*

cut-and-dried fixed; determined beforehand; usual and uninteresting. (Fixed order.) □ *I find your writing quite boring. It's too cut-and-dried.* □ *The lecture was, as usual, cut-and-dried. It was the same thing we've heard for years.*

cut and paste (Fixed order.) **1.** to cut something out of paper with scissors and paste it onto something else. □ *The teacher told the little children that it was time to cut and paste, and they all ran to the worktables.* □ *Mary made a*

tiny house by cutting and pasting little strips of paper. **2.** something trivial, simple, or childish. □ *I hate this job. It's nothing but cut and paste.* □ *I don't mind doing things that have to be done, but I hate to waste my time on cut and paste.*

cut and run to get free and run away. (Slang. As in cutting loose a ship's or boat's anchor and sailing away in a hurry. Fixed order.) □ *Max decided to cut and run when he heard the police sirens.* □ *As soon as I finish what I am doing here, I'm going to cut and run. I've got to get home by six o'clock.*

cut back (on something) to reduce something; to use less of something. □ *The government has to cut back on its spending.* □ *It's very difficult for the government to cut back.*

cut both ways to affect both sides of an issue equally. □ *Remember that your suggestion that costs should be shared cuts both ways. You will have to pay as well.* □ *If our side cannot take along supporters to the game, then yours cannot either. The rule has to cut both ways.*

cut class to skip going to class. (Informal.) □ *If Mary keeps cutting classes, she'll fail the course.* □ *I can't cut that class. I've missed too many already.*

cut corners to reduce efforts or expenditures; to do things poorly or incompletely. (From the phrase *cut the corner* meaning to avoid going to an intersection to make a turn.) □ *You cannot cut corners when you are dealing with public safety.* □ *Don't cut corners, Sally. Let's do the job right.*

cut loose (from someone or something) to break away from someone or something; to break ties with someone or something; to act in a free manner. (Compare with *break loose (from someone or something).*) □ *Jane is finding it hard to cut loose from her family.* □ *Cutting loose is part of growing up.* □ *When those farm boys get to town, they really cut loose from convention.* □ *They sure are wild when they cut loose.*

cut loose (with something) See *let go (with something)*.

cut no ice (with someone) to fail to change the mind of someone; to have no influence on someone. (Informal.) □ *What you just said will cut no ice with the manager.* □ *All that may be true, but it cuts no ice with me.* □ *That idea cuts no ice. It won't help at all.* □ *It cuts no ice that your mother is the mayor.*

cut off to stop by itself or oneself. (Informal.) □ *The machine got hot and cut off.* □ *Bob cut off in midsentence.*

cut off one's nose to spite one's face a phrase meaning that one harms oneself in trying to punish another person. (The phrase is variable in form. Note the examples.) □ *Billy loves the zoo, but he refused to go with his mother because he was mad at her. He cut off his nose to spite his face.* □ *Find a better way to be angry. It is silly to cut your nose off to spite your face.*

cut one's eyeteeth on something to have done something since one was very young; to have much experience at something. (Folksy.) □ *Do I know about cars? I cut my eyeteeth on cars.* □ *I cut my eyeteeth on Bach. I can whistle everything he wrote.*

cut one's losses to reduce someone's losses of money, goods, or other things of value. □ *I sold the stock as it went down, thus cutting my losses.* □ *He cut his losses by putting better locks on the doors. There were fewer robberies.* □ *The mayor's reputation suffered because of the scandal. He finally resigned to cut his losses.*

cut one's (own) throat [for someone] to experience certain failure; to do damage to someone. (Informal. Also literal.) □ *If I were to run for office, I'd just be cutting my throat.* □ *Judges who take bribes are cutting their own throats.*

cut out for something well-suited for something; with a talent for something. (Compare with *cut out to be something*.) □ *Tom was not cut out for banking.* □ *Sally was cut out for the medical profession.*

cut out the deadwood to remove unproductive persons from employment. (Also literal = to prune away dead branches or deadwood.) □ *This company would be more profitable if management would cut out the deadwood.* □ *When we cut out the deadwood, all our departments will run more smoothly.*

cut out to be something well-suited for a particular role or a particular occupation. (Compare with *cut out for something*.) □ *Tom was not cut out to be a banker.* □ *Sally was cut out to be a doctor.*

cut (someone) a check to write a check; to have a computer print a check. □ *We will cut a check for the balance due you later this afternoon.* □ *We will cut you a check as soon as possible.*

cut someone dead to ignore someone totally. □ *Joan was just about to speak to James when he cut her dead.* □ *Jean cut her former husband dead.*

cut someone down (to size) AND **take someone down (to size)** to make a person humble; to *put one in one's place*. (See also *beat someone down (to size)*.) □ *John's remarks really cut me down to size.* □ *Jane is too conceited. I think her new boss will take her down to size.* □ *The boss's angry stare will really cut her down.*

cut someone in to give someone a share of something. (Informal or slang.) □ *Shall we cut Bill in on this deal?* □ *I don't think we should cut anybody in.* ⊤ *Pretty soon we'll have to cut in the whole town.*

cut someone off without a penny to end someone's allowance; to fail to leave someone money in one's will. □ *Mr. and Mrs. Franklin cut their son off without a penny after he quit school.* ⊤ *They cut off both of their sons without a penny.* ⊤ *We learned, when Uncle Sam's will was read, that he cut off his own flesh and blood without a penny.*

cut someone or something to the bone
1. to slice deep to a bone. □ *The knife cut John to the bone. He had to be sewed up.* □ *Cut each slice of ham to the bone. Then each slice will be as big as possible.* **2.** [with *something*] to cut down severely (on something). □ *We cut our expenses to the bone and are still losing money.* □ *Congress had to cut the budget to the bone in order to balance it.*

cut someone or something up to criticize someone or something severely. (Slang. Also literal.) □ *Jane is such a gossip. She was really cutting Mrs. Jones up.* T *The professor really cut up my essay.*

cut someone to the quick to hurt someone's feelings very badly. (Can be used literally when *quick* refers to the tender flesh at the base of fingernails and toenails.) □ *Your criticism cut me to the quick.* □ *Tom's sharp words to Mary cut her to the quick.*

cut teeth [for a baby or young person] to grow teeth. □ *Billy is cranky because he's cutting teeth.* □ *Ann cut her first tooth this week.*

cut the ground out from under someone to destroy the foundation of someone's plans or someone's argument. □ *The politician cut the ground out from under his opponent.* T *Congress cut out the ground from under the president.*

cut up to act wildly; to show off and be troublesome; to act like a clown. (Slang. See also *cut someone or something up*.) □ *Tom, Billy! Stop cutting up, or I'll send you to the principal's office.* □ *If you spent more time studying than cutting up, you'd get better grades.*

D

daily dozen physical exercises done every day. (Informal.) □ *My brother always feels better after his daily dozen.* □ *She would rather do a daily dozen than go on a diet.*

damn someone or something with faint praise to criticize someone or something indirectly by not praising enthusiastically. □ *The critic did not say that he disliked the play, but he damned it with faint praise.* □ *Mrs. Brown is very proud of her son's achievements, but damns her daughter's with faint praise.*

dance to another tune to shift quickly to different behavior; to change one's behavior or attitude. (See also *change someone's tune; sing a different tune.*) □ *After being yelled at, Ann danced to another tune.* □ *A stern talking-to will make her dance to another tune.*

dance with death to attempt to do something that is very risky. □ *The crossing of the border into Adonia was like dancing with death.* □ *You are dancing with death in your effort to cross that narrow ledge.*

dare someone (to do something) to challenge someone to do something. □ *Sally dared Jane to race her to the corner.* □ *You wouldn't do that, would you? I dare you.*

dark horse someone or something whose abilities, plans, or feelings are little known to others. (From horse racing.) □ *It's difficult to predict who will win the prize—there are two or three dark horses in the tournament.* □ *Everyone was surprised at the results of the election. The dark horse won.*

darken someone's door [for an unwelcome person] to come to someone's door seeking entry. (As if the visitor were casting a shadow on the door. Formal, or even jocular.) □ *Who is this who has come to darken my door?* □ *Is that you, John, darkening my door again? I thought you were out of town.* □ *The heroine of the drama told the villain never to darken her door again.* □ *She touched the back of her hand to her forehead and said, "Go and never darken my door again!"*

dash cold water on something See *pour cold water on something.*

dash something off to send something off, usually quickly. □ *I'll dash a quick note off to Aunt Mary.* ⊤ *Ann just dashed off a message to her parents.*

date back (to sometime) to extend back to a particular time; to have been alive at a particular time in the past. □ *My late grandmother dated back to the Civil War.* □ *This record dates back to the sixties.* □ *How far do you date back?*

Davy Jones's locker the bottom of the sea, especially when it is a grave. (From the seamen's name for the evil spirit of the sea. See also *go to Davy Jones's locker.*) □ *They were going to sail around the world, but ended up in Davy Jones's locker.* □ *Most of the gold from that trading ship is in Davy Jones's locker.*

dawn on someone to occur to someone; to *cross someone's mind.* □ *It just dawned on me that I forgot my books.* □ *When will it dawn on him that his audience is bored?*

day after day every day; daily; all the time. □ *He wears the same clothes day after day.* □ *She visits her husband in the hospital day after day.*

day and night AND **night and day** all the time; around the clock. (Reversible.) □ *The nurse was with her day and night.* □ *The house is guarded night and day.*

day in and day out AND **day in, day out** on every day; for each day. (Fixed order.) □ *She smokes day in and day out.* □ *They eat nothing but vegetables, day in, day out.*

day in, day out See the previous entry.

day-to-day daily; everyday; common. □ *They update their accounts on a day-to-day basis.* □ *Just wear your regular day-to-day clothing.*

daylight robbery the practice of blatantly or grossly overcharging. □ *It's daylight robbery to charge that amount of money for a hotel room!* □ *The cost of renting a car at that place is daylight robbery.*

dead ahead straight ahead; directly ahead. □ *Look out! There is a cow in the road dead ahead.* □ *The farmer said that the town we wanted was dead ahead.*

dead and buried gone forever. (Refers literally to persons and figuratively to ideas and other things. Fixed order.) □ *Now that Uncle Bill is dead and buried, we can read his will.* □ *That kind of thinking is dead and buried.*

dead and gone dead and buried, and probably forgotten. (Fixed order.) □ *John is dead and gone. There is no reason to fear him anymore.* □ *Her husband is dead and gone, but she is getting along fine.*

dead as a dodo See *(as) dead as a dodo.*

dead as a doornail See *(as) dead as a doornail.*

dead duck someone or something that is failed, finished, or dead. □ *He missed the exam. He's a dead duck.* □

Yes, John's a dead duck. He drove his car into a tree.

dead in someone's or something's tracks exactly where someone or something is at the moment; at this instant. (This does not usually have anything to do with death. The phrase is often used with *stop.*) □ *Her unkind words stopped me dead in my tracks.* □ *When I heard the rattlesnake, I stopped dead in my tracks.* □ *The project came to a halt dead in its tracks.*

dead letter 1. a piece of mail that is returned to the post office as both undeliverable and unreturnable. □ *At the end of the year, the post office usually has bushels of dead letters.* □ *Some of the dead letters are opened to see if there is an address inside.* **2.** an issue, law, or matter that is no longer important or that no longer has force or power. (Could also be used for a person.) □ *His point about the need for education reform is a dead letter. It is being done now.* □ *This point of law is a dead letter since the last Supreme Court ruling on this matter.*

dead loss a total loss. □ *My investment was a dead loss.* □ *This car is a dead loss. It was a waste of money.*

dead on one's or its feet exhausted; worn out; no longer useful. □ *Ann is so tired. She's really dead on her feet.* □ *He can't teach well anymore. He's dead on his feet.* □ *This inefficient company is dead on its feet.*

dead set against someone or something totally opposed to someone or something. □ *I'm dead set against the new tax proposal.* □ *Everyone is dead set against the mayor.*

dead to the world tired; exhausted; sleeping soundly. (Compare with *dead on one's or its feet.*) □ *I've had such a hard day. I'm really dead to the world.* □ *Look at her sleep. She's dead to the world.*

deaf and dumb unable to hear or speak. (Used without any intended malice, but no longer considered polite. Sometimes euphemized as "hearing and speech impaired." Fixed order.) □ *Fred objected to being called deaf and dumb.* □ *Aunt Clara—she was deaf and dumb, you know—lived to be over 100.*

deal in something to buy and sell something. □ *My uncle is a stockbroker. He deals in stocks and bonds.* □ *My aunt deals in antiques.*

death and taxes death, which is inevitable, and the payment of taxes, which is unavoidable. (A saying that emphasizes the rigor with which taxes are collected. Fixed order.) □ *There is nothing as certain on this old planet as death and taxes.* □ *Max said he could get out of anything except death and taxes.*

death on someone or something 1. very effective in acting against someone or something. □ *This road is terribly bumpy. It's death on tires.* □ *The sergeant is death on lazy soldiers.* **2.** [with *something*] accurate or deadly at doing something requiring skill or great effort. □ *John is death on curve balls. He's our best pitcher.* □ *The boxing champ is really death on those fast punches.*

decide in favor of someone or something to determine that someone or something is the winner. □ *The judge decided in favor of the defendant.* □ *I decided in favor of the red one.*

deep-six someone or something to get rid of someone or something; to dispose of someone or something. (Slang. Means to bury someone or something six feet deep, the standard depth for a grave.) □ *Take this horrible food out and deep-six it.* □ *That guy is a pain. Deep-six him so the cops will never find him.*

desert a sinking ship AND **leave a sinking ship** to leave a place, a person, or a situation when things become difficult or unpleasant. (Rats are said to be the first to leave a ship that is sinking.) □ *I hate to be the one to desert a sinking ship, but I can't stand it around here anymore.* □ *There goes Tom. Wouldn't you know he'd leave a sinking ship rather than stay around and try to help?*

devil-may-care attitude AND **devil-may-care manner** a very casual attitude; a worry-free or carefree attitude. □ *You must get rid of your devil-may-care attitude if you want to succeed.* □ *She acts so thoughtless with her devil-may-care manner.*

devil-may-care manner See the previous entry.

devil of a job AND **the devil's own job** the most difficult task. (Informal. The first entry is usually with *a*.) □ *We had a devil of a job fixing the car.* □ *It was the devil's own job finding a hotel with vacancies.*

diamond in the rough a valuable or potentially excellent person or thing hidden by an unpolished or rough exterior. □ *Ann looks like a stupid woman, but she's a fine person—a real diamond in the rough.* □ *That piece of property is a diamond in the rough. Someday it will be valuable.*

die a natural death 1. [for someone] to die by disease or old age rather than by violence or foul play. □ *I hope to live to 100 and die a natural death.* □ *The police say she didn't die a natural death, and they are investigating.* **2.** [for something] to fade away or die down. □ *I expect that all this excitement about computers will die a natural death.* □ *Most fads die a natural death.*

die in one's boots AND **die with one's boots on** to go down fighting; to die in some fashion other than in bed; to die fighting. (A cliché popularized by western movies. The villains of these movies said they preferred death by gunshot or hanging to dying in bed. See also *go down fighting.*) □ *I won't let him get me. I'll die in my boots.* □ *He may give me a hard time, but I won't be overcome. I'll fight him and die with my boots on.*

die is cast some process is past the point of no return. (The *die* is one of a pair of dice. The *cast* means "thrown.") □ *After that speech favoring reform of* *the education system, the die is cast. This is now a campaign issue.* □ *The die is cast. There is no turning back on this point.*

die laughing 1. to meet one's death laughing—in good spirits, revenge, or irony. □ *Sally is such an optimist that she'll probably die laughing.* □ *Bob tried to poison his rich aunt, who then died laughing because she had taken Bob out of her will.* **2.** to laugh very long and hard. (Informal.) □ *The joke was so funny that I almost died laughing.* □ *The play was meant to be funny, but the audience didn't exactly die laughing.*

die of a broken heart 1. to die of emotional distress. □ *I was not surprised to hear of her death. They say she died of a broken heart.* □ *In the movie, the heroine appeared to die of a broken heart, but the audience knew she was poisoned.* **2.** to suffer from emotional distress, especially from a failed romance. □ *Tom and Mary broke off their romance and both died of broken hearts.* □ *Please don't leave me. I know I'll die of a broken heart.*

die of boredom to suffer from boredom; to be very bored. □ *No one has ever really died of boredom.* □ *We sat there and listened politely, even though we almost died of boredom.*

die on the vine See *wither on the vine.*

die with one's boots on See *die in one's boots.*

different as night and day See *(as) different as night and day.*

dig in 1. to eat a meal; to begin eating a meal. (Informal. Out of place in formal situations. See also *Come and get it!* Also literal.) □ *Dinner's ready, Tom. Sit down and dig in.* □ *The cowboy helped himself to some beans and dug in.* **2.** to apply oneself to a task; to tackle (something) vigorously. □ *Sally looked at the big job ahead of her. Then she rolled up her sleeves and dug in.* □ *"Tom," hollered Mrs. Smith, "you get to that pile of homework and dig in this very minute."*

dig one's heels in to refuse to alter one's course of action or opinions; to be obstinate or determined. □ *The student dug her heels in and refused to obey the instructions.* □ *I'm digging in my heels. I'm not going back.*

dig one's own grave to be responsible for one's own downfall or ruin. □ *The manager tried to get rid of his assistant, but he dug his own grave. He got fired himself for trying.* □ *The committee has dug its own grave with the new tax bill.*

dig some dirt up on someone to find out something bad about someone. (Informal.) □ *If you don't stop trying to dig some dirt up on me, I'll get a lawyer and sue you.* ⊤ *The citizens' group dug up some dirt on the mayor and used it against her at election time.*

dig someone or something to understand something; to relate to a person or a thing. (Slang.) □ *I really dig Tom. He's a special guy.* □ *I really dig rock music.*

dig someone or something up to go to great effort to find someone or something. (There is an implication that the thing or person dug up is not the most desirable, but is all that could be found.) □ *Mary dug a date up for the dance next Friday.* ⊤ *I dug up a recipe for roast pork with pineapple.* ⊤ *I dug up a carpenter who doesn't charge very much.*

dig something out to work hard to locate something and bring it forth. (Also literal.) □ *They dug the contract out of the file cabinet.* □ *I dug this old suit out of a box in the attic.* ⊤ *I dug out an old dress and wore it to the fifties party.*

dime a dozen abundant; cheap and common. □ *People who can write good books are not a dime a dozen.* □ *Romantic movies are a dime a dozen.*

dine out See *eat (a meal) out.*

dip in(to something) to take or borrow from a supply of something, especially a supply of money. (Also literal.) □ *I had to dip into my savings account to* pay for the car. □ *I hate to dip in like that.* □ *She put out her hand and dipped into the chocolate box.*

dirt cheap extremely cheap. (Informal.) □ *Buy some more of those plums. They're dirt cheap.* □ *In Italy, the peaches are dirt cheap.*

dirty old man an older man who is excessively interested in sex. □ *Tell your daughter to stay away from him. He's a dirty old man and might attack her.* □ *There were several dirty old men looking at pornographic magazines in the park.*

dirty one's hands See *get one's hands dirty.*

dirty work 1. unpleasant or uninteresting work. □ *My boss does all the traveling. I get all the dirty work to do.* □ *She's tired of doing all the dirty work at the office.* **2.** dishonest or underhanded actions; treachery. □ *She knew there was some dirty work going on when she saw her opponents whispering together.* □ *The company seems respectable enough, but there's a lot of dirty work that goes on.*

divide and conquer to cause the enemy to divide and separate into two or more warring factions, and then move in to conquer all of them. (Fixed order.) □ *Mary thought she could divide and conquer the board of directors, but they had survived such tactics many times, and her efforts failed.* □ *Sam led his men to divide and conquer the enemy platoon, and his strategy succeeded.*

divide something fifty-fifty AND **split something fifty-fifty** to divide something into two equal parts. (Informal. The *fifty* means 50 percent.) □ *Tommy and Billy divided the candy fifty-fifty.* □ *The robbers split the money fifty-fifty.*

do a double take to react with surprise; to have to look twice to make sure that one really saw correctly. (Informal.) □ *When the boy led a goat into the park, everyone did a double take.* □ *When the nurse saw that the man had six toes, she did a double take.*

do a flip-flop (on something) AND **do an about-face** to make a total reversal of opinion. (Informal or slang.) □ *Without warning, the government did a flip-flop on taxation.* □ *It had done an about-face on the question of deductions last year.*

do a job on someone or something 1. to damage someone or something; to mess up someone or something. (Informal or slang.) □ *The robbers really did a job on the bank guard. They beat him when they robbed the bank.* □ *The puppy did a job on my shoes. They are all chewed to pieces.* **2.** [with *something*] to defecate on something. (Informal and euphemistic. Note the variation in the second example.) □ *The puppy did a job on the living-room carpet.* □ *It's supposed to do its job on the newspapers in the basement.*

do a land-office business to do a large amount of business in a short period of time. □ *The ice cream shop always does a land-office business on a hot day.* □ *The tax collector's office did a land-office business on the day that taxes were due.*

do a number on someone or something to damage or harm someone or something. (Slang.) □ *The teacher did a number on the whole class. That test was terrible.* □ *Tom did a number on Mary when he went out with Ann.*

do a snow job on someone to deceive or confuse someone. (Informal or slang.) □ *Tom did a snow job on the teacher when he said that he was sick yesterday.* □ *I hate it when someone does a snow job on me. I find it harder and harder to trust people.*

do an about-face See *do a flip-flop (on something).*

do away with someone or something 1. [with *someone*] to kill someone; to dispose of someone or something. □ *The crooks did away with the witness.* □ *I was there, too. I hope they don't try to do away with me.* **2.** [with *something*] to get rid of something; to dispose of something. □ *This chemical will do away with the stain in your sink.* □ *The* *time has come to do away with that old building.*

do credit to someone AND **do someone credit** to add to the reputation of someone. (See also *do someone proud.*) □ *Your new job really does credit to you.* □ *Yes, it really does you credit.*

do justice to something 1. to do something well; to represent or portray something accurately. □ *Sally did justice to the contract negotiations.* □ *This photograph doesn't do justice to the beauty of the mountains.* **2.** to eat or drink a great deal. □ *Bill always does justice to the turkey on Thanksgiving.* □ *The party didn't do justice to the roast pig. There were nearly ten pounds left over.*

do one's bit See *do one's part.*

do one's duty to do one's job; to do what is expected of one. □ *Please don't thank me. I'm just doing my duty.* □ *Soldiers who fight in wars are doing their duty.*

do one's (level) best to do (something) as well as one can. □ *Just do your level best. That's all we can ask of you.* □ *Tom isn't doing his best. We may have to replace him.*

do one's (own) thing to do what one likes or what one pleases. (Informal or slang.) □ *Tom doesn't like being told what to do. He prefers to do his own thing.* □ *When you do your thing, you have no one but yourself to blame if things don't work out.*

do one's part AND **do one's bit** to do one's share of the work; to do whatever one can do to help. □ *All people everywhere must do their part to help get things under control.* □ *I always try to do my bit. How can I help this time?*

do or die do something or die trying. (Literal or figurative. Refers to an attitude or frame of mind that one can adopt when one must do something whether one wants to or not. Also occurs as a noun or an adjective. Fixed order.) □ *It was do or die. There was no turning back now.* □ *He simply had*

to get to the airport on time. It was a case of do or die.

do so See *do too.*

do somehow by someone to treat someone in a particular manner. (Informal. Do not confuse this with a passive construction. The *someone* is not the actor but the object.) □ *Tom did all right by Ann when he brought her red roses.* □ *I did badly by Tom. I fired him.*

do someone a good turn to do something that is helpful to someone. □ *My neighbor did me a good turn by lending me his car.* □ *The teacher did me a good turn when he told me to work harder.*

do someone credit See *do credit to someone.*

do someone damage to harm someone. (Informal.) □ *I hope she doesn't plan to do me damage.* □ *They did us damage by telling the whole story to the newspapers.*

do someone good to benefit someone. (Informal.) □ *A nice hot bath really does me good.* □ *A few years in the army would do you good.*

do someone one better See *go someone one better.*

do someone or something in 1. [with *someone*] to make someone tired. □ *That tennis game really did me in.* □ *Yes, hard activity will do you in.* **2.** [with *someone*] to cheat someone; to *take someone in.* □ *The crooks did the widow in.* ⊤ *They did in the widow by talking her into giving them all the money in her bank account.* **3.** [with *someone*] to kill someone. ⊤ *The crooks did in the bank guard.* ⊤ *They'll probably do in the witnesses soon.* **4.** [with *something*] to destroy something. ⊤ *The huge waves totally did in the seaside community.* □ *The fire did the wooden building in.*

do someone or something over AND **make someone or something over** (See also *make a fuss (over someone or something).*) **1.** [with *someone*] to buy a new wardrobe for someone; to redo someone's hair. □ *Sally's mother did Sally over for the play tryouts.* □ *It's very expensive to do a person over completely.* □ *The designer did Sally over completely.* **2.** [with *something*] to rebuild, redesign, or redecorate something. □ *We did our living room over for the holidays.* ⊤ *We made over the family room because it was looking shabby.*

do someone out of something to cheat someone out of something. (Informal or slang.) □ *They did the widow out of her life savings.* □ *I won't let anyone do me out of anything. I'm a very cautious and suspicious person.*

do someone proud to make someone proud. (Folksy. See *do credit to someone.*) □ *Well, Bill really did himself proud in the horse race.* □ *That fine-looking, prizewinning hog ought to do you proud. Did you raise it all by yourself?*

do someone's heart good to make someone feel good emotionally. (Informal. Also literal.) □ *It does my heart good to hear you talk that way.* □ *When she sent me a get-well card, it really did my heart good.*

do something by hand to do something with one's hands rather than with a machine. □ *The computer was broken so I had to do the calculations by hand.* □ *All this tiny stitching was done by hand. Machines cannot do this kind of work.*

do something fair and square to do something fairly. (Folksy. See also *fair and square.* Fixed order.) □ *He always plays the game fair and square.* □ *I try to treat all people fair and square.*

do something hands down to do something easily and without opposition. □ *The mayor won the election hands down.* □ *She was the choice of the people hands down.*

do something in person to appear somewhere and do something oneself rather than sending someone or doing

something over the telephone or by mail. □ *I know the money should be in his account. I saw him put it there in person.* □ *The famous actor came to the hospital and greeted each patient in person.*

do something in public to do something where anyone looking could see it. (Compare with *in private.*) □ *You should dress neatly when you appear in public.* □ *I wish that you wouldn't talk to me so rudely in public.* □ *Bob, you must behave properly in public.*

do something in secret to do something privately or secretly. □ *Why do you always do things like that in secret?* □ *There is no need to count your money in secret.*

do something in vain to do something for no purpose; to do something that fails. □ *They rushed her to the hospital, but they did it in vain.* □ *We tried in vain to get her there on time.*

do something on the fly to do something while one is moving; to do something (to something that is in motion). (Slang. This has nothing to do with actual flight.) □ *We can't stop the machine to oil it now. You'll have to do it on the fly.* □ *We will have to find the break in the film on the fly—while we are showing it.*

do something on the run to do something while one is moving hurriedly; to do something while one is going rapidly from one place to another. (Informal.) □ *I was very busy today and had to eat on the run.* □ *I didn't have time to meet with Bill, but I was able to talk to him on the run.*

do something on the sly to do something slyly or sneakily. (Informal.) □ *He was seeing Mrs. Smith on the sly.* □ *She was supposed to be losing weight, but she was snacking on the sly.*

do something over (again) to redo something; to repeat the doing of something. □ *This isn't right. You'll have to do it over again.* □ *The teacher made me do my paper over.*

do something the hard way 1. to accomplish something in the most difficult manner, rather than by an easier way. □ *I made it to this job the hard way. I came up through the ranks.* □ *She did it the hard way. She had no help from her parents.* **2.** to do something the wrong way. □ *No, you can't pound in nails like that. You're doing it the hard way.* □ *I'm sorry. I learn things the hard way.*

do something up to repair or redecorate something. □ *If we're going to sell the house, we'll have to do it up.* □ *I'm going to do up the kitchen.*

do something up brown to do something just right. (Folksy. As if one were cooking and trying to make something to have just the right amount of brownish color.) □ *Of course I can do it right. I'll really do it up brown.* □ *Come on, Bob. Let's do it right this time. I know you can do it up brown.*

do something with a vengeance to do something with vigor; to do something energetically as if one were angry with it. (Folksy.) □ *Bob is building that fence with a vengeance.* □ *Mary is really weeding her garden with a vengeance.*

do the dishes to wash the dishes; to wash and dry the dishes. □ *Bill, you cannot go out and play until you've done the dishes.* □ *Why am I always the one who has to do the dishes?*

do the honors to act as host or hostess and serve one's guests by pouring drinks, slicing meat, making (drinking) toasts, etc. □ *All the guests were seated, and a huge juicy turkey sat on the table. Jane Thomas turned to her husband and said, "Bob, will you do the honors?" Mr. Jones smiled and began slicing thick slices of meat from the turkey.* □ *The mayor stood up and addressed the people who were still eating their salads. "I'm delighted to do the honors this evening and propose a toast to your friend and mine, Bill Jones. Bill, good luck and best wishes in your new job in Washington." And everyone sipped a bit of wine.*

do the trick to do exactly what needs to be done. (Folksy.) □ *Push it just a little more to the left. There, that does the trick.* □ *If you lend me five dollars, I'll have enough to do the trick.*

do too AND **do so** to do something (despite anything to the contrary). (An emphatic way of saying *do*. See *be too*, *have too*.) □ BOB: *You don't have your money with you.* BILL: *I do too!* □ *He does so! I saw him put it in his pocket.* □ *She did too. I saw her do it.*

do without (someone or something) to manage to get through life without someone or something that you want or need. □ *I guess I'll just have to do without a car.* □ *I don't know how I can do without.* □ *The boss can't do without a secretary.*

Do you read me? Do you understand what I am telling you? (Typically asked of someone receiving a radio communication, such as from an airplane or an airport control tower. Also used as an emphatic way of asking if one is understood.) □ *This is Delta heavy 54. Do you read me?* □ *I have said no twenty times already! The answer is still no! Do you read me?*

dog and pony show a display, demonstration, or exhibition of something—such as something one is selling. (Also literal. From the image of a circus act where trained dogs leap onto and off of trained ponies, in exactly the same sequence each time the show is performed. Fixed order.) □ *Gary was there with his dog and pony show, trying to sell his ideas to whomever would listen to him.* □ *Don't you get tired of running through the same old dog and pony show, week after week?*

dog-eat-dog a situation in which one has to act ruthlessly in order to survive or succeed; ruthless competition. □ *It is dog-eat-dog in the world of business these days.* □ *Universities are not quiet peaceful places. It's dog-eat-dog to get a promotion.*

dog in the manger one who prevents other people from doing or having what one does not wish them to do or have. (From one of Aesop's fables in which a dog — which cannot eat hay — lay in the hayrack [manger] and prevented the other animals from eating the hay.) □ *Jane is a real dog in the manger. She cannot drive, but she will not lend anyone her car.* □ *If Martin were not such a dog in the manger, he would let his brother have that dinner jacket he never wears.*

dollar for dollar considering the amount of money involved; considering the cost. (Informal. Often seen in advertising.) □ *Dollar for dollar, you cannot buy a better car.* □ *Dollar for dollar, this laundry detergent washes cleaner and brighter than any other product on the market.*

done in tired; exhausted; terminated; killed. □ *I am really done in after all that exercise.* □ *The project was done in by a vote of the board.* □ *The witness was afraid he would be done in by the mobsters.*

done to a T AND **done to a turn** cooked just right. (Folksy. See also *fit someone to a T; suit someone to a T.*) □ *Yummy! This meat is done to a T.* □ *I like it done to a turn, not too done and not too raw.*

done to a turn See the previous entry.

Don't hold your breath. Do not stop breathing (while waiting for something to happen). (Informal.) □ *You think he'll get a job? Ha! Don't hold your breath.* □ *I'll finish building the fence as soon as I have time, but don't hold your breath.*

Don't let someone or something get you down. Do not allow yourself to be overcome by someone or something. □ *Don't let their constant teasing get you down.* □ *Don't let Tom get you down. He's not always unpleasant.*

doomed to failure certain to fail, usually because of some obvious flaw. □ *This project was doomed to failure from the very beginning.* □ *The play is doomed to failure because there is not a good story line.*

door-to-door 1. having to do with movement from one door to another or from one house to another. (See also *from door to door.*) □ *John is a door-to-door salesman.* □ *We spent two weeks making a door-to-door survey.* 2. by moving from one door to another or one house to another. □ *Anne is selling books door-to-door.* □ *We went door-to-door, collecting money.*

dose of one's own medicine the same kind of treatment that one gives to other people. (Often with *get* or *have.*) □ *Sally never is very friendly. Someone is going to give her a dose of her own medicine someday.* □ *He didn't like getting a dose of his own medicine.*

double back (on someone or something) [for a person or animal] to reverse motion, moving toward someone or something (rather than away from someone or something). (Refers primarily to a person or animal that is being pursued by someone or something.) □ *The deer doubled back on the hunter.* □ *The robber doubled back on the police, and they lost track of him.* □ *He doubled back on his trail.*

double-cross someone to betray someone by doing the opposite of what was promised; to betray a person by not doing what was promised. (Slang. Originally criminal slang.) □ *If you double-cross me again, I'll kill you.* □ *Tom is mad at Jane because she double-crossed him on the sale of his car.*

double in brass to serve two purposes; to be useful for two different things. (Refers to a musician who can play a trumpet or trombone, etc., in addition to some other instrument.) □ *The English teacher also doubles in brass as the football coach.* □ *The drummer doubles in brass as a violinist.*

double up (with someone) to share something with someone. □ *We don't have enough books. Tom, will you double up with Jane?* □ *When we get* more books, we won't have to double up anymore. □ We'll share hotel rooms to save money. Tom and Bill will double up in room twenty.

doubting Thomas someone who will not easily believe something without strong proof or evidence. (From the biblical account of the apostle Thomas, who would not believe that Christ had risen from the grave until he had touched Him.) □ Mary won't believe that I have a dog until she sees it. She's such a doubting Thomas. □ Bill's school is full of doubting Thomases. They want to see his new bike with their own eyes.

down-and-dirty sneaky, unfair, low-down, and nasty. (Slang. Fixed order.) □ The boys played a real down-and-dirty trick on the teacher. □ A political campaign provides a lot of down-and-dirty speeches that only confuse the voters.

down-and-out having no money or means of support. (Fixed order.) □ There are many young people down-and-out in Los Angeles just now. □ John gambled away all his fortune and is now completely down-and-out.

down-at-the-heels shabby; poorly dressed. (Refers to shoes that are worn down at the heels.) □ The hobo was really down-at-the-heels. □ Tom's house needs paint. It looks down-at-the-heels.

down for the count finished for the time being. (From boxing, where a fallen fighter remains down [resting] until the last count, or even beyond.) □ After the professor rebuked me in class, I knew I was down for the count. □ I am down for the count, but I'll try again tomorrow.

down in the dumps sad or depressed. (Informal.) □ I've been down in the dumps for the past few days. □ Try to cheer Jane up. She's down in the dumps for some reason.

down in the mouth sad-faced; depressed and unsmiling. □ Since her dog died, Barbara has been down in the mouth. □ Bob has been down in the mouth since the car wreck.

down on one's luck without any money; unlucky. (Euphemistic for broke.) □ Can you lend me twenty dollars? I've been down on my luck lately. □ The gambler had to get a job because he had been down on his luck and didn't earn enough money to live on.

down on someone or something against someone or something; negative about someone or something. □ I've been down on red meat lately. It's better to eat chicken or fish. □ The teacher was down on Tom because he's always talking in class.

down South to or at the southeastern United States. (See also back East; out West; up North.) □ I used to live down South. □ We are going down South for the winter.

down the drain lost forever; wasted. (Informal. Also literal.) □ I just hate to see all that money go down the drain. □ Well, there goes the whole project, right down the drain.

down the hatch [to] swallow (something). (Informal or slang. Sometimes said when someone takes a drink of alcohol.) □ Come on, Billy. Eat your dinner. Down the hatch! □ John raised his glass of beer and said, "Down the hatch."

down the street a short distance away on this same street. □ Sally lives just down the street. □ There is a drugstore down the street. It's very convenient.

down the tubes ruined; wasted. (Slang.) □ His political career went down the tubes after the scandal. He's lost his job. □ The business went down the tubes.

down-to-earth 1. direct, frank, and honest. □ You can depend on Ann. She's very down-to-earth. □ It's good that she's down-to-earth and will give us a frank response. 2. practical; not theoretical; not fanciful. □ Her ideas for the boutique are always very down-to-earth. □ The committee's plans for the village are anything but down-to-earth.

down to the last detail considering all of the details. (Fixed order.) □ *Jean planned the party very carefully, down to the last detail.* □ *Mary wanted to be in charge of everything right down to the last detail.*

down to the wire at the very last minute; up to the very last instant. (Refers to a wire that marks the end of a horse race.) □ *I have to turn this in tomorrow, and I'll be working down to the wire.* □ *When we get down to the wire, we'll know better what to do.*

down with a disease ill; sick at home. (Can be said about many diseases.) □ *Tom isn't here. He's down with a cold.* □ *Sally is down with the flu.* □ *The whole office has come down with something.*

downhill all the way easy all the way. (Informal.) □ *Don't worry about your algebra course. It's downhill all the way.* □ *The mayor said that the job of mayor is easy—in fact, downhill all the way.*

downhill from here on easy from this point on. (Informal.) □ *The worst part is over. It's downhill from here on.* □ *The painful part of this procedure is over. It's downhill from here on.*

drag one's feet to act very slowly, often deliberately. □ *The government is dragging its feet on this bill because it costs too much.* □ *If the planning department hadn't dragged their feet, the building would have been built by now.*

draw a bead on someone or something to aim at someone or something; to pick out someone or something for special treatment. (Informal.) □ *Ann wants a new car, and she has drawn a bead on a red convertible.* □ *Jane wants to get married, and she has drawn a bead on Tom.*

draw a blank (Informal.) **1.** to get no response; to find nothing. □ *I asked him about Tom's financial problems, and I just drew a blank.* □ *We looked in the files for an hour, but we drew a blank.* **2.** to fail to remember (something). □ *I tried to remember her telephone number, but I could only draw a blank.* □ *It was a very hard test with just one question to answer, and I drew a blank.*

draw a line between something and something else to separate two things; to distinguish or differentiate between two things. (The *a* can be replaced with *the*. See also *draw the line (at something)*.) □ *It's necessary to draw a line between bumping into people and striking them.* □ *It's very hard to draw the line between slamming a door and just closing it loudly.*

draw blood 1. to hit or bite (a person or an animal) and make a wound that bleeds. □ *The dog chased me and bit me hard, but it didn't draw blood.* □ *The boxer landed just one punch and drew blood immediately.* **2.** to anger or insult a person. □ *Sally screamed out a terrible insult at Tom. Judging by the look on his face, she really drew blood.* □ *Tom started yelling and cursing, trying to insult Sally. He wouldn't be satisfied until he had drawn blood, too.*

draw interest 1. to appear interesting and get (someone's) attention. (Note the variation in the examples.) □ *This kind of event isn't likely to draw a lot of interest.* □ *What kind of thing will draw interest?* **2.** [for money] to earn interest while on deposit. □ *Put your money in the bank so it will draw interest.* □ *The cash value of some insurance policies also draws interest.*

draw someone or something out 1. [with *someone*] to coax someone to speak or answer; to bring someone into a conversation or other social interaction. □ *Jane is usually very shy with older men, but Tom really drew her out last evening.* ⊤ *John drew out Mr. Smith on the question of tax increases.* **2.** [with *something*] to make something longer (literally or figuratively.) ⊤ *Jane drew out the conversation for more than twenty minutes.* □ *Bill drew the taffy candy out into a long string.*

draw (someone's) fire (away from someone or something) to make oneself a target in order to protect someone or something. (Refers literally to gunfire or figuratively to any kind of attack.) □ *The mother bird drew fire away from her chicks.* □ *The hen drew the hunter's fire away from her nest.* □ *Birds draw fire by flapping their wings to get attention.* □ *The president drew fire away from Congress by proposing a compromise.* □ *The airplanes drew the soldier's fire away from the ships in the harbor.*

draw something to a close to make something end. □ *It is now time to draw this evening to a close.* □ *What a lovely vacation. It's a shame that we must draw it to a close.*

draw something up to put something into writing; to prepare a written document; to put plans on paper. (Used especially with legal documents prepared by a lawyer. Also literal.) □ *You should draw a will up as soon as you can.* Ⓣ *I went to see my lawyer this morning about drawing up a will.* Ⓣ *The architect is drawing up plans for the new city hall.*

draw the line (at something) to set a limit at something; to decide when a limit has been reached. (See also *hold the line (at someone or something).*) □ *You can make as much noise as you want, but I draw the line at fighting.* □ *It's hard to keep young people under control, but you have to draw the line somewhere.*

draw to a close to end; to come to an end. □ *This evening is drawing to a close.* □ *It's a shame that our vacation is drawing to a close.*

drawn and quartered dealt with very severely. (Also literal, referring to a practice of torturing someone guilty of treason, usually a male, by disembowling and dividing the body into four parts. Fixed order.) □ *Todd was practically drawn and quartered for losing the Wilson contract.* □ *You were much too harsh with Jean. No matter what she did, she didn't need to be drawn and quartered for it!*

dream come true a wish or a dream that has become real. □ *Going to Hawaii is like having a dream come true.* □ *Having you for a friend is a dream come true.*

dress someone down to bawl someone out; to give someone a good scolding. (Primarily military.) □ *The sergeant dressed the soldier down severely.* □ *I know they'll dress me down when I get home.*

dressed to kill dressed in fancy or stylish clothes. (Slang.) □ *Wow, look at Sally! She's really dressed to kill.* □ *A person doesn't go to church dressed to kill.*

dressed to the nines dressed very well. (What *nines* means is not known.) □ *Tom showed up at the dance dressed to the nines.* □ *Sally is even dressed to the nines at the office.*

dressed up See *(all) dressed up.*

dribs and drabs in small irregular quantities. (Especially with *in* and *by*.) □ *The checks for the charity are coming in in dribs and drabs.* □ *The members of the orchestra arrived by dribs and drabs.* □ *All her fortune was spent in dribs and drabs on silly things—like clothes and fine wines.*

drink to excess to drink too much alcohol; to drink alcohol continually. □ *Mr. Franklin drinks to excess.* □ *Some people drink to excess only at parties.*

drive a hard bargain to work hard to negotiate prices or agreements in one's own favor. (Informal.) □ *I saved $200 by driving a hard bargain when I bought my new car.* □ *All right, sir, you drive a hard bargain. I'll sell you this car for $12,450.* □ *You drive a hard bargain, Jane, but I'll sign the contract.*

drive at something to be making a point; to be approaching the making of a point. □ *I do not understand what you are telling me. What are you driving at?* □ *She was driving at how important it is to get an education.*

drive someone crazy AND **drive someone mad** (Informal.) **1.** to make someone insane. □ *He's so strange that he actually drove his wife crazy.* □ *Doctor, there are little green people following me around trying to drive me mad.* **2.** to annoy or irritate someone. □ *This itch is driving me crazy.* □ *All these telephone calls are driving me mad.*

drive someone mad See the previous entry.

drive someone out (of office) See *force someone out (of office).*

drive someone to the wall See *force someone to the wall.*

drive someone up the wall (Slang.) **1.** to make someone insane. □ *Mr. Franklin drove his wife up the wall.* □ *All my problems will drive me up the wall someday.* **2.** to annoy or irritate someone. □ *Stop whistling that tune. You're driving me up the wall.* □ *All his talk about moving to California nearly drove me up the wall.*

drive something home to make something clearly understood. □ *Why do I always have to shout at you to drive something home?* ⊤ *Sometimes you have to be forceful to drive home a point.*

drive something into the ground See *run something into the ground.*

driving force (behind someone or something) a person or a thing that motivates or directs someone or something. □ *Money is the driving force behind most businesses.* □ *Ambition is the driving force behind Tom.* □ *Love can also be a driving force.*

drop a bomb(shell) AND **explode a bombshell; drop a brick** to announce shocking or startling news. (Informal or slang.) □ *They really dropped a bombshell when they announced that the mayor had cancer.* □ *Friday is a good day to drop a bomb like that. It gives the business world the weekend to recover.* □ *They must speak very carefully when they explode a bombshell like that.* □ *They really dropped a brick when they told the cause of her illness.*

drop a brick See the previous entry.

drop around (sometime) AND **drop by (sometime)** to come and visit (someone) at some future time. (Similar to *drop in (on someone).*) □ *Nice to see you, Mary. You and Bob must drop around sometime.* □ *Please do drop around when you're out driving.* □ *We'd love to have you drop by.*

drop by (sometime) See the previous entry.

drop by the wayside See *fall by the wayside.*

drop dead **1.** to die suddenly. □ *I understand that Tom Anderson dropped dead at his desk yesterday.* □ *No one knows why Uncle Bob suddenly dropped dead.* **2.** Go away and stop bothering me. (Rude slang.) □ *If you think I'm going to put up with your rudeness all afternoon, you can just drop dead!* □ *Drop dead! I'm not your slave!*

drop in (on someone) AND **drop in (to say hello)** to pay someone a casual visit, perhaps a surprise visit. □ *I hate to drop in on people when they aren't expecting me.* □ *You're welcome to drop in at any time.* □ *We won't stay a minute. We just dropped in to say hello.*

drop in one's tracks to stop or collapse from exhaustion; to die suddenly. □ *If I keep working this way, I'll drop in my tracks.* □ *Uncle Bob was working in the garden and dropped in his tracks. We are all sorry that he's dead.*

drop in the bucket See the following entry.

drop in the ocean AND **drop in the bucket** just a little bit; not enough of something to make a difference. □ *But one dollar isn't enough! That's just a drop in the ocean.* □ *At this point your help is nothing more than a drop in the ocean. I need far more help than twenty people could give.* □ *I won't accept your offer. It's just a drop in the bucket.*

drop in (to say hello) See *drop in (on someone).*

drop off (to sleep) to go to sleep without difficulty; to fall asleep. □ *I sat in* *the warm room for five minutes, and then I dropped off to sleep.* □ *After I've eaten dinner, I can drop off with no trouble at all.*

drop out (of something) to stop being a member of something; to stop attending or participating in something. (Also literal.) □ *I'm working part time so that I won't have to drop out of college.* □ *I don't want to drop out at this time.*

drop someone to stop being friends with someone, especially with one's boyfriend or girlfriend. □ *Bob finally dropped Jane. I don't know what he saw in her.* □ *I'm surprised that she didn't drop him first.*

drop someone a few lines See the following entry.

drop someone a line AND **drop someone a few lines** to write a letter or a note to someone. (The *line* refers to lines of writing.) □ *I dropped Aunt Jane a line last Thanksgiving.* □ *She usually drops me a few lines around the first of the year.*

drop someone's name to mention the name of an important or famous person as if the person was a personal friend. □ *Mary always tries to impress people by dropping a well-known movie star's name.* □ *Joan is such a snob. Leave it to her to drop some social leader's name.*

drop the ball to make a blunder; to fail in some way. (Also literal as in sports: to drop a ball in error.) □ *Everything was going fine in the election until my campaign manager dropped the ball.* □ *You can't trust John to do the job right. He's always dropping the ball.*

drop the other shoe to do the deed that completes something; to do the expected remaining part of something. (Refers to the removal of shoes at bedtime. One shoe is dropped, and then the process is completed when the second shoe drops.) □ *Mr. Franklin has left his wife. Soon he'll drop the other shoe and divorce her.* □ *Tommy has just failed three classes in school.*

We expect him to drop the other shoe and quit altogether any day now.

drown one's sorrows See the following entry.

drown one's troubles AND **drown one's sorrows** to try to forget one's problems by drinking a lot of alcohol. (Informal.) □ *Bill is in the bar, drowning his troubles.* □ *Jane is at home, drowning her sorrows.*

drown someone or something out to make so much noise that someone or something cannot be heard. □ *I can't hear what you said. The radio drowned you out.* Ⓣ *We couldn't hear all the concert because the airplanes drowned out the quiet parts.*

drug on the market on the market in great abundance; a glut on the market. □ *Right now, small computers are a drug on the market.* □ *Ten years ago, small transistor radios were a drug on the market.*

drum some business up to stimulate people to buy what you are selling. □ *I need to do something to drum some business up.* Ⓣ *A little bit of advertising would drum up some business.*

drum someone out of something to expel or send someone away from something, especially in a formal or public fashion. (From the military use of drums on such occasions.) □ *The officer was drummed out of the regiment for misconduct.* □ *I heard that he was drummed out of the country club for cheating on his golf score.*

drum something into someone('s head) to make someone learn something through persistent repetition. □ *Yes, I know that. They drummed it into me as a child.* □ *Now I'm drumming it into my own children.* □ *I will drum it into their heads day and night.*

drunk and disorderly a criminal charge for public drunkenness accompanied by bad or offensive behavior. (Fixed order.) □ *The judge fined Max for being drunk and disorderly.* □ *In addition to being convicted for driving* while intoxicated, Max was found guilty of being drunk and disorderly.

dry as dust See *(as) dry as dust.*

dry run an attempt; a rehearsal. □ *We had better have a dry run for the official ceremony tomorrow.* □ *The children will need a dry run before their procession in the pageant.*

dry someone out to help a drunk person get sober. □ *We had to call the doctor to help dry Mr. Franklin out.* Ⓣ *It takes time to dry out someone who has been drinking for a week.*

dry up to become silent; to stop talking. (Informal. Also literal.) □ *The young lecturer was so nervous that he forgot what he was going to say and dried up.* □ *Actors have a fear of drying up on stage.* □ *Oh, dry up! I'm sick of listening to you.*

duck and cover 1. to dodge something, such as an issue or a difficult question, and attempt to shield oneself against similar issues or questions. (Also literal, referring to ducking down and taking cover to protect oneself. Fixed order.) □ *The candidate's first reaction to the question was to duck and cover.* □ *The debaters were ducking and covering throughout the evening.* **2.** dodging something, such as an issue or a difficult question, and attempting to shield oneself against similar issues or questions. (Typically **duck-and-cover.**) □ *These politicians are experts at duck-and-cover.* □ *When in doubt, turn to duck-and-cover.*

dull as ditchwater See *(as) dull as dishwater.*

Dutch auction an auction or sale that starts off with a high asking price that is then reduced until a buyer is found. □ *Dutch auctions are rare—most auc-*

tioneers start with a lower price than they hope to obtain. □ *My real estate agent advised me to ask a reasonable price for my house rather than get involved with a Dutch auction.*

Dutch courage unusual or artificial courage arising from the influence of alcohol. □ *It was Dutch courage that made the football fan attack the policeman.* □ *It will take a bit of Dutch courage to make an after-dinner speech.*

Dutch treat a social occasion where one pays for oneself. (See also *go Dutch.*) □ *"It's nice of you to ask me out to dinner," she said, "but could we make it a Dutch treat?"* □ *The office outing is always a Dutch treat.*

Dutch uncle a man who gives frank and direct advice to someone in the manner of a parent or relative. □ *I would not have to lecture you like a Dutch uncle if you were not so extravagant.* □ *He acts more like a Dutch uncle than a husband. He's forever telling her what to do in public.*

duty bound (to do something) forced by a sense of duty and honor to do something. □ *Good evening, madam. I'm duty bound to inform you that we have arrested your husband.* □ *No one made me say that. I was duty bound.*

dyed-in-the-wool permanent; indelible; stubborn. (Usually said of a person.) □ *My uncle was a dyed-in-the-wool farmer. He wouldn't change for anything.* □ *Sally is a dyed-in-the-wool socialist.*

dying to do something very anxious to do something. □ *I'm just dying to go sailing in your new boat.* □ *After a long hot day like this one, I'm just dying for a cool drink of water.*

E

eager beaver someone who is very enthusiastic; someone who works very hard. □ *New volunteers are always eager beavers.* □ *The young assistant gets to work very early. She's a real eager beaver.*

eagle eye careful attention; an intently watchful eye. (From the sharp eyesight of the eagle.) □ *The students wrote their essays under the eagle eye of the headmaster.* □ *The umpire kept his eagle eye on the tennis match.*

early bird someone who gets up or arrives early or starts something very promptly, especially someone who gains an advantage of some kind by so doing. (See also *The early bird gets the worm.*) □ *The members of the Smith family are all early birds. They caught the first bus to town.* □ *I was an early bird and got the best selection of flowers.*

early on early; at an early stage. □ *We recognized the problem early on, but we waited too long to do something about it.* □ *This doesn't surprise me. I knew about it early on.*

Early to bed, early to rise(, makes a man healthy, wealthy, and wise.) a proverb that claims that going to bed early and getting up early is good for you. (Sometimes said to explain why a person is going to bed early. The last part of the saying is sometimes left out.) □ *Tom left the party at ten o'clock, saying "Early to bed, early to rise, makes a man healthy, wealthy, and wise."* □ *I always get up at dawn. After all, early to bed, early to rise.*

earn one's keep to help out with chores in return for food and a place to live; to earn one's pay by doing what is expected. □ *I earn my keep at college by shoveling snow in the winter.* □ *Tom hardly earns his keep around here. He should be fired.*

ease off (on someone or something) AND **ease up (on someone or something)** to reduce the urgency with which one deals with someone or something; to put less pressure on someone or something. □ *Ease off on John. He has been yelled at enough today.* □ *Yes, please ease off. I can't stand any more.* □ *Tell them to ease up on the horses. They are getting tired.* □ *Tell them to ease up now! They are making the horses work too hard.*

ease up (on someone or something) See the previous entry.

easier said than done said of a task that is easier to talk about than to do. □ *Yes, we must find a cure for cancer, but it's easier said than done.* □ *Finding a good job is easier said than done.*

easy as (apple) pie See *(as) easy as (apple) pie.*

easy as duck soup See *(as) easy as duck soup.*

easy as rolling off a log See *(as) easy as rolling off a log.*

easy come, easy go said to explain the loss of something that required only a small amount of effort to get in the first place. (Fixed order.) □ *Ann found twenty dollars in the morning and spent it foolishly at noon. "Easy come,* easy go," she said. □ *John spends his money as fast as he can earn it. With John it's easy come, easy go.*

Easy does it. Act with care. (Informal.) □ *Be careful with that glass vase. Easy does it!* □ *Now, now, Tom. Don't get angry. Easy does it.*

easy to come by easily found; easily purchased; readily available. □ *Please be careful with that phonograph record. It was not easy to come by.* □ *A good dictionary is very easy to come by.*

eat (a meal) out AND **dine out** to eat a meal at a restaurant. □ *I like to eat a meal out every now and then.* □ *Yes, it's good to eat out and try different kinds of food.* □ *It costs a lot of money to dine out often.*

eat and run to eat a meal or a snack and then leave. (Fixed order.) □ *Well, I hate to eat and run but I have to take care of some errands.* □ *I don't invite John to dinner anymore because he always has some excuse to eat and run.*

eat away at someone or something 1. to remove parts, bit by bit. □ *John's disease was eating away at him.* □ *The acid in the rain slowly ate away at the stone wall.* **2.** [with *someone*] to bother or worry someone. □ *Her failure to pass the exam was eating away at her.* □ *Fear of appearing in court was eating away at Tom.*

eat high on the hog to eat good or expensive food. (Folksy. Compare with *live high on the hog*. Note the *so* in the second example.) □ *The Smith family has been eating pretty high on the hog since they had a good corn harvest.* □ *John would have more money to spend on clothing if he didn't eat so high on the hog.*

eat humble pie (Informal.) **1.** to act very humbly when one is shown to be wrong. □ *I think I'm right, but if I'm wrong, I'll eat humble pie.* □ *You think you're so smart. I hope you have to eat humble pie.* **2.** to accept insults and humiliation. □ *John, stand up for your rights. You don't have to eat humble pie*

all the time. □ *Beth seems quite happy to eat humble pie. She should stand up for her rights.*

eat like a bird to eat only small amounts of food; to peck at one's food. □ *Jane is very slim because she eats like a bird.* □ *Bill is trying to lose weight by eating like a bird.*

eat like a horse to eat large amounts of food. (Informal.) □ *No wonder he's so fat. He eats like a horse.* □ *John works like a horse and eats like a horse, so he never gets fat.*

eat one's cake and have it too See *have one's cake and eat it too.*

eat one's hat a phrase telling the kind of thing that one would do if a very unlikely event really happens. (Informal. Always used with an *if*-clause. Not literal.) □ *If we get there on time, I'll eat my hat.* □ *I'll eat my hat if you get a raise.* □ *He said he'd eat his hat if she got elected.*

eat one's heart out 1. to be very sad (about someone or something). □ *Bill spent a lot of time eating his heart out after his divorce.* □ *Sally ate her heart out when she had to sell her house.* **2.** to be envious (of someone or something). (Informal.) □ *Do you like my new watch? Well, eat your heart out. It was the last one in the store.* □ *Don't eat your heart out about my new car. Go get one of your own.*

eat one's words to have to take back one's statements; to confess that one's predictions were wrong. □ *You shouldn't say that to me. I'll make you eat your words.* □ *John was wrong about the election and had to eat his words.*

eat out of someone's hands to do what someone else wants; to obey someone eagerly. (Often with *have*.) □ *Just wait! I'll have everyone eating out of my hands. They'll do whatever I ask.* □ *The president has Congress eating out of his hands.* □ *A lot of people are eating out of his hands.*

eat someone out See *chew someone out.*

eat someone out of house and home to eat a lot of food (in someone's home); to eat all the food in the house. (Fixed order.) □ *Billy has a huge appetite. He almost eats us out of house and home.* □ *When the kids come home from college, they always eat us out of house and home.*

eat something up to enjoy, absorb, or appreciate. (Informal. Also literal.) □ *The audience loved the comedian. They ate his act up and demanded more.* T *The children ate up Grandfather's stories. They listened to him for hours.*

ebb and flow to decrease and then increase, as with tides; a decrease followed by an increase, as with tides. (Also literal. Fixed order.) □ *The fortunes of the major political parties tend to ebb and flow over time.* □ *The ebb and flow of democracy through history is a fascinating subject.*

edge someone out to remove a person from a job, office, or position, usually by beating the person in competition. □ *The vice president edged the president out during the last election.* T *Tom edged out Bob as the new cook at the restaurant.*

egg someone on to encourage, urge, or dare someone to continue doing something, usually something unwise. □ *John wouldn't have done the dangerous experiment if his brother hadn't egged him on.* □ *The two boys kept throwing stones because the other children were egging them on.*

either feast or famine either too much (of something) or not enough (of something). (Also without *either.* Fixed order.) □ *This month is very dry, and last month it rained almost every day. Our weather is either feast or famine.* □ *Sometimes we are busy, and sometimes we have nothing to do. It's feast or famine.*

elbow someone out (of something) to force or pressure someone out of something, such as an office, post, or status. (Also literal, with the elbows.) □ *The old head of the company was elbowed out of office by a young vice president.* □ *They tried to elbow me out, but I held on to what was mine.*

eleventh-hour decision a decision made at the last possible minute. (See also *at the eleventh hour.*) □ *Eleventh-hour decisions are seldom satisfactory.* □ *The president's eleventh-hour decision was made in a great hurry, but it turned out to be correct.*

end in itself for its own sake; toward its own ends; toward no purpose but its own. □ *For Bob, art is an end in itself. He doesn't hope to make any money from it.* □ *Learning is an end in itself. Knowledge does not have to have a practical application.*

end of the line See the following entry.

end of the road AND **end of the line** the end; the end of the whole process; death. (*Line* originally referred to railroad tracks.) □ *Our house is at the end of the road.* □ *We rode the train to the end of the line.* □ *When we reach the end of the road on this project, we'll get paid.* □ *You've come to the end of the line. I'll not lend you another penny.* □ *When I reach the end of the road, I wish to be buried in a quiet place, near some trees.*

end something up to bring something to an end. (Informal. Also without *up.*) □ *I want you to end your game up and come in for dinner.* T *We can't end up the game until someone scores.*

end up by doing something to conclude something by doing something. (Compare with *end up doing something.*) □ *We ended up by going back to my house.* □ *They danced until midnight and ended up by having pizza in the front room.*

end up doing something AND **wind up doing something** to have to do something that one had not planned to do. (Compare with *end up by doing something.*) □ *We ended up going back to my house after all.* □ *Todd wound up inviting everyone to his house, even though he planned to spend the evening at home alone.*

end up (somehow) to end something at a particular place, in a particular state, or by having to do something. (Compare with *end up by doing something.*) □ *I ended up having to pay for everyone's dinner.* □ *After paying for dinner, I ended up broke.* □ *We all ended up at my house.* □ *After playing in the rain, we all ended up with colds.*

end up somewhere AND **wind up somewhere** to finish at a certain place. □ *If you don't get straightened out, you'll end up in jail.* □ *I fell and hurt myself, and I wound up in the hospital.*

end up with the short end of the stick See *get the short end of the stick.*

engage in small talk to talk only about minor matters rather than important matters or personal matters. □ *All the people at the party were engaging in small talk.* □ *They chatted about the weather and otherwise engaged in small talk.*

Enough is enough. That is enough, and there should be no more. □ *Stop asking for money! Enough is enough!* □ *I've heard all the complaining from you that I can take. Stop! Enough is enough!*

enough to go (a)round a supply adequate to serve everyone. (Informal.) □ *Don't take too much. There's not enough to go around.* □ *I cooked some extra potatoes, so there should be enough to go around.*

enter one's mind to come to one's mind; [for an idea or memory] to come into one's consciousness. □ *Leave you behind? The thought never even entered my mind.* □ *A very interesting idea just entered my mind. What if I ran for Congress?*

equal to someone or something able to handle or deal with someone or something. (Also literal.) □ *I'm afraid that I'm not equal to Mrs. Smith's problem right now. Please ask her to come back later.* □ *That's a very difficult task, but I'm sure Bill is equal to it.*

escape someone's notice to go unnoticed; not to have been noticed.

(Usually a way to point out that someone has failed to see or respond to something.) □ *I suppose my earlier request escaped your notice, so I'm writing again.* □ *I'm sorry. Your letter escaped my notice.*

even in the best of times even when things are good; even when things are going well. (Fixed order.) □ *It is hard to get high-quality leather even in the best of times.* □ *John had difficulty getting a loan even in the best of times because of his poor credit record.*

ever and anon now and then; occasionally. (Literary and archaic. Fixed order.) □ *Ever and anon the princess would pay a visit to the sorcerer in the small walled garden directly behind the castle.* □ *We eat swan ever and anon, but not when we can get wild boar.*

Every cloud has a silver lining. a proverb meaning that there is something good in every bad thing. □ *Jane was upset when she saw that all her flowers had died from the frost. But when she saw that the weeds had died too, she said, "Every cloud has a silver lining."* □ *Sally had a sore throat and had to stay home from school. When she learned she missed a math test, she said, "Every cloud has a silver lining."*

Every dog has his day. See the following entry.

Every dog has its day. AND **Every dog has his day.** a proverb meaning that everyone will get a chance. □ *Don't worry, you'll get chosen for the team. Every dog has its day.* □ *You may become famous someday. Every dog has his day.*

every inch a something AND **every inch the something** completely; in every way. (With the force of an attributive adjective.) □ *Mary is every inch the schoolteacher.* □ *Her father is every inch a gentleman.*

every inch the something See the previous entry.

every last one every one; every single one. (Informal.) □ *You must eat all your peas! Every last one!* □ *Each of* *you — every last one — has to take some medicine.*

every living soul every person. (Informal.) □ *I expect every living soul to be there and be there on time.* □ *This is the kind of problem that affects every living soul.*

every minute counts AND **every moment counts** time is very important. □ *Doctor, please try to get here quickly. Every minute counts.* □ *When you take a test, you must work rapidly because every minute counts.* □ *When you're trying to meet a deadline, every moment counts.*

every moment counts See the previous entry.

(every) now and again See the following entry.

(every) now and then AND **(every) now and again; (every) once in a while** occasionally; infrequently. □ *We eat lamb every now and then.* □ *We eat pork now and then.* □ *I read a novel every now and again.* □ *We don't go to the movies except maybe every now and then.* □ *I drink coffee every once in a while.* □ *I drink tea once in a while.*

(every) once in a while See the previous entry.

every time one turns around frequently; at every turn; with annoying frequency. (Informal.) □ *Somebody asks me for money every time I turn around.* □ *Something goes wrong with Bill's car every time he turns around.*

(every) Tom, Dick, and Harry everyone without discrimination; ordinary people. (Not necessarily males. Fixed order.) □ *The golf club is very exclusive. They don't let any Tom, Dick, or Harry join.* □ *Mary's sending out very few invitations. She doesn't want every Tom, Dick, and Harry turning up.*

every which way in all directions. (Folksy.) □ *The children were all running every which way.* □ *The wind scattered the leaves every which way.*

everything but the kitchen sink almost everything one can think of. □ *When Sally went off to college, she took everything but the kitchen sink.* □ *John orders everything but the kitchen sink when he goes out to dinner, especially if someone else is paying for it.*

everything from A to Z See the following entry.

everything from soup to nuts AND **everything from A to Z** almost everything one can think of. □ *For dinner we had everything from soup to nuts.* □ *In college I studied everything from soup to nuts.* □ *She mentioned everything from A to Z.*

exception that proves the rule a saying claiming that when an exception has to be made to a particular rule or guideline, this simply emphasizes the existence of the rule. (The exception tests for the existence of a rule. Usually with *the*.) □ *Sixth-graders do not have to wear school uniforms, but they're the exception that proves the rule.* □ *The youngest dog is allowed in the house. He's the exception that proves the rule.*

exchange more than ___ words with someone to say hardly anything to someone. (Always negated.) □ *I know Tom was there, but I am sure that I didn't exchange more than three words with him before he left.* □ *We hardly exchanged more than two words the whole evening.* □ *Sally and Liz didn't have enough time to exchange more than five words.*

excuse someone 1. to forgive someone. (Usually with *me*. Said when interrupting or when some other minor offense has been committed. There are many mannerly uses of this expression.) □ *John came in late and said, "Excuse me, please."* □ *John said "excuse me" when he interrupted our conversation.* □ *When John made a strange noise at the table, he said quietly, "Excuse me."* □ *John suddenly left the room saying, "Excuse me. I'll be right back." 2.* to permit someone to leave; to permit someone to remain away from an event. □ *The coach excused John from practice yesterday.* □ *The teacher* *excused John, and he ran quickly from the room.*

expecting (a child) pregnant. (A euphemism.) □ *Tommy's mother is expecting a child.* □ *Oh, I didn't know she was expecting.*

expense is no object See *money is no object.*

explain oneself 1. to explain what one has said or done or what one thinks or feels. (Formal and polite.) □ *Please take a moment to explain yourself. I'm sure we are interested in your ideas.* □ *Yes, if you give me a moment to explain myself, I think you'll agree with my idea.* **2.** to give an explanation or excuse for something wrong that one may have done. (Usually said in anger.) □ *Young man! Come in here and explain yourself this instant.* □ *Why did you do that, Tom Smith? You had better explain yourself, and it had better be good.*

explain something away to give a good explanation for something; to explain something so that it seems less important; to make excuses for something. □ *This is a very serious matter, and you cannot just explain it away.* ⊤ *John couldn't explain away his low grades.*

explode a bombshell See *drop a bomb-(shell).*

extend credit (to someone) AND **extend someone credit** to allow someone to purchase something on credit. □ *I'm sorry, Mr. Smith, but because of your poor record of payment, we are no longer able to extend credit to you.* □ *Look at this letter, Jane. The store won't extend credit anymore.* □ *We are unable to extend that company credit any longer.*

extend one's sympathy (to someone) to express sympathy to someone. (A very polite and formal way to tell someone that you are sorry about a misfortune.) □ *Please permit me to extend my sympathy to you and your children. I'm very sorry to hear of the death of your husband.* □ *Let's extend our sympathy to Bill Jones, who is in the hospital with a broken leg. We should send him some flowers.*

extend someone credit See *extend credit (to someone).*

extenuating circumstances special circumstances that account for an irregular or improper way of doing something. □ *Mary was permitted to arrive late because of extenuating circumstances.* □ *Due to extenuating circumstances, the teacher will not meet class today.*

eyeball-to-eyeball person to person; face to face. □ *The discussions will have to be eyeball-to-eyeball to be effective.* □ *Telephone conversations are a waste of time. We need to talk eyeball-to-eyeball.*

F

face someone down to overcome someone by being bold; to disconcert someone by displaying great confidence. □ *The teacher faced the angry student down without saying anything.* T *The mayor couldn't face down the entire city council.*

face the music to receive punishment; to accept the unpleasant results of one's actions. □ *Mary broke a dining-room window and had to face the music when her father got home.* □ *After failing a math test, Tom had to go home and face the music.*

face-to-face **1.** in person; in the same location. (Said only of people. An adverb.) □ *Let's talk about this face-to-face. I don't like talking over the telephone.* □ *Many people prefer to talk face-to-face.* **2.** facing one another; in the same location. □ *I prefer to have a face-to-face meeting.* □ *They work better on a face-to-face basis.*

facts of life **1.** the facts of sex and reproduction, especially human reproduction. (See also *birds and the bees*.) □ *My parents told me the facts of life when I was nine years old.* □ *Bill learned the facts of life from his classmates.* **2.** the truth about the unpleasant ways that the world works. □ *Mary really learned the facts of life when she got her first job.* □ *Tom couldn't accept the facts of life in business, so he quit.*

fair and impartial fair and unbiased. (Usually referring to some aspect of the legal system, such as a jury, a hearing, or a judge.) □ *Gary felt that he had not received a fair and impartial hearing.* □ *We demand that all of our judges be fair and impartial in every instance.*

fair and square completely fair(ly). (Fixed order.) □ *She won the game fair and square.* □ *The division of the money should be fair and square.*

fair game someone or something that it is quite permissible to attack. □ *I don't like seeing articles exposing people's private lives, but politicians are fair game.* □ *Journalists always regard movie stars as fair game.*

fair to middling only fair or okay; a little better than acceptable. (Folksy.) □ *I don't feel sick, just fair to middling.* □ *The play wasn't really good. It was just fair to middling.*

fair-weather friend someone who is your friend only when things are going well for you. (This person will desert you when things go badly for you. Compare with *A friend in need is a friend indeed*.) □ *Bill wouldn't help me with my homework. He's just a fair-weather friend.* □ *A fair-weather friend isn't much help in an emergency.*

fall afoul of someone or something AND **run afoul of someone or something** to get into a situation where one is opposed to someone or something; to get into trouble with someone or something. □ *Dan fell afoul of the law at an early age.* □ *I hope that you will avoid falling afoul of the district manager. She can be a formidable enemy.* □ *I hope I don't run afoul of your sister. She doesn't like me.*

fall (all) over oneself to behave awkwardly and eagerly in an attempt to please someone. (See also *fall over* backwards *(to do something).)* □ *Tom fell all over himself trying to make Jane feel at home.* □ *I fall over myself when I'm doing something that makes me nervous.*

fall all over someone to give a lot of attention, affection, or praise to someone. (Informal.) □ *My aunt falls all over me whenever she comes to visit.* □ *I hate for someone to fall all over me. It embarrasses me.*

fall apart at the seams to break into pieces; to fall apart; for material that is sewn together to separate at the seams. (Both literal and figurative uses. See also *come apart at the seams*.) □ *My new jacket fell apart at the seams.* □ *This old car is about ready to fall apart at the seams.*

fall asleep to go to sleep. □ *The baby cried and cried and finally fell asleep.* □ *Tom fell asleep in class yesterday.*

fall back on someone or something to turn to someone or something for help. (Also literal.) □ *Bill fell back on his brother for help.* □ *John ran out of ink and had to fall back on his pencil.*

fall between two stools to come somewhere between two possibilities and so fail to meet the requirements of either. □ *The material is not suitable for an academic book or for a popular one. It falls between two stools.* □ *He tries to be both teacher and friend, but falls between two stools.*

fall by the wayside AND **drop by the wayside** to give up and quit before the end (of something). (As if one became exhausted and couldn't finish a footrace. Also literal.) □ *John fell by the wayside and didn't finish college.* □ *Many people start out to train for a career in medicine, but some of them drop by the wayside.* □ *All of her projects fall by the wayside when she tires of them.*

fall down on the job to fail to do something properly; to fail to do one's job adequately. (Also literal.) □ *The team kept losing because the coach was fall-*ing down on the job. □ *Tom was fired because he fell down on the job.*

fall flat (on its face) See the following entry.

fall flat (on one's face) AND **fall flat (on its face)** to be completely unsuccessful. (Informal.) □ *I fell flat on my face when I tried to give my speech.* □ *The play fell flat on its face.* □ *My jokes fall flat most of the time.*

fall for someone or something 1. [with *someone*] to fall in love with someone. □ *Tom fell for Ann after only two dates. He wants to marry her.* □ *Some men always fall for women with blond hair.* **2.** [with *something*] to be deceived by something. □ *I can't believe you fell for that old trick.* □ *Jane didn't fall for Ann's story.*

fall from grace to cease to be held in favor, especially because of some wrong or foolish action. □ *He was the teacher's pet until he fell from grace by failing the history test.* □ *Mary was the favorite grandchild until she fell from grace by running away from home.*

fall head over heels to fall down, perhaps turning over or rolling. (Also literal.) □ *Fred tripped on the rug and fell head over heels into the center of the room.* □ *Slow down or you will fall down — head over heels.*

fall head over heels in love (with someone) to fall deeply in love with someone, perhaps suddenly. □ *Roger fell head over heels in love with Maggie, and they were married within the month.* □ *Very few people actually fall head over heels in love with each other.* □ *She fell head over heels in love and thought she was dreaming.*

fall in to line up in a row, standing shoulder to shoulder. (Usually refers to people in scouting or the military. Compare with *fall in(to) line* and *fall out*. Also literal.) □ *The Boy Scouts were told to fall in behind the scoutmaster.* □ *The soldiers fell in quickly.*

fall in for something See *come in for something*.

fall in love (with someone) to develop the emotion of love for someone. □ *Tom fell in love with Mary, but she only wanted to be friends.* □ *John is too young to really fall in love.*

fall in with someone or something 1. [with *someone*] to meet someone by accident; to join with someone. □ *John has fallen in with a strange group of people.* □ *We fell in with some people from our hometown when we went on vacation.* **2.** to agree with someone or something. □ *Bill was not able to fall in with our ideas about painting the house red.* □ *Bob fell in with Mary's plans to move to Texas.*

fall into a trap AND **fall into the trap; fall into someone's trap** to become caught in someone's scheme; to be deceived into doing or thinking something. (Also literal.) □ *We fell into a trap by asking for an explanation.* □ *I fell into his trap when I agreed to drive him home.* □ *We fell into the trap of thinking he was honest.*

fall in(to) line 1. to line up with each person (except the first person) standing behind someone. (Compare with *fall in.*) □ *The teacher told the students to fall in line for lunch.* □ *Hungry students fall into line very quickly.* **2.** to conform; to *fall in(to) place.* □ *All the parts of the problem finally fell into line.* □ *Bill's behavior began to fall in line.*

fall in(to) place to fit together; to become organized. □ *After we heard the whole story, things began to fall in place.* □ *When you get older, the different parts of your life begin to fall into place.*

fall into someone's trap See *fall into a trap.*

fall into the trap See *fall into a trap.*

fall off to decline or diminish. □ *Business falls off during the summer months.* □ *My interest in school fell off when I became twenty.*

fall on deaf ears [for talk or ideas] to be ignored by the persons they were intended for. □ *Her pleas for mercy fell on deaf ears.* □ *All of Sally's good*

advice fell on deaf ears. Walter had made up his own mind.

fall out 1. to happen; to result. □ *As things fell out, we had a wonderful trip.* □ *What fell out of our discussion was a decision to continue.* **2.** to leave one's place in a formation when dismissed. (Usually in scouting or the military. The opposite of *fall in.*) □ *The scouts fell out and ran to the campfire.* □ *All the soldiers fell out and talked among themselves.*

fall out (with someone about something) See the following entry.

fall out (with someone over something) AND **fall out (with someone about something)** to quarrel or disagree about something. □ *Bill fell out with Sally over the question of buying a new car.* □ *Bill fell out with John about who would sleep on the bottom bunk.* □ *They are always arguing. They fall out about once a week.*

fall over backwards (to do something) AND **bend over backwards (to do something); lean over backwards (to do something)** to do everything possible to please someone. (Informal. See also *fall (all) over oneself.*) □ *The taxi driver fell over backwards to be helpful.* □ *The teacher bent over backwards to help the students understand.* □ *The principal said that it was not necessary to bend over backwards.* □ *You don't have to lean over backwards to get me to help. Just ask.*

fall short (of something) 1. to lack something; to lack enough of something. □ *We fell short of money at the end of the month.* □ *When baking a cake, the cook fell short of eggs and had to go to the store for more.* **2.** to fail to achieve a goal. □ *We fell short of our goal of collecting a thousand dollars.* □ *Ann ran a fast race, but fell short of the record.*

fall through not to happen; to come to nothing. (Informal.) □ *Our plans fell through, and we won't be going to Texas after all.* □ *The party fell through at the last minute.*

fall to to begin (to do something). (Compare with *turn to*.) □ *The hungry children took their knives and forks and fell to.* □ *The carpenter unpacked his saw and hammer and fell to.* □ *The boys wanted to fight, so the coach put boxing gloves on them and told them to fall to.* □ *John fell to and cleaned up his room after he got yelled at.*

fall (up)on someone or something 1. to attack someone or something. (Also literal.) □ *The cat fell upon the mouse and killed it.* □ *The children fell on the birthday cake and ate it all.* **2.** [with *someone*] [for a task] to become the duty of someone. □ *The task of telling Mother about the broken vase fell upon Jane.* □ *The job of cleaning up the spill fell upon Tom.*

Familiarity breeds contempt. a proverb meaning that knowing a person closely for a long time leads to bad feelings. □ *Bill and his brothers are always fighting. As they say: "Familiarity breeds contempt."* □ *Mary and John were good friends for many years. Finally they got into a big argument and became enemies. That just shows that familiarity breeds contempt.*

fan the flames (of something) to make something more intense; to make a situation worse. □ *The riot fanned the flames of racial hatred even more.* □ *The hostility in the school is bad enough without anyone fanning the flames.*

far and away the best unquestionably the best. (Fixed order.) □ *This soap is far and away the best.* □ *Sally is good, but Ann is far and away the best.*

far be it from me to do something it is not really my place to do something. (Always with *but*, as in the examples.) □ *Far be it from me to tell you what to do, but I think you should buy the book.* □ *Far be it from me to attempt to advise you, but you're making a big mistake.*

far cry from something a thing that is very different from something else. (Informal.) □ *What you did was a far cry from what you said you were going*

to do. □ *The song they played was a far cry from what I call music.*

far from it not it at all; not at all. □ *Do I think you need a new car? Far from it. The old one is fine.* □ BILL: *Does this hat look strange?* TOM: *Far from it. It looks good.*

far into the night late into the night; late. □ *She sat up and read far into the night.* □ *The party went on far into the night.*

far out 1. far from the center of things; far from town. □ *The Smiths live sort of far out.* □ *The restaurant is nice, but too far out.* **2.** strange. (Slang.) □ *Ann acts pretty far out sometimes.* □ *The whole group of people seemed pretty far out.*

farm someone or something out 1. [with *someone*] to send someone (somewhere) for care or development. □ *When my mother died, they farmed me out to my aunt and uncle.* Ⓣ *The team manager farmed out the baseball player to the minor leagues until he improved.* **2.** [with *something*] to send something (elsewhere) to be dealt with. □ *Bill farmed his chores out to his brothers and sisters and went to a movie.* Ⓣ *I farmed out various parts of the work to different people.*

fast and furious very rapidly and with unrestrained energy. (Fixed order.) □ *Her work in the kitchen was fast and furious, and it looked lovely when she finished.* □ *Everything was going so fast and furious at the store during the Christmas rush that we never had time to eat lunch.*

fat and happy well-fed and content. (Fixed order.) □ *Since all the employees were fat and happy, there was little incentive to improve productivity.* □ *You look fat and happy. Has life been treating you well?*

fat chance very little likelihood. (Informal.) □ *Fat chance he has of getting a promotion.* □ *You think she'll lend you the money? Fat chance!*

feast one's eyes (on someone or something) to look at someone or something with pleasure, envy, or admiration. □ *Just feast your eyes on that beautiful juicy steak!* □ *Yes, feast your eyes. You won't see one like that again for a long time.*

feather in one's cap an honor; a reward for something. □ *Getting a new client was really a feather in my cap.* □ *John earned a feather in his cap by getting an A in physics.*

feather one's (own) nest 1. to decorate and furnish one's home in style and comfort. (Birds line their nests with feathers to make them warm and comfortable.) □ *Mr. and Mrs. Simpson have feathered their nest quite comfortably.* □ *It costs a great deal of money to feather one's nest these days.* **2.** to use power and prestige to provide for oneself selfishly. (Said especially of politicians who use their offices to make money for themselves.) □ *The mayor seemed to be helping people, but she was really feathering her own nest.* □ *The building contractor used a lot of public money to feather his nest.*

fed up (to some place) (with someone or something) bored with or disgusted with someone or something. (Informal. The *some place* can be *here, the teeth, the gills,* or other places.) □ *I'm fed up with Tom and his silly tricks.* □ *I'm fed up to here with high taxes.* □ *They are fed up to the teeth with screaming children.* □ *I'm really fed up!*

feed one's face to eat. (Slang.) □ *Come on, everyone. It's time to feed your faces.* □ *Bill, if you keep feeding your face all the time, you'll get fat.*

feed someone a line See *give someone a line.*

feed the kitty to contribute money. (See also *pass the hat.*) □ *Please feed the kitty. Make a contribution to help sick children.* □ *Come on, Bill. Feed the kitty. You can afford a dollar for a good cause.*

feel at home to feel as if one belongs; to feel as if one were in one's home; to

feel accepted. (See also *at home with someone or something.*) □ *I liked my dormitory room. I really felt at home there.* □ *We will do whatever we can to make you feel at home.*

feel dragged out to feel exhausted. (Informal.) □ *What a day! I really feel dragged out.* □ *If he runs too much, he ends up feeling dragged out.*

feel fit to feel well and healthy. □ *If you want to feel fit, you must eat the proper food and get enough rest.* □ *I hope I still feel fit when I get old.*

feel free (to do something) to feel like one is permitted to do something or take something. □ *Please feel free to stay for dinner.* □ *If you see something you want in the refrigerator, please feel free.*

feel it beneath one (to do something) to feel that one would be lowering oneself to do something. □ *Tom feels it beneath him to scrub the floor.* □ *Ann feels it beneath her to carry her own luggage.* □ *I would do it, but I feel it beneath me.*

feel like a million (dollars) to feel well and healthy, both physically and mentally. □ *A quick swim in the morning makes me feel like a million dollars.* □ *What a beautiful day! It makes you feel like a million.*

feel like a new person to feel refreshed and renewed, especially after getting well or getting dressed up. □ *I bought a new suit, and now I feel like a new person.* □ *Bob felt like a new person when he got out of the hospital.*

feel like something 1. to feel well enough to do something. □ *I believe I'm getting well. I feel like getting out of bed.* □ *I don't feel like going to the party. I have a headache.* **2.** to want to have something or do something. □ *I feel like having a nice cool drink.* □ *I feel like a nice cool drink.* □ *I don't feel like going to the party. It sounds boring.*

feel on top of the world to feel very good, as if one were ruling the world. □ *I feel on top of the world this morn-*

ing. □ *I do not actually feel on top of the world, but I have felt worse.*

feel out of place to feel that one does not belong in a place. □ *I feel out of place at formal dances.* □ *Bob and Ann felt out of place at the picnic, so they went home.*

feel put-upon to feel taken advantage of or exploited. □ *Bill refused to help because he felt put-upon.* □ *Sally's mother felt put-upon, but she took each of the children home after the birthday party.*

feel someone out to try to find out how someone feels (about something). (Informal. This does not involve touching anyone.) □ *Sally tried to feel Tom out on whether he'd make a contribution.* Ⓣ *The students felt out their parents to find out what they thought about the proposed party.*

feel something in one's bones AND **know something in one's bones** (Informal.) to sense something; to have an intuition about something. □ *The train will be late. I feel it in my bones.* □ *I failed the test. I know it in my bones.*

feel up to something to feel well enough or prepared enough to do something. (Often in the negative.) □ *I don't feel up to jogging today.* □ *Aunt Mary didn't feel up to making the visit.* □ *Do you feel up to going out today?*

fence someone in to restrict someone in some way. (Informal. See also *hem someone or something in.* Also literal.) □ *I don't want to fence you in, but you have to get home earlier at night.* □ *Don't try to fence me in. I need a lot of freedom.*

fend for oneself See *shift for oneself.*

ferret something out of someone or something to remove or retrieve something from someone or something, usually with cunning and persistence. □ *I tried very hard, but I couldn't ferret the information out of the clerk.* □ *I had to ferret out the answer from a book in the library.*

few and far between very few; few and widely scattered. (Informal. Fixed order.) □ *Get some gasoline now. Service stations on this highway are few and far between.* □ *Some people think that good movies are few and far between.*

fiddle about (with someone or something) See the following entry.

fiddle around (with someone or something) AND **fiddle about (with someone or something)** (See also *mess around (with someone or something).*) **1.** [with *someone*] to tease, annoy, or play with someone; to waste someone's time. □ *All right, stop fiddling around with me and tell me how much you will give me for my car.* □ *Now it's time for all of you to quit fiddling around and get to work.* □ *Tom, you have to stop spending your time fiddling about with your friends. It's time to get serious with your studies.* **2.** [with *something*] to play with something; to tinker with something ineptly. □ *My brother is outside fiddling around with his car engine.* □ *He should stop fiddling around and go out and get a job.* □ *Stop fiddling about with that stick. You're going to hurt someone.*

fiddle while Rome burns to do nothing or something trivial while something disastrous happens. (From a legend that the emperor Nero played the lyre while Rome was burning.) □ *The lobbyists don't seem to be doing anything to stop this tax bill. They're fiddling while Rome burns.* □ *The doctor should have sent for an ambulance right away instead of examining the woman. In fact, he was just fiddling while Rome burned.*

fight against time to hurry to meet a deadline or to do something quickly. □ *The ambulance sped through the city to reach the accident, fighting against time.* □ *All the students fought against time to complete the test.*

fight someone or something hammer and tongs AND **fight someone or something tooth and nail; go at it hammer and tongs; go at it tooth and nail** to fight against someone or something energetically and with great determination. (All have fixed order.) □ *They fought against the robber tooth and nail.* □ *The dogs were fighting each other hammer and tongs.* □ *The mayor fought the new law hammer and tongs.* □ *We'll fight this zoning ordinance tooth and nail.*

fight someone or something tooth and nail See the previous entry.

fighting chance a good possibility of success, especially if every effort is made. (See also *sporting chance*.) □ *They have at least a fighting chance of winning the race.* □ *The patient could die, but he has a fighting chance since the operation.*

figure in something [for a person] to play a role in something. □ *Tom figures in our plans for a new building.* □ *I don't wish to figure in your future.*

figure on something to plan on something; to make arrangements for something. (Informal.) □ *We figured on twenty guests at our party.* □ *I didn't figure on so much trouble.*

figure someone or something out to understand someone or something; to find an explanation for someone or something. □ *It's hard to figure John out. I don't know what he means.* ⊤ *I can't figure out this recipe.*

fill someone in (on someone or something) to inform someone about someone or something. □ *Please fill me in on what is happening in Washington.* □ *Please fill me in on Ann. How is she doing?* □ *Sit down, and I'll fill you in.* ⊤ *Later, I'll fill in everyone else.*

fill someone's shoes to take the place of some other person and do that person's work satisfactorily. (As if you were wearing the other person's shoes.) □ *I don't know how we'll be able to do without you. No one can fill your shoes.* □ *It'll be difficult to fill Jane's shoes. She did her job very well.*

fill the bill to be exactly the thing that is needed. □ *Ah, this steak is great. It really fills the bill.* □ *This new pair of shoes fills the bill nicely.*

filled to the brim filled all the way full; filled up to the top edge. □ *I like my coffee cup filled to the brim.* □ *If the glass is filled to the brim, I can't drink without spilling the contents.*

final fling the last act or period of enjoyment before a change in one's circumstances or life-style. □ *You might as well have a final fling before the baby's born.* □ *Mary's going out with her girlfriends for a final fling. She's getting married next week.*

find fault (with someone or something) to find things wrong with someone or something. □ *We were unable to find fault with the meal.* □ *Sally's father was always finding fault with her.* □ *Some people are always finding fault.*

find it in one's heart (to do something) to have the courage or compassion to do something. □ *She couldn't find it in her heart to refuse to come home to him.* □ *I can't do it! I can't find it in my heart.*

find one's or something's way somewhere 1. [with *one's*] to discover the route to a place. □ *Mr. Smith found his way to the museum.* □ *Can you find your way home?* **2.** [with *something's*] to end up in a place. (This expression avoids accusing someone of moving the thing to the place.) □ *The money found its way into the mayor's pocket.* □ *The secret plans found their way into the enemy's hands.*

find one's own level to find the position or rank to which one is best suited. (As water "seeks its own level.") □ *You cannot force clerks to be ambitious. They will all find their own level.* □ *The new student is happier in the beginning class. It was just a question of letting her find her own level.*

find one's tongue to be able to talk. (Informal.) □ *Tom was speechless for a moment. Then he found his tongue.* □ *Ann was unable to find her tongue. She sat there in silence.*

find one's way (around) to be able to move about an area satisfactorily. □ *I can go downtown by myself. I can find my way around.* □ *I know the area well enough to find my way.* □ *He can find his way around when it comes to car engines.*

find oneself to discover what one's talents and preferences are. □ *Bill did better in school after he found himself.* □ *John tried a number of different jobs. He finally found himself when he became a cook.*

find someone or something out 1. [with *something*] to discover facts about someone or something; to learn a fact. □ *I found something out that you might be interested in.* Ⓣ *We found out that the Smiths are going to sell their house.* **2.** [with *someone*] to discover something bad about someone. □ *John thought he could get away with smoking, but his mother found him out.* □ *Jane was taking a two-hour lunch period until the manager found her out.*

find (something) out the hard way See *learn something the hard way.*

Finders keepers(, losers weepers). a phrase said when something is found. (The person who finds something gets to keep it. The person who loses it can only weep. Fixed order.) □ *John lost a quarter in the dining room yesterday. Ann found the quarter there today. Ann claimed that since she found it, it was hers. She said, "Finders keepers, losers weepers."* □ *John said, "I'll say finders keepers when I find something of yours!"*

fine and dandy all right; okay; really fine. (Fixed order.) □ *Everything is fine and dandy at work. No special problems at the present time.* □ *I feel fine and dandy. The new medicine seems to be working.*

fine kettle of fish a real mess; an unsatisfactory situation. □ *The dog has eaten the steak we were going to have for dinner. This is a fine kettle of fish!* □ *This is a fine kettle of fish. It's below freezing outside, and the furnace won't work.*

fine state of affairs See *pretty state of affairs.*

fire away at someone or something 1. to shoot at someone or something. □ *The hunters fired away at the ducks.* □ *On television, somebody is always firing away at somebody else.* **2.** [with *someone*] to ask many questions of someone; to criticize someone severely. □ *When it came time for questions, the reporters began firing away at the mayor.* □ *Members of the opposite party are always firing away at the president.*

firing on all cylinders AND **hitting on all cylinders** working at full strength; making every possible effort. (From an internal combustion engine.) □ *The team is firing on all cylinders under the new coach.* □ *The factory is hitting on all cylinders to finish the orders on time.*

first and foremost first and most important. (Fixed order.) □ *First and foremost, I think you should work harder on your biology.* □ *Have this in mind first and foremost: Keep smiling!*

first and ten [in football] the first down [of four] with ten yards needed to earn another first down. (Fixed order.) □ *It is first and ten on the forty-yard line, and Army has the ball.* □ *There will be no first and ten on the last play because there was a flag on the play.*

First come, first served. The first people to arrive will be served first. (Fixed order.) □ *They ran out of tickets before we got there. It was first come, first served, but we didn't know that.* □ *Please line up and take your turn. It's first come, first served.*

first of all the very first thing; before anything else. □ *First of all, put your name on this piece of paper.* □ *First of all, we'll try to find a place to live.*

first off first; the first thing. (Almost the same as *first of all.*) □ *He ordered soup first off.* □ *First off, we'll find a place to live.*

first thing (in the morning) before anything else in the morning. □ *Please* call me first thing in the morning. I can't help you now. □ I'll do that first thing.

first things first the most important things must be taken care of first. □ *It's more important to get a job than to buy new clothes. First things first!* □ *Do your homework now. Go out and play later. First things first.*

fish for a compliment to try to get someone to pay you a compliment. (Informal.) □ *When she showed me her new dress, I could tell that she was fishing for a compliment.* □ *Tom was certainly fishing for a compliment when he modeled his fancy haircut for his friends.*

fish for something to try to get information (from someone). (Also literal.) □ *The lawyer was fishing for evidence.* □ *The teacher spent a lot of time fishing for the right answer from the students.*

fish in troubled waters to involve oneself in a difficult, confused, or dangerous situation, especially with a view to gaining an advantage. □ *Frank is fishing in troubled waters by buying more shares of that company. They are supposed to be in financial difficulties.* □ *The company could make more money by selling armaments abroad, but they would be fishing in troubled waters.*

fish or cut bait either do the job you are supposed to be doing or quit and let someone else do it. (Fixed order.) □ *Mary is doing much better on the job since her manager told her to fish or cut bait.* □ *The boss told Tom, "Quit wasting time! Fish or cut bait!"*

fit and trim slim and in good physical shape. (Fixed order.) □ *Jean tried to keep herself fit and trim at all times.* □ *For some people, keeping fit and trim requires time, effort, and self-discipline.*

fit as a fiddle See *(as) fit as a fiddle.*

fit for a king totally suitable. □ *What a delicious meal. It was fit for a king.* □ *Our room at the hotel was fit for a king.*

fit in someone See *fit someone in(to something).*

fit in (with someone or something) to be comfortable with someone or something; to be in accord or harmony with someone or something. □ *I really feel as if I fit in with that group of people.* □ *It's good that you fit in.* □ *This chair doesn't fit in with the style of furniture in my house.* □ *I won't buy it if it doesn't fit in.*

fit like a glove to fit very well; to fit tightly or snugly. □ *My new shoes fit like a glove.* □ *My new coat is a little tight. It fits like a glove.*

fit someone in(to something) AND **fit in someone** to manage to put someone into a schedule. □ *The doctor is busy, but I can fit you into the schedule.* □ *Yes, here's an opening in the schedule. I can fit you in.*

fit someone or something out (with something) to provide or furnish someone or something with something. □ *They fit the camper out with everything they needed.* □ *They fit them out for only $140.* □ *He fit his car out with lots of chrome.* Ⓣ *He fit out his car with too much chrome.*

fit someone to a T **1.** See *suit someone to a T.* **2.** [for something] to fit a person very well. □ *His new jacket fits him to a T.* □ *My new shoes fit me to a T.*

fit to be tied very angry and excited. (Folksy. To be so angry that one has to be restrained with ropes.) □ *If I'm not home on time, my parents will be fit to be tied.* □ *When Ann saw the bill, she was fit to be tied.*

fit to kill dressed up to look very fancy or sexy. (Folksy.) □ *Mary put on her best clothes and looked fit to kill.* □ *John looked fit to kill in his tuxedo.*

fix someone up (with someone or something) **1.** [with *something*] to supply a person with something. (Informal.) □ *The usher fixed us up with seats at the front of the theater.* Ⓣ *We fixed up the visitors with a cold drink.* **2.** [with *someone*] AND **line someone up with some-**

one to supply a person with a date or a companion. (Informal.) □ *They lined John up with my cousin, Jane.* □ *John didn't want us to fix him up.* Ⓣ *We fixed up Bob with a date.*

fix someone's wagon to punish someone; to get even with someone; to plot against someone. (Informal.) □ *If you ever do that again, I'll fix your wagon!* □ *Tommy! You clean up your room this instant, or I'll fix your wagon!* □ *He reported me to the boss, but I fixed his wagon. I knocked his lunch on the floor.*

fizzle out to die out; to come to a stop shortly after starting; to fail. □ *It started to rain, and the fire fizzled out.* □ *The car started in the cold weather, but it fizzled out before we got very far.* □ *My attempt to run for mayor fizzled out.* □ *She started off her job very well, but fizzled out after about a month.*

flare up to grow intense for a brief period. (Usually said of a flame, someone's anger, or a chronic disease. Also literal, as with flames.) □ *Just when we thought we had put the fire out, it flared up again.* □ *Mr. Jones always flares up whenever anyone mentions taxes.* □ *My hay fever usually flares up in August.*

flash in the pan someone or something that draws a lot of attention for a very brief time. (Informal.) □ *I'm afraid that my success as a painter was just a flash in the pan.* □ *Tom had hoped to be a singer, but his career was only a flash in the pan.*

flat as a pancake See *(as) flat as a pancake.*

flat broke completely broke; with no money at all. (Informal.) □ *I spent my last dollar, and I'm flat broke.* □ *The bank closed its doors to the public. It was flat broke!*

flat out 1. clearly and definitely; holding nothing back. (Informal.) □ *I told her flat out that I didn't like her.* □ *They reported flat out that the operation was a failure.* 2. at top speed. (Slang.) □ *How fast will this car go flat out?* □ *This car will hit about 110 miles per hour flat out.*

flesh and blood (Fixed order.) 1. a living human body, especially with reference to its natural limitations; a human being. □ *This cold weather is more than flesh and blood can stand.* □ *Carrying 300 pounds is beyond mere flesh and blood.* 2. the quality of being alive. □ *The paintings of this artist are lifeless. They lack flesh and blood.* □ *This play needs flesh and blood, not the mumbling of intensely dull actors.* 3. one's own relatives; one's own kin. □ *That's no way to treat one's own flesh and blood.* □ *I want to leave my money to my own flesh and blood.* □ *Grandmother was happier living with her flesh and blood.*

flesh something out to make something more detailed, bigger, or fuller. (As if one were adding flesh to a skeleton.) □ *This is basically a good outline. Now you'll have to flesh it out.* Ⓣ *The play was good, except that the author needed to flesh out the third act. It was too short.*

flight of fancy an idea or suggestion that is out of touch with reality or possibility. □ *What is the point in indulging in flights of fancy about foreign vacations when you cannot even afford the rent?* □ *We are tired of her flights of fancy about marrying a millionaire.*

fling oneself at someone See *throw oneself at someone.*

flip one's lid See the following entry.

flip one's wig AND **flip one's lid** to suddenly become angry, crazy, or enthusiastic. (Slang.) □ *Whenever anyone mentions taxes, Mr. Jones absolutely flips his wig.* □ *Stop whistling. You're going to make me flip my lid.* □ *When I saw that brand-new car and learned it was mine, I just flipped my wig.*

float a loan to get a loan; to arrange for a loan. □ *I couldn't afford to pay cash for the car, so I floated a loan.* □ *They needed money, so they had to float a loan.*

flora and fauna plants and animals. (Latin. Fixed order.) □ *The magazine story described the flora and fauna of Panama.* □ *We went for a hike in the Finnish wilderness hoping to learn all about the local flora and fauna.*

flotsam and jetsam worthless matter; worthless encumbrances. (Also literal for the floating wreckage of a ship and its cargo and floating cargo deliberately cast overboard to stabilize a ship in a rough sea. Fixed order.) □ *His mind is burdened with the flotsam and jetsam of many years of poor instruction and lax study habits.* □ *Your report would be better if you could get rid of a lot of the flotsam and jetsam and clean up the grammar a bit.*

fluff one's lines AND **blow one's lines; muff one's lines** to speak one's speech badly or forget one's lines when one is in a play. (Informal.) □ *The actress fluffed her lines badly in the last act.* □ *I was in a play once, and I muffed my lines over and over.* □ *It's okay to blow your lines in rehearsal.*

flunk out to fail a course; to fail out of school. □ *Tom didn't study, and he finally flunked out.* □ *Bill is about to flunk out of geometry.*

flunk someone out to cause someone to leave school by giving a failing grade. □ *The teacher flunked Tom out.* ⊤ *The professor wanted to flunk out the whole class.*

fly-by-night irresponsible; untrustworthy. (Refers to a person who sneaks away secretly in the night.) □ *The carpenter we hired was a fly-by-night worker who did a very bad job.* □ *You shouldn't deal with a fly-by-night merchant.*

fly in the face of someone or something AND **fly in the teeth of someone or something** to disregard, defy, or show disrespect for someone or something. □ *John loves to fly in the face of tradition.* □ *Ann made it a practice to fly in the face of standard procedures.* □ *John finds great pleasure in flying in the teeth of his father.*

fly in the ointment a small, unpleasant matter that spoils something; a drawback. □ *We enjoyed the play, but the fly in the ointment was not being able to find our car afterward.* □ *It sounds like a good idea, but there must be a fly in the ointment somewhere.*

fly in the teeth of someone or something See *fly in the face of someone or something.*

fly into the face of danger to take great risks; to threaten or challenge danger, as if danger were a person. (This may refer to flying, as in an airplane, but not necessarily.) □ *John plans to go bungee-jumping this weekend. He really likes flying into the face of danger.* □ *Willard was not exactly the type to fly into the face of danger, but tonight was an exception, and he ordered enchiladas.*

fly off the handle to lose one's temper. (Informal.) □ *Every time anyone mentions taxes, Mrs. Brown flies off the handle.* □ *If she keeps flying off the handle like that, she'll have a heart attack.*

fly the coop to escape; to get out or get away. (Informal. Refers to a chicken escaping from a chicken coop.) □ *I couldn't stand the party, so I flew the coop.* □ *The prisoner flew the coop at the first opportunity.*

foam at the mouth to be very angry. (Informal. Related to a "mad dog" — a dog with rabies — which foams at the mouth.) □ *Bob was raving — foaming at the mouth. I've never seen anyone so angry.* □ *Bill foamed at the mouth in anger.*

fob something off (on someone) to trick someone into accepting something that is worthless. (Informal.) □ *The car dealer fobbed a junky car off on Tom.* ⊤ *He also fobbed off a bad car on Jane.* □ *Some car dealers are always trying to fob something off.*

fold something up to put an end to something; to close something. (Also literal.) □ *Mr. Jones was going broke, so he folded his business up.* ⊤ *The* *producer decided to fold up the play early. It was losing money.*

fold, spindle, or mutilate to harm or disfigure a machine-readable document, such as a computer punch card. (Such a document, if folded, placed on a bill spike, or otherwise punctured, would no longer be machine-readable. Now rarely seen on a bill but the expression is sometimes used in a figurative sense. Fixed order.) □ *At the bottom of the bill, it said "do not fold, spindle, or mutilate," and Jane, in her anger, did all three.* □ *Look here, chum, if you don't want to get folded, spindled, or mutilated, you had better do what you are told!*

fold up to close up; to end. (Also literal.) □ *The play folded up after two days.* □ *It's time to fold up and go home.*

follow in someone's footsteps See the following entry.

follow in someone's tracks AND **follow in someone's footsteps** to follow someone's example; to assume someone else's role or occupation. □ *The vice president was following in the president's footsteps when he called for budget cuts.* □ *She followed in her father's footsteps and went into medicine.*

follow one's heart to act according to one's feelings; to obey one's sympathetic or compassionate inclinations. □ *I couldn't decide what to do, so I just followed my heart.* □ *I trust that you will follow your heart in this matter.*

follow one's nose **1.** to go straight ahead, the direction that one's nose is pointing. (Folksy.) □ *The town that you want is straight ahead on this highway. Just follow your nose.* □ *The chief's office is right around the corner. Turn left and follow your nose.* **2.** to follow an odor to its source. (Informal.) □ *The kitchen is at the back of the building. Just follow your nose.* □ *There was a bad smell in the basement — probably a dead mouse. I followed my nose until I found it.*

follow someone or something up **1.** [with *something*] to add more information or detail to something; to follow something through. □ *Bill had to follow my suggestion up.* ⊤ *The police followed up my story.* **2.** [with *someone*] to review someone's work and check it over. □ *The person who follows you up will make sure you're doing the right thing.* ⊤ *When I followed up Mary, I found errors in her work.*

follow suit to follow in the same pattern; to follow someone else's example. (From card games.) □ *Mary went to work for a bank, and Jane followed suit. Now they are both head cashiers.* □ *The Smiths went out to dinner, but the Browns didn't follow suit. They stayed home.*

follow the crowd to do what everyone else is doing. □ *I am an independent thinker. I could never just follow the crowd.* □ *When in doubt, I follow the crowd. At least I don't stand out like a fool.*

follow through (on something) AND **carry through (on something)** to complete a task; to see a task through to its completion. □ *You must follow through on the things that you start.* □ *Don't start the job if you can't follow through.* □ *Ask Sally to carry through on her project.*

follow up (on someone or something) to find out more about someone or something. □ *Please follow up on Mr. Brown and his activities.* □ *Bill, Mr. Smith has a complaint. Would you please follow up on it?* □ *We can take care of that when we follow up.*

fond of someone or something to like someone or something. □ *I'm fond of chocolate.* □ *Mary isn't fond of me, but I'm fond of her.*

food for thought something to think about. □ *I don't like your idea very much, but it's food for thought.* □ *Your lecture was very good. It contained much food for thought.*

fool around (with someone or something) to fiddle, play, or mess with someone or something; to waste time with someone or something. (Informal.) □ *John is out fooling around with his friends again.* □ *That child spends most of his time fooling around.* □ *Please don't fool around with the light switch. You'll break it.* □ *There are lots of interesting things in here, but you must leave them alone. Don't fool around.*

fool's paradise a condition of seeming happiness that is based on false assumptions and will not last. (Treated as a place grammatically.) □ *They think they can live on love alone, but they are living in a fool's paradise.* □ *The inhabitants of the island feel politically secure, but they are living in a fool's paradise. They could be invaded at any time.*

fools rush in (where angels fear to tread) people with little experience or knowledge often get involved in difficult or delicate situations that wiser people would avoid. □ *I wouldn't ask Jean about her divorce, but Kate did. Fools rush in, as they say.* □ *Only the newest member of the committee questioned the chairman's decision. Fools rush in where angels fear to tread.*

foot the bill to pay the bill; to pay (for something). □ *Let's go out and eat. I'll foot the bill.* □ *If the bank goes broke, don't worry. The government will foot the bill.*

footloose and fancy-free without responsibilities or commitments. (Fixed order.) □ *All the rest of them have wives, but John is footloose and fancy-free.* □ *Mary never stays long in any job. She likes being footloose and fancy-free.*

for all I care I don't care if (something happens). (Informal.) □ *For all I care, the whole city council can go to the devil.* □ *They can all starve for all I care.*

for all I know according to the information I have; I think; probably. (Informal.) □ *For all I know, the mayor has resigned already.* □ *She may have gone to town for all I know.*

for all intents and purposes virtually; practically speaking. (Sometimes this expression has very little meaning. Fixed order.) □ *He entered the room, looking for all intents and purposes as if he would burst into song.* □ *She said that for all intents and purposes she had completed her assignment.*

for all it's worth AND **for what(ever) it's worth** if it has any value. □ *My idea —for all it's worth—is to offer them only $300.* □ *Here is my thinking, for whatever it's worth.* □ *Ask her to give us her opinion, for what it's worth.*

for all practical purposes as might be reasonably expected; essentially. □ *For all practical purposes, this is simply a matter of right and wrong.* □ *This should be considered final, for all practical purposes.*

for all something in spite of something. □ *For all her complaining, she still seems to be a happy person.* □ *For all my aches and pains, I'm still rather healthy.*

for all the world 1. exactly; precisely. (Especially with *look*.) □ *She sat there looking for all the world as if she was going to cry.* □ *It started out seeming for all the world like a beautiful day. Then a storm came up.* **2.** everything. (Usually in the negative.) □ *I wouldn't give up my baby for all the world.* □ *They wouldn't sell their property for all the world.*

for better or for worse under any conditions; no matter what happens. (Fixed order.) □ *I married you for better or for worse.* □ *For better or for worse, I'm going to quit my job.*

for chicken feed AND **for peanuts** for nearly nothing; for very little money. (Informal. Also used without *for*.) □ *Bob doesn't get paid much. He works for chicken feed.* □ *You can buy an old car for chicken feed.* □ *I won't do that kind of work for peanuts!*

For crying out loud! For heaven's sake!; I am amazed! (An exclamation of surprise and mild shock.) □ *For crying out loud! I didn't expect to see you here.* □ *For crying out loud! What a time to call someone on the telephone.*

for days on end for many days. □ *We kept on traveling for days on end.* □ *Doctor, I've had this pain for days on end.*

for fear of something out of fear of something; because of fear of something. □ *He doesn't drive for fear of an accident.* □ *They lock their doors for fear of being robbed.*

for good forever; permanently. □ *I finally left home for good.* □ *They tried to repair it many times before they fixed it for good.*

for good measure as extra; (adding) a little more to make sure there is enough. □ *When I bought a pound of nails, the clerk threw in a few extra nails for good measure.* □ *I always put a little extra salt in the soup for good measure.*

for hours on end for many hours. □ *We sat and waited for the doctor for hours on end.* □ *We listened to the speaker for hours on end.*

for keeps forever; permanently. (Informal. See also *play for keeps.* Compare with *for good.*) □ *When I get married, it'll be for keeps.* □ *We've moved around a lot. Now I think we'll stay here for keeps.*

for kicks for fun; just for entertainment; for no good reason. (Slang.) □ *They didn't mean any harm. They just did it for kicks.* □ *We drove over to the next town for kicks.*

for one's (own) part as far as one is concerned; from one's point of view. □ *For my own part, I wish to stay here.* □ *For her part, she prefers chocolate.*

for one's (own) sake for one's good or benefit; in honor of someone. □ *I have to earn a living for my family's sake.* □ *I did it for my mother's sake.* □ *I didn't do it for my own sake.*

for openers AND **for starters** to start with. (Informal.) □ *For openers, they*

played a song everyone knows. □ *For starters, I'll serve a delicious soup.*

for peanuts See *for chicken feed.*

for real authentic; genuine; really. (Informal or slang.) □ *Is this diamond for real?* □ *Are you for real?* □ *Are we there for real?*

for sale available for purchase; buyable. (Compare with *on sale.*) □ *Is this item for sale?* □ *How long has this house been for sale?* □ *My car is for sale. Are you interested?*

for short in a short form. (Usually refers to names.) □ *My name is William. They call me Bill for short.* □ *Almost everyone who is named Robert is called Bob for short.*

for starters See *for openers.*

for sure certainly; surely. (Informal or slang.) □ MARY: *Do you like my new jacket?* JANE: *For sure.* □ *For sure, I want to go on the picnic.*

for that matter besides; in addition. □ *If you're hungry, take one of my doughnuts. For that matter, take two.* □ *I don't like this house. The roof leaks. For that matter, the whole place is falling apart.* □ *Tom is quite arrogant. So is his sister, for that matter.*

for the asking if one just asks (for something); simply by asking; on request. □ *Do you want to use my car? It's yours for the asking.* □ *I have an extra winter coat that's yours for the asking.*

for the best See *(all) for the best.*

for the better better; an improvement. (See also *take a turn for the better.*) □ *A change of government would be for the better.* □ *A new winter coat would certainly be for the better.*

for the birds worthless; undesirable. (Slang.) □ *This television program is for the birds.* □ *Winter weather is for the birds.*

for the devil of it AND **for the heck of it; for the hell of it** just for fun; because it is slightly evil; for no good reason. (Informal. Use *hell* with caution.) □

We filled their garage with leaves just for the devil of it. □ *Tom tripped Bill for the heck of it.* □ *John picked a fight with Tom just for the hell of it.*

for the heck of it See the previous entry.

for the hell of it See *for the devil of it.*

for the life of one even if one's life were threatened; even in exchange for one's life. (Informal. Always with a negative, and usually having to do with one's memory.) □ *For the life of me, I don't remember your name.* □ *She couldn't recall the correct numbers for the life of her.* □ *For the life of them, they couldn't remember the way home.*

for the moment AND **for the time being** for the present; for now; temporarily. □ *This will have to do for the moment.* □ *This is all right for the time being. It'll have to be improved next week, however.* □ *This good feeling will last only for the time being.* □ *This solution is satisfactory for the moment.*

for the most part mostly; in general. □ *For the most part, the class is enjoying geometry.* □ *I like working here for the most part.*

for the odds to be against one for things to be against one generally; for one's chances to be slim. □ *You can give it a try, but the odds are against you.* □ *I know the odds are against me, but I wish to run in the race anyway.*

for the record so that (one's own version of) the facts will be known; so there will be a record of a particular fact. (This often is said when there are reporters present.) □ *I'd like to say—for the record—that at no time have I ever accepted a bribe from anyone.* □ *For the record, I've never been able to get anything done around city hall without bribing someone.*

for the sake of someone or something for the good of someone or something; for the honor or recognition of someone or something. (Compare with *for one's own sake.*) □ *I did it for the sake of all those people who helped me get through school.* □ *I'm investing*

in a house for the sake of my children. □ *For the sake of honesty, Bill shared all the information he had.*

for the time being See *for the moment.*

for what(ever) it's worth See *for all it's worth.*

forbidden fruit someone or something that one finds attractive or desirable partly because having the person or thing is immoral or illegal. (From the apple in the Garden of Eden that was forbidden to Adam by God.) □ *Jim flirts with his sister-in-law only because she's forbidden fruit.* □ *The boy watches that program only when his parents are out. It's forbidden fruit.*

force someone or something down someone's throat See *shove someone or something down someone's throat.*

force someone out (of office) AND **drive someone out (of office)** to drive someone out of an elective office. □ *The city council forced the mayor out of office.* □ *Please resign immediately, or I'll have to drive you out.*

force someone to the wall AND **drive someone to the wall** to push someone to an extreme position; to put someone into an awkward position. □ *He wouldn't tell the truth until we forced him to the wall.* □ *They don't pay their bills until you drive them to the wall.*

force someone's hand to force a person to reveal plans, strategies, or secrets. (Refers to a handful of cards in card playing.) □ *We didn't know what she was doing until Tom forced her hand.* □ *We couldn't plan our game until we forced the other team's hand in the last play.*

force to be reckoned with someone or something that is important and powerful and must not be ignored. □ *Walter is a force to be reckoned with. Be prepared to deal with him.* □ *The growing discontent with the political system is a powerful force to be reckoned with.*

fore and aft at the front and the back, usually of a boat or ship. (Fixed order.) □ *They had to attach new lights fore and aft because the old ones were not bright enough to meet the new regulations.* □ *The captain ordered a watch stationed fore and aft.*

forever and a day See the following entry.

forever and ever AND **forever and a day** forever. (Fixed order.) □ *I will love you forever and ever.* □ *This car won't keep running forever and ever. We'll have to get a new one sometime.* □ *We have enough money to last forever and a day.*

forget oneself to forget one's manners or training. (Said in formal situations in reference to belching, bad table manners, and, in the case of very young children, pants-wetting.) □ *Sorry, Mother, I forgot myself.* □ *John, we are going out to dinner tonight. Please don't forget yourself.*

forgive and forget to forgive someone (for something) and forget that it ever happened. (Fixed order.) □ *I'm sorry, John. Let's forgive and forget. What do you say?* □ *It was nothing. We'll just have to forgive and forget.*

fork money out (for something) to pay (perhaps unwillingly) for something. (Informal. Often mention is made of the amount of money. See the examples.) □ *Do you think I'm going to fork twenty dollars out for that book?* □ *Forking money out to everyone is part of life in a busy economy.* T *I like that stereo, but I don't want to fork out a lot of money.*

fork something over to give something to someone. (Slang. Often refers to money. Usually used in a command.) □ *Now! Fork it over now!* T *Okay, Joe. Fork over that twenty dollars you owe me.*

form an opinion to think up or decide on an opinion. (Note the variations in the examples.) □ *I don't know enough about the issue to form an opinion.* □ *Don't tell me how to think! I can form my own opinion.* □ *I don't form opinions without careful consideration.*

form and substance meaningful content; structure and meaningful content. (Fixed order. See also *sum and substance*.) □ *The first act of the play was one screaming match after another. It lacked form and substance throughout.* □ *Jane's report was good. The teacher commented on the excellent form and substance of the paper.*

forty winks a short sleep; a nap. (Informal. See also *catch forty winks*.) □ *I had forty winks on the plane.* □ *If you're lucky you'll get forty winks while the children are out.*

foul one's own nest to harm one's own interests; to bring disadvantage upon oneself. □ *He tried to discredit a fellow senator with the president, but just succeeded in fouling his own nest.* □ *The boss really dislikes Mary. She certainly fouled her own nest when she spread those rumors about him.*

foul play illegal activity; bad practices. □ *The police investigating the death suspect foul play.* □ *Each student got an A on the test, and the teacher imagined it was the result of foul play.*

foul someone or something up to cause disorder and confusion for someone or something; to tangle up someone or something; to *mess someone or something up*. (Informal.) □ *Go away! Don't foul me up anymore.* T *You've fouled up my whole day.* T *Watch out! You're going to foul up my kite strings.* T *Stay off the field. You're going to foul up the coach.*

foul up to do (something) badly; to mess something up. (Informal.) □ *At the last minute, he fouled up and failed the course.* □ *Take your time. Plan your moves, and don't foul up.*

fouled up messed up. □ *My fishing line is all fouled up.* □ *The football team got fouled up and lost the game.*

free and clear without encumbrance, particularly in regard to the ownership of something. (Fixed order.) □ *After the last payment, Jane owned the car free and clear.* □ *If you can't prove* *that you own the house and the land it stands on free and clear, you can't sell it.*

free and easy casual. (Fixed order.) □ *John is so free and easy. How can anyone be so relaxed?* □ *Now, take it easy. Just act free and easy. No one will know you're nervous.*

free as a bird See *(as) free as a bird.*

free-for-all a disorganized fight or contest involving everyone; a brawl. □ *The picnic turned into a free-for-all after midnight.* □ *The race started out in an organized manner, but ended up being a free-for-all.*

fresh as a daisy See *(as) fresh as a daisy.*

fresh out (of something) AND **clean out (of something)** just now having sold or used up the last of something. (Folksy.) □ *Sorry, I can't serve you scrambled eggs. We are fresh out of eggs.* □ *We are fresh out of nails. I sold the last box just ten minutes ago.* □ *Lettuce? Sorry. I'm fresh out.* □ *Sorry. We are clean out of dried beans.*

friend or foe a friend or an enemy. (Fixed order.) □ *I can't tell whether Jim is friend or foe.* □ *"Who goes there? Friend or foe?" asked the sentry.*

frighten one out of one's wits AND **scare one out of one's wits** to frighten one very badly. (See also *frighten the wits out of someone.*) □ *Oh! That loud noise scared me out of my wits.* □ *I'll give him a good scolding and frighten him out of his wits.*

frighten someone to death AND **scare someone to death** to frighten someone severely. (Also literal.) □ *The dentist always frightens me to death.* □ *She scared me to death when she screamed.*

frighten the living daylights out of someone See the following entry.

frighten the wits out of someone AND **frighten the living daylights out of someone; scare the living daylights out of someone; scare the wits out of someone** to frighten someone very

badly. (The *living* can be left out.) □ *We nearly had an accident. It frightened the living daylights out of me.* □ *The incident scared the wits out of me.*

frightened to death AND **scared to death** severely frightened. (Also literal.) □ *I don't want to go to the dentist today. I'm frightened to death.* □ *I'm frightened to death of dogs.* □ *She's scared to death she'll fail algebra.*

fritter something away to waste something little by little, especially time or money. (Folksy.) □ *Don't stand around and fritter the whole day away.* Ⓣ *Stop frittering away my hard-earned money!*

from day to day on a daily basis; one day at a time; occasionally. □ *We face this kind of problem from day to day.* □ *I'll have to check into this matter from day to day.* □ *When you're very poor, you live from day to day.*

from door to door moving from one door to another—typically, from one house to another. (See also *door-to-door.*) □ *Anne went from door to door, selling books, to earn money for college.* □ *The children went from door to door, saying "Trick or treat!" at each one.*

from far and near AND **from near and far** all around, both close by and farther away. (Reversible, but with a preference for *from far and near.*) □ *All the young people from far and near gathered at the high school for the game.* □ *The eagles gathered from near and far at the river where the salmon were spawning.*

from hand to hand from one person to a series of other persons. □ *The book traveled from hand to hand until it got back to its owner.* □ *By the time the baby had been passed from hand to hand, it was crying.*

from head to toe from the top of one's head to one's feet. (See also *from tip to toe.* Fixed order.) □ *She was decked out in flowers from head to toe.* □ *The huge parka covered the small* child from head to toe, assuring that she would be well protected against the cold.

from pillar to post from one place to a series of other places; (figuratively) from person to person, as with gossip. □ *My father was in the army, and we moved from pillar to post year after year.* □ *After I told one person my secret, it went quickly from pillar to post.*

from rags to riches from poverty to wealth; from modesty to elegance. □ *The princess used to be quite poor. She certainly moved from rags to riches.* □ *After I inherited the money, I went from rags to riches.*

from start to finish from the beginning to the end; throughout. □ *I disliked the whole business from start to finish.* □ *Mary caused problems from start to finish.*

from stem to stern from one end to another. (Refers to the front and back ends of a ship. Also literal in reference to ships. Fixed order.) □ *Now, I have to clean the house from stem to stern.* □ *I polished my car carefully from stem to stern.*

from the bottom of one's heart sincerely. (Compare with *with all one's heart and soul*.) □ *When I returned the lost kitten to Mrs. Brown, she thanked me from the bottom of her heart.* □ *Oh, thank you! I'm grateful from the bottom of my heart.*

from the cradle to the grave from birth to death. □ *The government promised to take care of us from the cradle to the grave.* □ *You can feel secure and well protected from the cradle to the grave.*

from the ground up from the beginning; from start to finish. (Literal in reference to building a house or other building.) □ *We must plan our sales campaign carefully from the ground up.* □ *Sorry, but you'll have to start all over again from the ground up.*

from the heart from a deep and sincere emotional source. □ *I know that your*

kind words come from the heart. □ *We don't want your gift unless it comes from the heart.*

from the horse's mouth See *(straight) from the horse's mouth.*

from the outset from the beginning. □ *We had problems with this machine from the outset.* □ *We knew about the unfriendly judge from the outset of our trial.*

from the word go from the beginning. (Informal.) □ *I knew about the problem from the word go.* □ *She was failing the class from the word go.*

from this day forward See the following entry.

from this day on AND **from this day forward** from today into the future. (Formal.) □ *We'll live in love and peace from this day on.* □ *I'll treasure your gift from this day forward.*

from time to time occasionally. □ *We have pizza from time to time.* □ *From time to time, a visitor comes to our door.*

from tip to toe from the top to the bottom. (Not necessarily of a person. See also *from head to toe*. Fixed order.) □ *She is wearing all new clothes from tip to toe.* □ *The house needs to be cleaned thoroughly from tip to toe.*

from top to bottom from the highest point to the lowest point; throughout. (Compare with *from stem to stern*.) □ *I have to clean the house from top to bottom today.* □ *We need to replace our elected officials from top to bottom.*

from way back from far in the past; from an earlier time. (Informal.) □ *Grandfather comes from way back.* □ *This antique clock is from way back.*

full blast See *(at) full blast.*

full of beans See *full of hot air.*

full of bull See the following entry.

full of hot air AND **full of beans; full of bull; full of it; full of prunes** full of nonsense; talking nonsense. (Slang.) □ *Oh, shut up, Mary. You're full of hot air.* □ *Don't pay any attention to Bill.*

He's full of beans. □ *My English professor is full of bull.* □ *You're full of it.* □ *She doesn't know what she's talking about. She's just full of prunes.*

full of it See the previous entry.

full of Old Nick See *full of the devil.*

full of oneself conceited; self-important. □ *Mary is very unpopular because she's so full of herself.* □ *She doesn't care about other people's feelings. She's too full of herself.*

full of prunes See *full of hot air.*

full of the devil AND **full of Old Nick** always making mischief. (Informal. *Old Nick* is another name for the devil.) □ *Tom is a lot of fun, but he's sure full of the devil.* □ *I've never seen a child get into so much mischief. He's really full of Old Nick.*

full steam ahead forward at the greatest speed possible; with as much energy and enthusiasm as possible. (From an instruction given to engineers on steamships.) □ *It will have to* be full steam ahead for everybody if the factory gets this order. □ *It's going to be full steam ahead for me this year. I take my final exams.*

fun and games playing around; doing worthless things. (Informal. Fixed order.) □ *All right, Bill, the fun and games are over. It's time to get down to work.* □ *This isn't a serious course. It's nothing but fun and games.*

funny as a crutch See *(as) funny as a crutch.*

funny ha-ha amusing; comical. (Informal. Compare with *funny peculiar.*) □ *I didn't mean that Mrs. Peters is funny ha-ha. She's weird—funny peculiar in fact.* □ *Mike thinks his jokes are funny ha-ha, but we laugh because they are so silly.*

funny peculiar odd; eccentric. (Informal. Compare with *funny ha-ha.*) □ *I didn't mean that Mrs. Peters is funny ha-ha. She's weird—funny peculiar in fact.* □ *His face is sort of funny—funny peculiar, that is.*

G

gain ground to make progress; to advance; to become more important or popular. □ *Our new product is gaining ground against that of our competitor.* □ *Since the government announced the new policies, the stock market is gaining ground.*

game that two can play a manner of competing that two competitors can use; a strategy that competing sides can both use. □ *The mayor shouted at the city council, "Politics is a game that two can play."* □ *"Flattery is a game that two can play," said John as he returned Mary's compliment.*

gang up (on someone) to form into a group and attack someone. (Usually a physical attack, but it can also be a verbal attack.) □ *We can't win against the robber unless we gang up on him.* □ *All right, you guys, don't gang up on me. Play fair!*

gas up to fill up one's gasoline tank with gasoline. (Informal.) □ *I have to stop at the next service station and gas up.* □ *The next time you gas up, try some of the gasoline with alcohol in it.*

gear (oneself) up (for something) to prepare for something; to get into shape for something. □ *We are gearing up for a very busy summer season.* □ *We are not ready yet. We have to gear up.* □ *Tom is gearing himself up for his exams.*

generous to a fault too generous; overly generous. □ *My favorite uncle is generous to a fault.* □ *Sally — always generous to a fault — gave away her sandwiches.*

get a bang out of someone or something See *get a charge out of someone or something.*

get a bee in one's bonnet to get an idea or a thought that remains in one's mind; to get an obsession. (Also with *have*. See the note at *get a big send-off*. See also *put a bee in someone's bonnet*.) □ *I have a bee in my bonnet that you'd be a good manager.* □ *I got a bee in my bonnet about swimming. I couldn't stop wanting to go swimming.*

get a big send-off to receive or enjoy a happy celebration before departing. (Also with *have*. Note: *Get* can be replaced with *have*. Note variations in the examples. *Get* usually means to become, to acquire, or to cause. *Have* usually means to possess, to be, or to have resulted in. See also *give someone a big send-off*.) □ *I had a wonderful send-off before I left.* □ *John got a fine send-off as he left for Europe.*

get a black eye (Also with *have*. See the note at *get a big send-off*.) **1.** to get a bruise near the eye from being struck. □ *I got a black eye from walking into a door.* □ *I have a black eye where John hit me.* **2.** to have one's character or reputation harmed. □ *Mary got a black eye because of her complaining.* □ *The whole group now has a black eye.*

get a break to have good fortune; to receive a bit of luck. (Often with *lucky, nice*, etc. Also with *have*. See the note at *get a big send-off*.) □ *Mary is going to get a break.* □ *I wish I'd get a lucky break.* □ *Why don't I have a lucky break when I need one?* □ *She's got a lucky break and doesn't even know it.*

get a bright idea for a clever thought or idea to occur (to someone). (Also with *have*. See the note at *get a big send-off.*) □ *Now and then I get a bright idea.* □ *John hardly ever gets a bright idea.* □ *Listen here! I have a bright idea!*

get a charge out of someone or something AND **get a bang out of someone or something; get a kick out of someone or something** to receive special pleasure from someone or something. (Informal.) □ *Tom is really funny. I always get a kick out of his jokes.* □ *Bill really got a bang out of the present we gave him.* □ *Mary got a charge out of Bob's visit.*

get a charley horse to develop a cramp in the arm or leg, usually from strain. (Also with *have*. See the note at *get a big send-off.*) □ *Don't work too hard or you'll get a charley horse.* □ *Poor Tom is always getting a charley horse in his leg.* □ *Sally can't play. She has a charley horse.*

get a checkup to have a physical examination by a physician. (Also with *have*. See the note at *get a big send-off.*) □ *She got a checkup yesterday.* □ *I going to have a checkup in the morning. I hope I'm okay.*

get a clean bill of health [for someone] to be pronounced healthy by a physician. (Also with *have*. See the note at *get a big send-off.*) □ *Sally got a clean bill of health from the doctor.* □ *Now that Sally has a clean bill of health, she can go back to work.*

get a crush on someone to become infatuated with someone. (Also with *have*. See the note at *get a big send-off.*) □ *Mary thinks she's getting a crush on Bill.* □ *Sally says she'll never get a crush on anyone again.* □ *John has a crush on Mary.*

get a dirty look from someone to get frowned at by someone. □ *I stopped whistling when I got a dirty look from Ann.* □ *I got a dirty look from the teacher. I don't know why.*

get a fix on something (Also with *have*. See the note at *get a big send-off*. See also *give someone a fix on something.*) **1.** to find out the exact location of something. □ *I can't get a fix on your location. Where are you?* □ *We are trying to get a fix on your radio transmission.* □ *I have a fix on them now.* **2.** to begin to understand the direction of a discussion. □ *I can't quite get a fix on what you're trying to say.* □ *I can't get a fix on where you're going with this argument.*

get a free hand (with someone or something) to be granted complete control over something. (Also with *have*. See the note at *get a big send-off*. See also *give someone a free hand (with something).*) □ *I didn't get a free hand with the last project.* □ *John was in charge then, but he didn't have a free hand either.* □ *I demand to have a free hand with my own child!*

get a frog in one's throat to get soreness or something else in one's throat that prevents one from talking well. (This often leads to one clearing one's throat. Also with *have*. See the note at *get a big send-off.*) □ *The speaker got a frog in his throat and had to stop talking for a while.* □ *Excuse me. I have a frog in my throat.*

get a grasp of something to understand something. (Also with *good, solid, sound,* as in the examples. Also with *have*. See the note at *get a big send-off.*) □ *Try to get a grasp of the basic rules.* □ *You don't have a good grasp of the principles yet.* □ *John was unable to get a solid grasp of the methods used in his work, and we had to let him go.*

get a hand with something to receive assistance with something. (Also with *have*. See the note at *get a big send-off.*) □ *Mary would really like to get a hand with that. It's too much for one person.* □ *I'd like to have a hand with this.*

get a handle on something to find a way to understand something; to find an aid to understanding something.

(Informal. Also with *have*. See the note at *get a big send-off*.) □ *Let me try to get a handle on this.* □ *You can't seem to get a handle on what I'm saying.* □ *Now that I have a handle on the concept, I can begin to understand it.*

get a head start (on someone or something) 1. [with *someone*] to start (something) earlier than someone else. (Also with *have*. See the note at *get a big send-off*.) □ *Bill always gets there first because he gets a head start on everybody else.* □ *I'm doing well in my class because I have a head start.* **2.** [with *something*] to start something earlier (than someone else). □ *I was able to get a head start on my reading during the holidays.* □ *If I hadn't had a head start, I'd be behind in my reading.*

get a hurry on AND **get a move on** to start to hurry. (Informal.) □ *We are going to leave in five minutes, Jane. Get a hurry on!* □ *Mary! Get a move on! We can't wait all day.*

get a jump(start) See under *get a start*.

get a kick out of someone or something See *get a charge out of someone or something*.

get a licking AND **take a licking** to get a spanking; to get beat in a fight. (Folksy.) □ *Billy, you had better get in here if you don't want to get a licking.* □ *Bob took a real licking in the stock market.* □ *Tom took a licking in the fight he was in.*

Get a life! don't act so stupid; get some purpose for existing. (Slang. Usually rude.) □ *Hey, stupid! You want to get run over? Get a life!* □ *You worthless jerk! Get a life!*

get a line on someone or something to get an idea on how to locate someone or something; to find out about someone who can help find someone or something. (Also with *have*. See the note at *get a big send-off*.) □ *I got a line on a book that might help explain what you want to know.* □ *Sally has a line on someone who could help you fix up your apartment.*

get a load of someone or something look at someone or something. (Informal or slang.) □ *Get a load of that guy. Have you ever seen such arrogance?* □ *Get a load of that car. It's got real wire wheels.*

get a load off one's feet AND **take a load off one's feet** to sit down; to enjoy the results of sitting down. (Informal.) □ *Come in, John. Sit down and take a load off your feet.* □ *Yes, I need to get a load off my feet. I'm really tired.*

get a load off one's mind to say what one is thinking; to *speak one's mind*. (Informal.) □ *He sure talked a long time. I guess he had to get a load off his mind.* □ *You aren't going to like what I'm going to say, but I have to get a load off my mind.*

get a lump in one's throat to have the feeling of something in one's throat — as if one were going to cry. (Also with *have*. See the note at *get a big send-off*.) □ *Whenever they play the national anthem, I get a lump in my throat.* □ *I have a lump in my throat because I'm frightened.*

get a move on See *get a hurry on*.

get a rain check (on something) AND **take a rain check (on something)** (Also with *have*. See the note at *get a big send-off*.) **1.** to accept a piece of paper allowing one to see an event — which has been canceled — at a later time. (Originally said of sporting events that had to be canceled because of rain.) □ *The game was canceled because of the storm, but we all got rain checks on it.* □ *I didn't take a rain check because I'm leaving town for a month.* **2.** to accept (or request) a reissuance of an invitation at a later date. (Said to someone who has invited you to something that you cannot attend now, but would like to attend at a later time.) □ *We would love to come to your house, but we are busy next Saturday. Could we take a rain check on your kind invitation?* □ *Oh, yes. You have a rain check that's good anytime you can come by and visit.* **3.** to accept a piece of paper that allows one to purchase an item on sale at a later date. (Stores issue these pieces of paper when they run out of specially priced sale merchandise.) □ *The store was all out of the shampoo they advertised, but I got a rain check.* □ *Yes, you should always take a rain check so you can get it at the sale price later when they have more.*

get a raw deal to receive unfair or bad treatment. (Slang. Also with *have*. See the note at *get a big send-off*. See also *give someone a raw deal*.) □ *Mary got a raw deal on her traffic ticket. She was innocent, but she had to pay a big fine.* □ *I bought a used T.V. that worked for two days and then quit. I sure got a raw deal.* □ *You sure had a raw deal.*

get a reputation (as a something) to become recognized for being something. (Can be a good or a bad reputation. Also with *have*. See the note at *get a big send-off*.) □ *You'll get a reputation as a cheater.* □ *She once had a reputation as a singer.* □ *Behave yourself, or you'll get a reputation.* □ *Unfortunately, Tom's got a reputation.*

get a reputation (for doing something) to become recognized for doing something. (Often a bad reputation, as in the examples. Also with *have*. See the note at *get a big send-off*.) □ *You'll get a reputation for cheating.* □ *I don't want to get a reputation.* □ *He's got a bad reputation.* □ *I have a reputation for being honest.*

get a rise out of someone to get a response from someone, usually anger or laughter. (Informal.) □ *Mary really liked my joke. I knew I could get a rise out of her.* □ *I got a rise out of him by telling him to go home.*

get a rough idea (about something) AND **get a rough idea (of something)** to receive a general idea; to receive an estimate. (Also with *have*. See the note at *get a big send-off*.) □ *I need to get a rough idea of how many people will be there.* □ *I don't need to know exactly. Just get a rough idea.* □ *Judy has got a rough idea about who'll be there.* □ *I have a rough idea. That's good enough.*

get a rough idea (of something) See the previous entry.

get a run for one's money (See also *give one a run for one's money*.) **1.** to receive what one deserves, expects, or wants. □ *I get a run for my money at a high school football game.* □ *I get a run for my money in the stock market.* **2.** to receive a challenge. □ *Bob got a run for his money when he tried to convince Mary to go to college.* □ *Bill got a run for his money playing cards with John.*

get a shellacking AND **take a shellacking** (Slang.) **1.** to receive a beating. □ *The boxer took a shellacking and lost the fight.* □ *I got a shellacking when I broke the window.* **2.** to be beaten — as in sports. □ *Our team played well, but got a shellacking anyway.* □ *I practiced my tennis game so I wouldn't take a shellacking in the tournament.*

get a slap on the wrist to get a light punishment (for doing something wrong). (Also with *have*. See the note at *get a big send-off*. See also *give someone a slap on the wrist*.) □ *He created quite a disturbance, but he only got a slap on the wrist.* □ *I thought I'd get a slap on the wrist for speeding, but I got fined $200.* □ *She had a slap on the wrist about that before.*

get a start 1. AND **get a jump(start)** to receive help starting one's car. □ *My car is stalled. I need to get a start.* □ *I got my car going. I got a jump from John.* **2.** to receive training or a big opportunity in beginning one's career. (The same as *get one's start*. Also with *have*. See the note at *get a big send-off*.) □ *She got a start in show business in Cincinnati.* □ *She had a start when she was only four.*

get a taste of one's own medicine [for one] to receive difficulties of the same kind that one has been causing other people. (Also with *have*. See the note at *get a big send-off*. See also *dose of one's own medicine*.) □ *Now you see how it feels to have someone call you names! You are getting a taste of your own medicine!* □ *John, who is often* rude and abrupt with people, was devastated when the teacher treated him rudely. He doesn't like having a taste of his own medicine.

get a thing about someone or something to get strong likes or dislikes about someone or something. (Also with *have*. See the note at *get a big send-off*.) □ *I have a thing about celery. I can't stand it.* □ *John can't get enough celery. He's got a thing about it.* □ *John has a thing about Mary. He thinks he's in love.*

get a tongue-lashing to receive a severe scolding. (Folksy. Also with *have*. See the note at *get a big send-off*. See also *give someone a tongue-lashing*.) □ *I really got a tongue-lashing when I got home.* □ *Ted will have a tongue-lashing at home.* □ *I never had a tongue-lashing like that before.*

get a word in edgeways See the following entry.

get a word in edgewise AND **get a word in edgeways** to manage to say something when other people are talking and ignoring you. (Often in the negative.) □ *It was such an exciting conversation that I could hardly get a word in edgewise.* □ *Mary talks so fast that nobody can get a word in edgeways.*

get after someone to remind, scold, or nag someone (to do something). (Informal. See also *keep after someone*.) □ *John hasn't taken out the garbage. I'll have to get after him.* □ *Mary's mother will get after her if she doesn't do the dishes.*

get (a)hold of someone or something (See also *get one's hands on someone or something; get in touch (with someone)*. Also with *have*. See the note at *get a big send-off*.) **1.** [with *someone*] to make contact with someone; to call someone on the telephone. □ *I'll try to get hold of you in the morning.* □ *It's very hard to get ahold of John. He's so busy.* **2.** [with *something*] to obtain something. □ *I'm trying to get hold of a glass jar. I need it for school.* □ *Does anyone know where I can get ahold of a spare tire?* □ *I have hold of a very large*

piece of land. **3.** See *take (a)hold of someone or something*.

get (all) dolled up to dress (oneself) up. (Informal. Usually used for females.) □ *I have to get all dolled up for the dance tonight.* □ *I just love to get dolled up in my best clothes.*

get along (in years) to grow older. □ *Grandfather is getting along in years.* □ *Yes, he's really getting along.*

get along (on a shoestring) to be able to afford to live on very little money. □ *For the last two years, we have had to get along on a shoestring.* □ *With so little money, it's hard to get along.*

get along (with someone) AND **get on (with someone)** to be friends with someone; to cooperate with someone. (See also *get on (with someone or something)*.) □ *I just can't seem to get along with you.* □ *We must try harder to get along.* □ *How do you get on with John?* □ *Oh, we get on.*

get along (with someone or something) See *get on (with someone or something)*.

get along (without (someone or something)) to manage without someone or something; to do without someone or something. □ *I don't think I can get along without my secretary.* □ *My secretary just quit, and I don't think I will be able to get along.* □ *I like steak, but I can't afford it. I guess I'll have to get along without.*

get an in (with someone) to develop a way to request a special favor from someone; to gain influence with someone. (The *in* is a noun. Also with *have*. See the note at *get a big send-off*.) □ *Did you get an in with the mayor? I have to ask him a favor.* □ *Sorry, I don't have an in, but I know someone who does.*

get another guess coming See the following entry.

get another think coming AND **get another guess coming** to have to rethink something because one was wrong the first time. (Folksy. *Think* is a noun here. Also with *have*. See the note at *get a big send-off*.) □ *She's quite wrong. She's got another think coming if she wants to walk in here like that.* □ *You have another guess coming if you think you can treat me like that!*

get ants in one's pants to become nervous and agitated. (Slang. As if ants had crawled into one's pants. Also with *have*. See the note at *get a big send-off*.) □ *I always get ants in my pants before a test.* □ *I wonder if all actors get ants in their pants before they go on stage.*

get around to be experienced; to know a lot about life. (Informal. Use with caution — especially with females — since this can also refer to sexual experience. See also *have been around*.) □ *That's a hard question. I'll ask Jane. She gets around.* □ *John knows a lot about New York City. He gets around.*

get around to doing something to find time to do something; to do something after a long delay. (Compare with *get (around) to something*.) □ *I finally got around to buying a new coat.* □ *It takes Sally years to get around to visiting her aunt.* □ *I finally got around to doing the breakfast dishes.*

get (around) to something to manage to deal with someone or something after a delay. (Compare with *get around to doing something*.) □ *It was noon before I got around to the breakfast dishes.* □ *The doctor was not able to get to John, even though John waited for three hours.* □ *I can't get around to you until tomorrow.*

get at someone or something 1. to attack or strike someone or something. (Compare with *go at someone or something*. Also with *have*.) □ *The cat jumped over the wall to get at the mouse.* □ *Ok, you guys. There he is. Have at him!* **2.** [with *something*] to eat food; to gobble up food. (Informal.) □ *I can't wait to get at that cake.* □ *Dinner's ready. Sit down and have at it.* **3.** [with *someone*] to find a way to irritate someone; to manage to wound someone, physically or emotionally. □

Mr. Smith found a way to get at his wife. □ *John kept trying to get at his teacher.* **4.** [with *something*] to explain or try to explain something; to hint at something. □ *We spent a long time trying to get at the answer.* □ *I can't understand what you're trying to get at.* **5.** [with *something*] to begin to do something; to *get (around) to something*. □ *I won't be able to get at it until the weekend.* □ *I'll get at it first thing in the morning.*

get at the heart of the matter See *get to the heart of the matter*.

get away (from it all) to get away from one's work or daily routine; to go on a vacation. □ *I just love the summer when I can take time off and get away from it all.* □ *Yes, that's the best time to get away.*

get away with something to do something bad and not get punished or found out. (Informal when the *something* refers figuratively to murder.) □ *Tom did it again and didn't get punished. He's always getting away with murder.* □ *Just because she's so popular, she thinks she can get away with anything.* □ *You'll never get away with it.*

get back (at someone) AND **have back at someone** to repay one for a bad deed; to *get even (with someone)*. (*Have back at someone* is informal or folksy. Compare with *have at someone or something* at *get at someone or something*.) □ *Tom called me a jerk, but I'll get back at him.* □ *I don't know how I'll get back, but I will.* □ *Just wait. I'll have back at you!*

get back into circulation to start being social with people again after a period of being by oneself; to start dating again, especially after a divorce or breakup with a lover. □ *Sally is anxious to get back into circulation after the nasty divorce she went through.* □ *Todd could not bring himself to get back into circulation after the death of his wife.*

get back into harness to return to one's workplace, such as after a vacation or a period of illness. (Refers to harnessing a horse so it can return to work.) □ *I am not at all anxious to get back into harness after spending two weeks in Mexico.* □ *Tom was eager to get back into harness after his illness.*

get back on one's feet to become independent again; to become able to *get around* again. (Note the variations with *own* and *two* in the examples.) □ *He was sick for a while, but now he's getting back on his feet.* □ *My parents helped a lot when I lost my job. I'm glad I'm back on my own feet now.* □ *It feels great to be back on my own two feet again.*

get back (to someone) to continue talking with someone (at a later time); to find out information and tell it to a person (at a later time). □ *I don't have the answer to that question right now. Let me find out and get back to you.* □ *Okay. Please try to get back early tomorrow.*

get better to improve. □ *I had a bad cold, but it's getting better.* □ *Business was bad last week, but it's getting better.* □ *I'm sorry you're ill. I hope you get better.*

get busy to start working; to work harder or faster. □ *The boss is coming. You'd better get busy.* □ *I've got to get busy and clean this house up.* □ *Come on, everybody. Let's get busy and get this job done.*

get butterflies in one's stomach to get a nervous feeling in one's stomach. (Informal. Also with *have.* See the note at *get a big send-off.* See also *give one butterflies in one's stomach.*) □ *Whenever I have to go on stage, I get butterflies in my stomach.* □ *She always has butterflies in her stomach before a test.*

get by (on something) to manage on the least amount. (Compare with *get along (on a shoestring).*) □ *We don't have much money. Can we get by on love?* □ *I'll get by as long as I have you.* □ *We don't have very much money, but we'll get by.*

get by (with something) 1. to satisfy the minimum requirements. □ *I was failing geometry, but managed to get by with a D.* □ *I took the bar exam and just barely got by.* 2. to do something bad and not get caught or punished; to *get away with something.* □ *Tom cheated on the test and got by with it.* □ *Maybe you can get by like that once or twice, but you'll get caught.*

get carried away to be overcome by emotion or enthusiasm (in one's thinking or actions). (Also literal.) □ *Calm down, Jane. Don't get carried away.* □ *Here, Bill. Take this money and go to the candy store, but don't get carried away.*

get close (to someone or something) (Also literal.) 1. [with *someone*] to be close friends with someone; to get to know someone well. □ *I would really like to get close to Jane, but she's so unfriendly.* □ *We talked for hours and hours, but I never felt that we were getting close.* □ *It's very hard to get next to someone who won't talk to you.* 2. [with *something*] to almost equal something; to be almost as good as something. (Often in the negative.) □ *I practiced and practiced, but my bowling couldn't get close to Mary's.* □ *Her performance was so good that I couldn't get close.*

get cold feet to be fearful about doing something. (Also with *have.* See the note at *get a big send-off.*) □ *Todd got cold feet at the last moment.* □ *He can't do it. He has cold feet. Someone else will have to tell the police.* □ *I usually get cold feet when I have to speak in public.*

get cracking to get moving; to *get busy.* (Folksy.) □ *Let's go. Come on, get cracking!* □ *Move it! We don't have all day. Let's get cracking!* □ *We'll never get finished if you don't get cracking.*

get credit (for something) to receive praise or recognition for one's role in something. (Especially with *a lot of, much,* etc., as in the examples.) □ *Mary should get a lot of credit for the team's success.* □ *Each of the team captains should get credit.*

get down to brass tacks to begin to talk about important things; to *get down to business*. □ *Let's get down to brass tacks. We've wasted too much time chatting.* □ *Don't you think that it's about time to get down to brass tacks?*

get down to business AND **get down to work** to begin to get serious; to begin to negotiate or conduct business. □ *All right, everyone. Let's get down to business. There has been enough playing around.* □ *When the president and vice president arrive, we can get down to business.* □ *They're here. Let's get down to work.*

get down to cases to begin to discuss specific matters; to *get down to business*. □ *When we've finished the general discussion, we'll get down to cases.* □ *Now that everyone is here, we can get down to cases.*

get down to something to begin doing some kind of work in earnest. □ *I have to get down to my typing.* □ *John, you get in here this minute and get down to that homework!*

get down to the facts to begin to talk about things that matter; to get to the truth. □ *The judge told the lawyer that the time had come to get down to the facts.* □ *Let's get down to the facts, Mrs. Brown. Where were you on the night of January 16?*

get down to the nitty-gritty to *get down to the facts*; to *get down to cases*. (Slang.) □ *Stop fooling around. Get down to the nitty-gritty.* □ *Let's stop wasting time. We have to get down to the nitty-gritty.*

get down to work See *get down to business*.

get even (with someone) to repay someone's bad deed; to *get back (at someone)*. □ *Bill hit Bob, and Bob got even with Bill by hitting him back.* □ *Some people always have to get even.*

get fresh (with someone) to become overly bold or impertinent. □ *When I tried to kiss Mary, she slapped me and shouted, "Don't get fresh with me!"* □ *I can't stand people who get fresh.*

get goose bumps AND **get goose pimples** for one's skin to feel prickly or become bumpy due to fear or excitement. (Also with *have*. See the note at *get a big send-off*.) □ *When he sings, I get goose bumps.* □ *I never get goose pimples.* □ *That really scared her. Now she's got goose pimples.*

get goose pimples See the previous entry.

get gray hair(s) to have one's hair turn gray from stress or frustration. (Also with *have*. See the note at *get a big send-off*.) □ *I'm getting gray hair because I have three teenage boys.* □ *Oh, Tom, stop it! I'm going to get gray hairs.* □ *I have gray hairs from raising four kids.*

get hell See *get the devil*.

get hold of someone or something See *get (a)hold of someone or something*.

get in on something to become associated with something, such as an organization or an idea; to find out or be told about special plans. (Also with *be*, as in the final example.) □ *There is a party upstairs, and I want to get in on it.* □ *I want to get in on your club's activities.* □ *Mary and Jane know a secret, and I want to get in on it.* □ *I'm happy to be in on your celebration.* □ *There is going to be a surprise party, and I'm in on it.*

get in (on the ground floor) to become associated with something at its start. □ *If you move fast, you can still get in on the ground floor.* □ *A new business is starting up, and I want to get in early.*

get in someone's hair to bother or irritate someone. □ *Billy is always getting in his mother's hair.* □ *I wish you'd stop getting in my hair.*

get in touch (with someone) to communicate with someone; to telephone or write to someone. (See also *keep in touch (with someone)*.) □ *I have to get in touch with John and ask him to come over for a visit.* □ *Yes, you must try to get in touch.*

get into a jam See the following entry.

get into a mess AND **get into a jam** to get into difficulty or confusion. (Informal. Compare with *get out of a mess*.) □ *Try to keep from getting into a mess.* □ *"Hello, Mom," said John on the telephone. "I'm at the police station. I got into a jam."*

get into an argument (with someone) to begin to argue with someone. □ *Let's try to discuss this calmly. I don't want to get into an argument with you.* □ *Tom got into an argument with John.* □ *Tom and John got into an argument.* □ *Let's not get into an argument.*

get into full swing AND **get into high gear** to move into the peak of activity; to start moving fast or efficiently. (Informal.) □ *In the summer months, things really get into full swing around here.* □ *We go skiing in the mountains each winter. Things get into high gear there in November.*

get into high gear See the previous entry.

get in(to) hot water to get into trouble or difficulty; to get involved in something that is complicated or troublesome. □ *When you start trying to build your own computer, you are getting into hot water.* □ *When Fred was caught cheating on his exam, he got into hot water.*

get into the act to try to be part of whatever is going on. (As if someone were trying to get on stage and participate in a performance.) □ *I can do this by myself. There is no need for you to get into the act.* □ *Everyone wants to get into the act. Please let us do it. We don't need your help!*

get into the swing of things to join into the routine or the activities. □ *Come on, Bill. Try to get into the swing of things.* □ *John just couldn't seem to get into the swing of things.*

get involved (with someone) to become associated with someone. (Sometimes romantically involved.) □ *Sally is getting involved with Bill. They've been see-ing a lot of each other.* □ *I hope they don't get too involved.* □ *He didn't want his son involved with the gangs.*

get it See *get something*.

get it (all) together to become fit or organized; to organize one's thinking; to become relaxed and rational. (Slang. Also with *have*. See the note at *get a big send-off*.) □ *Bill seems to be acting more normal now. I think he's getting it all together.* □ *I hope he gets it together soon. His life is a mess.* □ *When Jane has it all together, she really makes sense.* □ *Sally is a lovely person. She really has it together.*

get it in the neck to receive something bad, such as punishment or criticism. (Slang. Compare with *get it.*) □ *I don't know why I should get it in the neck. I didn't break the window.* □ *Bill got it in the neck for being late.*

get lost **1.** to become lost; to lose one's way. □ *We got lost on the way home.* □ *Follow the path, or you might get lost.* **2.** Go away!; Stop being an annoyance! (Slang. Always a command.) □ *Stop bothering me. Get lost!* □ *Get lost! I don't need your help.* □ *Stop following me. Get lost!*

get mad (at someone or something) **1.** to become angry at someone or something. □ *Don't get mad at me. I didn't do it.* □ *I got mad at my car. It won't start.* □ *I get mad every time I think about it.* **2.** [with *something*] to muster all one's physical and mental resources in order to do something. (Informal or slang.) □ *Come on, Bill. If you're going to lift your end of the piano, you're going to have to get mad at it.* □ *The sergeant keep yelling, "Work, work! Push, push! Come on, you guys, get mad!"*

get mixed-up to get confused. □ *I get mixed-up easily whenever I take a test.* □ *Sorry, I didn't say the right thing. I got mixed-up.*

get nowhere fast not to make progress; to get nowhere. (Informal or slang.) □ *I can't seem to make any progress. No matter what I do, I'm just getting* *nowhere fast.* □ *Come on. Speed up this car. We're getting nowhere fast.*

get off 1. to escape or avoid punishment (for doing something wrong). (Also literal.) □ *It was a serious crime, but Mary got off with a light sentence.* □ *I was afraid that the robber was going to get off completely.* **2.** to start off (on a friendship). (See also *get off on the wrong foot; get off to a bad start.* Compare with *get along (with someone).*) □ *Tom and Bill had never met before. They seemed to get off all right, though.* □ *I'm glad they got off so well.* **3.** to leave; to depart. □ *The plane did not get off on time.* □ *We have to get off early in the morning before the traffic gets heavy.*

get off easy AND **get off lightly** to receive very little punishment (for doing something wrong). (See also *get a slap on the wrist.*) □ *It was a serious crime, but Mary got off easy.* □ *Billy's punishment was very light. Considering what he did, he got off lightly.*

Get off it! don't talk nonsense; don't talk like that. (Usually a command.) □ *Get off it, Tom! You don't know that for a fact.* □ *Oh, get off it! You sound so conceited!*

get off lightly See *get off easy.*

get off on the wrong foot AND **get off to a bad start** to start something (such as a friendship) with negative factors. (See also *get off; be off on the wrong foot; be off to a bad start; start off on the wrong foot.*) □ *Bill and Tom got off on the wrong foot. They had a minor car accident just before they were introduced.* □ *Let's work hard to be friends. I hate to get off on the wrong foot.* □ *Bill is getting off to a bad start in geometry. He failed the first test.*

get off scot-free See *go scot-free.*

Get off someone's back! See the following entry.

Get off someone's case! AND **Get off someone's back!; Get off someone's tail!** Leave someone alone!; Stop picking on someone! (Slang. Usually a command.) □ *I'm tired of your criticism, Bill. Get off my case!* □ *Quit picking on her. Get off her back!* □ *Leave me alone! Get off my tail!*

Get off someone's tail! See the previous entry.

get off to a bad start See *get off on the wrong foot.*

get off to a flying start to have a very successful beginning to something. □ *The new business got off to a flying start with those export orders.* □ *We shall need a large donation from the local citizens if the charity is to get off to a flying start.*

get on someone to pester someone (about something); to pressure someone. (Also literal.) □ *John is supposed to empty the trash every day. He didn't do it, so I will have to get on him.* □ *It's time to get on Bill about his homework. He's falling behind.*

get on someone's nerves to irritate someone. □ *Please stop whistling. It's getting on my nerves.* □ *All this arguing is getting on their nerves.*

get on the bandwagon AND **jump on the bandwagon** to join the popular side (of an issue); to take a popular position. □ *You really should get on the bandwagon. Everyone else is.* □ *Jane has always had her own ideas about things. She's not the kind of person to jump on the bandwagon.*

get on the good side of someone to get in someone's favor. □ *You had better behave properly if you want to get on the good side of Mary.* □ *If you want to get on the good side of your teacher, you must do your homework.*

get on (with someone) See *get along (with someone).*

get on (with someone or something) AND **get along (with someone or something) 1.** [with *someone*] to be friends with someone; to have a good relationship with someone. (The friendship is always assumed to be good unless it is stated to be otherwise.) □ *How do you get on with John?* □ *I get along with John just fine.* □ *We get* along. □ *I don't get on with John.* □ *We don't get along.* **2.** [with *something*] to continue with something. □ *I must get on with my work.* □ *Now that the crisis is over, I'll get on with my life.*

get one's act together to get oneself organized, especially mentally. (Slang. Originally from theatrical use. Also with *have.* See the note at *get a big send-off.*) □ *I'm so confused about life. I have to get my act together.* □ *Bill Smith had a hard time getting his act together after his mother's death.* □ *Mary really has her act together. She handles herself very well.*

get one's bearings to determine where one is; to determine how one is oriented to one's immediate environment. (Also with *have.* See the note at *get a big send-off.*) □ *After he fell, it took Ted a few minutes to get his bearings.* □ *Jean found her compass and got her bearings almost immediately.* □ *I don't have my bearings yet. Wait a minute.*

get one's comeuppance to get a reprimand; to get the punishment one deserves. (Folksy.) □ *Tom is always insulting people, but he finally got his comeuppance. Bill hit him.* □ *I hope I don't get my comeuppance like that.*

get one's ducks in a row to get something into order or into line; to put one's affairs in order; to get things ready. (Informal. Also with *have.* See the note at *get a big send-off.* Imagine a mother duck leading a row of ducklings.) □ *Jane is organized. She really has all her ducks in a row.* □ *You can't hope to go into a company and sell something until you get your ducks in a row.* □ *As soon as you people get your ducks in a row, we'll leave.*

get one's feet on the ground to get firmly established or reestablished. (Also with *have.* See the note at *get a big send-off.* See also *keep one's feet on the ground.*) □ *He's new at the job, but soon he'll get his feet on the ground.* □ *Her productivity will improve after she gets her feet on the ground again.* □

Don't worry about Sally. She has her feet on the ground.

get one's feet wet to begin something; to have one's first experience of something. (Informal. As if one were wading into water. Also with *have.* See the note at *get a big send-off.*) □ *Of course he can't do the job right. He's hardly got his feet wet yet.* □ *I'm looking forward to learning to drive. I can't wait to get behind the steering wheel and get my feet wet.* □ *I've only been at this job for a month, and I don't have my feet wet yet.*

get one's fill of someone or something to receive enough of someone or something. (Also with *have.* See the note at *get a big send-off.*) □ *You'll soon get your fill of Tom. He can be quite a pest.* □ *I can never get my fill of shrimp. I love it.* □ *Three weeks of visiting grandchildren is enough. I've had my fill of them.*

get one's fingers burned to have a bad experience. (Also literal. Also with *have.* See the note at *get a big send-off.*) □ *I had my fingers burned the last time I did this.* □ *I tried that once before and got my fingers burned. I won't try it again.* □ *If you go swimming and get your fingers burned, you won't want to swim again.*

get one's foot in the door to achieve a favorable position (for further action); to take the first step in a process. (From people selling things from door to door who block the door with a foot so it cannot be closed on them. Also with *have.* See the note at *get a big send-off.*) □ *I think I could get the job if I could only get my foot in the door.* □ *It pays to get your foot in the door. Try to get an appointment with the boss.* □ *I have a better chance now that I have my foot in the door.*

get one's hands dirty AND **dirty one's hands; soil one's hands** to become involved with something illegal; to do a shameful thing; to do something that is beneath one. (Also literal.) □ *The mayor would never get his hands dirty by giving away political favors.* □ *I will* *not dirty my hands by breaking the law.* □ *Sally felt that to talk to the hobo was to soil her hands.*

get one's hands on someone or something AND **lay one's hands on someone or something** to get (a)hold of someone or something; to get someone or something in one's grasp. (Informal. Sometimes said in anger, as if one may wish to do harm.) □ *Just wait until I get my hands on Tom. I'll really give him something to think about.* □ *When I lay my hands on my book again, I'll never lend it to anyone.*

get one's head above water to get ahead of one's problems; to catch up with one's work or responsibilities. (Also literal. Also with *have*. See the note at *get a big send-off.*) □ *I can't seem to get my head above water. Work just keeps piling up.* □ *I'll be glad when I have my head above water.*

get one's hooks into someone or something to grasp someone or something; to acquire someone or something; to get someone or something in one's grasp. (Said of someone who is grasping and acquisitive and who will not let go easily. Usually said about a person or about something that is small enough to grasp in one's hand.) □ *I want to get my hooks into a copy of that book.* □ *She can't wait until she gets her hooks into George.*

get one's just deserts to get what one deserves. □ *I feel better now that Jane got her just deserts. She really insulted me.* □ *Bill got back exactly the treatment that he gave out. He got his just deserts.*

get one's knuckles rapped to receive punishment. (Also with *have*. See the note at *get a big send-off.*) □ *I got my knuckles rapped for whispering too much.* □ *You will have your knuckles rapped if you are not careful.*

get one's money's worth to get everything that has been paid for; to get the best quality for the money paid. (Also with *have*. See the note at *get a big send-off.*) □ *Weigh that package of meat before you buy it. Be sure you're*

getting your money's worth. □ *I didn't get my money's worth with my new camera, so I took it back.* □ *I will stay here and watch the movie over and over until I get my money's worth.*

get one's nose out of someone's business to stop interfering in someone else's business; to mind one's own business. (See also *keep one's nose out of someone's business.*) □ *Go away! Get your nose out of my business!* □ *Bob just can't seem to get his nose out of other people's business.*

get one's (own) way (with someone or something) to have someone or something follow one's plans; to control someone or something. (Also with *have*. See the note at *get a big send-off.*) □ *The mayor got his way with the city council.* □ *He seldom gets his own way.* □ *How often do you have your way with your own money?* □ *Parents usually have their way with their children.*

get one's say to be able to state one's position; to be able to say what one thinks. (Also with *have*. See the note at *get a big send-off.* See also *have a voice (in something).*) □ *I want to have my say on this matter.* □ *He got his say, and then he was happy.*

get one's sea legs to become accustomed to the movement of a ship at sea; to be able to walk steadily on the constantly rolling and pitching decks of a ship. (Also with *have*. See the note at *get a big send-off.*) □ *Jean was a little awkward at first, but in a few days she got her sea legs and was fine.* □ *You may feel a little sick until you get your sea legs.* □ *I will feel better when I have my sea legs.*

get one's second wind (Also with *have*. See the note at *get a big send-off.*) **1.** for one's breathing to become stabilized after exerting oneself for a short time. □ *John was having a hard time running until he got his second wind.* □ *Bill had to quit the race because he never got his second wind.* □ *"At last,"* thought Ann, *"I have my second wind. Now I can really swim fast."* **2.** to become more active or productive (after starting off slowly). □ *I usually get my second wind early in the afternoon.* □ *Mary is a better worker now that she has her second wind.*

get one's start to receive the first major opportunity of one's career. □ *I had my start in painting when I was thirty.* □ *She helped me get my start by recommending me to the manager.*

get one's teeth into something to start on something seriously, especially a difficult task. (Informal.) □ *Come on, Bill. You have to get your teeth into your biology.* □ *I can't wait to get my teeth into this problem.*

get one's walking papers to get fired. (Informal. See also *give one one's walking papers.*) □ *Well, I'm through. I got my walking papers today.* □ *They are closing down my department. I guess I'll get my walking papers soon.*

get one's wires crossed to get confused about something. (Informal. As if one's brain were an electrical circuit. Also with *have.* See the note at *get a big send-off.*) □ *You don't know what you are talking about. You really have your wires crossed!* □ *Joan got her wires crossed about who arrived first. It was Bob, not Gary.*

get one's wits about one to pull oneself together for action; to set one's mind to work, especially in a time of stress. (Also with *have.* See the note at *get a big send-off.*) □ *Let me get my wits about me so I can figure this out.* □ *I don't have my wits about me at this time of the morning.*

get (oneself) into a stew (over someone or something) to be worried or upset about someone or something. □ *Please don't get yourself into a stew over Walter.* □ *Liz is the kind of person who gets into a stew over someone else's business.*

get out from under someone or something 1. [with *someone*] to get free of someone's control. □ *Mary wanted to get out from under her mother.* □ *We started our own business because we*

needed to get out from under our employer. **2.** [with *something*] to get free of a burdensome problem. □ *I can't go out tonight until I get out from under this pile of homework.* □ *There is so much work to do! I don't know when I'll ever get out from under it.*

get out of a jam to get free from a problem or a bad situation. □ *Would you lend me five dollars? I need it to get out of a jam.* □ *I need some help getting out of a jam.*

get out of a mess to get free of a bad situation. (Informal. Also with *this, such a,* etc. See the examples. Compare to *get into a mess.*) □ *How can anyone get out of a mess like this?* □ *Please help me get out of this mess!*

get out of the wrong side of the bed See *get up on the wrong side of the bed.*

get out while the getting is good to leave a place while it is still possible to do so; to withdraw from a place, position, or some organization at an opportune time. □ *The party was getting noisy enough that one of the neighbors was bound to call the police, so we left. We always get out while the getting is good.* □ *Everyone at my office was being required to do more and more work. I decided to get out while the getting was good. I quit.*

get over someone or something to recover from someone or something. □ *Now that Bob has left me, I have to learn to get over him.* □ *It was a horrible shock. I don't know when I'll get over it.* □ *It was a serious illness. It took two weeks to get over it.*

get physical (with someone) 1. to use physical force against someone. □ *The coach got in trouble for getting physical with some members of the team.* □ *When the suspect wouldn't cooperate, the police were forced to get physical.* **2.** to touch someone in lovemaking. □ *I've heard that Bill tends to get physical with his dates.* □ *I don't care if he gets physical—within reason.*

get ready (to do something) to prepare to do something. □ *Get ready to jump!* □ *It's time to get ready to go to work.* □ *It's time to get ready.*

get religion to become serious (about something), usually after a powerful experience; to develop a strong religious belief. (Folksy. Also with *have.* See the note at *get a big send-off.*) □ *I've always had religion. I don't need a crisis to make me get it.* □ *When I had an automobile accident, I really got religion. Now I'm a very safe driver.* □ *Soldiers often say they got religion in the midst of a battle.*

get rid of someone or something to get free of someone or something; to dispose of or destroy someone or something. (Also with *be,* as in the examples.) □ *I'm trying to get rid of Mr. Smith. He's bothering me.* □ *I'll be happy when I get rid of my old car.*

get rolling to get started. (Informal.) □ *Come on. It's time to leave. Let's get rolling!* □ *Bill, it's 6:30. Time to get up and get rolling!*

get second thoughts about someone or something to have doubts about someone or something. (Also with *have.* See the note at *get a big send-off.*) □ *I'm beginning to get second thoughts about Tom.* □ *Tom is getting second thoughts about it, too.* □ *We now have second thoughts about going to Canada.*

get set get ready; get organized. (Also with *be,* as in the examples.) □ *We are going to start. Please get set.* □ *We are set. Let's go.* □ *Hurry up and get set!*

get sick 1. to become ill (perhaps with vomiting). □ *I got sick and couldn't go to school.* □ *My whole family got sick with the flu.* **2.** to vomit. (A euphemism.) □ *Mommy, the dog just got sick on the carpet.* □ *Bill got sick in the hallway.*

get (someone) off the hook to free someone from an obligation. (Informal. When *someone* is missing, this refers to oneself.) □ *Thanks for getting me off the hook. I didn't want to at-tend that meeting.* □ *I couldn't get off the hook by myself.*

get someone or something across See *put someone or something across.*

get someone or something down 1. [with *something*] to manage to swallow something, especially something large or unpleasant. □ *The pill was huge, but I got it down.* □ *It was the worst food I have ever had, but I got it down somehow.* **2.** [with *someone*] to depress a person; to make a person very sad. (Also with *have.* See the note at *get a big send-off.*) □ *My dog ran away, and it really got me down.* □ *Oh, that's too bad. Don't let it get you down.* □ *All my troubles really have me down.*

get someone or something out of one's head See the following entry.

get someone or something out of one's mind AND **get someone or something out of one's head** to manage to forget someone or something; to stop thinking about or wanting someone or something. (Almost the same as *put someone or something out of one's mind.*) □ *I can't get him out of my mind.* □ *Mary couldn't get the song out of her mind.* □ *Get that silly idea out of your head!*

get someone out of a jam to free someone from a problem or a bad situation. (Informal. Compare with *in a jam.*) □ *I like John. He got me out of a jam once.* □ *I would be glad to help get you out of a jam.*

get someone over a barrel AND **get someone under one's thumb** for someone to be put *at the mercy of someone;* to get control over someone. (Informal. Also with *have.* See the note at *get a big send-off.*) □ *He got me over a barrel, and I had to do what he said.* □ *Ann will do exactly what I say. I've got her over a barrel.* □ *All right, John. You've got me under your thumb. What do you want me to do?*

get someone under one's thumb See the previous entry.

get someone's back up See the following entry.

get someone's dander up AND **get someone's back up; get someone's hackles up; get someone's Irish up** to make someone get angry. (Informal. Also with *have*. See the note at *get a big send-off*.) □ *Now, don't get your dander up. Calm down.* □ *I insulted him and really got his hackles up.* □ *Bob had his Irish up all day yesterday. I don't know what was wrong.* □ *She really got her back up when I asked her for money.* □ *Now, now, don't get your hackles up. I didn't mean any harm.*

get someone's ear to get someone to listen (to you). (Also with *have*. See the note at *get a big send-off*. Compare with *bend someone's ear*.) □ *He got my ear and talked for an hour.* □ *While I have your ear, I'd like to tell you about something I'm selling.*

get someone's eye See *catch someone's eye*.

get someone's goat to irritate someone; to annoy and arouse someone to anger. (Also with *have*. See the note at *get a big send-off*.) □ *I'm sorry. I didn't mean to get your goat.* □ *Jean got Sally's goat and Sally made quite a fuss about it.* □ *Tom really had her goat for a while.*

get someone's hackles up See *get someone's dander up*.

get someone's Irish up See *get someone's dander up*.

get someone's number (Also with *have*. See the note at *get a big send-off*.) **1.** to find out someone's telephone number. □ *As soon as I get Mary's number, I'll call her.* □ *I have her number. Do you want me to write it down for you?* **2.** to find out about a person; to learn the key to understanding a person. (Informal.) □ *I'm going to get your number if I can. You're a real puzzle.* □ *I've got Tom's number. He's ambitious.*

get something AND **get it 1.** to receive punishment. (Also literal.) □ *Bill broke the window, and he's really going to get it.* □ *John got it for arriving late*

at school. **2.** to receive the meaning of a joke; to understand a joke. □ *John told a joke, but I didn't get it.* □ *Bob laughed very hard, but Mary didn't get it.*

get something across (to someone) to convey information to someone; to teach someone. □ *I'm trying to get this across to you. Please pay attention.* □ *I'll keep trying until I get it across.*

get something into someone's thick head See *get something through someone's thick skull*.

get something off one's chest to tell something that has been bothering you. (Also with *have*. See the note at *get a big send-off*.) □ *I have to get this off my chest. I broke your window with a stone.* □ *I knew I'd feel better when I had that off my chest.*

get something off (the ground) to get something started. □ *I can relax after I get this project off the ground.* □ *You'll have a lot of free time when you get the project off.*

get something on someone to learn something potentially damaging to a person. (Also with *have*. See the note at *get a big send-off*.) □ *Tom is always trying to get something on me. I can't imagine why.* □ *If he has something on you, he'll have you over a barrel.* □ *If he gets something on you, you ought to get something on him.*

get something out in the open to make something public; to stop hiding a fact or a secret. □ *We had better get this out in the open before the press gets wind of it.* □ *I'll feel better when it's out in the open. I can't stand all of this secrecy.*

get something out of one's system 1. to get something like food or medicine out of one's body, usually through natural elimination. □ *He'll be more active once he gets the medicine out of his system.* □ *My baby, Mary, ate applesauce and has been crying for three hours. She'll stop when she gets the applesauce out of her system.* **2.** to be rid of the desire to do something; to do something that you have been wanting to do so that you aren't bothered by wanting to do it anymore. □ *I bought a new car. I've been wanting to for a long time. I'm glad I finally got that out of my system.* □ *I can't get it out of my system! I want to go back to school and earn a degree.*

get something out of something to get some kind of benefit from something. □ *I didn't get anything out of the lecture.* □ *I'm always able to get something helpful out of our conversations.*

get something over (with) to complete something, especially something you have dreaded. (Also with *have*. See the note at *get a big send-off.*) □ *Oh, please hurry and get it over with. It hurts.* □ *Please get it over.* □ *When I have this over with, I can relax.*

get something sewed up AND **get something wrapped up** to have something settled or finished. (See also *wrap something up.* Also with *have.* See the note at *get a big send-off.*) □ *I'll take the contract to the mayor tomorrow morning. I'll get the whole deal sewed up by noon.* □ *Don't worry about the car loan. I'll have it sewed up in time to make the purchase.* □ *I'll get the loan wrapped up, and you'll have the car this week.*

get something straight to understand something clearly. (Informal. Also with *have.* See the note at *get a big send-off.*) □ *Now get this straight. You're going to fail history.* □ *Let me get this straight. I'm supposed to go there in the morning?* □ *Let me make sure I have this straight.*

get something through someone's thick skull AND **get something into someone's thick head** to manage to get someone, including oneself, to understand something. (Informal.) □ *He can't seem to get it through his thick skull.* □ *If I could get this into my thick head once, I'd remember it.*

get something to go See *buy something to go.*

get something under one's belt (Informal. Also with *have.* See the note at *get a big send-off.*) **1.** to eat or drink something. (This means the food goes into one's stomach and is under one's belt.) □ *I'd feel a lot better if I had a cool drink under my belt.* □ *Come in out of the cold and get a nice warm meal under your belt.* **2.** to learn something well; to assimilate some information. □ *I have to study tonight. I have to get a lot of algebra under my belt.* □ *Now that I have my lessons under my belt, I can rest easy.*

get something under way to get something started. (Also with *have.* See the note at *get a big send-off.*) □ *The time has come to get this meeting under way.* □ *Now that the president has the meeting under way, I can relax.*

get something wrapped up See *get something sewed up.*

get stars in one's eyes to be obsessed with show business; to be stagestruck. (Also with *have.* See the note at *get a big send-off.*) □ *Many young people get stars in their eyes at this age.* □ *Ann has stars in her eyes. She wants to go to Hollywood.*

get the advantage of someone AND **get the advantage over someone; get the edge on someone; get the edge over someone** to achieve a position superior to someone else. (The word *the* can be replaced with *an.* Also with *have.* See the note at *get a big send-off.* See also *take advantage of someone or something.*) □ *Toward the end of the race, I got the advantage over Mary.* □ *She'd had an advantage over me since the start of the competition.* □ *I got an edge on Sally, too, and she came in second.* □ *It's speed that counts. You can have the edge over everyone, but if you don't have speed, you lose.*

get the advantage over someone See the previous entry.

get the air to be ignored or sent away. (See also *give someone the air.*) □ *Whenever I get around Tom, I end up* *getting the air.* □ *I hate to get the air. It makes me feel unwanted.*

get the ax See *get the sack.*

get the ball rolling AND **set the ball rolling; start the ball rolling** to start something; to get some process going. (Informal. Also with *have*. See the note at *get a big send-off.*) □ *If I could just get the ball rolling, then other people would help.* □ *Who else would start the ball rolling?* □ *I had the ball rolling, but no one helped me with the project.* □ *Ann set the ball rolling, but didn't follow through.*

get the benefit of the doubt to receive a judgment in your favor when the evidence is neither for you nor against you. (Also with *have*. See the note at *get a big send-off.* See also *give someone the benefit of the doubt.*) □ *I was right between a B and an A. I got the benefit of the doubt — an A.* □ *I thought I should have had the benefit of the doubt, but the judge made me pay a fine.*

get the best of someone See the following entry.

get the better of someone AND **get the best of someone** to win out over someone in a competition or bargain. (Also with *have*. See the note at *get a big send-off.*) □ *Bill got the best of John in the boxing match.* □ *I tried to get the better of John, but he won anyway.* □ *I set out to have the better of Sally, but I didn't have enough skill.*

get the blues to become sad or depressed. (Also with *have*. See the note at *get a big send-off.*) □ *You'll have to excuse Bill. He has the blues tonight.* □ *I get the blues every time I hear that song.*

get the boot to be sent away (from somewhere); to be dismissed from one's employment; to be kicked out (of a place). (Slang. See also *get the sack; give someone the boot.*) □ *I guess I wasn't dressed well enough to go in there. I got the boot.* □ *I'll work harder at my job today. I nearly got the boot yesterday.*

get the brush-off to be ignored or sent away; to be rejected. (Slang.) □ *Don't talk to Tom. You'll just get the brush-off.* □ *I went up to her and asked for a date, but I got the brush-off.*

get the cold shoulder to be ignored; to be rejected. (Informal. See also *give someone the cold shoulder.*) □ *If you invite her to a party, you'll just get the cold shoulder.* □ *I thought that Sally and I were friends, but lately I've been getting the cold shoulder.*

get the creeps AND **get the willies** to become frightened; to become uneasy. (Slang. Also with *have*. See the note at *get a big send-off.*) □ *I get the creeps when I see that old house.* □ *I really had the willies when I went down into the basement.*

get the day off to have a day free from working. (Also with *have*. See the note at *get a big send-off.* See also *take the day off.*) □ *The next time I get a day off, we'll go to the zoo.* □ *I have the day off. Let's go to the zoo.*

get the devil AND **catch hell; catch the devil; get hell** to receive a severe scolding. (Informal. Use *hell* with caution.) □ *Bill is always getting the devil about something.* □ *I'm late. If I don't get home soon, I'll catch hell!* □ *I caught the devil yesterday for being late.*

get the edge on someone See *get the advantage of someone.*

get the edge over someone See *get the advantage of someone.*

get the feel of something [for someone] to learn the way something feels (when it is used). (Also with *have*. See the note at *get a big send-off.* See also the special sense at *have the feel of something.*) □ *I haven't yet got the feel of this bat. I hope I don't strike out.* □ *I can drive better now that I have the feel of this car's steering.*

get the final word See *get the last word.*

get the floor to receive official permission to address the audience. (Also with *have*. See the note at *get a big* send-off.) □ *When I get the floor, I'll make a short speech.* □ *The last time you had the floor, you talked for an hour.*

get the gate to be sent away; to be rejected. (Slang. See also *give someone the gate.*) □ *I thought he liked me, but I got the gate.* □ *I was afraid I'd get the gate, and I was right.*

get the glad hand to receive an overly friendly welcome; to receive insincere attention. (Informal.) □ *Whenever I go into that store, I get the glad hand.* □ *I hate to go to a party and get the glad hand.*

get the go-ahead AND **get the green light** to receive a signal to start or continue. (Also with *have.* See the note at *get a big send-off.* See also *give someone the go-ahead.*) □ *We have to wait here until we have the go-ahead.* □ *I hope we get the green light on our project soon.*

get the go-by to be ignored or passed by. (Slang.) □ *It was my turn, but I got the go-by.* □ *Tom stood on the road for fifteen minutes trying to get a ride, but all he could get was the go-by.*

get the goods on someone to find out something potentially damaging or embarrassing about someone. (Slang. Also with *have.* See the note at *get a big send-off.*) □ *John beat me unfairly in tennis, but I'll get even. I'll get the goods on him and his cheating.* □ *The authorities have the goods on Mr. Smith. He has been selling worthless land again.*

get the green light See *get the go-ahead.*

get the hang of something to learn how to do something; to learn how something works. (Informal. Also with *have.* See the note at *get a big send-off.*) □ *As soon as I get the hang of this computer, I'll be able to work faster.* □ *Now that I have the hang of starting the car in cold weather, I won't have to get up so early.*

get the hard sell to receive considerable pressure to buy or accept (something). (Informal.) □ *I won't go to that store again. I really got the hard sell.* □ *You'll probably get the hard sell if you go to a used-car dealer.*

get the high sign to receive a prearranged signal. (Often refers to a hand signal or some other visual signal.) □ *When I got the high sign, I pulled cautiously out into the roadway.* □ *The train's engineer got the high sign and began to move the train out of the station.*

get the inside track to get the advantage (over someone) because of special connections, special knowledge, or favoritism. (Also with *have.* See the note at *get a big send-off.*) □ *If I could get the inside track, I could win the contract.* □ *The boss likes me. Since I have the inside track, I'll probably be the new office manager.*

get the jump on someone to do something before someone; to get ahead of someone. (Also with *have.* See the note at *get a big send-off.*) □ *I got the jump on Tom and got a place in line ahead of him.* □ *We'll have to work hard to get the contract, because they have the jump on us.*

get the last laugh to laugh at or ridicule someone who has laughed at or ridiculed you; to put someone in the same bad position that you were once in; to *turn the tables (on someone).* (Also with *have.* See the note at *get a big send-off.* See also *He who laughs last, laughs longest.*) □ *John laughed when I got a D on the final exam. I got the last laugh, though. He failed the course.* □ *Mr. Smith said I was foolish when I bought an old building. I had the last laugh when I sold it a month later for twice what I paid for it.*

get the last word AND **get the final word** to get to make the final point (in an argument); to get to make the final decision (in some matter). (Also with *have.* See the note at *get a big send-off.*) □ *The boss gets the last word in hiring.* □ *Why do you always have to have the final word in an argument?*

get the lead out AND **shake the lead out** to hurry; to move faster. (Slang. This means to get the lead weights out of your pants so you can move faster.) □ *Come on, you guys. Get the lead out!* □ *If you're going to sell cars, you're going to have to shake the lead out.*

get the low-down (on someone or something) to receive the full story about someone or something. (Slang. Also with *have*. See the note at *get a big send-off*. See also *give someone the low-down (on someone or something).*) □ *I need to get the low-down on John. Is he still an accountant?* □ *Sally wants to get the low-down on the new expressway. Please tell her all about it.* □ *Now I have the low-down on the princess!*

get the message See *get the word.*

get the nod to get chosen. (Informal. Also with *have*. See the note at *get a big send-off*.) □ *The manager is going to pick the new sales manager. I think Ann will get the nod.* □ *I had the nod for captain of the team, but I decided not to do it.*

get the (old) heave-ho to get thrown out (of a place); to get dismissed (from one's employment). (Informal. From nautical use, where sailors used *heave-ho* to coordinate hard physical labor. One sailor called "Heave-ho," and all the sailors would pull at the same time on the *ho*. Also with *have*. See the note at *get a big send-off*. See also *give someone or something the (old) heave-ho.*) □ *I went there to buy a record album, but I got the old heave-ho. That's right. They threw me out!* □ *They fired a number of people today, but I didn't get the heave-ho.* □ *John had the old heave-ho last week. Now he's unemployed.*

get the once-over to receive a quick visual examination. (With variations, as in the examples. See also *give someone the once-over.*) □ *Every time John walks by I get the once-over. Does he like me?* □ *I went to the doctor yesterday, but I only had a once-over.* □ *I*

wanted a complete examination, not just a once-over.

get the picture to understand the whole situation. (Informal or slang.) □ *Okay, Bob. That's the whole explanation. You get the picture?* □ *Yes, I got the picture.*

get the red-carpet treatment to receive very special treatment; to receive royal treatment. (This refers—sometimes literally—to the rolling out of a clean red carpet for someone to walk on. Also with *have*. See the note at *get a big send-off*. See also *give someone the red-carpet treatment; roll out the red carpet for someone.*) □ *I love to go to fancy stores where I get the red-carpet treatment.* □ *The queen expects to get the red-carpet treatment wherever she goes.* □ *And she will have the red-carpet treatment*

get the runaround to receive a series of excuses, delays, and referrals. □ *You'll get the runaround if you ask to see the manager.* □ *I hate it when I get the runaround.*

get the sack AND **get the ax** to get fired; to be dismissed (from one's employment). (Slang. See also *give someone the ax.*) □ *I got the sack yesterday. Now I have to find a new job.* □ *I tried to work harder, but I got the ax anyway.*

get the shock of one's life to receive a serious (emotional) shock. (Also with *have*. See the note at *get a big send-off*.) □ *I opened the telegram and got the shock of my life.* □ *I had the shock of my life when I won $5,000.*

get the short end of the stick AND **end up with the short end of the stick** to end up with less (than someone else); to end up cheated or deceived. (Also with *have*. See the note at *get a big send-off*.) □ *Why do I always get the short end of the stick? I want my fair share!* □ *She's unhappy because she has the short end of the stick again.* □ *I hate to end up with the short end of the stick.*

get the show on the road to get (something) started. (Slang.) □ *Hurry up,*

you guys. Let's get the show on the road.
□ *If you don't get the show on the road right now, we'll never finish today.*

get the slip [for someone] to elude or escape (someone). (Slang.) □ *We followed her for two blocks, and then got the slip.* □ *The police got the slip, and the criminal got away.*

get the third degree to be questioned in great detail for a long period. (Slang. See also *give someone the third degree.*) □ *Why is it I get the third degree from you every time I come home late?* □ *Poor Sally spent all night at the police station getting the third degree.*

get the upper hand (on someone) to get into a position superior to someone; to *get the advantage of someone.* (Also with *have.* See the note at *get a big send-off.*) □ *John is always trying to get the upper hand on someone.* □ *He never ends up having the upper hand, though.*

get the willies See *get the creeps.*

get the word AND **get the message** to receive an explanation; to receive the final and authoritative explanation. (Informal. Also with *have.* See the note at *get a big send-off.*) □ *I'm sorry, I didn't get the word. I didn't know the matter had been settled.* □ *Now that I have the message, I can be more effective in answering questions.*

get the works to receive a lot of something. (Slang. *The works* can be a lot of food, good treatment, bad treatment, etc. See also *give someone the works.*) □ BILL: *Shall we order a snack or a big meal?* JANE: *I'm hungry. Let's get the works.* □ *But, your honor. I shouldn't get the works. I only drove too fast!*

get the worst of something to experience the worst aspects of something. (Also with *have.* See the note at *get a big send-off.*) □ *No matter what happens at the office, I seem to get the worst of it.* □ *He always gets the worst of the bargain.* □ *I got to choose which one I wanted, but I still got the worst of the two.*

get through something 1. to finish something; to work one's way through something. (Compare with *get through with something.*) □ *If I read fast, I can get through this book in an hour.* □ *I don't think I can get through all this work by quitting time.* **2.** to survive something; to *go through something.* □ *This is a busy day. I don't know how I'll get through it.* □ *Sally hopes to get through college in three years.*

get through (to someone) 1. to reach someone; to manage to communicate to someone. □ *I called her on the telephone time after time, but I couldn't get through to her.* □ *I tried every kind of communication, but I couldn't get through.* **2.** to pass through (something). □ *The crowd was so thick that I couldn't get through to him.* □ *I tried, but I couldn't get through. The crowd was too heavy.* **3.** to make someone understand something; to *get something through someone's thick skull.* □ *Why don't you try to understand me? What do I have to do to get through to you?* □ *Can anybody get through, or are you just stubborn?* □ *Ann is still too sick to understand what I'm saying. Maybe I can get through to her tomorrow.*

get through with something to get finished with something. (Compare with *get through something.*) □ *You can use this pencil when I get through with it.* □ *Can I have the salt when you get through with it?*

get time off to receive a period of time that is free from employment. (Compare with *get the day off.* See *take time off.* Also with *have.* See the note at *get a big send-off.*) □ *I'll have to get time off for jury duty.* □ *I got time off to go downtown and shop.* □ *I don't have time off from work very often.*

get time off for good behavior to have one's prison sentence shortened because of good behavior. (Also with *have.* See the note at *get a big send-off.*) □ *Bob will get out of jail* tomorrow rather than next week. He got time off for good behavior. □ I know I will have time off for good behavior.

get time to catch one's breath to find enough time to relax or behave normally. (Also with *have*. See the note at *get a big send-off*.) □ *When things slow down around here, I'll get time to catch my breath.* □ *Sally was so busy she didn't even have time to catch her breath.*

get to first base (with someone or something) AND **reach first base (with someone or something)** to make a major advance with someone or something. (Informal. *First base* refers to baseball.) □ *I wish I could get to first base with this business deal.* □ *John adores Sally, but he can't even reach first base with her. She won't even speak to him.* □ *He smiles and acts friendly, but he can't get to first base.*

get to one's feet to stand up. □ *On a signal from the director, the singers got to their feet.* □ *I was so weak, I could hardly get to my feet.*

get to the bottom of something to get an understanding of the causes of something. □ *We must get to the bottom of this problem immediately.* □ *There is clearly something wrong here, and I want to get to the bottom of it.*

get to the heart of the matter AND **get at the heart of the matter** to get to the essentials of a matter. □ *We have to stop wasting time and get to the heart of the matter.* □ *You've been very helpful. You really seem to be able to get to the heart of the matter.*

get to the point See *come to the point.*

get tough (with someone) to become firm with someone; to use physical force against someone. (Compare with *get physical (with someone)*.) □ *The teacher had to get tough with the class because the students were acting badly.* □ *I've tried to get you to behave, but it looks like I'll have to get tough.*

get two strikes against one to get a number of things against one; to be in a position where success is unlikely.

(From baseball where one is "out" after three strikes. Also with *have*. See the note at *get a big send-off*.) □ *Poor Bob got two strikes against him when he tried to explain where he was last night.* □ *I can't win. I've got two strikes against me before I start.*

get under someone's skin to bother or irritate someone. (Informal.) □ *John is so annoying. He really gets under my skin.* □ *I know he's bothersome, but don't let him get under your skin.*

get under way to start going; to start. (The word *get* can be replaced with *be*. Compare with *get something under way*.) □ *The ship is leaving soon. It's about to get under way.* □ *Let us get our journey under way.* □ *I'm glad our project is under way.*

get-up-and-go energy; motivation. (Fixed order.) □ *I must be getting old. I just don't have my old get-up-and-go.* □ *A good breakfast will give you lots of get-up-and-go.*

get up enough nerve (to do something) to get brave enough to do something. □ *I could never get up enough nerve to sing in public.* □ *I'd do it if I could get up enough nerve, but I'm shy.*

get up on the wrong side of the bed AND **get out of the wrong side of the bed** to get up in the morning in a bad mood. □ *What's wrong with you? Did you get up on the wrong side of the bed today?* □ *Excuse me for being grouchy. I got out of the wrong side of the bed.*

get used to someone or something to become accustomed to someone or something. □ *I got used to being short many years ago.* □ *John is nice, but I really can't get used to him. He talks too much.*

get well to become healthy again. □ *Ann had a cold for a week, and then she got well.* □ *Hurry up and get well!*

get wet to become soaked with water. (See also *all wet*.) □ *Get out of the rain or you'll get wet.* □ *Don't get wet, or you'll catch a cold.*

get what's coming to one to get what one deserves. (See also *give one what's coming to one*.) □ *If you cheat, you'll get in trouble. You'll get what's coming to you.* □ *Billy got what was coming to him.*

get wind of something to hear about something; to receive information about something. (Informal.) □ *I just got wind of your marriage. Congratulations.* □ *Wait until the boss gets wind of this. Somebody is going to get in trouble.*

get wise (to someone or something) to find out about someone or something; to see through the deception of someone or something. (Informal or slang.) □ *Watch out, John. Your friends are getting wise to your tricks.* □ *John's friends are getting wise. He had better watch out.*

get with something (Slang. Usually with *it*.) **1.** to become alert. □ *Hey, stupid. Get with it!* □ *Wake up, Bill. Get with what's going on!* **2.** to get up to date on something. □ *You're too old-fashioned, Mary. Get with it!* □ *Tom just couldn't get with the newest dance fad.*

get worked up (about something) See the following entry.

get worked up (over something) AND **get worked up (about something)** to get excited or emotionally distressed about something. (See also *all worked up (over something)*.) □ *Please don't get worked up over this matter.* □ *They get worked up about these things very easily.* □ *I try not to get worked up.*

ghost of a chance even the slightest chance. (Slang.) □ *She can't do it. She doesn't have a ghost of a chance.* □ *There is just a ghost of a chance that I'll be there on time.*

gild the lily to add ornament or decoration to something that is pleasing in its original state; to attempt to improve something that is already fine the way it is. (Often refers to flattery or exaggeration.) □ *Your house has lovely brickwork. Don't paint it. That*

would be gilding the lily. □ *Oh, Sally. You're beautiful the way you are. You don't need makeup. You would be gilding the lily.*

gird (up) one's loins to get ready; to prepare oneself (for something). □ *Well, I guess I had better gird up my loins and go to work.* □ *Somebody has to do something about the problem. Why don't you gird your loins and do something?*

give a blank check to someone See *give someone a blank check.*

give a good account of oneself to do (something) well or thoroughly. □ *John gave a good account of himself when he gave his speech last night.* □ *Mary was not hungry, and she didn't give a good account of herself at dinner.*

give (an) ear to someone or something AND **give one's ear to someone or something** to listen to someone or to what someone is saying. (Compare with *get someone's ear.*) □ *I gave an ear to Mary so she could tell me her problems.* □ *She wouldn't give her ear to my story.* □ *He gave ear to the man's request.*

give-and-take flexibility; willingness to compromise. (Fixed order.) □ *Don't expect any give-and-take when you are negotiating with Roger.* □ *There was no question of give-and-take in the contract talks. They would not budge on their demands one little bit.*

give as good as one gets to give as much as one receives; to pay someone back *in kind.* (Usually in the present tense.) □ *John can take care of himself in a fight. He can give as good as he gets.* □ *Sally usually wins a formal debate. She gives as good as she gets.*

give birth to something to give rise to or start something. □ *The composer gave birth to a new kind of music.* □ *They gave birth to a new view of language.*

give carte blanche to someone See *give someone carte blanche.*

give chase (to someone or something) to chase someone or something. □ *The dogs gave chase to the fox.* □ *A mouse ran by, but the cat was too tired to give chase.* □ *The police gave chase to the robber.*

give credence to something to believe something. □ *He tells lies. Don't give credence to what he says.* □ *Please don't give credence to Mary. She doesn't know what she's talking about.*

give credit where credit is due to give credit to someone who deserves it; to acknowledge or thank someone who deserves it. □ *We must give credit where credit is due. Thank you very much, Sally.* □ *Let's give credit where credit is due. Mary is the one who wrote the report, not Jane.*

give free rein to someone AND **give someone free rein** to allow someone to be completely in charge (of something). (See also *get a free hand (with someone or something).*) □ *The boss gave the manager free rein with the new project.* □ *The principal gave free rein to Mrs. Brown in her classes.*

give ground to retreat (literally or figuratively). □ *When I argue with Mary, she never gives ground.* □ *I approached the barking dog, but it wouldn't give ground.*

give her the gun See *give it the gun.*

give in (to someone or something) to yield to someone or something; to give up to someone or something. □ *He argued and argued and finally gave in to my demands.* □ *I thought he'd never give in.*

give it the gun AND **give her the gun** to make a motor or engine run faster; to rev up an engine. (Informal or slang. The *her* is often pronounced "er.") □ BILL: □ *How fast will this thing go?* BOB: *I'll give it the gun and see.* □ *Hurry up, driver. Give 'er the gun. I've got to get there immediately.*

give it to someone (straight) to tell something to someone clearly and directly. (Informal.) □ *Come on, give it to me straight. I want to know exactly what happened.* □ *Quit wasting time, and tell me. Give it to me straight.*

give of oneself to be generous with one's time and concern. □ *Tom is very good with children because he gives of himself.* □ *If you want to have more friends, you have to learn to give of yourself.*

give one a run for one's money (See also *get a run for one's money.*) **1.** to give one what one deserves, expects, or wants. □ *High school football gives me a run for my money.* □ *I invest in the stock market, and that really gives me a run for my money.* **2.** give one a challenge. □ *That was some argument. Bill gave John a run for his money.* □ *Tom likes to play cards with Mary because she always gives him a run for his money.*

Give one an inch, and one will take a mile. a proverb meaning that a person who is granted a little of something (such as a reprieve or lenience) will want more. □ *I told John he could turn in his paper one day late, but he turned it in three days late. Give him an inch, and he'll take a mile.* □ *First we let John borrow our car for a day. Now he wants to go on a two-week vacation. If you give him an inch, he'll take a mile.*

give one butterflies in one's stomach to cause someone to have a nervous stomach. (See also *get butterflies in one's stomach.*) □ *Tests give me butterflies in my stomach.* □ *It was not frightening enough to give me butterflies in my stomach, but it made me a little apprehensive.*

give one one's freedom to set someone free; to divorce someone. □ *Mrs. Brown wanted to give her husband his freedom.* □ *Well, Tom, I hate to break it to you this way, but I have decided to give you your freedom.*

give one one's walking papers to fire someone; to *give someone the sack.* (Informal. See also *get one's walking papers.*) □ *Tom has proved unsatisfactory. I decided to give him his* walking papers. □ *We might even give Sally her walking papers, too.*

give one what's coming to one to give one what one deserves, either a punishment or a reward. (See also *get what's coming to one.*) □ *I'm here to be paid. Give me what's coming to me.* □ *Thank you. I will see that you get what's coming to you.*

give one's ear to someone or something See *give (an) ear to someone or something.*

give one's right arm (for someone or something) to be willing to give something of great value for someone or something. (Never literal.) □ *I'd give my right arm for a nice cool drink.* □ *I'd give my right arm to be there.* □ *Tom really admires John. Tom would give his right arm for John.*

give out to wear out; to become exhausted and stop. □ *The old lady's heart finally gave out.* □ *Our television set gave out right in the middle of my favorite program.* □ *Bill gave out in the middle of the race.*

give out with something to utter or say something. (Informal. Also with *have.* See the examples.) □ *Suddenly, the dog gave out with a horrible growl.* □ *At that point, John gave out with a comment about how boring it all was.* □ *Come on, tell me. Have out with it!*

give rise to something to cause something. □ *The bad performance gave rise to many complaints.* □ *The new law gave rise to violence in the cities.*

give someone a bang AND **give someone a charge; give someone a kick** to give someone a bit of excitement. (Informal.) □ *John always gives me a bang.* □ *The whole afternoon, with all its silliness, gave me a charge anyway.*

give someone a big send-off to see someone off on a journey with celebration and encouragement. (See also *get a big send-off.*) □ *When I left for college, all my brothers and sisters came to the airport to give me a big send-off.* □ *When the sailors left, every-*

one went down to the docks and gave them a big send-off.

give someone a black eye 1. to hit someone near the eye so that a dark bruise appears. □ *John became angry and gave me a black eye.* □ *The door began to swing closed as I approached and it gave me a black eye.* **2.** to harm the character or reputation of someone. (See also *get a black eye*) □ *The constant complaining gave the whole group a black eye.* □ *His behavior gave him a black eye with the manager.*

give someone a blank check AND **give a blank check to someone** to give someone freedom or permission to act as one wishes or thinks necessary. (From a signed bank check with the amount left blank. Also literal.) □ *He's been given a blank check with regard to reorganizing the work force.* □ *The manager has been given no instructions about how to train the staff. The owner just gave him a blank check.* □ *Jean gave the decorator a blank check and said she wanted the whole house done.*

give someone a break to give someone a chance; to give someone another chance or a second chance. □ *I'm sorry. Don't send me home. Give me a break!* □ *They gave me a nice break. They didn't send me home.*

give someone a bright idea to give someone a clever thought or idea. □ *That gives me a bright idea!* □ *Thank you for giving me a bright idea.*

give someone a bum steer to give someone misleading instructions or guidance; to make a misleading suggestion. (Slang. *Bum* = false; phony. *Steer* = guidance, as in the steering of a car.) □ *Max gave Ted a bum steer and Ted ended up in the wrong town.* □ *Someone gave me a bum steer and I paid far more than I needed to for a used car.*

give someone a buzz See *give someone a ring.*

give someone a charge See *give someone a bang.*

give someone a clean bill of health [for a doctor] to pronounce someone well and healthy. □ *The doctor gave Sally a clean bill of health.* □ *I had hoped to be given a clean bill of health, but there was something wrong with my blood test results.*

give someone a dirty look [for a person] to frown or make an angry face at someone. □ *Ann gave me a dirty look.* □ *I gave her a dirty look back.*

give someone a fair shake to give someone fair treatment. □ *He's unpleasant, but we have to give him a fair shake.* □ *We give all our people a fair shake.*

give someone a fix on something to tell someone the location of something. (See also *get a fix on something.*) □ *Please give me a fix on your location.* □ *If you give the tower a fix on where you are, they can advise you on runway selection.*

give someone a free hand (with something) to give someone complete control over something. (See also *get a free hand (with someone or something).*) □ *They gave me a free hand with the project.* □ *I feel proud that they gave me a free hand. That means that they trust my judgment.*

give someone a (good) dressing-down a scolding. □ *After that dressing-down I won't be late again.* □ *The boss gave Fred a real dressing-down for breaking the machine.*

give someone a hand (for something) to applaud someone for something. □ *After she sang, they gave her a nice hand.* □ *Come on, give them a hand. They did very well.*

give someone a hand (with someone or something) to help someone with someone or something, often with the hands. □ *Will somebody please give me a hand with this?* □ *Can you give me a hand with the baby?*

give someone a hard time to give someone unnecessary difficulty. □ *Please don't give me a hard time.* □ *The clerk gave me a hard time, so I walked out.*

give someone a head start (on someone or something) 1. [with *someone*] to allow someone to start (something) earlier than someone else. □ *They gave Bill a head start on everyone else, so he arrived early.* □ *Please give me a head start on Charles. He is too fast!* 2. [with *something*] to allow someone to start something earlier (than someone else). □ *We'll give you a head start on the project.* □ *I need a head start on the test because I lost my glasses.*

give someone a kick See *give someone a bang.*

give someone a licking to beat someone. □ *Bill give Tom a licking in a fight.* □ *I'll give you a good licking if you don't leave me alone.*

give someone a line AND **feed someone a line** to lead someone on; to deceive someone with false talk. □ *Don't pay any attention to John. He gives everybody a line.* □ *He's always feeding us a line.*

give someone a pain to annoy or bother someone. (Slang.) □ *Here comes Sally. Oh, she gives me a pain.* □ *She's such a pest. She really gives me a pain.*

give someone a pat on the back See *pat someone on the back.*

give someone a piece of one's mind to bawl someone out; to *tell someone off.* □ *I've had enough from John. I'm going to give him a piece of my mind.* □ *Sally, stop it, or I'll give you a piece of my mind.*

give someone a rain check (on something) 1. to give someone a piece of paper allowing admission to an event —which has been canceled—at a later time. □ *The game was canceled because of the rain, but they gave everyone rain checks.* □ *They were not able to show the film, so everyone was given a rain check.* 2. to tell someone that an invitation to a social event will be reissued at a later date. □ *We couldn't go to the Smiths' party, so they gave us a rain check.* □ *We are sorry we cannot attend, but we would love for you to give us a rain check on another date.* 3. to issue a piece of paper that allows one to purchase an item on sale at a later date. □ *If you have no more of the sale shampoo, will you give me a rain check on it, please?* □ *Can I have a rain check on this item? You don't have enough of it in stock.*

give someone a raw deal to treat someone unfairly or badly. (See also *get a raw deal.*) □ *The judge gave Mary a raw deal.* □ *The students think that the teacher gave them a raw deal.*

give someone a reputation (as a something) to cause someone to be known for being something. □ *That evening gave him a reputation as a flirt.* □ *Yes, it gave him a reputation.*

give someone a reputation (for doing something) to cause someone to be known for doing something. □ *Her excellent parties gave Jane a reputation for entertaining well.* □ *You had better be careful or your behavior will give you a reputation.*

give someone a ring AND **give someone a buzz** to call someone on the telephone. (Informal.) □ *Nice talking to you. Give me a ring sometime.* □ *Give me a buzz when you're in town.*

give someone a rough idea (about something) AND **give someone a rough idea (of something)** to give someone a general idea or an estimate about something. □ *I don't need to know exactly. Just give me a rough idea about how big it should be.* □ *Let me give you a rough idea about my plan.*

give someone a rough idea (of something) See the previous entry.

give someone a shellacking (See also *get a shellacking.*) **1.** to beat someone. □ *My dad gave me a shellacking when I broke his fishing rod.* □ *If you do that again, I will give you a shellacking.* **2.** to beat someone (in a contest). □ *The other team gave us a shellacking.* □ *The Bears gave the Packers a shellacking.*

give someone a slap on the wrist AND **slap someone on the wrist; slap someone's wrist** to give someone a light

punishment (for doing something wrong). (See also *get a slap on the wrist.*) □ *The judge gave her a slap on the wrist for speeding.* □ *The judge should have done more than slap her wrist.* □ *They should do more than just slap his wrist.*

give someone a start **1.** to help start someone's car. □ *John gave me a start when my car was stalled.* □ *Won't someone please give me a start?* **2.** to give someone training or a big opportunity in beginning one's career. □ *No one gave me a start in the theater, and I eventually gave up trying.* □ *My career began when my father gave me a start in his act.* **3.** to startle someone; to make someone jerk or jump from a sudden fright. (Often with *quite.*) □ *The thunderclap gave me quite a start.* □ *I didn't mean to give you a start. I should have knocked before I entered.*

give someone a swelled head to make someone conceited. □ *Fame gave John a swelled head.* □ *Don't let this success give you a swelled head.*

give someone a tongue-lashing to give someone a severe scolding. (Folksy. See also *get a tongue-lashing.*) □ *I gave Bill a real tongue-lashing when he got home late.* □ *I will give you a real tongue-lashing if you ever do that again.*

give someone carte blanche AND **give carte blanch to someone** to give someone freedom or permission to act as one wishes or thinks necessary. (Almost the same as *give someone a blank check.*) □ *He's been given carte blanche with the reorganization of the work force.* □ *The manager has been given no instructions about how to train the staff. The owner just gave him carte blanche.* □ *Jean gave carte blanche to the decorator and said she wanted the whole house done.*

give someone credit (for something) to praise or recognize someone for doing something. □ *The coach gave Mary a lot of credit.* □ *The director gave John much credit for his fine performance.*

give someone free rein See *give free rein to someone.*

give someone gray hair(s) to cause someone's hair to turn gray from stress or frustration. □ *My three teenage boys are giving me gray hair.* □ *Your behavior is giving me gray hairs.*

give someone hell See *give someone the devil.*

give someone or something a wide berth to keep a reasonable distance from someone or something; to *steer clear (of someone or something).* (Originally referred to sailing ships.) □ *The dog we are approaching is very mean. Better give it a wide berth.* □ *Give Mary a wide berth. She's in a very bad mood.*

give someone or something the (old) heave-ho to throw someone or something out; to get rid of someone or something; to fire someone. (Informal. See also *get the (old) heave-ho.*) □ *We gave Jane the old heave-ho today.* □ *John was behaving badly at our party, so my father gave him the heave-ho.* □ *This chair is completely worn out. Shall I give it the old heave-ho?*

give someone pause to cause someone to stop and think. □ *When I see a golden sunrise, it gives me pause.* □ *Witnessing an accident is likely to give all of us pause.*

give someone some skin [for two people] to touch two hands together in a special greeting, like a handshake. (Slang. One hand may be slapped down on top of the other, or they may be slapped together palm to palm with the arms held vertically. Usually said as a command.) □ *Hey, Bob, give me some skin!* □ *Come over here, you guys. I want you to meet my brother and give him some skin!*

give someone the air to ignore someone; to dismiss someone. (See also *get the air.*) □ *Tom always gives me the air. Is there something wrong with me?* □ *Why is she giving him the air? What did he do?*

give someone the ax AND **give someone the sack** to fire someone; to terminate someone's employment. (See also *get the sack.*) □ *I gave Tom the sack, and he has to find a new job.* □ *I had to give three people the ax yesterday. We are having to reduce our office staff.*

give someone the benefit of the doubt to make a judgment in someone's favor when the evidence is neither for nor against the person. (See also *get the benefit of the doubt.*) □ *I'm glad the teacher gave me the benefit of the doubt.* □ *Please, judge. Give me the benefit of the doubt.*

give someone the boot to dismiss someone; to kick someone out (of a place). (Slang. See also *get the boot.*) □ *You had better behave, or they'll give you the boot.* □ *I will give him the boot if he doesn't straighten up.*

give someone the brush-off to send someone away; to reject someone. (Slang.) □ *Tom wouldn't talk to her. He just gave her the brush-off.* □ *Please don't give me the brush-off!*

give someone the bum's rush to hurry someone into leaving; to usher someone out of a place quickly. (As someone might quickly escort a vagrant from a fancy restaurant.) □ *The young customer in the jewelry store was being given the bum's rush, so he pulled out an enormous roll of bills and the clerk became much more helpful.* □ *The doorman gave Bill the bum's rush at the restaurant because Bill did not have a tie on.*

give someone the business to harass someone; to give someone a bad time. (Informal.) □ *The people in that office can't answer your question. They just give you the business.* □ *I'll get rid of her. I'll give her the business.*

give someone the cold shoulder to ignore someone; to reject someone. (Informal. See also *get the cold shoulder.*) □ *She gave me the cold shoulder when I asked her to the party.* □ *Sally has been giving me the cold shoulder.*

give someone the creeps AND **give someone the willies** to make someone uneasy; to frighten someone. (Informal.

See also *get the creeps*.) □ *That old house gives me the creeps.* □ *That strange old man gives him the willies.*

give someone the devil AND **give someone hell** to scold someone severely. (Informal. Use *hell* with caution.) □ *I'm going to give Bill hell when he gets home. He's late again.* □ *Bill, why do I always have to give you the devil?*

give someone the eye to look at someone in a way that communicates romantic interest. (Informal. See also *catch someone's eye*.) □ *Ann gave John the eye. It really surprised him.* □ *Tom kept giving Sally the eye. She finally left.*

give someone the gate to send someone away; to reject someone. (Slang. See also *get the gate*.) □ *Not only was he not friendly, he gave me the gate.* □ *He was rude, so we gave him the gate.*

give someone the glad hand to give someone an overly friendly welcome; to give someone insincere attention. (Informal.) □ *Here comes Tom. Watch him give us the glad hand and leave.* □ *These politicians give you the glad hand and ignore you after they are elected.*

give someone the go-ahead AND **give someone the green light** to give someone the signal to start or continue. (See also *get the go-ahead*.) □ *It's time to start work. Give everybody the go-ahead.* □ *They gave us the green light to start.*

give someone the go-by to pass by or ignore someone. (Slang.) □ *I could see that Tom wanted a ride, but I gave him the go-by.* □ *There was no reason to give the me go-by!*

give someone the green light See *give someone the go-ahead*.

give someone the hard sell to put pressure on someone to buy or accept (something). (Informal.) □ *They gave me the hard sell, but I still wouldn't buy the car.* □ *The clerk gave the customer the hard sell.*

give someone the high sign to give someone a prearranged signal. □ *As the robber walked past me, I gave the police officer a high sign. Then the officer arrested the robber.* □ *Things got started when I gave the conductor the high sign.*

give someone the low-down (on someone or something) to tell someone the full story about someone or something. (Slang. See also *get the low-down (on someone or something)*.) □ *Please give Sally the low-down on the new expressway.* □ *I do not know what's going on. Please give me the low-down.*

give someone the once-over to examine someone visually quickly. (See also *get the once-over*.) □ *John gives me the once-over every time he walks by me.* □ *Why does he just give me the once-over? Why doesn't he say hello?*

give someone the red-carpet treatment to give someone very special treatment; to give someone royal treatment. (See also *get the red-carpet treatment*.) □ *We always give the queen the red-carpet treatment when she comes to visit.* □ *They never give me the red-carpet treatment.*

give someone the runaround to give someone a series of excuses, delays, and referrals. □ *If you ask to see the manager, they'll give you the runaround.* □ *Stop giving me the runaround!*

give someone the sack See *give someone the ax*.

give someone the shirt off one's back to be very generous or solicitous to someone. □ *Tom really likes Bill. He'd give Bill the shirt off his back.* □ *John is so friendly that he'd give anyone the shirt off his back.*

give someone the slip to escape from or elude someone. (Slang.) □ *We followed her for two blocks, and then she gave us the slip.* □ *Max gave Lefty the slip.*

give someone the third degree to question someone in great detail for a long period. (Slang. See also *get the third* degree.) □ *The police gave Sally the third degree.* □ *Stop giving me the third degree. I told you what I know.*

give someone the willies See *give someone the creeps.*

give someone the works to give someone the full amount or the full treatment. (Slang. See also *get the works.*) □ *The judge gave her the works for driving too fast.* □ *I want everything. Give me the works.*

give someone tit for tat to give someone something equal to what was given you; to exchange a series of things, one by one, with someone. (Informal.) □ *They gave me the same kind of difficulty that I gave them. They gave me tit for tat.* □ *He punched me, so I punched him. Every time he hit me, I hit him. I just gave him tit for tat.*

give someone to understand something to explain something to someone; to imply something to someone. (This may mislead someone, accidentally or intentionally.) □ *Mr. Smith gave Sally to understand that she should be home by midnight.* □ *The mayor gave the citizens to understand that there would be no tax increase. He didn't promise, though.*

give someone what for to scold someone. (Folksy.) □ *Billy's mother gave him what for because he didn't get home on time.* □ *I will really give you what for if you don't straighten up.*

give something a lick and a promise to do something poorly—quickly and carelessly. (Informal. Fixed order.) □ *John! You didn't clean your room! You just gave it a lick and a promise.* □ *This time, Tom, comb your hair. It looks as if you just gave it a lick and a promise.*

give something one's best shot to give a task one's best effort. □ *I gave the project my best shot.* □ *Sure, try it. Give it your best shot!*

give the bride away [for a bride's father] to accompany the bride to the groom in a wedding ceremony. □ *Mr. Brown is ill. Who'll give the bride away?*

□ *In the traditional wedding ceremony, the bride's father gives the bride away.*

give the devil her due See the following entry.

give the devil his due AND **give the devil her due** to give your foe proper credit (for something). (This usually refers to a person who has been evil—like the devil.) □ *She's generally impossible, but I have to give the devil her due. She bakes a terrific cherry pie.* □ *John may cheat on his taxes and yell at his wife, but he keeps his car polished. I'll give the devil his due.*

give the game away to reveal a plan or strategy. (Informal.) □ *Now, all of you have to keep quiet. Please don't give the game away.* □ *If you keep giving out hints, you'll give the game away.*

give up the ghost to die; to release one's spirit. (Considered formal or humorous.) □ *The old man sighed, rolled over, and gave up the ghost.* □ *I'm too young to give up the ghost.*

give vent to something to express anger. (The *something* is usually anger, ire, irritation, etc.) □ *John gave vent to his anger by yelling at Sally.* □ *Bill couldn't give vent to his frustration because he had been warned to keep quiet.*

give voice to something to express a feeling or an opinion in words; to speak out about something. □ *The bird gave voice to its joy in the golden sunshine.* □ *All the people gave voice to their anger at Congress.*

given to understand made to believe. □ *They were given to understand that there would be no tax increase, but after the election taxes went up.* □ *She was given to understand that she had to be home by midnight.*

gloss something over to cover up or conceal an error; to make something appear right by minimizing or concealing the flaws. □ *When I asked him not to gloss the flaws over, he got angry.* Ⓣ *When Mr. Brown was selling me the car, he tried to gloss over its defects.*

glutton for punishment someone who seems to like doing or seeking out difficult, unpleasant, or badly paid tasks. □ *If you want to work for this charity, you'll have to be a glutton for punishment and work long hours for nothing.* □ *Jane must be a real glutton for punishment. She's typing Bill's manuscript free of charge, and he doesn't even thank her.*

go a long way in doing something See the following entry.

go a long way toward doing something AND **go a long way in doing something** almost to satisfy specific conditions; to be almost right. □ *This machine goes a long way toward meeting our needs.* □ *Your plan went a long way in helping us with our problem.*

go about one's business to mind one's business; to move elsewhere and mind one's own business. □ *Leave me alone! Just go about your business!* □ *I have no more to say. I would be pleased if you would go about your business.*

go against the grain to go against the natural direction or inclination. (See also *rub someone('s fur) the wrong way*.) □ *You can't expect me to help you cheat. That goes against the grain.* □ *Would it go against the grain for you to call in sick for me?*

go all out to use all one's resources; to be very thorough. (Informal. Compare with *make an all-out effort*.) □ *Whenever they have a party, they really go all out.* □ *My cousin is coming for a visit, and she expects us to go all out.*

go all the way (with someone) AND **go to bed (with someone)** to have sexual intercourse with someone. (Euphemistic. Use with caution.) □ *If you go all the way, you stand a chance of getting pregnant.* □ *I've heard that they go to bed all the time.*

go along for the ride to accompany (someone) for the pleasure of riding along. □ *Join us. You can go along for the ride.* □ *I don't really need to go to the grocery store, but I'll go along for the ride.*

go along (with someone or something) 1. [with *something*] to agree to something. (Also literal.) □ *All right. I'll go along with your plan.* □ *I'm sure that John won't want to go along with it.* **2.** [with *someone*] to agree with someone. (Also literal.) □ *I go along with Sally. I'm sure she's right.* □ *I can't go along with John. He doesn't know what he's talking about.*

go ape (over someone or something) to become very excited and enthusiastic about someone or something. (Slang.) □ *I really go ape over chocolate ice cream.* □ *Tom really goes ape over Mary.*

go (a)round in circles 1. to keep going over the same ideas or repeating the same actions, often resulting in confusion, without reaching a satisfactory decision or conclusion. □ *We're just going round in circles discussing the problems of the party. We need to consult someone else to get a new point of view.* □ *Fred's trying to find out what's happened but he's going round in circles. No one will tell him anything useful.* **2.** to be or act confused. (Informal.) □ *I'm so busy I'm going around in circles.* □ *I can't work anymore. I'm so tired that I'm going round in circles.*

go (a)round the bend 1. to go around a turn or a curve; to make a turn or a curve. □ *You'll see the house you're looking for as you go round the bend.* □ *John waved to his father until the car went round the bend.* **2.** to go crazy; to lose one's mind. (Informal.) □ *If I don't get some rest, I'll go round the bend.* □ *Poor Bob. He has been having trouble for a long time. He finally went around the bend.*

go around with someone See *hang around (with someone); run around with someone.*

go astray to leave the proper path (literally or figuratively). □ *Stay right on the road. Don't go astray and get lost.* □ *Follow the rules I've given you and don't go astray. That'll keep you out of trouble.*

go at it hammer and tongs See *fight someone or something hammer and tongs.*

go at it tooth and nail See *fight someone or something hammer and tongs.*

go at someone or something to attack someone or something; to move or lunge toward someone or something. □ *The dog went at the visitor and almost bit him.* □ *He went at the door and tried to break it down.*

go away empty-handed to depart with nothing. (Compare with *come away empty-handed.*) □ *I hate for you to go away empty-handed, but I cannot afford to contribute any money.* □ *They came hoping for some food, but they had to go away empty-handed.*

go AWOL to become absent without leave. (See also *absent without leave.*) □ *Private Smith went AWOL last Wednesday. Now he's in a military prison.* □ *Tom went AWOL once too often.*

go back on one's word to break a promise that one has made. □ *I hate to go back on my word, but I won't pay you $100 after all.* □ *Going back on your word makes you a liar.*

go bad to become rotten, undesirable, evil, etc. □ *I'm afraid that this milk has gone bad.* □ *Life used to be wonderful. Now it has gone bad.*

go bananas to go crazy or become silly. (Slang.) □ *Whenever I see Sally, I just go bananas! She's fantastic.* □ *This was a horrible day! I almost went bananas.*

go begging to be unwanted or unused. (As if a thing were begging for an owner or a user.) □ *There is still food left. A whole lobster is going begging. Please eat some more.* □ *There are many excellent books in the library just going begging because people don't know they are there.*

go broke to completely run out of money and other assets. □ *This company is going to go broke if you don't stop spending money foolishly.* □ *I made some bad investments last year, and it looks as if I may go broke this year.*

go by the board to get ruined or lost. (This is a nautical expression meaning "to fall or be washed overboard.") □ *I hate to see good food go by the board. Please eat up so we won't have to throw it out.* □ *Your plan has gone by the board. The entire project has been canceled.*

go by the book to follow the rules exactly. (Refers to a book of rules.) □ *The judge of the contest went by the rules and disqualified us in the first round.* □ *Everyone insisted that the chairman go by the book and rule against the questionable motion.*

go chase oneself to go away (and stop being a bother). (Slang.) □ *He was bothering me, so I told him to go chase himself.* □ *Get out, you pest! Go chase yourself!*

go cold turkey to stop (doing something) without tapering off. (Slang. Originally drug slang. Now concerned with breaking any habit.) □ *I had to stop smoking, so I went cold turkey. It's awful!* □ *When heroin addicts go cold turkey, they get terribly sick.*

go down fighting to continue the struggle until one is completely defeated. □ *I won't give up easily. I'll go down fighting.* □ *Sally, who is very determined, went down fighting.*

go down in history to be remembered as historically important. □ *Bill is so great. I'm sure that he'll go down in history.* □ *This is the greatest party of the century. I bet it'll go down in history.*

go downhill [for something] to decline and grow worse and worse. (Also literal.) □ *This industry is going downhill. We lose money every year.* □ *As one gets older, one tends to go downhill.*

go Dutch to share the cost of a meal or some other event. (See also *Dutch treat.*) □ JANE: *Let's go out and eat.* MARY: *Okay, but let's go Dutch.* □ *It's getting expensive to have Sally for a friend. She never wants to go Dutch.*

go easy (on someone or something) **1.** to be kind or gentle with someone or something. (See also *take it easy (on someone or something).*) □ *Go easy on Tom. He just got out of the hospital.* □ *Go easy on the cat. It doesn't like to be roughed up.* □ *Okay, I'll go easy.* **2.** [with *something*] to use something sparingly. □ *Go easy on the mustard. That's all there is.* □ *Please go easy on the onions. I don't like them very well.*

go fifty-fifty (on something) to divide the cost of something in half with someone. □ *Todd and Jean decided to go fifty-fifty on dinner.* □ *The two brothers went fifty-fifty on a replacement for the broken lamp.*

Go fly a kite! go away and stop bothering me. (Slang.) □ *You're bothering me. Go fly a kite!* □ *If you think I'm going to waste my time talking to you, go fly a kite.*

go for broke to risk everything; to try as hard as possible. (Slang.) □ *Okay, this is my last chance. I'm going for broke.* □ *Look at Mary starting to move in the final hundred yards of the race! She is really going for broke.*

go for it to make a try for something; to decide to do something. (Slang.) □ *I have an offer of a new job. I think I'm going to go for it.* □ *Hey, great. Go for it!*

go for someone or something to desire someone or something. (Usually with *could*, as in the examples. Also literal.) □ *Look at that cute guy. I could really go for him.* □ *I could go for a nice cool glass of iced tea.*

go from bad to worse to progress from a bad state to a worse state. □ *This is a terrible day. Things are going from bad to worse.* □ *My cold is awful. It went from bad to worse in just an hour.*

go great guns to go fast or energetically. (Folksy.) □ *I'm over my cold and going great guns.* □ *Business is great. We are going great guns selling ice cream.*

go haywire to go wrong; to malfunction; to break down. (Folksy.) □ *I* was talking to Mary when suddenly the telephone went haywire. I haven't heard from her since. □ *There we were, driving along, when the engine went haywire. It was two hours before the tow truck came.*

go hog-wild to behave wildly. (Folksy.) □ *Have a good time at the party, but don't go hog-wild.* □ *The teacher cannot control a class that is going hog-wild.*

go in a body to move in a group. □ *The whole team went in a body to talk to the coach.* □ *Each of us was afraid to go alone, so we went in a body.*

go in for something to take part in something; to enjoy (doing) something. □ *John doesn't go in for sports.* □ *None of them seems to go in for swimming.*

go in one ear and out the other [for something] to be heard and then forgotten. (See also *in one ear and out (of) the other.*) □ *Everything I say to you seems to go in one ear and out the other. Why don't you pay attention?* □ *I can't concentrate. Things people say to me just go in one ear and out the other.*

go into a nosedive AND **take a nosedive** **1.** [for an airplane] suddenly to dive toward the ground, nose first. □ *It was a bad day for flying, and I was afraid we'd go into a nosedive.* □ *The small plane took a nosedive. The pilot was able to bring it out at the last minute, so the plane didn't crash.* **2.** to go into a rapid emotional or financial decline, or a decline in health. (Informal.) □ *Our profits took a nosedive last year.* □ *After he broke his hip, Mr. Brown's health went into a nosedive, and he never recovered.*

go into a tailspin **1.** [for an airplane] to lose control and spin to the earth, nose first. □ *The plane shook and then suddenly went into a tailspin.* □ *The pilot was not able to bring the plane out of the tailspin, and it crashed into the sea.* **2.** [for someone] to become disoriented or panicked; [for someone's life] to fall apart. (Informal.) □ *Although John was a great success, his* life went into a tailspin. It took him a year to get straightened out. □ After her father died, Mary's world fell apart, and she went into a tailspin.

go into action AND **swing into action** to start doing something. □ I usually get to work at 7:45, and I go into action at 8:00. □ When the ball is hit in my direction, you should see me swing into action.

go into effect AND **take effect** [for a law or a rule] to become effective. □ When does this new law go into effect? □ The new tax laws won't go into effect until next year. □ This law takes effect almost immediately.

go into one's song and dance (about something) to start giving one's explanations and excuses about something. (One's can be replaced by the same old. Fixed order.) □ Please don't go into your song and dance about how you always tried to do what was right. □ John went into his song and dance about how he won the war all by himself. □ He always goes into the same old song and dance every time he makes a mistake.

go into orbit to get very excited; to be in ecstasy. (Slang. Also literal.) □ When I got a letter from my boyfriend in England, I almost went into orbit. □ Tom goes into orbit every time the football team scores.

go into something to start something new. (Especially a new career, project, product line, etc. Compare with be into something.) □ I may quit selling and go into management. □ We are shifting production away from glass bottles, and we are going into vases and other decorative containers. □ After she graduated, she went into law.

go it alone to do something by oneself. (Informal.) □ Do you need help, or will you go it alone? □ I think I need a little more experience before I go it alone.

go like clockwork to progress with regularity and dependability. (Informal.) □ The building project is pro-

gressing nicely. Everything is going like clockwork. □ The elaborate pageant was a great success. It went like clockwork from start to finish.

go off [for something] to explode. □ The fireworks didn't go off when they were supposed to. □ There was a bomb in the building, but it didn't go off.

go off half-cocked to proceed without proper preparation; to speak (about something) without adequate knowledge. (Informal or slang.) □ Don't pay any attention to what John says. He's always going off half-cocked. □ Get your facts straight before you make your presentation. There is nothing worse than going off half-cocked.

go off on a tangent to go off suddenly in another direction; suddenly to change one's line of thought, course of action, etc. (A reference to geometry. Plural: **go off on tangents**.) □ Please stick to one subject and don't go off on a tangent. □ If Mary would settle down and deal with one subject she would be all right, but she keeps going off on tangents.

go off the deep end AND **jump off the deep end** to become deeply involved (with someone or something) before one is ready; to follow one's emotions into a situation. (Informal. Refers to going into a swimming pool at the deep end—rather than the shallow end—and finding oneself in deep water. Applies especially to falling in love.) □ Look at the way Bill is looking at Sally. I think he's about to go off the deep end. □ Now, John, I know you really want to go to Australia, but don't go jumping off the deep end. It isn't all perfect there.

go on stop saying those things; not so; I don't believe you. (Always as a command. Also literal.) □ Go on! You don't know what you're talking about! □ Oh, go on! You're just trying to flatter me.

go on a binge to do too much of something. (Slang. Especially to drink too much.) □ Jane went on a binge last *night and is very sick this morning.* □ *Bill loves to spend money on clothes. He's out on a binge right now—buying everything in sight.*

go on a fishing expedition to attempt to discover information. (Also literal.) □ *We are going to have to go on a fishing expedition to try to find the facts.* □ *One lawyer went on a fishing expedition in court, and the other lawyer objected.*

go on an errand See *run an errand.*

go on and on to (seem to) last or go forever. (Folksy.) □ *You talk too much, Bob. You just go on and on.* □ *The road to their house is very boring. It goes on and on with nothing interesting to look at.*

go out (for something) to try out for something. (Usually refers to sports. Also literal.) □ *Mary went out for the soccer team.* □ *Tom went out for baseball.* □ *He didn't go out last year.*

go out of fashion AND **go out of style** to become unfashionable; to become obsolete. □ *That kind of furniture went out of style years ago.* □ *I hope this kind of thing never goes out of fashion.*

go out of one's way (to do something) **1.** to travel an indirect route in order to do something. □ *I'll have to go out of my way to give you a ride home.* □ *I'll give you a ride even though I have to go out of my way.* **2.** to make an effort to do something; to accept the bother of doing something. □ *We went out of our way to please the visitor.* □ *We appreciate anything you can do, but don't go out of your way.*

go out of style See *go out of fashion.*

go (out) on strike [for a group of people] to quit working at their jobs until certain demands are met. □ *If we don't have a contract by noon tomorrow, we'll go out on strike.* □ *The entire work force went on strike at noon today.*

go out (with someone) **1.** to go out with someone for entertainment. □ *The Smiths went out with the Franklins to a movie.* □ *Those guys don't have much*

time to go out. **2.** to go on a date with someone; to date someone regularly. □ *Is Bob still going out with Sally?* □ *No, they've stopped going out.*

go over to succeed; to be accepted. □ *His idea went over well.* □ *How did my joke go over?*

go over big with someone to be very much appreciated by someone. □ *Your jokes did not exactly go over big with my parents.* □ *We hope that the musical will go over big with the audience.*

go over like a lead balloon to fail; to *go over* badly. (Slang. See also *go over with a bang.*) □ *Your joke went like a lead balloon.* □ *If that play was supposed to be a comedy, it went over like a lead balloon.* □ *Her suggestion went over like a lead balloon.*

go over someone's head [for the intellectual content of something] to be too difficult for someone to understand. □ *All that talk about computers went over my head.* □ *I hope my lecture didn't go over the students' heads.*

go over something to review or explain something. (Also literal.) □ *The teacher went over the lesson.* □ *Will you please go over this form? I don't understand it.*

go over something with a fine-tooth comb AND **search something with a fine-tooth comb** to search through something very carefully. □ *I can't find my calculus book. I went over the whole place with a fine-tooth comb.* □ *I searched this place with a fine-tooth comb and didn't find my ring.*

go over with a bang to succeed spectacularly. (Informal. Compare with *go over like a lead balloon.*) □ *The play was a success. It really went over with a bang.* □ *That's a great joke. It went over with a bang.*

go overboard to do too much; to be extravagant. (Also literal.) □ *Look, Sally, let's have a nice party, but don't go overboard. It doesn't need to be fancy.* □ *Okay, you can buy a big comfortable car, but don't go overboard.*

go places to have a good future. (Informal.) □ *Sally shows great promise as a scholar. She's really going to go places.* □ *Tom is as good as we thought. He's certainly going places now.*

go right through someone [for food] to pass through and out of the body very rapidly. (Informal. Use with caution.) □ *Those little apples go right through me, but I love them.* □ *I can't eat onions. They go right through me.*

go scot-free AND **get off scot-free** to go unpunished; to be acquitted of a crime. (This *scot* is an old word meaning "tax" or "tax burden.") □ *The thief went scot-free.* □ *Jane cheated on the test and got caught, but she got off scot-free.*

go sky-high to go very high. (Informal.) □ *Prices go sky-high whenever there is inflation.* □ *Oh, it's so hot. The temperature went sky-high about noon.*

go so far as to say something to put something into words; to risk saying something. □ *I think that Bob is dishonest, but I wouldn't go so far as to say he's a thief.* □ *Red meat may be harmful, but I can't go so far as to say it causes cancer.*

go someone one better AND **do someone one better** to do something superior to what someone else has done; to top someone. □ *That was a great joke, but I can go you one better.* □ *Your last song was beautifully sung, but Mary can do you one better.*

go (somewhere) by shank's mare to travel by foot; to go somewhere on foot. □ *The car wouldn't start so I had to go to work by shank's mare.* □ *We enjoy walking and go by shank's mare whenever we can.*

go stag to go to an event (which is meant for couples) without a member of the opposite sex. (Informal. Originally referred only to males.) □ *Is Tom going to take you, or are you going stag?* □ *Bob didn't want to go stag, so he took his sister to the party.*

go steady (with someone) to date someone on a regular basis. □ *Mary is going steady with John.* □ *Bill went steady for two years before he got married.*

go stir-crazy to become anxious because one is confined. (Slang. *Stir* is an old criminal word for "prison.") □ *If I stay around this house much longer, I'm going to go stir-crazy.* □ *John left school. He said he was going stir-crazy.*

go straight to begin to obey the law; to become law-abiding. (Slang. Primarily criminal slang. Also literal.) □ *When John got out of prison, he decided to go straight.* □ *I promised the teacher that I would go straight and that I would never cheat again.*

go the distance to do the whole amount; to play the entire game; to run the whole race. (Informal. Originally sports use.) □ *That horse runs fast. I hope it can go the distance.* □ *This is going to be a long, hard project. I hope I can go the distance.*

go the limit to do as much as possible. (Compare with *go whole hog*.) □ *What do I want on my hamburger? Go the limit!* □ *Don't hold anything back. Go the limit.*

go through to be approved; to succeed in getting through the approval process. (See also *go through something*.) □ *I sent the board of directors a proposal. I hope it goes through.* □ *We all hope that the new law goes through.*

go through channels to proceed by consulting the proper persons or offices. (See also *work through channels*.) □ *If you want an answer to your questions, you'll have to go through channels.* □ *If you know the answers, why do I have to go through channels?*

go through something 1. to examine something. □ *Give me a day or two to go through this contract, and then I'll call you with advice.* □ *Don't go through it too fast. Read it carefully, or you might miss something.* **2.** to experience something; to endure something unpleasant; to *get through something.*

□ *It was a terrible thing. I don't know how I went through it.* □ *It'll take four years to go through college.*

go through the changes to experience a rough period in one's life. (Slang.) □ *Sally's pretty upset. She's really going through the changes.* □ *Most teenagers spend their time going through the changes.*

go through the motions to make a feeble effort to do something; to do something insincerely. □ *Jane isn't doing her best. She's just going through the motions.* □ *Bill was supposed to be raking the yard, but he was just going through the motions.*

go through the roof to go very high; to reach a very high degree (of something). (Informal.) □ *It's so hot! The temperature is going through the roof.* □ *Mr. Brown got so angry he almost went through the roof.*

go through with something to decide to do something; to finish something. □ *We decided to go through with the new highway.* □ *I can't do it. I just can't go through with it.*

go to any length to do whatever is necessary. □ *I'll go to any length to secure this contract.* □ *I want to get a college degree, but I won't go to any length to get one.*

go to bat for someone to support or help someone. (Informal. From baseball. See *pinch-hit (for someone).*) □ *I tried to go to bat for Bill, but he said he didn't want any help.* □ *I heard them gossiping about Sally, so I went to bat for her.*

go to bed (with someone) See *go all the way (with someone).*

go to bed with the chickens to go to bed at sundown; to go to bed very early (when the chickens do). □ *Of course I get enough sleep. I go to bed with the chickens.* □ *Mr. Brown goes to bed with the chickens and gets up with them, too.*

go to Davy Jones's locker to go to the bottom of the sea. (Thought of as a nautical expression.) □ *My camera fell overboard and went to Davy Jones's locker.* □ *My uncle was a sailor. He went to Davy Jones's locker during a terrible storm.*

go to (hell) AND **go to (the devil)** to become ruined; to go away and stop bothering (someone). (Informal. Use *hell* with caution.) □ *This old house is just going to hell. It's falling apart everywhere.* □ *Leave me alone! Go to the devil!* □ *Oh, go to, yourself!*

go to hell in a handbasket to become totally worthless; to *go to (hell).* (Informal. Use *hell* with caution. Not used as a command.) □ *The whole country is going to hell in a handbasket.* □ *Look at my lawn — full of weeds. It's going to hell in a handbasket.*

go to pieces **1.** to break into pieces; to fall apart. □ *My old winter coat is going to pieces.* □ *I don't want to see a nice vase like that go to pieces.* **2.** to break out in tears; to break down mentally. □ *On hearing of the death, we just went to pieces.* □ *I couldn't talk about it any longer. I went to pieces.*

go to pot AND **go to the dogs** to go to ruin; to deteriorate. (Informal.) □ *My whole life seems to be going to pot.* □ *My lawn is going to pot. I had better weed it.* □ *The government is going to the dogs.*

go to rack and ruin AND **go to wrack and ruin** to go to ruin. (The words *rack* and *wrack* mean "wreckage" and are found only in this expression. Fixed order.) □ *That lovely old house on the corner is going to go to rack and ruin.* □ *My lawn is going to wrack and ruin.*

go to seed See *run to seed.*

go to someone's head to make someone conceited; to make someone overly proud. □ *You did a fine job, but don't let it go to your head.* □ *He let his success go to his head, and soon he became a complete failure.*

go to the bathroom **1.** to go into a rest room, bathroom, or toilet. □ BILL: *Where is Bob?* JANE: *He went to the* bathroom. □ *John went to the bathroom to brush his teeth.* **2.** to eliminate bodily wastes through defecation and urination. □ *Mommy! The dog went to the bathroom on the carpet!* □ *Billy's in there going to the bathroom. Don't disturb him.*

go to (the devil) See *go to (hell).*

go to the dogs See *go to pot.*

go to the expense (of doing something) to pay the (large) cost of doing something. □ *I hate to have to go to the expense of painting the house.* □ *It needs to be done, so you'll have to go to the expense.*

go to the limit to do as much as is possible to do. (Compare with *go the limit.*) □ *Okay, we can't afford it, but we'll go to the limit.* □ *How far shall I go? Shall I go to the limit?*

go to the trouble (of doing something) AND **go to the trouble (to do something)** to endure the bother of doing something. □ *I really don't want to go to the trouble to cook.* □ *Should I go to the trouble of cooking something for her to eat?* □ *Don't go to the trouble. She can eat a sandwich.*

go to the trouble (to do something) See the previous entry.

go to the wall to be defeated; to fail in business. (Informal.) □ *We really went to the wall on that deal.* □ *The company went to the wall because of that contract. Now it's broke.*

go to town to work hard or fast. (Informal. Also literal.) □ *Look at all those ants working. They are really going to town.* □ *Come on, you guys. Let's go to town. We have to finish this job before noon.*

go to waste to be wasted; to be unused (and therefore thrown away). □ *Eat your potatoes! Don't let them go to waste.* □ *We shouldn't let all those nice flowers go to waste. Let's pick some.*

go to wrack and ruin See *go to rack and ruin.*

go together 1. [for two things] to look, sound, or taste good together. □ *Do you think that this pink one and this purple one go together?* □ *Milk and grapefruit don't go together.* **2.** [for two people] to date each other regularly. □ *Bob and Ann have been going together for months.* □ *Tom and Jane want to go together, but they live too far apart.*

go too far to do more than is acceptable. □ *I didn't mind at first, but now you've gone too far.* □ *If you go too far, I'll slap you.*

go under to fail. (Also literal.) □ *The company was weak from the start, and it finally went under.* □ *Tom had a lot of trouble in school, and finally he went under.*

go under the knife to have a surgical operation. (Informal.) □ *Mary didn't want to go under the knife, but the doctor insisted.* □ *If I go under the knife, I want to be completely asleep.*

go up in flames AND **go up in smoke** to burn up. □ *The whole museum went up in flames.* □ *My paintings — my whole life's work — went up in flames.* □ *What a shame for all that to go up in smoke.*

go up in smoke See the previous entry.

go whole hog to do everything possible; to be extravagant. (Informal. Compare with *go the limit.*) □ *Let's go whole hog. Order steak and lobster.* □ *Show some restraint. Don't go whole hog all the time.*

go window-shopping to go about looking at goods in store windows without actually buying anything. □ *The clerks do a lot of window-shopping in their lunch hour, looking for things to buy when they get paid.* □ *Joan said she was just window-shopping, but she bought a new coat.*

go with something 1. to go well with something. □ *Milk doesn't go with grapefruit.* □ *Pink doesn't go with orange.* **2.** to choose something (over something else). (Informal.) □ *I think I'll go with the yellow one.* □ *We decided to go with the oak table rather than the walnut one.*

go without (something) to manage to get along without something. (Compare with *do without (someone or something)*.) □ *I went without food for three days.* □ *Some people have to go without a lot longer than that.*

go wrong to fail; [for something bad] to happen. □ *The project failed. I don't know what went wrong.* □ *I'm afraid that everything will go wrong.*

goes to show you [something] serves to prove something to you. □ *It just goes to show you that too much sugar is bad for you.* □ *Of course you shouldn't have married her. It goes to show you that your parents are always right.*

goes without saying [something] is so obvious that it need not be said. □ *It goes without saying that you are to wear formal clothing to dinner each evening.* □ *Of course. That goes without saying.*

gold mine of information someone or something that is full of information. □ *Grandfather is a gold mine of information about World War I.* □ *The new encyclopedia is a positive gold mine of useful information.*

gone but not forgotten gone or dead and still remembered. (Fixed order.) □ *The good days we used to have together are gone, but not forgotten.* □ *Uncle Harry is gone but not forgotten. The stain where he spilled the wine is still visible in the parlor carpet.*

gone goose someone or something that has departed or run away. □ *Surely, the burglar is a gone goose by now.* □ *The child was a gone goose, and we did not know where to look for him.*

gone on died. (Euphemistic.) □ *My husband, Tom—he's gone on, you know—was a great one for golf.* □ *Let us remember those who have gone on before.*

gone with the wind gone; mysteriously gone. (A phrase made famous by the Margaret Mitchell novel and film *Gone with the Wind*. The phrase is used to make *gone* have a stronger force. Also literal.) □ *Everything we worked for was gone with the wind.* □ *Jean was nowhere to be found. She was gone with the wind.*

good and something very something. (The *something* can be *ready, mad, tired, worn-out,* etc. Fixed order.) □ *Now I'm good and mad, and I'm going to fight back.* □ *I'll be there when I'm good and ready.* □ *He'll go to bed when he's good and tired.*

good as done See *(as) good as done.*

good as gold See *(as) good as gold.*

good enough for someone or something adequate for someone or something. □ *This seat is good enough for me. I don't want to move.* □ *I'm happy. It's good enough for me.* □ *That table is good enough for my office.*

good-for-nothing 1. worthless. □ *Here comes that good-for-nothing boy now.* □ *Where is that good-for-nothing pen of mine?* **2.** a worthless person. □ *Tell that good-for-nothing to go home at once.* □ *Bob can't get a job. He's such a good-for-nothing.*

good riddance (to bad rubbish) [it is] good to be rid (of worthless persons or things). □ *She slammed the door behind me and said, "Good riddance to bad rubbish!"* □ *"Good riddance to you, madam," thought I.*

goof off to waste time. (Informal or slang.) □ *John is always goofing off.* □ *Quit goofing off and get to work!*

grasp at straws to depend on something that is useless; to make a futile attempt at something. □ *John couldn't answer the teacher's question. He was just grasping at straws.* □ *There I was, grasping at straws, with no one to help me.*

gray area an area of a subject, etc., that is difficult to put into a particular category as it is not clearly defined and may have connections or associations with more than one category. □ *The responsibility for social studies in the college is a gray area. Several depart-*

ments are involved. □ *Publicity is a gray area in that company. It is shared between the marketing and design divisions.*

gray matter intelligence; brains; power of thought. (Informal.) □ *Use your gray matter and think what will happen if the committee resigns.* □ *Surely they'll come up with an acceptable solution if they use some gray matter.*

grease someone's palm AND **oil someone's palm** to bribe someone. (Slang.) □ *If you want to get something done around here, you have to grease someone's palm.* □ *I'd never oil a police officer's palm. That's illegal.*

greatest thing since sliced bread the best thing there ever was. (Usually sarcastic.) □ *To hear her talk, you would think she had found the greatest thing since sliced bread.* □ *Todd thinks he is the greatest thing since sliced bread.*

Greek to me See *(all) Greek to me.*

green around the gills See *pale around the gills.*

green with envy envious; jealous. □ *When Sally saw me with Tom, she turned green with envy. She likes him a lot.* □ *I feel green with envy whenever I see you in your new car.*

grin and bear it to endure something unpleasant in good humor. (Fixed order.) □ *There is nothing you can do but grin and bear it.* □ *I hate having to work for rude people. I guess I have to grin and bear it.*

grind to a halt to slow to a stop; to run down. □ *By the end of the day, the factory had ground to a halt.* □ *The car ground to a halt, and we got out to stretch our legs.*

grist for someone's mill something that can be put to good use or that can bring advantage or profit. (Grist was corn brought to a mill to be ground and so kept the mill operating.) □ *Some of the jobs that we are offered are*

more interesting than others, but each one is grist for my mill. □ *The company is having to sell some tacky-looking dresses, but they are grist for their mill and keep the company in business.*

grit one's teeth to grind one's teeth together in anger or determination. □ *I was so mad, all I could do was stand there and grit my teeth.* □ *All through the race, Sally was gritting her teeth. She was really determined.*

gross someone out to revolt someone; to make someone sick. (Slang.) □ *Oh, look at his face. Doesn't it gross you out?* Ⓣ *That teacher is such a creep. He grosses out the whole class.*

ground someone to take away someone's privileges. (Informal. Usually said of a teenager.) □ *My father said that if I didn't get at least C's, he'd ground me.* □ *Guess what! He grounded me!*

grow on someone [for someone or something] to become commonplace to a person. (The *someone* is usually one, someone, a person, etc., not a specific person.) □ *That music is strange, but it grows on you.* □ *I didn't think I could ever get used to this town, but after a while it grows on one.*

grow out of something to abandon something as one matures. (Also literal.) □ *I used to have a lot of allergies, but I grew out of them.* □ *She grew out of the habit of biting her nails.*

guard against someone or something to take care to avoid someone or something. □ *Try to guard against getting a cold.* □ *You should guard against pickpockets.*

gum something up AND **gum up the works** to make something inoperable; to ruin someone's plans. (Informal.) □ *Please, Bill, be careful and don't gum up the works.* □ *Tom sure gummed it up.* Ⓣ *Tom sure gummed up the whole plan.*

gum up the works See the previous entry.

gun for someone to be looking for someone, presumably to harm them. (Informal. Rarely literal. Originally from western and gangster movies.) □ *The coach is gunning for you. I think he's going to bawl you out.* □ *I've heard that the sheriff is gunning for me, so I'm getting out of town.*

H

hack something to endure something; to deal with something. (Slang. The *something* is usually *it*.) □ *I don't know if I can hack it.* □ *John works very hard, but he can't seem to hack it.*

had as soon do something AND **would as soon do something** prefer to do something else; to be content to do something. (The *would* or *had* is usually *'d*. Also with *just*, as in the examples.) □ *They want me to go into town. I'd as soon stay home.* □ *If you're cooking stew tonight, we'd as soon eat somewhere else.* □ *I would just as soon stay home as see a bad movie.* □ *If that's what we're having for dinner, I'd just as soon starve.*

had best do something ought to do something. (Informal. Almost the same as the following entry.) □ *You had best get that fixed right away.* □ *You had best be at school on time every day.*

had better do something ought to do something (or face the consequences). (Almost the same as the previous entry.) □ *I had better get home for dinner, or I'll get yelled at.* □ *You had better do your homework right now.*

had rather do something AND **had sooner do something** prefer to do something. (The *had* is usually expressed in a contraction, *'d*.) □ *I'd rather go to town than sit here all evening.* □ *They'd rather not.* □ *I'd sooner not make the trip.*

had sooner do something See the previous entry.

hail-fellow-well-met friendly to everyone; falsely friendly to everyone. (Us-ually said of males. See also *get the glad hand*.) □ *Yes, he's friendly, sort of hail-fellow-well-met.* □ *He's not a very sincere person. hail-fellow-well-met — you know the type.* □ *What a pain he is. Good old Mr. Hail-fellow-well-met. What a phony!*

hail from somewhere [for someone] to come originally from somewhere. □ *I'm from Kansas. Where do you hail from?* □ *I hail from the Southwest.*

hair of the dog that bit one a drink of liquor taken when one has a hangover; a drink of liquor taken when one is recovering from drinking too much liquor. (Informal.) □ *Oh, I'm miserable. I need some of the hair of the dog that bit me.* □ *That's some hangover you've got there, Bob. Here, drink this. It's some of the hair of the dog that bit you.*

hale and hearty well and healthy. (Fixed order.) □ *Doesn't Ann look hale and hearty?* □ *I don't feel hale and hearty. I'm really tired.*

Half a loaf is better than none. a proverb meaning that having part of something is better than having nothing. □ *When my raise was smaller than I wanted, Sally said, "Half a loaf is better than none."* □ *People who keep saying "Half a loaf is better than none" usually have as much as they need.*

half-and-half **1.** a liquid that is half milk and half cream. □ *Harry would always pour half-and-half on his breakfast cereal in spite of what his doctor told him.* □ *There is less fat in half-and-half than there is in cream.* **2.** a substance composed half of one thing and half of another. □ *This coffee is half-and-half, so there isn't quite as much caffeine as in regular coffee. I can't decide between a chocolate sundae and a pineapple sundae, so make mine half-and-half.*

halfhearted (about someone or something) unenthusiastic about someone or something. □ *Ann was halfhearted about the choice of Sally for president.* □ *She didn't look halfhearted to me. She looked angry.*

ham something up to make a performance seem silly by showing off or exaggerating one's part. (Informal. A show-off actor is known as a *ham*.) □ *Come on, Bob. Don't ham it up!* ⊤ *The play was going fine until Bob got out there and hammed up his part.*

hammer away (at someone or something) to keep trying to accomplish something with someone or something. (Also literal.) □ *John, you've got to keep hammering away at your geometry.* □ *They hammered away at the prisoner until he confessed.* □ *They kept hammering away.*

hammer something home to try extremely hard to make someone understand or realize something. □ *The teacher hammered the dates home.* ⊤ *I tried to hammer home to Anne the fact that she would have to get a job.* ⊤ *The boss hopes to hammer home the company's precarious financial position to the staff.*

hammer something out 1. to work hard at writing up an agreement; to work hard at writing something. (As if one were hammering at the keys of a typewriter. Also literal.) □ *I'm busy hammering my latest novel out.* ⊤ *The lawyers sat down to hammer out a contract.* **2.** to play something on the piano. □ *She hammered the song out loudly and without feeling.* ⊤ *Listen to John hammer out that song on the piano.*

hand in glove (with someone) very close to someone. □ *John is really hand in glove with Sally.* □ *The teacher and the principal work hand in glove.*

hand in hand 1. holding hands. □ *They walked down the street hand in hand.* □ *Bob and Mary sat there quietly, hand in hand.* **2.** together, one with the other. (Said of two things, the presence of either of which implies the other.) □ *Cookies and milk seem to go hand in hand.* □ *Teenagers and back talk go hand in hand.*

hand it to someone give credit to someone. (Informal. Often with *have to* or *must*.) □ *I'll hand it to you. You did a fine job.* □ *We must hand it to Sally. She helped us a lot.*

hand-me-down something, such as an article of used clothing, that has been handed down from someone. (See *hand something down (to someone.)*) □ *Why do I always have to wear my brother's hand-me-downs? I want some new clothes.* □ *This is a nice shirt. It doesn't look like a hand-me-down at all.*

hand over fist [for money and merchandise to be exchanged] very rapidly. □ *What a busy day. We took in money hand over fist.* □ *They were buying things hand over fist.*

hand over hand [moving] one hand after the other (again and again). □ *Sally pulled in the rope hand over hand.* □ *The man climbed the rope hand over hand.*

hand something down (to someone) 1. to give something to a younger person. (Either at death or during life. See also *hand-me-down.*) □ *John handed his old shirts down to his younger brother.* ⊤ *I hope my uncle will hand down his golf clubs to me when he dies.* **2.** to announce or deliver a (legal) verdict or indictment. ⊤ *The grand jury handed down seven indictments last week.* ⊤ *The jury handed down a guilty verdict.*

handle someone with kid gloves to be very careful with a touchy person. □ *Bill has become so sensitive. You really have to handle him with kid gloves.*

☐ *You don't have to handle me with kid gloves. I can take it.*

hands down without a doubt. (Usually regarding a choice or a winner.) ☐ *Jean was our choice for the new manager hands down.* ☐ *Todd won the race hands down.* ☐ *Sharon was the favorite librarian of all the people there hands down.*

Hands off! Do not touch (someone or something). ☐ *Careful! Don't touch that wire. Hands off!* ☐ *The sign says, "Hands off!" and you had better do what it says.*

Hands up! AND **Stick 'em up!** Put your hands in the air. (Slang. Said by robbers and police officers.) ☐ *All right, you, hands up!* ☐ *Stick 'em up! I got you covered.*

hang a left to turn to the left. (Slang. See also the following entry.) ☐ *Hang a left up at that light.* ☐ *Go three blocks and hang a left.*

hang a right to turn to the right. (Slang. See the previous entry.) ☐ *At the next corner, hang a right.* ☐ *Hang a right at the stop sign.*

hang around (with someone) AND **go around with someone** to spend a lot of time with someone; to waste away time with someone. (See also *run around with someone.*) ☐ *John hangs around with Bill a lot.* ☐ *They've been going around with the Smiths.* ☐ *I've asked them all to stop hanging around.*

hang back to stay behind (the others); to hold back (from the others). ☐ *Walk with the group, Bob. Don't hang back. You'll get left behind.* ☐ *Three of the marchers hung back and talked to each other.*

hang by a hair AND **hang by a thread** to be in an uncertain position; to depend on something very insubstantial; to *hang in the balance.* (Informal. Also with *on,* as in the second example.) ☐ *Your whole argument is hanging by a thread.* ☐ *John isn't failing geometry, but he's just hanging on by a hair.*

hang by a thread See the previous entry.

hang fire to delay or wait; to be delayed. ☐ *I think we should hang fire and wait for other information.* ☐ *Our plans have to hang fire until we get planning permission.*

hang in the balance to be in an undecided state; to be between two equal possibilities. ☐ *The prisoner stood before the judge with his life hanging in the balance.* ☐ *This whole issue will have to hang in the balance until Jane gets back from her vacation.*

hang in there to keep trying; to persevere. (Slang.) ☐ *I know things are tough, John, but hang in there.* ☐ *I know if I hang in there, things will come out okay.*

hang loose to relax; to remain calm. (Slang.) ☐ *I know I can pass this test if I just hang loose.* ☐ *Hang loose, Bob. Everything is going to be all right.*

hang on someone's coattails See *ride on someone's coattails.*

hang on someone's every word to listen carefully to everything someone says. ☐ *He gave a great lecture. We hung on his every word.* ☐ *Look at the way John hangs on Mary's every word. He must be in love with her.*

hang on (to someone or something) AND **hold on (to someone or something)** to remember someone or something for a long time; to be affected very much by someone or something in the past. (Never with the literal sense of grasping or holding.) ☐ *That's a nice thought, Bob. Hang on to it.* ☐ *You've been holding on to those bad memories for too long. It's time to let them go.* ☐ *Yes, I can't keep hanging on.*

hang out (somewhere) to spend time somewhere; to waste time somewhere. ☐ *I wish you guys wouldn't hang out around the bowling alley.* ☐ *Why do you have to hang out near our house?*

hang out (with someone) to waste time in the company of someone. ☐ *I hope*

Bob isn't hanging out with the wrong people. □ *He needs to spend more time studying and less time hanging out.*

hang someone in effigy to hang a dummy or some other figure of a hated person. (See also *burn someone in effigy.*) □ *They hanged the dictator in effigy.* □ *The angry mob hanged the president in effigy.*

hang tough to be firm in one's position; to stick to one's position. (Slang. Compare with *hang in there.*) □ *I know that your parents don't want you to go out tonight, but hang tough. They may change their minds.* □ *Hang tough, Mary. You'll get your way!*

hang up to replace the telephone receiver. □ *If you have called a wrong number, you should apologize before you hang up.* □ *When you hear the busy signal, you're supposed to hang up.*

happen (up)on someone or something to find someone or something unexpectedly. □ *I happened on this nice little restaurant on Elm Street yesterday.* □ *Mr. Simpson and I happened on one another in the bank last week.*

happy as a clam See *(as) happy as a clam.*

happy as a lark See *(as) happy as a lark.*

hard-and-fast rigid, especially when applied to rules, laws, or regulations. (Fixed order.) □ *The rule isn't hard-and-fast, but we expect you to obey it anyway.* □ *The company has a hard-and-fast rule about the use of radios, even in private offices.*

hard as nails See *(as) hard as nails.*

hard nut to crack AND **tough nut to crack** difficult person or thing to deal with. (Informal.) □ *This problem is getting me down. It's a hard nut to crack.* □ *Tom sure is a hard nut to crack. I can't figure him out.* □ *He sure is a tough nut to crack.*

hard on someone's heels following someone very closely; following very closely to someone's heels. (Informal.) □ *I ran as fast as I could, but the dog*

was still hard on my heels. □ *Here comes Sally, and John is hard on her heels.*

hard pressed (to do something) See the following entry.

hard put (to do something) AND **hard pressed (to do something)** able to do something only with great difficulty. □ *I'm hard put to come up with enough money to pay the rent.* □ *I get hard put like that about once a month.*

hard up (for something) greatly in need of something. (Informal.) □ *Ann was hard up for cash to pay the bills.* □ *I was so hard up, I couldn't afford to buy food.*

hardly have time to breathe to be very busy. □ *This was such a busy day. I hardly had time to breathe.* □ *They made him work so hard that he hardly had time to breathe.*

hark(en) back to something (*Harken* is an older word meaning "pay heed to.") **1.** to have originated as something; to have started out as something. □ *The word* icebox *harks back to refrigerators that were cooled by ice.* □ *Our modern breakfast cereals hark back to the porridge and gruel of our ancestors.* **2.** to remind one of something. □ *Seeing a horse and buggy in the park harks back to the time when horses drew milk wagons.* □ *Sally says it harkens back to the time when everything was delivered by a horse-drawn wagon.*

harp on something to keep talking or complaining about something; to refer to something again and again. □ *Mary's always harping on being poor, but she has more than enough money.* □ *Jack has been harping on high taxes for years.*

hash something over to discuss something in great detail. (Informal.) □ *Okay, we can hash it over this afternoon.* Ⓣ *Why don't you come to my office so we can hash over this contract?*

Haste makes waste. a proverb meaning that time gained in doing something rapidly and carelessly will be lost when one has to do the thing over again correctly. □ *Now, take your time. Haste makes waste.* □ *Haste makes waste, so be careful as you work.*

hat in hand See *(with) hat in hand.*

hate someone's guts to hate someone very much. (Informal and rude.) □ *Oh, Bob is terrible. I hate his guts!* □ *You may hate my guts for saying so, but I think you're getting gray hair.*

haul someone in to arrest someone; [for a police officer] to take someone to the police station. (Slang.) □ *The cop hauled the crook in.* ⊤ *They hauled in the suspects.* □ *The traffic officer said, "Do you want me to haul you in?"*

haul someone over the coals See *rake someone over the coals.*

haul up (somewhere) AND **pull up (somewhere)** to stop somewhere; to come to rest somewhere. □ *The car hauled up in front of the house.* □ *My hat blew away just as the bus pulled up.* □ *The attackers hauled up at the city gates.*

have a bad effect (on someone or something) to be bad for someone or something. □ *Aspirin has a bad effect on me.* □ *Cold weather has a bad effect on roses.*

have a ball have a really great time. (Slang. This *ball* is a formal, social dancing party.) □ *The picnic was fantastic. We had a ball!* □ *Hey, Mary! Have a ball at the party tonight!*

have a big mouth to be a gossiper; to be a person who tells secrets. (Informal.) □ *Mary has a big mouth. She told Bob what I was getting him for his birthday.* □ *You shouldn't say things like that about people all the time. Everyone will say you have a big mouth.*

have a blowout 1. [for one's car tire] to burst. □ *I had a blowout on the way here. I nearly lost control of the car.* □ *If you have a blowout in one tire, you should check the other tires.* **2.** to have a big, wild party; to enjoy oneself at a big party. □ *Mary and Bill had quite a*

blowout at their house Friday night. □ *Fred and Tom had quite a blowout last night.*

have a bone to pick (with someone) to have a matter to discuss with someone; to have something to argue about with someone. (See also *bone of contention.*) □ *Hey, Bill. I've got a bone to pick with you. Where is the money you owe me?* □ *I had a bone to pick with her, but she was so sweet that I forgot about it.* □ *You always have a bone to pick.*

have a brush with something to have a brief contact with something; to have an experience with something. (Especially with the law. Sometimes a *close* brush. Compare with *have a scrape (with someone or something).*) □ *Ann had a close brush with the law. She was nearly arrested for speeding.* □ *When I was younger, I had a brush with scarlet fever, but I got over it.*

have a case (against someone) to have much evidence that can be used against someone in court. (*Have* can be replaced with *build, gather, assemble,* etc.) □ *Do the police have a case against John?* □ *No, they don't have a case.* □ *They are trying to build a case against him.* □ *My lawyer is busy assembling a case against the other driver.*

have a change of heart to change one's attitude or decision, usually from a negative to a positive position. □ *I had a change of heart at the last minute and gave the old lady some money.* □ *Since I talked to you last, I have had a change of heart. I now approve of your marrying Sam.*

have a chip on one's shoulder to be tempting someone to an argument or a fight. □ *Who are you mad at? You always seem to have a chip on your shoulder.* □ *John has had a chip on his shoulder ever since he got his speeding ticket.*

have a clean conscience (about someone or something) See the following entry.

have a clear conscience (about someone or something) AND **have a clean conscience (about someone or something)** to be free of guilt about someone or something. □ *I'm sorry that John got the blame. I have a clean conscience about the whole affair.* □ *I have a clear conscience about John and his problems.* □ *I didn't do it. I have a clean conscience.* □ *She can't sleep at night because she doesn't have a clear conscience.*

have a close call See the following entry.

have a close shave AND **have a close call** to have a narrow escape from something dangerous. (See also *have a brush with something.*) □ *What a close shave I had! I nearly fell off the roof when I was working there.* □ *I almost got struck by a speeding car. It was a close shave.*

have a clue (about something) to know anything about something; to have even a hint about someone or something. (Usually negative.) □ *I don't have a clue about where to start looking for Jim.* □ *Why do you think I have a clue about Tom's disappearance?*

have a conniption (fit) to get angry or hysterical. (Folksy. See also *have a fit.*) □ *I got so mad I thought I was going to have a conniption.* □ *My father had a conniption fit when I got home this morning.*

have a crack at something See *have a try at something.*

have a familiar ring [for a story or an explanation] to sound familiar. □ *Your excuse has a familiar ring. Have you done this before?* □ *This term paper has a familiar ring. I think it has been copied.*

have a field day to experience freedom from one's usually work schedule; to have a wild time. (As with children who are released from classes to take part in sports and athletic contests. Also literal.) □ *The boss was gone and we had a field day today. No one got anything done.* □ *The air was fresh and clear and everyone had a field day in the park during the lunch hour.*

have a finger in the pie AND **have one's finger in the pie** to have a role in something; to be involved in something. □ *Tess wants to have a finger in the pie. She doesn't think we can do it by ourselves.* □ *Sally always wants to have a finger in the pie.*

have a fit to be very angry. (Informal.) □ *The teacher had a fit when the dog ran through the classroom.* □ *John had a fit when he found his car had been damaged.*

have a foot in both camps to have an interest in or to support each of two opposing groups of people. □ *The shop steward had been promised a promotion and so had a foot in both camps during the strike — workers and management.* □ *Mr. Smith has a foot in both camps in the parent-teacher dispute. He teaches math, but he has a son at the school.*

have a glass jaw to be susceptible to collapsing when struck on the head. (Informal. Said only of boxers who are frequently knocked down by a blow to the head.) □ *When the prizefighter was knocked out in his third fight, the newspapers said he had a glass jaw.* □ *Once a fighter has a glass jaw, he's finished as a boxer.*

have a go (at something) to make a try at something. (See also *take a try at something.*) □ *I've never fished before, but I'd like to have a go at it.* □ *Great, have a go right now. Take my fishing pole and give it a try.*

have a good command of something to know something well. □ *Bill has a good command of French.* □ *Jane has a good command of economic theory.*

have a good head on one's shoulders to have common sense; to be sensible and intelligent. □ *Mary doesn't do well in school, but she's got a good head on her shoulders.* □ *John has a good head on his shoulders and can be depended on to give good advice.*

have a (good) mind to do something to be tempted to do something; to be on the verge of doing something that one has thought about. □ *I have a good mind to tell her just exactly what I think of her.* □ *She had a mind to leave the room right then and there.*

have a good thing going to have something arranged for one's benefit. (Informal.) □ *Sally paints pictures and sells them at art fairs. She has a good thing going, and she makes good money.* □ *John inherited a fortune and doesn't have to work for a living anymore. He's got a good thing going.*

have a green thumb to have the ability to grow plants well. □ *Just look at Mr. Simpson's garden. He has a green thumb.* □ *My mother has a green thumb when it comes to houseplants.*

have a grudge against someone See *bear a grudge (against someone).*

have a hand in something to play a part in (doing) something. (Also literal.) □ *I had a hand in the picnic plans.* □ *I want to have a hand in any revision of the script.*

have a hard time to experience unnecessary difficulties. (Also with *have*. See the note at *get a big send-off.*) □ *I get a hard time every time I come to this store.* □ *I never have a hard time at the store across the street.*

have a heart to be compassionate; to be generous and forgiving. □ *Oh, have a heart! Give me some help!* □ *If Ann had a heart, she'd have made us feel more welcome.*

have a heart of gold to be generous, sincere, and friendly. □ *Mary is such a lovely person. She has a heart of gold.* □ *You think Tom stole your watch? Impossible! He has a heart of gold.*

have a heart of stone to be cold and unfriendly. □ *Sally has a heart of stone. She never even smiles.* □ *The villain in the play had a heart of stone. He was an ideal villain.*

have a heart-to-heart (talk) to have a sincere and intimate talk. □ *I had a heart-to-heart talk with my father before I went off to college.* □ *I have a problem, John. Let's sit down and have a heart-to-heart.*

have a lot going (for one) to have many things working to one's benefit. □ *Jane is so lucky. She has a lot going for her.* □ *She has a good job and a nice family. She has a lot going.*

have a lot of promise to be very promising; to have a good future ahead. □ *Sally is quite young, but she has a lot of promise.* □ *This bush is small, but it has a lot of promise.*

have a lot on one's mind to have many things to worry about; to be preoccupied. □ *I'm sorry that I'm so grouchy. I have a lot on my mind.* □ *He forgot to go to his appointment because he had a lot on his mind.*

have a low boiling point to anger easily. (Informal.) □ *Be nice to John. He's upset and has a low boiling point.* □ *Mr. Jones sure has a low boiling point. I hardly said anything, and he got angry.*

have a mind like a steel trap to have a very sharp and agile mind; to have a mind capable of fast, incisive thought. □ *Sally can handle the questioning. She has a mind like a steel trap.* □ *If I had a mind like a steel trap, I wouldn't have so much trouble concentrating.*

have a near miss to nearly crash or collide. □ *The airplanes—flying much too close—had a near miss.* □ *I had a near miss while driving over here.*

have a penchant for doing something to have a taste, desire, or inclination for doing something. □ *John has a penchant for eating fattening foods.* □ *Ann has a penchant for buying clothes.*

have a pick-me-up to eat or drink something stimulating. (The *have* can be replaced with *need, want,* etc. The *me* does not change.) □ *I'd like to have a pick-me-up. I think I'll have a bottle of pop.* □ *You look tired. You need a pick-me-up.*

have a price on one's head to be wanted by the authorities, who have offered a reward for one's capture. (Informal or folksy. Usually limited to western and gangster movies.) □ *We captured a thief who had a price on his head, and the sheriff gave us the reward.* □ *The crook was so mean, he turned in his own brother, who had a price on his head.*

have a right to do something AND **have the right to do something** to have the freedom to do something; to possess legal or moral permission or license to do something. □ *You don't have the right to enter my home without my permission.* □ *I have a right to grow anything I want on my farmland.*

have a rough time (of it) to experience a difficult period. □ *Since his wife died, Mr. Brown has been having a rough time of it.* □ *Be nice to Bob. He's been having a rough time.*

have a run of bad luck to have bad luck repeatedly; to have bad luck happen a number of times. □ *I have had a run of bad luck, and I have no more money to spend.* □ *The company had a run of bad luck over the last few years.*

have a say (in something) See *have a voice (in something).*

have a score to settle (with someone) to have a problem to clear up with someone; to have to get even with someone about something. (See also *settle a score with someone.*) □ *I have a score to settle with John.* □ *John and I have a score to settle.*

have a scrape (with someone or something) to come into contact with someone or something; to have a small battle with someone or something. (Compare with *have a brush with something.*) □ *I had a scrape with the county sheriff.* □ *John and Bill had a scrape, but they are friends again now.*

have a screw loose to act silly or crazy. (Slang.) □ *John is such a clown. He acts as if he has a screw loose.* □ *What's the matter with you? Do you have a screw loose or something?*

have a shot at something See *have a try at something.*

have a smoke to smoke a cigarette, cigar, or pipe. (The *have* can be replaced with *need, want,* etc.) □ *Can I have a smoke? I'm very nervous.* □ *Do you have a cigarette? I need a smoke.*

have a snowball's chance in hell to have no chance at all; to have a chance no greater than that of a snowball in hell. (A snowball would melt in hell and have no chance of surviving. Use *hell* with caution.) □ *He has a snowball's chance in hell of passing the test.* □ *You don't have a snowball's chance in hell of her agreeing to marry you.*

have a soft spot in one's heart for someone or something to be fond of someone or something. □ *John has a soft spot in his heart for Mary.* □ *I have a soft spot in my heart for chocolate cake.*

have a spaz to get angry or hysterical; to *have a conniption (fit).* (Slang.) □ *Relax, Bob. Don't have a spaz.* □ *My father had a spaz when I came in late last night.*

have a stroke to experience sudden unconsciousness or paralysis due to an interruption in the blood supply to the brain. (Also used as an exaggeration. See the last two examples.) □ *The patient who received an artificial heart had a stroke two days after the operation.* □ *My great-uncle Bill—who is very old—had a stroke last May.* □ *Calm down, Bob. You're going to have a stroke.* □ *My father almost had a stroke when I came home at three o'clock this morning.*

have a sweet tooth to desire to eat many sweet foods—especially candy and pastries. □ *I have a sweet tooth, and if I don't watch it, I'll really get fat.* □ *John eats candy all the time. He must have a sweet tooth.*

have a thing going (with someone) AND **have something going (with someone)** to have a romance or a love affair with someone. (Informal.) □ *John* *amd Mary have a thing going.* □ *Bill has a thing going with Ann.* □ *They have something going.*

have a try at something AND **have a shot at something; have a crack at something** to take a turn at trying to do something. (The expressions with *shot* and *crack* are more colloquial than the main entry phrase. See also the variants at *take a try at something.*) □ *You don't seem to be having a lot of luck with this. Can I have a try at it?* □ *Let Sally have a shot at it.* □ *If you let me have a crack at it, maybe I can be successful.*

have a vested interest in something to have a personal or biased interest, often financial, in something. □ *Margaret has a vested interest in wanting her father to sell the family firm. She has shares in it and would make a large profit.* □ *Jack has a vested interest in keeping the village traffic-free.*

have a voice (in something) AND **have a say (in something)** to have a part in making a decision. □ *I'd like to have a voice in choosing the carpet.* □ *John wanted to have a say in the issue also.* □ *He says he seldom gets to have a say.*

have a way with someone or something to handle or deal well with someone or something. □ *John has a way with hamburger. It's always delicious.* □ *Mother has a way with Father. She'll get him to paint the house.*

have a weakness for someone or something to be unable to resist someone or something; to be fond of someone or something; to be (figuratively) powerless against someone or something. (Compare with *have a soft spot in one's heart for someone or something.*) □ *I have a weakness for chocolate.* □ *John has a weakness for Mary. I think he's in love.*

have a whale of a time to have an exciting time; to have a big time. (Slang. *Whale* is a way of saying *big.*) □ *We had a whale of a time at Sally's birthday party.* □ *Enjoy your vacation! I hope you have a whale of a time.*

have a word with someone to speak to someone, usually privately. □ *The manager asked to have a word with me when I was not busy.* □ *John, could I have a word with you? We need to discuss something.*

have an accident **1.** to experience something that was not foreseen or intended. □ *Traffic is very bad. I almost had an accident.* □ *Drive carefully. Try to avoid having an accident.* **2.** to lose control of the bowels or the bladder. (Euphemistic. Usually said of a young child.) □ *"Oh, Ann," cried Mother. "It looks like you've had an accident!"* □ *Mother asked Billy to go to the bathroom before they left so that he wouldn't have an accident in the car.*

have an ace up one's sleeve to have a secret or concealed means of accomplishing something. (Also literal, as with cheating in card games.) □ *I think that Liz has an ace up her sleeve and will surprise us with success at the last minute.* □ *I have done all I can do. I have no idea what to do next. I don't have an ace up my sleeve, and I can't work miracles.*

have an ax to grind (with someone) to have something to complain about. (Informal.) □ *Tom, I need to talk to you. I have an ax to grind with you.* □ *Bill and Bob went into the other room to argue. They had an ax to grind.*

have an eye for someone or something to have a taste or an inclination for someone or something. □ *Bob has an eye for beauty.* □ *He has an eye for color.* □ *Ann has an eye for well-dressed men.*

have an eye on someone or something AND **keep an eye on someone or something** to keep watch on someone or something; to keep track of someone or something. (The *an* can be replaced by *one's.*) □ *I have my eye on the apple tree. When the apples ripen, I'll harvest them.* □ *Please keep an eye on the baby.* □ *Will you please keep your eye on my house while I'm on vacation?*

have an eye out (for someone or something) AND **keep an eye out (for**

someone or something) to watch for the arrival or appearance of someone or something. (The *an* can be replaced by *one's*.) □ *Please try to have an eye out for the bus.* □ *Keep an eye out for rain.* □ *Have your eye out for a raincoat on sale.* □ *Okay. I'll keep my eye out.*

have an itching palm See the following entry.

have an itchy palm AND **have an itching palm** to be in need of a tip; to tend to ask for tips. (As if placing money in the palm would stop the itching.) □ *All the waiters at that restaurant have itchy palms.* □ *The cabdriver was troubled by an itching palm. Since he refused to carry my bags, I gave him nothing.*

have an out to have an excuse; to have a (literal or figurative) means of escape or avoiding something. (Informal. The *out* is a noun.) □ *He's very clever. No matter what happens, he always has an out.* □ *I agreed to go to a party that I don't want to go to now. I'm looking for an out.*

have at someone or something See under *get at someone or something*.

have back at someone See *get back (at someone)*.

have bats in one's belfry to be slightly crazy. □ *Poor old Tom has bats in his belfry.* □ *Don't act so silly, John. People will think you have bats in your belfry.*

have been around to be experienced in life. (Informal. Use with caution — especially with females — since this can also refer to sexual experience. See also *get around*.) □ *Ask Sally about how the government works. She's been around.* □ *They all know a lot about life. They've been around.*

have broad shoulders to have the ability to take on unpleasant responsibilities; to have the ability to accept criticism or rebuke. (Also literal.) □ *No need to apologize to me. I can take it. I have broad shoulders.* □ *Karen may have broad shoulders, but she can't endure endless criticism.*

have clean hands to be guiltless. (As if the guilty person would have bloody hands.) □ *Don't look at me. I have clean hands.* □ *The police took him in, but let him go again because he had clean hands.*

have come a long way 1. to have traveled a long distance. □ *You've come a long way. You must be tired and hungry.* □ *I've come a long way. Please let me rest.* **2.** to have accomplished much; to have advanced much. □ *My, how famous you are. You've come a long way.* □ *Tom has come a long way in a short time.*

have designs on someone or something to have plans for someone or something. □ *Mrs. Brown has designs on my apple tree. I think she's going to cut off the part that hangs over her fence.* □ *Mary has designs on Bill. I think she'll try to date him.*

have dibs on something to reserve something for oneself; to claim something for oneself. (Informal. See also *put (one's) dibs on something*.) □ *I have dibs on the last piece of cake.* □ *John has dibs on the last piece again. It isn't fair.*

have egg on one's face to be embarrassed because of an error that is obvious to everyone. (Rarely literal.) □ *Bob has egg on his face because he wore jeans to the party and everyone else wore formal clothing.* □ *John was completely wrong about the weather for the picnic. It snowed! Now he has egg on his face.*

have eyes bigger than one's stomach to have a desire for more food than one could possibly eat. (See also *one's eyes are bigger then one's stomach*.) □ *I know I have eyes bigger than my stomach, so I won't take a lot of food.* □ *Todd has eyes bigger than his stomach.*

have eyes in the back of one's head to seem to be able to sense what is going on outside of one's vision. □ *My teacher seems to have eyes in the back of her head.* □ *My teacher doesn't* *need to have eyes in the back of his head. He watches us very carefully.*

have feet of clay [for a strong person] to have a defect of character. □ *All human beings have feet of clay. No one is perfect.* □ *Sally was popular and successful. She was nearly fifty before she learned that she, too, had feet of clay.*

have foot-in-mouth disease to embarrass oneself through a silly blunder. (Informal. This is a parody on *foot-and-mouth disease* or *hoof-and-mouth disease,* which affects cattle and deer. See also *put one's foot in one's mouth.* Fixed order.) □ *I'm sorry I keep saying stupid things. I guess I have foot-in-mouth disease.* □ *Yes, you really have foot-in-mouth disease tonight.*

have growing pains 1. [for a child] to have pains—which are attributed to growth—in the muscles and joints. □ *The doctor said that all Mary had were growing pains and that nothing was really wrong.* □ *Not everyone has growing pains.* **2.** [for an organization] to have difficulties in its growth. □ *The banker apologized for losing my check and said the bank was having growing pains.* □ *Governments have terrible growing pains.*

have had enough to have had as much of something as is needed or will be tolerated. (Compare with *have had it (up to here).*) □ *Stop yelling at me. I've had enough.* □ *No more potatoes, please. I've had enough.* □ *I'm leaving you, Bill. I've had enough!*

have had it (up to here) to have reached the end of one's endurance or tolerance. (Informal.) □ *Okay, I've had it. You kids go to bed this instant.* □ *We've all had it with you, John. Get out!* □ *I've had it. I've got to go to bed before I drop dead.* □ *Tom is disgusted. He said that he has had it up to here.*

have had its day to be no longer useful or successful. □ *Streetcars have had their day in most American cities.* □ *Some people think that radio has had its day, but others prefer it to television.*

have half a mind to do something See the following entry.

have half a notion to do something AND **have half a mind to do something** to have almost decided to do something, especially something unpleasant. (Informal.) □ *I have half a mind to go off and leave you here.* □ *The cook had half a notion to serve cold chicken.*

have hell to pay See *have the devil to pay.*

have it all over someone or something to be much better than someone or something. □ *This cake has it all over that one.* □ *My car has it all over yours.* □ *Sally can really run. She has it all over Bill.*

have it both ways to have both of two incompatible things. (Also literal. See also *have one's cake and eat it too.*) □ *John wants the security of marriage and the freedom of being single. He wants to have it both ways.* □ *John thinks he can have it both ways—the wisdom of age and the vigor of youth.*

have it in for someone to *have something against someone;* to plan to scold or punish someone. □ *Don't go near Bob. He has it in for you.* □ *Billy! You had better go home. Your mom really has it in for you.*

have method in one's madness to have a purpose in what one is doing, even though it seems to be mad. □ *What I'm doing may look strange, but there is method in my madness.* □ *Wait until she finishes; then you'll see that there is method in her madness.*

have mixed feelings (about someone or something) to be uncertain about someone or something. □ *I have mixed feelings about Bob. Sometimes I think he likes me; other times I don't.* □ *I have mixed feelings about my trip to England. I love the people, but the climate upsets me.* □ *Yes, I also have mixed feelings.*

have money to burn to have lots of money; to have more money than one needs. (See also *Money burns a hole in someone's pocket.*) □ *Look at the* *way Tom buys things. You'd think he had money to burn. □ If I had money to burn, I'd just put it in the bank.*

(have) never had it so good have never had so much good fortune. (Informal.) □ *No, I'm not complaining. I've never had it so good. □ Mary is pleased with her new job. She's never had it so good.*

have no business doing something to be wrong to do something; to be extremely unwise to do something. □ *You have no business bursting in on me like that! □ You have no business spending money like that!*

have no staying power to lack endurance; not to be able to last. □ *Sally can swim fast for a short distance, but she has no staying power. □ That horse can race fairly well, but it has no staying power.*

have none of something to tolerate or endure no amount of something. □ *I'll have none of your talk about quitting school. □ We'll have none of your gossip. □ I wish to have none of the sweet potatoes, please.*

have nothing on someone or something 1. [with *someone*] to lack evidence against someone. (Informal.) □ *The police had nothing on Bob, so they let him loose. □ You've got nothing on me! Let me go!* **2.** to have no information about someone or something. □ *The dictionary had nothing on the word I looked up. □ The librarian said that the library has nothing on the Jones brothers.*

have nothing to do with someone or something 1. not to be related to or concerned with someone or something. (Also literal.) □ *Your wants and needs have nothing to do with my wants and needs. □ Waterloo? That has nothing to do with water!* **2.** to avoid being associated with someone or something. □ *She will have nothing to do with me anymore. □ I have nothing to do with computers after I found out how hard they are to operate.*

have one foot in the grave to be near death, either because of old age or be-

cause of illness. □ *Fred's uncle is ninety. He has one foot in the grave and may not live another two months. □ Terry has one foot in the grave and will perish unless he receives treatment soon.*

have one's back to the wall to be in a defensive position. (Informal. See also *push someone to the wall*.) □ *He'll have to give in. He has his back to the wall. □ How can I bargain when I've got my back to the wall?*

have one's cake and eat it too AND **eat one's cake and have it too** to enjoy both having something and using it up; to *have it both ways*. (Usually stated in the negative.) □ *Tom wants to have his cake and eat it too. It can't be done. □ Don't buy a car if you want to walk and stay healthy. You can't eat your cake and have it too.*

have one's druthers to get one's choice; to be permitted to have one's preference. (Folksy. The *druthers* is from *rather*.) □ *If I had my druthers, I'd go to France. □ Tom said that if he had his druthers, he'd choose to stay home.*

have one's ear to the ground AND **keep one's ear to the ground** to listen carefully, hoping to get advance warning of something. (Not literal.) □ *John had his ear to the ground, hoping to find out about new ideas in computers. □ His boss told him to keep his ear to the ground so that he'd be the first to know of a new idea.*

have one's finger in the pie See *have a finger in the pie*.

have one's hand in the till to be stealing money from a company or an organization. (The till is a cash box or drawer.) □ *Mr. Jones had his hand in the till for years before he was caught. □ I think that the new clerk has her hand in the till. There is cash missing every morning.*

have one's hands full (with someone or something) to be busy or totally occupied with someone or something. □ *I have my hands full with my three children. □ You have your hands full with* the store. □ *We both have our hands full.*

have one's hands tied to be prevented from doing something. (See also *tie someone's hands.*) □ *I can't help you. I was told not to, so I have my hands tied.* □ *John can help. He doesn't have his hands tied.*

have one's head in the clouds to be unaware of what is going on. □ *"Bob, do you have your head in the clouds?" said the teacher.* □ *She walks around all day with her head in the clouds. She must be in love.*

have one's heart go out to someone to have compassion for someone. □ *I can't have my heart go out to everyone.* □ *To have compassion is to have one's heart go out to those who are suffering.*

have one's heart in the right place to have good intentions, even if there are bad results. (See also *one's heart is in the right place.*) □ *I don't always do what is right, but my heart is in the right place.* □ *Good old Tom. His heart's in the right place.* □ *It doesn't matter if she lost the game. She has her heart in the right place.*

have one's heart on one's sleeve See *wear one's heart on one's sleeve.*

have one's heart set against something to be totally against something. (Also with *dead,* as in the example. See also *dead set against someone or something; set one's heart against something.*) □ *Jane has her heart dead set against going to Australia.* □ *John has his heart set against going to college.*

have one's heart set on something to be desiring and expecting something. □ *Jane has her heart set on going to London.* □ *Bob will be disappointed. He had his heart set on going to college this year.* □ *She had her heart set on it.*

have one's heart stand still one's heart (figuratively) stops beating because one is feeling strong emotions. □ *I had my heart stand still once when I was overcome with joy.* □ *Lovers — at least the ones in love songs — usually have their hearts stand still.*

have one's luck run out for one's good luck to stop; for one's good fortune to come to an end. □ *I had my luck run out when I was in South America. I nearly starved.* □ *I hate to have my luck run out just when I need it.*

have one's nose in a book to be reading a book; to read books all the time. □ *Bob has his nose in a book every time I see him.* □ *His nose is always in a book. He never gets any exercise.*

have one's nose in the air to be conceited or aloof. (See also *one's nose is in the air.*) □ *Mary always seems to have her nose in the air.* □ *I wonder if she knows that she has her nose in the air.*

have one's words stick in one's throat to be so overcome by emotion that one can hardly speak. □ *I sometimes have my words stick in my throat.* □ *John said that he never had his words stick in his throat.*

have one's work cut out for one to have a large and difficult task prepared for one. (See also *one's work is cut out for one.*) □ *They sure have their work cut out for them, and it's going to be hard.* □ *There is a lot for Bob to do. He has his work cut out for him.*

have oneself something to select, use, or consume something. (Folksy. Also with nonreflexive pronouns, *me, him, her,* etc., as in the last example.) □ *He had himself a two-hour nap.* □ *I'll have myself one of those red ones.* □ *I think I'll have me a big, cold drink.*

have other fish to fry to have other things to do; to have more important things to do. (*Other* can be replaced by *bigger, better, more important,* etc. The literal sense is not used.) □ *I can't take time for your problem. I have other fish to fry.* □ *I won't waste time on your question. I have bigger fish to fry.*

have pull with someone to have influence with someone. (Slang. Also with *some, much, lots,* etc.) □ *Let's ask Ann to help us. She has pull with the mayor.* □ *Do you know anyone who* *has some pull with the bank president? I need a loan.*

have rocks in one's head to be silly or crazy. (Slang.) □ *John is a real nut. He has rocks in his head.* □ *I don't have rocks in my head—I'm just different.*

have seen better days to be worn or worn out. (Informal.) □ *This coat has seen better days. I need a new one.* □ *Oh, my old legs ache. I've seen better days, but everyone has to grow old.*

have so See *have too.*

have someone dead to rights to have proven someone unquestionably guilty. □ *The police burst in on the robbers while they were at work. They had the robbers dead to rights.* □ *All right, Tom! I've got you dead to rights! Get your hands out of the cookie jar.*

have someone in one's pocket to have control over someone. (Informal.) □ *Don't worry about the mayor. She'll cooperate. I've got her in my pocket.* □ *John will do just what I tell him. I've got him and his brother in my pocket.*

have someone on the string to have someone waiting for your decision. (Informal.) □ *Sally has John on the string. He has asked her to marry him, but she hasn't replied yet.* □ *Yes, it sounds like she has him on the string.*

have someone or something in one's hands to have control of or responsibility for someone or something. (*Have* can be replaced with *leave* or *put.* Also literal.) □ *You have the whole project in your hands.* □ *The boss put the whole project in your hands.* □ *I have to leave the baby in your hands while I go to the doctor.*

have someone or something in tow to lead, pull, or tow someone or something around. □ *Mrs. Smith has her son in tow.* □ *That car has a boat in tow.*

have someone or something on one's hands to be burdened with someone or something. (*Have* can be replaced with *leave.* Also literal.) □ *I run a re-*cord store. I sometimes have a large number of unwanted records on my hands.* □ *Please don't leave the children on my hands.*

have someone or something on one's mind to think often about someone or something; to be obsessed with someone or something. □ *Bill has chocolate on his mind.* □ *John has Mary on his mind every minute.*

have someone's hide to scold or punish someone. (Slang. Refers to skinning an animal. Not literal. Compare to *skin someone alive.*) □ *If you ever do that again, I'll have your hide.* □ *He said he'd have my hide if I entered his garage again.*

have something against someone or something to possess something (such as prejudice or knowledge) that is harmful to someone or something. (Note the variation in the examples.) □ *I have something against John. He was rude to me.* □ *Do you have something against North Americans?* □ *What do you have against me?* □ *I don't have anything against eating beef.*

have something at hand See the following entry.

have something at one's fingertips AND **have something at hand** to have something within (one's) reach. (*Have* can be replaced with *keep.*) □ *I have a dictionary at my fingertips.* □ *I try to have everything I need at hand.* □ *I keep my medicine at my fingertips.*

have something coming (to one) to deserve punishment (for something). (Informal. Also literal.) □ *Bill broke a window, so he has a spanking coming to him.* □ *That's it, Bill. Now you've got it coming!*

have something doing AND **have something on** to have plans for an event. (Informal. Note the variation with *anything* in the examples.) □ BOB: *Are you busy Saturday night?* BILL: *Yes, I've got something doing.* □ *I don't have anything doing Sunday night.* □ *I have something on almost every Saturday.*

have something going (for oneself) [for someone] to have a scheme or operation going. (Informal.) □ *John really has something going for himself. He's a travel agent, and he gets to travel everywhere for free.* □ *I wish I could have something like that going.*

have something going (with someone) (Informal.) **1.** to have a business deal with someone. □ *Sally has a new business project going with Ann. They'll announce a new product in the spring.* □ *John and Tom work as stockbrokers. I've heard that they have a business deal going.* **2.** See *have a thing going (with someone).*

have something hanging over one's head to have something bothering or worrying one; to have a deadline worrying one. (Informal. Also literal.) □ *I keep worrying about getting drafted. I hate to have something like that hanging over my head.* □ *I have a history paper that is hanging over my head.*

have something in common (with someone or something) [for groups of people or things] to resemble one another in specific ways. □ *Bill and Bob both have red hair. They have that in common with each other.* □ *Bob and Mary have a lot in common. I can see why they like each other.*

have something in hand to have something in one's hand or close by. (Compare with *have something at hand.*) □ *I have your letter of May tenth in hand.* □ *I have my pen in hand, and I'm ready to write.*

have something in mind to think of something; to have an idea or image (of something) in one's mind. □ BILL: *I would like to purchase some boots.* CLERK: *Yes, sir. Did you have something in mind?* □ *I have something in mind, but I don't see it here. Good day.*

have something in stock to have merchandise available and ready for sale. □ *Do you have extra large sizes in stock?* □ *Of course, we have all sizes and colors in stock.*

have something in store (for someone) to have something planned for one's future. □ *Tom has a large inheritance in store for him when his uncle dies.* □ *I wish I had something like that in store.*

have something made 1. to hire someone to make something. □ *Isn't it a lovely coat? I had to have it made because I couldn't find one I liked in a store.* □ *We had the cake made at the bakery. Our oven isn't big enough for a cake that size.* **2.** to have achieved a successful state. (Slang. Usually with *it.*) □ *Mary really has it made. She inherited one million dollars.* □ *I wish I had it made like that.*

have something on See *have something doing.*

have something on file to have a written record of something in storage. □ *I'm sure I have your letter on file. I'll check again.* □ *We have your application on file somewhere.*

have something on the ball to be smart and clever. (Slang.) □ *Both John and Mary have a lot on the ball. They should go far.* □ *I think I'd do better in school if I had more on the ball. I learn slowly.*

have something on the brain to be obsessed with something. (Slang.) □ *Bob has chocolate on the brain.* □ *Mary has money on the brain. She wants to earn as much as possible.*

have something on the tip of one's tongue to be on the verge of remembering a specific fact, such as someone's name; to have just forgotten a specific fact. (See also *on the tip of one's tongue.*) □ *Just give me a minute. I have her name on the tip of my tongue!* □ *I had her name on the tip of my tongue, but you made me forget it when you called.*

have something out (with someone) to settle a disagreement or a complaint. (Informal.) □ *John has been mad at Mary for a week. He finally had it out with her today.* □ *I'm glad we are having this out today.*

have something stick in one's craw to have something irritate or displease someone. (Folksy.) □ *I don't like to have someone's words stick in my craw.* □ *He meant to have the problem stick in my craw and upset me.*

have something to go See *buy something to go.*

have something to spare to have more than enough of something. (Informal. See also *and something to spare.*) □ *Ask John for some firewood. He has firewood to spare.* □ *Do you have any candy to spare?*

have something up one's sleeve to have a secret or surprise plan or solution (to a problem). (Slang. Refers to cheating at cards by having a card hidden in one's sleeve.) □ *I've got something up my sleeve, and it should solve all your problems. I'll tell you what it is after I'm elected.* □ *The manager has something up her sleeve. She'll surprise us with it later.*

have sticky fingers to have a tendency to steal. (Slang.) □ *The clerk—who had sticky fingers—got fired.* □ *The little boy had sticky fingers and was always taking his father's small change.*

have the ball in one's court to be responsible for the next move in some process; to have to make a response to something that someone else has started. □ *You have the ball in your court now. You have to answer the attorney's questions.* □ *There was no way that Liz could avoid acting. She had the ball in her court.*

have the best of both worlds to be in a situation where one can enjoy two different opportunities. □ *When Donna was a fellow at the university, she had the privileges of a professor and the freedom of a student. She definitely had the best of both worlds.* □ *Don hated to have to choose between retirement and continuing working. He wanted to do both so he could have the best of both worlds.*

have the cards stacked against one to have luck against one. (Informal. See also *the cards are stacked against one.*) □ *You can't get very far in life if you have the cards stacked against you.* □ *I can't seem to get ahead. I always have the cards stacked against me.*

have the courage of one's convictions to have enough courage and determination to carry out one's goals. □ *It's fine to have noble goals in life and to believe in great things. If you don't have the courage of your convictions, you'll never reach your goals.* □ *Jane was successful because she had the courage of her convictions.*

have the devil to pay AND **have hell to pay** to have a great deal of trouble. (Informal. Use *hell* with caution.) □ *If you cheat on your income taxes, you'll have the devil to pay.* □ *I came home after three in the morning and had hell to pay.*

have the feel of something 1. [for something] to feel like something (else). □ *This plastic has the feel of fine leather.* □ *The little car has the feel of a much larger one.* **2.** See *get the feel of something.*

have the gift of gab to have a great facility with language; to be able to use language very effectively. (Slang.) □ *My brother really has the gift of gab. He can convince anyone of anything.* □ *If I had the gift of gab like you do, I'd achieve more in life.*

have the Midas touch to have the ability to be successful, especially the ability to make money easily. (From the name of a legendary king whose touch turned everything to gold.) □ *Bob is a merchant banker and really has the Midas touch.* □ *The poverty-stricken boy turned out to have the Midas touch and was a millionaire by the time he was twenty-five.*

have the right-of-way to possess the legal right to occupy a particular space on a public roadway. (See also *yield the right-of-way.*) □ *I had a traffic accident yesterday, but it wasn't my fault. I had the right-of-way.* □ *Don't pull out onto a highway if you don't have the right-of-way.*

have the right to do something See *have a right to do something.*

have the shoe on the other foot to experience the opposite situation (from a previous situation). (Informal. Also with *be* instead of *have*. See the examples. See the proverb *The shoe is on the other foot.* Compare with *in someone else's shoes.*) □ *I used to be a student, and now I'm the teacher. Now I have the shoe on the other foot.* □ *You were mean to me when you thought I was cheating. Now that I have caught you cheating, the shoe is on the other foot.*

have the time of one's life to have a very good time; to have the most exciting time in one's life. □ *What a great party! I had the time of my life.* □ *We went to Florida last winter and had the time of our lives.*

have the wherewithal (to do something) to have the means to do something, especially energy or money. □ *He has good ideas, but he doesn't have the wherewithal to carry them out.* □ *I could do a lot if only I had the wherewithal.*

have them rolling in the aisles to make an audience roll in the aisles with laughter. (Slang. Never literal.) □ *I have the best jokes you've ever heard. I'll have them rolling in the aisles.* □ *What a great performance. We had them rolling in the aisles.*

have to live with something to have to endure something. (See also *learn to live with something.*) □ *I have a slight limp in the leg that I broke last year. The doctor says I'll have to live with it.* □ *We don't like the new carpeting in the living room, but we'll have to live with it.*

have too AND **have so** to have done something (despite anything to the contrary). (This is an emphatic way of affirming that something has happened.) □ BILL: *You haven't made your bed.* BOB: *I have too!* □ *I have so turned in my paper! If you don't have it, you lost it!*

have too many irons in the fire to be doing too many things at once. □ *Tom had too many irons in the fire and missed some important deadlines.* □ *It's better if you don't have too many irons in the fire.*

have turned the corner to have passed a critical point in a process. (Also literal.) □ *The patient has turned the corner. She should begin to show improvement now.* □ *The project has turned the corner. The rest should be easy.*

have what it takes to have the courage or stamina (to do something). □ *Bill has what it takes. He can swim for miles.* □ *Tom won't succeed. He doesn't have what it takes.*

He laughs best who laughs last. See the following entry.

He who laughs last, laughs longest. AND **He laughs best who laughs last.** a proverb meaning that whoever succeeds in making the last move or pulling the last trick has the most enjoyment. □ *Bill had pulled many silly tricks on Tom. Finally Tom pulled a very funny trick on Bill and said, "He who laughs last, laughs longest."* □ *Bill pulled another, even bigger, trick on Tom and said, laughing, "He laughs best who laughs last."*

He who pays the piper calls the tune. a saying meaning that the person who is paying for something has control over how the money is used. □ *Fred's father is paying his way through college, and wants to help him choose his courses. He says that he who pays the piper calls the tune.* □ *The bride's parents should have a say in where the wedding is held since they're paying for it. He who pays the piper calls the tune.*

head and shoulders above someone or something clearly superior to someone or something. (Often with *stand,* as in the example. Fixed order.) □ *This wine is head and shoulders above that one.* □ *John stands head and shoulders above Bob.*

head for someone or something to aim for or move toward someone or something. □ *She waved good-bye as she headed for the door.* □ *Ann came in and headed for her mother.*

head for the last roundup to reach the end of something. (Originally said of a dying cowboy.) □ *This ballpoint pen is headed for the last roundup. I have to get another one.* □ *I am so weak. I think I'm headed for the last roundup.*

head over heels in debt deeply in debt. (Fixed order.) □ *Finally, when she was head over heels in debt, she tore up her credit cards.* □ *I couldn't stand being head over heels in debt, so I always pay off my bills immediately.*

head over heels in love (with someone) very much in love with someone. (Fixed order. See also *fall head over heels in love (with someone)*.) □ *John is head over heels in love with Mary.* □ *They are head over heels in love with each other.* □ *They are head over heels in love.*

head someone or something off to prevent someone or something from arriving. □ *The doctors worked round the clock to head the epidemic off.* □ *Bill headed his mother off so that we had time to clean up the mess before she saw it.* ⊤ *The farmer headed off the herd of sheep before it ruined our picnic.*

head something up to serve as leader or head of something. □ *I had already agreed to head the fund-raising campaign up.* ⊤ *They asked me to head up the meeting.*

heads or tails the face of a coin or the other side of a coin. (Often used in an act of coin tossing, where one circumstance is valid if the front of a coin appears and another circumstance is valid if the other side appears. Fixed order.) □ *Jim looked at Jane as he flipped the coin into the air. "Heads or tails?" he asked.* □ *It doesn't matter whether the result of the toss is heads or tails. I won't like the outcome in any case.*

heads will roll someone will get into severe trouble. (Informal. From the use of the guillotine to execute people.) □ *When the company's year-end results are known, heads will roll.* □ *Heads will roll when the principal sees the damaged classroom.*

hear a peep out of someone to get some sort of a response from someone; to hear the smallest word from someone. (Usually in the negative.) □ *I don't want to hear another peep out of you.* □ *I didn't know they were there. I didn't hear a peep out of them.*

hear of something to tolerate something; to permit something. (Usually negative.) □ *No, you cannot go to the movies! I won't hear of it!* □ *My mother wouldn't hear of my marrying Bill.*

heart and soul the central core [of someone or something]. (Also literal. Fixed order.) □ *My very heart and soul was made sad by her hurtful attitude.* □ *Now we are getting to the heart and soul of the matter.* □ *This feature is the heart and soul of my invention.*

heavy going difficult to do, understand, or make progress with. (Informal.) □ *Jim finds math heavy going.* □ *Talking to Mary is heavy going. She has nothing to say.*

hedge one's bets to reduce one's loss on a bet or on an investment by counterbalancing the loss in some way. (Slang.) □ *Bob bet Ann that the plane would be late. He usually hedges his bets. This time he called the airline and asked about the plane before he made the bet.* □ *John bought some stock and then bet Mary that the stock would go down in value in one year. He has hedged his bets perfectly. If the stock goes up, he sells it, pays off Mary, and still makes a profit. If it goes down, he reduces his loss by winning the bet he made with Mary.*

hell-bent for leather moving or behaving recklessly; riding a horse fast and recklessly. (Informal. Typically found in western movies.) □ *They took off after the horse thief, riding hell-bent for* *leather.* □ *Here comes the boss. She's not just angry; she's hell-bent for leather.*

help oneself to take whatever one wants or needs. □ *Please have some candy. Help yourself.* □ *When you go to a cafeteria, you help yourself to the food.* □ *Bill helped himself to dessert.*

help someone or something out (with someone or something) to assist someone or something with a person or a thing. □ *Can you help me out with my geometry?* □ *Yes, I can help you out.* Ⓣ *Please help out my son with his geometry.* □ *Please help me out around the house.* Ⓣ *We helped out the school with its fund-raising.*

hem and haw (around) to be uncertain about something; to be evasive; to say "ah" and "eh" when speaking — avoiding saying something meaningful. (Folksy. Fixed order.) □ *Stop hemming and hawing around. I want an answer.* □ *Don't just hem and haw around. Speak up. We want to hear what you think.*

hem someone or something in to trap or enclose someone or something. □ *The large city buildings hem me in.* Ⓣ *Don't hem in the bird. Let it have a way to escape.*

here and there at this place and that; from place to place. (Could imply a casual search. See also *here, there, and everywhere; hither and thither.* Fixed order.) □ *We find rare books in used-book stores here and there.* □ *She didn't make a systematic search. She just looked here and there.*

Here goes nothing. I am beginning to do something that will fail or be poorly done. (Informal.) □ *Sally stood on the diving board and said, "Here goes nothing."* □ *As Ann walked onto the stage, she whispered, "Here goes nothing."*

Here (it) goes. Something is going to start.; I will start now.; I will do it now. (Informal or slang.) □ *I'm ready to start now. Here goes.* □ *Okay, it's my turn to kick the ball. Here it goes!*

here, there, and everywhere everywhere; at all points. (See also *hither, thither, and yon.* Compare with *here and there.* Fixed order.) □ *Fred searched here, there, and everywhere, frantically looking for the lost check.* □ *She did not rest until she had been hear, there, and everywhere, shopping for just the right gift.*

here's to someone or something an expression used as a toast to someone or something to wish someone or something well. □ *Here's to Jim and Mary! May they be very happy!* □ *Here's to your new job!*

hide-and-seek a guessing game where one has to find something or figure out something that is concealed or disguised. (Also literal when referring to a game where a person hides and another person tries to find the hidden person. Fixed order.) □ *I am tired of running up against a game of hide-and-seek every time I ask to see the financial records of this company.* □ *I have been trying to see the manager for two days. Where is she? I refuse to play hide-and-seek any longer. I want to see her now!*

hide one's face in shame to cover one's face because of shame or embarrassment. □ *Mary was so embarrassed. She could only hide her face in shame.* □ *When Tom broke Ann's crystal vase, he wanted to hide his face in shame.*

hide one's head in the sand See *bury one's head in the sand.*

hide one's light under a bushel to conceal one's good ideas or talents. (A biblical theme.) □ *Jane has some good ideas, but she doesn't speak very often. She hides her light under a bushel.* □ *Don't hide your light under a bushel. Share your gifts with other people.*

high and dry 1. safe; unbothered by difficulties; unscathed. (As if someone or something were safe from the flood. Also literal. Fixed order.) □ *While the riot was going on, I was high and dry in my apartment.* □ *Liz came out of the argument high and dry.* **2.**

abandoned; unsupported and helpless. (See also *leave someone high and dry*.) □ *Everyone else on the committee quit, leaving me high and dry.* □ *The company moved to Chicago, and I was left high and dry in Dallas.*

high-and-mighty important and arrogant. (Fixed order.) □ *I don't know why Albert is so high-and-mighty. He's no better than the rest of us.* □ *The boss acts high-and-mighty because he can fire us all.*

high as the sky See *(as) high as a kite*.

high man on the totem pole the person at the top of the hierarchy; the person in charge of an organization. (Informal. Compare with *low man on the totem pole*.) □ *I don't want to talk to a secretary. I demand to talk to the high man on the totem pole.* □ *Who's in charge around here? Who's high man on the totem pole?*

high on something (Slang.) **1.** intoxicated with some drug. □ *He got thrown out of the movie because he was high on something.* □ *Bill was high on marijuana and was singing loudly.* **2.** enthusiastic about something. □ *Jane quit eating red meat. She's really high on fish, however.* □ *Bob is high on meditation. He sits and meditates for an hour each day.*

highflier a person who is ambitious or who is very likely to be successful. (Informal.) □ *Jack was one of the highfliers of our university year, and he is now in the foreign office.* □ *Tom is a highflier and has applied for the post of managing director.*

hightail it out of somewhere to run or ride a horse away from somewhere fast. (Folksy. Typically heard in western movies.) □ *Here comes the sheriff. We'd better hightail it out of here.* □ *Look at that guy go. He really hightailed it out of town.*

highways and byways [all the] roads; the major and minor roads and routes. (Both literal and figurative. Fixed order.) □ *I hope I meet you again some day on life's highways and byways.* □

The city council voted to plant new trees along all the highways and byways of the town.

hinge on something to depend on something. □ *This all hinges on how much risk you're willing to take.* □ *Whether we have the picnic hinges on the weather.*

hit a happy medium See *strike a happy medium*.

hit a snag to run into a problem. (Informal.) □ *We've hit a snag with the building project.* □ *I stopped working on the roof when I hit a snag.*

hit a sour note See *strike a sour note*.

hit-and-miss AND **hit-or-miss** carelessly; aimlessly; without plan or direction. (Fixed order.) □ *There was no planning. It was just hit-and-miss.* □ *We handed out the free tickets hit-or-miss. Some people got one; others got five or six.*

hit-and-run an accident where the driver of a car strikes a person or another vehicle and speeds away without admitting to the deed or stopping to help. (Fixed order.) □ *Fred was injured in a hit-and-run accident.* □ *The state passed a law making any kind of hit-and-run accident a felony.*

hit bottom to reach the lowest or worst point. (Informal.) □ *Our profits have hit bottom. This is our worst year ever.* □ *When my life hit bottom, I began to feel much better. I knew that if there was going to be any change, it would be for the better.*

hit it off (with someone) to quickly become good friends with someone. □ *Look how John hit it off with Mary.* □ *Yes, they really hit it off.*

hit one close to home See the following entry.

hit one where one lives AND **hit one close to home** to affect one personally and intimately. (Informal.) □ *Her comments really hit me where I live. Her words seemed to apply directly o me.* □ *I listened carefully and didn't think she hit close to home at all.*

hit one's stride See *reach one's stride.*

hit-or-miss See *hit-and-miss.*

hit pay dirt to discover something of value. (Slang. Refers to discovering valuable ore.) □ *Sally tried a number of different jobs until she hit pay dirt.* □ *I tried to borrow money from a lot of different people. They all said no. Then when I went to the bank, I hit pay dirt.*

hit (someone) below the belt to do something unfair or unsporting to someone. (Informal. From boxing, where a blow below the belt line is not permitted. Also literal.) □ *You really hit me below the belt when you told the boss about my tax problems.* □ *In business Bill is difficult to deal with. He hits below the belt.*

hit (someone) like a ton of bricks to surprise, startle, or shock someone. (Informal. Also literal.) □ *Suddenly, the truth hit me like a ton of bricks.* □ *The sudden tax increase hit like a ton of bricks. Everyone became angry.*

hit someone (right) between the eyes to become completely apparent; to surprise or impress someone. (Informal. Also literal.) □ *Suddenly, it hit me right between the eyes. John and Mary were in love.* □ *Then—as he was talking—the exact nature of the evil plan hit me between the eyes.*

hit someone up (for something) to ask someone for something. (Informal.) □ *John hit me up for a loan.* T *I told him to go hit up someone else.*

hit the books to begin to study; to study. (Slang.) □ *Well, time to hit the books.* □ *John, if you don't start hitting the books, you're going to fail.*

hit the bottle to drink alcohol to excess. (As if drinking directly from the bottle. Also literal = to strike a bottle; to take a drink from a bottle.) □ *Fred goes home and hits the bottle every night.* □ *Bill has been hitting the bottle a lot lately. I think he has a problem.*

hit the bricks to start walking; to go out into the streets. (Slang.) □ *If you want to get a job, you had better get out*
there and hit the bricks. □ *I got fired today. The boss came by and told me to hit the bricks.*

hit the bull's-eye 1. to hit the center area of a circular target. □ *The archer hit the bull's-eye three times in a row.* □ *I didn't hit the bull's-eye even once.* **2.** to achieve the goal perfectly. (Informal.) □ *Your idea really hit the bull's-eye. Thank you!* □ *Jill has a lot of insight. She knows how to hit the bull's-eye.*

hit the ceiling to become very angry. (Informal.) □ *My father hit the ceiling when I damaged the car.* □ *Our employer hit the ceiling when we lost an important contract.*

hit the hay AND **hit the sack** to go to bed and get some sleep. (Slang. Compare with *sack out.*) □ *Look at the clock. It's time to hit the hay.* □ *I like to hit the sack before midnight.*

hit the high spots to do only the important, obvious, or good things. (Informal.) □ *I won't discuss the entire report. I'll just hit the high spots.* □ *First, let me hit the high spots; then I'll tell you about everything.*

hit the jackpot (Slang.) **1.** to win at gambling. (Refers to the "jack" in playing cards.) □ *Bob hit the jackpot three times in one night.* □ *I've never hit the jackpot even once.* **2.** to have a success. □ *I hit the jackpot on a business deal.* □ *I really hit the jackpot in the library. I found just what I needed.*

hit the nail on the head to do exactly the right thing; to do something in the most effective and efficient way. (Also with *right*, as in the second example.) □ *You've spotted the flaw, Sally. You hit the nail on the head.* □ *Bob doesn't say much, but every now and then he hits the nail right on the head.*

hit the road (Slang.) to depart; to begin one's journey, especially on a road trip; to leave for home. □ *It's time to hit the road. I'll see you.* □ *We have to hit the road very early in the morning.*

hit the sack See *hit the hay.*

hit the skids to decline; to decrease in value. (Slang.) □ *Business usually hits the skids in the summer.* □ *Tom hit the skids after he lost his job.*

hit the spot to be exactly right; to be refreshing. (Informal.) □ *This cool drink really hits the spot.* □ *That was a delicious meal, dear. It hit the spot.*

hit (up)on something to discover or think up something. (Informal.) □ *Ann hit on the idea of baking lots of bread and freezing it.* □ *John hit upon a new way of planting corn.*

hitch a ride See *thumb a ride.*

hither and thither *here and there.* (Formal and archaic. Fixed order.) □ *The dog chased the poor bunny hither and thither, failing at every turn to capture it.* □ *Sharon searched hither and thither, hoping to find her lost Persian cat.*

hither, thither, and yon everywhere; *here, there, and everywhere.* (Formal and archaic. Fixed order.) □ *The prince looked hither, thither, and yon for the beautiful woman who had lost the glass slipper.* □ *The terrible wizard had sown the seeds of his evil vine hither, thither, and yon, and soon, the evil, twisted plants began to sprout in all the land.*

hitting on all cylinders See *firing on all cylinders.*

Hobson's choice the choice between taking what is offered and getting nothing at all. (From the name of a stable owner in the seventeenth century who offered customers the hire of the horse nearest the door.) □ *We didn't really want that particular hotel, but it was a case of Hobson's choice. We booked very late and there was nothing else left.* □ *If you want a yellow car, it's Hobson's choice. The garage has only one.*

hoist with one's own petard to be harmed or disadvantaged by an action of one's own which was meant to harm someone else. (From a line in Shakespeare's *Hamlet.*) □ *She intended to murder her brother but was hoist with her own petard when she ate the poisoned food intended for him.* □ *The vandals were hoist with their own petard when they tried to make an emergency call from the pay phone they had broken.*

hold a grudge against someone See *bear a grudge (against someone).*

hold a meeting to meet; to have a meeting (of an organization). □ *We'll have to hold a meeting to make a decision.* □ *Our club held a meeting to talk about future projects.*

hold all the aces to be in a favorable position; to be in a controlling position. (Slang. Refers to having possession of all four aces in a card game.) □ *How can I advance in my job when my enemy holds all the aces?* □ *If I held all the aces, I'd be able to do great things.*

hold forth to speak at length. (Informal.) □ *I've never seen anyone who could hold forth so long.* □ *The professor held forth about economic theory for nearly an hour.*

hold no brief for someone or something not to care about someone or something; to dislike someone or something. □ *I hold no brief for bad typists.* □ *My father says he holds no brief for sweet potatoes.*

hold on (to someone or something) See *hang on (to someone or something).*

hold one's breath 1. to stop breathing for a short period, on purpose. □ *Do you hold your breath when you dive into the water?* □ *I can't hold my breath for very long.* **2.** to stop breathing until something special happens. (Informal. Usually in the negative.) □ BOB: *The bus is going to come soon.* BILL: *Don't hold your breath until it does.* □ *I expect the mail to be delivered soon, but I'm not holding my breath.*

hold one's end (of the bargain) up to do one's part as agreed; to attend to one's responsibilities as agreed. □ *If you don't hold your end up, the whole project will fail.* ⊤ *Tom has to learn to* *cooperate. He must hold up his end of the bargain.*

hold one's fire 1. to refrain from shooting (a gun, etc.). □ *The sergeant told the soldiers to hold their fire.* □ *Please hold your fire until I get out of the way.* **2.** to postpone one's criticism or commentary. (Informal.) □ *Now, now, hold your fire until I've had a chance to explain.* □ *Hold your fire, Bill. You're too quick to complain.*

hold one's ground See *stand one's ground.*

hold one's head up to have one's self-respect; to retain or display one's dignity. (Also literal.) □ *I've done nothing wrong. I can hold my head up in public.* ⊤ *I'm so embarrassed and ashamed. I'll never be able to hold up my head again.*

hold one's own to do as well as anyone else. □ *I can hold my own in a footrace any day.* □ *She was unable to hold her own, and she had to quit.*

hold one's peace to remain silent. □ *Bill was unable to hold his peace any longer. "Don't do it!" he cried.* □ *Quiet, John. Hold your peace for a little while longer.*

hold one's temper See *keep one's temper.*

hold one's tongue to refrain from speaking; to refrain from saying something unpleasant. (See also the fixed phrase *Hold your tongue!*) □ *I felt like scolding her, but I held my tongue.* □ *You must learn to hold your tongue, John. You can't talk to people that way.*

hold out (for someone or something) to wait for someone or something; to forgo everything for someone or something. □ BOB: *Would you like some of this chocolate ice cream?* BILL: *No, I'll hold out for the vanilla.* □ *How long will you hold out?*

hold out the olive branch to offer to end a dispute and be friendly; to offer reconciliation. (The olive branch is a symbol of peace and reconciliation. A biblical reference.) □ *Jill was the first*

to hold out the olive branch after our argument. □ *I always try to hold out the olive branch to someone I have hurt. Life is too short for a person to bear grudges for very long.*

hold someone down to try to keep someone from succeeding. (Also literal.) □ *I still think you're trying to hold him down.* ⊤ *I'm not trying to hold down my brother.*

hold someone or something in check See *keep someone or something in check.*

hold someone or something over to retain someone or something (for a period of time). □ *The storm held John over for another day.* □ *The manager held the movie over for another week.*

hold someone or something still See under *keep someone or something still.*

hold someone or something up 1. [with *someone*] to rob someone (figuratively or literally). □ *I don't eat at that restaurant any more. The food is too expensive. They really held me up the last time I ate there.* □ *That's the one who held me up at gunpoint.* ⊤ *The thug held up the old lady.* **2.** to detain someone or something; to make someone or something late. (Also literal.) □ *The traffic on the expressway held me up.* ⊤ *A storm in Boston held up our plane.*

hold someone or something up (as an example) to point out someone or something as a good example. (See also *make an example of someone.*) □ *I was embarrassed when the boss held me up as an example.* □ *I don't like for anyone to hold me up like that.* ⊤ *The teacher held up the leaf as an example of a typical compound leaf.*

hold something against someone to blame something on someone; to bear a grudge against someone; to resent someone. (Also literal.) □ *Your brother is mean to me, but I can't hold it against you.* □ *You're holding something against me. What is it?*

hold still See under *keep still.*

hold still for something See *stand still for something.*

hold the fort to take care of a place, such as a store or one's home. (Informal. From western movies.) □ *I'm going next door to visit Mrs. Jones. You stay here and hold the fort.* □ *You should open the store at eight o'clock and hold the fort until I get there at ten.*

hold the line (at someone or something) to limit the number or degree of someone or something; to limit (something) to someone or something. (See also *draw the line (at something).*) □ *The room will seat fifty, but I think you should hold the line at forty.* □ *The Browns and the Smiths could be invited, but I think we ought to hold the line at the Browns.* □ *Okay, we'll hold the line.*

hold true [for something] to be true; [for something] to remain true. □ *Does this rule hold true all the time?* □ *Yes, it holds true no matter what.*

hold up to endure; to last a long time. □ *How long will this cloth hold up?* □ *I want my money back for this chair. It isn't holding up well.*

hold up (for someone or something) See under *wait up (for someone or something).*

hold up on something to delay doing something. □ *Please hold up on the project. We've run out of money.* □ *I have to hold up on my reading because I broke my glasses.*

hold water to be able to be proved; to be correct or true. (Also literal.) □ *Jack's story won't hold water. It sounds too unlikely.* □ *The police's theory will not hold water. The suspect has an iron-clad alibi.*

hold with something to accept or agree with something. (Folksy. Usually in the negative.) □ *My father doesn't hold with fancy clothes.* □ *I don't hold with too many X rays.*

Hold your horses! wait a minute and be reasonable; do not run off wildly. (Folksy. From western movies.) □ *Now, hold your horses, John. Be reasonable for a change.* □ *Don't get so mad. Just hold your horses.*

Hold your tongue! Be quiet!; Stop saying what you are saying! □ *Hold your tongue! I've heard enough of your insults.* □ *That's enough rudeness for today! Hold your tongue!*

hole in one (Informal.) **1.** an instance of hitting a golf ball into a hole in only one try. (From the game of golf.) □ *John made a hole in one yesterday.* □ *I've never gotten a hole in one.* **2.** an instance of succeeding the first time. □ *It worked the first time I tried it — a hole in one.* □ *Bob got a hole in one on that sale. A lady walked in the door, and he sold her a car in five minutes.*

hole up (somewhere) to hide somewhere; to live in hiding somewhere. (Slang. Typically in western or gangster movies.) □ *The old man is holed up in the mountains, waiting for the war to end.* □ *If we are going to hole up for the winter, we'll need lots of food.*

holier-than-thou excessively pious; acting as though one is more virtuous than other people. □ *Jack always adopts a holier-than-thou attitude to other people, but people say he has been in prison.* □ *Jane used to be holier-than-thou, but she is marrying Tom, who is a crook.*

home in (on someone or something) to aim exactly at something and move toward it. □ *The sheriff walked into the room and homed in on the horse thief.* □ *The plane homed in on the beacon at the airport.* □ *First, you must set your goal and then home in.*

honest and aboveboard See *aboveboard.*

Honest to God. See *Honest to goodness.*

honest-to-God See *honest-to-goodness.*

Honest to goodness. AND **Honest to God.; Honest to Pete.** I speak the truth. (Some people may object to the use of *God* in this phrase.) □ *Did he really say that? Honest to goodness?* □ *Honest to Pete, I've been to the moon.* □ *I've been there, too—honest to God.*

honest-to-goodness AND **honest-to-God; honest-to-Pete** truthful; genuine. □ *Is that an honest-to-goodness leather jacket, or is it vinyl?* □ *It's honest-to-goodness vinyl.*

Honest to Pete. See *Honest to goodness.*

honest-to-Pete See *honest-to-goodness.*

honor someone's check to accept someone's personal check. □ *The clerk at the store wouldn't honor my check. I had to pay cash.* □ *The bank didn't honor your check when I tried to deposit it. Please give me cash.*

hooked (on something) (Slang.) **1.** addicted to a drug or something similar. □ *Jenny is hooked on cocaine.* □ *She was not hooked on anything before that.* □ *John is hooked on coffee.* **2.** enthusiastic about something; supportive of something. □ *Mary is hooked on football. She never misses a game.* □ *Jane is so happy! She's hooked on life.*

hoot and holler to shout in disapproval; to call and shout one's displeasure. (Fixed order.) □ *After the umpire rendered his decision, the spectators hooted and hollered their thoughts on the matter.* □ *It's hard to play a good game of basketball when the fans are hooting and hollering at everything you do.*

hop, skip, and a jump a short distance. (Also literal. Fixed order.) □ *Her house was just a hop, skip, and a jump away from mine, so we visited often.* □ *Our town is just a hop, skip, and a jump from a big city, so we get the advantages of the city and of country life.*

Hop to it! move fast; get started. (Slang.) □ *Come on, you guys, move it! Hop to it!* □ *Hop to it, Bill. You look like you're loafing.*

hope against (all) hope to have hope even when the situation appears to be

hopeless. □ *We hope against all hope that she'll see the right thing to do and do it.* □ *There is little point in hoping against hope, except that it makes you feel better.*

hopeless at doing something incapable of doing something. □ *Tom is hopeless at cooking.* □ *Sally is hopeless at dusting. She hates it.*

hopped up (Slang.) **1.** intoxicated with drugs or alcohol; stimulated by drugs or alcohol. □ *The old man was hopped up again. He was addicted to opium.* □ *John usually gets hopped up on the weekends.* **2.** excited; enthusiastic. □ *What are you hopped up about now? You're certainly cheery.* □ *I always get hopped up when I think of mountain climbing.*

horn in (on someone or something) **1.** [with *someone*] to attempt to displace someone. (Informal.) □ *I'm going to ask Sally to the party. Don't you dare try to horn in on me!* □ *I wouldn't think of horning in.* **2.** [with *something*] to attempt to participate in something without invitation or consent. □ *Are you trying to horn in on my conversation with Sally?* □ *I hope you are not trying to horn in on our party.*

horse and buggy AND **horse and carriage** a carriage pulled by a horse, as opposed to a modern automobile. (A symbol of old-fashionedness or out-of-dateness. Particularly with *go out with,* as in the examples. Fixed order.) □ *That kind of clothing went out with the horse and buggy.* □ *I thought suspenders went out with the horse and carriage, but I see them everywhere now.*

horse and carriage See the previous entry.

horse around to play around; to waste time in frivolous activities. (Informal.) □ *Stop horsing around and get to work.* □ *The children were on the playground horsing around when the bell rang.*

horse of a different color See the following entry.

horse of another color AND **horse of a different color** another matter altogether. □ *I was talking about trees, not bushes. Bushes are a horse of another color.* □ *Gambling is not the same as investing in the stock market. It's a horse of a different color.*

horse sense common sense; practical thinking. □ *Jack is no scholar but he has a lot of horse sense.* □ *Horse sense tells me I should not be involved in that project.*

horseplay physically active and frivolous play. (Informal. See also *horse around*.) □ *Stop that horseplay and get to work.* □ *I won't tolerate horseplay in my living room.*

hot and bothered 1. excited; anxious. (Informal. Fixed order.) □ *Now don't get hot and bothered. Take it easy.* □ *John is hot and bothered about the tax increase.* 2. amorous; interested in romance or sex. (Informal and euphemistic. Use with caution.) □ *John gets hot and bothered whenever Mary comes into the room.* □ *The dog seems hot and bothered. I think it's that time of the year again.*

hot and heavy referring to serious passion or emotions. (Fixed order.) □ *Things were getting a little hot and heavy so Ellen asked to be taken home.* □ *The movie had one hot and heavy scene after another. Pretty soon it got to be a joke.*

hot as hell See *(as) hot as hell.*

hot on something enthusiastic about something; very much interested in something; knowledgeable about something. (Informal.) □ *Meg's hot on animal rights.* □ *Jean is hot on modern ballet just now.*

hot under the collar very angry. □ *The boss was really hot under the collar when you told him you lost the contract.* □ *I get hot under the collar every time I think about it.*

hotfoot it out of somewhere to run away from a place. (Folksy. Compare with *high tail it out of somewhere.*) □ *Did you see Tom hotfoot it out of the office*

when the boss came in? □ *Things are looking bad. I think we had better hotfoot it out of here.*

hue and cry a loud public protest or opposition. (Fixed order.) □ *There was a hue and cry when the city government tried to build houses on the playing field.* □ *The decision to close the local school started a real hue and cry.*

hung up (on someone or something) obsessed with someone or something; devoted to someone or something. (Slang.) □ *John is really hung up on Mary.* □ *She's hung up, too. See how she smiles at him.*

hungry as a bear See *(as) hungry as a bear.*

hunt-and-peck a slow "system" of typing where one searches for a letter and then presses it. (From the movement used by fowls when feeding. Fixed order.) □ *I never learned to type right. All I do is hunt-and-peck.* □ *I can't type. I just hunt-and-peck, but I get the job done — eventually.*

hunt high and low (for someone or something) AND **look high and low (for someone or something); search high and low (for someone or something)** to look carefully in every possible place for someone or something. □ *We looked high and low for the right teacher.* □ *The Smiths are searching high and low for the home of their dreams.*

hunt someone or something up See *look someone or something up.*

hush money money paid as a bribe to persuade someone to remain silent and not reveal certain information. □ *Bob gave his younger sister hush money so that she wouldn't tell Jane that he had gone to the movies with Sue.* □ *The crooks paid Fred hush money to keep their whereabouts secret.*

hustle and bustle confusion, hurry, and bother. (Fixed order.) □ *The hustle and bustle of the big city is especially annoying in the hot days of summer.* □ *Fred seems to enjoy the hustle and bustle of traffic during rush hour, so he is a very happy bus driver.*

I

if push comes to shove if the situation really becomes difficult; if matters escalate into a strong argument. (See also *when push comes to shove.*) □ *If push comes to shove, I am ready to be more aggressive.* □ *If push comes to shove, I am sure that our senator will help out.*

If the shoe fits, wear it. a proverb meaning that you should pay attention to something if it applies to you. □ *Some people here need to be quiet. If the shoe fits, wear it.* □ *This doesn't apply to everyone. If the shoe fits, wear it.*

if worst comes to worst in the worst possible situation; if things really get bad. □ *If worst comes to worst, we'll hire someone to help you.* □ *If worst comes to worst, I'll have to borrow some money.*

ill at ease uneasy; anxious. □ *I feel ill at ease about the interview.* □ *You look ill at ease. Please relax.*

ill-gotten gains money or other possessions acquired in a dishonest or illegal fashion. □ *Fred cheated at cards and is now living on his ill-gotten gains.* □ *Mary is also enjoying her ill-gotten gains. She deceived an old lady into leaving her money in her will.*

in a bad mood sad; depressed; grouchy; with low spirits. □ *He's in a bad mood. He may yell at you.* □ *Please try to cheer me up. I'm in a bad mood.*

in a bad way in a critical or bad state. (Can refer to health, finances, mood, etc.) □ *Mr. Smith is in a bad way. He may have to go to the hospital.* □ *My bank account is in a bad way. It needs some help from a millionaire.* □ *My*

life is in a bad way, and I'm depressed about it.

in a bind AND **in a jam** in a tight or difficult situation; stuck on a problem. (*In* can be replaced with *into* to show movement toward or into the state described by *bind* or *jam*. Especially *get into*. See the examples.) □ *I'm in a bind. I owe a lot of money.* □ *Whenever I get into a jam, I ask my supervisor for help.* □ *When things get busy around here, we get in a bind. We could use another helper.*

in a coon's age AND **in a month of Sundays** in a very long time. (Folksy. The *coon* is a *raccoon.*) □ *How are you? I haven't seen you in a coon's age.* □ *I haven't had a piece of apple pie this good in a coon's age.* □ *John hasn't seen a movie in a month of Sundays.*

in a dead heat [finishing a race] at exactly the same time; tied. □ *The two horses finished the race in a dead heat.* □ *They ended the contest in a dead heat.*

in a family way AND **in the family way** pregnant. (Informal.) □ *I've heard that Mrs. Smith is in a family way.* □ *Our dog is in the family way.*

in a fix in a bad situation. (Informal. *In* can be replaced with *into*. See *in a bind* and the examples.) □ *I really got myself into a fix. I owe a lot of money on my taxes.* □ *John is in a fix because he lost his wallet.* □ *John got into a fix.*

in a flash quickly; immediately. (Informal.) □ *I'll be there in a flash.* □ *It happened in a flash. Suddenly my wallet was gone.*

in a fog preoccupied; not paying attention to what is going on around one; not alert. □ *Jane always seems to be in a fog.* □ *When I get up, I'm in a fog for an hour.*

in a huff in an angry or offended manner. (Informal. *In* can be replaced with *into.* See *in a bind* and the examples.) □ *He heard what we had to say, then left in a huff.* □ *She came in a huff and ordered us to bring her something to eat.* □ *She gets into a huff very easily.*

in a jam See *in a bind.*

in a jiffy very fast; very soon. (Slang.) □ *Just wait a minute. I'll be there in a jiffy.* □ *I'll be finished in a jiffy.*

in a lather flustered; excited and agitated. (Slang. *In* can be replaced with *into.* See *in a bind* and the examples.) □ *Now, calm down. Don't be in a lather.* □ *I always get in a lather when I'm late.* □ *I get into a lather easily.*

in a mad rush in a hurry. □ *I ran around all day today in a mad rush, looking for a present for Bill.* □ *Why are you always in a mad rush?*

in a month of Sundays See *in a coon's age.*

in a nutshell in a few words; briefly; concisely. (Informal.) □ *I don't have time for the whole explanation. Please give it to me in a nutshell.* □ *Well, in a nutshell, we have to work late.*

in a pinch in a situation where there is but one choice; in a situation where there is not time to locate another choice. □ *I don't care for this kind of paint, but it will do in a pinch.* □ *Tom is not the best choice around, but he will have to do in a pinch.*

in a (pretty) pickle in a mess; in trouble. (Informal. *In* can be replaced with *into.* See *in a bind* and the examples.) □ *John has gotten himself into a pickle. He has two dates for the party.* □ *Now we are in a pretty pickle. We are out of gas.*

in a quandary uncertain about what to do; confused. (*In* can be replaced with *into.* See *in a bind* and the examples.) □ *Mary was in a quandary about what college to go to.* □ *I couldn't decide what to do. I was in such a quandary.* □ *I got myself into a quandary.*

in a sense in a way; sort of. □ *In a sense, cars make life better.* □ *But, in a sense, they also make life worse.*

in a snit in a fit of anger or irritation. (Slang. *In* can be replaced with *into.* See *in a bind* and the examples.) □ *Mrs. Smith threw on her coat and left in a snit.* □ *Here comes John—in a snit again—as usual.* □ *Don't get into a snit.*

in a split second in just an instant. (Informal.) □ *The lightning struck, and in a split second the house burst into flames.* □ *Just wait. I'll be there in a split second.*

in a stage whisper in a loud whisper that everyone can hear. □ *John said in a stage whisper, "This play is boring."* □ *"When do we eat?" asked Billy in a stage whisper.*

in a stew (about someone or something) upset or bothered about someone or something. (Informal. *In* can be replaced with *into.* See *in a bind* and the examples.) □ *I'm in such a stew about my dog. She ran away last night.* □ *Now, now. Don't be in a stew. She'll be back when she gets hungry.* □ *I hate to get into a stew about my friends.*

in a (tight) spot caught in a problem; *in a jam.* (Informal. *In* can be replaced with *into.* See *in a bind* and the examples.) □ *Look, John, I'm in a tight spot. Can you lend me twenty dollars?* □ *I'm in a spot too. I need $300.* □ *I have never gotten into a tight spot.*

in a vicious circle in a situation in which the solution of one problem leads to a second problem, and the solution of the second problem brings back the first problem, etc. (*In* can be replaced with *into.* See *in a bind* and the examples.) □ *Life is so strange. I seem to be in a vicious circle most of the time.* □ *I put lemon in my tea to make* *it sour, then sugar to make it sweet. I'm in a vicious circle.* □ *Don't let your life get into a vicious circle.*

in a word said simply; concisely said. □ *Mrs. Smith is — in a word — haughty.* □ *In a word, the play flopped.*

in a world of one's own aloof; detached; self-centered. (*In* can be replaced with *into*. See *in a bind* and the examples.) □ *John lives in a world of his own. He has very few friends.* □ *Mary walks around in a world of her own, but she's very intelligent.* □ *When she's thinking, she drifts into a world of her own.*

in (all) good conscience having good motives; displaying motives that will not result in a guilty conscience. □ *In all good conscience, I could not recommend that you buy this car.* □ *In good conscience, she could not accept the reward. She had only been acting as a good citizen should.*

in all one's born days ever; in all one's life. (Folksy.) □ *I've never been so angry in all my born days.* □ *Have you ever heard such a thing in all your born days?*

in all probability very likely; almost certainly. □ *He'll be here on time in all probability.* □ *In all probability, they'll finish the work today.*

in and of itself considering it alone. (Fixed order.) □ *The idea in and of itself is not bad, but the side issues introduce many difficulties.* □ *Her action, in and of itself, caused us no problem.*

in any case AND **in any event** no matter what happens. □ *I intend to be home by supper time, but in any case by eight o'clock.* □ *In any event, I'll see you this evening.*

in any event See the previous entry.

in apple-pie order in very good order; very well organized. (Folksy. *In* can be replaced with *into*. See *in a bind* and the examples.) □ *Please put everything in apple-pie order before you leave.* □ *I always put my desk in apple-pie order*

every evening. □ *I've put my entire life into apple-pie order.*

in arrears overdue; late, especially in reference to bills and money. □ *This bill is three months in arrears. It must be paid immediately.* □ *I was in arrears on my car payments, so the bank threatened to take my car away.*

in at the kill See *in on the kill.*

in awe (of someone or something) fearful and respectful of someone or something. □ *Everyone in the country was in awe of the king and queen.* □ *I love my new car. In fact, I'm in awe of it.* □ *When I first saw the house, I just stood there in awe.*

in bad faith without sincerity; with bad or dishonest intent; with duplicity. (Compare with *in good faith.*) □ *It appears that you acted in bad faith and didn't live up to the terms of our agreement.* □ *If you do things in bad faith, you'll get a bad reputation.*

in bad sorts in a bad humor. □ *Bill is in bad sorts today. He's very grouchy.* □ *I try to be extra nice to people when I'm in bad sorts.*

in bad taste AND **in poor taste** rude; vulgar; obscene. □ *Mrs. Franklin felt that your joke was in bad taste.* □ *We found the play to be in poor taste, so we walked out in the middle of the second act.*

in bad (with someone) to have someone against you; to have gotten into trouble with someone. (Informal. Compare with *in good (with someone).*) □ *Sally is in bad with her parents for failing algebra.* □ *She's really in bad. She has real trouble.*

in behalf of someone AND **in someone's behalf; on behalf of someone; on someone's behalf; in someone's name** [doing something] as someone's agent; [doing something] in place of someone; for the benefit of someone. □ *I'm writing in behalf of Mr. Smith, who has applied for a job with your company.* □ *I'm calling on behalf of my client, who wishes to complain about* your actions. □ *I'm calling in her behalf.* □ *I'm acting on your behalf.*

in black and white official, in writing or printing. (Said of something, such as an agreement or a statement, which has been recorded in writing. *In* can be replaced with *into*. See *in a bind* and the examples. Fixed order.) □ *I have it in black and white that I'm entitled to three weeks of vacation each year.* □ *It says right here in black and white that oak trees make acorns.* □ *Please put the agreement into black and white.*

in brief briefly; concisely. □ *The whole story, in brief, is that Bob failed algebra because he did not study.* □ *Please tell me in brief why you want this job.*

in broad daylight publicly visible in the daytime. □ *The thief stole the car in broad daylight.* □ *There they were, selling drugs in broad daylight.*

in cahoots (with someone) in conspiracy with someone; in league with someone. (Folksy.) □ *The mayor is in cahoots with the construction company that got the contract for the new building.* □ *Those two have been in cahoots before.*

in care of someone [to be delivered to someone] through someone or by way of someone. (Indicates that mail is to be delivered to a person at some other person's address.) □ *Bill Jones is living at his father's house. Address the letter to Bill in care of Mr. John Jones.* □ *Bill said, "Please send me my mail in care of my father at his address."*

in case of something in the event of something. (Compare with *in the case of someone or something; in case something happens.*) □ *Please leave the building at once in case of fire.* □ *Please take your raincoat in case of rain.*

in case something happens in the event that something takes place. (Compare with *in case of something.*) □ *She carries an umbrella in case it rains.* □ *I have some aspirin in my office in case I get a headache.*

in character typical of someone's behavior. □ *For Tom to shout that way wasn't at all in character. He's usually quite pleasant.* □ *It was quite in character for Sally to walk away angry.*

in clover with good fortune; in a very good situation, especially financially. (Slang.) □ *If I get this contract, I'll be in clover for the rest of my life.* □ *I have very little money saved, so when I retire I won't exactly be in clover.*

in cold blood without feeling; with cruel intent. (Informal or slang. Frequently said of a crime, especially murder.) □ *The killer walked up and shot the woman in cold blood.* □ *How insulting! For a person to say something like that in cold blood is just horrible.*

in cold storage stored away for future use; in an out-of-the-way place. (Also literal.) □ *I have had this special gift in cold storage for an occasion such as this.* □ *Todd had been keeping himself in cold storage, trying to study for his exams.*

in concert (with someone) in cooperation with someone; with the aid of someone. □ *Mrs. Smith planned the party in concert with her sister.* □ *In concert they planned a lovely event.*

in condition AND **in shape** in good health; strong and healthy. (Used only with people. Compare with *in good shape. In* can be replaced with *into*. See *in a bind* and the examples.) □ *Bob exercises frequently, so he's in condition.* □ *If I were in shape, I could run faster and farther.* □ *I'm not healthy. I have to try to get into shape.*

in consequence (of something) as a result of something; because of something. □ *In consequence of the storm, there was no electricity.* □ *The wind blew down the wires. In consequence, we had no electricity.*

in consideration of something in return for something; as a result of something. (Compare with *out of consideration (for someone or something).*) □ *In consideration of your many years of* service, we are pleased to present you with this gold watch. □ *In consideration of your efforts, here is a check for $3,000.*

in creation See *on earth*.

in deep (Slang.) **1.** deeply involved. □ *John and Mary have been seeing each other for months now. They are really in deep.* □ *Bill loves the theater. He's definitely in deep. He tries out for all the plays and gets into many of them.* **2.** deeply in debt. □ *Bill owes a lot of money to the bank. He's really in deep.* □ *John is in deep with his stockbroker.*

in deep water in a dangerous or vulnerable situation; in a serious situation; in trouble. (As if one were swimming in or fell into water that is over one's head. See also *go off the deep end. In* can be replaced with *into.* See *in a bind* and the examples.) □ *John is having trouble with his taxes. He's in deep water.* □ *Bill is in deep water in algebra class. He's almost failing.* □ *He really got himself into deep water.*

in defiance (of someone or something) against someone's will or against instructions; in bold resistance to someone or someone's orders. □ *Jane spent the afternoon in the park in defiance of her mother's instructions.* □ *She did it in defiance of her mother.* □ *She has done a number of things in defiance lately.*

in due course AND **in due time; in good time; in the course of time; in time** in a normal or expected amount of time. □ *The roses will bloom in due course.* □ *The vice president will become president in due course.* □ *I'll retire in due time.* □ *Just wait, my dear. All in good time.* □ *It'll all work out in the course of time.* □ *In time, things will improve.*

in due time See the previous entry.

in Dutch (with someone) in trouble with someone. (Informal. *In* can be replaced with *into.* See *in a bind* and the examples.) □ *I'm in Dutch with my parents for my low grades.* □ *You're in Dutch quite a bit.* □ *Don't get into Dutch with anyone.*

in earnest sincerely. □ *This time I'll try in earnest.* □ *She spoke in earnest, and many people believed her.*

in exchange (for someone or something) in return for someone or something. □ *They gave us two of our prisoners in exchange for two of theirs.* □ *I gave him chocolate in exchange for some licorice.* □ *John gave Mary a book and got a sweater in exchange.*

in fact in reality; really; actually. □ *I'm over forty. In fact, I'm forty-six.* □ *This is a very good computer. In fact, it's the best.*

in favor of someone See under *in someone's favor*.

in favor (of someone or something) 1. approving, supporting, or endorsing someone or something. □ *Are you in favor of lower taxes?* □ *Of course, I'm in favor.* **2.** [with *someone*] See *in someone's favor*.

in fear and trembling with anxiety or fear; with dread. (Fixed order.) □ *In fear and trembling, I went into the room to take the test.* □ *The witness left the courtroom in fear and trembling.*

in fine feather in good humor; in good health. (*In* can be replaced with *into.* See *in a bind* and the examples.) □ *Hello, John. You appear to be in fine feather.* □ *Of course I'm in fine feather. I get lots of sleep.* □ *Good food and lots of sleep put me into fine feather.*

in for something due to receive a surprise; due to receive punishment. (When the *something* is *it*, the *it* usually means punishment.) □ *I hope I'm not in for any surprises when I get home.* □ *Tommy, you broke my baseball bat. You're really in for it!*

in force in a very large group. (See also *out in force*.) □ *The entire group arrived in force.* □ *The mosquitoes will attack in force this evening.*

in full swing in progress; operating or running without restraint. (*In* can be replaced with *into.* See *in a bind* and the examples.) □ *We can't leave now!*

The party is in full swing. □ *Our program to help the starving people is in full swing. You should see results soon.* □ *Just wait until our project gets into full swing.*

in good condition See *in good shape.*

in good faith with good and honest intent; with sincerity. (Compare with *in bad faith.*) □ *We are convinced you were acting in good faith, even though you made a serious error.* □ *I think you didn't sign the contract in good faith. You never intended to carry out our agreement.*

in good hands in the safe, competent care of someone. (Also literal.) □ *Don't worry. Your children are in good hands. Sally is a good baby-sitter.* □ *Your car is in good hands. My mechanics are factory-trained.*

in good repair in good condition; operating well; well taken care of. (Usually said of a thing rather than a person.) □ *The house is in good repair and ought to attract a number of potential buyers.* □ *If the car were in good repair, it would run more smoothly.*

in good shape AND **in good condition** physically and functionally sound and sturdy. (Used for both people and things. Compare with *in condition. In* can be replaced with *into.* See *in a bind* and the examples.) □ *This car isn't in good shape. I'd like to have one that's in better condition.* □ *Mary is in good condition. She works hard to keep healthy.* □ *You have to make an effort to get into good shape.*

in good spirits happy and cheerful; positive and looking toward the future, despite unhappy circumstances. □ *The patient is in good spirits and that will speed her recovery.* □ *Tom wasn't in very good spirits after he heard the bad news.*

in good time 1. quickly; in a short amount of time. □ *We traveled from Mexico to Texas in good time.* □ *I've never been able to make that trip in good time.* 2. See *in due course.*

in good (with someone) in someone's favor; to *have pull with someone.* (Compare with *in bad (with someone).*) □ *I can ask Mary a favor. I'm in good with her.* □ *Well, I'm not in good with her.* □ *I don't know Mary. How do I go about getting in good?*

in great demand wanted by many people; eagerly sought after. □ *Liz is in great demand as a singer.* □ *Mary's paintings are in great demand.*

in great haste very fast; in a big hurry. □ *John always did his homework in great haste.* □ *Why not take time and do it right? Don't do everything in great haste.*

in heat in a period of sexual excitement; in estrus. (*Estrus* is the period of time in which females are most willing to breed. This expression is usually used for animals. It has been used for humans in a joking sense. *In* can be replaced with *into.* See *in a bind* and the examples.) □ *Our dog is in heat.* □ *She goes into heat every year at this time.* □ *When my dog is in heat, I have to keep her locked in the house.*

in high dudgeon feeling or exhibiting great resentment; taking great offense at something. (Often with *leave.*) □ *After the rude remarks, the person who was insulted left in high dudgeon.* □ *Dennis strode from the room in high dudgeon, and we knew he would get his revenge eventually.*

in high gear (*In* can be replaced with *into.* See *in a bind* and the examples.) 1. [for a machine, such as a car] to be set in its highest gear, giving the greatest speed. □ *When my car is in high gear, it goes very fast.* □ *You can't start out in high gear. You must work up through the low ones.* □ *You don't go into high gear soon enough.* 2. very fast and active. (Informal.) □ *Don't leave now. The party is just now in high gear.* □ *When Jane is in high gear, she's a superb athlete.* □ *When Jane moved into high gear, I knew she'd win the race.*

in honor of someone or something showing respect or admiration for someone or something. □ *Our club gave a party in honor of the club's president.* □ *I wrote a poem in honor of John and Mary's marriage.*

in hopes of something expecting something. (Also with *high*, as in the example.) □ *I was in hopes of getting there early.* □ *We are in high hopes that John and Mary will have a girl.*

in hot water in trouble. (Slang. *In* can be replaced with *into*. See *in a bind* and the examples.) □ *John got himself into hot water by being late.* □ *I'm in hot water at home for coming in late last night.* □ *I get into hot water a lot.*

in its prime See *in one's prime.*

in (just) a second in a very short period of time. □ *I'll be there in a second.* □ *I'll be with you in just a second. I'm on the phone.*

in keeping (with something) AND **in line with something** in accord or harmony with something; following the rules of something. □ *In keeping with your instructions, I've canceled your order.* □ *I'm disappointed with your behavior. It really wasn't in keeping.* □ *It was not in line with the kind of behavior we expect here.*

in kind **1.** in goods rather than in money. □ *The country doctor was usually paid in kind. He accepted two pigs as payment for an operation.* □ *Do you have to pay tax on payments made in kind?* **2.** similarly; [giving] something similar to what was received. □ *John punched Bill, and Bill gave it back in kind.* □ *She spoke rudely to me, so I spoke to her in kind.*

in league (with someone) in cooperation with someone; in a conspiracy with someone. □ *The mayor is in league with the city treasurer. They are misusing public money.* □ *Those two have been in league for years.*

in less than no time very quickly. □ *I'll be there in less than no time.* □ *Don't worry. This won't take long. It'll be over with in less than no time.*

in lieu of something in place of something; instead of something. (The word *lieu* occurs only in this phrase.) □ *They gave me roast beef in lieu of beefsteak.* □ *We gave money to charity in lieu of sending flowers to the funeral.*

in light of something because of certain knowledge; considering something. (As if knowledge or information shed light on something.) □ *In light of what you have told us, I think we must abandon the project.* □ *In light of the clerk's rudeness, we didn't return to that shop.*

in limbo (*In* can be replaced with *into*. See *in a bind* and the examples.) **1.** a region on the border of hell. (In some Christian religions, there is a *limbo* set aside for souls that do not go to either heaven or hell. This sense is used only in this religious context.) □ *The baby's soul was in limbo because she had not been baptized.* □ *Considering all things, getting into limbo is probably better than going to hell.* **2.** in a state of neglect; in a state of oblivion; in an indefinite state. □ *We'll have to leave the project in limbo for a month or two.* □ *After I got hit on the head, I was in limbo for about ten minutes.*

in line AND **on line** standing and waiting in a line of people. (*On line* is used in the New York City area.) □ *I've been in line for an hour.* □ *Get in line if you want to buy a ticket.* □ *We waited on line to see the movie.*

in line with something See *in keeping (with something).*

in love (with someone or something) feeling love for someone or something; experiencing a strong affectionate emotion for someone or something. □ *Mary was in love with her new car! It was perfect for her.* □ *John is deeply in love with Mary.* □ *Those two are really in love.*

in luck fortunate; lucky. □ *You want a red one? You're in luck. There is one red one left.* □ *I had an accident, but I was in luck. It was not serious.*

in mint condition in perfect condition. (Refers to the perfect state of a coin that has just been minted. *In* can be replaced with *into*. See *in a bind* and the examples.) □ *This is a fine car. It runs well and is in mint condition.* □ *We went through a house in mint condition and decided to buy it.* □ *We put our house into mint condition before we sold it.*

in name only nominally; not actual, only by terminology. □ *The president is head of the country in name only. Congress makes the laws.* □ *Mr. Smith is the boss of the Smith Company in name only. Mrs. Smith handles all the business affairs.*

in no mood to do something not to feel like doing something; to wish not to do something. □ *I'm in no mood to cook dinner tonight.* □ *Mother is in no mood to put up with our arguing.*

in no time (at all) very quickly. (Compare with *in less than no time.*) □ *I'll be there in no time.* □ *It won't take long. I'll be finished in no time at all.*

in no uncertain terms in very specific and direct language. (*In* can be replaced with *into*. See *in a bind* and the examples.) □ *I was so mad. I told her in no uncertain terms to leave and never come back.* □ *I told him in no uncertain terms to stop it.* □ *He put his demands into no uncertain terms, and then they listened to him.*

in nothing flat in exactly no time at all. (Informal.) □ *Of course I can get there in a hurry. I'll be there in nothing flat.* □ *We covered the distance between New York and Philadelphia in nothing flat.*

in on the kill AND **in at the kill** present at the end of some activity, usually an activity with negative results. (Literally, present when a hunted animal is put to death. Informal when used about any other activity.) □ *Congress was due to defeat the bill, and I went to Washington so I could be in on the kill.* □ *The judge will sentence the criminal today, and I'm going to be in at the kill.*

in one breath See *(all) in one breath.*

in one ear and out (of) the other [for something to be] ignored; [for some-thing to be] unheard or unheeded. (*In* can be replaced with *into*. See the explanation at *in a bind* and the examples. See also *go in one ear and out the other.*) □ *Bill just doesn't pay attention. Everything is in one ear and out the other.* □ *I told Billy to be home by dinnertime, but I am sure it's just in one ear and out the other.*

in one fell swoop See *at one fell swoop.*

in one's birthday suit naked; nude. (Informal. In the "clothes" in which one was born. *In* can be replaced with *into*. See *in a bind* and the examples.) □ *I've heard that John sleeps in his birthday suit.* □ *We used to go down to the river and swim in our birthday suits.* □ *You have to get into your birthday suit to bathe.*

in one's blood See *in the blood.*

in one's book according to one's own opinion. (Informal.) □ *He's okay in my book.* □ *In my book, this is the best that money can buy.*

in one's cups drunk. (Euphemistic.) □ *She doesn't make much sense when she's in her cups.* □ *The speaker—who was in his cups—could hardly be understood.*

in one's element in a natural or comfortable situation or environment. (Compare with *out of one's element*. *In* can be replaced with *into*. See *in a bind* and the examples.) □ *Sally is in her element when she's working with algebra or calculus.* □ *Bob loves to work with color and texture. When he's painting, he's in his element.* □ *He's most comfortable when he can get into his element.*

in one's glory at one's happiest or best. □ *When I go to the beach on vacation, I'm in my glory.* □ *Sally is a good teacher. She's in her glory in the classroom.*

in one's mind's eye in one's mind. (Refers to visualizing something in one's mind.) □ *In my mind's eye, I can see trouble ahead.* □ *In her mind's eye, she could see a beautiful building* *beside the river. She decided to design such a building.*

in one's opinion according to one's belief or judgment. □ *In my opinion, that is a very ugly picture.* □ *That isn't a good idea in my opinion.*

in one's (own) backyard [figuratively] very close to one. (Also literal.) □ *That kind of thing is quite rare. Imagine it happening right in your backyard.* □ *You always think of something like that happening to someone else. You never expect to find it in your own backyard.*

in one's (own) (best) interest(s) to one's advantage; as a benefit to oneself. □ *It is not in your own interests to share your ideas with Jack. He will say that they are his.* □ *Jane thought it was in the best interest of her friend to tell his mother about his illness.*

in one's prime AND **in its prime** at one's or its peak or best time. (Compare with *in the prime of life.*) □ *Our dog — which is in its prime — is very active.* □ *The program ended in its prime when we ran out of money.* □ *I could work long hours when I was in my prime.*

in one's right mind sane; rational and sensible. (Often in the negative.) □ *That was a stupid thing to do. You're not in your right mind.* □ *You can't be in your right mind! That sounds crazy!*

in one's salad days in one's youth. (Usually formal or literary. Comparing the greenness of a salad with the greenness, or freshness and inexperience, of youth.) □ *I recall the joys I experienced in the warm summer air in my salad days.* □ *In our salad days, we were apt to get into all sorts of mischief on the weekends.*

in one's second childhood being interested in things or people that normally interest children. □ *My father bought himself a toy train, and my mother said he was in his second childhood.* □ *Whenever I go to the river and throw stones, I feel as if I'm in my second childhood.*

in one's spare time in one's extra time; in the time not reserved for doing something else. □ *I write novels in my spare time.* □ *I'll try to paint the house in my spare time.*

in one's Sunday best in one's best Sunday clothes; in the clothes one wears to church. (Folksy. See also *Sunday-go-to-meeting clothes. In* can be replaced with *into.* See *in a bind* and the examples.) □ *All the children were dressed up in their Sunday best.* □ *I like to be in my Sunday best whenever I go out.* □ *Let's get into our Sunday best and go out for dinner.*

in orbit (*In* can be replaced with *into.* See *in a bind* and the examples.) **1.** [for something] to circle a heavenly body. (Planets, moons, and stars are heavenly bodies.) □ *The moon is in orbit around the earth.* □ *They put the satellite into orbit.* **2.** ecstatic; thrilled; emotionally high. (Slang.) □ *Jane is in orbit about her new job.* □ *John went into orbit when he got the check in the mail.*

in order to do something for the purpose of doing something; as a means of doing something. □ *I went to college in order to further my education.* □ *I gave John three dollars in order to buy lunch.*

in other words said in another, simpler way. □ BOB: *Cease! Desist!* BILL: *In other words you want me to stop?* □ *Our cash flow is negative, and our assets are worthless. In other words, we are broke.*

in over one's head with more difficulties than one can manage. (Informal. See also *in deep; in deep water.*) □ *Calculus is very hard for me. I'm in over my head.* □ *Ann is too busy. She's really in over her head.*

in part partly; to a lesser degree or extent. □ *I was not there, in part because of my disagreement about the purpose of the meeting. I also had a previous appointment.* □ *I hope to win, in part because I want the prize money.*

in particular specifically; especially. □ *I'm not going anywhere in particular.*

□ *Of the three ideas, there is one I like in particular.*

in passing casually; as an aside. (See also *mention someone or something in passing.*) □ *I just heard your name in passing. I didn't hear more than that.* □ *The lecturer referred to George Washington in passing.*

in place (*In* can be replaced with *into.* See *in a bind* and the examples.) **1.** in (someone's or something's) proper place or location. (See also *out of place.*) □ *The maid came into the room and put everything into place.* □ *It's good to see everything in place again.* **2.** proper. □ *Your remark was not in place.* □ *The presentation was quite in place and nicely done.*

in place of someone or something instead of someone or something. □ *John went in place of Mary.* □ *We had vegetables in place of meat.*

in plain English See the following entry.

in plain language AND **in plain English** in simple, clear, and straightforward language. (*In* can be replaced with *into.* See *in a bind* and the examples.) □ *That's too confusing. Please say it again in plain English.* □ *Tell me again in plain language.* □ *Please put it into plain language.*

in poor taste See *in bad taste.*

in practice (*In* can be replaced with *into.* See *in a bind* and the examples.) **1.** in an application (of a principle, etc.); in the actual doing of something. □ *Our policy is to be very particular, but in practice we don't care that much.* □ *The instructions say not to set it too high. In practice I always set it as high as possible.* **2.** well-rehearsed; well-practiced; well-exercised. □ *The swimmer was not in practice and almost drowned.* □ *I play the piano for a living, and I have to keep in practice.*

in print available in printed form. (Compare with *out of print.* See also *put something into print.*) □ *I think I can get that book for you. It's still in*

print. □ *This is the only book in print on this subject.*

in private privately. □ *I'd like to speak to you in private.* □ *I enjoy spending the evening in private.*

in progress happening now; taking place at this time. □ *You can't go into that room. There is a meeting in progress.* □ *Please tell me about the work you have in progress.*

in pursuit of something chasing after something. □ *Bill spends most of his time in pursuit of money.* □ *Every year Bob goes into the countryside in pursuit of butterflies.*

in quest of someone or something AND **in search of someone or something** seeking or hunting something; trying to find something. □ *They went into town in quest of a reasonably priced restaurant.* □ *Monday morning I'll go out in search of a job.*

in rags in worn-out and torn clothing. □ *Oh, look at my clothing. I can't go to the party in rags!* □ *I think the new casual fashions make you look as if you're in rags.*

in round figures See the following entry.

in round numbers AND **in round figures** as an estimated number; a figure that has been rounded off. (*In* can be replaced with *into.* See *in a bind* and the examples.) □ *Please tell me in round numbers what it'll cost.* □ *I don't need the exact amount. Just give it to me in round figures.*

in search of someone or something See *in quest of someone or something.*

in season **1.** currently available for selling. (Some foods and other things are available only at certain seasons. Compare with *out of season. In* can be replaced with *into,* especially when used with *come.* See *in a bind* and the examples.) □ *Oysters are available in season.* □ *Strawberries aren't in season in January.* □ *When do strawberries come into season?* **2.** legally able to be caught or hunted. □ *Catfish are in* *season all year round.* □ *When are salmon in season?*

in seventh heaven in a very happy state. □ *Ann was really in seventh heaven when she got a car of her own.* □ *I'd be in seventh heaven if I had a million dollars.*

in shape See *in condition.*

in short stated briefly. □ *At the end of the financial report, the board president said, "In short, we are okay."* □ *My remarks, in short, indicate that we are in good financial shape.*

in short order very quickly. □ *I can straighten out this mess in short order.* □ *The people came in and cleaned the place up in short order.*

in short supply scarce. (*In* can be replaced with *into.* See *in a bind* and the examples.) □ *Fresh vegetables are in short supply in the winter.* □ *Yellow cars are in short supply because everyone likes them and buys them.* □ *At this time of the year, fresh vegetables go into short supply.*

(in) single file lined up, one behind the other; in a line, one person or one thing wide. (*In* can be replaced with *into.* See *in a bind* and the examples.) □ *Have you ever seen ducks walking in single file?* □ *No, do they usually walk single file?* □ *Please march in single file.* □ *Please get into single file.*

in so many words exactly; explicitly; literally. □ *I told her in so many words to leave me alone.* □ *He said yes, but not in so many words.*

in some neck of the woods in some remote place. (Folksy. The *some* is usually *this, that, your, their,* etc. Can be used literally to refer to some section of a forest.) □ *I think that the Smiths live in your neck of the woods.* □ *What's happening over in that neck of the woods?*

in someone else's place See the following entry.

in someone else's shoes AND **in someone else's place** seeing or experiencing something from someone else's point of view. (See *in a bind* and the examples. See *put oneself in someone else's place.*) □ *You might feel different if you were in her shoes.* □ *Pretend you're in Tom's place, and then try to figure out why he acts the way he does.*

in someone's behalf See *in behalf of someone.*

in someone's favor 1. to someone's advantage or credit. (Especially in sports scores, as in the examples.) □ *The score was ten to twelve in our favor.* □ *At the end of the second half, the score was forty to three in the other team's favor.* **2.** liked by someone; approved of by someone. (*In* can be replaced with *into.* See *in a bind* and the examples.) □ *John might be able to help me. I hope I'm currently in his favor.* □ *My mother is mad at me. I'm certainly not in her favor.* □ *I'll try to get into her favor.* **3.** AND **in favor of someone** to someone, as when writing a check. (See also *honor someone's check.*) □ *Please make out a check for $300 in Tom's favor.* □ *I'm making out the check in favor of Mr. Brown.*

in someone's name 1. See *in behalf of someone.* **2.** in someone's ownership; as someone's property. (*In* can be replaced with *into.* See *in a bind* and the examples.) □ *The house is in my name. I own all of it.* □ *I put the house into my husband's name.* □ *The car is in our names.*

in someone's name See *in behalf of someone.*

in spite of someone or something regardless of someone or something; in defiance of someone or something. □ *In spite of what you said, I still like you.* □ *He went to the concert in spite of his parents.*

in step (with someone or something) (*In* can be replaced with *into.* See *in a bind* and the examples.) **1.** [with *someone*] [marching or dancing] in cadence with another person. □ *Please keep in step with Jane.* □ *You two, back there. You aren't in step.* □ *Get into step!* **2.** AND **in time** [with *something*] keeping in time with music. □ *John, your violin isn't in step with the beat. Sit up straight and try it again.* □ *I'm trying to play in time.* **3.** as up to date as someone or something. □ *Bob is not in step with the times.* □ *We try to keep in step with the fashion of the day.*

in stock readily available, as with goods in a store. □ *I'm sorry, I don't have that in stock. I'll have to order it for you.* □ *We have all our Christmas merchandise in stock now.*

in style 1. in fashion; fashionable. (Compare with *out of style. In* can be replaced with *into*, especially with *come*. See *in a bind* and the examples.) □ *This old coat isn't in style anymore.* □ *I don't care if it's not in style. It's warm.* □ *I hope this coat comes into style again.* **2.** in elegance; in luxury. (Informal.) □ *If I had a million dollars, I could really live in style.* □ *If he saves his money, someday he'll be able to live in style.*

in terms of something regarding something; concerning something. □ *I don't know what to do in terms of John's problem.* □ *Now, in terms of your proposal, don't you think you're asking for too much?*

in the absence of someone or something while someone or something isn't here; without someone or something. □ *In the absence of the cook, I'll prepare dinner.* □ *In the absence of opposition, she won easily.*

in the act (of doing something) while doing something. (See also *catch someone in the act (of doing something).*) □ *There he was, in the act of opening the door.* □ *I tripped while in the act of climbing.* □ *It happened in the act, not before or after.*

in the air everywhere; all about. (Also literal.) □ *There is such a feeling of joy in the air.* □ *We felt a sense of tension in the air.*

in the altogether AND **in the buff; in the raw** naked; nude. (Informal. *In* can be replaced with *into*. See *in a bind* and the examples.) □ *We often went swimming in the altogether down at the creek.* □ *The museum has a painting of some ladies in the buff.* □ *Mary felt a little shy about getting into the altogether.* □ *Bill says he sleeps in the raw.*

in the balance in an undecided state. (See also *hang in the balance.*) □ *He stood on the edge of the cliff, his life in the balance.* □ *With his fortune in the balance, John rolled the dice.*

in the bargain in addition to what was agreed on. (*In* can be replaced with *into*. See *in a bind* and the examples.) □ *I bought a car, and they threw an air conditioner into the bargain.* □ *When I bought a house, I asked the seller to include the furniture in the bargain.*

in the best of health very healthy. □ *Bill is in the best of health. He eats well and exercises.* □ *I haven't been in the best of health. I think I have the flu.*

in the black not in debt; in a financially profitable condition. (Compare with *in the red. In* can be replaced with *into*. See *in a bind* and the examples.) □ *I wish my accounts were in the black.* □ *Sally moved the company into the black.*

in the blood AND **in one's blood** built into one's personality or character. □ *John's a great runner. It's in his blood.* □ *The whole family is very athletic. It's in the blood.*

in the buff See *in the altogether.*

in the bullpen [for a baseball pitcher to be] in a special place near a baseball playing field, warming up to pitch. (*In* can be replaced with *into*. See *in a bind* and the examples.) □ *You can tell who is pitching next by seeing who is in the bullpen.* □ *Our best pitcher just went into the bullpen. He'll be pitching soon.*

in the cards in the future. (Informal.) □ *Well, what do you think is in the cards for tomorrow?* □ *I asked the boss if there was a raise in the cards for me.*

in the care of someone AND **in the charge of someone** in the keeping of someone. (*In* can be replaced with *into*. See *in a bind* and the examples.) □ *I left the baby in the care of my mother.* □ *I placed the house into the care of my friend.* □ *Bill left the office in the charge of his assistant.*

in the case of someone or something 1. in the matter of someone or something; in the instance of someone or something. (See also *in case of something.* Compare with *in the event of something.*) □ *In the case of John, I think we had better allow his request.* □ *In the case of this woman, we'll not grant permission.* **2.** [with *someone*] in the legal proceedings relating to someone. (The *someone* may be contained in the official name of a legal case.) □ *I recall a similar situation in the case of* Ohio *vs.* Jane Smith. □ *Have they found any new facts in the case of Bill Wilson?*

in the charge of someone See *in the care of someone.*

in the chips wealthy; with much money. (Slang. *In* can be replaced with *into.* See *in a bind* and the examples.) □ *John is a stock trader, and occasionally he's in the chips.* □ *Bill really came into the chips when his uncle died.*

in the clear (*In* can be replaced with *into.* See *in a bind* and the examples.) **1.** not obstructed; not enclosed. □ *You're in the clear. Go ahead and back up.* □ *Once the deer got into the clear, it ran away.* **2.** innocent; not guilty. □ *Don't worry, Tom. I'm sure you're in the clear.* □ *I'll feel better when I get into the clear.*

in the course of time See *in due course.*

in the dark (about someone or something) uninformed about someone or something; ignorant about someone or something. □ *I'm in the dark about who is in charge around here.* □ *I can't imagine why they are keeping me in the dark.* □ *You won't be in the dark long. I'm in charge.* □ *She's in the dark about how this machine works.*

in the doghouse in trouble; in (someone's) disfavor. (Informal. *In* can be replaced with *into.* See *in a bind* and the examples.) □ *I'm really in the doghouse. I was late for an appointment.* □ *I hate being in the doghouse all the time. I don't know why I can't stay out of trouble.*

in the doldrums sluggish; inactive; in low spirits. (*In* can be replaced with *into.* See *in a bind* and the examples.) □ *He's usually in the doldrums in the winter.* □ *I had some bad news yesterday, which put me into the doldrums.*

in the driver's seat in control. (Also literal. As if one were driving and controlling the vehicle.) □ *Now that Fred is in the driver's seat, there is a lot less criticism about how things are being done.* □ *Joan can't wait to get into the driver's seat and do what she can to turn things around.*

in the event of something if something happens. (Compare with *in the case of someone or something.*) □ *In the event of fire, please leave quickly and quietly.* □ *The picnic will be canceled in the event of rain.*

in the family See *(all) in the family.*

in the family way See *in a family way.*

in the final analysis AND **in the last analysis** in truth; when all the facts are known; when the truth becomes known. (Usually used when someone is speculating about what the final truth is.) □ *In the final analysis, it is usually the children who suffer most in a situation like this.* □ *In the last analysis, you simply do not want to do as you are told!*

in the first instance See the following entry.

in the first place AND **in the first instance** initially; to begin with. (Compare with *in the second place.*) □ *In the first place, you don't have enough money to buy one. In the second place, you don't need one.* □ *In the first instance, I don't have the time. In the second place, I'm not interested.*

in the flesh really present; in person. □ *I've heard that the queen is coming here* *in the flesh.* □ *Is she really here? In the flesh?* □ *I've wanted a color television for years, and now I've got one right here in the flesh.*

in the gutter [for a person to be] in a low state; depraved. (*In* can be replaced with *into*. See *in a bind* and the examples.) □ *You had better straighten out your life, or you'll end in the gutter.* □ *His bad habits put him into the gutter.*

in the hole in debt. (Informal. *In* can be replaced with *into* with *go*. See *in a bind* and the examples. Also literal.) □ *I'm $200 in the hole.* □ *Our finances end in the hole every month.* □ *We went into the hole on that deal.*

in the hot seat See *on the hot seat.*

in the interest of someone or something as an advantage or benefit to someone or something; in order to advance or improve someone or something. (Formal.) □ *In the interest of health, people are asked not to smoke.* □ *The police imprisoned the suspects in the interest of the safety of the public.*

in the know knowledgeable. (Informal. *In* can be replaced with *into*. See *in a bind* and the examples.) □ *Let's ask Bob. He's in the know.* □ *I have no knowledge of how to work this machine. I think I can get into the know very quickly though.*

in the lap of luxury in luxurious surroundings. (See the explanation at *in a bind* and the examples.) □ *John lives in the lap of luxury because his family is very wealthy.* □ *When I retire, I'd like to live in the lap of luxury.*

in the last analysis See *in the final analysis.*

in the limelight AND **in the spotlight** at the center of attention. (*In* can be replaced with *into*. See *in a bind* and the examples. The literal sense is also used. *Limelight* refers to an obsolete type of spotlight, and the word occurs only in this phrase.) □ *John will do almost anything to get himself into the limelight.* □ *I love being in the spot-*

light. □ *All elected officials spend a lot of time in the limelight.*

in the line of duty as part of the expected (military or police) duties. □ *When soldiers fight people in a war, it's in the line of duty.* □ *Police officers have to do things they may not like in the line of duty.*

in the long run over a long period of time; ultimately. (Compare with *in the short run*.) □ *We'd be better off in the long run buying one instead of renting one.* □ *In the long run, we'd be happier in the South.*

in the market (for something) wanting to buy something. □ *I'm in the market for a video recorder.* □ *If you have a boat for sale, we're in the market.*

in the middle of nowhere in a very remote place. (Informal. *In* can be replaced with *into*. See *in a bind* and the examples.) □ *To get to my house, you have to drive into the middle of nowhere.* □ *We found a nice place to eat, but it's out in the middle of nowhere.*

in the money (Informal. See also *on the money.*) **1.** wealthy. □ *John is really in the money. He's worth millions.* □ *If I am ever in the money, I'll be generous.* **2.** in the winning position in a race or contest. (As if one had won the prize money.) □ *I knew when Jane came around the final turn that she was in the money.* □ *The horses coming in first, second, and third are said to be in the money.*

in the near future in the time immediately ahead. (*In* can be replaced with *into*. See *in a bind* and the examples.) □ *I don't plan to go to Florida in the near future.* □ *Today's prices won't extend into the near future.* □ *What do you intend to do in the near future?*

in the offing happening at some time in the future. (See *in a bind* and the examples.) □ *There is a big investigation in the offing, but I don't know when.* □ *It's hard to tell what's in the offing if you don't keep track of things.*

in the pink (of condition) in very good health; in very good condition, physically and emotionally. (Informal. *In* can be replaced with *into*. See *in a bind* and the examples.) □ *The garden is lovely. All the flowers are in the pink of condition.* □ *Jane has to exercise hard to get into the pink of condition.* □ *I'd like to be in the pink, but I don't have the time.*

in the prime of life in the best and most productive and healthy period of life. (See also *in one's prime. In* can be replaced with *into*. See *in a bind* and the examples.) □ *The good health of one's youth can carry over into the prime of life.* □ *He was struck down by a heart attack in the prime of life.*

in the public eye publicly; visible to all; conspicuous. (*In* can be replaced with *into*. See *in a bind* and the examples.) □ *Elected officials find themselves constantly in the public eye.* □ *The mayor made it a practice to get into the public eye as much as possible.*

in the raw See *in the altogether.*

in the red in debt. (Compare with *in the black* and *out of the red. In* can be replaced with *into*. See *in a bind* and the examples.) □ *My accounts are in the red at the end of every month.* □ *It's easy to get into the red if you don't pay close attention to the amount of money you spend.*

in the right on the moral or legal side of an issue; on the right side of an issue. (Compare with *in the wrong*.) □ *I felt I was in the right, but the judge ruled against me.* □ *It's hard to argue with Jane. She always believes that she's in the right.*

in the running in competition; competing and having a chance to win. (Compare with *out of the running. In* can be replaced with *into*. See *in a bind* and the examples.) □ *Is Tom still in the running? Does he still have a chance to be elected?* □ *I'm glad I didn't get into the running.*

in the same boat (as someone) in the same situation; having the same problem. (*In* can be replaced with *into*. See the explanation at *in a bind* and the examples.) □ TOM: *I'm broke. Can you lend me twenty dollars?* BILL: *Sorry. I'm in the same boat.* □ *Jane and Mary are both in the same boat. They have been called for jury duty.* □ *I am in the same boat as Mary.*

in the same breath [stated or said] almost at the same time. □ *He told me I was lazy, but then in the same breath he said I was doing a good job.* □ *The teacher said that the students were working hard and, in the same breath, that they were not working hard enough.*

in the second place secondly; in addition. (Usually said after one has said *in the first place*.) □ *In the first place, you don't have enough money to buy one. In the second place, you don't need one.* □ *In the first place, I don't have the time. In the second place, I'm not interested.*

in the short run for the immediate future. (Compare with *in the long run.*) □ *In the short run, we'd be better off saving our money.* □ *We decided to rent an apartment in the short run. We can buy a house later.*

in the soup in a bad situation. (Slang. *In* can be replaced with *into*. See *in a bind* and the examples.) □ *Now I'm really in the soup. I broke Mrs. Franklin's window.* □ *I make a lot of mistakes. It's easy for me to get into the soup.*

in the spotlight See *in the limelight.*

in the swim of things involved in or participating in events or happenings. (The *in* can be replaced with *into*. See the explanation at *in a bind* and the examples. The opposite of *out of the swim of things*.) □ *I've been ill, but soon I'll be back in the swim of things.* □ *I can't wait to settle down and get into the swim of things.*

in the twinkling of an eye very quickly. (A biblical reference.) □ *In the twinkling of an eye, the deer had disappeared into the forest.* □ *I gave Bill ten dollars and, in the twinkling of an eye, he spent it.*

in the unlikely event of something if something—which probably will not happen—actually happens. (Compare with *in the event of something*.) □ *In the unlikely event of my getting the job, I'll have to buy a car to get there every day.* □ *In the unlikely event of a fire, please walk quickly to an exit.*

in the (very) nick of time just in time; at the last possible instant; just before it's too late. □ *The doctor arrived in the nick of time. The patient's life was saved.* □ *I reached the airport in the very nick of time.*

in the wake of something after something; as a result of some event. (Also literal, as with the wake of a boat.) □ *We had no place to live in the wake of the fire.* □ *In the wake of the storm, there were many broken tree limbs.*

in the way of something kind of something; style of something. □ *What do you have in the way of leather shoes?* □ *We have nothing in the way of raincoats.* □ *I've seen nothing in the way of nice weather in this part of the country.*

in the wind about to happen. (Also literal.) □ *There are some major changes in the wind. Expect these changes to happen soon.* □ *There is something in the wind. We'll find out what it is soon.*

in the works being prepared; being planned; being done. (Informal.) □ *There are some new laws in the works that will affect all of us.* □ *I have some ideas in the works that you might be interested in.*

in the world See *on earth*.

in the worst way very much. (Informal. Also literal.) □ *I want a new car in the worst way.* □ *Bob wants to retire in the worst way.*

in the wrong on the wrong or illegal side of an issue; guilty or in error. (Compare with *in the right*.) □ *I felt she was in the wrong, but the judge ruled in her favor.* □ *It's hard to argue with Jane. She always believes that everyone else is in the wrong.*

in there pitching trying very hard. (Informal.) □ *Bob is always in there pitching.* □ *Just stay in there pitching. You'll make some progress eventually.*

in this day and age presently; currently; nowadays. (Folksy. Fixed order.) □ *You don't expect people to be polite in this day and age.* □ *Young folks don't take care of their parents in this day and age.*

in time 1. See *in due course*. 2. See under *in step (with someone or something)*. 3. before the deadline; before the last minute. □ *Did you turn in your paper in time?* □ *I didn't go to Florida. I didn't get to the airport in time.*

in tune with someone or something (*In* can be replaced with *into*. See *in a bind* and the examples.) 1. at the same or a harmonizing musical pitch. □ *The violin isn't in tune with the piano.* □ *Bill, please get into tune with John.* 2. [with *something*] keeping up with something. □ *Tom, your clothes are old-fashioned. You aren't in tune with the times.* □ *Come on, Sally. Get into tune with what's going on around you.*

in turn one at a time in sequence. □ *Each of us can read the book in turn.* □ *We cut the hair of every child in turn.*

in two shakes of a lamb's tail very quickly. □ *I'll be there in two shakes of a lamb's tail.* □ *In two shakes of a lamb's tail, the bird flew away.*

in view of something in consideration of something; because of something. □ *In view of the high cost of gasoline, I sold my car.* □ *I won't invite John to the meeting in view of his attitude.*

in with someone friends with someone; having influence with someone. □ *Are you in with John? I need to ask him for a favor.* □ *I've heard that the mayor is in with the county treasurer.*

inch along (something) to move slowly along something little by little. □ *The cat inched along the carpet toward the mouse.* □ *Traffic was inching along.*

inch by inch one inch at a time; little by little. □ *Traffic moved along inch by* inch. □ *Inch by inch, the snail moved across the stone.*

incumbent upon someone to do something necessary for someone to do something. (*Upon* can be replaced with *on.*) □ *It's incumbent upon you to do the work.* □ *It was incumbent on me to make the presentation of the first prize.*

innocent as a lamb See *(as) innocent as a lamb.*

ins and outs of something the correct and successful way to do something; the special things that one needs to know to do something. (Fixed order.) □ *I don't understand the ins and outs of politics.* □ *Jane knows the ins and outs of working with computers.*

instrumental in doing something playing an important part in doing something. □ *John was instrumental in getting the contract to build the new building.* □ *Our senator was instrumental in defeating the bill.*

iron something out to solve a problem; to straighten out a problem; to smooth out a difficulty. (Also literal.) □ *The principal had to iron a classroom problem out.* 🔟 *I just have to iron out this little problem; then I'll be able to see you.*

it behooves one to do something it is necessary for one to do something; it is *incumbent upon someone to do something.* □ *It behooves me to report the crime.* □ *It behooves you to pay for the window that you broke.*

It never rains but it pours. a proverb meaning that a lot of bad things tend to happen at the same time. □ *The car won't start, the stairs broke, and the dog died. It never rains but it pours.* □ *More bad news? It never rains but it pours.*

It (only) stands to reason. It is only reasonable to hold a certain opinion. □ *It stands to reason that most people will not buy a new car if they don't think they can pay for it.* □ *I think he will come back to pick up his check. It only stands to reason.*

It takes (some) getting used to. It is so unpleasant that you will have to get used to it, and then it won't bother you so much. (Said in recognition of the unpleasantness of something.) □ *I never ate duck's feet before. It takes some getting used to.* □ *These hot Mexican dishes seem impossible at first. They take some getting used to, I agree. But it's worth it.*

It'll never fly. It will never work!; It will never be approved! (Also literal. Refers to an evaluation of an unlikely-looking aircraft of some type.) □ *I have read your report and studied your proposal. It'll never fly.* □ *Your design for a new electric automobile is interesting, but it'll never fly!*

It's about time! It is almost too late!; I've been waiting a long time! (Informal. See also the following entry.) □ *So you finally got here! It's about time!* □ *They finally paid me my money. It's about time!*

It's high time! it is past time (for something); (something) is overdue. (Informal. See also the previous entry.) □ *It's high time that you got recognition for what you do!* □ *They sent me my check, and it's high time, too.*

it's no use (doing something) it is hopeless to do something; it is pointless to do something. □ *It's no use trying to call on the telephone. The line is always busy.* □ *They tried and tried, but it was no use.*

J

jack-of-all-trades someone who can do several different jobs instead of specializing in one. □ *John can do plumbing, carpentry, and roofing—a real jack-of-all-trades. He isn't very good at any of them.* □ *Take your car to a trained mechanic, not a jack-of-all-trades.*

jack someone or something up 1. [with *someone*] to motivate someone; to stimulate someone to do something. (Slang.) □ *The mail is late again today. We'll have to jack those people up at the post office.* ⊤ *I guess I'll have to jack up the carpenter again to repair my stairs.* **2.** [with *something*] to raise the price. □ *The grocery store jacks the price of meat up on the weekend.* ⊤ *The electric company jacked up the price of electricity.*

jazz something up to make something more exciting, colorful, or lively. (Slang. Said especially of music.) □ *When we play the music this time, let's jazz it up a bit.* ⊤ *I think we need to jazz up this room. It looks so drab.*

Jekyll and Hyde someone with both an evil and a good personality. (From the novel *The Strange Case of Dr. Jekyll and Mr. Hyde* by Robert Louis Stevenson. Fixed order.) □ *Bill thinks Mary is so soft and gentle, but she can be very cruel—she is a real Jekyll and Hyde.* □ *Jane doesn't know that Fred is a Jekyll and Hyde. She sees him only when he is being kind and generous, but he can be very cruel.*

jockey for position to try to push or maneuver one's way into an advantageous position at the expense of others. □ *All the workers in the com-pany are jockeying for position. They all want the manager's job.* □ *It is unpleasant working for a company where people are always jockeying for position.*

Johnny-come-lately someone who joins in (something) after it is under way. □ *Don't pay any attention to Sally. She's just a Johnny-come-lately and doesn't know what she's talking about.* □ *We've been here for thirty years. Why should some Johnny-come-lately tell us what to do?*

Johnny-on-the-spot someone who is in the right place at the right time. □ *Here I am, Johnny-on-the-spot. I told you I would be here at 12:20.* □ *Bill is late again. You can hardly call him Johnny-on-the-spot.*

join forces (with someone) to unite with someone. □ *We joined forces with the police to search for the lost child.* □ *The choirs joined forces to sing the song.*

Join the club! an expression indicating that the person spoken to is in the same, or a similar, unfortunate state as the speaker. (Informal.) □ *You don't have anyplace to stay? Join the club! Neither do we.* □ *Did you get fired too? Join the club!*

judge one on one's own merit(s) to judge or evaluate one on one's own achievements and virtues, not someone else's. (See the following entry.) □ *Please judge me on my own merits, not on those of my family.* □ *You should judge Sally on her own merit. Forget that her mother is a famous opera star.*

judge something on its own merit(s) to judge or evaluate a thing on its own good points and usefulness. (See the previous entry.) □ *You have to judge each painting on its own merits. Not every painting by a famous painter is superior.* □ *Each rose must be judged on its own merit.*

judging by something considering something; using something as an indication (of something else). □ *Judging by your wet clothing, it must be raining.* □ *Judging by the looks of this house, I would guess there has been a party here.*

juice and cookies trivial and uninteresting snacks or refreshments. (Also literal. Fixed order.) □ *The party was not much. They might as well have served juice and cookies.* □ *After juice and cookies, we all went back into the meeting room for another hour of talk, talk, talk.*

jump all over someone AND **jump down someone's throat; jump on someone** to scold someone severely. (Slang. Also literal.) □ *If I don't get home on time, my parents will jump all over me.* □ *Don't jump on me! I didn't do it!* □ *Please don't jump all over John. He wasn't the one who broke the window.* □ *Why are you jumping down my throat? I wasn't even in the house when it happened.*

jump at something to seize the opportunity to do something. (Usually with *it*. See *jump at the chance*, from which this phrase comes.) □ *When I heard about John's chance to go to England, I knew he'd jump at it.* □ *If something you really want to do comes your way, jump at it.*

jump at the chance AND **jump at the opportunity; leap at the opportunity** to take advantage of a chance to do something. □ *John jumped at the chance to go to England.* □ *I don't know why I didn't jump at the opportunity myself.* □ *I should have leaped at the chance.*

jump at the opportunity See the previous entry.

jump bail AND **skip bail** to fail to appear in court for trial and give up one's bail bond. (Slang.) □ *Not only was Bob arrested for theft, he skipped bail and left town. He's in a lot of trouble.* □ *I thought only criminals jumped bail.*

jump down someone's throat See *jump all over someone.*

jump off the deep end See *go off the deep end.*

jump on someone See *jump all over someone.*

jump on the bandwagon See *get on the bandwagon.*

jump out of one's skin to react strongly to shock or surprise. (Informal. Usually with *nearly, almost,* etc. Not literal.) □ *Oh! You really scared me. I nearly jumped out of my skin.* □ *Bill was so startled he almost jumped out of his skin.*

jump the gun to start before the starting signal. (Originally used in sports contests that are started by firing a gun.) □ *We all had to start the race again because Jane jumped the gun.* □ *When we took the test, Tom jumped the gun and started early.*

jump the track 1. [for something] to fall or jump off the rails or guides. (Usually said about a train.) □ *The train jumped the track, causing many injuries to the passengers.* □ *The engine jumped the track, but the other cars stayed on.* 2. to change suddenly from one thing, thought, plan, or activity to another. □ *The entire project jumped the track, and we finally had to give up.* □ *John's mind jumped the track while he was in the play, and he forgot his lines.*

jump through a hoop AND **jump through hoops** to do everything possible to obey or please someone; to bend over backwards (to do something). (Informal. Trained animals jump through hoops.) □ *She expects us to jump through hoops for her.* □ *What do you want me to do—jump through a hoop?*

jump through hoops See the previous entry.

jump to conclusions AND **leap to conclusions** to judge or decide something without having all the facts; to reach unwarranted conclusions. □ *Now don't jump to conclusions. Wait until you hear what I have to say.* □ *Please find out all the facts so you won't leap to conclusions.*

jumping-off place See the following entry.

jumping-off point AND **jumping-off place** a point or place from which to begin something. □ *The local library is a good jumping-off point for your research.* □ *The office job in that company would be a good jumping-off place for a job in advertising.*

(just) a stone's throw away See *within a stone's throw (of something).*

just in case if (something happens). (Compare with *in case something happens.*) □ *All right. I'll take it just in case.* □ *I'll take along some aspirin, just in case.*

just one of those things something that couldn't have been prevented; something caused by fate. □ *I'm sorry, too. It's not your fault. It's just one of those things.* □ *I feel terrible that I didn't pass the bar exam. I guess it was just one of those things.*

just so 1. in perfect order; neat and tidy. □ *Her hair is always just so.* □ *Their front yard is just so.* **2.** (Usually **Just so!**) Precisely right!; Quite right! □ BILL: *The letter should arrive tomorrow.* TOM: *Just so!* □ JANE: *We must always try our best.* MARTIN: *Just so!*

just the same See *all the same.*

just the same (to someone) See *all the same (to someone).*

just what the doctor ordered exactly what is required, especially for health or comfort. □ *That meal was delicious, Bob. Just what the doctor ordered.* □ BOB: *Would you like something to drink?* MARY: *Yes, a cold glass of water would be just what the doctor ordered.*

K

keel over [for a person] to fall over or fall down in a faint or in death. □ *Suddenly, Mr. Franklin keeled over. He had had a heart attack.* □ *It was so hot in the room that two people just keeled over.*

keen about someone or something See the following entry.

keen on someone or something AND **keen about someone or something** to be enthusiastic about someone or something. □ *I'm not too keen on going to Denver.* □ *Sally is fairly keen about getting a new job.* □ *Mary isn't keen on her new boss.*

keep a civil tongue (in one's head) to speak decently and politely. (Also with *have.* See the note at *keep a straight face.*) □ *Please, John. Don't talk like that. Keep a civil tongue in your head.* □ *John seems unable to keep a civil tongue.* □ *He'd be welcome here if he had a civil tongue in his head.*

keep a stiff upper lip to be cool and unmoved by unsettling events. (Also with *have.* See the note at *keep a straight face.*) □ *John always keeps a stiff upper lip.* □ *Now, Billy, don't cry. Keep a stiff upper lip.* □ *Bill can take it. He has a stiff upper lip.*

keep a straight face to make one's face stay free from laughter. (Note: *Keep* can be replaced with *have. Keep* implies the exercise of effort, and *have* means that a state exists.) □ *It's hard to keep a straight face when someone tells a funny joke.* □ *I knew it was John who played the trick. He couldn't keep a straight face.* □ *John didn't have a straight face.*

keep abreast (of something) to keep informed about something; to *keep up (with the times).* (Also with *be* instead of *keep,* as in the examples.) □ *I try to keep abreast of the financial markets.* □ *I believe that I'm abreast of foreign events.* □ *Yes, I try to keep abreast by reading the papers every day.*

keep after someone AND **keep at someone; keep on someone; stay after someone** to remind or nag someone over and over to do something. (See also *get after someone.*) □ *I'll keep after you until you do it!* □ *Mother stayed after Bill until he did the dishes.* □ *She kept at him until he dried them and put them away.* □ *She kept on him for forty minutes before he finally finished.*

keep an eye on someone or something See *have an eye on someone or something.*

keep an eye out (for someone or something) See *have an eye out (for someone or something).*

Keep at it! Keep doing what you are doing!; Keep trying! (Encouragement to keep working at something.) □ *The boss told me to keep at it every time he passed my desk.* □ *Keep at it, Tom! You can do it!*

keep at someone See *keep after someone.*

keep at someone or something 1. [with *someone*] See *keep after someone.* 2. [with *something*] to continue doing something; to continue trying to do something. □ *John kept at his painting until the whole house was done.*

□ *Keep at the job if you want to get it finished.*

keep body and soul together to feed, clothe, and house oneself. (Fixed order.) □ *I hardly have enough money to keep body and soul together.* □ *How the old man was able to keep body and soul together is beyond me.*

keep (close) watch (on someone or something) to monitor someone or something; to observe someone or something. □ *Keep close watch on Bill. I think he's loafing.* □ *Okay. I'll keep watch, but I think he's a good worker.*

keep (close) watch (over someone or something) to guard or care for someone or something. □ *I'm keeping watch over my children to make sure they have the things they need.* □ *I think that an angel is keeping close watch over her to make sure nothing bad happens to her.* □ *Angels don't have much to do except to keep watch.*

keep company (with someone) to spend much time with someone; to associate with or consort with someone. (Compare with *keep someone company.*) □ *Bill has been keeping company with Ann for three months.* □ *Bob has been keeping company with a tough-looking bunch of boys.*

keep cool to stay calm and undisturbed. (Informal or slang. Also literal.) □ *Relax man, keep cool!* □ *If Sally could just keep cool before a race, she could probably win.*

keep good time [for a watch] to be accurate. (See also *keep time.*) □ *I have to return my watch to the store because it doesn't keep good time.* □ *Mine keeps good time.*

keep house to manage a household. □ *I hate to keep house. I'd rather live in a tent than keep house.* □ *My grandmother kept house for nearly sixty years.*

keep in touch (with someone) AND **stay in touch (with someone)** to remain in friendly communication with someone. (See also *get in touch (with someone).*) □ *I try to keep in touch with my*

cousins. □ *All our family tries to stay in touch.*

keep late hours to stay up or stay out until very late. □ *I'm always tired because I keep late hours.* □ *If I didn't keep late hours, I wouldn't sleep so late in the morning.*

keep off (something) to stay off someone's land; not to trespass. □ *You had better keep off my property.* □ *The sign says "Keep off."*

keep on an even keel to remain cool and calm. (Originally nautical. See also *keep something on an even keel.*) □ *If Jane can keep on an even keel and not panic, she will be all right.* □ *Try to keep on an even keel and not get upset so easily.*

keep on one's toes to stay alert and watchful. □ *If you want to be a success at this job, you will have to keep on your toes.* □ *Please keep on your toes and report anything strange that you see.*

keep on someone See *keep after someone.*

keep one's chin up to keep one's spirits high; to act brave and confident. (Informal.) □ *Keep your chin up, John. Things will get better.* □ *Just keep your chin up and tell the judge exactly what happened.*

keep one's cool to remain calm, even when provoked. □ *I have a hard time keeping my cool when someone is yelling at me.* □ *Whatever you do, try to keep your cool.*

keep one's distance (from someone or something) to maintain a respectful or cautious distance from someone or something. (The distance can be figurative or literal.) □ *Keep your distance from John. He's in a bad mood.* □ *Keep your distance from the fire.* □ *Okay. I'll tell Sally to keep her distance, too.*

keep one's ear to the ground See *have one's ear to the ground.*

keep one's eye on the ball 1. to watch or follow the ball carefully, especially when one is playing a ball game; to follow the details of a ball game very carefully. □ *John, if you can't keep your eye on the ball, I'll have to take you out of the game.* □ *"Keep your eye on the ball," the coach roared at the players.* **2.** to remain alert to the events occurring around one. (Informal.) □ *If you want to get along in this office, you're going to have to keep your eye on the ball.* □ *Bill would do better in his classes if he would just keep his eye on the ball.*

keep one's eyes open (for someone or something) AND **keep one's eyes peeled (for someone or something)** to remain alert and watchful for someone or something. (The entries with *peeled* are informal. *Peel* refers to moving the eyelids back.) □ *I'm keeping my eyes open for a sale on winter coats.* □ *Please keep your eyes peeled for Mary. She's due to arrive here any time.* □ *Okay. I'll keep my eyes open.*

keep one's eyes peeled (for someone or something) See the previous entry.

keep one's feet on the ground to remain firmly established. (See also *get one's feet on the ground.*) □ *Sally will have no trouble keeping her feet on the ground.* □ *If you can keep your feet on the ground, there should be no problem.*

keep one's fingers crossed (for someone or something) AND **cross one's fingers** to wish for luck for someone or something, often by crossing one's fingers; to hope for a good outcome for someone or something. □ *I hope you win the race Saturday. I'm keeping my fingers crossed for you.* □ *I'm trying out for a play. Keep your fingers crossed!*

keep one's hand in (something) to retain one's control of something. (See also *take a hand in something.*) □ *I want to keep my hand in the running of the business.* □ *Mrs. Johnson has retired from the library, but she still wants to keep her hand in.*

keep one's hands off (someone or something) to refrain from touching or handling something. □ *I'm going to put these cookies here. You keep your hands off them.* □ *Get your hands off my book, and keep them off.*

keep one's head to remain calm and sensible when in an awkward situation that might cause a person to panic or go out of control. □ *She was very angry. We had to calm her down and encourage her to keep her head.* □ *Always try to keep your head when others are panicking.*

keep one's head above water to stay ahead of one's responsibilities; to remain financially solvent. (Also literal.) □ *Now that I have more space to work in, I can easily keep my head above water.* □ *While I was out of work, I could hardly keep my head above water.*

keep one's mouth shut (about someone or something) to keep quiet about someone or something; to keep a secret about someone or something. (Informal.) □ *They told me to keep my mouth shut about the boss or I'd be in big trouble.* □ *I think I'll keep my mouth shut.*

keep one's nose clean to keep out of trouble, especially trouble with the law. (Slang.) □ *I'm trying to keep my nose clean by staying away from those rough guys.* □ *John, if you don't learn how to keep your nose clean, you're going to end up in jail.*

keep one's nose out of someone's business to refrain from interfering in someone else's business. (See also *get one's nose out of someone's business.*) □ *Let John have his privacy, and keep your nose out of my business, too!* □ *Keep your nose out of my business!*

keep one's nose to the grindstone to keep busy continuously over a period of time. (See also *put one's nose to the grindstone.*) □ *The manager told me to keep my nose to the grindstone or be fired.* □ *Keep your nose to the grindstone, and you will prosper.*

keep one's own counsel to keep one's thoughts and plans to oneself; not to tell other people about one's thoughts and plans. □ *Jane is very quiet. She* *tends to keep her own counsel.* □ *I advise you to keep your own counsel.*

keep one's place to exhibit only the behavior appropriate to one's position or status in life. (Also literal.) □ *When I complained about the food, they told me to keep my place!* □ *I suggest you keep your place until you're in a position to change things.*

keep one's temper AND **hold one's temper** not to get angry; to hold back an expression of anger. (The opposite of *lose one's temper.*) □ *She should have learned to keep her temper when she was a child.* □ *Sally got thrown off the team because she couldn't hold her temper.*

keep one's weather eye open to watch for something (to happen); to be on the alert (for something); to be on guard. □ *Some trouble is brewing. Keep your weather eye open.* □ *Try to be more alert. Learn to keep your weather eye open.*

keep one's wits about one to keep one's mind operating in a time of stress. □ *If Jane hadn't kept her wits about her during the fire, things would have been much worse.* □ *I could hardly keep my wits about me.*

keep one's word to uphold one's promise. (The opposite of *break one's word.*) □ *I told her I'd be there to pick her up, and I intend to keep my word.* □ *Keeping one's word is necessary in the legal profession.*

keep pace (with someone or something) to move at the same speed as someone or something; to *keep up (with someone or something).* □ *The black horse was having a hard time keeping pace with the brown one.* □ *Bill can't keep pace with the geometry class.* □ *You've just got to keep pace.*

keep quiet (about someone or something) AND **keep still (about someone or something)** not to reveal something about someone or something; to keep a secret about someone or something. □ *Please keep quiet about the missing money.* □ *Please keep still*

about Mr. Smith's illness. □ *All right. I'll keep still.*

keep someone company to sit or stay with someone, especially someone who is lonely. □ *I kept my uncle company for a few hours.* □ *He was very grateful for someone to keep him company. He gets very lonely.*

keep someone in line to make certain that someone behaves properly. (Informal. Also literal.) □ *It's very hard to keep Bill in line. He's sort of rowdy.* □ *The teacher had to struggle to keep the class in line.*

keep someone in stitches to cause someone to laugh loud and hard, over and over. (Informal. Also with *have.* See the note at *keep a straight face.*) □ *The comedian kept us in stitches for nearly an hour.* □ *The teacher kept the class in stitches, but the students didn't learn anything.* □ *She had us in stitches for ten minutes.*

keep someone on tenterhooks to keep someone anxious or in suspense. (Also with *have.* See the note at *keep a straight face.*) □ *Please tell me now. Don't keep me on tenterhooks any longer!* □ *Now that we have her on tenterhooks, shall we let her worry, or shall we tell her?*

keep someone or something hanging in midair See *leave someone or something hanging in midair.*

keep someone or something in check AND **hold someone or something in check** to keep someone or something under control; to restrain someone or something. □ *Hang on to this rope to keep the dog in check.* □ *I was so angry I could hardly hold myself in check.*

keep someone or something in mind AND **bear someone or something in mind** to remember and think about someone or something. □ *When you're driving a car, you must bear this in mind at all times: Keep your eyes on the road.* □ *As you leave home, keep your family in mind.*

keep someone or something quiet See under *keep someone or something still.*

keep someone or something still 1. AND **keep someone or something quiet** to make someone or something silent or less noisy. □ *Can you please keep the baby quiet?* □ *Keep that stereo still!* **2.** [with *something*] AND **keep something quiet** to keep something a secret. (See also *keep quiet (about someone or something).*) □ *I'm quitting my job, but my boss doesn't know yet. Please keep it quiet.* □ *Okay. I'll keep it still.* **3.** AND **hold someone or something still** to restrain or control someone or something so that the person or thing cannot move. (See also *keep still.*) □ *Please keep your foot still. It makes me nervous when you wiggle it.* □ *You have to hold the nail still if you want to hit it.*

keep someone or something up 1. [with *someone*] to prevent someone from going to bed; to keep someone awake. □ *Their party kept me up all night.* Ⓣ *The noise kept up the entire household.* **2.** [with *something*] to continue doing something. □ *I don't know how long I can keep this up.* Ⓣ *I can't keep up working this way much longer.*

keep someone out in the cold to prevent someone from coming in; to prevent someone from being informed. (Also literal.) □ *Please don't keep me out in the cold. Tell me what's going on.* □ *Don't keep your supervisor out in the cold. Tell her what's going on.*

keep someone posted to keep someone informed (of what is happening); to keep someone up to date. □ *If the price of corn goes up, I need to know. Please keep me posted.* □ *Keep her posted about the patient's status.*

keep something down to keep food in one's stomach (without vomiting it up). □ *I don't know how I managed to keep the pill down.* □ *The food must have been spoiled. I couldn't keep it down.* □ *Sally is ill. She can't keep solid food down.*

keep something for another occasion See *leave something for another occasion.*

keep something on an even keel to keep something in a steady and untroubled state. (See *keep on an even keel.*) □ *The manager cannot keep the company on an even keel any longer.* □ *When the workers are unhappy, it is difficult to keep the factory on an even keel.*

keep something quiet See under *keep someone or something still.*

keep something to oneself to keep something a secret. (Notice the use of *but* in the examples.) □ *I'm quitting my job, but please keep that to yourself.* □ *Keep it to yourself, but I'm quitting my job.* □ *John is always gossiping. He can't keep anything to himself.*

keep something under one's hat to keep something a secret; to keep something in one's mind (only). (Informal. If the secret stays under your hat, it stays in your mind. Note the use of *but* in the examples.) □ *Keep this under your hat, but I'm getting married.* □ *I'm getting married, but keep it under your hat.*

keep something under wraps to keep something concealed (until some future time). □ *We kept the plan under wraps until after the election.* □ *The automobile company kept the new model under wraps until most of the old models had been sold.*

keep still 1. AND **hold still** do not move. □ *Quit wiggling. Keep still!* □ *"Hold still. I can't examine your ear if you're moving," said the doctor.* **2.** See *keep quiet (about someone or something).*

keep still (about someone or something) See *keep quiet (about someone or something).*

keep tabs (on someone or something) AND **keep track (of someone or something)** to monitor someone or something; to follow the activities of someone or something. (*Tabs* can be replaced by *tab*.) □ *I'm supposed to* *keep track of my books.* □ *Try to keep tabs on everyone who works for you.* □ *It's hard to keep tabs when you have a lot of other work to do.* □ *I can't keep track of the money I earn. Maybe someone else is spending it.*

keep the ball rolling to cause something that is in progress to continue. (Also literal. See also *get the ball rolling*.) □ *Tom started the project, and we kept the ball rolling.* □ *Who will keep the ball rolling now that she is gone?*

keep the home fires burning to keep things going at one's home or other central location. (From a World War I song.) □ *My uncle kept the home fires burning when my sister and I went to school.* □ *The manager stays at the office and keeps the home fires burning while I'm out selling our products.*

keep the lid on something to restrain something; to keep something quiet. (Informal. Also literal.) □ *The politician worked hard to keep the lid on the scandal.* □ *The party was noisy because they weren't trying to keep the lid on it. It got louder and louder.*

keep the wolf from the door to maintain oneself at a minimal level; to keep from starving, freezing, etc. □ *I don't make a lot of money, just enough to keep the wolf from the door.* □ *We have a small amount of money saved, hardly enough to keep the wolf from the door.*

keep time 1. to maintain a musical rhythm. □ *Bob had to drop out of the band because he couldn't keep time.* □ *Since he can't keep time, he can't march, and he can't play the drums.* **2.** to keep watch over the time in a game or an athletic contest. □ *Ann kept time at all the basketball games.* □ *Whoever keeps time has to watch the referee very carefully.* **3.** [for a clock or a watch] to keep track of time accurately. (See also *keep good time*.) □ *This watch doesn't keep time.* □ *My other watch kept time better.*

keep to oneself to be solitary; to stay away from other people. □ *Ann tends*

to keep to herself. She doesn't have many friends. □ *I try to keep to myself each morning so I can get some work done.*

keep track (of someone or something) See *keep tabs (on someone or something)*.

keep up an act AND **keep up one's act** to maintain a false front; to act in a special way that is different from one's natural behavior. □ *Most of the time John kept up an act. He was really not a friendly person.* □ *He works hard to keep up his act.*

keep up appearances to keep oneself looking calm or happy despite serious problems. □ *Even with all the trouble Dave was having at home, he still managed to keep up appearances.* □ *She was trained from childhood to keep up appearances no matter how bad she really felt.*

keep up one's act See *keep up an act*.

keep up (with someone or something) to *keep pace (with someone or something);* to advance at the same rate as someone or something. (See the following two entries.) □ *You're running so fast that I cannot keep up with you.* □ *I don't make enough money to keep up with your spending.* □ *You don't even try to keep up.*

keep up (with the Joneses) to stay financially even with one's peers; to work hard to get the same amount of material goods that one's friends and neighbors have. □ *Mr. and Mrs. Brown bought a new car simply to keep up with the Joneses.* □ *Keeping up with the Joneses can take all your money.*

keep up (with the times) to stay in fashion; to keep up with the news; to be contemporary or modern. □ *I try to keep up with the times. I want to know what's going on.* □ *I bought a whole new wardrobe because I want to keep up with the times.* □ *Sally learns all the new dances. She likes to keep up.*

Keep your shirt on! Be patient! (Slang. Usually considered rude.) □ *Hey, keep your shirt on! I'll be with you in a* minute. □ *I'll bring you your hamburger when it's cooked. Just keep your shirt on, friend.*

keyed up anxious; tense and expectant. (Informal.) □ *I don't know why I'm so keyed up all the time. I can't even sleep.* □ *Ann gets keyed up before a test.*

kick a habit AND **kick the habit** to break a habit. (Slang.) □ *It's hard to kick a habit, but it can be done. I stopped biting my nails.* □ *I used to drink coffee every morning, but I kicked the habit.*

kick off 1. to start a football game by kicking the ball a great distance. □ *Tom kicked off in the last game. Now it's my turn.* □ *John tripped when he was kicking off.* **2.** AND **kick the bucket** to die. (Slang. Impolite.) □ *Don't say that George Washington "kicked off." Say that he "passed away."* □ *My cat kicked off last night. She was tough as a lion.* □ *When I kick the bucket, I want a huge funeral with lots of flowers and crying.*

kick oneself (for doing something) to regret doing something. (Informal.) □ *I could just kick myself for going off and not locking the car door. Now the car has been stolen.* □ *Don't kick yourself. It's insured.*

kick over See *turn over.*

kick someone or something around (Slang.) **1.** to treat someone or something badly. (Also literal.) □ *I finally quit my job. My boss wouldn't stop kicking me around.* □ *Stop kicking my car around. It does everything I ask it.* **2.** [with *something*] to discuss an idea or a proposal. □ *That sounds like a good idea to me. Let's kick it around in our meeting tomorrow.* Ⓣ *We kicked around John's idea for a while.*

kick someone or something out AND **boot someone or something out** □ *I lived at home until I was eighteen and my father kicked me out.* Ⓣ *He kicked out his own child?* Ⓣ *Yes. He booted out my brother when he was twenty.*

kick something in to contribute some money (to a cause). (Informal. Also literal.) □ *John kicked five dollars in.* Ⓣ *I'd be happy to kick in a dollar, but no more.*

kick something off to start something; to start off an event. (Also literal.) □ *They kicked the picnic off with a footrace.* Ⓣ *We kicked off the party by singing rowdy songs.* Ⓣ *That was a great way to kick off a weekend.*

kick the bucket See under *kick off.*

kick the habit See *kick a habit.*

kick up to cause trouble or discomfort. □ *The ignition in my car is kicking up again. I will have to have it looked into.* □ *Aunt Jane's arthritis is kicking up. She needs to see the doctor again.*

kick up a fuss AND **kick up a row; kick up a storm** to become a nuisance; to misbehave and disturb (someone). (Informal. *Row* rhymes with *cow.* Note the variations in the examples.) □ *The customer kicked up such a fuss about the food that the manager came to apologize.* □ *I kicked up such a row that they kicked me out.* □ *Oh, what pain! My arthritis is kicking up a storm.*

kick up a row See the previous entry.

kick up a storm See *kick up a fuss.*

kick up one's heels to act frisky; to be lively and have fun. (Informal.) □ *I like to go to an old-fashioned square dance and really kick up my heels.* □ *For an old man, your uncle is really kicking up his heels.*

kid around (with someone) to tease and joke with someone. (Informal.) □ *I like to kid around with John. We are great friends.* □ *Yes, John and I used to kid around a lot.*

kid stuff a very easy task. (Informal.) □ *Climbing that hill is kid stuff.* □ *Driving an automatic car is kid stuff.*

kidding aside See *(all) kidding aside.*

kill the fatted calf to prepare an elaborate banquet (in someone's honor). (From the biblical story recounting the return of the prodigal son.) □ *When Bob got back from college, his parents killed the fatted calf and threw a great* party. □ *Sorry this meal isn't much, John. We didn't have time to kill the fatted calf.*

kill time to waste time. (Informal.) □ *Stop killing time. Get to work!* □ *We went over to the record shop just to kill time.*

kill two birds with one stone to solve two problems with one solution. □ *John learned the words to his part in the play while peeling potatoes. He was killing two birds with one stone.* □ *I have to cash a check and make a payment on my bank loan. I'll kill two birds with one stone by doing them both in one trip to the bank.*

kind of something See *sort of something.*

kiss and make up to forgive (someone) and be friends again. (Also literal.) □ *They were very angry, but in the end they kissed and made up.* □ *I'm sorry. Let's kiss and make up.*

kiss and tell to participate in something secret and private, and then tell other people about it. (Also literal. In actual use, it usually refers to a person of the opposite sex even when it does not refer to actual kissing. Fixed order.) □ *The project was supposed to be a secret between Jane and me, but she spread it all around. I didn't think she was the type to kiss and tell.* □ *I am willing to discuss it with you, but only if you promise not to kiss and tell.*

kiss of death an act that puts an end to someone or something. (Informal.) □ *The mayor's veto was the kiss of death for the new law.* □ *Fainting on stage was the kiss of death for my acting career.*

kiss something good-bye to anticipate or experience the loss of something. (Not literal.) □ *If you leave your camera on a park bench, you can kiss it good-bye.* □ *You kissed your wallet good-bye when you left it in the store.*

kit and caboodle the entire amount; everyone; everything. (Folksy. Fixed order.) □ *Everybody in the family was there — the whole kit and caboodle.* □

The sheriff came and threw the crook out of town, kit and caboodle.

kith and kin friends and relatives; people known to someone. (Fixed order.) □ *I was delighted to find all my kith and kin waiting for me at the airport to welcome me home.* □ *I sent cards to my kith and kin, telling them of my arrival.*

knee-high to a grasshopper not very tall; short and small, as a child. (Folksy.) □ *Hello, Billy. I haven't seen you since you were knee-high to a grasshopper.* □ *I have two grandchildren, both knee-high to a grasshopper.*

knit one's brow to wrinkle one's brow, especially by frowning. □ *The woman knit her brow and asked us what we wanted from her.* □ *While he read his book, John knit his brow occasionally. He must not have agreed with what he was reading.*

knock about (somewhere) to travel around; to act as a vagabond. (Informal.) □ *I'd like to take off a year and knock about Europe.* □ *If you're going to knock about, you should do it when you're young.*

knock-down-drag-out fight a serious fight; a serious argument. (Folksy.) □ *Boy, they really had a knock-down-drag-out fight.* □ *Stop calling each other names, or you're going to end up with a real knock-down-drag-out fight.*

knock it off to stop something; to cease something. (Slang.) □ *Shut up, you guys. Knock it off!* □ *Knock it off. I've heard enough of your music.*

knock off work to quit work (for the day). (Informal.) □ *It's time to knock off work.* □ *It's too early to knock off work.*

knock on wood a phrase said to cancel out imaginary bad luck. (The same as the British "touch wood.") □ *My stereo as never given me any trouble — knock on wood.* □ *We plan to be in Florida by tomorrow evening — knock on wood.*

knock one off one's feet See *sweep one off one's feet.*

knock oneself out (to do something) to go to a great deal of trouble to do something. (Informal. As if one had worked oneself into unconsciousness.) □ *I knocked myself out to prepare this meal for you, and you won't even taste it!* □ *I don't know why I knock myself out to do these things for you. You are not at all appreciative.*

knock some heads together to scold some people; to get some people to do what they are supposed to be doing. (Slang.) □ *If you kids don't quiet down and go to sleep, I'm going to come up there and knock some heads together.* □ *The government is in a mess. We need to go to Washington and knock some heads together.*

knock someone dead to put on a stunning performance or display for someone. (Informal. *Someone* is often replaced by *'em* from *them.*) □ *This band is going to do great tonight. We're going to knock them dead.* □ *"See how your sister is all dressed up!" said Bill. "She's going to knock 'em dead."*

knock someone down (to size) See *beat someone down (to size).*

knock someone for a loop See *throw someone for a loop.*

knock someone off See *bump someone off.*

knock someone or something about See the following entry.

knock someone or something around AND **knock someone or something about** to mistreat someone or something physically. □ *They knocked my baggage around on the flight to Mexico.* □ *The tough guys knocked me around a little.* □ *They knocked my brother about a bit also.*

knock someone out (cold) 1. to knock someone unconscious. (Informal.) □ *The blow knocked the boxer out cold.* □ *The attacker knocked the old man out cold.* 2. to overwhelm someone. (*Someone* includes *oneself.* See also *knock oneself out (to do something).*) □ *The bad news really knocked me out.* □ *Her story was great. It just knocked me out cold!*

knock someone over with a feather to push over a person who is stunned, surprised, or awed by something extraordinary. (Folksy. Not literal.) □ *I was so surprised you could have knocked me over with a feather.* □ *When she heard the news, you could have knocked her over with a feather.*

knock someone's block off to strike someone hard, especially in the head. (Slang. Used in threats, but never literally.) □ *If you touch me again, I'll knock your block off.* □ *John punched Bob so hard that he almost knocked his block off.*

knock something back See the following entry.

knock something down AND **knock something back** to drink down a drink of something, especially something alcoholic. (Slang. Also literal.) □ *I don't see how he can knock that stuff down.* Ⓣ *John knocked back two beers in ten minutes.*

knock something off to finish something, especially in haste or carelessly. (Slang. Also literal.) □ *I knocked it off with the help of Bob.* Ⓣ *I knocked off the last chapter of my book in four hours.*

knock the props out from under someone to destroy someone's emotional, financial, or moral underpinnings; to destroy someone's confidence. □ *When you told Sally that she was due to be fired, you really knocked the props out from under her.* □ *I don't want to knock the props out from under you, but the bank is foreclosing on your mortgage.*

know a thing or two (about someone or something) to be well informed about someone or something; to know something unpleasant about someone or something. (Informal.) □ *I know a thing or two about cars.* □ *I know a thing or two about Mary that would really shock you.*

know a trick or two to know some special way of dealing with a problem. □ *I think I can handle all of this with no trouble. I know a trick or two.* □ *I may be a senior citizen, but I still know a trick or two. I think I can help you with this.*

know (all) the tricks of the trade to possess the skills and knowledge necessary to do something. □ *Tom can repair car engines. He knows the tricks of the trade.* □ *If I knew all the tricks of the trade, I could be a better plumber.*

know better to be wise, experienced, or well taught. □ *Mary should have known better than to accept a lift from a stranger.* □ *Children should know better than to play in the road.*

know-how knowledge and skill. (Informal.) □ *Peter doesn't have the know-how to mend that car.* □ *Mary hasn't the know-how to work the computer.*

know one's ABCs to know the alphabet; to know the most basic things (about something). (Informal.) □ *Bill can't do it. He doesn't even know his ABCs.* □ *You can't expect to write novels when you don't even know your ABCs.*

know one's onions See *know one's stuff.*

know one's place to know the behavior appropriate to one's position or status in life. (See also *put one in one's place.*) □ *I know· my place. I won't speak unless spoken to.* □ *People around here are expected to know their place. You have to follow all the rules.*

know one's stuff AND **know one's onions** to know what one is expected to know. (Informal or slang. See also *know the score.*) □ *I know my stuff. I can do my job.* □ *She can't handle the assignment. She doesn't know her onions.*

know one's way about See the following entry.

know one's way around AND **know one's way about** to know the techniques of getting something done, especially in a bureaucracy. (Also literal.) □ *Sally can get the job done. She knows her way around.* □ *Since Sally worked at city hall for a year, she really knows her way about.*

know someone by sight to know the name and recognize the face of someone. □ *I've never met the man, but I know him by sight.* □ BOB: *Have you ever met Mary?* JANE: *No, but I know her by sight.*

know someone or something like a book See *know someone or something like the palm of one's hand.*

know someone or something like the back of one's hand See the following entry.

know someone or something like the palm of one's hand AND **know someone or something like the back of one's hand; know someone or something like a book** to know someone or something very well. □ *Of course I know John. I know him like the back of my hand.* □ *I know him like a book.*

know something backwards and forwards AND **know something forwards and backwards** to know something very well; to know a passage of language so well that one could recite it backwards as well as forwards. (Reversible.) □ *Of course I've memorized my speech. I know it backwards and forwards.* □ *Todd knows the skeletal structure of the frog backwards and forwards.*

know something by heart to know something perfectly; to have memorized something perfectly. □ *I know my speech by heart.* □ *I went over and over it until I knew it by heart.*

know something forwards and backwards See *know something backwards and forwards.*

know something from memory to have memorized something so that one does not have to consult a written version; to know something well from seeing it very often. (Almost the same as *know something by heart.*) □ *Mary didn't need the script because she knew the play from memory.* □ *The conduc-*

*tor went through the entire concert with-
out music. He knew it from memory.*

know something in one's bones See
feel something in one's bones.

know something inside out to know
something thoroughly; to know about
something thoroughly. (Informal.) □
I know my geometry inside out. □ *I
studied and studied for my driver's test
until I knew the rules inside out.*

know something only too well to know
something very well; to know something from unpleasant experience.
(Note the variation in the examples.)
□ *I know the problem only too well.* □
*I know only too well the kind of prob-
lem you must face.*

know the ropes to know how to do
something. (Informal. See also *learn
the ropes.*) □ *I can't do the job because I don't know the ropes.* □ *Ask
Sally to do it. She knows the ropes.*

know the score AND **know what's what**
to know the facts; to know the facts
about life and its difficulties. (Informal. Also literal.) □ *Bob is so naive.
He sure doesn't know the score.* □ *I
know what you're trying to do. Oh, yes, I
know what's what.*

know what's what See *the previous
entry.*

**know where someone stands (on some-
one or something)** to know what
someone thinks or feels about something. □ *I don't know where John
stands on this issue.* □ *I don't even
know where I stand.*

know which is which AND **tell which is
which** to be able to distinguish one
person or thing from another person
or thing. □ *I have an old one and a
new one, but I don't know which is
which.* □ *I know that Bill and Bob are
twins, but I can't tell which is which.*

**know which side one's bread is buttered
on** to know what is most advantageous for one. □ *He'll do it if his
boss tells him to. He knows which side
his bread is buttered on.* □ *Since John
knows which side his bread is buttered
on, he'll be there on time.*

knuckle down (to something) to get
busy doing something; to get serious
about one's work. (Informal.) □ *It's
time you knuckled down to your studies.*
□ *You must knuckle down if you want
to succeed.*

**knuckle under (to someone or some-
thing)** to submit to someone or something; to yield or give in to someone or
something. (Informal.) □ *You have to
knuckle under to your boss if you expect
to keep your job.* □ *I'm too stubborn to
knuckle under.*

L

labor of love a task that is either unpaid or badly paid and that one does simply for one's own satisfaction or pleasure or to please someone whom one likes or loves. □ *Jane made no money out of the biography she wrote. She was writing about the life of a friend and the book was a labor of love.* □ *Mary hates knitting, but she made a sweater for her boyfriend. What a labor of love.*

lace into someone or something AND **light into someone or something** to attack, devour, or scold someone or something. (Informal.) □ *We laced into a big meal of pork and beans.* □ *The bully punched John once, and then John really laced into him.* □ *John lit into him with both fists.* □ *My father really lit into me when I came in late. He yelled at me for ten minutes.*

laid-back relaxed and unperplexed by difficulties. (Slang.) □ *John is so laid-back. Nothing seems to disturb him.* □ *I wish I could be more laid-back. I get so tense.*

laid up immobilized for recuperation or repairs. (Said of people and things.) □ *I was laid up for two weeks after my accident.* □ *My car is laid up for repairs.* □ *I was laid up with the flu for a week.* □ *Todd was laid up for a month.*

land of Nod sleep. (Humorous. From the fact that people sometimes nod when they are falling asleep.) □ *The baby is in the land of Nod.* □ *Look at the clock! It's time we were all in the land of Nod.*

land on both feet See the following entry.

land on one's feet AND **land on both feet** to recover satisfactorily from a trying situation or a setback. (Informal. Also literal.) □ *Her first year was terrible, but she landed on both feet.* □ *It's going to be a hard day. I only hope I land on my feet.*

land up somehow or somewhere to finish somehow or somewhere; to come to be in a certain state or place at the end. (Usually in the wrong place or in a bad situation. See also *end up somewhere*.) □ *We set out for Denver but landed up in Salt Lake City.* □ *He's so extravagant that he landed up in debt.*

lap something up to believe something, especially something untrue. (Informal. Also literal.) □ *Did she believe it? She just lapped it up.* Ⓣ *I can't imagine why she lapped up that ridiculous story.*

large as life See *(as) large as life*.

last but not least last in sequence, but not last in importance. (Often said when introducing people. Fixed order.) □ *The speaker said, "And now, last but not least, I'd like to present Bill Smith, who will give us some final words."* □ *And last but not least, here is the loser of the race.*

last-ditch effort a final effort; the last possible attempt. □ *I made one last-ditch effort to get her to stay.* □ *It was a last-ditch effort. I didn't expect it to work.*

last will and testament a will; the last edition of someone's will. (Fixed

214

order.) □ *The lawyer read Uncle Charles's last will and testament to a group of expectant relatives.* □ *Fred dictated his last will and testament on his deathbed.*

late in life when one is old. □ *She injured her hip running. She's exercising rather late in life.* □ *Isn't it rather late in life to buy a house?*

late in the day far along in a project or activity; too late in a project or activity for action, decisions, etc., to be taken. □ *It was a bit late in the day for him to apologize.* □ *It's late in the day to try to change the plans.*

laugh out of the other side of one's mouth to change sharply from happiness to sadness. □ *Now that you know the truth, you'll laugh out of the other side of your mouth.* □ *He was so proud that he won the election. He's laughing out of the other side of his mouth since they recounted the ballots and found out that he lost.*

laugh something off to avoid or reject a serious problem by laughing at it. □ *Tom suffered an injury to his leg, but he laughed it off and kept playing ball.* Ⓣ *Mary just laughed off her bad experience.*

laugh up one's sleeve to laugh secretly; to laugh quietly to oneself. (Informal.) □ *Jane looked very serious, but I knew she was laughing up her sleeve.* □ *I told Sally that her dress was darling, but I was laughing up my sleeve because it was too small.*

launch forth (on something) See *set forth (on something); take off (on something).*

law unto oneself one who makes one's own laws or rules; one who sets one's own standards of behavior. □ *You can't get Bill to follow the rules. He's a law unto himself.* □ *Jane is a law unto herself. She's totally unwilling to cooperate.*

lay a finger on someone or something to touch someone or something, even slightly. (Usually in the negative. Compare with *put one's finger on something.*) □ *Don't you dare lay a finger on my pencil. Go get your own!* □ *If you lay a finger on me, I'll scream.*

lay an egg to give a bad performance. (Informal. Also literal.) □ *The cast of the play really laid an egg last night.* □ *I hope I don't lay an egg when it's my turn to sing.*

lay down on the job See *lie down on the job.*

lay down one's life (for someone or something) to sacrifice one's life for someone or something. □ *Would you lay down your life for your country?* □ *There aren't many things for which I'd lay down my life.*

lay down the law 1. to state firmly what the rules are (for something). □ *Before the meeting, the boss laid down the law. We all knew exactly what to do.* □ *The way she laid down the law means that I'll remember her rules.* **2.** to scold someone for misbehaving. (Informal.) □ *When the teacher caught us, he really laid down the law.* □ *Poor Bob. He really got it when his mother laid down the law.*

lay eyes on someone or something See *set eyes on someone or something.*

lay hold of someone or something to grasp someone or something with the hands. (Informal. Compare with *get one's hands on someone or something; get (a)hold of someone or something.*) □ *Just wait till I lay hold of Bill!* □ *I can't wait to lay hold of that fishing pole. I'm ready to catch a huge fish.*

lay into someone or something to attack, consume, or scold someone or something. □ *Bob laid into the big plate of fried chicken.* □ *The bear laid into the hunter.* □ *My father really laid into me when I got home.*

lay it on thick AND **lay it on with a trowel; pour it on thick; spread it on thick** to exaggerate praise, excuses, or blame. □ *Sally was laying it on thick when she said that Tom was the best singer she had ever heard.* □ *After Bob finished making his excuses, Sally said* *that he was pouring it on thick.* □ *Bob always spreads it on thick.*

lay it on with a trowel See *the previous entry.*

lay low See *lie low.*

lay off (someone or something) to leave someone or something alone; to stop bothering someone or something; to *take it easy (on someone or something).* (Slang. See also *lay someone off.*) □ *Lay off Bill. He didn't mean any harm!* □ *Hey! I said lay off!* □ *Lay off the butter. Don't use it all up.*

lay one's cards on the table See *put one's cards on the table.*

lay one's hands on someone or something See *get one's hands on someone or something.*

lay over (somewhere) to pause some place during one's journey. (Compare with *stop over (some place).*) □ *I had to lay over in San Antonio for a few hours before my plane left.* □ *I want a bus that goes straight through. I don't want to lay over.*

lay someone off to put an employee out of work, possibly temporarily. □ *They even laid the president off.* Ⓣ *The computer factory laid off two thousand workers.*

lay someone or something away 1. [with *someone*] to bury someone. □ *They laid my uncle away last week.* □ *They laid him away with a quiet ceremony.* **2.** [with *something*] [for a store clerk] to accept a deposit for merchandise that is held until it is paid for in full. □ *I wanted the dress, but I didn't have enough money. The clerk took ten dollars and laid the dress away for me.* Ⓣ *I never lay away anything. I always charge it.*

lay someone up to cause someone to be ill in bed. □ *A broken leg laid me up for two months.* Ⓣ *Flu laid up everyone at work for a week or more.*

lay something by See *put something by.*

lay something in to get something and store it for future use. □ *They laid a*

lot of food in for the holidays. Ⓣ *We always lay in a large supply of firewood each November.*

lay something on someone to direct blame, guilt, or verbal abuse at someone. (Slang. See also *put the blame on someone or something.*) □ *Don't lay that stuff on me! It's not my fault.* □ *The boss is in the conference room laying a lot of anger on the sales staff.*

lay something on the line See *put something on the line.*

lay something to rest See *put something to rest.*

lay something to waste AND **lay waste to something** to destroy something (literally or figuratively). □ *The invaders laid the village to waste.* □ *The kids came in and laid waste to my clean house.*

lay the blame on someone or something See *put the blame on someone or something.*

lay the finger on someone See *put the finger on someone.*

lay waste to something See *lay something to waste.*

lead a dog's life AND **live a dog's life** to lead a miserable life. □ *Poor Jane really leads a dog's life.* □ *I've been working so hard. I'm tired of living a dog's life.*

lead off to begin; to start (assuming that others will follow). □ *We were waiting for someone to start dancing. Finally, Bob and Jane led off.* □ *The hunter led off, and the dogs followed.* □ *The first baseman will lead off as the first batter in the baseball game.*

lead someone by the nose to force someone to go somewhere (with you); to lead someone by coercion. (Informal.) □ *John had to lead Tom by the nose to get him to the opera.* □ *I'll go, but you'll have to lead me by the nose.*

lead someone down the garden path to deceive someone. □ *Now, be honest with me. Don't lead me down the garden path.* □ *That cheater really led her down the garden path.*

lead someone on a merry chase to lead someone in a purposeless pursuit. □ *What a waste of time. You really led me on a merry chase.* □ *Jane led Bill on a merry chase trying to find an antique lamp.*

lead someone to believe something to imply something to someone; to cause someone to believe something untrue, without lying. □ *But you led me to believe that this watch was guaranteed!* □ *Did you lead her to believe that she was hired as a clerk?*

lead someone to do something to cause someone to do someone. □ *This agent led me to purchase a worthless piece of land.* □ *My illness led me to quit my job.*

lead the life of Riley to live in luxury. (Informal. No one knows who Riley is.) □ *If I had a million dollars, I could live the life of Riley.* □ *The treasurer took our money to Mexico, where he lived the life of Riley until the police caught him.*

lead up to something to prepare the way for something. □ *His compliments were his way of leading up to asking for money.* □ *What were his actions leading up to?*

leaf through something See *thumb through something.*

leak something (out) AND **let something (get) out** to disclose special information to the press so that the resulting publicity will accomplish something. (Usually said of government disclosures. Also used for accidental disclosures. Also literal.) □ *Don't leak that information out.* □ *I don't want to be the one to leak it.* □ *They let it get out on purpose.*

lean on someone to try to make someone do something; to coerce someone to do something. (Informal. Also literal.) □ *If she refuses to do it, lean on her a bit.* □ *Don't lean on me! I don't have to do it if I don't want to.*

lean over backwards (to do something) See *fall over backwards (to do something).*

leap at the opportunity See *jump at the chance.*

leap to conclusions See *jump to conclusions.*

learn something by heart to learn something so well that it can be written or recited without thinking; to memorize something. □ *The director told me to learn my speech by heart.* □ *I had to go over it many times before I learned it by heart.*

learn something by rote to learn something without giving any thought to what is being learned. □ *I learned history by rote; then I couldn't pass the test that required me to think.* □ *If you learn things by rote, you'll never understand them.*

learn something from the bottom up to learn something thoroughly, from the very beginning; to learn all aspects of something, even the most lowly. (Informal.) □ *I learned my business from the bottom up.* □ *I started out sweeping the floors and learned everything from the bottom up.*

learn (something) the hard way AND **find (something) out the hard way** to learn something by experience, especially by an unpleasant experience. □ *She learned how to make investments the hard way.* □ *I wish I didn't have to learn things the hard way.* □ *I found out the hard way that it's difficult to work and go to school at the same time.* □ *Investing in real estate is tricky. I found that out the hard way.*

learn the ropes to learn how to do something; to learn how to work something. (Informal. See also *know the ropes; show someone the ropes.*) □ *I'll be able to do my job very well as soon as I learn the ropes.* □ *John is very slow to learn the ropes.*

learn to live with something to learn to adapt to something unpleasant or painful. (See also *have to live with something.*) □ *Finally the doctor told Marion that she was going to have to learn to live with her arthritis.* □ *The floor plan of the house we bought is not* *as handy as we had thought, but we will learn to live with it.*

least of all least; of smallest importance. (Informal.) □ *There were many things wrong with the new house. Least of all, the water faucets leaked.* □ *What a bad day. Many things went wrong, but least of all, I tore my shirt.*

leave a bad taste in someone's mouth [for someone or something] to leave a bad feeling or memory with someone. (Informal. Also literal.) □ *The whole business about the missing money left a bad taste in his mouth.* □ *It was a very nice party, but something about it left a bad taste in my mouth.* □ *I'm sorry that Bill was there. He always leaves a bad taste in my mouth.*

leave a lot to be desired to be lacking something important; to be inadequate. (A polite way of saying that something is bad.) □ *This report leaves a lot to be desired.* □ *I'm sorry to have to fire you, Mary, but your work leaves a lot to be desired.*

leave a sinking ship See *desert a sinking ship.*

leave no stone unturned to search in all possible places. (As if one might find something under a rock.) □ *Don't worry. We'll find your stolen car. We'll leave no stone unturned.* □ *In searching for a nice place to live, we left no stone unturned.*

leave one to one's fate to abandon someone to whatever may happen — possibly death or some other unpleasant event. □ *We couldn't rescue the miners and were forced to leave them to their fate.* □ *Please don't try to help. Just go away and leave me to my fate.*

leave oneself wide open for something AND **leave oneself wide open to something** to invite criticism or joking about oneself; to fail to protect oneself from criticism or ridicule. □ *Yes, that was a harsh remark, Jane, but you left yourself wide open to it.* □ *I can't complain about your joke. I left myself wide open for it.*

leave oneself wide open to something See the previous entry.

leave someone flat (Informal.) **1.** to fail to entertain or stimulate someone. □ *Your joke left me flat.* □ *We listened carefully to his lecture, but it left us flat.* **2.** to leave someone without any money — flat broke. □ *Paying all my bills left me flat.* □ *The robber took all my money and left me flat.* **3.** to leave someone completely alone. □ *I was at the dance with Harry, but when he met Alice, he left me flat.* □ *They just walked off and left us flat.*

leave someone for dead to abandon someone as being dead. (The abandoned person may actually be alive.) □ *He looked so bad that they almost left him for dead.* □ *As the soldiers turned — leaving the enemy captain for dead — the captain fired at them.*

leave someone high and dry (Informal.) **1.** to leave someone unsupported and unable to maneuver; to leave someone helpless. (See also *high and dry.*) □ *All my workers quit and left me high and dry.* □ *All the children ran away and left Billy high and dry to take the blame for the broken window.* **2.** to leave someone *flat broke.* □ *Mrs. Franklin took all the money out of the bank and left Mr. Franklin high and dry.* □ *Paying the bills always leaves me high and dry.*

leave someone holding the bag to leave someone to take all the blame; to leave someone appearing guilty. (Informal.) □ *They all ran off and left me holding the bag. It wasn't even my fault.* □ *It was the mayor's fault, but he wasn't left holding the bag.*

leave someone in peace to stop bothering someone; to go away and leave someone in peace. (Does not necessarily mean to go away from a person.) □ *Please go — leave me in peace.* □ *Can't you see that you're upsetting her? Leave her in peace.*

leave someone in the lurch to leave someone waiting for or anticipating your actions. □ *Where were you,*

John? You really left me in the lurch. □ *I didn't mean to leave you in the lurch. I thought we had canceled our meeting.*

leave someone or something hanging in midair AND **keep someone or something hanging in midair** to suspend dealing with someone or something; to leave someone or something waiting to be finished or continued. (Also literal.) □ *She left her sentence hanging in midair.* □ *She left us hanging in midair when she paused.* □ *Tell me the rest of the story. Don't leave me hanging in midair.* □ *Don't leave the story hanging in midair.*

leave someone out in the cold to fail to inform someone; to exclude someone. (Informal. Compare with the previous entry. Also literal.) □ *I don't know what's going on. They left me out in the cold.* □ *Tom wasn't invited. They left him out in the cold.*

leave something for another occasion AND **keep something for another occasion** to hold back something for later. (*Occasion* can be replaced with *time, day, person,* etc.) □ *Please leave some cake for me.* □ *Don't eat all the turkey. Leave some for another day.* □ *I have to keep some of my paycheck for next month.*

leave something on to leave something running or operating. (Also literal in reference to wearing clothes.) □ *Please don't leave the light on.* □ *Ann went to school and left her radio on.*

leave something open to leave a date or time unscheduled. □ *I left something open on Friday, just in case we want to leave work early.* □ *Please leave something open for Mrs. Wallace next week. She will be calling in to our office for an appointment.*

leave well enough alone See *let well enough alone.*

leave word (with someone) to leave a message with someone (who will pass the message on to someone else). □ *If you decide to go to the convention, please leave word with my secretary.* □ *Leave word before you go.* □ *I left*

word with your brother. Didn't he give you the message?

left and right See *right and left.*

lend a hand (to someone) See *lend (someone) a hand.*

lend an ear (to someone) to listen to someone. □ *Lend an ear to John. Hear what he has to say.* □ *I'd be delighted to lend an ear. I find great wisdom in everything John has to say.*

lend color to something to provide an interesting accompaniment for something. □ *Your clever comments lent a great deal of color to the slide show of your vacation.* □ *The excellent master of ceremonies will lend color to an otherwise dry and uninteresting dance recital.*

lend oneself or itself to something [for someone or something] to be adaptable to something; [for someone or something] to be useful for something. □ *This room doesn't lend itself to bright colors.* □ *John doesn't lend himself to casual conversation.*

lend (someone) a hand AND **lend a hand (to someone)** to give someone some help, not necessarily with the hands. □ *Could you lend me a hand with this piano? I need to move it across the room.* □ *Could you lend a hand with this math assignment?* □ *I'd be happy to lend a hand.*

less than pleased displeased. □ *We were less than pleased to learn of your comments.* □ *Bill was less than pleased at the outcome of the election.*

let alone someone or something not to mention or think of someone or something; not even to take someone or something into account. □ *Do I have a dollar? I don't even have a dime, let alone a dollar.* □ *I didn't invite John, let alone the rest of his family.*

Let bygones be bygones. a proverb meaning that one should forget the problems of the past. □ *Okay, Sally, let bygones be bygones. Let's forgive and forget.* □ *Jane was unwilling to let* *bygones be bygones. She still won't speak to me.*

let go (with something) AND **cut loose (with something)**; **let loose (with something)** to shout something out or expel something; to shout or express something wildly. (Slang.) □ *The audience cut loose with a loud cheer.* □ *The whole team let go with a loud shout.* □ *John let loose with a horrendous belch.* □ *I wish you wouldn't let loose like that!*

let grass grow under one's feet to do nothing; to stand still. □ *Mary doesn't let the grass grow under her feet. She's always busy.* □ *Bob is too lazy. He's letting the grass grow under his feet.*

let her rip AND **let it roll** to go ahead and start something; let something begin. (Informal or slang. *Her* is usually *'er.*) □ *When Bill was ready for John to start the engine, he said, "Okay, John, let 'er rip."* □ *When Sally heard Bob say "Let 'er rip," she let the anchor go to the bottom of the lake.* □ *Let's go, Bill. Let it roll!*

let it all hang out to tell or reveal everything and hold back nothing (because one is relaxed or carefree). (Slang.) □ *Sally has no secrets. She lets it all hang out all the time.* □ *Relax, John. Let it all hang out.*

let it roll See *let her rip.*

let loose (with something) See *let go (with something).*

let off steam AND **blow off steam** to release excess energy or anger. (Informal. Also literal.) □ *Whenever John gets a little angry, he blows off steam.* □ *Don't worry about John. He's just letting off steam.*

let one's hair down to become more intimate and begin to speak frankly. (Informal.) □ *Come on, Jane, let your hair down and tell me all about it.* Ⓣ *I have a problem. Do you mind if I let down my hair?*

let oneself go to become less constrained; to get excited and have a good time. □ *I love to dance and just*

let myself go. □ *Let yourself go, John. Learn to enjoy life.*

Let sleeping dogs lie. a proverb meaning that one should not search for trouble or that one should leave well enough alone. □ *Don't mention that problem with Tom again. It's almost forgotten. Let sleeping dogs lie.* □ *You'll never be able to reform Bill. Leave him alone. Let sleeping dogs lie.*

let someone down to disappoint someone; to fail someone. (Also literal.) □ *I'm sorry I let you down. Something came up, and I couldn't meet you.* □ *I don't want to let you down, but I can't support you in the election.*

let someone go to dismiss someone from employment; to fire someone. □ *John was not working as well as we had hoped, and we had to let him go.* □ *They let a number of the older workers go and were faced with an age discrimination suit.*

let someone have it (with both barrels) to strike someone or attack someone verbally. (Informal. *With both barrels* simply intensifies the phrase.) □ *I really let Tom have it with both barrels. I told him he had better not do that again if he knows what's good for him.* □ *Bob let John have it—right on the chin.*

let someone in on something to tell someone the secret. (Informal. The *something* can be a *plan, arrangements, scheme, trick,* or anything else that might be kept a secret.) □ *Should we let John in on the secret?* □ *Please let me in on the plan.*

let someone off (the hook) to release someone from a responsibility. □ *Please let me off the hook for Saturday. I have other plans.* □ *Okay, I'll let you off.*

let someone or something off 1. [with *someone*] to release or dismiss someone without punishment. (See *get off easy.*) □ *The judge didn't let me off.* Ⓣ *The judge let off Mary with a warning.* **2.** [with *someone*] to permit someone to disembark or leave a means of transportation. □ *The driver let Mary off the bus.* □ *"I can't let you off at this corner," said the driver.* **3.** [with *something*] to release something; to give something off. ⊤ *The engine was letting off some kind of smoke.* ⊤ *The flower let off a wonderful smell.*

let something (get) out See *leak something (out).*

let something out to reveal something that is a secret. (Also literal.) □ *Please don't let this out, but I'm quitting my job.* ⊤ *John let out the secret by accident.*

let something ride to allow something to continue or remain as it is. (Informal.) □ *It isn't the best plan, but we'll let it ride.* □ *I disagree with you, but I'll let it ride.*

let something slide to neglect something. (Informal.) □ *John let his lessons slide.* □ *Jane doesn't let her work slide.*

let something slide by See the following entry.

let something slip by AND **let something slide by 1.** to forget or miss an important time or date. □ *I'm sorry I just let your birthday slip by.* □ *I let it slide by accidentally.* **2.** to waste a period of time. □ *You wasted the whole day by letting it slip by.* □ *We were having fun, and we let the time slide by.*

let something slip (out) to tell a secret by accident. □ *I didn't let it slip out on purpose. It was an accident.* □ *John let the plans slip when he was talking to Bill.*

let the cat out of the bag AND **spill the beans** to reveal a secret or a surprise by accident. □ *When Bill glanced at the door, he let the cat out of the bag. We knew then that he was expecting someone to arrive.* □ *We are planning a surprise party for Jane. Don't let the cat out of the bag.* □ *It's a secret. Try not to spill the beans.*

let the chance slip by to lose the opportunity (to do something). □ *When I*

was younger, I wanted to become a doctor, but I let the chance slip by.* □ *Don't let the chance slip by. Do it now!*

let things slide to ignore the things that one is supposed to do; to fall behind in the doing of one's work. □ *I am afraid that I have let things slide while I was recovering from my operation.* □ *If I let things slide for even one day, I get hopelessly behind in my work.*

let up (on someone or something) to take the pressure off someone or something; to *take it easy (on someone or something).* □ *Please let up on me. I can't work any faster, and you're making me nervous.* □ *Let up on the project. You're working too hard.* □ *Yes, I guess I had better let up.*

let well enough alone AND **leave well enough alone** to leave things as they are (and not try to improve them). □ *There isn't much more you can accomplish here. Why don't you just let well enough alone?* □ *This is as good as I can do. I'll stop and leave well enough alone.*

level with someone to be honest with someone. (Slang.) □ *Come on, Bill. Level with me. Did you do it?* □ *I'm leveling with you. I wasn't even in town. I couldn't have done it.*

lick one's chops to show one's eagerness to do something, especially to eat something. (This can be literal to some degree when it refers to the licking of one's lips in expectation of eating. Some animals, but not people, really do lick their chops.) □ *We could tell from the way the boys were licking their chops that they really wanted a turn at riding the motorcycle.* □ *Fred started licking his chops when he smelled the turkey roasting in the oven.*

lick one's lips to show eagerness or pleasure about a future event. (Informal. From the habit of people licking their lips when they are about to enjoy eating something.) □ *The children licked their lips at the sight of the cake.* □ *The author's readers were licking their lips in anticipation of her new* novel. □ *The journalist was licking his lips when he went off to interview the disgraced politician.*

lick something into shape AND **whip something into shape** to put something into good condition. (Informal.) □ *I have to lick this report into shape this morning.* □ *Let's all lend a hand and whip this house into shape. It's a mess.*

lie down on the job AND **lay down on the job** to do one's job poorly or not at all. (*Lay* is a common error for *lie.*) □ *Tom was fired because he was laying down on the job.* □ *You mean he was lying down on the job, don't you?* □ *Sorry, I was lying down on the job in English class.*

lie in state [for a corpse] to be on display in a public place. □ *The dead leader lay in state for three days in the country's main city.* □ *While the king lay in state, many people walked by and paid their respects.*

lie in wait for someone or something to wait quietly in ambush for someone or something. □ *The lion lay in wait for the zebra.* □ *The robber was lying in wait for a victim.*

lie low AND **lay low** to keep quiet and not be noticed; to avoid being conspicuous. (Informal. *Lay* is a common error for *lie.*) □ *I suggest you lie low for a few days.* □ *The robber said that he would lay low for a short time after the robbery.*

lie through one's teeth to lie boldly. □ *I knew she was lying through her teeth, but I didn't want to say so just then.* □ *I'm not lying through my teeth! I never do!*

life is too short life is short and there is no point in wasting it on things like worry, hatred, vengeance, etc. □ *I am not going to spend any more time trying to get even with Wally. Life's too short.* □ *It's a waste of time worrying about money. Life is too short for that.*

life of the party the type of person who is lively and helps make a party fun and exciting. □ *Bill is always the life of*

the party. Be sure to invite him. □ *Bob isn't exactly the life of the party, but he's polite.*

lift a hand (against someone or something) AND **raise a hand (against someone or something)** to threaten (to strike) someone or something. (Often in the negative. The *a hand* can be replaced with *one's hand.*) □ *She's very peaceful. She wouldn't lift a hand against a fly.* □ *That's right. She wouldn't lift a hand.* □ *Would you raise your hand against your own brother?*

light as a feather See *(as) light as a feather.*

light into someone or something See *lace into someone or something.*

light out (for somewhere) to depart in haste for somewhere. (Informal.) □ *The bus pulled away and lit out for the next stop.* □ *It's time I lit out for home.* □ *I should have lit out ten minutes ago.*

light out (of somewhere) to depart somewhere in haste. (Informal.) □ *It's time I lit out of here. I'm late for my next appointment.* □ *Look at that horse go. He really lit out of the starting gate.*

Lightning never strikes twice (in the same place). a saying meaning that it is extremely unlikely that the same misfortune will occur again in the same set of circumstances or to the same people. □ *Ever since the fire, Jean has been afraid that her house will catch fire again, but they say that lightning never strikes twice.* □ *Supposedly lightning never strikes twice, but the Smiths' house has been robbed twice this year.*

like a bat out of hell with great speed and force. (Use *hell* with caution.) □ *Did you see her leave? She left like a bat out of hell.* □ *The car sped down the street like a bat out of hell.*

like a bolt out of the blue suddenly and without warning. (Refers to a bolt of lightning coming out of a clear blue sky. See also *out of a clear blue sky.*)

□ *The news came to us like a bolt out of the blue.* □ *Like a bolt out of the blue, the boss came and fired us all.*

like a bump on a log unresponsive; immobile. □ *I spoke to him, but he just sat there like a bump on a log.* □ *Don't stand there like a bump on a log. Give me a hand!*

like a fish out of water appearing to be completely out of place; in a very awkward manner. □ *Vincent stood there in his rented tuxedo, looking like a fish out of water.* □ *Whenever I am with your friends, I feel like a fish out of water. What on earth do you see in them — or me?* □ *At a formal dance, John is like a fish out of water.*

like a house afire See the following entry.

like a house on fire AND **like a house afire** rapidly and with force. (Folksy.) □ *The truck came roaring down the road like a house on fire.* □ *The crowd burst through the gate like a house afire.*

like a sitting duck AND **like sitting ducks** unguarded; unsuspecting and unaware. (The second phrase is the plural form. See *be a sitting duck.*) □ *He was waiting there like a sitting duck — a perfect target for a mugger.* □ *The soldiers were standing at the top of the hill like sitting ducks. It's a wonder they weren't all killed.*

like a three-ring circus chaotic; exciting and busy. □ *Our household is like a three-ring circus on Monday mornings.* □ *This meeting is like a three-ring circus. Quiet down and listen!*

like crazy AND **like mad** furiously; very much, fast, many, or actively. (Slang.) □ *People are coming in here like crazy. There isn't enough room for them all.* □ *We sold ice cream like crazy. It was a very hot day.* □ *When she stubbed her toe, she started screaming like mad.*

like greased lightning very fast. (Folksy. Informal. See also *(as) quick as greased lightning.*) □ *He left the room like greased lightning.* □ *They fled the burning building like greased lightning.*

like it or lump it either accept it or drop dead. (Slang and fairly rude. Fixed order.) □ *I don't care whether you care for my attitude or not. You can just like it or lump it.* □ *This is all the food you get. Like it or lump it!*

like lambs to the slaughter quietly and without seeming to realize or complain about the likely difficulties or dangers of a situation. □ *Young men fighting in World War I simply went like lambs to the slaughter.* □ *Our team went on the football field like lambs to the slaughter to meet the league-leaders.*

like looking for a needle in a haystack engaged in a hopeless search. □ *Trying to find a white dog in the snow is like looking for a needle in a haystack.* □ *I tried to find my lost contact lens on the beach, but it was like looking for a needle in a haystack.*

like mad See *like crazy.*

like nothing on earth **1.** very untidy or very unattractive. (Informal.) □ *Joan arrived at the office looking like nothing on earth. She had fallen in the mud.* □ *Alice was like nothing on earth in that electric yellow dress.* **2.** very unusual; otherworldly. □ *The new car models look like nothing on earth this year.* □ *This cake is so good! It's like nothing on earth!*

like one of the family as if someone (or a pet) were a member of one's family. (Informal.) □ *We treat our dog like one of the family.* □ *We are very happy to have you stay with us, Bill. I hope you don't mind if we treat you like one of the family.*

like sitting ducks See *like a sitting duck.*

like water off a duck's back easily; without any apparent effect. □ *Insults rolled off John like water off a duck's back.* □ *The bullets had no effect on the steel door. They fell away like water off a duck's back.*

likely as not See *(as) likely as not.*

line of least resistance the course of action that will cause least trouble or effort. (Compare with *path of least resistance*.) □ *Jane won't stand up for her rights. She always takes the line of least resistance.* □ *Joan never states her point of view. She takes the line of least resistance and agrees with everyone else.*

line one's own pockets to make money for oneself in a greedy or dishonest fashion. (Slang.) □ *When it was discovered that the sales manager was lining her own pockets with commissions, she was fired.* □ *If you line your pockets while in public office, you'll get in serious trouble.*

line someone or something up with something to position someone or something (or a group) in reference to other things. (See also *fix someone up (with someone or something)*.) □ *Please line the chairs up with the floor tiles.* Ⓣ *Line up this brick with the bricks below and at both sides. That's the way you lay bricks.* Ⓣ *Line up the boys with the row of trees.*

line someone up (for something) to schedule someone for something; to arrange for someone to do or be something. □ *I lined gardeners up for the summer work on the gardens.* Ⓣ *I lined up four of my best friends to serve as ushers at my wedding.*

lion's share (of something) the larger share of something. □ *The elder boy always takes the lion's share of the food.* □ *Jim was supposed to divide the cake in two equal pieces but he took the lion's share.*

listen to reason to yield to a reasonable argument; to take the reasonable course. □ *Please listen to reason, and don't do something you'll regret.* □ *She got into trouble because she wouldn't listen to reason.*

little by little slowly, a bit at a time. □ *Little by little, he began to understand what we were talking about.* □ *The snail crossed the stone little by little.*

live a dog's life See *lead a dog's life.*

live and learn to increase one's knowledge by experience. (Also informal and folksy. Usually said when one is surprised to learn something. Fixed order.) □ *I didn't know that snakes could swim. Well, live and learn!* □ *John didn't know he should water his houseplants a little extra in the dry winter months. When they all died, he said, "Live and learn."*

live and let live not to interfere with other people's business or preferences. (Fixed order.) □ *I don't care what they do! Live and let live, I always say.* □ *Your parents are strict. Mine just live and let live.*

live beyond one's means to spend more money than one can afford. (Compare with *live within one's means*.) □ *The Browns are deeply in debt because they are living beyond their means.* □ *I keep a budget so that I don't live beyond my means.*

live by one's wits to survive by being clever. □ *When you're in the kind of business I'm in, you have to live by your wits.* □ *John was orphaned at the age of ten and grew up living by his wits.*

live for the moment to live without planning for the future. □ *John has no health or life insurance. He lives only for the moment.* □ *When you're young, you tend to live for the moment and not plan for your future security.*

live from hand to mouth to live in poor circumstances. (Informal.) □ *When both my parents were out of work, we lived from hand to mouth.* □ *We lived from hand to mouth during the war. Things were very difficult.*

live happily ever after to live in happiness after a specific event. (Usually found in fairy tales.) □ *The prince and the princess lived happily ever after.* □ *They went away from the horrible haunted castle and lived happily ever after.*

live high off the hog AND **live high on the hog; eat high on the hog** to live well and eat good food. (Folksy. Note the variation with *pretty*.) □ *After they discovered oil on their land, they lived pretty high on the hog.* □ *Looks like* *we're eating high on the hog tonight. What's the occasion?*

live high on the hog See the previous entry.

live in to live at the residence at which one works. (Said of servants.) □ *In order to be here early enough to prepare breakfast, the cook has to live in.* □ *Mr. Simpson has a valet, but he doesn't live in.*

live in an ivory tower to be aloof from the realities of living. (*Live* can be replaced by a number of expressions meaning to dwell or spend time, as in the first example.) □ *If you didn't spend so much time in your ivory tower, you'd know what people really think!* □ *Many professors are said to live in ivory towers. They don't know what the real world is like.*

live it up to have an exciting time; to do what one pleases—regardless of cost—to please oneself. □ *At the party, John was really living it up.* □ *Come on! Have fun! Live it up!* □ *They spent a week in Mexico living it up and then came home broke.*

live off the fat of the land to grow one's own food; to live on stored-up resources or abundant resources. □ *If I had a million dollars, I'd invest it and live off the fat of the land.* □ *I'll be happy to retire soon and live off the fat of the land.* □ *Many farmers live off the fat of the land.*

live on borrowed time to live longer than circumstances warrant. □ *John has a terminal disease, and he's living on borrowed time.* □ *This project is living on borrowed time. It is overdue for completion.*

live out of a suitcase to live briefly in a place, never unpacking one's luggage. □ *I hate living out of a suitcase. For my next vacation, I want to go to just one place and stay there the whole time.* □ *We were living out of suitcases in a motel while they repaired the damage the fire caused to our house.*

live something down to overcome the shame or embarrassment of some-

thing. □ *You'll live it down someday.* ⊤ *Max will never be able to live down what happened at the party last night.*

live through something to endure something. □ *I thought I'd never be able to live through the lecture. It was so boring.* □ *I just can't live through another day like this.*

live up to something to fulfill expectations; to satisfy a set of goals. (Often with *one's reputation, promise, word, standards,* etc.) □ *I hope I can live up to my reputation.* □ *The class lives up to its reputation of being exciting and interesting.* □ *He never lives up to his promises.* □ *She was unable to live up to her own high standards.*

live within one's means to spend no more money than one has. (Compare with *live beyond one's means.*) □ *We have to struggle to live within our means, but we manage.* □ *John is unable to live within his means.*

loaded for bear (Slang and folksy.) **1.** angry. □ *He left here in a rage. He was really loaded for bear.* □ *When I got home from work, I was really loaded for bear. What a horrible day!* **2.** drunk. (An elaboration of *loaded,* which means "drunk.") □ *By the end of the party, Bill was loaded for bear.* □ *The whole gang drank for an hour until they were loaded for bear.*

lock horns (with someone) to get into an argument with someone. (Informal.) □ *Let's settle this peacefully. I don't want to lock horns with the boss.* □ *The boss doesn't want to lock horns either.*

lock something in to make something, such as a rate of interest, permanent over a period of time. (Informal.) □ *We locked in an 11 percent rate on our mortgage.* □ *You should try to lock in a high percentage rate on your bonds.*

lock, stock, and barrel everything. (Fixed order.) □ *We had to move everything out of the house—lock, stock, and barrel.* □ *We lost everything—lock, stock, and barrel—in the fire.*

long and (the) short of it the whole story; all the necessary facts. (Fixed order.) □ *I was late and I missed my train, and that's the long and short of it.* □ *Soon after the big green frog turned into a handsome prince, Princess Ellen and her newfound love went to live happily ever after in a kingdom by the sea, and that's the long and the short of it.*

Long time no see. not to have seen someone for a long time. (Informal.) □ *Hello, John. Long time no see.* □ *When John and Mary met on the street, they both said, "Long time no see."*

look as if butter wouldn't melt in one's mouth to appear to be cold and unfeeling (despite any information to the contrary). □ *Sally looks as if butter wouldn't melt in her mouth. She can be so cruel.* □ *What a sour face. He looks as if butter wouldn't melt in his mouth.*

look at someone cross-eyed to do something slightly provocative. (Informal.) □ *Bob is very excitable. He'd lose his temper if anyone so much as looked at him cross-eyed.* Ⓣ *Don't even look cross-eyed at the boss this morning unless you want trouble.*

look daggers at someone to give someone a dirty look. (Compare with *look at someone cross-eyed*.) □ *Tom must have been mad at Ann from the way he was looking daggers at her.* □ *Don't you dare look daggers at me! Don't even look cross-eyed at me!*

look down on someone or something AND **look down one's nose at someone or something** to regard someone or something with contempt or displeasure. □ *I think that John liked Mary, although he did seem to look down on her.* □ *Don't look down your nose at my car just because it's rusty and noisy.*

look down one's nose at someone or something See the previous entry.

look for trouble See *ask for trouble.*

look forward to something to anticipate something with pleasure. □ *I'm really looking forward to your visit next week.* □ *We all look forward to your new book on gardening.*

look high and low (for someone or something) See *hunt high and low (for someone or something).*

look in (on someone or something) AND **check in (on someone or something)** to see to the welfare of someone or something; to visit someone or something. □ *I'll stop by your house and look in on things while you're on vacation.* □ *Yes, just look in and make sure nothing is wrong.* □ *I checked in on John yesterday. He's almost over his illness.* □ *He was glad I checked in.*

look into something AND **check into something; see into something** to investigate something. □ *I'll have to look into that matter.* □ *The police checked into her story.* □ *Don't worry about your problem. I'll see into it.*

look like a million dollars to look very good. □ *Oh, Sally, you look like a million dollars.* □ *Your new hairdo looks like a million dollars.*

look like death warmed over to look quite ill; to look as pale as a dead person. □ *Poor Tom had quite a shock. He looks like death warmed over.* □ *After her long ordeal with chemotherapy, she looked like death warmed over.*

look like something to give the appearance of predicting (something). □ *The sky looks like rain.* □ *No, it looks like snow.* □ *Oh, oh. This looks like trouble. Let's go.*

look like something the cat dragged in to look very shabby, worn, exhausted, or abused. (Informal. Sometimes with *drug.*) □ *That new sofa of theirs looks like something the cat dragged in.* □ *Poor Dave looks like something the cat drug in. He must have been out late last night.*

look like the cat that swallowed the canary to appear as if one had just had a great success. □ *After the meeting John looked like the cat that swallowed the canary. I knew he must have been a success.* □ *What happened? You look like the cat that swallowed the canary.*

look on someone as something to view or think of someone as something. □ *I look on you as a very thoughtful person.* □ *Mary looked on Jane as a good friend.*

look out See under *watch out for someone or something.*

look out for someone or something See *watch out for someone or something.*

look someone in the eye See the following entry.

look someone in the face AND **look someone in the eye; stare someone in the face** to face someone directly. (Facing someone this way should assure sincerity.) □ *I don't believe you. Look me in the eye and say that.* □ *She looked him in the face and said she never wanted to see him again.* □ *I dare you to stare him in the face and say that!*

look someone or something over to examine someone or something carefully. □ *She looked him over and decided to hire him.* T *Please look over this report.*

look someone or something up AND **hunt someone or something up** to search for and find someone or something. □ *I don't know where the hammer is. I'll have to hunt it up.* □ *Ann looked the word up in the dictionary.* T *Would you please look up John? I need to talk to him.*

look the other way to ignore (something) on purpose. (Also literal.) □ *John could have prevented the problem, but he looked the other way.* □ *By looking the other way, he actually made the problem worse.*

look to one's laurels to take care not to lower or diminish one's reputation or position, especially in relation to that of someone else potentially better. □ *With the arrival of the new member of the football team, James will have to look to his laurels to remain as the highest scorer.* □ *The older members of the team will have to look to their laurels when young people join.*

look to someone or something (for something) to expect someone or something to supply something. □ *Children look to their parents for help.* □ *Tom looked to the bank for a loan.* □ *Most people who need to borrow money look to a bank.*

look up to someone to view someone with respect and admiration. □ *Bill really looks up to his father.* □ *Everyone in the class looked up to the teacher.*

loom large (on the horizon) to be of great importance, especially when referring to a possible problem, danger, or threat. □ *The exams were looming large on the horizon.* □ *Eviction was looming large when the students could not pay their rent.*

lord it over someone to dominate someone; to direct and control someone. □ *Mr. Smith seems to lord it over his wife.* □ *The boss lords it over everyone in the office.*

lose face to lose status; to become less respectable. □ *John is more afraid of losing face than losing money.* □ *Things will go better if you can explain to him where he was wrong without making him lose face.*

lose ground to fall behind; to fall back. □ *She was recovering nicely yesterday, but she lost ground last night.* □ *We are losing ground in our fight against mosquitoes.*

lose heart to lose one's courage or confidence. □ *Now, don't lose heart. Keep trying.* □ *What a disappointment! It's enough to make one lose heart.*

lose one's cool AND **blow one's cool** to lose one's temper; to lose one's nerve. (Slang.) □ *Wow, he really lost his cool! What a tantrum!* □ *Whatever you do, don't blow your cool.*

lose one's grip 1. to lose one's grasp (of something). □ *I'm holding on to the rope as tightly as I can. I hope I don't lose my grip.* □ *This hammer is slippery. Try not to lose your grip.* **2.** to lose control (over something). □ *I can't seem to run things the way I used to.*

I'm losing my grip. □ *They replaced the board of directors because it was losing its grip.*

lose one's head (over someone or something) to become confused or "crazy" about someone or something. (Refers especially to emotional attachments.) □ *Don't lose your head over John. He isn't worth it.* □ *I'm sorry. I got upset and lost my head.*

lose one's marbles AND **lose one's mind** to go crazy; to go out of one's mind. (The first phrase is slang. See also *not have all one's marbles.*) □ *What a silly thing to say! Have you lost your marbles?* □ *I can't seem to remember anything. I think I'm losing my mind.*

lose one's mind See the previous entry.

lose one's reason to lose one's power of reasoning, possibly in anger. □ *I was so confused that I almost lost my reason.* □ *Bob seems to have lost his reason when he struck John.*

lose one's shirt to lose all of one's assets (including one's shirt). (Slang. Never literal.) □ *I almost lost my shirt on that deal. I have to invest more wisely.* □ *No, I can't loan you $200. I just lost my shirt at the racetrack.*

lose one's temper to become angry. □ *Please don't lose your temper. It's not good for you.* □ *I'm sorry that I lost my temper.*

lose one's touch (with someone or something) to lose one's ability to handle someone or something. □ *I seem to have lost my touch with my children. They won't mind me anymore.* □ *We've both lost our touch as far as managing people goes.* □ *Tom said that he had lost his touch with the stock market.*

lose one's train of thought to forget what one was talking or thinking about. (See also *train of thought.*) □ *Excuse me, I lost my train of thought. What was I talking about?* □ *You made the speaker lose her train of thought.*

lose oneself (in something) to become deeply involved in something (so that everything else is forgotten). □ *Jane has a tendency to lose herself in her work.* □ *I often lose myself in thought.* □ *Excuse me, I lost myself for a moment.*

lose out (on something) See *miss out (on something).*

lose out to someone or something to lose a competition to someone or something. □ *Our team lost out to the other team.* □ *Bill lost out to Sally in the contest.*

lose sleep (over someone or something) to worry about someone or something. □ *I keep losing sleep over my son, who is in the army.* □ *Do you lose sleep over your investments?* □ *No, I don't lose sleep, and I never worry.*

lose touch (with someone or something) to lose contact with someone or something. (Compare with *keep in touch (with someone).*) □ *Poor Sally has lost touch with reality.* □ *I've lost touch with all my relatives.* □ *Jane didn't mean to lose touch, but she did.*

lose track (of someone or something) to forget where someone or something is; to lose or misplace someone or something. □ *I've lost track of the time.* □ *The mother lost track of her child and started calling her.* □ *When I get tired, I tend to lose track.*

lost-and-found an office or department that handles items that someone has lost that have been found by someone. (Each item is both lost by someone and found by someone. Fixed order.) □ *The lost-and-found office had an enormous collection of umbrellas and four sets of false teeth!* □ *I found a book on the seat of the bus. I turned it in to the driver, who gave it to the lost-and-found office.*

lost and gone forever lost; permanently lost. (Fixed order.) □ *My poor doggy is lost and gone forever.* □ *My money fell out of my pocket and I am sure that it is lost and gone forever.*

lost cause a futile attempt; a hopeless matter. □ *Our campaign to have the new party on the ballot was a lost cause.* □ *Todd gave it up as a lost cause.*

lost in thought busy thinking. □ *I'm sorry, I didn't hear what you said. I was lost in thought.* □ *Bill — lost in thought as always — went into the wrong room.*

lost on someone having no effect on someone; wasted on someone. (Informal.) □ *The joke was lost on Jean. She didn't understand it.* □ *The humor of the situation was lost on Mary. She was too upset to see it.*

loud and clear clear and distinctly. (Originally said of radio reception that is heard clearly and distinctly. Fixed order.) □ TOM: *If I've told you once, I've told you a thousand times: Stop it! Do you hear me?* BILL: *Yes, loud and clear.* □ *I hear you loud and clear.*

louse something up to mess up or ruin something. (Slang.) □ *I've worked hard on this. Please don't louse it up.* ⊤ *You've loused up all my plans.*

lousy with something with something in abundance. (Slang.) □ *This place is lousy with cops.* □ *Our picnic table was lousy with ants.*

love at first sight love established when two people first see one another. □ *Bill was standing at the door when Ann opened it. It was love at first sight.* □ *It was love at first sight when they met, but it didn't last long.*

lovely weather for ducks rainy weather. □ BOB: *Not very nice out today, is it?* BILL: *It's lovely weather for ducks.* □ *I don't like this weather, but it's lovely weather for ducks.*

low man on the totem pole the least important person. (Compare with *high man on the totem pole.*) □ *I was the last to find out because I'm low man on the totem pole.* □ *I can't be of any help. I'm low man on the totem pole.*

lower one's sights to set one's goals lower. □ *Even though you get frustrated, don't lower your sights.* □ *I shouldn't lower my sights. If I work hard, I can do what I want.*

lower one's voice to speak more softly. □ *Please lower your voice, or you'll disturb the people who are working.* □ *He wouldn't lower his voice, so everyone heard what he said.*

lower the boom on someone to scold or punish someone severely; to crack down on someone; to *throw the book at someone.* (Informal.) □ *If Bob won't behave better, I'll have to lower the boom on him.* □ *The teacher lowered the boom on the whole class for misbehaving.*

luck out to get lucky (about something). (Slang.) □ *I won $100 in the lottery. I really lucked out.* □ *Bob lucked out when he got an easy teacher for geometry.*

lull someone into a false sense of security to lead someone into believing that all is well before attacking or doing someone bad. □ *We lulled the enemy into a false sense of security by pretending to retreat. Then we launched an attack.* □ *The boss lulled us into a false sense of security by saying that our jobs were safe and then let half the staff go.*

M

mad about someone or something See *crazy about someone or something*.

mad as a hatter See *(as) mad as a hatter*.

mad as a hornet See *(as) mad as a hornet*.

mad as a March hare See *(as) mad as a March hare*.

mad as a wet hen See *(as) mad as a wet hen*.

mad as hell See *(as) mad as hell*.

made for each other [for two people] to be very well suited romantically. □ *Bill and Jane were made for each other.* □ *Mr. and Mrs. Smith were not exactly made for each other. They really don't get along.*

made to measure [of clothing] made especially to fit the measurements of a particular person. □ *Jack has his suits made to measure because he's rather large.* □ *Having clothes made to measure is rather expensive.*

made to order put together on request. (Compare with *in stock*.) □ *This suit fits so well because it's made to order.* □ *His feet are so big that all his shoes have to be made to order.*

maiden voyage the first voyage of a ship or boat. □ *The liner sank on its maiden voyage.* □ *Jim is taking his yacht on its maiden voyage.*

main strength and awkwardness great force; brute force. (Folksy. Fixed order.) □ *They finally got the piano moved in to the living room by main strength and awkwardness.* □ *Lifting the table must be done carefully. This is* not a job requiring main strength and awkwardness.

make a beeline for someone or something to head straight toward someone or something. (Informal. Also literal for bees in flight.) □ *Billy came into the kitchen and made a beeline for the cookies.* □ *After the game, we all made a beeline for John, who was serving cold drinks.*

make a big deal about something See *make a federal case out of something*.

make a break for something or somewhere to move or run quickly to something or somewhere. (Informal.) □ *Before we could stop her, she made a break for the door and got away.* □ *The mouse got frightened and made a break for a hole in the wall.*

make a bundle AND **make a pile** to make a lot of money. (Slang.) □ *John really made a bundle on that deal.* □ *I'd like to make a pile and retire.*

make a check out (to someone) to write a check naming someone as payee. □ *Please make a check out to John Jones.* ⊤ *Do you want cash, or should I make out a check?*

make a clean breast of something to confess something; to *get something off one's chest*. □ *You'll feel better if you make a clean breast of it. Now tell us what happened.* □ *I was forced to make a clean breast of the whole affair.*

make a clean sweep to do something completely or thoroughly, with no exceptions. (Informal.) □ *The boss decided to fire everybody, so he made a clean sweep.* □ *They made a clean* *sweep through the neighborhood, repairing all the sidewalks.*

make a comeback to return to one's former (successful) career. (Informal.) □ *After ten years in retirement, the singer made a comeback.* □ *You're never too old to make a comeback.*

make a day of doing something AND **make a day of it** to spend the whole day doing something. □ *We went to the museum to see the new exhibit and then decided to make a day of it.* □ *They made a day of cleaning the attic.*

make a day of it See the previous entry.

make a dent in something to begin to consume or accomplish something. (Informal. Also literal.) □ *Bob, you've hardly made a dent in your dinner!* □ *There is a lot of rice left. We hardly made a dent in it all week.* □ *Get busy! You haven't even made a dent in your work.*

make a face (at someone) 1. to make a face at someone in ridicule. □ *Mother, Billy made a face at me!* □ *The teacher sent Jane to the principal for making a face in class.* 2. to attempt to communicate to someone through facial gestures, usually an attempt to say "no" or "stop." □ *I started to tell John where I was last night, but Bill made a face so I didn't.* □ *John made a face at me as I was testifying, so I avoided telling everything.*

make a fast buck AND **make a quick buck** to make money with little effort. (Slang.) □ *Tom is always ready to make a fast buck.* □ *I made a quick buck selling used cars.*

make a federal case out of something AND **make a big deal about something** to exaggerate the seriousness of something. (Slang.) □ *Come on. It was nothing! Don't make a federal case out of it.* □ *I only stepped on your toe. Don't make a big deal about it.*

make a fool out of someone AND **make a monkey out of someone** to make someone look foolish. □ *John made a monkey out of himself while trying to make a fool out of Jim.* □ *John made*

a fool out of himself at the party. □ *Are you trying to make a monkey out of me?*

make a fuss (over someone or something) AND **make over someone or something** 1. to worry about or make a bother about someone or something. □ *Why do you fuss over a problem like that?* □ *Please don't make a fuss. Everything will be all right.* □ *Don't make over me so much!* 2. to be very solicitous and helpful toward a person or a pet. □ *How can anyone make a fuss over a cat?* □ *Billy was embarrassed when his mother made a fuss over him.* 3. to argue about someone or something. □ *Please don't make a fuss over who gets the last cookie.* □ *Please discuss it. Don't fuss about it!*

make a go of it to make something work out all right. (Informal.) □ *It's a tough situation, but Ann is trying to make a go of it.* □ *We don't like living here, but we have to make a go of it.*

make a great show of something to make something obvious; to do something in a showy fashion. □ *Ann made a great show of wiping up the drink that John spilled.* □ *Jane displayed her irritation at our late arrival by making a great show of serving the cold dinner.*

make a hit (with someone or something) to please someone. (Informal.) □ *The singer made a hit with the audience.* □ *She was afraid she wouldn't make a hit.* □ *John made a hit with my parents last evening.*

make a killing to have a great success, especially in making money. (Slang.) □ *John has got a job selling insurance. He's not exactly making a killing.* □ *Bill made a killing at the racetrack yesterday.*

make a laughingstock of oneself or something AND **make oneself or something a laughingstock** to make oneself a source of ridicule or laughter; to do something that invites ridicule. □ *Laura made herself a laughingstock by arriving at the fast-food restaurant in full evening dress.* □ *The board of directors made the company a* *laughingstock by hiring an ex-convict as president.*

make a living to earn enough money to live on. □ *I'll be glad when I get a job and can make a living.* □ *I can hardly make a living with the skills I have.*

make a long story short to bring a story to an end. (A formula that introduces a summary of a story or a joke.) □ *And—to make a long story short—I never got back the money that I lent him.* □ *If I can make a long story short, let me say that everything worked out fine.*

make a meal of something to eat only a large portion of one kind of food as an entire meal. □ *There were lots of salad makings, so we fixed a large salad and made a meal of it.* □ *We had tons of leftover turkey after the festival, so the next day we sat down and made a meal of it.*

make a monkey out of someone See *make a fool out of someone.*

make a mountain out of a molehill to make a major issue out of a minor one; to exaggerate the importance of something. □ *Come on, don't make a mountain out of a molehill. It's not that important.* □ *Mary is always making mountains out of molehills.*

make a name (for oneself) to become famous. □ *Sally wants to work hard and make a name for herself.* □ *It's hard to make a name without a lot of talent and hard work.*

make a night of doing something to do something for the entire night. □ *We partied until three in the morning and then decided to make a night of it.* □ *Once or twice in the early spring we make a night of fishing.*

make a note of something to write something down. □ *Please make a note of this address.* □ *This is important. Make a note of it.*

make a nuisance of oneself to be a constant bother. □ *I'm sorry to make a nuisance of myself, but I do need an answer to my question.* □ *Stop making a nuisance of yourself and wait your turn.*

make a pass at someone to flirt with someone; to make a romantic advance at someone. (This often has sexual implications. Compare with *make a play (for someone).)* □ *I was shocked when Ann made a pass at me.* □ *I think Bob was making a pass at me, but he did it very subtly.*

make a pile See *make a bundle.*

make a pitch (for someone or something) to say something in support of someone or something; to attempt to promote or advance someone or something. (Informal.) □ *Bill is making a pitch for his friend's new product again.* □ *The theatrical agent came in and made a pitch for her client.* □ *Every time I turn on the television set, someone is making a pitch.*

make a play (for someone) to attempt to attract the romantic interest of someone. (Informal. Compare with *make a pass at someone.)* □ *Ann made a play for Bill, but he wasn't interested in her.* □ *I knew he liked me, but I never thought he'd make a play.*

make a point to state an item of importance. (Also literal, as in sports and games.) □ *You made a point that we all should remember.* □ *He spoke for an hour without making a point.*

make a point of doing something to make an effort to do something. □ *Please make a point of mailing this letter. It's very important.* □ *The hostess made a point of thanking me for bringing flowers.*

make a point of someone or something AND **make an issue of someone or something** to turn someone or something into an important matter. □ *Please don't make a point of John's comment. It wasn't that important.* □ *I hope you make an issue of Tom's success and the reasons for it.* □ *Tom has a lot of problems. Please don't make an issue of him.*

make a practice of something AND **make something a practice** to turn something into a habitual activity. □ *Jane makes a practice of planting daisies every summer.* □ *Her mother also made it a practice.*

make a quick buck See *make a fast buck.*

make a run for it to run fast to get away or get somewhere. (Informal. Compare with *make a break for something or somewhere.*) □ *When the guard wasn't looking, the prisoner made a run for it.* □ *In the baseball game, the player on first base made a run for it, but he didn't make it to second base.*

make a scene AND **create a scene** to make a public display or disturbance. □ *When John found a fly in his drink, he started to create a scene.* □ *Oh, John, please don't make a scene. Just forget about it.*

make a silk purse out of a sow's ear to create something of value out of something of no value. (Often in the negative.) □ *Don't bother trying to fix up this old bicycle. You can't make a silk purse out of a sow's ear.* □ *My mother made a lovely jacket out of an old coat. She succeeded in making a silk purse out of a sow's ear.*

make a stink (about something) See *create a stink (about something).*

make allowance(s) (for someone or something) 1. to allow time, space, food, etc., for someone or something. □ *When planning the party, please make allowances for John and his family.* □ *I'm making allowance for ten extra guests.* 2. to make excuses or explanations for someone or something; to take into consideration the negative effects of someone or something. □ *You're very late even when we make allowance for the weather.* □ *We have to make allowance for the age of the house when we judge its condition.*

make an all-out effort to make a thorough and energetic effort. (See also *all-out effort.*) □ *Sally made an all-out effort to get to class on time.* □ *In my job, I have to make an all-out effort every day.*

make an appearance to appear; to appear in a performance. (Compare with *put in an appearance.*) □ *We waited for thirty minutes for the professor to make an appearance, then we went home.* □ *The famous singing star made an appearance in Detroit last August.*

make an appointment (with someone) to schedule a meeting with someone. □ *I made an appointment with the doctor for late today.* □ *The professor wouldn't see me unless I made an appointment.*

make an example of someone to make a public issue out of someone's bad behavior. □ *The judge decided to make an example of John, so he fined him the full amount.* □ *The teacher made an example of Mary, who disturbed the class constantly with her whispering.*

make an exception (for someone) to suspend a rule or practice for someone in a single instance. □ *Please make an exception just this once.* □ *The rule is a good one, and I will not make an exception for anyone.*

make an exhibition of oneself to embarrass oneself by showing off or doing something daring in public. (Sometimes under the influence of alcohol.) □ *You can be certain that Joan will have too much to drink and make an exhibition of herself.* □ *Sit down and be quiet. Stop making an exhibition of yourself.*

make an impression (on someone) to produce a memorable effect on someone. (Often with *good, bad,* or some other adjective.) □ *Tom made a bad impression on the banker.* □ *I'm afraid that you haven't made a very good impression on our visitors.* □ *You made quite an impression on my father.*

make an issue of someone or something See *make a point of someone or something.*

make an uproar See *create an uproar.*

make arrangements (for someone or something) 1. to make plans for someone or something. □ *I'm making arrangements for the convention.* □ *It starts next week, and I hardly have time to make arrangements.* **2.** [with *someone*] to plan accommodations for someone. □ *John is coming for a visit next week. Please make arrangements for him at the hotel.* □ *I will make arrangements for everyone when I call the hotel.*

make as if to do something to act as if one were about to do something. □ *The thief made as if to run away but changed his mind.* □ *Jane made as if to smack the child.*

make away with someone or something AND **make off with someone or something** to take someone or something away; to make someone or something disappear. □ *The robber made away with the jewelry.* □ *The maid quickly made off with the children. We only saw them for a moment.*

make book on something to make or accept bets on something. (Slang.) □ *It looks as if it will rain, but I wouldn't make book on it.* □ *John's making book on the football game this Saturday.*

make (both) ends meet to manage to live on a small amount of money. □ *It's hard these days to make ends meet.* □ *I have to work overtime to make both ends meet.*

make chin music to talk or chatter. (Slang.) □ *We sat around all evening making chin music.* □ *You were making chin music when you should have been listening.*

make cracks (about someone or something) to ridicule or make jokes about someone or something. (Informal.) □ *Please stop making cracks about my haircut. It's the new style.* □ *Some people can't help making cracks. They are just rude.*

make do (with someone or something) to do as well as possible with someone or something. □ *You'll have to make do with less money next year. The economy is very weak.* □ *We'll have to*

make do with John even though he's a slow worker. □ *Yes, we'll have to make do.*

make eyes (at someone) to flirt with someone. □ *Tom spent all afternoon making eyes at Ann.* □ *How could they sit there in class making eyes?*

make fast work of someone or something See *make short work of someone or something*.

make for somewhere to run or travel to somewhere. (Slang, especially criminal slang.) □ *When I got out of class, I made for the gym.* □ *When he got out of jail, he made for Toledo.*

make free with someone or something **1.** [with *someone*] See *take liberties with someone or something.* **2.** [with *something*] to take advantage of or use something as if it were one's own. (Compare with *take liberties with someone or something.*) □ *I wish you wouldn't come into my house and make free with my food and drink.* □ *Please make free with my car while I'm gone.*

make fun (of someone or something) to ridicule someone or something. □ *Please stop making fun of me. It hurts my feelings.* □ *Billy teases and makes fun a lot, but he means no harm.*

make good as something to succeed in a particular role. □ *I hope I make good as a teacher.* □ *John made good as a football player.*

make good (at something) to succeed at something. □ *Bob worked hard to make good at selling.* □ *Jane was determined to make good.*

make good money to earn a large amount of money. (Informal.) □ *Ann makes good money at her job.* □ *I don't know what she does, but she makes good money.*

make good on something **1.** to fulfill a promise. □ *Tom made good on his pledge to donate $1,000.* □ *Bill refused to make good on his promise.* **2.** to repay a debt. (See also *make something good.*) □ *I couldn't make good on my debts, and I got in a lot of trouble.* □ *If* *you don't make good on this bill, I'll have to take back your car.*

make good time to proceed at a fast or reasonable rate. (Informal.) □ *On our trip to Toledo, we made good time.* □ *I'm making good time, but I have a long way to go.*

make good time to travel fast; to progress rapidly. □ *I am making good time. My report is almost finished.* □ *Now that we are clear of the city traffic, we can make good time.*

make hamburger out of someone or something AND **make mincemeat out of someone or something** to beat up or overcome someone or something. (Slang. Literal when referring to foodstuffs. Figurative with people.) □ *Stop acting silly, or I'll make hamburger out of you.* □ *Our team made mincemeat out of the other team.*

make it to succeed. (See also *make something.*) □ *I hope Bob's new business makes it.* □ *Donna wants to graduate this year. I hope she makes it.*

make it hot for someone to make things difficult for someone; to put someone under pressure. (Slang.) □ *Maybe if we make it hot for them, they'll leave.* □ *John likes making it hot for people. He's sort of mean.*

make it one's business to do something AND **take it upon oneself to do something** to do something on one's own even if it means interfering in something that does not directly concern one. (As opposed to minding one's own business.) □ *I know I doesn't concern me, but I made it my business to call city hall because someone had to.* □ *Jane took it upon herself to find out exactly what had happened to the old lady.*

make it (until something) AND **make it to something; make it as far as something** to endure until something; to last until some time. □ *I hope my car can make it to the next town.* □ *Do you think you can make it until we come to a stopping point?* □ *I made it*

as far as the first turn and decided to give up.

make it worth someone's while to make something profitable enough for someone to do. (See also *worth someone's while.*) □ *If you deliver this parcel for me, I'll make it worth your while.* □ *The boss said he'd make it worth our while if we worked late.*

make life miserable for someone to make someone unhappy over a long period of time. □ *My shoes are tight, and they are making life miserable for me.* □ *Jane's boss is making life miserable for her.*

make light of something to treat something as if it were unimportant or humorous. □ *I wish you wouldn't make light of his problems. They're quite serious.* □ *I make light of my problems, and that makes me feel better.*

make little of someone or something to minimize someone or something; to *play someone or something down;* to belittle someone or something. □ *John made little of my efforts to collect money for charity.* □ *The neighbors made little of John and thought he would amount to nothing.*

make love (to someone) to share physical or emotional love (or both) with someone. (This phrase usually has a sexual meaning.) □ *Tom and Ann turned out the lights and made love.* □ *The actress refused to make love to the leading man on stage.*

make merry to have fun; to have an enjoyable time. □ *The guests certainly made merry at the wedding.* □ *The children were making merry in the backyard.*

make mincemeat out of someone or something See *make hamburger out of someone or something.*

make mischief to cause trouble. □ *Bob loves to make mischief and get other people into trouble.* □ *Don't believe what Mary says. She's just trying to make mischief.*

make no bones about it to *make no mistake (about it);* no need to doubt it; absolutely. (Folksy.) □ *This is the greatest cake I've ever eaten. Make no bones about it.* □ *Make no bones about it, Mary is a great singer.*

make no difference (to someone) not to matter to someone; for someone not to care (about something). □ *It makes no difference to me what you do.* □ *Do whatever you want. It really makes no difference.*

make no mistake (about it) without a doubt; certainly. (Informal.) □ *This car is a great buy. Make no mistake about it.* □ *We support your candidacy — make no mistake.*

make nothing of something to ignore something as if it had not happened; to think no more about something. (Often with *it*.) □ *My father caught me throwing the snowball, but he made nothing of it.* □ *I made nothing of the remark, even though it seemed quite rude.* □ *I saw him leave, but I made nothing of it.*

make off with someone or something See *make away with someone or something.*

make one's mind up to decide. □ *Please make your mind up. Which do you want?* Ⓣ *Would you help me make up my mind?*

make one's way through something See *pick one's way through something.*

make oneself at home to make oneself comfortable as if one were in one's own home. □ *Please come in and make yourself at home.* □ *I'm glad you're here. During your visit, just make yourself at home.*

make oneself conspicuous to attract attention to oneself. □ *Please don't make yourself conspicuous. It embarrasses me.* □ *Ann makes herself conspicuous by wearing brightly colored clothing.*

make oneself or something a laughingstock See *make a laughingstock of oneself or something.*

make oneself scarce to go away. (Slang.) □ *Hey, kid, go away. Make*

yourself scarce. □ *When there is work to be done, I make myself scarce.*

make (oneself) up to put makeup on oneself. □ *I have to make up now. I go on stage in ten minutes.* □ *I will make myself up. I don't need your help.*

make or break someone either to improve or ruin someone. (Fixed order.) □ *The army will either make or break him.* □ *It's a tough assignment, and it will either make or break her.*

make out (with someone or something) 1. to manage to do (something) with someone or something. □ *I think I can make out with this hammer.* □ *If I can't make out with John, I'll have to ask for more help.* 2. [with *someone*] to flirt with, kiss, or hug someone; to make love (to someone). (Slang.) □ *Bob was trying to make out with Sally all evening.* □ *She didn't want to make out, so she left.*

make over someone or something See *make a fuss (over someone or something).*

make peace (with someone) to end a quarrel with someone. (Compare with *kiss and make up*.) □ *Don't you think it's time to make peace with your brother? There is no point in arguing anymore.* □ *Yes, it's time we made peace.*

make points (with someone) to gain favor with someone. (Slang.) □ *Tom is trying to make points with Ann. He wants to ask her out.* □ *He's trying to make points by smiling and telling her how nice she looks.*

make sense to be understandable. □ *John doesn't make sense.* □ *What John says makes sense.*

make sense out of someone or something to understand or interpret someone or something. (Also with *some*, as in the second example.) □ *I can hardly make sense out of John.* □ *I'm trying to make some sense out of what John is saying.*

make short work of someone or something AND **make fast work of someone or something** to finish with someone or something quickly. □ *I made short work of Tom so I could leave the office to play golf.* □ *Billy made fast work of his dinner so he could go out and play.*

make someone eat crow to cause someone to retract a statement or admit an error. (Informal.) □ *Because Mary was completely wrong, we made her eat crow.* □ *They won't make me eat crow. They don't know I was wrong.*

make someone look good to cause someone to appear successful or competent (especially when this is not the case). (Also literal.) □ *John arranges all his affairs to make himself look good.* □ *The manager didn't like the quarterly report because it didn't make her look good.*

make someone look ridiculous to make someone look foolish (not funny). □ *This hat makes me look ridiculous.* □ *Please make me look good. Don't make me look ridiculous!*

make someone or something available to someone to supply someone with someone or something. □ *I made my car available to Bob.* □ *They made their maid available to us.*

make someone or something over See *do someone or something over.*

make someone or something tick to cause someone or something to run or function. (Informal. Usually with *what.*) □ *I don't know what makes it tick.* □ *What makes John tick? I just don't understand him.* □ *I took apart the radio to find out what made it tick.*

make someone or something up 1. [with *something*] to repay or redo something. Ⓣ *Can I make up the test I missed?* Ⓣ *Please make up the payment you missed.* □ *You can make it up.* **2.** [with *something*] to think up something; to make and tell a lie. □ *That's not true! You just made that up!* □ *I didn't make it up!* Ⓣ *You made up that story!* **3.** to mix something up; to assemble something. □ JOHN: *Is my prescription ready?* DRUGGIST: *No, I haven't made it up yet.* Ⓣ *I'll make up your prescription in a minute.* Ⓣ

How long does it take to make up a cheese sandwich? **4.** [with *someone*] to put makeup on someone. □ *She made herself up before leaving the house.* Ⓣ *The crew made up the cast before the play.*

make someone the scapegoat for something to make someone take the blame for something. □ *They made Tom the scapegoat for the whole affair. It wasn't all his fault.* □ *Don't try to make me the scapegoat. I'll tell who really did it.*

make someone's bed See *make the bed.*

make someone's blood boil to make someone very angry. (Informal.) □ *It just makes my blood boil to think of the amount of food that gets wasted around here.* □ *Whenever I think of that dishonest mess, it makes my blood boil.*

make someone's blood run cold to shock or horrify someone. □ *The terrible story in the newspaper made my blood run cold.* □ *I could tell you things about prisons that would make your blood run cold.*

make someone's hair curl See *curl someone's hair.*

make someone's hair stand on end to cause someone to be very frightened. (Informal.) □ *The horrible scream made my hair stand on end.* □ *The ghost story made our hair stand on end.*

make someone's head spin See the following entry.

make someone's head swim AND **make someone's head spin 1.** to make someone dizzy or disoriented. □ *Riding in your car makes my head spin.* □ *Breathing the gas made my head swim.* **2.** to confuse or overwhelm someone. □ *All these numbers make my head swim.* □ *The physics lecture made my head spin.*

make someone's mouth water to make someone hungry (for something). (Informal.) □ *That beautiful salad makes my mouth water.* □ *Talking about food makes my mouth water.*

make someone's position clear to clarify where someone stands on an issue. □ *I don't think you understand what I said. Let me make my position clear.* □ *I can't tell whether you are in favor of or against the proposal. Please make your position clear.*

make something to attend an event. (See also *make it.*) □ *I hope you can make our party.* □ *I am sorry, but I won't be able to make it.*

make something a practice See *make a practice of something.*

make something from scratch to make something by starting with the basic ingredients. (Informal.) □ *We made the cake from scratch, using no prepared ingredients.* □ *I didn't have a ladder, so I made one from scratch.*

make something good AND **make something right** to replace or restore something. (Informal. See also *set something right.*) □ *I know I owe you some money, but don't worry, I'll make it good.* □ *I'm sorry I broke your window. I'll make it right, though.*

make something out of nothing 1. to make an issue of something of little importance. (See also *make a mountain out of a molehill.*) □ *Relax, John, you're making a big problem out of nothing.* □ *You have no evidence. You're making a case out of nothing.* **2.** to create something of value from nearly worthless parts. □ *My uncle—he sells sand—made a fortune out of nothing.* □ *My model airplane won the contest even though I made it out of nothing.*

make something (out) of something 1. to make an interpretation of something. □ *Can you make anything out of this message? I don't understand it.* □ *I'm sorry, I can't make any sense out of it.* **2.** to interpret something negatively. (Informal. Compare with *make nothing of something.*) □ *So, I'm wrong! You want to make something of it?* □ *The hostess made too much out of my absence.*

make something right See *make something good.*

make something to order to put something together only when someone requests it. (Usually said about clothing. See also *build something to order.*) □ *This store only makes suits to order.* □ *Our shirts fit perfectly because each one is made to order.*

make something up out of whole cloth to create a story or a lie from no facts at all. □ *I don't believe you. I think you made that up out of whole cloth.* ⊤ *Ann made up her explanation out of whole cloth. There was not a bit of truth in it.*

make something up to someone to repay someone; to make amends to someone. □ *I'm so sorry I've insulted you. How can I make it up to you?* □ *I'm sorry I broke our date. I'll make it up to you, I promise.*

make the bed AND **make someone's bed** to restore a bed to an unslept-in condition. □ *I make my bed every morning.* □ *The maid goes to all the rooms to make the beds.*

make the best of something to try to make a bad situation work out well. (Compare with *make the most of something.*) □ *It's not good, but we'll have to make the best of it.* □ *Ann is clever enough to make the best of a bad situation.*

make the feathers fly See the following entry.

make the fur fly AND **make the feathers fly** to cause a fight or an argument; to *create an uproar* (about something). (Informal.) □ *When your mother gets home and sees what you've done, she'll really make the fur fly.* □ *When those two get together, they'll make the feathers fly. They hate each other.*

make the grade to be satisfactory; to be what is expected. (Informal.) □ *I'm sorry, but your work doesn't exactly make the grade.* □ *This meal doesn't just make the grade. It is excellent.*

make the most of something to make something appear as good as possible; to exploit something; to get as much out of something as is possible.

(Compare with *make the best of something*.) □ *Mary knows how to make the most of her talents.* □ *They designed the advertisements to make the most of the product's features.*

make the scene to appear somewhere. (Slang.) □ *I hope I can make the scene Saturday night.* □ *Man, I've got to make the scene. The whole world will be there!*

make time (for someone or something) to schedule time to see someone or do something. □ *I can make time for you tomorrow morning.* □ *I am very busy, but I can make time.* □ *You are going to have to start making time for balanced meals.*

make time (with someone) to flirt with, date, or hang around with someone. (Informal.) □ *I hear that Tom's been making time with Ann.* □ *I hear they've been making time for months.*

make up for lost time to do much of something; to do something fast. □ *Because we took so long eating lunch, we have to drive faster to make up for lost time. Otherwise we won't arrive on time.* □ *At the age of sixty, Bill learned to play golf. Now he plays it every day. He's making up for lost time.*

make up for someone or something to take the place of someone or something. □ *John can't play in the game Saturday, but I think I can make up for him.* □ *Do you think that this cat can make up for the one that ran away?*

make waves to make trouble or difficulties. (Informal. Compare with *rock the boat*.) □ *I don't want to make waves, but this just isn't right.* □ *Why do you always have to make waves? Can't you be constructive?*

make way to make progress; to move ahead. (Originally nautical.) □ *Is this project making way?* □ *A sailboat can't make way if there is no wind.*

make way (for someone or something) to clear a path for someone or something. □ *Make way for the stretcher.* □ *Please make way for the nurse.* □ *Here comes the doctor—make way!*

man-about-town a fashionable man who leads a sophisticated life. □ *He prefers wine bars to pubs—quite a man-about-town.* □ *Jack's too much of a man-about-town to go to a football game.*

man in the street the ordinary person. □ *Politicians rarely care what the man in the street thinks.* □ *The man in the street has little interest in literature.*

man to man AND **woman to woman** speaking frankly and directly, one person to another. □ *Let's discuss this man to man so we know what each other thinks.* □ *The two mothers discussed their child-raising problems woman to woman.*

many is the time on many occasions. □ *Many is the time I wanted to complain, but I just kept quiet.* □ *Many is the time that we don't have enough to eat.*

march to a different drummer to believe in a different set of principles. □ *John is marching to a different drummer, and he doesn't come to our parties anymore.* □ *Since Sally started marching to a different drummer, she has had a lot of great new ideas.*

mark my word(s) remember what I'm telling you. □ *Mark my word, you'll regret this.* □ *This whole project will fail—mark my words.*

mark someone or something down 1. [with *someone*] to make a note about someone; to note a fact about someone. □ *I'm going to the party. Please mark me down.* □ *Mark me down, too.* **2.** [with *someone*] [for a teacher] to give someone a low score. □ *He'll mark you down for misspelled words.* ⊺ *I marked down Tom for bad spelling.* **3.** [with *something*] to lower the price of something. □ *Okay, we'll mark it down.* ⊺ *Let's mark down this price so it'll sell faster.*

mark something up 1. to mess something up with marks. ⊺ *Don't mark up your book!* □ *Who marked this book up?* **2.** to grade a paper and make lots of informative marks and comments on it. ⊺ *The teacher really marked up* *my term paper.* □ *Why did you mark my test up so much? I hardly made any errors.* **3.** to raise the price of something. □ *The grocery store seems to mark the price of food up every week.* Ⓣ *They don't mark up the price of turkey at Thanksgiving.*

matter-of-fact businesslike; unfeeling. (See also *as a matter of fact.*) □ *Don't expect a lot of sympathy from Ann. She's very matter-of-fact.* □ *Don't be so matter-of-fact. It hurts my feelings.*

matter of life and death a matter of great urgency; an issue that will decide between living and dying. (Often an exaggeration. Fixed order.) □ *We must find a doctor. It's a matter of life and death.* □ *I must have some water. It's a matter of life and death.*

matter of opinion the question of how good or bad someone or something is. □ *It's a matter of opinion how good the company is. John thinks it's great and Fred thinks it's poor.* □ *How efficient the committee is is a matter of opinion.*

mealymouthed not frank or direct. (Informal.) □ *Jane is too mealymouthed to tell Frank she dislikes him. She just avoids him.* □ *Don't be so mealymouthed. It's better to speak plainly.*

mean nothing (to someone) 1. not to make sense to someone. □ *This sentence means nothing to me. It isn't clearly written.* □ *I'm sorry. This message means nothing.* **2.** [for someone] not to have feeling for (someone or something). □ *Do I mean nothing to you after all these years?* □ *Do all those years mean nothing?*

mean something (to someone) 1. to make sense to someone. (See also the preceding entry.) □ *Does this line mean anything to you?* □ *Yes, it means something.* **2.** for someone to have feeling for (someone or something). □ *You mean a lot to me.* □ *This job means a lot to Ann.*

mean to (do something) to intend to do something. □ *Did you mean to do*

that? □ *No, it was an accident. I didn't mean to.*

measure up (to someone or something) to be equal to someone or something. □ *Ann is good, but she doesn't measure up to Mary.* □ *This measures up to my standards quite nicely.* □ *Yes, it measures up.*

measure up (to someone's expectations) to be as good as one expects. □ *This meal doesn't measure up to my expectations.* □ *Why doesn't it measure up?*

meat-and-potatoes basic, sturdy, and hearty. (Often refers to a robust person, usually a man, with simple tastes in food and other things. Also literal as a noun compound. Fixed order.) □ *Fred was your meat-and-potatoes kind of guy. No creamy sauces for him.* □ *There is no point in trying to cook up something special for the Wilsons. They are strictly meat-and-potatoes.*

Mecca for someone a place that is frequently visited by a particular group of people because it is important to them for some reason. (From the city of Mecca, the religious center of Islam.) □ *New York City is a Mecca for theatergoers.* □ *St. Andrews is a Mecca for golf enthusiasts because of its famous course.*

meet one's end to die. □ *The dog met his end under the wheels of a car.* □ *I don't intend to meet my end until I'm 100 years old.*

meet one's match to meet one's equal. □ *John played tennis with Bill yesterday, and it looks as if John has finally met his match.* □ *Listen to Jane and Mary argue. I always thought that Jane was loud, but she has finally met her match.*

meet one's Waterloo to meet one's final and insurmountable challenge. (Refers to Napoleon at Waterloo.) □ *The boss is being very hard on Bill. It seems that Bill has finally met his Waterloo.* □ *John was more than Sally could handle. She has finally met her Waterloo.*

meet someone halfway to offer to compromise with someone. (Also literal.) □ *No, I won't give in, but I'll meet you halfway.* □ *They settled the argument by agreeing to meet each other halfway.*

meet the requirements (for something) to fulfill the requirements for something. □ *Sally was unable to meet the requirements for the job.* □ *Jane met the requirements and was told to report to work the next day.*

melt in one's mouth to taste very good. □ *This cake is so good it'll melt in your mouth.* □ *John said that the food didn't exactly melt in his mouth.*

mend (one's) fences to restore good relations (with someone). (Also literal.) □ *I think I had better get home and mend my fences. I had an argument with my daughter this morning.* □ *Sally called up her uncle to apologize and try to mend fences.*

mend one's ways to improve one's behavior. □ *John used to be very wild, but he's mended his ways.* □ *You'll have to mend your ways if you go out with Mary. She hates people to be late.*

mention someone or something in passing to mention someone or something casually; to mention someone or something while talking about someone or something else. □ *He just happened to mention in passing that the mayor had resigned.* □ *John mentioned in passing that he was nearly eighty years old.*

mess about (with someone or something) See the following entry.

mess around (with someone or something) AND **mess about (with someone or something); monkey around (with someone or something); screw around (with someone or something)** to play with or waste time with someone or something. (Slang.) □ *Will you please stop messing around with that old car!* □ *Stop messing about! Get busy!* □ *Tom wastes a lot of time messing around with Bill.* □ *Don't monkey*

around with my computer! □ *John is always screwing around with his stereo.*

mess someone or something up 1. [with *someone*] to rough someone up; to beat someone up. (Slang.) □ *The robbers threatened to mess Bob up if he didn't cooperate.* Ⓣ *John messed up Bill a little, but no real harm was done.* **2.** [with *something*] to make something disorderly. □ *You really messed this place up!* Ⓣ *Who messed up my bed?*

middle-of-the-road halfway between two extremes, especially political extremes. □ *Jane is very left-wing, but her husband is politically middle-of-the-road.* □ *I don't want to vote for either the left-wing or the right-wing candidate. I prefer someone with more middle-of-the-road views.*

might and main great physical strength; great force. (Fixed order.) □ *The huge warrior, with all his might and main, could not break his way through the castle gates.* □ *The incredible might and main of the sea crushed the ship against the cliff.*

milestone in someone's life a very important event or point in one's life. (From the stone at the side of a road showing the distance to or from a place.) □ *Joan's wedding was a milestone in her mother's life.* □ *The birth of a child is a milestone in every parent's life.*

milk of human kindness natural kindness and sympathy shown to others. (From Shakespeare's play *Macbeth*, I. v.) □ *Mary is completely hard and selfish — she has no milk of human kindness in her.* □ *Roger is too full of the milk of human kindness and people take advantage of him.*

millstone about one's neck a continual burden or handicap. □ *This huge and expensive house is a millstone about my neck.* □ *Bill's inability to read is a millstone about his neck.*

mince (one's) words to lessen the force of one's statement by choosing weak or polite words; to be euphemistic. (Formal.) □ *I won't mince words. You* *did a rotten job.* □ *I'm not one to mince words, so I have to say that you behaved very badly.*

mind one's own business to attend only to the things that concern one. □ *Leave me alone, Bill. Mind your own business.* □ *I'd be fine if John would mind his own business.*

mind one's p's and q's to mind one's manners. (Fixed order.) □ *When we go to the mayor's reception, please mind your p's and q's.* □ *I always mind my p's and q's when I eat at a restaurant with white tablecloths.*

mind the store to take care of local matters. (Informal. Also literal.) □ *Please stay here in the office and mind the store while I go to the conference.* □ *I had to stay home and mind the store when Ann went to Boston.*

miscarriage of justice a wrong or mistaken decision, especially one made in a court of law. □ *Sentencing the old man on a charge of murder proved to be a miscarriage of justice.* □ *Punishing the student for cheating was a miscarriage of justice. He was innocent.*

miss out (on something) AND **lose out (on something)** to fail to participate in something; to fail to take part in something. □ *I'm sorry I missed out on the ice cream.* □ *I lost out on it, too.* □ *We both missed out.*

miss (something) by a mile to fail to hit something by a great distance; to land wide of the mark. □ *Ann shot the arrow and missed the target by a mile.* □ *"Good grief, you missed by a mile," shouted Sally.*

miss the boat to miss out (on something); to be ignorant (of something). (Slang. Also literal.) □ *Pay attention, John, or you'll miss the boat.* □ *Tom really missed the boat when it came to making friends.*

miss the point to fail to understand the important part of something. □ *I'm afraid you missed the point. Let me explain it again.* □ *You keep explaining, and I keep missing the point.*

mistake someone for someone else AND **mix someone up with someone else** to confuse someone with someone else; to think that one person is another person. □ *I'm sorry. I mistook you for John.* □ *Tom is always mistaking Bill for me. We don't look a thing alike, though.* □ *Try not to mix Bill up with Bob.*

mix and match (Fixed order.) **1.** to assemble a limited number of items, usually clothing, in a number of different ways. □ *Alice was very good at mixing and matching her skirts, blouses, and sweaters so that she always could be attractively dressed on a limited budget.* □ *Gary always bought black, blue, and gray trousers and shirts so he could mix and match without too many bad combinations.* **2.** to select a number of items from an assemblage, often in order to get a quantity discount. (As opposed to getting a quantity discount for buying a lot of only one item.) □ *The candles were 25 percent off, and you could mix and match colors, sizes, and length.* □ *I found a good sale on shirts. They were four for fifty dollars, and the store would let you mix and match.*

mix it up to argue or fight. (Slang. Also literal.) □ *First they were just talking, then suddenly one of them got mad and they really began to mix it up.* □ *Look at you, Bill! Your face is bleeding. Have you been mixing it up with John again?*

mix someone or something up **1.** to confuse two things or two people with each other. □ *Please don't mix these ideas up. They are quite distinct.* ⊤ *I always mix up Bill and Bob.* □ *Why do you mix them up?* **2.** [with *someone*] to cause someone to be confused or puzzled. □ *I'm confused as it is. Don't mix me up anymore.* ⊤ *They mixed up my uncle by giving him too many things to remember.* **3.** [with *something*] to blend the ingredients of something; to assemble and mix the parts of something. (Usually refers to fluid matter such as paint, gasoline, or milk.) □ *The glue will be ready to use as soon as I mix it up.* ⊤ *Now, mix up the eggs,* *water, and salt; then add the mixture to the flour and sugar.*

mix someone up with someone else See *mistake someone for someone else.*

mixed bag a varied collection of people or things. (Refers to a bag of game brought home after a day's hunting.) □ *The new students in my class are a mixed bag—some bright, some positively stupid.* □ *The furniture I bought is a mixed bag. Some of it is valuable and the rest is worthless.*

moment of truth the point at which someone has to face the reality or facts of a situation. □ *The moment of truth is here. Turn over your test papers and begin.* □ *Now for the moment of truth when we find out whether we have got permission or not.*

Money burns a hole in someone's pocket. someone spends as much money as possible. (Informal. See also *have money to burn.*) □ *Sally can't seem to save anything. Money burns a hole in her pocket.* □ *If money burns a hole in your pocket, you never have any for emergencies.*

money is no object AND **expense is no object** it does not matter how much something costs. □ *Please show me your finest automobile. Money is no object.* □ *I want the finest earrings you have. Don't worry about how much they cost because expense is no object.*

Money is the root of all evil. a proverb meaning that money is the basic cause of all wrongdoing. □ *Why do you work so hard to make money? It will just cause you trouble. Money is the root of all evil.* □ *Any thief in prison can tell you that money is the root of all evil.*

money talks money gives one power and influence to help get things done or get one's own way. (Informal.) □ *Don't worry. I have a way of getting things done. Money talks.* □ *I can't compete against rich old Mrs. Jones. She'll get her way because money talks.*

monkey around (with someone or something) See *mess around (with someone or something).*

monkey business playful or out of the ordinary activities; mischievous or illegal activities. □ *There's been some monkey business in connection with the bank's accounts.* □ *Bob left the company quite suddenly. I think there was some monkey business between him and the boss's wife.*

mop the floor up with someone to overwhelm and physically subdue someone; to beat someone. (Slang.) □ *Stop talking like that, or I'll mop the floor up with you!* T *Did you hear that? He threatened to mop up the floor with me!*

mope around to go about in a depressed state. (Informal.) □ *Since her dog ran away, Sally mopes around all day.* □ *Don't mope around. Cheer up!*

more dead than alive exhausted; in very bad condition; near death. (Almost always an exaggeration.) □ *We arrived at the top of the mountain more dead than alive.* □ *The marathon runners stumbled one by one over the finish line, more dead than alive.*

more fun than a barrel of monkeys See *(as) funny as a barrel of monkeys.*

more often than not usually. □ *These flowers will live through the winter more often than not.* □ *This kind of dog will grow up to be a good watchdog more often than not.*

more or less to some extent; approximately; sort of. (Fixed order.) □ *This one will do all right, more or less.* □ *We'll be there at eight, more or less.*

more someone or something than one can shake a stick at a lot; too many to count. (Folksy.) □ *There were more snakes than you could shake a stick at.* □ *There are lots of flowers in the field —more than one can shake a stick at.*

more than someone bargained for more than one thought one would get. (Usually in reference to trouble or difficulty.) □ *When Betsy brought home the sweet little puppy for a companion, she got more than she bargained for. That animal has cost her hundreds of* dollars in medical bills. □ *I got more than I bargained for when I took this job.*

more (to something) than meets the eye [there are] hidden values or facts in something. □ *There is more to that problem than the eye.* □ *What makes you think that there is more than meets the eye?*

morning after (the night before) the morning after a night spent drinking, when one has a hangover. □ *Oh, I've got a headache. Talk about the morning after the night before!* □ *It looked like a case of the morning after the night before, and Frank asked for some aspirin.*

move heaven and earth to do something to make a major effort to do something. (Fixed order.) □ *"I'll move heaven and earth to be with you, Mary," said Bill.* □ *I had to move heaven and earth to get there on time.* □ *Your father and I had to move heaven and earth to pay for your braces and your college bills, and what thanks do we get?*

move in (on someone or something) 1. [with *someone*] to attempt to displace someone or take over someone's property, interests, or relationships. (Slang, especially criminal slang. Compare with *muscle in (on someone or something)*.) □ *Look here, pal, Sally's my girl. Are you trying to move in on me?* □ *It looks like the south-side gang is trying to move in. We'll have to teach them as lesson.* 2. [with *someone*] to move into someone's household. □ *My mother-in-law moved in on us for two months.* □ *I wouldn't move in on you without an invitation.* 3. to move closer to someone or something, especially with a camera. □ *Now, slowly move in on the cereal box. This will be a great advertisement.* □ *Hold the camera very steady and move in on the baby.*

move into something to get started in a new enterprise, job, etc. (Also literal.) □ *I moved into a new job last week. It's very exciting work.* □ *John moved into a new line of work, too.*

move up (in the world) to advance (oneself) and become successful. □ *The harder I work, the more I move up in the world.* □ *Keep your eye on John. He's really moving up.*

movers and shakers people who get things done; people who are productive and cause other people to be productive; people who create and produce. (Fixed order.) □ *The trouble with the ABC Company is that all the movers and shakers are leaving to take jobs elsewhere.* □ *It seems as if all the movers and shakers of the world are employed by a very small number of large firms.*

much ado about nothing a lot of excitement about nothing. (This is the title of a play by Shakespeare. Do not confuse *ado* with *adieu*.) □ *All the commotion about the new tax law turned out to be much ado about nothing.* □ *Your promises always turn out to be much ado about nothing.*

much in evidence very visible or evident. □ *John was much in evidence during the conference.* □ *Your influence is much in evidence. I appreciate your efforts.*

much sought after wanted or desired very much. □ *This kind of crystal is much sought after. It's very rare.* □ *Sally is a great singer. She's much sought after.*

muddy the water to make something less clear; to make matters confusing; to create difficulty where there was none before. (Also literal.) □ *Things were going along quite smoothly until you came along and muddied the water.* □ *The events of the past month have muddied the water as far as our proposed joint venture is concerned.*

muff one's lines See *fluff one's lines.*

mull something over to think about something; to ponder or worry about something. □ *That's an interesting idea, but I'll mull it over.* Ⓣ *I'll mull over your suggestions and report to you next week.*

mum's the word don't spread the secret. □ *Don't tell anyone what I told you. Remember, mum's the word.* □ *Okay, mum's the word. Your secret is safe with me.*

muscle in (on someone or something) to try forcefully to displace someone or take over someone's property, interests, or relationships. (Slang, especially criminal slang. Compare with *move in (on someone or something).*) □ *Are you trying to muscle in on my scheme?* □ *If you try to muscle in, you'll be facing big trouble.*

N

nail in someone's or something's coffin See *(another) nail in someone's or something's coffin.*

nail someone or something down 1. [with *someone*] to get a firm and final decision from someone (on something). (Informal. Also literal.) □ *I want you to find Bob and get an answer from him. Nail him down one way or the other.* ⊤ *Please nail down John on the question of signing the contract.* **2.** [with *something*] to get a firm and final decision (from someone) on something. (Informal.) ⊤ *Find Bob and nail down an answer.* □ *Let's get in touch with John and nail down this contract.*

naked as a jaybird See *(as) naked as a jaybird.*

naked eye the human eye, unassisted by optics, such as a telescope, microscope, or spectacles. (Especially with *to* or *with*.) □ *I can't see the bird's markings with the naked eye.* □ *The scientist could see nothing in the liquid with the naked eye, but with the aid of a microscope, she identified the bacteria.* □ *That's how it appears to the naked eye.*

name of the game goal or purpose. (Slang.) □ *The name of the game is sell. You must sell, sell, sell if you want to make a living.* □ *Around here, the name of the game is look out for yourself.*

name someone after someone else AND **name someone for someone else** to give someone (usually a baby) the name of another person. □ *We*

named our baby after my aunt. □ *My parents named me for my grandfather.*

name someone for someone else See the previous entry.

near at hand close or handy (to someone). (See also *at hand; close at hand.*) □ *Do you have a pencil near at hand?* □ *My dictionary isn't near at hand.*

neck and neck exactly even, especially in a race or a contest. (Informal.) □ *John and Tom finished the race neck and neck.* □ *Mary and Ann were neck and neck in the spelling contest. Their scores were tied.*

neither fish nor fowl not any recognizable thing. □ *The car that they drove up in was neither fish nor fowl. It must have been made out of spare parts.* □ *This proposal is neither fish nor fowl. I can't tell what you're proposing.*

neither here nor there of no consequence or meaning; irrelevant and immaterial. □ *Whether you go to the movie or stay at home is neither here nor there.* □ *Your comment—though interesting—is neither here nor there.*

neither hide nor hair no sign or indication (of someone or something). (Fixed order.) □ *We could find neither hide nor hair of him. I don't know where he is.* □ *There has been no one here—neither hide nor hair—for the last three days.*

never fear do not worry; have confidence. □ *I'll be there on time—never fear.* □ *I'll help you, never fear.*

never had it so good See *(have) never had it so good.*

never in one's life not in one's experience. □ *Never in my life have I been so insulted!* □ *He said that never in his life had he seen such an ugly painting.*

never mind forget it; pay no more attention (to something). □ *I wanted to talk to you, but never mind. It wasn't important.* □ *Never mind. I'm sorry to bother you.*

new ball game a new set of circumstances. (Slang. Originally from sports. Often with *whole.*) □ *It's a whole new ball game since Jane took over the office.* □ *You can't do the things you used to do around here. It's a new ball game.*

new blood See *(some) new blood.*

new lease on life a renewed and revitalized outlook on life. □ *Getting the job offer was a new lease on life.* □ *When I got out of the hospital, I felt as if I had a new lease on life.*

new one on someone something one has not heard before and that one is not ready to believe. (Informal. The *someone* is often *me.*) □ *Jack's poverty is a new one on me. He always seems to have plenty of money.* □ *The city's difficulties are a new one on me.*

next to nothing hardly anything; almost nothing. □ *This car's worth next to nothing. It's full of rust.* □ *I bought this antique chair for next to nothing.*

nickel and dime someone to charge someone many small amounts of money; to assess many small fees against someone. (Fixed order.) □ *We will not stay at that resort again. They nickel and dime you to death in that place. There is a charge for everything.* □ *Tuition at the university hasn't gone up in two years but other small fees have. They really nickel and dime you there.*

night and day See *day and night.*

night on the town a night of celebrating (at one or more places in a town). □ *Did you enjoy your night on the town?* □ *After we got the contract signed, we celebrated with a night on the town.*

night owl someone who usually stays up very late. □ *Anne's a real night owl. She never goes to bed before 2 A.M. and sleeps till midday.* □ *Jack's a night owl and is at his best after midnight.*

nine days' wonder something that is of interest to people only for a short time. □ *Don't worry about the story about you in the newspaper. It'll be a nine days' wonder, and then people will forget.* □ *The elopement of Jack and Anne was a nine days' wonder. Now people never mention it.*

nine-to-five job a job with regular and normal hours. □ *I wouldn't want a nine-to-five job. I like the freedom I have as my own boss.* □ *I used to work nights, but now I have a nine-to-five job.*

nip and tuck almost even; almost tied. (Informal. Fixed order.) □ *The horses ran nip and tuck for the first half of the race. Then my horse pulled ahead.* □ *In the football game last Saturday, both teams were nip and tuck throughout the game.*

nip something in the bud to put an end to something at an early stage. □ *John is getting into bad habits, and it's best to nip them in the bud.* □ *There was trouble in the classroom, but the teacher nipped it in the bud.*

no buts about it See *no ifs, ands, or buts about it.*

no can do cannot do (something). (Slang.) □ *Sorry, John. No can do. I can't sell you this one. I've promised it to Mrs. Smith.* □ BILL: *Please fix this clock today.* BOB: *No can do. It'll take a week to get the parts.*

no doubt surely; without a doubt; undoubtedly. □ *He will be here again tomorrow, no doubt.* □ *No doubt you will require a ride home?*

no end of something lots of something. (Informal.) □ *It was a wonderful banquet. They had no end of good food.* □ *Tom is a real problem. He's no end of trouble.*

no flies on someone someone is not slow; someone is not wasting time.

□ *Of course I work fast. I go as fast as I can. There are no flies on me.* □ *There are no flies on Robert. He does his work very fast and very well.*

no great shakes nothing important or worth noticing. (Slang.) □ *It's okay, but it's no great shakes.* □ *I like John, but he's no great shakes when it comes to sports.*

no hard feelings no anger or resentment. (Informal. *No* can be replaced with *any.*) □ *I hope you don't have any hard feelings.* □ *No, I have no hard feelings.*

no holds barred with no restraints. (Slang. From wrestling.) □ *I intend to argue it out with Mary, no holds barred.* □ *When Ann negotiates a contract, she goes in with no holds barred and comes out with a good contract.*

no ifs, ands, or buts about it AND **no buts about it** absolutely no discussion, dissension, or doubt about something. □ *I want you there exactly at eight, no ifs, ands, or buts about it.* □ *This is the best television set available for the money, no buts about it.*

no joke a serious matter. (Informal.) □ *It's no joke when you miss the last train.* □ *It's certainly no joke when you have to walk home.*

no kidding [spoken] honestly; [someone is] not joking or lying. (Slang.) □ *No kidding, you really got an A in geometry?* □ *I really did, no kidding.*

no laughing matter a serious matter. □ *Be serious. This is no laughing matter.* □ *This disease is no laughing matter. It's quite deadly.*

no love lost (between someone and someone else) no friendship wasted between someone and someone else (because they are enemies). □ *Ever since their big argument, there has been no love lost between Tom and Bill.* □ *You can tell by the way that Jane is acting toward Ann that there is no love lost.*

no matter what happens in any event; without regard to what happens (in the future). □ *We'll be there on time,* no matter what. □ *No matter what happens, we'll still be friends.*

No news is good news. a saying meaning if one has not had any information about someone or something for some time, it means that all is well, since one would have heard if anything bad or unfortunate had occurred. □ *I haven't heard from my son since he left for college, but I suppose no news is good news.* □ *I think Joan would have heard by now if she hadn't got the job. No news is good news.*

no problem See *no sweat.*

no skin off someone's nose See the following entry.

no skin off someone's teeth AND **no skin off someone's nose** no difficulty for someone; no concern of someone. □ *It's no skin off my nose if she wants to act that way.* □ *She said it was no skin off her teeth if we wanted to sell the house.*

no sooner said than done done quickly and obediently. (Informal.) □ *When Sally asked for someone to open the window, it was no sooner said than done.* □ *As Jane opened the window, she said, "No sooner said than done."*

no spring chicken not young (anymore). (Informal.) □ *I don't get around very well anymore. I'm no spring chicken, you know.* □ *Even though John is no spring chicken, he still plays tennis twice a week.*

no sweat AND **no problem** no difficulty; do not worry. (Slang.) □ *Of course I can have your car repaired by noon. No sweat.* □ *You'd like a red one? No problem.*

no trespassing do not enter. (Usually seen on a sign. Not usually spoken.) □ *The sign on the tree said, "No Trespassing." So we didn't go in.* □ *The angry farmer chased us out of the field shouting, "Get out! Don't you see the no trespassing sign?"*

no two ways about it no choice about it; no other interpretation of it. (Folksy. Note the form *there's* rather than *there are.*) □ *You have to go to the doctor* *whether you like it or not. There's no two ways about it.* □ *This letter means you're in trouble with the tax people. There's no two ways about it.*

no way not any means (to do something). (Slang.) □ *You think I'm going to sit around here while you're having fun at the picnic? No way!* □ BOB: *Will you please take this to the post office for me?* BILL: *No way.*

no-win situation a situation where there is no correct or satisfactory solution. □ *The general was too weak to fight and too proud to surrender. It was a no-win situation.* □ *The huge dog my father gave us as a gift eats too much. If we get rid of the dog, my father will be insulted. If we keep it, we will go broke buying food for it. This is a classic no-win situation.*

no wonder [something is] not surprising. (Informal.) □ *No wonder the baby is crying. She's wet.* □ *It's no wonder that plant died. You watered it too much.*

nobody's fool a sensible and wise person who is not easily deceived. □ *Mary's nobody's fool. She knows Jack would try to cheat her.* □ *Anne looks as though she's not very bright, but she's nobody's fool.*

nod off to fall asleep. (Informal.) □ *Jack nodded off during the minister's sermon.* □ *Father always nods off after Sunday lunch.*

none of someone's beeswax none of someone's business. (Slang.) □ *The answer to that question is none of your beeswax.* □ *It's none of your beeswax what I do with my spare time.*

none other than someone the very person. □ *The new building was opened by none other than the mayor.* □ *Jack's wife turned out to be none other than my cousin.*

none the wiser not knowing any more. □ *I was none the wiser about the project after the lecture. It was a complete waste of time.* □ *Anne tried to explain the situation tactfully to Jack, but in the end, he was none the wiser.*

none the worse for wear no worse because of use or effort. □ *I lent my car to John. When I got it back, it was none the worse for wear.* □ *I had a hard day today, but I'm none the worse for wear.*

none too something not very something; not at all something. □ *The towels in the bathroom were none too clean.* □ *It was none too warm in their house.*

nook and cranny small, out-of-the-way places or places where something can be hidden. (Usually with *every*. Fixed order.) □ *We looked for the tickets in every nook and cranny. They were lost. There was no doubt.* □ *The decorator had placed flowers in every nook and cranny.*

nose about See the following entry.

nose around AND **nose about** to investigate; to check (into something). (Informal.) □ *I don't have an answer to your question, but I'll nose around and see what I can find out.* □ *I'll nose about, too. Who knows what we'll find out?*

nose in(to something) to move into something, front end first. □ *Slowly the car nosed into its parking place.* □ *You must nose in very carefully.*

nose someone out to push someone away; to exclude someone. □ *Where I work someone is always trying to nose me out. I'd hate to lose my job.* Ⓣ *John nosed out Bill from the team.*

not a bit none at all. □ *Am I unhappy? Not a bit.* □ *I don't want any mashed potatoes. Not a bit!*

not a living soul nobody. (Informal. See some of the possible variations in the examples.) □ *I won't tell anybody — not a living soul.* □ *I won't tell a living soul.* □ *They wouldn't think of telling a living soul.*

not able See the expressions listed at *can't* as well as those listed below.

not able to call one's time one's own too busy; so busy as not to be in charge of one's own schedule. (Informal. *Not able to* is often expressed as *can't.*) □ *It's been so busy around here that I haven't been able to call my time my own.* □ *She can't call her time her own these days.*

not able to go on unable to continue (doing something — even living). (*Not able to* is often expressed as *can't.*) □ *I just can't go on this way.* □ *Before her death, she left a note saying she was not able to go on.*

not able to help something unable to prevent or control something. (*Not able to* is often expressed as *can't.*) □ *I'm sorry about being late. I wasn't able to help it.* □ *Bob can't help being boring.*

not able to make anything out of someone or something unable to understand someone or something. (*Not able to* is often expressed as *can't.* The *anything* may refer to something specific, as in the first example.) □ *I can't make sense out of what you just said.* □ *We were not able to make anything out of the message.*

not able to see the forest for the trees allowing many details of a problem to obscure the problem as a whole. (*Not able to* is often expressed as *can't.*) □ *The solution is obvious. You missed it because you can't see the forest for the trees.* □ *She suddenly realized that she hadn't been able to see the forest for the trees.*

not able to wait to have to *go to the bathroom* urgently. (Informal. Also literal.) □ *Mom, I can't wait.* □ *Driver, stop the bus! My little boy can't wait.*

not agree with someone to make someone ill; to give someone minor stomach distress. □ *Fried foods don't agree with Tom.* □ *I always have onions in my garden, but I never eat them. They just don't agree with me.*

not all something is cracked up to be AND **not what something is cracked up to be** not as good as something is supposed to be. (Informal. Not always in the negative.) □ *This isn't a very good pen. It's not all it's cracked up to be.* □ *Is this one all it's cracked up to be?* □

This restaurant isn't what it's cracked up to be.

not all there not mentally adequate; crazy or silly. (Informal.) □ *Sometimes I think you're not all there.* □ *Be nice to Sally. She's not all there.*

not at all certainly not; absolutely not. □ *No, it doesn't bother me — not at all.* □ *I'm not complaining. Not me. Not at all.*

not bat an eyelid to show no signs of distress even when something bad happens or something shocking is said. □ *Sam didn't bat an eyelid when the mechanic told him how much the car repairs would cost.* □ *The pain of the broken arm must have hurt Sally terribly, but she did not bat an eyelid.*

not believe one's eyes not to believe what one is seeing; to be shocked or dumbfounded at what one is seeing. □ *I walked into the room and I couldn't believe my eyes. All the furniture had been stolen!* □ *When Jimmy opened his birthday present, he could hardly believe his eyes. Just what he wanted!*

not born yesterday experienced; knowledgeable in the ways of the world. □ *I know what's going on. I wasn't born yesterday.* □ *Sally knows the score. She wasn't born yesterday.*

not breathe a word (about someone or something) to keep a secret about someone or something. □ *Don't worry. I won't breathe a word about it.* □ *Please don't breathe a word about Bob and his problems.*

not breathe a word of (something) not to tell something (to anyone). □ *Don't worry. I won't breathe a word of it.* □ *Tom won't breathe a word.*

not buy something not accept something (to be true). (Slang. Also literal.) □ *You may think so, but I don't buy it.* □ *The police wouldn't buy his story.*

not by a long shot not by a great amount; not. (Informal.) □ *Did I win the race? Not by a long shot.* □ *Not by a long shot did she complete the assignment.*

not care two hoots about someone or something AND **not give two hoots about someone or something; not give a hang about someone or something; not give a hoot about someone or something** not to care at all about someone or something. (Folksy. The *someone* and the *something* are *anyone* and *anything* in the negative.) □ *I don't care two hoots about whether you go to the picnic or not.* □ *She doesn't give a hoot about me. Why should I care?* □ *I don't give a hang about it.*

not dry behind the ears See *wet behind the ears*.

not enough room to swing a cat not very much space. (Folksy.) □ *Their living room was very small. There wasn't enough room to swing a cat.* □ *How can you work in a small room like this? There's not enough room to swing a cat.*

not for a moment not at all; not even for a short amount of time; never. □ *I don't want you to leave. Not for a moment!* □ *I could not wish such a horrible punishment on anyone. Not for a moment!*

not for (anything in) the world AND **not for love nor money; not on your life** not for anything (no matter what its value). (Note the variation in the examples. The order of *love nor money* is fixed.) □ *I won't do it for love nor money.* □ *He said he wouldn't do it—not for the world.* □ *She said no, not for anything in the world.* □ *Me, go there? Not on your life!*

not for love nor money See the previous entry.

not give a hang about someone or something See *not care two hoots about someone or something*.

not give a hoot about someone or something See *not care two hoots about someone or something*.

not give anyone the time of day to ignore someone (usually out of dislike). (Informal.) □ *Mary won't speak to Sally. She won't give her the time of day.* □ *I couldn't get an appointment with Mr. Smith. He wouldn't even give me the time of day.*

not give two hoots about someone or something See *not care two hoots about someone or something*.

not half bad okay; pretty good. (Folksy.) □ *Say, this roast beef isn't half bad.* □ *Hey, Sally! You're not half bad!*

not have a care in the world free and casual; unworried and carefree. □ *I really feel good today—as if I didn't have a care in the world.* □ *Ann always acts as if she doesn't have a care in the world.*

not have a leg to stand on [for an argument or a case] to have no support. (Informal.) □ *You may think you're in the right, but you don't have a leg to stand on.* □ *My lawyer said I didn't have a leg to stand on, so I shouldn't sue the company.*

not have all one's marbles not to have all one's mental capacities. (Informal.) □ *John acts as if he doesn't have all his marbles.* □ *I'm afraid that I don't have all my marbles all the time.*

not hold a candle to someone or something See the following entry.

not hold a stick to someone or something AND **not hold a candle to someone or something** not to be nearly as good as someone or something. (Informal.) □ *Sally is much faster than Bob. Bob doesn't hold a stick to Sally.* □ *This T.V. doesn't hold a candle to that one. That one is much better.*

not hold water to make no sense; to be illogical. (Informal. Said of ideas, arguments, etc., not people. It means that the idea has holes in it. See also *won't hold water*.) □ *Your argument doesn't hold water.* □ *This scheme won't work because it can't hold water.*

not hurt a flea not to harm anything or anyone, even a tiny insect. (Also with other forms of negation.) □ *Ted would not even hurt a flea. He could not have struck Bill* □ *Ted would never hurt a flea, and he would not hit anyone as you claim.*

not in the same league with someone or something not anywhere nearly as good as someone or something. □ *John isn't in the same league with Bob and his friends.* □ *This house isn't in the same league with our old one.*

not know beans (about someone or something) to know nothing about someone or something. (Slang.) □ *Bill doesn't know beans about flying an airplane.* □ *When it comes to flying, I don't know beans.* □ *Nobody knows beans about Bill.*

not know enough to come in out of the rain to be very stupid. □ *Bob is so stupid he doesn't know enough to come in out of the rain.* □ *You can't expect very much from somebody who doesn't know enough to come in out of the rain.*

not know from nothing to be stupid, innocent, and naive. (Slang. This *nothing* is not replaced with *something*. Usually with *don't*, as in the examples.) □ *Old John—he don't know from nothing.* □ *What do you expect from somebody who don't know from nothing?*

not know if one is coming or going See *not know whether one is coming or going.*

not know someone from Adam not to know someone at all. □ *I wouldn't recognize John if I saw him. I don't know him from Adam.* □ *What does she look like? I don't know her from Adam.*

not know the first thing about someone or something not to know anything about someone or something. □ *I don't know the first thing about flying an airplane.* □ *She doesn't know the first thing about John.*

not know where to turn AND **not know which way to turn** to have no idea about what to do (about something). □ *I was so confused I didn't know where to turn.* □ *We needed help, but we didn't know which way to turn.*

not know whether one is coming or going AND **not know if one is coming or going** to be very confused. (Fixed order.) □ *I'm so busy that I don't know if I'm coming or going.* □ *You look as if you don't know whether you're coming or going.*

not know which way to turn See *not know where to turn.*

not let someone catch someone doing something AND **not want to catch someone doing something** to find someone doing something wrong. (The idea is that the person ought not to do the wrong thing again, not that the person simply avoid getting caught.) □ *How many times have I told you not to play ball in the house? Don't let me catch you doing that again.* □ *If I've told you once, I've told you a thousand times: Don't do that! I don't want to catch you doing it again!*

not lift a finger (to help someone) AND **not lift a hand (to help someone)** to do nothing to help someone. (The *someone* is *anyone* in the negative.) □ *They wouldn't lift a finger to help us.* □ *Can you imagine that they wouldn't lift a finger?* □ *Sally refused to lift a hand to help her own sister.*

not long for this world to be about to die. □ *Our dog is nearly twelve years old and not long for this world.* □ *I'm so tired. I think I'm not long for this world.*

not miss much 1. AND **not miss a thing** not to miss observing any part of what is going on. (Usually with *do* as in the examples.) □ *Ted doesn't miss much. He is very alert.* □ *The puppy doesn't miss a think. He sees every move you make.* **2.** not to miss experiencing something that really was not worth experiencing anyway. (Sarcastic. Usually with *do* as in the examples.) □ *I missed the big sales meeting last week, but I understand I didn't miss much.* □ BILL: *I didn't see that new movie that is showing at the theater.* TOM: *You didn't miss much.*

not move a muscle to remain perfectly motionless. □ *Be quiet. Sit there and don't move a muscle.* □ *I was so tired I couldn't move a muscle.*

not on any account See *on no account.*

not on your life See *not for (anything in) the world.*

not one iota not even a tiny bit. □ *I won't give you any at all! Not one iota! □ I did not get one iota of encouragement from any of those people.*

not one's cup of tea not the kind of thing that one is interested in. □ *I turned down an invitation to the opera. It's just not my cup of tea. □ It's not that I find historical novels unpleasant. They're just not my cup of tea.*

not open one's mouth AND **not utter a word** not to say anything at all; not to tell something (to anyone). □ *Don't worry, I'll keep your secret. I won't even open my mouth. □ Have no fear. I won't utter a word. □ I don't know how they found out. I didn't even open my mouth.*

not see any objection (to something) See *see no objection (to something).*

not see farther than the end of one's nose AND **not see past the end of one's nose** not to care about what is not actually present or obvious; not to care about the future or about what is happening elsewhere or to other people. □ *Mary can't see past the end of her nose. She doesn't care about what will happen in the future as long as she's comfortable now. □ Jack's been accused of not seeing farther than the end of his nose. He refuses to expand the company and look for new markets.*

not see past the end of one's nose See the previous entry.

not set foot somewhere not to go somewhere. □ *I wouldn't set foot in John's room. I'm very angry at him. □ He never set foot here.*

not show one's face not to appear (somewhere). □ *After what she said, she had better not show her face around here again. □ If I don't say I'm sorry, I'll never be able to show my face again.*

not sleep a wink not to sleep at all. (Informal.) □ *I couldn't sleep a wink last night. □ Ann hasn't been able to sleep a wink for a week.*

not someone's cup of tea not something one prefers. □ *Playing cards isn't her cup of tea. □ Sorry, that's not my cup of tea.*

not take no for an answer not to accept someone's refusal. (Informal. A polite way of being insistent.) □ *Now, you must drop over and see us tomorrow. We won't take no for an answer. □ I had to go. They just wouldn't take no for an answer.*

not take stock in something See *take no stock in something.*

not up to scratch AND **not up to snuff** not adequate. (Informal. See also *up to snuff; up to scratch.*) □ *Sorry, your paper isn't up to scratch. Please do it over again. □ The performance was not up to snuff.*

not up to snuff See the previous entry.

not utter a word See *not open one's mouth.*

not want to catch someone doing something See *not let someone catch someone doing something.*

not what something is cracked up to be See *not all something is cracked up to be.*

not worth a dime AND **not worth a red cent** worthless. (Informal.) □ *This land is all swampy. It's not worth a dime. □ This pen I bought isn't worth a dime. It has no ink. □ It's not worth a red cent.*

not worth a hill of beans AND **not worth a plugged nickel** worthless. (Folksy.) □ *Your advice isn't worth a hill of beans. □ This old cow isn't worth a plugged nickel.*

not worth a plugged nickel See the previous entry.

not worth a red cent See *not worth a dime.*

nothing but skin and bones AND **(all) skin and bones** very thin or emaciated. (Informal. Fixed order.) □ *Bill has lost so much weight. He's nothing* *but skin and bones.* □ *Look at Bill. He's just skin and bones.* □ *That old horse is all skin and bones. I won't ride it.*

nothing but something only; just. □ *Joan drinks nothing but milk.* □ *Fred buys nothing but expensive clothes.*

nothing doing no. (Informal.) □ *No, I won't do that. Nothing doing.* □ BOB: *Will you help me with this?* BILL: *Nothing doing.*

nothing down requiring no down payment. □ *You can have this car for nothing down and $140 a month.* □ *I bought a winter coat for nothing down and no payments due until February.*

nothing of the kind 1. no; absolutely not. □ *I didn't tear your jacket — nothing of the kind!* □ *Did I break your vase? Nothing of the kind!* **2.** nothing like that. □ *That's not true. We did nothing of the kind!* □ *She did nothing of the kind! She wasn't even there!*

nothing short of something more or less the same as something bad; as bad as something. □ *His behavior was nothing short of criminal.* □ *Climbing those mountains alone is nothing short of suicide.*

nothing to choose from no choice; no choice in the selection; not enough of something to make a choice. □ *I went to the store looking for new shoes, but there was nothing to choose from.* □ *By the time I got around to selecting a team of helpers, there was nothing to choose from.*

nothing to complain about all right. (Folksy. Said in answer to the question "How are you?") □ *Bob said he has nothing to complain about.* □ BILL: *How're you doing, Bob?* BOB: *Nothing to complain about, Bill. Yourself?*

nothing to it it is easy; no difficulty involved. □ *Driving a car is easy. There's nothing to it.* □ *Geometry is fun to learn. There's nothing to it.*

nothing to sneeze at nothing small or unimportant. (Informal.) □ *It's not a lot of money, but it's nothing to sneeze at.* □ *Our house isn't a mansion, but it's nothing to sneeze at.*

nothing to speak of not many; not much. (Informal.) □ JOHN: *What's happening around here?* BILL: *Nothing to speak of.* □ MARY: *Has there been any rain in the last week?* SALLY: *Nothing to speak of.*

nothing to write home about nothing exciting or interesting. (Folksy.) □ *I've been busy, but nothing to write home about.* □ *I had a dull week — nothing to write home about.*

Nothing ventured, nothing gained. a proverb meaning that you cannot achieve anything if you do not try. (Fixed order.) □ *Come on, John. Give it a try. Nothing ventured, nothing gained.* □ *I felt as if I had to take the chance. Nothing ventured, nothing gained.*

now and again See *(every) now and again.*

now and then See *(every) now and then.*

now or never at this time and no other. (Fixed order.) □ *This is your only chance, John. It's now or never.* □ *I decided that it was now or never and jumped.*

nowhere near not nearly. □ *We have nowhere near enough wood for the winter.* □ *They're nowhere near ready for the game.*

null and void canceled; worthless. (Fixed order.) □ *I tore the contract up, and the entire agreement became null and void.* □ *The judge declared the whole business null and void.*

nurse a grudge (against someone) to keep resenting and disliking someone over a period of time. (See also *bear a grudge (against someone)*.) □ *Sally is still nursing a grudge against Mary.* □ *How long can anyone nurse a grudge?*

nuts about someone or something See *crazy about someone or something.*

nuts and bolts (of something) the basic facts about something; the practical details of something. (Fixed order.) □ *Tom knows all about the nuts and bolts of the chemical process.* □ *Ann is familiar with the nuts and bolts of public relations.*

nutty as a fruitcake See *(as) nutty as a fruitcake.*

O

occur to someone [for an idea or thought] to come into someone's mind. □ *It occurred to me that you might be hungry after your long journey.* □ *Would it ever occur to you that I want to be left alone?*

odd man out an unusual or atypical person or thing. □ *I'm odd man out because I'm not wearing a tie.* □ *You had better learn to work a computer unless you want to be odd man out.*

odds and ends small, miscellaneous things. (Fixed order.) □ *There were lots of odds and ends in the attic, but nothing of real value.* □ *I had the whole house cleaned up except for a few odds and ends that didn't seem to belong anywhere.*

odor of sanctity an atmosphere of excessive holiness or piety. (Derogatory.) □ *I hate their house. There's such an odor of sanctity, with Bibles and religious pictures everywhere.* □ *People are made nervous by Jane's odor of sanctity. She's always praying for people or doing good works and never has any fun.*

of all the nerve how shocking; how dare (someone). (Informal. The speaker is exclaiming that someone is being very cheeky or rude.) □ *How dare you talk to me that way! Of all the nerve!* □ *Imagine anyone coming to a formal dance in jeans. Of all the nerve!*

of all things Can you imagine?; Imagine that! (Folksy.) □ *She wore jeans to the dance. Of all things!* □ *Billy, stop eating the houseplant! Of all things!*

of benefit (to someone) serving someone well; to the good of someone. □

I can't believe that this proposal is of benefit to anyone. □ *Oh, I'm sure it's of benefit.*

of late lately. (Formal.) □ *Have you seen Sally of late?* □ *We haven't had an opportunity to eat out of late.*

of no avail See *to no avail.*

of one's own accord AND **of one's own free will** by one's own choice, without coercion. □ *I wish that Sally would choose to do it of her own accord.* □ *I'll have to order her to do it because she won't do it of her own free will.*

of one's own free will See the previous entry.

of the first water of the finest quality. □ *This is a very fine pearl—a pearl of the first water.* □ *Tom is of the first water—a true gentleman.*

of the old school holding attitudes or ideas that were popular and important in the past, but which are no longer considered relevant or in line with modern trends. □ *Grammar was not much taught in my son's school, but fortunately he had a teacher of the old school.* □ *Aunt Jane is of the old school. She never goes out without wearing a hat and gloves.*

off again, on again See *on again, off again.*

off and on See *on and off.*

off and running started up and going. (Also literal, as in a footrace. Fixed order.) □ *The car was finally loaded by 9:30, and we were off and running.* □ *The construction of the building was going to take two years, but we were off* *and running, and it appeared we would finish on schedule.*

off base unrealistic; inexact; wrong. (Also literal in baseball.) □ *I'm afraid you're off base when you state that this problem will take care of itself.* □ *You're way off base!*

off-center not exactly in the center or middle. □ *The arrow hit the target a little off-center.* □ *The picture hanging over the chair is a little off-center.*

off-color 1. not the exact color (that one wants). □ *The book cover used to be red, but now it's a little off-color.* □ *The wall was painted off-color. I think it was meant to be orange.* **2.** in bad taste; rude, vulgar, or impolite. □ *That joke you told was off-color and embarrassed me.* □ *The nightclub act was a bit off-color.*

off duty not working at one's job. (The opposite of *on duty*.) □ *I'm sorry, I can't talk to you until I'm off duty.* □ *The police officer couldn't help me because he was off duty.*

off like a shot away [from a place] very quickly. □ *He finished his dinner and was off like a shot.* □ *The thief grabbed the lady's purse and was off like a shot.*

off limits AND **out of bounds** forbidden. □ *This area is off limits. You can't go in there.* □ *Don't go there. It's out of bounds.* □ *That kind of behavior is off limits. Stop it!*

off one's nut See the following entry.

off one's rocker AND **off one's nut; off one's trolley** crazy; silly. (Slang.) □ *Sometimes, Bob, I think you're off your rocker.* □ *Good grief, John. You're off your nut.* □ *About this time of the day I go off my trolley. I get so tired.*

off one's trolley See the previous entry.

off season not in the busy time of the year. □ *We don't have much to do off season.* □ *Things are very quiet around here off season.*

off someone or something goes someone or something is leaving. (Said on the departure of someone or something.) □ *It's time to leave. Off I go.* □

Sally looked at the airplane taking off and said, "Off it goes."

off the air not broadcasting (a radio or television program). □ *The radio audience won't hear what you say when you're off the air.* □ *When the performers were off the air, the director told them how well they had done.*

off the (beaten) track in an unfamiliar place; on a route that is not often traveled. (See also *off the track.*) □ *Their home is in a quiet neighborhood, off the beaten track.* □ *We like to stop there and admire the scenery. It's off the track, but it's worth the trip.*

off-the-cuff spontaneous; without preparation or rehearsal. (Informal.) □ *Her remarks were off-the-cuff, but very sensible.* □ *I'm not very good at making speeches off-the-cuff.*

off the mark not quite exactly right. □ *Her answer was a little off the mark.* □ *You were off the mark when you said we would be a little late to the party. It was yesterday, in fact!*

off the record unofficial; informal. □ *This is off the record, but I disagree with the mayor on this matter.* □ *Although her comments were off the record, the newspaper published them anyway.*

off the top of one's head [to state something] rapidly and without having to think or remember. (Informal.) □ *I can't think of the answer off the top of my head.* □ *Jane can tell you the correct amount off the top of her head.*

off the track 1. See *off the (beaten) track.* **2.** irrelevant and immaterial (comments). □ *I'm afraid you're off the track, John. Try again.* □ *I'm sorry. I was thinking about dinner, and I got off the track.*

off-the-wall odd; silly; unusual. (Slang.) □ *Why are you so off-the-wall today?* □ *This book is strange. It's really off-the-wall.*

off to a running start with a good, fast beginning, possibly a head start. □ *I got off to a running start in math this year.* □ *The horses got off to a running start.*

off to one side beside (something); (moved) slightly away from something. □ *Our garden has roses in the middle and a spruce tree off to one side.* □ *He took me off to one side to tell me the bad news.*

oil someone's palm See *grease someone's palm.*

old as the hills See *(as) old as the hills.*

old enough to be someone's father See the following entry.

old enough to be someone's mother AND **old enough to be someone's father** as old as someone's parents. (Usually a way of saying that a person is too old. Not literal.) □ *You can't go out with Bill. He's old enough to be your father!* □ *He married a woman who is old enough to be his mother.*

old hand at doing something someone who is experienced at doing something. □ *I'm an old hand at fixing clocks.* □ *He's an old hand at changing diapers.*

on a diet trying to lose weight by eating less food or specific foods. □ *I didn't eat any cake because I'm on a diet.* □ *I'm getting too heavy. I'll have to go on a diet.*

on a first-name basis (with someone) knowing someone very well; good friends with someone. □ *I'm on a first-name basis with John.* □ *John and I are on a first-name basis.*

on a fool's errand involved in a useless journey or task. □ *Bill went for an interview, but he was on a fool's errand. The job had already been filled.* □ *I was sent on a fool's errand to buy some flowers. I knew the shop would be closed by then.*

on a waiting list [with one's name] on a list of people waiting for an opportunity to do something. (*A* can be replaced with *the.*) □ *I couldn't get a seat on the plane, but I got on a waiting list.* □ *There is no room for you, but we can put your name on the waiting list.*

on account [money paid or owed] on a debt. □ *I paid twelve dollars on ac-*

count last month. Wasn't that enough? □ *I still have $100 due on account.*

on active duty in battle or ready to go into battle. (Military.) □ *The soldier was on active duty for ten months.* □ *That was a long time to be on active duty.*

on again, off again AND **off again, on again** uncertain; indecisive. (Reversible.) □ *I don't know about the picnic. It's on again, off again. It depends on the weather.* □ *Jane doesn't know if she's going to the picnic. She's off again, on again about it.*

on all fours on one's hands and knees. □ *I dropped a contact lens and spent an hour on all fours looking for it.* □ *The baby can walk, but is on all fours most of the time anyway.*

on and off AND **off and on** occasionally; erratically; *now and again.* (Reversible.) □ *I feel better off and on, but I'm not well yet.* □ *He only came to class on and off.*

on any account for any purpose; for any reason; no matter what. (Compare with *on no account.*) □ *On any account, I'll be there on time.* □ *This doesn't make sense on any account.*

on approval for examination, with the privilege of return. □ *I ordered the merchandise on approval so I could send it back if I didn't like it.* □ *Sorry, you can't buy this on approval. All sales are final.*

on behalf of someone See *in behalf of someone.*

on bended knee kneeling, as in supplication. (Usually hypothetical. Also literal. The verb form is obsolescent and occurs now only in this phrase.) □ *Do you expect me to come to you on bended knee and ask you for forgiveness?* □ *The suitors came on bended knee and begged the attention of the princess.*

on board 1. aboard (on or in) a ship, bus, airplane, etc. □ *Is there a doctor on board? We have a sick passenger.* □ *When everyone is on board, we will* *leave.* **2.** employed by (someone); working with (someone). (Informal.) □ *Our company has a computer specialist on board to advise us about automation.* □ *Welcome to the company, Tom. We're all glad you're on board now.*

on call ready to serve when called. □ *I live a very hard life. I'm on call twenty hours a day.* □ *I'm sorry, but I can't go out tonight. I'm on call at the hospital.*

on cloud nine very happy. (Informal.) □ *When I got my promotion, I was on cloud nine.* □ *When the check came, I was on cloud nine for days.*

on dead center 1. at the exact center of something. □ *The arrow hit the target on dead center.* □ *When you put the flowers on the table, put them on dead center.* **2.** exactly correct. □ *Mary is quite observant. Her analysis is on dead center.* □ *My view isn't on dead center, but it's sensible.*

on deck 1. on the deck of a boat or a ship. □ *Everyone except the cook was on deck when the storm hit.* □ *Just pull up the anchor and leave it on deck.* **2.** ready (to do something); ready to be next (at something). □ *Ann, get on deck. You're next.* □ *Who's on deck now?*

on deposit deposited or stored in a safe place. □ *I have $10,000 on deposit in that bank.* □ *We have some gold coins on deposit in the bank's vault.*

on duty at work; currently doing one's work. (The opposite of *off duty*.) □ *I can't help you now, but I'll be on duty in about an hour.* □ *Who is on duty here? I need some help.*

on earth AND **in creation; in the world** really; indeed; in fact. (Used as an intensifier after *who, what, when, where, how.*) □ *What on earth do you mean?* □ *How in creation do you expect me to do that?* □ *Who in the world do you think you are?* □ *When on earth do you expect me to do this?*

on easy street in luxury. (Slang.) □ *If I had a million dollars, I'd be on easy*

street. □ *Everyone has problems, even people who live on easy street.*

on edge 1. on (something's own) edge. □ *Can you stand a dime on edge?* □ *You should store your records on edge, not flat.* **2.** nervous. □ *I have really been on edge lately.* □ *Why are you so on edge?*

on foot by walking. □ *My bicycle is broken, so I'll have to travel on foot.* □ *You can't expect me to get there on foot! It's twelve miles!*

on good terms (with someone) friendly with someone. □ *I'm on good terms with Ann. I'll ask her to help.* □ *We're on good terms now. Last week we were not.*

on hold (See also *put someone or something on hold.*) **1.** waiting; temporarily halted. □ *The building project is on hold while we try to find money to complete it.* □ *We put our plans on hold until we finished school.* **2.** left waiting on a telephone line. □ *I hate to call up someone and then end up on hold.* □ *I waited on hold for ten minutes when I called city hall.*

on in years See *up in years.*

on line 1. See *in line.* **2.** connected to a computer. □ *As soon as I get on line, I can check the balance of your account.* □ *I was on line for an hour before I found out what I wanted to know.*

on no account AND **not on any account** for no reason; absolutely not. □ *On no account will I lend you the money.* □ *Will I say I'm sorry? Not on any account.*

on occasion occasionally. □ *We go out for dinner on occasion.* □ *I enjoy going to a movie on occasion.*

on one's best behavior being as polite as possible. □ *When we went out, the children were on their best behavior.* □ *I try to be on my best behavior all the time.*

on one's feet 1. standing up. □ *Get on your feet. They are playing the national anthem.* □ *I've been on my feet all day, and they hurt.* **2.** well and healthy, especially after an illness. □ *I hope to be back on my feet next week.* □ *I can help out as soon as I'm back on my feet.*

on (one's) guard cautious; watchful. □ *Be on guard. There are pickpockets around here.* □ *You had better be on your guard.*

on one's honor on one's solemn oath; sincerely. □ *On my honor, I'll be there on time.* □ *He promised on his honor that he'd pay me back next week.*

on one's mind occupying one's thoughts; currently being thought about. □ *You've been on my mind all day.* □ *Do you have something on your mind? You look so serious.*

on one's own by oneself. □ *Did you do this on your own, or did you have help?* □ *I have to learn to do this kind of thing on my own.*

on one's own time not while one is at work. □ *The boss made me write the report on my own time. That's not fair.* □ *Please make your personal telephone calls on your own time.*

on one's toes alert. (See also *step on someone's toes.*) □ *You have to be on your toes if you want to be in this business.* □ *My boss keeps me on my toes.*

on one's way (somewhere) See *on the way (somewhere).*

on one's way to doing something See *on the way to doing something.*

on order ordered with delivery expected. □ *Your car is on order. It'll be here in a few weeks.* □ *I don't have the part in stock, but it's on order.*

on par (with someone or something) equal to someone or something. □ *Your effort is simply not on par with what's expected from you.* □ *These two reports are right on par.*

on pins and needles anxious; in suspense. (Fixed order.) □ *I've been on pins and needles all day, waiting for you to call with the news.* □ *We were on pins and needles until we heard that your plane landed safely.*

on sale offered for sale at a special low price. □ *I won't buy anything that's not on sale.* □ *I need a new coat, but I want to find a nice one on sale.*

on schedule at the expected or desired time. □ *The plane came in right on schedule.* □ *Things have to happen on schedule in a theatrical performance.*

on second thought having given something more thought; having reconsidered something. □ *On second thought, maybe you should sell your house and move into an apartment.* □ *On second thought, let's not go to a movie.*

on someone's account because of someone. □ *Don't do it on my account.* □ *They were late on Jane's account.*

on someone's back See *on someone's case.*

on someone's behalf See *in behalf of someone.*

on someone's case AND **on someone's back** constantly criticizing someone. (Slang. See also *Get off someone's case!*) □ *I'm tired of your being on my case all the time.* □ *It seems as if someone is always on his back.*

on someone's doorstep See *at someone's doorstep.*

on someone's head on someone's own self. (Usually with *blame. On* can be replaced with *upon.*) □ *All the blame fell on their heads.* □ *I don't think that all the criticism should be on my head.*

on someone's or something's last legs for someone or something to be almost finished. (Informal.) □ *This building is on its last legs. It should be torn down.* □ *I feel as if I'm on my last legs. I'm really tired.*

on someone's say-so on someone's authority; with someone's permission. □ *I can't do it on your say-so. I'll have to get a written request.* □ BILL: *I canceled the contract with the A.B.C. Company.* BOB: *On whose say-so?*

on someone's shoulders on someone's own self. (Usually with *responsibility. On* can be replaced with *upon.*)

□ *Why should all the responsibility fall on my shoulders?* □ *She carries a tremendous amount of responsibility on her shoulders.*

on speaking terms (with someone) on friendly terms with someone. (Often in the negative. Compare with *on good terms (with someone).*) □ *I'm not on speaking terms with Mary. We had a serious disagreement.* □ *We're not on speaking terms.*

on target on schedule; exactly as predicted. □ *Your estimate of the cost was right on target.* □ *My prediction was not on target.*

on the air broadcasting (a radio or television program). □ *The radio station came back on the air shortly after the storm.* □ *We were on the air for two hours.*

on the alert (for someone or something) watchful and attentive for someone or something. □ *Be on the alert for pickpockets.* □ *You should be on the alert when you cross the street in heavy traffic.*

on the average generally; usually. □ *On the average, you can expect about a 10 percent failure rate.* □ *This report looks okay, on the average.*

on the ball alert, effective, and efficient. (Slang.) □ *Sally has a lot on the ball.* □ *You've got to be on the ball if you want to succeed in this business.*

on the beam exactly right; thinking along the correct lines. (Informal. Also literal.) □ *That's the right idea. Now you're on the beam!* □ *She's not on the beam yet. Explain it to her again.*

on the bench **1.** directing a session of court. (Said of a judge.) □ *I have to go to court tomorrow. Who's on the bench?* □ *It doesn't matter who's on the bench. You'll get a fair hearing.* **2.** sitting, waiting for a chance to play in a game. (In sports, such as basketball, football, soccer, etc.) □ *Bill is on the bench now. I hope he gets to play.* □ *John played during the first quarter, but now he's on the bench.*

on the blink See *on the fritz.*

on the block **1.** on a city block. □ *John is the biggest kid on the block.* □ *We had a party on the block last weekend.* **2.** on sale at auction; on the auction block. □ *We couldn't afford to keep up the house, so it was put on the block to pay the taxes.* □ *That's the finest painting I've ever seen on the block.*

on the button exactly right; in exactly the right place; at exactly the right time. (Informal.) □ *That's it! You're right on the button.* □ *He got here at one o'clock on the button.*

on the contrary as the opposite. (Compare with *to the contrary.*) □ *I'm not ill. On the contrary, I'm very healthy.* □ *She's not in a bad mood. On the contrary, she's as happy as a lark.*

on the dot at exactly the right time. (Informal. Compare with *at sometime sharp.*) □ *I'll be there at noon on the dot.* □ *I expect to see you here at eight o'clock on the dot.*

on the double very fast. (Informal.) □ *Okay, you guys. Get over here on the double.* □ *Get yourself into this house on the double.*

on the eve of something just before something, possibly the evening before something. □ *John decided to leave school on the eve of his graduation.* □ *The team held a party on the eve of the tournament.*

on the face of it superficially; from the way it looks. □ *This looks like a serious problem on the face of it. It probably is minor, however.* □ *On the face of it, it seems worthless.*

on the fence (about something) undecided. (Informal.) □ *Ann is on the fence about going to Mexico.* □ *I wouldn't be on the fence. I'd love to go.*

on the fritz AND **on the blink** not operating; not operating correctly. (Slang.) □ *This vacuum cleaner is on the fritz. Let's get it fixed.* □ *How long has it been on the blink?*

on the go busy; moving about busily. (Informal.) □ *I'm usually on the go all* day long. □ *I hate being on the go all the time.*

on the heels of something soon after something. (Informal.) □ *There was a rainstorm on the heels of the windstorm.* □ *The team held a victory celebration on the heels of their winning season.*

on the horizon soon to happen. (Also literal. See also *in the offing.*) □ *Do you know what's on the horizon?* □ *Who can tell what's on the horizon?*

on the horns of a dilemma having to decide between two things, people, etc. □ *Mary found herself on the horns of a dilemma. She didn't know which to choose.* □ *I make up my mind easily. I'm not on the horns of a dilemma very often.*

on the hot seat AND **in the hot seat** in a difficult position; subject to much criticism. (Slang.) □ *I was really in the hot seat for a while.* □ *Now that John is on the hot seat, no one is paying any attention to what I do.*

on the hour at each hour on the hour mark. □ *I have to take this medicine every hour on the hour.* □ *I expect to see you there on the hour, not one minute before and not one minute after.*

on the house [something that is] given away free by a merchant. (Informal. Also literal.) □ *"Here," said the waiter, "have a cup of coffee on the house."* □ *I went to a restaurant last night. I was the ten-thousandth customer, so my dinner was on the house.*

on the job working; doing what one is expected to do. □ *I'm always on the job when I should be.* □ *I can depend on my furnace to be on the job day and night.*

on the level honest; dependably open and fair. (Informal. Also with *strictly*. Compare with *on the up-and-up*.) □ *How can I be sure you're on the level?* □ *You can trust Sally. She's on the level.*

on the lookout (for someone or something) watchful for someone or something. □ *Be on the lookout for signs of a storm.* □ *I'm on the lookout for John, who is due here any minute.* □ *Okay, you remain on the lookout for another hour.*

on the loose running around free. (Informal.) □ *Look out! There is a bear on the loose from the zoo.* □ *Most kids enjoy being on the loose when they go to college.*

on the make **1.** building or developing; being made. (Informal.) □ *There is a company that is on the make.* □ *That was a very good sales strategy, John. You're a real-estate agent on the make.* **2.** making sexual advances; seeking sexual activities. (Slang.) □ *It seems like Bill is always on the make.* □ *He should meet Sally, who is also on the make.*

on the market available for sale; offered for sale. (Compare with *on the block*.) □ *I had to put my car on the market.* □ *This is the finest home computer on the market.*

on the mend getting well; healing. □ *My cold was terrible, but I'm on the mend now.* □ *What you need is some hot chicken soup. Then you'll really be on the mend.*

on the money AND **on the nose** in exactly the right place; in exactly the right amount (of money). (Slang.) □ *That's a good answer, Bob. You're right on the money.* □ *This project is going to be finished right on the nose.*

on the move moving; happening busily. □ *What a busy day. Things are really on the move at the store.* □ *When all the buffalo were on the move across the plains, it must have been very exciting.*

on the nose See *on the money.*

on the off-chance because of a slight possibility that something may happen, might be the case, etc.; just in case. □ *I went to the theater on the off-chance that there were tickets for the show left.* □ *We didn't think we would get into the stadium, but we went anyway on the off-chance.*

on (the) one hand from one point of view; as one side (of an issue). □ *On one hand, I really ought to support my team. On the other hand, I don't have to time to attend all the games.* □ *On the one hand, I need Ann's help. On the other hand, she and I don't get along very well.*

on the other hand from another point of view; as the other side (of an issue). See the examples for *on (the) one hand.*

on the point of doing something AND **at the point of doing something** ready to start doing something. (Compare with *on the verge (of doing something).*) □ *I was just on the point of going out the door.* □ *We were almost at the point of buying a new car.*

on the QT quietly; secretly. (Informal.) □ *The company president was making payments to his wife on the QT.* □ *The mayor accepted a bribe on the QT.*

on the rocks 1. in a state of destruction or wreckage. (As a ship, stranded on the rocks.) □ *I hear their marriage is on the rocks.* □ *The company is on the rocks and may not survive.* **2.** [poured] onto ice cubes in a glass. □ *Joan prefers her drinks on the rocks.* □ *Could I have a scotch on the rocks?*

on the spot (Informal.) **1.** at exactly the right place; at exactly the right time. (See also *Johnny-on-the-spot.*) □ *It's noon, and I'm glad you're all here on the spot. Now we can begin.* □ *I expect you to be on the spot when and where trouble arises.* **2.** in trouble; in a difficult situation. (Compare with *on the hot seat.*) □ *There is a problem in the department I manage, and I'm really on the spot.* □ *I hate to be on the spot when it's not my fault.*

on the spur of the moment suddenly; spontaneously. □ *We decided to go on the spur of the moment.* □ *I had to leave town on the spur of the moment.*

on the strength of something because of the support of something, such as a promise or evidence; due to something. □ *On the strength of your com-*ment, I decided to give John another chance.* □ *On the strength of my testimony, my case was dismissed.*

on the take accepting bribes. (Slang.) □ *I don't believe that the mayor is on the take.* □ *The county clerk has been on the take for years.*

on the tip of one's tongue about to be said; almost remembered. (See also *have something on the tip of one's tongue.*) □ *It's right on the tip of my tongue. I'll think of it in a second.* □ *The answer was on the tip of my tongue, but Ann said it first.*

on the track of someone or something See the following entry.

on the trail of someone or something AND **on the track of someone or something** seeking someone or something; about to find someone or something. □ *I'm on the trail of a new can opener that is supposed to be easier to use.* □ *I spent all morning on the track of the new secretary, who got lost on the way to work.*

on the up-and-up See *(strictly) on the up-and-up.*

on the verge (of doing something) just about to do something, usually something important. (Compare with *on the point of doing something.*) □ *I'm on the verge of opening a shoe store.* □ *Tom was on the verge of quitting school when he became interested in physics.* □ *I haven't done it yet, but I'm on the verge.*

on the wagon not drinking alcohol; no longer drinking alcohol. (Also literal.) □ *None for me, thanks. I'm on the wagon.* □ *Look at John. I don't think he's on the wagon anymore.*

on the warpath angry and upset (at someone). (Informal.) □ *Oh, oh. Here comes Mrs. Smith. She's on the warpath again.* □ *Why are you always on the warpath? What's wrong?*

on the way (somewhere) AND **on someone's way (somewhere)** along the route to somewhere. □ *She's now on the way to San Francisco.* □ *Yes, she's on the way.*

on the way to doing something AND **on one's way to doing something** in the process of doing something. □ *You're on the way to becoming a very good carpenter.* □ *She's on her way to becoming a first-class sculptor.*

on the whole generally; considering everything. □ *On the whole, this was a very good day.* □ *Your work—on the whole—is quite good.*

on the wing while flying; while in flight. (Formal. Usually refers to birds, fowl, etc., not people or planes.) □ *There is nothing as pretty as a bird on the wing.* □ *The hawk caught the sparrow on the wing.*

on the wrong track going the wrong way; following the wrong set of assumptions. (Also literal.) □ *You'll never get the right answer. You're on the wrong track.* □ *They won't get it figured out because they are on the wrong track.*

on thin ice in a risky situation. □ *If you try that you'll really be on thin ice. That's too risky.* □ *If you don't want to find yourself on thin ice, you must be sure of your facts.*

on time at the scheduled time; at the predicted time. □ *The plane landed right on time.* □ *We'll have to hurry to get there on time.*

on tiptoe standing or walking on the front part of the feet (the balls of the feet) with no weight put on the heels. (This is done to gain height or to walk quietly.) □ *I had to stand on tiptoe in order to see over the fence.* □ *I came in late and walked on tiptoe so I wouldn't wake anybody up.*

on top victorious over something; famous or notorious for something. □ *I have to study day and night to keep on top.* □ *Bill is on top in his field.*

on top of something 1. up-to-date on something; knowing about the current state of something. (Informal.) □ *Ask Mary. She's on top of this issue.* □ *This issue is constantly changing. She has to pay attention to it to stay on top of things.* **2.** in addition to something. □

Jane told Bill he was dull. On top of that, she said he was unfriendly. □ *On top of being dull, he's unfriendly.*

on top of the world See *(sitting) on top of the world.*

on trial being tried in court. □ *My sister is on trial today, so I have to go to court.* □ *They placed the suspected thief on trial.*

on vacation away, taking a vacation; on holiday. □ *Where are you going on vacation this year?* □ *I'll be away on vacation for three weeks.*

on view visible; on public display. □ *The painting will be on view at the museum.* □ *I'll pull the shades so that we won't be on view.*

once and for all finally and irreversibly. (Fixed order.) □ *I want to get this problem settled once and for all.* □ *I told him once and for all that he has to start studying.*

once in a blue moon very rarely. □ *I seldom go to a movie—maybe once in a blue moon.* □ *I don't go into the city except once in a blue moon.*

once-in-a-lifetime chance a chance that will never occur again in one's lifetime. □ *This is a once-in-a-lifetime chance. Don't miss it.* □ *She offered me a once-in-a-lifetime chance, but I turned it down.*

once in a while See *(every) now and then.*

once-over-lightly 1. a quick and careless treatment. (A noun. Said of an act of cleaning, studying, examination, or appraisal.) □ *Bill gave his geometry the once-over-lightly and then quit studying.* □ *Ann, you didn't wash the dishes properly. They only got a once-over-lightly.* **2.** cursory; in a quick and careless manner. (An adverb.) □ *Tom studied geometry once-over-lightly.* □ *Ann washed the dishes once-over-lightly.*

once upon a time once in the past. (A formula used to begin a fairy tale.) □ *Once upon a time, there were three* bears. □ *Once upon a time, I had a puppy of my own.*

one and all everyone. (Fixed order.) □ *"Good morning to one and all," said Jane as she walked through the outer office.* □ *Let's hope that this turns out to be a wonderful party for one and all.*

one and only (Fixed order.) **1.** the famous and talented (person). (Used in theatrical introductions.) □ *And now — the one and only — Jane Smith!* □ *Let's have a big hand for the one and only Bob Jones!* **2.** one's spouse. (Informal.) □ *Look at the time. I've got to get home to my one and only.* □ *You're my one and only. There is no one else for me.*

one and the same the very same person or thing. (Fixed order.) □ *John Jones and J. Jones are one and the same.* □ *Men's socks and men's stockings are almost one and the same.*

one at a time See the following entry.

one by one AND **one at a time** the first one, then the next one, then the next one, etc.; one at a time; each in turn. □ *I have to deal with problems one by one. I can't handle them all at once.* □ *Okay, just take things one at a time.* □ *The children came into the room one by one.* □ *Fred peeled potatoes one by one, hating every minute of it.*

one for the (record) books a record-breaking act. □ *What a dive! That's one for the record books.* □ *I've never heard such a funny joke. That's really one for the books.*

One good turn deserves another. a proverb meaning that a good deed should be repaid with another good deed. □ *If he does you a favor, you should do him a favor. One good turn deserves another.* □ *Glad to help you out. One good turn deserves another.*

one in a hundred See *one in a thousand.*

one in a million See the following entry.

one in a thousand AND **one in a hundred; one in a million** unique; one of a very few. □ *He's a great guy. He's one in a million.* □ *Mary's one in a hundred — such a hard worker.*

one jump ahead (of someone or something) AND **one move ahead (of someone or something)** one step in advance of someone or something. □ *Try to stay one jump ahead of the customer.* □ *If you're one move ahead, you're well prepared to deal with problems. Then, nothing is a surprise.*

one little bit any at all; at all. (Also literal.) □ *Jean could not be persuaded to change her mind one little bit.* □ *I don't want to hear anything more about it. Not even one little bit.*

One man's meat is another man's poison. a proverb meaning that one person's preference may be disliked by another person. □ *John just loves his new fur hat, but I think it is horrible. Oh, well, one man's meat is another man's poison.* □ *The neighbors are very fond of their dog even though it's ugly, loud, and smelly. I guess one man's meat is another man's poison.*

one means business one is very serious. (Informal.) □ *Billy, get into this house and do your homework, and I mean business.* □ *We mean business when we say you must stop all this nonsense.*

one move ahead (of someone or something) See *one jump ahead (of someone or something).*

one-night stand an activity lasting one night. (Informal. Often refers to a musical performance or to sexual activity.) □ *Our band has played a lot of one-night stands.* □ *What we want is an engagement for a week, not just a one-night stand.*

one of these days someday; in some situation like this one. □ *One of these days, someone is going to steal your purse if you don't take better care of it.* □ *You're going to get in trouble one of these days.*

one to a customer each person can have or receive only one. (As in sales restrictions where each customer is permitted to buy only one. Also literal, in reference to sales.) □ *"Only one to a customer!" said the chef as he handed out the hamburgers.* □ *Is it one to a customer, or can I take two now?*

one-track mind a mind that thinks entirely or almost entirely about one subject, often sex. □ *Adolescent boys often have one-track minds. All they're interested in is the opposite sex.* □ *Bob has a one-track mind. He can only talk about football.*

one up (on someone) ahead of someone; with an advantage over someone. □ *Tom is one up on Sally because he got a job and she didn't.* □ *Yes, it sounds like Tom is one up.*

one way or another somehow. □ *I'll do it one way or another.* □ *One way or another, I'll get through school.*

One's bark is worse than one's bite. a proverb meaning that one may threaten, but not do much damage. □ *Don't worry about Bob. He won't hurt you. His bark is worse than his bite.* □ *She may scream and yell, but have no fear. Her bark is worse than her bite.*

one's better half one's spouse. (Usually refers to a wife.) □ *I think we'd like to come for dinner, but I'll have to ask my better half.* □ *I have to go home now to my better half. We are going out tonight.*

one's days are numbered [for someone] to face death or dismissal. □ *If I don't get this contract, my days are numbered at this company.* □ *Uncle Tom has a terminal disease. His days are numbered.*

one's eyes are bigger than one's stomach [for one] to take more food than one can eat. □ *I can't eat all this. I'm afraid that my eyes were bigger than my stomach.* □ *Try to take less food. Your eyes are bigger than your stomach at every meal.*

one's for the asking can become one's property if one asks for it. □ *I have a cherry pie here. A slice is yours for the asking if you want it.* □ *Uncle Mac said we could have his old car if we wanted it. It was ours for the asking.*

one's heart goes out to someone one feels compassion for someone. □ *My heart goes out to those starving children I see on television.* □ *We are so sorry. Our hearts go out to you.*

one's heart is in one's mouth to feel strongly emotional (about someone or something). □ *"Gosh, Mary," said John, "my heart is in my mouth whenever I see you."* □ *My heart is in my mouth whenever I hear the national anthem.* □ *It was a touching scene. My heart was in my mouth the whole time.*

one's heart is in the right place [for one] to have good intentions, even if the results are bad. (See also have one's heart in the right place.) □ *She gave it a good try. Her heart was in the right place.* □ *He is awkward, but his heart is in the right place.*

one's heart is set against something one is totally against something. □ *Jane's heart is set against going there.*

one's heart is set on something to desire and expect something. □ *Jane's heart is set on going to London.* □ *My heart is set on returning home.*

one's heart misses a beat AND **one's heart skips a beat** for one's heart to flutter or palpitate. □ *Whenever I'm near you, my heart skips a beat.* □ *When the racehorse fell, my heart missed a beat.*

one's heart skips a beat See the previous entry.

one's heart stands still for one's heart to (figuratively) stop beating because of strong emotions. □ *When I first saw you, my heart stood still.* □ *My heart will stand still until you answer.*

one's luck runs out one's good luck stops. □ *My luck ran out, so I had to come home.* □ *She will quit gambling when her luck runs out.*

one's name is mud for one to be in trouble or humiliated. (Slang.) □ *If I can't get this contract signed, my name will be mud.* □ *His name is mud ever since he broke the crystal vase.*

one's nose is in the air one is acting conceited or aloof. (Note the variation with *always*. See also *have one's nose in the air*.) ☐ *Mary's nose is always in the air.* ☐ *Her mother's nose was always in the ar, too.*

one's number is up one's time to die — or to suffer some other unpleasantness — has come. (Informal.) ☐ *John is worried. He thinks his number is up.* ☐ *When my number is up, I hope it all goes fast.*

one's old stamping ground the place where one was raised or where one has spent a lot of time. (Folksy. There are variants with *stomping* and *grounds*.) ☐ *Ann should know about that place. It's near her old stamping ground.* ☐ *I can't wait to get back to my old stomping grounds.*

one's way of life one's life-style; one's pattern of living. ☐ *That kind of thing just doesn't fit into my way of life.* ☐ *Our way of life includes contributing to worthy causes.*

one's work is cut out for one one's task is prepared for one; one has a lot of work to do. (See also *have one's work cut out for one*.) ☐ *This is a big job. My work is cut out for me.* ☐ *The new president's work is cut out for him.*

only have eyes for someone to be loyal to only one person, in the context of romance. ☐ *Oh, Jane! I only have eyes for you!* ☐ *Don't waste any time on Tom. He only has eyes for Ann.*

onto someone or something having discovered the truth about someone or something. (Informal.) ☐ *The police are onto John's plot.* ☐ *Yes, they are onto him, and they are onto the plot.*

open a can of worms to uncover a set of problems; to create unnecessary complications. (Informal. *Can of worms* means "mess." Also with *open up* and with various modifiers such as *new, whole, another*, as in the examples. Compare with *open Pandora's box*.) ☐ *Now you are opening a whole new can of worms.* ☐ *How about* cleaning up this mess before you open up a new can of worms?

open and aboveboard See *aboveboard*.

open-and-shut case something, usually a legal matter, that is simple and straightforward without complications. (Fixed order.) ☐ *The murder trial was an open-and-shut case. The defendant was caught with the murder weapon.* ☐ *Jack's death was an open-and-shut case of suicide. He left a suicide note.*

open fire (on someone) to start (doing something, such as asking questions or criticizing). (Informal. Also literal = to begin shooting at someone.) ☐ *The reporters opened fire on the mayor.* ☐ *When the reporters opened fire, the mayor was smiling, but not for long.*

open one's heart (to someone) to reveal one's inmost thoughts to someone. ☐ *I always open my heart to my spouse when I have a problem.* ☐ *It's a good idea to open your heart every now and then.*

open Pandora's box to uncover a lot of unsuspected problems. ☐ *When I asked Jane about her problems, I didn't know I had opened Pandora's box.* ☐ *You should be cautious with people who are upset. You don't want to open Pandora's box.*

open season (on someone or something) 1. [with *something*] unrestricted hunting of a particular game animal. ☐ *It's always open season on rabbits around here.* ☐ *Is it ever open season on deer?* 2. [with *someone*] a time when everyone is criticizing someone. (Informal. See *open fire (on someone)*.) ☐ *It seems as if it's always open season on politicians.* ☐ *At the news conference, it was open season on the mayor.*

open someone's eyes (to something) 1. to become aware of something. ☐ *He finally opened his eyes to what was going on.* ☐ *It was a long time before he opened his eyes and realized what had been happening.* 2. to cause someone to be aware of something. ☐ *I opened* *his eyes to what was happening at the office.* □ *Why can't I make you understand? Why don't you open your eyes?*

open something up 1. to unwrap something; to open something. □ *Yes, I want to open my presents up.* ⊤ *I can't wait to open up my presents.* ⊤ *Open up this door!* **2.** to begin examining or discussing something. □ *Do you really want to open it up now?* ⊤ *Now is the time to open up the question of taxes.* **3.** to reveal the possibilities of something; to reveal an opportunity. □ *Your letter opened new possibilities up.* ⊤ *Your comments opened up a whole new train of thought.* **4.** to start the use of something, such as land, a building, a business, etc. □ *They opened the coastal lands up to cotton planting.* ⊤ *We opened up a new store last March.* **5.** to make a vehicle go as fast as possible. (Informal.) □ *We took the new car out on the highway and opened it up.* ⊤ *I've never really opened up this truck. I don't know how fast it'll go.* **6.** to make something less congested. □ *They opened the yard up by cutting out a lot of old shrubbery.* ⊤ *We opened up the room by taking the piano out.*

open the door to something to permit or allow something to become a possibility. (Also literal.) □ *Your policy opens the door to cheating.* □ *Your statement opens the door to John's candidacy.*

open up 1. open your door. (A command.) □ *I want in. Open up!* □ *Open up! This is the police.* **2.** to become available. □ *A new job is opening up at my office.* □ *Let me know if any other opportunities open up.* **3.** to go as fast as possible. □ *I can't get this car to open up. Must be something wrong with the engine.* □ *Faster, Tom! Open up! Let's go!* **4.** to become clear, uncluttered, or open. □ *As we drove along, the forest opened up, and we entered into a grassy plain.* □ *The sky opened up, and the sun shone.*

open up (on someone or something) to attack someone or something; to fire a gun or other weapon at someone or

something. □ *The sergeant told the soldiers to open up on the enemy position.* □ *"Okay, you guys," shouted the sergeant. "Open up!"*

open up (to someone) AND **open up (with someone)** to talk frankly, truthfully, or intimately. □ *Finally Sally opened up to her sister and told her what the problem was.* □ *Bill wouldn't open up with me. He's still keeping quiet.* □ *At last, Sally opened up and told everything.*

open up (with someone) See the previous entry.

open with something to start out with something. (Usually said of a performance of some type.) □ *We'll open with a love song and then go on to something faster.* □ *The play opened with an exciting first act, and then it became very boring.*

order of the day something necessary or usual; an overriding necessity. □ *Warm clothes are the order of the day when camping in the winter.* □ *Going to bed early was the order of the day when we were young.*

order someone about AND **order someone around** to give commands to someone. □ *I don't like for someone to order me about.* □ *Don't order me around!*

order someone around See the previous entry.

order something to go See *buy something to go*.

other things being equal if things stay the way they are now; if there were no complications by other factors. □ *Other things being equal, we should have no trouble getting your order to you on time.* □ *I anticipate no problems, other things being equal.*

out and about able to go out and travel around; well enough to go out. (Fixed order.) □ *Beth has been ill, but now she's out and about.* □ *As soon as I feel better, I'll be able to get out and about.*

out-and-out something a complete or absolute something; an indisputable something. (Informal. The *something* must always be a specific thing.) □ *If he said that, he told you an out-and-out lie!* □ *You're an out-and-out liar!*

out cold AND **out like a light** unconscious. □ *I fell and hit my head. I was out cold for about a minute.* □ *Tom fainted! He's out like a light!*

out from under (something) free and clear of something; no longer bearing a (figurative) burden. □ *I'll feel much better when I'm out from under this project.* □ *Now that I'm out from under, I can relax.*

out front in the front of one's house. □ *Our mailbox is out front.* □ *We have a spruce tree out front and a maple tree in the back.*

out in force appearing in great numbers. (See also *in force*.) □ *What a night! The mosquitoes are out in force.* □ *The police were out in force over the holiday weekend.*

out in left field offbeat; unusual and eccentric. (Informal.) □ *Sally is a lot of fun, but she's sort of out in left field.* □ *What a strange idea. It's really out in left field.*

out like a light See *out cold*.

out of a clear blue sky AND **out of the blue** suddenly; without warning. (See also *like a bolt out of the blue*.) □ *Then, out of a clear blue sky, he told me he was leaving.* □ *Mary appeared on my doorstep out of the blue.*

out of all proportion of an exaggerated proportion; of an unrealistic proportion compared to something else; (figuratively) lopsided. (The *all* can be left out.) □ *This problem has grown out of all proportion.* □ *Yes, this thing is way out of proportion.*

out of bounds 1. outside the boundaries of the playing area. (In various sports.) □ *The ball went out of bounds, but the referee didn't notice.* □ *The play ended when Sally ran out of bounds.* **2.** unreasonable. (Informal.)

□ *Your demands are totally out of bounds.* □ *Your request for money is out of bounds.* **3.** See *off limits*.

out of breath breathing fast and hard. □ *I ran so much that I got out of breath.* □ *Mary gets out of breath when she climbs stairs.*

out of character 1. unlike one's usual behavior. □ *Ann's remark was quite out of character.* □ *It was out of character for Ann to act so stubborn.* **2.** inappropriate for the character that an actor is playing. □ *Bill went out of character when the audience started giggling.* □ *Bill played the part so well that it was hard for him to get out of character after the performance.*

out of circulation 1. no longer available for use or lending. (Usually said of library materials.) □ *I'm sorry, but the book you want is temporarily out of circulation.* □ *How long will it be out of circulation?* **2.** not interacting socially with other people. (Informal.) □ *I don't know what's happening because I've been out of circulation for a while.* □ *My cold has kept me out of circulation for a few weeks.*

out of commission 1. [for a ship] to be not currently in use or under command. □ *This vessel will remain out of commission for another month.* □ *The ship has been out of commission since repairs began.* **2.** broken, unserviceable, or inoperable. □ *My watch is out of commission and is running slow.* □ *I can't run in the marathon because my knees are out of commission.*

out of condition See *out of shape*.

out of consideration (for someone or something) with consideration for someone or something; with kind regard for someone or something. □ *Out of consideration for your past efforts, I will do what you ask.* □ *They let me do it out of consideration. It was very thoughtful of them.*

out of control AND **out of hand** uncontrollable; wild and unruly. □ *The party got out of control about midnight, and the neighbors called the police.*

□ *We tried to keep things from getting out of hand.*

out of courtesy (to someone) in order to be polite to someone; *out of consideration for someone.* □ *We invited Mary's brother out of courtesy to her.* □ *They invited me out of courtesy.*

out-of-date old-fashioned; *out of style;* obsolete. (See also *go out of style.*) □ *Isn't that suit sort of out-of-date?* □ *All my clothes are out-of-date.*

out of fashion See *out of style.*

out of favor (with someone) no longer desirable or preferred by someone. □ *I can't ask John to help. I'm out of favor with him.* □ *That kind of thing has been out of favor for years.*

out of gas 1. having no gasoline (in a car, truck, etc.). □ *We can't go any farther. We're out of gas.* □ *This car will be completely out of gas in a few more miles.* **2.** tired; exhausted; worn out. (Informal.) □ *What a day! I've been working since morning, and I'm really out of gas.* □ *This electric clock is out of gas. I'll have to get a new one.*

out of hand 1. See *out of control.* **2.** immediately and without consulting anyone; without delay. □ *I can't answer that out of hand. I'll check with the manager and call you back.* □ *The offer was so good that I accepted it out of hand.*

out of it See under *out to lunch.*

out of keeping (with something) not following the rules of something; out of accord with something. (Compare with *in keeping (with something).*) □ *The length of this report is out of keeping with your request.* □ *I didn't even read it because it was so much out of keeping.*

out of kilter (Slang.) **1.** out of balance; crooked or tilted. □ *John, your tie is sort of out of kilter. Let me fix it.* □ *Please straighten the picture on the wall. It's out of kilter.* **2.** malfunctioning; *on the fritz.* □ *My furnace is out of kilter. I have to call someone to fix it.* □ *This*

computer *is out of kilter. It doesn't work.*

out of line 1. See *out of line (with something).* **2.** improper. □ *I'm afraid that your behavior was quite out of line. I do not wish to speak further about this matter.* □ *Bill, that remark was out of line. Please be more respectful.*

out of line (with something) 1. not properly lined up in a line of things. □ *I told you not to get out of line. Now, get back in line.* □ *One of those books on the shelf is out of line with the others. Please fix it.* **2.** unreasonable when compared to something (else). □ *The cost of this meal is out of line with what other restaurants charge.* □ *Your request is out of line.*

out of luck without good luck; having bad fortune. (Informal.) □ *If you wanted some ice cream, you're out of luck.* □ *I was out of luck. I got there too late to get a seat.*

out of necessity because of necessity; due to need. □ *I bought this hat out of necessity. I needed one, and this was all there was.* □ *We sold our car out of necessity.*

out of one's element not in a natural or comfortable situation. (Compare with *in one's element.*) □ *When it comes to computers, I'm out of my element.* □ *Sally's out of her element in math.*

out of one's head See the following entry.

out of one's mind AND **out of one's head; out of one's senses** silly and senseless; crazy; irrational. □ *Why did you do that? You must be out of your mind!* □ *Good grief, Tom! You have to be out of your head!* □ *She's acting as if she were out of her senses.*

out of one's senses See the previous entry.

out of one's way See *out of the way.*

out of order 1. not in the correct order. □ *This book is out of order. Please put it in the right place on the shelf.* □ *You're out of order, John. Please get in line after Jane.* **2.** not following correct parliamentary procedure. □ *I was declared out of order by the president.* □ *Ann inquired, "Isn't a motion to table the question out of order at this time?"* **3.** not operating; broken. □ *The coffee machine is out of order. It takes your money and gives you no coffee.* □ *We will have to use the stairs. The elevator is out of order.*

out of place 1. not in a proper place. □ *The salt was out of place in the cupboard, so I couldn't find it.* □ *Billy, you're out of place. Please sit next to Tom.* **2.** improper and impertinent; *out of line.* □ *That kind of behavior is out of place in church.* □ *Your rude remark is quite out of place.*

out-of-pocket expenses the actual amount of money spent. (Refers to the money one person pays while doing something on someone else's behalf. One is usually paid back this money.) □ *My out-of-pocket expenses for the party were nearly $175.* □ *My employer usually pays all out-of-pocket expenses for a business trip.*

out of practice performing poorly due to a lack of practice. □ *I used to be able to play the piano extremely well, but now I'm out of practice.* □ *The baseball players lost the game because they were out of practice.*

out of print [for a book] to be no longer available for sale. □ *The book you want is out of print, but perhaps I can find a used copy for you.* □ *It was published nearly ten years ago, so it's probably out of print.*

out of reach 1. not near enough to be reached or touched. □ *Place the cookies out of reach, or Bob will eat them all.* □ *The mouse ran behind the piano, out of reach. The cat just sat and waited for it.* **2.** unattainable. □ *I wanted to be president, but I'm afraid that such a goal is out of reach.* □ *I shall choose a goal that is not out of reach.*

out of season (The opposite of *in season.* Compare with *off season.*) **1.** not now available for sale. □ *Sorry,*

oysters are out of season. We don't have any. □ *Watermelon is out of season in the winter.* **2.** not now legally able to be hunted or caught. □ *Are salmon out of season?* □ *I caught a trout out of season and had to pay a fine.*

out of service inoperable; not now operating. □ *Both elevators are out of service, so I had to use the stairs.* □ *The washroom is temporarily out of service.*

out of shape AND **out of condition** not in the best physical condition. □ *I get out of breath when I run because I'm out of shape.* □ *Keep exercising regularly, or you'll get out of condition.*

out of sight 1. not visible. (Especially with *get, keep,* or *stay.*) □ *The cat kept out of sight until the mouse came out.* □ *"Get out of sight, or they'll see you!" called John.* **2.** [for a price to be] very high. (Informal.) □ *I won't pay this bill. It's out of sight.* □ *The estimate was out of sight, so I didn't accept it.* **3.** figuratively stunning, unbelievable, or awesome. (Slang.) □ *Wow, this music is out of sight!* □ *What a wild party — out of sight!*

Out of sight, out of mind. a proverb meaning that if you do not see something, you will not think about it. (Fixed order.) □ *When I go home, I put my schoolbooks away so I won't worry about doing my homework. After all, out of sight, out of mind.* □ *Jane dented the fender on her car. It's on the right side, so she doesn't have to look at it. Like they say, out of sight, out of mind.*

out of sorts not feeling well; grumpy and irritable. □ *I've been out of sorts for a day or two. I think I'm coming down with something.* □ *The baby is out of sorts. Maybe she's getting a tooth.*

out of step (with someone or something) 1. AND **out of time (with someone or something)** [marching or dancing] out of cadence with someone else. □ *You're out of step with the music.* □ *Pay attention, Ann. You're out of time.* **2.** not as up-to-date as someone or something. □ *John is out of step with* *the times.* □ *Billy is out of step with the rest of the class.*

out of stock not immediately available in a store; [for goods] to be temporarily unavailable. □ *Those items are out of stock, but a new supply will be delivered on Thursday.* □ *I'm sorry, but the red ones are out of stock. Would a blue one do?*

out of style AND **out of fashion** not fashionable; old-fashioned; obsolete. □ *John's clothes are really out of style.* □ *He doesn't care if his clothes are out of fashion.*

out of the blue See *out of a clear blue sky.*

out of the corner of one's eye [seeing something] at a glance; glimpsing (something). □ *I saw someone do it out of the corner of my eye. It might have been Jane who did it.* □ *I only saw the accident out of the corner of my eye. I don't know who is at fault.*

out of the frying pan into the fire from a bad situation to a worse situation. (Often with *jump.*) □ *When I tried to argue about my fine for a traffic violation, the judge charged me with contempt of court. I really went out of the frying pan into the fire.* □ *I got deeply in debt. Then I really got out of the frying pan into the fire when I lost my job.*

out of the hole out of debt. (Informal. Also literal.) □ *I get paid next week, and then I can get out of the hole.* □ *I can't seem to get out of the hole. I keep spending more money than I earn.*

out of the ordinary unusual. □ *It was a good meal, but not out of the ordinary.* □ *Your report was nicely done, but nothing out of the ordinary.*

out of the question not possible; not permitted. □ *I'm sorry, but it's out of the question.* □ *You can't go to Florida this spring. We can't afford it. It's out of the question.*

out of the red out of debt. (Informal.) □ *This year our company is likely to get out of the red before fall.* □ *If we*

can cut down on expenses, we can get out of the red fairly soon.*

out of the running no longer being considered; eliminated from a contest. (Compare with *in the running.*) □ *After the first part of the diving meet, three members of our team were out of the running.* □ *After the scandal was made public, I was no longer in the running. I pulled out of the election.*

out of the swim of things not in the middle of activity; not involved in things. (Informal. The opposite of *in the swim of things.*) □ *While I had my cold, I was out of the swim of things.* □ *I've been out of the swim of things for a few weeks. Please bring me up to date.*

out of the way AND **out of one's way** **1.** not blocking or impeding the way. □ *Please get out of my way.* □ *Would you please get your foot out of the way?* **2.** not along the way. □ *I'm sorry, but I can't give you a ride home. It's out of the way.* □ *That route is out of my way.*

out-of-the-way difficult to get to. □ *They live on a quiet, out-of-the-way street.* □ *I know an out-of-the-way little restaurant on Maple Street.*

out of the woods past a critical phase; out of the unknown. (Informal.) □ *When the patient got out of the woods, everyone relaxed.* □ *I can give you a better prediction for your future health when you are out of the woods.*

out of thin air out of nowhere; out of nothing. (Informal.) □ *Suddenly— out of thin air—the messenger appeared.* □ *You just made that up out of thin air.*

out of this world wonderful; extraordinary. □ *This pie is just out of this world.* □ *Look at you! How lovely you look—simply out of this world.*

out of time (with someone or something) See under *out of step (with someone or something).*

out of touch (with someone or something) **1.** [with *someone*] no longer talking to or writing to someone;

knowing no news of someone. □ *I've been out of touch with my brother for many years.* □ *We've been out of touch for quite some time.* **2.** [with *something*] not keeping up with the developments of something. □ *I've been out of touch with automobile mechanics for many years.* □ *I couldn't go back into mechanics because I've been out of touch for too long.*

out of town temporarily not in one's own town. □ *I'll be out of town next week. I'm going to a conference.* □ *I take care of Mary's cat when she's out of town.*

out of tune (with someone or something) **1.** not in musical harmony with someone or something. □ *The oboe is out of tune with the flute.* □ *The flute is out of tune with John.* □ *They are all out of tune.* **2.** not in (figurative) harmony or agreement. □ *Your proposal is out of tune with my ideas of what we should be doing.* □ *Your ideas and mine are out of tune.*

out of turn not at the proper time; not in the proper order. (See also *speak out of turn.*) □ *We were permitted to be served out of turn because we had to leave early.* □ *Bill tried to register out of turn and was sent away.*

out of w(h)ack (Slang.) **1.** crazy; silly; irrational. □ *Why do you always act as if you're out of whack?* □ *I'm not out of wack. I'm eccentric.* **2.** out of adjustment; out of order. □ *I'm afraid that my watch is out of whack.* □ *The elevator is out of wack. We'll have to walk up.*

out of work unemployed, temporarily or permanently. □ *How long have you been out of work?* □ *My brother has been out of work for nearly a year.*

out on a limb in a dangerous position; taking a chance. □ *I don't want to go out on a limb, but I think I'd agree to your request.* □ *She really went out on a limb when she agreed.*

out on bail out of jail because bail bond money has been paid. (The money will be forfeited if the person who is *out on bail* does not appear in court at the proper time. See also *jump bail.*) □ *Bob is out on bail waiting for his trial.* □ *The robber committed another crime while out on bail.*

out on parole out of jail but still under police supervision. □ *Bob got out on parole after serving only a few years of his sentence.* □ *He was out on parole because of good behavior.*

out on the town celebrating at one or more places in a town. (See also *night on the town.*) □ *I'm really tired. I was out on the town until dawn.* □ *We went out on the town to celebrate our wedding anniversary.*

out to lunch **1.** eating lunch away from one's place of work or activity. □ *I'm sorry, but Sally Jones is out to lunch. May I take a message?* □ *She's been out to lunch for nearly two hours. When will she be back?* **2.** AND **out of it** not alert; giddy; uninformed. (Slang.) □ *Bill is really out of it. Why can't he pay attention?* □ *Don't be out of it, John. Wake up!* □ *Ann is really out to lunch these days.*

out West in the western part of the United States. (See also *back East, down South, up North.*) □ *We lived out West for nearly ten years.* □ *Do they really ride horses out West?*

outgrow something **1.** to get too big for something. □ *Tom outgrew all his clothes in two months.* □ *The plant outgrew its pot.* **2.** to become too mature for something. □ *I outgrew my allergies.* □ *The boys will outgrow their toys.*

outguess someone to guess what someone else might do; to predict what someone might do. □ *I can't outguess Bill. I just have to wait and see what happens.* □ *Don't try to outguess John. He's too sharp and tricky.*

outside of something except for something; besides something. (Also literal.) □ *Outside of the cost of my laundry, I have practically no expenses.* □ *Outside of some new shoes, I don't need any new clothing.*

over and above something more than something; in addition to something. (Informal. Fixed order.) □ *I'll need another twenty dollars over and above the amount you have already given me.* □ *You've been eating too much food over and above what is required for good nutrition. That's why you're gaining weight.*

over and done with finished. (Informal. Fixed order.) □ *I'm glad that's over and done with.* □ *Now that I have college over and done with, I can get a job.*

over and over (again) repeatedly. □ *She stamped her foot over and over again.* □ *Bill whistled the same song over and over.*

over my dead body not if I can stop you. (Slang. It means that you'll have to kill me to prevent me from keeping you from doing something.) □ *Over my dead body you'll sell this house!* □ *You want to quit college? Over my dead body!*

over someone's head too difficult or clever for someone to understand. (Treated grammatically as a distance above one's head. Also literal.) □ *The children have no idea what the new teacher is talking about. Her ideas are way over their heads.* □ *She enrolled in a physics course, but it turned out to be miles over her head.*

over the hill overage; too old to do something. (Informal.) □ *Now that Mary's forty, she thinks she's over the hill.* □ *My grandfather was over eighty before he felt as if he was over the hill.*

over the hump over the difficult part. (Informal.) □ *This is a difficult project, but we're over the hump now.* □ *I'm halfway through — over the hump — and it looks as if I may get finished after all.*

over the long haul for a relatively long period of time. □ *Over the long haul, it might be better to invest in stocks.* □ *Over the long haul, everything will turn out all right.*

over the short haul for the immediate future. □ *Over the short haul, you'd be better off to put your money in the bank.* □ *Over the short haul, you may wish you had done something different. But things will work out all right.*

over the top having gained more than one's goal. □ *Our fund-raising campaign went over the top by $3,000.* □ *We didn't go over the top. We didn't even get half of what we set out to collect.*

over with See *(all) over with.*

own up (to something) to confess to something. □ *I know you broke the window. Come on and own up to it.* □ *The boy holding the baseball bat owned up. What else could he do?*

P

pack a punch See the following entry.

pack a wallop AND **pack a punch** to provide a burst of energy, power, or excitement. (Informal.) □ *Wow, this spicy food really packs a wallop.* □ *I put a special kind of gasoline in my car because I thought it would pack a punch. It didn't.*

pack them in to draw a lot of people. (Informal.) □ *It was a good night at the theater. The play really packed them in.* □ *The circus manager knew he could pack them in if he advertised the lion tamer.*

packed (in) like sardines packed very tightly. (Many variations are possible, as in the examples.) □ *It was terribly crowded there. We were packed in like sardines.* □ *The bus was full. The passengers were packed like sardines.* □ *They packed us in like sardines.*

pad the bill to put unnecessary items on a bill to make the total cost higher. (Informal.) □ *The plumber had padded the bill with things we didn't need.* □ *I was falsely accused of padding the bill.*

paddle one's own canoe to do (something) by oneself; to be alone. (Could also be literal.) □ *I've been left to paddle my own canoe too many times.* □ *Sally isn't with us. She's off paddling her own canoe.*

pain in the neck a bother; an annoyance. (Slang.) □ *This assignment is a pain in the neck.* □ *Your little brother is a pain in the neck.*

paint the town red to have a wild celebration during a *night on the town.* □ *Let's all go out and paint the town red!* □ *Oh, do I feel awful. I was out all last night, painting the town red.*

pal around (with someone) to be friends with someone; to be the companion of someone. □ *Bill likes to pal around with Mary, but it's nothing serious.* □ *Ann and Jane still like to pal around.*

pale around the gills AND **blue around the gills; green around the gills** looking sick. (Informal. The *around* can be replaced with *about.*) □ *John is looking a little pale around the gills. What's wrong?* □ *Oh, I feel a little green about the gills.*

pan out See *turn out (all right).*

paper over the cracks (in something) to try to hide faults or difficulties, often in a hasty or not very successful way. □ *The politician tried to paper over the cracks in his party's economic policy.* □ *Tom tried to paper over the cracks in his relationship with the boss, but it was not possible.* □ *She didn't explain it. She just papered over the cracks.*

par for the course typical; about what one could expect. (This refers to golf courses, not school courses.) □ *So he went off and left you? Well that's about par for the course. He's no friend.* □ *I worked for days on this project, but it was rejected. That's par for the course around here.*

part and parcel (of something) part of something; an important part of something. (See also *bag and baggage.* Fixed order.) □ *This point is part and parcel of my whole argument.* □ *Get* *every part and parcel of this machine out of my living room.* □ *Come on! Move out—part and parcel!*

part company (with someone) to leave someone; to depart from someone. □ *Tom finally parted company with his brother.* □ *They parted company, and Tom got in his car and drove away.*

part someone's hair to come very close to someone. (Informal. Usually an exaggeration. Also literal.) □ *That plane flew so low that it nearly parted my hair.* □ *He punched at me and missed. He only parted my hair.*

partake of something to take something; to eat or drink something. (Formal.) □ *I don't usually partake of rich foods, but in this instance I'll make an exception.* □ *Good afternoon, Judge Smith, would you care to partake of some wine?*

parting of the ways a point at which people separate and go their own ways. (Often with *come to a, arrive at a, reach a,* etc.) □ *Jane and Bob finally came to a parting of the ways.* □ *Bill and his parents reached a parting of the ways.*

party line the official ideas and attitudes that are adopted by the leaders of a particular group and that the other members are expected to accept. □ *Tom has left the club. He refused to follow the party line.* □ *Many politicians agree with the party line without thinking.*

pass as someone or something to succeed in being accepted as someone or something. □ *The spy was able to pass as a regular citizen.* □ *The thief was arrested when he tried to pass as a priest.*

pass away AND **pass on** to die. (A euphemism.) □ *My aunt passed away last month.* □ *When I pass away, I want to have lots of flowers and a big funeral.* □ *When I pass on, I won't care about the funeral.*

pass muster to measure up to the required standards. (Folksy.) □ *I tried, but my efforts didn't pass muster.* □ *If you don't wear a suit, you won't*

pass muster at that fancy restaurant. They won't let you in.

pass on See *pass away.*

pass out to faint; to lose consciousness. □ *Oh, look! Tom has passed out.* □ *When he got the news, he passed out.*

pass the buck to pass the blame (to someone else); to give the responsibility (to someone else). (Informal.) □ *Don't try to pass the buck! It's your fault, and everybody knows it.* □ *Some people try to pass the buck whenever they can.*

pass the hat to attempt to collect money for some (charitable) project. □ *Bob is passing the hat to collect money to buy flowers for Ann.* □ *He's always passing the hat for something.*

pass the time to fill up time (by doing something). □ *I never know how to pass the time when I'm on vacation.* □ *What do you do to pass the time?*

pass the time of day (with someone) to chat or talk informally with someone. □ *I saw Mr. Brown in town yesterday. I stopped and passed the time of day with him.* □ *No, we didn't have a serious talk; we just passed the time of day.*

pass through someone's mind AND **cross someone's mind** to come to mind briefly; for an idea to occur to someone. (Compare with *come to mind.*) □ *Let me tell you what just crossed my mind.* □ *As you were speaking, something passed through my mind that I'd like to discuss.*

past someone's or something's prime beyond the most useful or productive period. □ *Joan was a wonderful singer, but she's past her prime now.* □ *This old car's past its prime. I'll need to get a new one.*

pat someone on the back AND **give someone a pat on the back** to congratulate someone; to encourage someone. (Also literal.) □ *We patted Ann on the back for a good performance.* □ *When people do a good job, you should give them a pat on the back.*

patch someone or something up 1. [with *someone*] to doctor someone; to dress someone's wounds. (Informal.) □ *They patched John up in the emergency room.* ⊤ *I patched up Ann's cuts with bandages and sent her home.* **2.** [with *something*] to (figuratively) repair the damage done by an argument or disagreement. (Also literal.) □ *Mr. and Mrs. Smith are trying to patch things up.* ⊤ *We patched up our argument, then kissed and made up.*

path of least resistance to do the easiest thing; to take the easiest route. (Often with *follow the* or *take the.* Compare with *line of least resistance.*) □ *John will follow the path of least resistance.* □ *I like challenges. I won't usually take the path of least resistance.*

pave the way (for someone or something) to prepare (someone or something) for someone or something. □ *The public doesn't understand the metric system. We need to pave the way for its introduction.* □ *They are paving the way in the schools.*

pay a king's ransom (for something) to pay a great deal for something. (To pay an amount as large as one might have to pay to get back a king held for ransom.) □ *I would like to buy a nice watch, but I don't want to pay a king's ransom for it.* □ *It's a lovely house. I had to pay a king's ransom, but it is worth it.*

pay an arm and a leg (for something) AND **pay through the nose (for something)** to pay too much [money] for something. (Informal.) □ *I hate to have to pay an arm and a leg for a tank of gas.* □ *If you shop around, you won't have to pay an arm and a leg.* □ *Why should you pay through the nose?*

pay as you go to pay costs as they occur; to pay for goods as they are bought (rather than charging them). □ *You ought to pay as you go. Then you won't be in debt.* □ *If you pay as you go, you'll never spend too much money.*

pay-as-you-go paying costs as they occur. □ *There is no charging allowed here. This store is strictly pay-as-you-go.* □ *I can't buy this then. I didn't know your policy was pay-as-you-go.*

pay attention (to someone or something) to be attentive to someone or something; to give one's attention or concentration to someone or something. □ *Pay attention to me!* □ *I'm paying attention!*

pay for something 1. to pay out money for something. □ *Did you pay for the magazine, or shall I?* □ *No, I'll pay for it.* **2.** to be punished for something. □ *The criminal will pay for his crimes.* □ *I don't like what you did to me, and I'm going to see that you pay for it.*

pay in advance to pay (for something) before it is received or delivered. □ *I want to make a special order. Will I have to pay in advance?* □ *Yes, please pay in advance.*

pay lip service (to something) to express loyalty, respect, or support for something insincerely. □ *You don't really care about politics. You're just paying lip service to the candidate.* □ *Don't sit here and pay lip service. Get busy!*

pay one's debt (to society) to serve a sentence for a crime, usually in prison. □ *The judge said that Mr. Simpson had to pay his debt to society.* □ *Mr. Brown paid his debt in state prison.*

pay one's dues 1. to pay the fees required to belong to an organization. □ *If you haven't paid your dues, you can't come to the club picnic.* □ *How many people have paid their dues?* **2.** to have earned one's right to something through hard work or suffering. (Informal.) □ *He worked hard to get to where he is today. He paid his dues and did what he was told.* □ *I have every right to be here. I paid my dues!*

pay someone a back-handed compliment AND **pay someone a left-handed compliment** to give someone a false compliment that is really an insult. □ *John said that he had never seen me looking better. I think he was paying me a left-handed compliment.* □ *I'd prefer* *that someone insulted me directly. I hate it when someone pays me a back-handed compliment — unless it's a joke.*

pay someone a compliment to compliment someone. □ *Sally thanked me for paying her a compliment.* □ *When Tom did his job well, I paid him a compliment.*

pay someone a left-handed compliment See *pay someone a back-handed compliment.*

pay (someone) a visit to visit someone. □ *I think I'll pay Mary a visit.* □ *We'd like to see you. When would be a good time to pay a visit?*

pay someone or something off 1. [with *someone*] to pay someone a bribe (for a favor already done). (Compare with *buy someone off.*) □ *The lawyer was put in prison for paying the judge off. The judge was imprisoned also.* T *The lawyer paid off the judge for deciding the case in the lawyer's favor.* **2.** to pay a debt; to pay a debtor; to pay the final payment for something bought on credit. □ *This month I'll pay the car off.* T *Did you pay off the plumber yet?*

pay someone's (own) way to pay the costs (of something) for a person. □ *I wanted to go to Florida this spring, but my parents say I have to pay my own way.* □ *My aunt is going to pay my way to Florida — only if I take her with me!*

pay the piper to face the results of one's actions; to receive punishment for something. □ *You can put off paying your debts only so long. Eventually you'll have to pay the piper.* □ *You can't get away with that forever. You'll have to pay the piper someday.*

pay through the nose (for something) See *pay an arm and a leg (for something).*

pay up Pay me now! (Slang.) □ *You owe me $200. Come on, pay up!* □ *If you don't pay up, I'll take you to court.*

peg away (at something) See *plug away (at something).*

penny-wise and pound-foolish a proverb meaning that it is foolish to lose a lot of money to save a little money. (Fixed order.) □ *Sally shops very carefully to save a few cents on food, then charges the food to a charge card that costs a lot in annual interest. That's being penny-wise and pound-foolish.* □ *John drives thirty miles to buy gas for three cents a gallon less than it costs here. He's really penny-wise and pound-foolish.*

pep someone or something up to make someone or something more sprightly and active. □ *I need a bottle of pop to pep me up.* □ *The third act of this play needs something to pep it up. How about a few good jokes?*

Perish the thought. Do not even consider thinking of something. (Formal.) □ *If you should become ill — perish the thought — I'd take care of you.* □ *I'm afraid that we need a new car. Perish the thought.*

perk someone or something up to make someone or something more cheery. □ *A nice cup of coffee would really perk me up.* T *Don't you think that new curtains would perk up this room?*

peter out [for something] to die or dwindle away; [for something] to become exhausted gradually. (Informal.) □ *When the fire petered out, I went to bed.* □ *My money finally petered out, and I had to come home.*

pick a quarrel (with someone) to start an argument with someone. □ *Are you trying to pick a quarrel with me?* □ *No, I'm not trying to pick a quarrel.*

pick and choose to choose very carefully from a number of possibilities; to be selective. (Fixed order.) □ *You must take what you are given. You cannot pick and choose.* □ *Meg is so beautiful. She can pick and choose from a whole range of boyfriends.*

pick at someone or something 1. to be very critical of someone or something; to *pick on someone or something.* (Informal.) □ *Why are you always picking at me?* □ *You always seem to be picking at your car.* **2.** [with *something*] to eat only little bits of something. □

You're only picking at your food. Don't you feel well? □ *Billy is only picking at his peas, and he usually eats all of them.*

pick holes in something AND **pick something to pieces** to criticize something severely; to find all the flaws or fallacies in an argument. (Also literal.) □ *The lawyer picked holes in the witness's story.* □ *They will pick holes in your argument.* □ *She picked my story to pieces.*

pick on someone or something to criticize someone or something; to abuse someone or something. □ *Stop picking on me!* □ *Why are you always picking on your dog?* □ *Don't pick on our house. It's old but we love it.*

pick on someone your own size to abuse someone who is big enough to fight back. (Also with *somebody*.) □ *Go pick on somebody your own size!* □ *Max should learn to pick on someone his own size.*

pick one's way through something AND **make one's way through something 1.** to work slowly and meticulously through something. □ *My teacher said he couldn't even pick his way through my report. It was just too confusing.* □ *I spent an hour picking my way through the state tax forms.* **2.** to move along a route full of obstacles; to travel through an area with care, avoiding obstacles. □ *When the grandchildren visit, I have to pick my way through the toys on the floor.* □ *We slowly picked our way through the thorny bushes to get to the ripe raspberries.*

pick someone or something off to kill someone or something with a carefully aimed gunshot. (Also literal.) □ *The hunter picked the deer off with great skill.* ⊤ *The killer tried to pick off the police officer.*

pick someone or something up 1. [with *someone*] to go to a place in a car, bus, etc., and take on a person as a passenger. □ *Please come to my office and pick me up at noon.* ⊤ *I have to pick up Billy at school.* **2.** [with *someone*] to stop one's car, bus, etc., and offer someone a ride. □ *Don't ever pick a stranger up when you're out driving!* ⊤ *I picked up a hitchhiker today, and we had a nice chat.* **3.** [with *someone*] to attempt to become acquainted with someone for romantic or sexual purposes. (Informal.) □ *Who are you anyway? Are you trying to pick me up?* ⊤ *No, I never picked up anybody in my life!* **4.** [with *someone*] [for the police] to find and bring someone to the police station for questioning or arrest. □ *I tried to pick her up, but she heard me coming and got away.* ⊤ *Sergeant Jones, go pick up Sally Franklin and bring her in to be questioned about the jewel robbery.* **5.** [with *something*] to tidy up or clean up a room or some other place. □ *Let's pick this room up in a hurry.* ⊤ *I want you to pick up the entire house.* **6.** [with *something*] to find, purchase, or acquire something. □ *Where did you pick that up?* ⊤ *I picked up this tool at the hardware store.* **7.** [with *something*] to learn something. □ *I pick languages up easily.* ⊤ *I picked up a lot of knowledge about music from my brother.* ⊤ *I picked up an interesting melody from a movie.* **8.** [with *something*] to cause something to go faster, especially music. □ *All right, let's pick this piece up and get it moving faster.* □ *Okay, get moving. Pick it up!* **9.** [with *something*] to resume something. □ *Pick it up right where you stopped.* ⊤ *I'll have to pick up my work where I left off.* **10.** [with *something*] to receive radio signals; to bring something into view. □ *I can just pick it up with a powerful telescope.* ⊤ *I can hardly pick up a signal.* ⊤ *We can pick up a pretty good television picture where we live.* **11.** [with *something*] to find a trail or route. ⊤ *The dogs finally picked up the scent.* ⊤ *You should pick up highway 80 in a few miles.*

pick someone's brain(s) to talk with someone to find out information about something. □ *I spent the afternoon with Donna, picking her brain for ideas to use in our celebration.* □ *Do you mind if I pick your brains? I need some fresh ideas.*

pick something over to sort through something; to rummage through something. □ *They picked all the records over.* T *The shoppers quickly picked over the sale merchandise.*

pick something to pieces See *pick holes in something.*

pick up 1. to tidy up. □ *When you finish playing, you have to pick up.* □ *Please pick up after yourself.* 2. to get busy; to go faster. □ *Things usually pick up around here about 8:00.* □ *I hope things pick up a little later. It's boring here.*

pick up the check See the following entry.

pick up the tab AND **pick up the check** to pay the bill. (Informal.) □ *Whenever we go out, my father picks up the tab.* □ *Order whatever you want. The company is picking up the check.*

picked over rejected; worn, dirty, or undesirable. □ *This merchandise looks worn and picked over. I don't want any of it.* □ *Everything in the store is picked over by the end of the month.*

pie in the sky a future reward, especially after death. □ *Are you nice to people just because of pie in the sky, or do you really like them?* □ *Don't hold out for a big reward. You know—pie in the sky.*

piece of cake very easy. (Slang.) □ *No, it won't be any trouble. It's a piece of cake.* □ *It's easy! Look here—piece of cake.*

piece of the action a share in a scheme or project; a degree of involvement. (Slang.) □ *If you guys are going to bet on the football game, I want a piece of the action, too.* □ *My brother wants in on it. Give him a piece of the action.*

pile in(to something) to climb in or get in roughly. □ *Okay, kids, pile in!* □ *The children piled into the car and slammed the door.*

pile out (of something) to get out of something roughly. □ *Okay, kids, pile out!* □ *The car door burst open, and the children piled out.*

pile something up to crash or wreck something. (Also literal = to heap something up.) □ *Drive carefully if you don't want to pile the car up.* T *The driver piled up the car against a tree.*

pile up to crash or wreck. (Also literal.) □ *The car piled up against the tree.* □ *The bus piled up on the curve.*

pin one's faith on someone or something to put one's hope, trust, or faith in someone or something. □ *I'm pinning my faith on your efforts.* □ *Don't pin your faith on Tom. He's not dependable.*

pin someone down (on something) to force someone to explain or clarify something. (Informal. Also literal.) □ *Try to pin her down on the time.* T *Pin down Jane on exactly what she means.* □ *Please find out exactly how much it costs. Pin them down on the price.*

pin someone's ears back to scold someone severely; to beat someone. (Slang.) □ *Tom pinned my ears back because I insulted him.* □ *I got very mad at John and wanted to pin his ears back, but I didn't.*

pin something on someone to place the blame for something on someone. (Slang. Also literal.) □ *I didn't take the money. Don't try to pin it on me. I wasn't even there.* □ *The police managed to pin the crime on Bob.*

pinch-hit (for someone) to substitute for someone. (Originally from baseball, where it refers to a substitute batter.) □ *Will you pinch-hit for me at band practice?* □ *Sorry, I can't pinch-hit. I don't have the time.*

pipe down to be quiet; to get quiet. (Slang.) □ *Okay, you guys, pipe down!* □ *I've heard enough out of you. Pipe down!*

pipe dream a wish or an idea that is impossible to achieve or carry out. (From the dreams or visions induced by the smoking of an opium pipe.) □ *Going to the West Indies is a pipe dream. We'll never have enough money.* □ *Your* *hopes of winning a lot of money are just a silly pipe dream.*

pipe up with something to speak up and say something, especially with a high-pitched voice. □ *Billy piped up with a silly remark.* □ *Did I hear somebody pipe up with an insult?*

pit someone or something against someone or something to set someone or something in opposition to someone or something. □ *The rules of the tournament pit their team against ours.* □ *John pitted Mary against Sally in the tennis match.* □ *In an interesting plowing match, Bill pitted himself against a small tractor.*

pitch in (and help) to get busy and help (with something). □ *Pick up a paintbrush and pitch in and help.* □ *Why don't some of you pitch in? We need all the help we can get.*

pitch someone a curve (ball) to surprise someone with an unexpected act or event. (Informal. Also literal, referring to a curve ball in baseball. It is the route of the ball that is curved, not the ball itself.) □ *You really pitched me a curve ball when you said I had done a poor job. I did my best.* □ *You asked Tom a hard question. You certainly pitched him a curve.*

place someone to recall someone's name; to recall the details about a person that would help you identify the person. □ *I am sorry, I can't seem to place you. Could you tell me your name again?* □ *I can't place her. Did I meet her once before?*

place the blame on someone or something See *put the blame on someone or something.*

plain and simple See *pure and simple.*

plain as day See *(as) plain as day.*

plain as the nose on one's face See *(as) plain as the nose on one's face.*

play about (with someone or something) See *play around (with someone or something).*

play along with someone or something to agree to cooperate or conspire with

someone or someone's plan; to pretend to agree to cooperate or conspire with someone or someone's plan. □ *I refused to play along with the treasurer when she outlined her plan.* □ *It might be wise to play along with the kidnappers, at least for a little while.* □ *I'll play along with your scheme until the others get here, but I don't like it.*

play around (with someone or something) AND **play about (with someone or something)** to engage in some amusing activity with someone or something; to tease someone or something. □ *Please don't play around with that vase. You'll break it.* □ *Don't play about with the parrot. It'll bite you.* □ *Bill and I were just playing around when we heard the sound of breaking glass.*

play ball (with someone) **1.** to play a ball game with someone. (Note the special baseball use in the second example.) □ *When will our team play ball with yours?* □ *Suddenly, the umpire shouted, "Play ball!" and the game began.* **2.** to cooperate with someone. (Informal.) □ *Look, friend, if you play ball with me, everything will work out all right.* □ *Things would go better for you if you'd learn to play ball.*

play both ends (against the middle) [for one] to scheme in a way that pits two sides against each other (for one's own gain). (Informal.) □ *I told my brother that Mary doesn't like him. Then I told Mary that my brother doesn't like her. They broke up, so now I can have the car this weekend. I succeeded in playing both ends against the middle.* □ *If you try to play both ends, you're likely to get in trouble with both sides.*

play by ear See under *play something by ear.*

play-by-play description a description of an event given as the event is taking place. (Usually in reference to a sporting event.) □ *And now here is Bill Jones with a play-by-play description of the baseball game.* □ *John was giving me a play-by-play description of the argument going on next door.*

play cat and mouse (with someone) to (literally or figuratively) capture and release someone over and over. (Fixed order.) □ *The police played cat and mouse with the suspect until they had sufficient evidence to make an arrest.* □ *Tom had been playing cat and mouse with Ann. Finally she got tired of it and broke up with him.*

play fair to do something by the rules; to play something in a fair and just manner. □ *John won't play with Bill anymore because Bill doesn't play fair.* □ *You moved the golf ball with your foot! That's not playing fair!*

play fast and loose (with someone or something) to act carelessly, thoughtlessly, and irresponsibly. (Informal. Fixed order.) □ *I'm tired of your playing fast and loose with me. Leave me alone.* □ *Bob got fired for playing fast and loose with the company's money.* □ *If you play fast and loose like that, you can get into a lot of trouble.*

play first chair 1. to be the leader of a section of instruments in an orchestra or a band. □ *Sally learned to play the violin so well that she now plays first chair in the orchestra.* □ *I'm going to practice my flute so I can play first chair.* 2. to act as a leader. □ *I need to get this job done. Who plays first chair around here?* □ *You're not the boss! You don't play first chair.*

play footsie (with someone) (Informal.) 1. to attract someone's attention by touching feet under the table; to flirt with someone. □ *Bill was trying to play footsie with Sally at the dinner table. The hostess was appalled.* □ *They shouldn't play footsie at a formal dinner.* 2. to get involved with someone; to collaborate with someone. (Informal.) □ *The treasurer got fired for playing footsie with the vice president.* □ *When politicians play footsie, there is usually something illegal going on.*

play for keeps to take an action that is permanent or final. (Slang.) □ *Mary told me that Tom wants to marry me. I didn't know he wanted to play for keeps.*

□ *I like to play cards and make money, but I don't like to play for keeps.*

play hard to get to be coy, shy, and fickle. (Usually refers to someone of the opposite sex.) □ *Why can't we go out? Why do you play hard to get?* □ *Sally annoys all the boys because she plays hard to get.*

play havoc (with someone or something) See *raise havoc (with someone or something).*

play hob with someone or something See *raise hob with someone or something.*

play hooky not to go to school or to some important meeting. (Slang.) □ *Why aren't you in school? Are you playing hooky?* □ *I don't have time for the sales meeting today, so I think I'll just play hooky.*

play into someone's hands [for a person one is scheming against] to assist one in one's scheming without realizing it. □ *John is doing exactly what I hoped he would. He's playing into my hands.* □ *John played into my hands by taking the coins he found in my desk. I caught him and had him arrested.*

play it cool to act calm and unconcerned. (Slang.) □ *No one will suspect anything if you play it cool.* □ *Don't get angry, Bob. Play it cool.*

play it safe to be or act safe; to do something safely. □ *You should play it safe and take your umbrella.* □ *If you have a cold or the flu, play it safe and go to bed.*

play on something to have an effect on something; to manage something for a desired effect. (The *on* can be replaced by *upon.*) □ *The clerk played on my sense of responsibility in trying to get me to buy the book.* □ *See if you can get her to confess by playing on her sense of guilt.*

play one's cards close to one's vest See the following entry.

play one's cards close to the chest AND **play one's cards close to one's vest**

[for someone] to work or negotiate in a careful and private manner. □ *It's hard to figure out what John is up to because he plays his cards close to his chest.* □ *Don't let them know what you're up to. Play your cards close to your vest.*

play one's cards right AND **play one's cards well** to work or negotiate correctly and skillfully. (Informal.) □ *If you play your cards right, you can get whatever you want.* □ *She didn't play her cards well, and she ended up with something less than what she wanted.*

play one's cards well See the previous entry.

play one's trump card to use a special trick; to use one's most powerful or effective strategy or device. (Informal.) □ *I won't play my trump card until I have tried everything else.* □ *I thought that the whole situation was hopeless until Mary played her trump card and solved the whole problem.*

play politics **1.** to negotiate politically. □ *Everybody at city hall is playing politics as usual.* □ *If you're elected as a member of a political party, you'll have to play politics.* **2.** to allow politics to dominate in matters where principle should prevail. □ *Look, I came here to discuss this trial, not play politics.* □ *They're not making reasonable decisions. They're playing politics.*

play possum to pretend to be inactive, unobservant, asleep, or dead. (Folksy. The *possum* is an opossum.) □ *I knew that Bob wasn't asleep. He was just playing possum.* □ *I can't tell if this animal is dead or just playing possum.*

play second fiddle (to someone) to be in a subordinate position to someone. □ *I'm tired of playing second fiddle to John.* □ *I'm better trained than he, and I have more experience. I shouldn't play second fiddle.*

play someone for something to treat someone like (a) something. (Slang. Compare with *take someone for someone or something.*) □ *Don't play me for a fool! I know what's going on.*

□ *They played her for a jerk, but were they surprised!*

play someone off against someone else to scheme in a manner that pits two of your adversaries against one another. □ *Bill wanted to beat me up and so did Bob. I did some fast talking, and they ended up fighting with each other. I really played Bill off against Bob.* □ *The president played the House off against the Senate and ended up getting his own way.*

play someone or something down to lessen the effect or importance of someone or something. □ *John is a famous actor, but the director tried to play him down as just another member of the cast.* T *They tried to play down her earlier arrest.*

play someone or something up to make someone or something seem to be more important. □ *The director tried to play Ann up, but she was not really a star.* T *Try to play up the good qualities of our product.*

play something by ear **1.** to be able to play a piece of music after just listening to it a few times, without looking at the notes. □ *I can play "Stardust" by ear.* □ *Some people can play Chopin's music by ear.* **2.** AND **play by ear** to play a musical instrument well, without formal training. □ *John can play the piano by ear.* □ *If I could play by ear, I wouldn't have to take lessons — or practice!* **3.** to improvise; to decide what to do after one is already involved in a situation. (Compare with *wing it.*) □ *When we get into the meeting we'll have to play everything by ear.* □ *He never prepared his presentations. He always played things by ear.*

play (the) devil's advocate to put forward arguments against or objections to a proposition — which one may actually agree with — purely to test the validity of the proposition. (The devil's advocate was given the role of opposing the canonization of a saint in the medieval Church in order to prove that the grounds for canonization were sound.) □ *I agree with your plan. I'm just playing the devil's advocate so you'll know what the opposition will say.* □ *Mary offered to play devil's advocate and argue against our case so that we would find out any flaws in it.*

play the field to date many different people rather than going steady. (Informal. See *go steady with someone*.) □ *When Tom told Ann good-bye, he said he wanted to play the field.* □ *He said he wanted to play the field while he was still young.*

play the fool to act in a silly manner in order to amuse other people. □ *The teacher told Tom to stop playing the fool and sit down.* □ *Fred likes playing the fool, but we didn't find him funny last night.*

play the market to invest in the stock market. (Informal. As if it were a game or as if it were gambling.) □ *Would you rather put your money in the bank or play the market?* □ *I've learned my lesson playing the market. I lost a fortune.*

play to the gallery to perform in a manner that will get the strong approval of the audience; to perform in a manner that will get the approval of the lower elements in the audience. □ *John is a competent actor, but he has a tendency to play to the gallery.* □ *When he made the rude remark, he was just playing to the gallery.*

play tricks (on someone) to trick or confuse someone. □ *I thought I saw a camel over there. I guess my eyes are playing tricks on me.* □ *Please don't play tricks on your little brother. It makes him cry.*

play up to someone to try to gain someone's favor. □ *Bill is always playing up to the teacher.* □ *Ann played up to Bill as if she wanted him to marry her.*

play with fire to take a big risk. (Informal. Also literal.) □ *If you accuse her of stealing, you'll be playing with fire.* □ *I wouldn't try that if I were you — unless you like playing with fire.*

played out worn out; spent; exhausted. □ *This charcoal is just about played out.* □ *The batteries in this flashlight are almost played out.*

pleased as punch See *(as) pleased as punch*.

plow into someone or something to crash into someone or something; to bump hard into someone or something. □ *The car plowed into the ditch.* □ *The runner plowed into another player.*

pluck up one's courage to increase one's courage a bit. □ *Come on, Ann, make the dive. Pluck up your courage and do it.* □ *Pluck up your courage, Ann! You can do it!*

plug away (at something) AND **peg away (at something)** to keep trying something; to keep working at something. □ *John kept pegging away at the trumpet until he became pretty good at it.* □ *I'm not very good at it, but I keep plugging away.*

plug something in to place a plug into a receptacle. (*In* can be replaced with *into*.) □ *This television set won't work unless you plug it in!* ⊤ *Please plug in this lamp.*

plug something up to stop or fill up a hole, crack, or gap. □ *Take out the nail and plug the hole up with something.* ⊤ *You have to plug up the cracks to keep out the cold.*

poetic justice the appropriate but chance receiving of rewards or punishments by those deserving them. □ *It was poetic justice that Jane won the race after Mary tried to get her banned.* □ *The car thieves stole a car with no gas. That's poetic justice.*

point someone or something out to select or indicate someone or something (from a group). □ *Everyone pointed the error out.* □ *She pointed the thief out to the police officer.* ⊤ *She pointed out the boy who took her purse.*

point something up to emphasize something; to demonstrate a fact. □ *I'd like to point your approach up by citing some authorities who agree with* *you.* T *This kind of incident points up the flaws in your system.*

point the finger at someone to blame someone; to identify someone as the guilty person. (See also *put the finger on someone.*) □ *Don't point the finger at me! I didn't take the money.* □ *The manager refused to point the finger at anyone in particular and said that everyone was sometimes guilty of being late.*

poke about See the following entry.

poke around AND **poke about** to look or search around. □ *I've been poking around in the library looking for some statistics.* □ *I don't mind if you look in my drawer for a paper clip, but please don't poke about.*

poke fun (at someone) to make fun of someone; to ridicule someone. □ *Stop poking fun at me! It's not nice.* □ *Bob is always poking fun.*

poke one's nose in(to something) AND **stick one's nose in(to something)** to interfere with something; to be nosy about something. □ *I wish you'd stop poking your nose into my business.* □ *She was too upset for me to stick my nose in and ask what was wrong.*

polish something off to finish something off. □ *There is just a little bit of work left. It won't take any time to polish it off.* T *Bob polished off the rest of the pie.*

poop out to quit; to wear out and stop. (Slang.) □ *I'm so tired I could poop out right here.* □ *My car sounded as if it were going to poop out.*

pooped out [for a person or animal to be] exhausted. (Slang.) □ *The horse was pooped out and could run no more.* □ *I can't go on. I'm pooped out.*

poor as a church mouse See *(as) poor as a church mouse.*

poor but clean having little money but clean and of good habits, nonetheless. (Either extremely condescending or jocular. Some people would consider it offensive. Fixed order.) □ *My salary isn't very high, and I only have two color*

TV sets. Anyway, I'm poor but clean. □ *When Fred uttered the phrase* poor but clean *in reference to some of the people working in the yard, Ellen went into a rage.*

pop off to make a wisecrack or smart-aleck remark. (Informal.) □ *If you pop off one more time, you'll have to stay after school.* □ *Bob keeps popping off at the worst times.*

pop one's cork (Slang.) **1.** to suddenly become mentally disturbed; to go crazy. □ *I was so upset that I nearly popped my cork.* □ *They put him away because he popped his cork.* **2.** to become very angry. □ *My mother popped her cork when she heard about my grades.* □ *Calm down! Don't pop your cork.*

pop the question to ask someone to marry you. (Informal.) □ *I was surprised when he popped the question.* □ *I've been waiting for years for someone to pop the question.*

pop up 1. [for a baseball batter] to hit a baseball that goes upward rather than outward. □ *The catcher came to bat and popped up.* □ *I hope I don't pop up this time.* **2.** [for a baseball] to fly upward rather than outward. □ *The ball popped up and went foul.* □ *The ball will always pop up if you hit it in a certain way.* **3.** to arise suddenly; to appear without warning. □ *New problems keep popping up all the time.* □ *Billy popped up out of nowhere and scared his mother.*

possessed by something under the control of something; obsessed with something. □ *She acted as if she were possessed by evil spirits.* □ *He was possessed by a powerful sense of guilt.*

possessed of something having something. (Formal.) □ *Bill was possessed of an enormous sense of self-worth.* □ *The Smiths were possessed of a great deal of fine ranch land.*

postage and handling charges for sending [something] through the mail and for wrapping and handling the item. (See also *shipping and handling.* Fixed order.) □ *The cost of the book was quite reasonable, but the postage and handling was outrageous.* □ *They did not charge postage and handling because I prepaid the order.*

pound a beat to walk a route. (Informal. Usually said of a police patrol officer.) □ *Officer Smith pounded the same beat for years and years.* □ *I don't want to pound a beat all my life.*

pound something out 1. to play something loudly on the piano. (Slang. Compare with *belt something out.* Also literal.) □ *Don't pound the music out! Just play it.* Ⓣ *Listen to her pound out that song.* **2.** to type something on a typewriter. (Slang.) □ *Please pound it out again. There are six errors.* Ⓣ *It'll take just a few hours to pound out this letter.*

pound the pavement to walk through the streets looking for a job. (Informal.) □ *I spent two months pounding the pavement after the factory I worked for closed.* □ *Hey, Bob. You'd better get busy pounding those nails unless you want to be out pounding the pavement.*

pour cold water on something AND **dash cold water on something; throw cold water on something** to discourage doing something; to reduce enthusiasm for something. □ *When my father said I couldn't have the car, he poured cold water on my plans.* □ *John threw cold water on the whole project by refusing to participate.* □ *I hate to dash cold water on your party, but you cannot use the house that night.*

pour it on thick See *lay it on thick.*

pour money down the drain to waste money; to throw money away. (Informal.) □ *What a waste! You're just pouring money down the drain.* □ *Don't buy any more of that low-quality merchandise. That's just throwing money down the drain.*

pour oil on troubled water(s) to calm things down. (If oil is poured onto rough seas during a storm, the water will become more calm.) □ *That was a good thing to say to John. It helped*

pour oil on troubled water. Now he looks happy. □ *Bob is the kind of person who pours oil on troubled waters.*

pour one's heart (out to someone) to tell all one's hopes, fears, and feelings to someone. □ *She was so upset. She poured her heart out to Sally.* Ⓣ *She sat there talking for over an hour — pouring out her heart.*

power behind the throne the person who controls the person who is apparently in charge. □ *Mr. Smith appears to run the shop, but his brother is the power behind the throne.* □ *They say that the vice president is the power behind the throne.*

powers that be the people who are in authority. □ *The powers that be have decided to send back the immigrants.* □ *I have applied for a license and the powers that be are considering my application.*

praise someone or something to the skies to give someone or something much praise. □ *He wasn't very good, but his friends praised him to the skies.* □ *They liked your pie. Everyone praised it to the skies.*

preach to the converted to praise or recommend something to someone who is already in favor of it. □ *Mary was preaching to the converted when she tried to persuade Jean to become a feminist. She's been one for years.* □ *Bob found himself preaching to the converted when he was telling Jane the advantages of living in the country. She hates city life.*

precious few AND **precious little** very few; very little. (Informal.) □ *We get precious few tourists here in the winter.* □ *There's precious little food in the house and there is no money.*

precious little See the previous entry.

presence of mind calmness and the ability to act sensibly in an emergency or difficult situation. □ *Jane had the presence of mind to phone the police when the child disappeared.* □ *The child had the presence of mind to take note of the car's license number.*

press one's luck See *push one's luck.*

press someone to the wall See *push someone to the wall.*

press the panic button See *push the panic button.*

pressed for time in a hurry. □ *I am sorry. I can't talk to you. I'm just too pressed for time.* □ *If you are pressed for time, you might want to stop for some food somewhere on the highway.*

pretty as a picture See *(as) pretty as a picture.*

Pretty is as pretty does. you should do pleasant things if you wish to be considered pleasant. □ *Now, Sally. Let's be nice. Pretty is as pretty does.* □ *My great-aunt always used to say "pretty is as pretty does" to my sister.*

pretty state of affairs AND **fine state of affairs** an unpleasant state of affairs. (See also *fine kettle of fish.*) □ *This is a pretty state of affairs, and it's all your fault.* □ *What a fine state of affairs you've got us into.*

prevail (up)on someone to ask or beg someone (for a favor). □ *Can I prevail upon you to give me some help?* □ *Perhaps you could prevail on my brother for a loan.*

prick up one's ears to listen more closely. (Informal.) □ *At the sound of my voice, my dog pricked up her ears.* □ *I pricked up my ears when I heard my name mentioned.*

pride and joy something or someone that one is very proud of. (Often in reference to a baby, a car, a house, etc. Fixed order.) □ *And this is our little pride and joy, Roger.* □ *Fred pulled up in his pride and joy and asked if I wanted a ride.*

Pride goes before a fall. a saying meaning that someone who behaves in an arrogant or vain way is likely to suffer misfortune. (From the Bible.) □ *Bert was so busy admiring his reflection in a shop window that he stepped in a puddle. Pride goes before a fall.* □ *Jean was boasting about how well she thought she'd done on her final exams,* but she failed them all. You know what they say. Pride goes before a fall.

pride oneself in something See the following entry.

pride oneself on something AND **pride oneself in something** to take special pride in something. □ *Ann prides herself on her apple pies.* □ *John prides himself in his ability to make people feel at ease.*

prime mover the force that sets something going; someone or something that starts something off. □ *The manager was the prime mover in getting the clerk fired.* □ *Discontent with his job was the prime mover in John's deciding to go to Alaska.*

promise someone the moon See the following entry.

promise the moon (to someone) AND **promise someone the moon** to make extravagant promises to someone. □ *Bill will promise you the moon, but he won't live up to his promises.* □ *My boss promised the moon, but only paid the minimum wage.*

proud as a peacock See *(as) proud as a peacock.*

psyche out to go crazy. (Slang. Pronounced as if it were spelled *sike.*) □ *I don't know what happened to me. Suddenly I psyched out and started yelling.* □ *Max nearly psyched out when he saw the bill.*

psyche someone out (Slang. Pronounced as if it were spelled *sike.*) **1.** to figure out someone psychologically. □ *Don't try to psyche me out. Just be my friend.* ⊤ *I think I've psyched out my opponent so I can beat him.* **2.** to confuse someone; to cause someone to go crazy. □ *All that bright light psyched me out. I couldn't think straight.* ⊤ *They psyched out the enemy soldiers, causing them to jump into the river.*

psyche someone up to cause someone to be enthusiastic about doing something. (Slang. Pronounced as if it were spelled *sike.*) ⊤ *The coach psyched up* the team before the game. □ *I need someone to psyche me up before I go on stage.*

psyched out confused and disoriented. (Slang. Pronounced as if it were spelled *siked*.) □ *What an upsetting day! I'm really psyched out.* □ *She is so psyched out she can't see straight.*

psyched up (for something) excited and enthusiastic. (Slang. Pronounced as if it were spelled *siked*.) □ *I can play a great tennis game if I'm psyched up.* □ *She is really psyched up for the game.*

publish or perish [for a professor] to publish many books or articles in scholarly journals or get released from a university or fall into disfavor in a university. (Also occurs in other parts of speech. See the examples. Fixed order.) □ *Alice knew she would have to publish or perish if she took the teaching job.* □ *This is a major research university and publish or perish is the order of the day.* □ *When Jane heard that publish or perish was the rule at her university, she was afraid that she would not get any professors who were interested in her intellectual advancement.*

pull a boner to do something stupid or silly. (Slang.) □ *Boy, I really pulled a boner! I'm so dumb.* □ *If you pull a boner like that again, you're fired!*

pull a fast one to succeed in an act of deception. (Slang.) □ *She was pulling a fast one when she said she had a headache and went home.* □ *Don't try to pull a fast one with me! I know what you're doing.*

pull a stunt (on someone) AND **pull a trick (on someone)** to deceive someone. □ *Let's pull a trick on the teacher.* □ *Don't you dare pull a stunt like that!*

pull a trick (on someone) See the previous entry.

pull one's (own) weight See *carry one's (own) weight.*

pull one's punches (Slang.) **1.** [for a boxer] to strike with light blows to enable the other boxer to win. □ *Bill*

has been barred from the boxing ring for pulling his punches. □ *"I never pulled my punches in my life!" cried Tom.* **2.** to hold back in one's criticism. (Usually in the negative. The *one's* can be replaced with *any*.) □ *I didn't pull any punches. I told her just what I thought of her.* □ *The teacher doesn't pull any punches when it comes to discipline.*

pull oneself together to become emotionally stabilized; to *regain one's composure.* □ *Now, calm down. Pull yourself together.* □ *I'll be all right as soon as I can pull myself together.*

pull oneself up (by one's own bootstraps) to achieve (something) through one's own efforts. □ *They simply don't have the resources to pull themselves up by their own bootstraps.* □ *If I could have pulled myself up, I'd have done it by now.*

pull out all the stops to use all one's energy and effort in order to achieve something. (From the stops of a pipe organ. The more that are pulled out, the louder it gets.) □ *You'll have to pull out all the stops if you're going to pass the course.* □ *The doctors will pull out all the stops to save the child's life.*

pull rank (on someone) to assert one's rank, authority, or position over someone when making a request or giving an order. □ *Don't pull rank on me! I don't have to do what you say!* □ *When she couldn't get her way politely, she pulled rank and really got some action.*

pull someone or something down **1.** [with *someone*] to degrade someone; to humiliate someone. (Also literal.) □ *I'm afraid that your friends are pulling you down. Your manners used to be much better.* □ *My bad habits are pulling me down.* Ⓣ *There is no need to pull down everyone.* **2.** [with *something*] to earn a certain amount of money. (Slang.) Ⓣ *She's able to pull down $400 a week.* Ⓣ *I wish I could pull down a salary like that.* □ *How much is she pulling down?* **3.** [with *something*] to demolish something; to raze something. □ *Why do they want to pull it down? Why not remodel it?* Ⓣ *They are going to pull down the old building today.* **4.** [with *something*] to lower or reduce the amount of something. □ *That last test pulled my grade down.* Ⓣ *Let's see if we can pull down your temperature.*

pull someone through (something) to help someone survive something. □ *With the help of the doctor, we pulled her through her illness.* □ *With lots of encouragement, we pulled her through.*

pull someone's leg to kid, fool, or trick someone. (Informal.) □ *You don't mean that. You're just pulling my leg.* □ *Don't believe him. He's just pulling your leg.*

pull someone's or something's teeth to reduce the power of someone or something. (Informal. Also literal.) □ *The mayor tried to pull the teeth of the new law.* □ *The city council pulled the teeth of the new mayor.*

pull something off to manage to make something happen. (Slang. Also literal.) □ *Yes, I can pull it off.* Ⓣ *Do you think you can pull off this deal?*

pull something on someone 1. to surprise someone with a weapon. □ *He pulled a knife on me!* □ *The robber pulled a gun on the bank teller.* **2.** to play a trick on someone; to deceive someone with a trick. (The word *something* is often used.) □ *You wouldn't pull a trick on me, would you?* □ *Who would pull something like that on an old lady?*

pull something out of a hat AND **pull something out of thin air** to produce something as if by magic. □ *This is a serious problem, and we just can't pull a solution out of a hat.* □ *I'm sorry, but I don't have a pen. What do you want me to do, pull one out of thin air?*

pull something out of thin air See the previous entry.

pull something together to organize something; to arrange something. (Compare with *scrape something together*.) □ *How about a party? I'll see if I can pull something together for Friday night.* □ *This place is a mess. Please pull things together.*

pull strings to use influence (with someone to get something done). □ *I can get it done easily by pulling strings.* □ *Is it possible to get anything done around here without pulling strings?*

pull the plug (on someone or something) 1. to cause someone or something to end; to reduce the power or effectiveness of someone or something. (Informal.) □ *Jane pulled the plug on the whole project.* □ *The mayor was doing a fine job until the treasurer pulled the plug because there was no more money.* **2.** [with *someone*] to turn off someone's life support system in a hospital. (This results in the death of person whose life support has been terminated.) □ *They had to get a court order to pull the plug on their father.* □ *Fred signed a living will making it possible to pull the plug on him without a court order.*

pull the rug out (from under someone) to make someone ineffective. □ *The treasurer pulled the rug out from under the mayor.* □ *Things were going along fine until the treasurer pulled the rug out.*

pull the wool over someone's eyes to deceive someone. □ *You can't pull the wool over my eyes. I know what's going on.* □ *Don't try to pull the wool over her eyes. She's too smart.*

pull through to get better; to recover from a serious illness or other problem. □ *She's very ill, but I think she'll pull through.* □ *Oh, I hope she pulls through.*

pull up (somewhere) See *haul up (somewhere)*.

pull up stakes to move to another place. (As if one were pulling up tent stakes.) □ *I've been here long enough. It's time to pull up stakes.* □ *I hate the thought of having to pull up stakes.*

pure and simple AND **plain and simple** absolutely; without further complication or elaboration. (Informal. Fixed order.) □ *I told you what you must do, and you must do it, pure and simple.* □ *Will you kindly explain to me what it is, pure and simple, that I am expected to do?* □ *Just tell me plain and simple, do you intend to go or don't you?* □ *I explained it to her plain and simple, but she still didn't understand.*

push off to go away. (Informal.) □ *We told the children to push off.* □ *Push off! We don't want you here.*

push one's luck AND **press one's luck** to expect continued good fortune; to expect to continue to escape bad luck. □ *You're okay so far, but don't push your luck.* □ *Bob pressed his luck too much and got into a lot of trouble.*

push someone to the wall AND **press someone to the wall** to force someone into a position where there is only one choice to make; to put someone in a defensive position. (Also literal.) □ *There was little else I could do. They pushed me to the wall.* □ *When we pressed him to the wall, he told us where the cookies were hidden.*

push the panic button AND **press the panic button** to panic; to become anxious or panicky. (Slang.) □ *I do okay taking tests as long as I don't push the panic button.* □ *Whatever you do, don't press the panic button.*

pushing up daisies dead. (Folksy.) □ *If you don't drive safely, you'll be pushing up daisies.* □ *We'll all be pushing up daisies in the long run.*

put a bee in someone's bonnet to give someone an idea (about something). (See also *get a bee in one's bonnet*.) □ *Somebody put a bee in my bonnet that we should go to a movie.* □ *Who put a bee in your bonnet?*

put a stop to something AND **put an end to something** to bring something to an end. □ *I want you to put a stop to all this bad behavior.* □ *Please put an end to this conversation.*

put all one's eggs in one basket to risk everything at once. (Often negative.) □ *Don't put all your eggs in one bas-*

ket. Then everything won't be lost if there is a catastrophe. □ *John only applied to the one college he wanted to go to. He put all his eggs in one basket.*

put an end to something See *put a stop to something.*

put ideas into someone's head to suggest something — usually something bad — to someone (who would not have thought of it otherwise). □ *Bill keeps getting into trouble. Please don't put ideas into his head.* □ *Bob would get along all right if other kids didn't put ideas into his head.*

put in a good word (for someone) to say something (to someone) in support of someone. □ *I hope you get the job. I'll put in a good word for you.* □ *Yes, I want the job. If you see the boss, please put in a good word.*

put in an appearance to appear (somewhere) for just a little while. (Compare with *make an appearance*.) □ *I couldn't stay for the whole party, so I just put in an appearance and left.* □ *Even if you can't stay for the whole thing, at least put in an appearance.*

put off by someone or something distressed or repelled by someone or something. □ *I was really put off by your behavior.* □ *We were all put off by the unfairness of the rules.*

put on to pretend; to act as if something were true. □ *Ann wasn't really angry. She was just putting on.* □ *I can't believe she was just putting on. She really looked mad.*

put on a brave face to try to appear happy or satisfied when faced with misfortune or danger. □ *We've lost all our money, but we must put on a brave face for the sake of the children.* □ *Jim has lost his job and is worried, but he's putting on a brave face.*

put on a (brave) front See *put up a (brave) front.*

put on airs to act superior. □ *Stop putting on airs. You're just human like the rest of us.* □ *Ann is always putting on airs. You'd think she was a queen.*

put on an act to pretend that one is something other than what one is. (See also *put on*.) □ *Be yourself, Ann. Stop putting on an act.* □ *You don't have to put on an act. We accept you the way you are.*

put on the dog to dress or entertain in an extravagant or showy manner. (Informal.) □ *The Smiths really put on the dog at their party last Saturday.* □ *They're always putting on the dog.*

put on the feed bag to eat a meal. (Folksy and slang.) □ *It's noon—time to put on the feed bag.* □ *I didn't put on the feed bag until about eight o'clock last night.*

put one in one's place to rebuke someone; to remind one of one's (lower) rank or station. □ *The boss put me in my place for criticizing her.* □ *Then her boss put her in her place for being rude.*

put one through one's paces to make one demonstrate what one can do; to make one do one's job thoroughly. (See also *put something through its paces*.) □ *The boss really put me through my paces today. I'm tired.* □ *I tried out for a part in the play, and the director really put me through my paces.*

put one's back (in)to something **1.** to apply great physical effort to lift or move something. □ *All right, you guys. Put your backs into moving this piano.* □ *You can lift it if you put your back to it.* **2.** to apply a lot of mental or creative effort to doing something. □ *If we put our backs to it, we can bake twelve dozen cookies today.* □ *The artist put his back into finishing the picture on time.*

put one's best foot forward to act or appear at one's best; to try to make a good impression. □ *When you apply for a job, you should always put your best foot forward.* □ *I try to put my best foot forward whenever I meet someone for the first time.*

put one's cards on the table AND **lay one's cards on the table** to reveal everything; to be open and honest with someone. (Informal.) □ *Come on, John, lay your cards on the table. Tell me what you really think.* □ *Why don't we both put our cards on the table?*

put (one's) dibs on something to lay a claim to something; to state one's claim to something. (See also *have dibs on something*.) □ *I put dibs on the last piece of cake.* □ *Mary put her dibs on the book you are reading. She gets it next.*

put one's finger on something to identify something as very important. (Informal. Also literal.) □ *Ann put her finger on the cause of the problem.* □ *Yes, she really put her finger on it.*

put one's foot down (about something) to become adamant about something. (Informal.) □ *Ann put her foot down about what kind of car she wanted.* □ *She doesn't put her foot down very often, but when she does, she really means it.*

put one's foot in it See the following entry.

put one's foot in one's mouth AND **put one's foot in it; stick one's foot in one's mouth** to say something that you regret; to say something stupid, insulting, or hurtful. □ *When I told Ann that her hair was more beautiful than I had ever seen it, I really put my foot in my mouth. It was a wig.* □ *I put my foot in it by telling John's secret.*

put one's hand to the plow to begin to do a big and important task; to undertake a major effort. □ *If John would only put his hand to the plow, he could do an excellent job.* □ *You'll never accomplish anything if you don't put your hand to the plow.*

put one's hand(s) on something to locate and acquire something. (Compare with *get one's hands on someone or something*.) □ *I wish I could put my hands on a 1954 Chevrolet.* □ *If I could put my hands on that book, I could find the information I need.*

put one's head on the block (for someone or something) to take great risks for someone or something; to go to a lot of trouble or difficulty for someone or something; to attempt to gain favor for someone or something. □ *I don't know why I should put my head on the block for Joan. What has she ever done for me?* □ *Sally tried to get me to put in a good word about her with the boss. You know, tell the boss what a great worker she is and how smart she is. The last time I put my head on the block for anyone, it all backfired, and when the person goofed up, I looked like an idiot!*

put one's house in order to put one's business or personal affairs into good order. (Not literal.) □ *There was some trouble at work and the manager was told to put his house in order.* □ *Every now and then, I have to put my house in order. Then life becomes more manageable.*

put one's nose to the grindstone to keep busy doing one's work. (Also with *have* and *get*, as in the examples. See also *keep one's nose to the grindstone*.) □ *The boss told me to put my nose to the grindstone.* □ *I've had my nose to the grindstone ever since I started working here.* □ *If the other people in this office would get their noses to the grindstone, more work would get done.*

put one's oar in to give help; to interfere by giving advice; to *put one's two cents worth in.* □ *You don't need to put your oar in. I don't need your advice.* ⊤ *I'm sorry. I shouldn't have put in my oar.*

put one's shoulder to the wheel to get busy. (Not literal.) □ *You won't accomplish anything unless you put your shoulder to the wheel.* □ *I put my shoulder to the wheel and finished the job quickly.*

put one's thinking cap on to start thinking in a serious manner. (Usually used with children.) □ *It's time to put our thinking caps on, children.* ⊤ *All right now, let's put on our thinking caps and do some arithmetic.*

put one's two cents (worth) in to add one's comments (to something). (Informal.) ⊤ *Can I put in my two cents*

worth? □ *Sure, go ahead—put your two cents in.*

put oneself in someone else's place AND **put oneself in someone else's shoes** to allow oneself to see or experience something from someone else's point of view. (See also *in someone else's place; in someone else's shoes.*) □ *Put yourself in someone else's place, and see how it feels.* □ *I put myself in Tom's shoes and realized that I would have made exactly the same choice.*

put oneself in someone else's shoes See the previous entry.

put out (about someone or something) irritated; bothered. □ *John behaved rudely at the party, and the hostess was quite put out.* □ *Liz was quite put out about the question.*

put out (some) feelers to attempt to find out something without being too obvious. □ *I wanted to get a new job, so I put out some feelers.* □ *The manager was mean to everyone in the office, so everyone put out feelers in an attempt to find new jobs.*

put someone away 1. to kill someone. (Slang. Also literal.) □ *The gangster threatened to put me away if I told the police.* ⊤ *They've put away witnesses in the past.* **2.** to bury someone. □ *My uncle died last week. They put him away on Saturday.* **3.** to have someone put into a mental institution. □ *My uncle became irrational, and they put him away.* ⊤ *They put away my aunt the year before.*

put someone down as something to assume that someone is something. (See also *put someone or something down.*) □ *He was so rude that I put him down as someone to be avoided.* □ *If you act silly all the time, people will put you down as a fool.*

put someone down (for something) to put someone's name on a list of people who volunteer to do something or give an amount of money. □ *Can I put you down for ten dollars?* □ *We're having a picnic, and you're invited.*

Everyone is bringing something. Can I put you down for potato salad?

put someone in the picture to give someone all the necessary facts about something. (Slang.) □ *They put the police in the picture about how the accident happened.* □ *Would someone put me in the picture about what went on in my absence?*

put someone on to tease or deceive someone. (Slang.) □ *Oh, you're not serious. You're putting me on.* □ *Stop putting me on!*

put someone on a pedestal to respect, admire, or worship a person. □ *He has put her on a pedestal and thinks she can do no wrong.* □ *Don't put me on a pedestal. I'm only human.*

put someone on the spot to ask someone embarrassing questions; to demand that someone produce as expected. □ *Don't put me on the spot. I can't give you an answer.* □ *The boss put Bob on the spot and demanded that he do everything he had promised.*

put someone or something across AND **get someone or something across 1.** [with *someone*] to present someone in a good way or a good light. □ *I don't want Tom to make the speech. He doesn't put himself across well.* □ *I get myself across in situations like this. I'll do it.* **2.** to make a clear explanation of something; to explain oneself clearly. □ *The teacher got the idea across with the help of pictures.* □ *I'm taking a course in public speaking to help put myself across better.* **3.** [with *something*] to convince someone of something; to get a plan accepted. □ *After many weeks of trying, we were unable to put our plan across. They refused to accept it.* □ *We just couldn't get it across.*

put someone or something at someone's disposal to make someone or something available to someone; to offer someone or something to someone. □ *I'd be glad to help you if you need me. I put myself at your disposal.* □ *I put my car at my neighbor's disposal.*

put someone or something down 1. to belittle or degrade someone or something. (Slang.) □ *It's an old car, but that's no reason to put it down.* □ *Please stop putting me down all the time. It hurts my feelings.* Ⓣ *You put down everything you don't understand!* **2.** [with *something*] to repress or (figuratively) crush something. Ⓣ *The army was called to put down the rebellion.* □ *The police used tear gas to put the riot down.* **3.** [with *something*] to write something down. □ *I'll give you the address. Please put it down.* Ⓣ *I'll put down the address in my address book.* **4.** [with *something*] to land an aircraft. □ *The pilot put the plane down exactly on time.* Ⓣ *I can't put down this plane in the rain.* **5.** [with *something*] to take the life of an animal, such as a pet that is suffering. (This is usually done by a veterinarian.) □ *We had to put our dog down. She was suffering so.* □ *It's very difficult to put down one's pet.*

put someone or something off 1. [with *someone*] to divert or avoid someone. □ *I don't wish to see Mr. Brown now. Please put him off.* □ *I won't talk to reporters. Tell them something that will put them off.* Ⓣ *Put off those annoying people.* **2.** [with *someone*] to upset or distress someone. □ *She always puts me off. She's so rude.* Ⓣ *I try not to put off people.* **3.** [with *something*] to delay something; to postpone something. Ⓣ *I had to put off my appointment with the doctor.* □ *It's raining, so we'll have to put the picnic off.*

put someone or something on hold (See also *on hold.*) **1.** [with *someone*] to stop all activity or communication with someone. □ *John put Ann on hold and started dating Mary.* □ *"You can't just put me on hold!" cried Ann.* **2.** [with *someone*] to leave someone waiting on a telephone call. □ *Please don't put me on hold. I'll call back later when you aren't so busy.* □ *I'll have to put you on hold while I look up the information.* **3.** [with *something*] to postpone something; to stop the progress of something. □ *They put the project* on hold until they got enough money to finish it. □ *Sorry, but we must put your plan on hold.*

put someone or something out 1. [with *something*] to extinguish something. Ⓣ *Put out the fire before you go to bed.* □ *My grandfather told me to put out the light and go to bed.* **2.** [with *someone*] to distress or inconvenience someone. □ *I'd like to have a ride home, but not if it puts you out.* Ⓣ *Don't worry. It won't put out anybody.* **3.** [with *something*] to publish something. □ *They are putting the book out next month.* Ⓣ *When did you put out the article?* **4.** [with *someone*] to make someone "out" in baseball. □ *The pitcher put the runner out.* Ⓣ *I thought the catcher put out the runner.*

put someone or something out of one's mind to forget someone or something; to make an effort to stop thinking about someone or something. (Almost the same as *get someone or something out of one's mind.*) □ *Try to put it out of your mind.* □ *I can't seem to put him out of my mind.*

put someone or something out to pasture to retire someone or something. (Informal. Originally said of a horse that was too old to work.) □ *Please don't put me out to pasture. I have lots of good years left.* □ *This car has reached the end of the line. It's time to put it out to pasture.*

put someone or something to bed 1. [with *someone*] to help someone — usually a child — get into a bed. □ *Come on, Billy, it's time for me to put you to bed.* □ *I want Grandpa to put me to bed.* **2.** [with *something*] to complete work on something and send it on to the next step in production, especially in publishing. □ *This edition is finished. Let's put it to bed.* □ *Finish the editing of this book and put it to bed.*

put someone or something to sleep 1. to kill someone or something. (Euphemistic.) □ *We had to put our dog to sleep.* □ *The robber said he'd put us to sleep forever if we didn't cooperate.* **2.**

to cause someone or something to sleep, perhaps through drugs or anesthesia. □ *The doctor put the patient to sleep before the operation.* □ *I put the cat to sleep by stroking its tummy.* **3.** [with *someone*] to bore someone. □ *That dull lecture put me to sleep.* □ *Her long story almost put me to sleep.*

put someone or something up 1. [with *someone*] to provide lodging for someone. □ *I hope I can find someone to put me up.* Ⓣ *They were able to put up John for the night.* **2.** [with *something*] to preserve and store food by canning or freezing. □ *This year we'll put some strawberries up.* Ⓣ *We put up a lot of food every year.* **3.** [with *something*] to offer something, such as an idea. □ *We need a better idea. Who'll put one up?* Ⓣ *Let me put up a different idea.* **4.** [with *someone*] to run someone as a candidate. □ *I think you should put someone else up.* Ⓣ *We're putting up Ann for treasurer.* **5.** [with *something*] to build a building, a sign, a fence, a wall, etc. □ *We'll put a garage up next month.* Ⓣ *The city put up a fence next to our house.* **6.** [with *something*] to provide the money for something. □ *The government put the money up for the cost of construction.* Ⓣ *Who will put up the money for my education?* **7.** [with *something*] to shape and arrange one's hair (with curlers, hairpins, etc.). □ *I can't go out because I just put my hair up.* Ⓣ *I put up my hair every night.* **8.** [with *something*] to make a struggle, a fight, etc. (Usually *put up something*, and not *put something up*.) Ⓣ *Did he put up a fight?* Ⓣ *No, he only put up a bit of a struggle.*

put someone through the wringer to give someone a difficult time. (Informal.) □ *They are really putting me through the wringer at school.* □ *The boss put Bob through the wringer over this contract.*

put someone to shame to show someone up; to embarrass someone; to make someone ashamed. □ *Your excellent efforts put us all to shame.* □ *I* *put him to shame by telling everyone about his bad behavior.*

put someone to the test to test someone; to see what someone can achieve. □ *I think I can jump that far, but no one has ever put me to the test.* □ *I'm going to put you to the test right now!*

put someone up to something to cause someone to do something; to bribe someone to do something; to give someone the idea of doing something. □ *Who put you up to it?* □ *Nobody put me up to it. I thought it up myself.*

put someone wise to someone or something to inform someone about someone or something. (Informal.) □ *I put her wise to the way we do things around here.* □ *I didn't know she was taking money. Mary put me wise to her.*

put someone's nose out of joint to offend someone; to cause someone to feel slighted or insulted. (Informal.) □ *I'm afraid I put his nose out of joint by not inviting him to the picnic.* □ *There is no reason to put your nose out of joint. I meant no harm.*

put something by AND **lay something by** to reserve a portion of something; to preserve and store something, such as food. (Folksy.) □ *I put some money by for a rainy day.* □ *I laid some eggs by for our use tomorrow.*

put something down in black and white to write down the terms of an agreement; to draw up a written contract; to put the details of something down on paper. (Refers to black ink and white paper.) □ *We agree on all the major points. Now, let's put it down in black and white.* □ *I think I understand what you are talking about, but we need to put it down in black and white.*

put something down to something AND **set something down to something** to explain something as being caused by something else. □ *I put his bad humor down to his illness.* □ *We set your failure down to your emotional upset.*

put something forward to state an idea; to advance an idea. (Also literal.) □ *Toward the end of the meeting, Sally put*

an idea forward. □ *Now, I'd like to put something forward.* Ⓣ *He put several suggestions forward.*

put something in 1. to submit something. (Also literal.) □ *In fact, I put the order in some time ago.* Ⓣ *I put in a request for a new typewriter.* 2. to spend an amount of time (doing something). □ *You put how much time in?* Ⓣ *I put in four months on that project.*

put something in mothballs to put something in storage. (Also literal. Often said of battleships.) □ *The navy put the old cruiser in mothballs and no one ever expected to see it again.* □ *Let's just put this small bicycle in mothballs until we hear of a child who can use it.*

put something into practice to start using a scheme or plan. □ *I hope we can put your idea into practice soon.* □ *The mayor hopes to put the new plan into practice after the next election.*

put something into print to have something printed and published. □ *It's true, but I never believed you'd put it into print.* □ *This is a very interesting story. I can't wait to put it into print.*

put something into words to state or utter a thought; to find a way to express a feeling with words. □ *I can hardly put my gratitude into words.* □ *John has a hard time putting his feelings into words.*

put something on ice AND **put something on the back burner** to delay or postpone something; to put something on hold. (Informal. Both phrases are also literal.) □ *I'm afraid that we'll have to put your project on ice for a while.* □ *Just put your idea on ice and keep it there till we get some money.*

put something on paper to write something down. □ *You have a great idea for a novel. Now put it on paper.* □ *I'm sorry, I can't discuss your offer until I see something in writing. Put it on paper, and then we'll talk.*

put something on the back burner See *put something on ice.*

put something on the cuff to buy something on credit; to add to one's credit balance. □ *I'll take two of those, and please put them on the cuff.* □ *I'm sorry, Tom. We can't put anything more on the cuff.*

put something on the line AND **lay something on the line** to speak very firmly and directly about something. □ *She was very mad. She put it on the line, and we had no doubt about what she meant.* □ *All right, you kids. I'm going to lay it on the line. Don't ever do that again if you know what's good for you.*

put something over to accomplish something; to put something across. □ *This is a very hard thing to explain to a large audience. I hope I can put it over.* □ *This is a big request for money. I go before the board of directors this afternoon, and I hope I can put it over.*

put something over (on someone) to manage to trick or deceive someone. □ *They really put one over on me.* □ *It's easy to put something over if you plan carefully.*

put something plainly to state something firmly and explicitly. □ *To put it plainly, I want you out of this house immediately.* □ *Thank you. I think you've put your feelings quite plainly.*

put something right See *set something right*.

put something straight AND **set something straight** to clarify something; to straighten something out. □ *He has made such a mess of this report. It'll take hours to put it straight.* □ *I'm sorry I confused you. Let me set it straight.*

put something through its paces to demonstrate how well something operates; to demonstrate all the things something can do. (Compare with *put one through one's paces*.) □ *I was down by the barn, watching Sally put her horse through its paces.* □ *This is an excellent can opener. Watch me put it through its paces.*

put something to (good) use to use something. □ *This is a very nice present. I'm sure I'll put it to good use.* □ *I hope you can put these old clothes to use.*

put something to rest AND **lay something to rest** to put an end to a rumor; to finish dealing with something and forget about it. (Also literal.) □ *I've heard enough about Ann and her illness. I'd like to put the whole matter to rest.* □ *I'll be happy to lay it to rest, but will Jane?*

put something together to consider some facts and arrive at a conclusion. (Also literal.) □ *I couldn't put everything together to figure out the answer in time.* ⊤ *When I put together all the facts, I found the answer.*

Put that in your pipe and smoke it! See how you like that!; It is final, and you have to live with it. □ *Well, I'm not going to do it, so put that in your pipe and smoke it!* □ *I'm sick of you, and I'm leaving. Put that in your pipe and smoke it!*

put the arm on someone to apply pressure to someone. (Slang.) □ *John's been putting the arm on Mary to get her to go out with him.* □ *John has been putting the arm on Bill to get him to co-operate.*

put the bite on someone AND **put the touch on someone** to try to get money from someone. (Slang.) □ *Tom put the bite on me for ten dollars.* □ *Bill put the touch on me, but I told him to drop dead.*

put the blame on someone or something AND **lay the blame on someone or something; place the blame on someone or something** to blame someone or something. □ *Don't put the blame on me. I didn't do it.* □ *We'll have to place the blame for the damage on the storm.*

put the cart before the horse to have things in the wrong order; to have things confused and mixed up. (Also with *have*.) □ *You're eating your dessert! You've put the cart before the* horse. □ *Slow down and get organized. Don't put the cart before the horse!* □ *John has the cart before the horse in most of his projects.*

put the clamps on (someone) to restrain or restrict someone. (Slang.) □ *Tom's parents put the clamps on him. They decided he was getting out of hand.* Ⓣ *They got mad and put on the clamps.*

put the finger on someone AND **lay the finger on someone** to accuse someone; to identify someone as the one who did something. (Slang. See also *point the finger at someone.*) □ *Tom put the finger on John, and John is really mad.* □ *He'd better not lay the finger on me. I didn't do it.*

put the heat on (someone) AND **put the screws on (someone); put the squeeze on (someone)** to put pressure on someone (to do something); to coerce someone. (Slang.) □ *John wouldn't talk, so the police were putting the heat on him to confess.* □ *When they put the screws on, they can be very unpleasant.* □ *The police know how to put the squeeze on.*

put the kibosh on something to put an end to something; to veto something. (Slang.) □ *The mayor put the kibosh on the project.* □ *It's a great idea, and I'm sorry that I had to put the kibosh on it.*

put the screws on (someone) See *put the heat on (someone).*

put the skids on (something) to cause something to fail. (Slang.) □ *They put the skids on the project when they refused to give us any more money.* □ *That's the end of our great idea! Somebody put the skids on.*

put the squeeze (on someone) See *put the heat on (someone).*

put the touch on someone See *put the bite on someone.*

put to bed with a shovel to kill someone; to kill and bury someone. (Slang.) □ *That guy'd better be careful, or somebody's going to put him to bed with*

a shovel. □ *"Watch out, wise guy,"* said the robber, *"or I'll put you to bed with a shovel."*

put to it in trouble or difficulty; hard up (for something such as money). (Slang.) □ *I'm in big trouble. I'm really put to it.* □ *John was put to it to get there on time.*

put two and two together to figure something out from the information available. □ *Well, I put two and two together and came up with an idea of who did it.* □ *Don't worry. John won't figure it out. He can't put two and two together.*

put up a (brave) front AND **put on a (brave) front** to appear to be brave (even if one is not). □ *Mary is frightened, but she's putting up a brave front.* □ *If she weren't putting on a front, I'd be more frightened than I am.*

Put up or shut up! (Fixed order.) **1.** a command to prove something or stop talking about it; to do something or stop promising to do it. (Slang.) □ *I'm tired of your telling everyone how fast you can run. Now, do it! Put up or shut up!* □ *Now's your chance to show us that you can run as fast as you can talk. Put up or shut up!* **2.** a command to bet money in support of what one advocates. (See also *Put your money where your mouth is!*) □ *If you think that your horse is faster than mine, then make a bet. Put up or shut up!* □ *You think you can beat me at cards? Twenty bucks says you're wrong. Put up or shut up!*

put up with someone or something to endure someone or something. □ *I can't put up with you anymore. I'm leaving.* □ *She couldn't put up with the smell, so she opened the window.*

put upon by someone to be made use of to an unreasonable degree. (Typically passive.) □ *My mother was always put upon by her neighbors. She was too nice to refuse their requests for help.* □ *Jane feels put upon by her husband's parents.* □ *They're always coming to stay with her.*

put weight on to gain weight; to grow fat. □ *I have to go on a diet because I've been putting on a little weight lately.* ⊤ *The doctor says I need to put on some weight.*

put words into someone's mouth to speak for another person without permission. □ *Stop putting words into my mouth. I can speak for myself.* □ *The lawyer was scolded for putting words into the witness's mouth.*

Put your money where your mouth is! a command to stop talking big and make a bet. □ *I'm tired of your bragging about your skill at betting. Put your money where your mouth is!* □ *You talk about betting, but you don't bet. Put your money where your mouth is!*

putty in someone's hands easily influenced by someone else; excessively willing to do what someone else wishes. □ *Bob's wife is putty in his hands. She never thinks for herself.* □ *Jane's putty in her mother's hands. She always does exactly what she is told.*

puzzle something out to figure something out; to try to figure something out. □ *I looked and looked at it, but I couldn't puzzle it out.* ⊤ *See if you can puzzle out this confusing mess.*

Q

quake in one's boots See *shake in one's boots.*

quick and dirty [done] fast and carelessly; [done] fast and cheaply. (Fixed order.) □ *I am not interested in a quick and dirty job. I want it done right.* □ *The contractor made a lot of money on quick and dirty projects that would never last very long.*

quick as a flash See *(as) quick as a flash.*

quick as greased lightning See *(as) quick as greased lightning.*

quick on the draw See the following entry.

quick on the trigger AND **quick on the draw** (Informal.) **1.** quick to draw a gun and shoot. □ *Some of the old cowboys were known to be quick on the trigger.* □ *Wyatt Earp was particularly quick on the draw.* **2.** quick to respond to anything. □ *John gets the right answer before anyone else. He's really quick on the trigger.* □ *Sally will pro-* bably win the quiz game. She's really quick on the draw.

quick on the uptake quick to understand (something). □ *Just because I'm not quick on the uptake, it doesn't mean I'm stupid.* □ *Mary understands jokes before anyone else because she's so quick on the uptake.*

quiet as a mouse See *(as) quiet as a mouse.*

quiet as the grave See *(as) quiet as the grave.*

quite a bit AND **quite a few; quite a little; quite a lot; quite a number** much or many. □ *Do you need one? I have quite a few.* □ *I have quite a little —enough to spare some.* □ *How many? Oh, quite a number.*

quite a few See the previous entry.

quite a little See *quite a bit.*

quite a lot See *quite a bit.*

quite a number See *quite a bit.*

R

race against time 1. a rush; rushing to beat a deadline. □ *We were in a race against time to beat the deadline.* □ *It was a race against time, but we made it.* **2.** to hurry to beat a deadline. □ *We had to race against time to finish before the deadline.* □ *You don't need to race against time. Take all the time you want.*

rack one's brain(s) to try very hard to think of something. (Informal.) □ *I racked my brains all afternoon, but couldn't remember where I put the book.* □ *Don't waste any more time racking your brain. Go borrow the book from the library.*

rain cats and dogs to rain very hard. (Fixed order.) □ *It's raining cats and dogs. Look at it pour!* □ *I'm not going out in that storm. It's raining cats and dogs.*

rain or shine no matter whether it rains or the sun shines. (Fixed order.) □ *Don't worry. I'll be there rain or shine.* □ *We'll hold the picnic — rain or shine.*

rain something out [for the weather] to spoil something by raining. □ *Oh, the weather looks awful. I hope it doesn't rain the picnic out.* Ⓣ *It's starting to sprinkle now. Do you think it will rain out the ball game?*

raise a hand (against someone or something) See *lift a hand (against someone or something).*

raise a stink (about something) See *create a stink (about something).*

raise an objection (to someone or something) to mention an objection about someone or something. (Also without *an,* as in the examples.) □ *I hope your family won't raise an objection to my staying for dinner.* □ *I'm certain no one will raise objection. We are delighted to have you.*

raise cain (with someone or something) See *raise the devil (with someone or something).*

raise havoc with someone or something AND **play havoc with someone or something** to create confusion or disruption for or among someone or something. □ *Your announcement raised havoc with the students.* □ *I didn't mean to play havoc with them.*

raise hell (with someone or something) See *raise the devil (with someone or something).*

raise hob with someone or something AND **play hob with someone or something** to do something devilish to someone or something; to cause trouble for someone or something. (A *hob* is a hobgoblin, a wicked little elf.) □ *Your sudden arrival is going to play hob with my dinner plans.* □ *Sorry, I didn't mean to raise hob with you.*

raise one's sights to set higher goals for oneself. □ *When you're young, you tend to raise your sights too high.* □ *On the other hand, some people need to raise their sights.*

raise one's voice (to someone) to speak loudly or shout at someone in anger. □ *Don't you dare raise your voice to me!* □ *I'm sorry. I didn't mean to raise my voice.*

raise some eyebrows to shock or surprise people mildly (by doing or saying something). (*Some* can be replaced with *a few, someone's, a lot of,* etc.) □ *What you just said may raise some eyebrows, but it shouldn't make anyone really angry.* □ *John's sudden marriage to Ann raised a few eyebrows.*

raise the devil (with someone or something) AND **raise hell (with someone or something); raise cain (with someone or something); raise the dickens (with someone or something)** to act in some extreme manner; to make trouble; to behave wildly; to be very angry. (Informal. Use *hell* with caution.) □ *John was out all night raising the devil.* □ *Don't come around here and raise hell with everybody.* □ *That cheap gas I bought really raised the dickens with my car's engine.*

raise the dickens (with someone or something) See the previous entry.

rake someone over the coals AND **haul someone over the coals** to give someone a severe scolding. □ *My mother hauled me over the coals for coming in late last night.* □ *The manager raked me over the coals for being late again.*

rake something off to steal or embezzle a portion of a payment. (Slang. Also literal.) □ *They claimed that no one was raking anything off and that the money was only mislaid.* T *The county treasurer was caught raking off some of the tax money.*

rake up something to uncover something unpleasant and remind people about it. □ *The young journalist raked up the old scandal about the senator.* □ *The politician's opponents are trying to rake up some unpleasant details about his past.*

rally (a)round someone or something to come together to support someone or something. □ *Everyone rallied around Jack when he lost his job.* □ *Former students rallied round their college when it was in danger of being closed.*

ram someone or something down someone's throat See *shove someone or something down someone's throat.*

ramble on (about someone or something) to talk aimlessly about someone or something. □ *John is so talkative. He's always rambling on about something.* □ *You're rambling on yourself.*

rank and file (Fixed order.) **1.** regular soldiers, not the officers. □ *I think there is some trouble with the rank and file, sir.* □ *The rank and file usually do exactly as they are told.* **2.** the members of a group, not the leaders. □ *The rank and file will vote on the proposed contract tomorrow.* □ *The last contract was turned down by the rank and file last year.*

rant and rave (about someone or something) to shout angrily and wildly about someone or something. (Fixed order.) □ *Bob rants and raves when anything displeases him.* □ *Bob rants and raves about anything that displeases him.* □ *Father rants and raves if we arrive home late.*

rap someone's knuckles to punish someone slightly. □ *She rapped his knuckles for whispering too much.* □ *Don't rap my knuckles. I didn't do it.*

rarin' to go to be extremely eager to act or do something. (Informal.) □ *Jane can't wait to start her job. She's rarin' to go.* □ *Mary is rarin' to go and can't wait for her university term to start.*

rat on someone to report someone's bad behavior; to tattle on someone. (Slang.) □ *John ratted on me, and I got in trouble.* □ *If he rats on me, I'll hit him!*

rat race a fierce struggle for success, especially in one's career or business. □ *Bob got tired of the rat race. He's retired and gone to the country.* □ *The money market is a rat race, and many people who work in it die of the stress.*

rate with someone to be in someone's favor; to be thought of highly by someone. □ *Ann is great. She really rates with me.* □ *She doesn't rate with me at all.*

rattle something off AND **reel something off** to recite something quickly and accurately. □ *She can really reel them off.* T *Listen to Mary rattle off those numbers.*

reach first base (with someone or something) See *get to first base (with someone or something).*

reach for the sky 1. to aspire to something; to set one's goals high. □ *It's a good idea to set high goals, but there is no point in reaching for the sky.* □ *Go ahead, you can do it! Reach for the sky!* **2.** a command to put one's hands up, as in a robbery. (Slang.) □ *Reach for the sky! This is a stickup!* □ *The sheriff told the bank robbers to reach for the sky.*

reach one's stride AND **hit one's stride** to do something at one's best level of ability. □ *When I reach my stride, things will go faster, and I'll be more efficient.* □ *Now that I've hit my stride, I can work more efficiently.*

read between the lines to infer something (from something). (Usually figurative. Does not necessarily refer to written or printed information.) □ *After listening to what she said, if you read between the lines, you can begin to see what she really means.* □ *Don't believe everything you hear. Learn to read between the lines.*

read one one's rights to make the required statement of legal rights to a person who has been arrested. □ *All right, read this guy his rights and book him on a charge of theft.* □ *You have to read them their rights before putting them in jail.*

read someone like a(n open) book to understand someone very well. □ *I've got John figured out. I can read him like a book.* □ *Of course I understand you. I read you like an open book.*

read someone out of something to expel someone from an organization, such as a political party. □ *Because of her statement, they read her out of the party.* □ *The officers tried to read me out of the society, but they didn't succeed.*

read someone the riot act to give someone a severe scolding. □ *The manager read me the riot act for coming in late.* □ *The teacher read the students the riot act for their failure to do their assignments.*

read someone's mind to guess what someone is thinking. □ *You'll have to tell me what you want. I can't read your mind, you know.* □ *If I could read your mind, I'd know what you expect of me.*

read something into something to attach or attribute a new or different meaning to something. □ *This statement means exactly what it says. Don't try to read anything else into it.* □ *Am I reading too much into your comments?*

read something over to read something. □ *When you have a chance, read this over.* T *Also, read over this report.*

read something through to read all of something. □ *Take this home and read it through.* T *Read through this report and see if you can find any errors.*

read the handwriting on the wall to anticipate what is going to happen by observing small hints and clues. □ *I know I am going to be fired. I can read the handwriting on the wall.* □ *Can't you read the handwriting on the wall? Can't you see what they are planning?*

read up (on someone or something) to find and read some information about someone or something. □ *Please go to the library and read up on George Washington.* □ *I don't know anything about that. I guess I need to read up.*

ready, willing, and able eager or at least willing [to do something]. (Fixed order.) □ *If you need someone to help you move furniture, I'm ready, willing, and able.* □ *Fred is ready, willing, and able to do anything you ask him.*

rear its ugly head [for something unpleasant] to appear or become obvious after lying hidden. □ *Jealousy reared its ugly head and destroyed their marriage.* □ *The question of money always rears its ugly head in matters of business.*

receive someone with open arms AND **welcome someone with open arms** to greet someone eagerly. (Used literally or figuratively.) □ *I'm sure they wanted us to stay for dinner. They received us with open arms.* □ *When I came home from school, the whole family welcomed me with open arms.*

reckon with someone or something to deal with someone or something; to confront someone or something. □ *Eventually you will have to reckon with getting a job.* □ *I really don't want to have to reckon with the manager when she's mad.*

red herring a piece of information or suggestion introduced to draw attention away from the real facts of a situation. (A red herring is a type of strong-smelling smoked fish that was once drawn across the trail of a scent to mislead hunting dogs and put them off the scent.) □ *The detectives were following a red herring, but they're on the right track now.* □ *Jack and Mary were hoping their friends would confuse their parents with a red herring so that they wouldn't realize that they had eloped.*

red in the face embarrassed. □ *After we found Ann hiding in the closet, she became red in the face.* □ *The speaker kept making errors and became red in the face.*

red tape over-strict attention to the wording and details of rules and regulations, especially by government workers. (From the color of the tape used by government departments in England to tie up bundles of documents.) □ *Because of red tape, Frank took weeks to get a visa.* □ *Red tape prevented Jack's wife from joining him abroad.*

reel something off See *rattle something off.*

regain one's composure to become calm and composed. □ *I found it difficult to regain my composure after the argument.* □ *Here, sit down and relax so that you can regain your composure.*

regain one's feet **1.** to stand up again after falling or stumbling. □ *I fell on the ice and almost couldn't regain my feet.* □ *I helped my uncle regain his feet as he tried to get up from the chair.* **2.** to become independent after financial difficulties. □ *I lent Bill $400 to help him regain his feet.* □ *I'll be able to pay my bills when I regain my feet.*

regular as clockwork See *(as) regular as clockwork.*

relative to someone or something **1.** concerning someone or something. □ *I have something to say relative to Bill.* □ *Do you have any information relative to the situation in South America?* **2.** in proportion to someone or something. □ *My happiness is relative to yours.* □ *I can spend an amount of money relative to the amount of money I earn.*

resign oneself to something to accept something reluctantly. □ *I finally resigned myself to going to Mexico even though I didn't want to.* □ *Mary resigned herself to her fate.*

rest assured to be assured; to be certain. □ *Rest assured that you'll receive the best of care.* □ *Please rest assured that we will do everything possible to help.*

rest on one's laurels to enjoy one's success and not try to achieve more. □ *Don't rest on your laurels. Try to continue to do great things!* □ *I think I'll rest on my laurels for a time before attempting anything new.*

result in something to cause something to happen. □ *The storm resulted in a lot of flooding.* □ *Her fall resulted in a broken leg.*

return someone's compliment See the following entry.

return the compliment AND **return someone's compliment** to pay a compliment to someone who has paid you a compliment. (See also *pay someone a compliment.*) □ *Mary told me that my hair looked nice, so I returned her compliment and told her that her hair was lovely.* □ *When someone says* *something nice, it is polite to return the compliment.*

return the favor to do a good deed for someone who has done a good deed for you. □ *You helped me last week, so I'll return the favor and help you this week.* □ *There is no point in helping Bill. He'll never return the favor.*

rev something up to make an idling engine run very fast, in short bursts of speed. □ *Hey! Stop revving it up!* T *I wish that Tom wouldn't sit out in front of our house in his car and rev up his engine.*

ride herd on someone or something to supervise someone or something. (Informal. Refers to a cowboy supervising cattle.) □ *I'm tired of having to ride herd on my kids all the time.* □ *My job is to ride herd on this project and make sure everything is done right.*

ride off in all directions to behave in a totally confused manner; to try to do everything at once. (Folksy.) □ *Bill has a tendency to ride off in all directions. He's not organized enough.* □ *Now, calm down. There is no sense in riding off in all directions.*

ride on someone's coattails AND **hang on someone's coattails** to make one's good fortune or success depend on another person. (Also with *else*, as in the examples.) □ *Bill isn't very creative, so he rides on John's coattails.* □ *Some people just have to hang on somebody else's coattails.*

ride roughshod over someone or something to treat someone or something with disdain or scorn. □ *Tom seems to ride roughshod over his friends.* □ *You shouldn't have come into our town to ride roughshod over our laws and our traditions.*

ride something out to endure something unpleasant. (Originally referred to ships lasting out a storm.) □ *It was a nasty situation, but the mayor tried to ride it out.* T *The mayor decided to ride out the scandal.*

ride the gravy train to live in luxury. (Informal.) □ *If I had a million dol-*

lars, I sure could ride the gravy train. □ *I wouldn't like loafing. I don't want to ride the gravy train.*

riding for a fall risking failure or an accident, usually due to overconfidence. □ *Tom drives too fast, and he seems too sure of himself. He's riding for a fall.* □ *Bill needs to eat better and get more sleep. He's riding for a fall.*

right and left AND **left and right** to both sides; on all sides; everywhere. (Reversible.) □ *I dropped the tennis balls, and they rolled right and left.* □ *There were children everywhere—running right and left.*

right as rain See *(as) right as rain.*

right away immediately. □ *Please do it right away!* □ *I'll be there right away. I'm leaving this instant.*

right down someone's alley AND **right up someone's alley** ideally suited to one's interests or abilities. (Informal.) □ *Skiing is right down my alley. I love it.* □ *This kind of thing is right up John's alley.*

right off the bat immediately; first thing. (Informal.) □ *When he was learning to ride a bicycle, he fell on his head right off the bat.* □ *The new manager demanded new office furniture right off the bat.*

right on time at the correct time; no later than the specified time. □ *Bill always shows up right on time.* □ *If you get there right on time, you'll get one of the free tickets.*

right side up with the correct side upwards, as with a box or some other container. □ *Keep this box right side up, or the contents will be crushed.* □ *Please set your coffee cup right side up so I can fill it.*

(right) under someone's (very) nose **1.** right in front of someone. □ *I thought I'd lost my purse, but it was sitting on the table under my very nose.* □ *How did Mary fail to see the book? It was right under her nose.* **2.** in someone's presence. (Note the variations in the examples.) □ *The thief stole Jim's* wallet right under his nose. □ *The jewels were stolen from under the very noses of the security guards.*

right up someone's alley See *right down someone's alley.*

ring a bell [for something] to cause someone to remember something or for it to seem familiar. (Informal.) □ *I've never met John Franklin, but his name rings a bell.* □ *Whenever I see a bee, it rings a bell. I remember when I was stung by one.*

ring down the curtain (on something) AND **bring down the curtain (on something)** to bring something to an end; to declare something to be at an end. □ *It's time to ring down the curtain on our relationship. We have nothing in common anymore.* □ *We've tried our best to make this company a success, but it's time to ring down the curtain.* □ *After many years the old man brought down the curtain and closed the restaurant.*

ring in the New Year to celebrate the beginning of the new year at midnight on December 31. □ *We are planning a big party to ring in the New Year.* □ *How did you ring in the New Year?*

ring something up to record the cost of an item on a cash register. □ *Please ring this chewing gum up first, and I'll put it in my purse.* ⊤ *The cashier rang up each item and told me how much money I owed.*

ring true to sound or seem true or likely. (From testing the quality of metal or glass by striking it and listening to the noise made.) □ *The student's excuse for being late doesn't ring true.* □ *Do you think that Mary's explanation for her absence rang true?*

rip into someone or something to attack someone or something, physically or verbally. (Informal.) □ *The bear ripped into the deer.* □ *The angry teacher ripped into the student.*

rip someone or something off (Slang.) **1.** [with *someone*] to cheat or deceive someone; to steal from someone. □ *That store operator ripped me off.* ⊤

They shouldn't rip off people like that. **2.** [with *something*] to steal something. □ *I bought it! I didn't rip it off!* ⊤ *The crooks ripped off a car in broad daylight.*

ripe old age a very old age. □ *Mr. Smith died last night, but he lived to a ripe old age — 99.* □ *All the Smiths seem to reach a ripe old age.*

Rise and shine! Get out of bed and be lively and energetic! (Informal. Often a command. Fixed order.) □ *Come on, children! Rise and shine! We're going to the beach.* □ *Father always calls "Rise and shine!" in the morning when we want to go on sleeping.*

rise to the bait to be lured by some kind of bait. (Also literal when referring to a fish.) □ *I threatened to take another job elsewhere, but the boss did not rise to the bait.* □ *When I said I was leaving, Ted rose to the bait and asked why.*

rise to the occasion to meet the challenge of an event; to try extra hard to do a task. □ *John was able to rise to the occasion and make the conference a success.* □ *It was a big challenge, but he rose to the occasion.*

risk one's neck (to do something) to risk physical harm in order to accomplish something. (Informal.) □ *Look at that traffic! I refuse to risk my neck just to cross the street to buy a paper.* □ *I refuse to risk my neck at all.*

rob Peter to pay Paul to take from one in order to give to another. □ *Why borrow money to pay your bills? That's just robbing Peter to pay Paul.* □ *There's no point in robbing Peter to pay Paul. You will still be in debt.*

rob the cradle to marry or date someone who is much younger than you are. (Informal.) □ *I hear that Bill is dating Ann. Isn't that sort of robbing the cradle? She's much younger than he is.* □ *Uncle Bill — who is nearly eighty — married a thirty-year-old woman. That is really robbing the cradle.*

rock the boat to cause trouble where none is welcome; to disturb a situation that is otherwise stable and satisfactory. (Often negative. Also literal.) □ *Look, Tom, everything is going fine here. Don't rock the boat!* □ *You can depend on Tom to mess things up by rocking the boat.*

roll in to come in large numbers or amounts. (Informal.) □ *We didn't expect many people at the party, but they just kept rolling in.* □ *Money is simply rolling in for our charity appeal.*

roll one's sleeves up to get ready to do some work. (Also literal.) □ *Roll your sleeves up and get busy. This isn't a picnic. This is work!* ⊤ *Come on, you guys, get busy. Roll up your sleeves and go to work.*

roll out the red carpet for someone to provide special treatment for someone. □ *There's no need to roll out the red carpet for me.* □ *We rolled out the red carpet for the king and queen.*

roll something back to reduce a price to a previous amount. (Also literal.) □ *The government forced the company to roll its prices back.* ⊤ *It wouldn't have rolled back its prices if the government hadn't forced it to.*

rolling in something having large amounts of something, usually money. (Informal.) □ *That family is rolling in money.* □ *Jack doesn't need to earn money. He's rolling in it.*

Rome wasn't built in a day. important things don't happen overnight. □ *Don't expect a lot to happen right away. Rome wasn't built in a day, you know.* □ *Don't be anxious about how fast you are growing. Rome wasn't built in a day.*

room and board food to eat and a place to live; the cost of food and lodging. (Fixed order.) □ *That college charges too much for room and board.* □ *How much is your room and board?*

root for someone or something to cheer and encourage someone or something. (Informal.) □ *Are you rooting for anyone in particular, or are you just shouting because you're excited?* □ *I'm rooting for the home team.*

rooted to the spot unable to move because of fear or surprise. □ *Joan stood rooted to the spot when she saw the ghostly figure.* □ *Mary was rooted to the spot as the mugger snatched her bag.*

rope someone into doing something to persuade or trick someone into doing something. (Informal.) □ *I don't know who roped me into this, but I don't want to do it.* □ *See if you can rope somebody into taking this to the post office.*

rotten to the core completely no good and worthless. (Also literal.) □ *Fred is rotten to the core. He will never be a good member of society.* □ *I hope that just because I made one little mistake with my life that you don't think I am rotten to the core.*

rough-and-ready strong, active, and ready for anything. (Fixed order.) □ *John is not exactly rough-and-ready, but he is a moderately good athlete.* □ *Ralph is very rough-and-ready, but his table manners are very bad.*

rough-and-tumble rough; overly active. (In reference to physical activity.) □ *The game got sort of rough-and-tumble, so I stopped playing.* □ *Jane runs with a rough-and-tumble crowd that's always involved in some sort of sport.*

rough it to live in discomfort; to live in uncomfortable conditions without the usual amenities. (Informal.) □ *The students are roughing it in a shack with no running water.* □ *Bob and Jack had nowhere to live and so they had to rough it in a tent till they found somewhere.*

rough someone up to beat or physically harass someone. (Slang.) □ *The gangsters roughed their victim up.* ⊤ *The police roughed up the suspect, and they got in trouble for it.*

round out something See under *round something off.*

round something off 1. to change a number to the next higher or lower whole number. □ *You should round 8.122 off.* ⊤ *I rounded off 8.789 to 9.* **2.** AND **round out something** to finish something (in a special way, by doing something). □ *She rounded her schooling off with a trip to Europe.* ⊤ *I like to round out the day with a period of meditation.*

round the clock See *(a)round the clock.*

round-the-clock See *(a)round-the-clock.*

round-trip ticket a ticket (for a plane, train, bus, etc.) that allows one to go to a destination and return. □ *A round-trip ticket is usually cheaper than a one-way ticket.* □ *How much is a round-trip ticket to San Francisco?*

rub elbows (with someone) AND **rub shoulders with someone** to associate with someone; to work closely with someone. □ *I don't care to rub elbows with someone who acts like that!* □ *I rub shoulders with John at work. We are good friends.*

rub off (on someone) [for a characteristic of one person] to seem to transfer to someone else. (Also literal.) □ *I'll sit by Ann. She has been lucky all evening. Maybe it'll rub off on me.* □ *Sorry. I don't think that luck rubs off.*

rub salt in the wound deliberately to make someone's unhappiness, shame, or misfortune worse. □ *Don't rub salt in the wound by telling me how enjoyable the party was.* □ *Jim is feeling miserable about losing his job, and Fred is rubbing salt into the wound by saying how good his replacement is.*

rub shoulders with someone See *rub elbows (with someone).*

rub someone out to kill someone. (Slang.) □ *The crook said, "Bill is getting to be a problem. We're going to have to rub him out."* ⊤ *The gangsters tried to rub out the witness.*

rub someone('s fur) the wrong way to irritate someone. (From the rubbing of a cat's or dog's fur the wrong way.) □ *I'm sorry I rubbed your fur the wrong way. I didn't mean to upset you.* □ *Don't rub her the wrong way!*

rub someone's nose in it to remind one of something one has done wrong; to remind one of something bad or unfortunate that has happened. (From a method of housebreaking pets.) □ *When Bob failed his exam, his brother rubbed his nose in it.* □ *Mary knows she shouldn't have broken off her engagement. Don't rub her nose in it.*

rub something in to keep reminding one of one's failures; to nag someone about something. (Informal. Also literal.) □ *I like to rub it in. You deserve it!* ⊤ *Why do you have to rub in everything I do wrong?*

ruffle someone's feathers to upset or annoy someone. (A bird's feathers become ruffled if it is angry or afraid.) □ *You certainly ruffled Mrs. Smith's feathers by criticizing her garden.* □ *Try to be tactful and not ruffle people's feathers.*

rule of thumb a rough or an inexact guide, rather than an exact measurement, used for quick calculations. (From the use of one's thumb to make quick and rough measurements.) □ *By rule of thumb, that table is about six feet long.* □ *I haven't measured that pole, but I guess according to rule of thumb that it's about ten feet high.*

rule someone or something out to prevent, disqualify, overrule, or cancel someone or something. □ *John's bad temper rules him out for the job.* ⊤ *The weather ruled out a picnic for the weekend.*

rule the roost to be the boss or manager, especially at home. (Informal.) □ *Who rules the roost at your house?* □ *Our new office manager really rules the roost.*

run a fever AND **run a temperature** to have a body temperature higher than normal; to have a fever. □ *I ran a fever when I had the flu.* □ *The baby is running a temperature and is grouchy.*

run a risk (of something) AND **run the risk (of something)** to take a chance that something (bad) will happen. □ *I don't want to run the risk of losing my* *job.* □ *Don't worry. You won't have to run a risk.*

run a taut ship See *run a tight ship.*

run a temperature See *run a fever.*

run a tight ship AND **run a taut ship** to run a ship or an organization in an orderly and disciplined manner. (*Taut* and *tight* mean the same thing. *Taut* is correct nautical use.) □ *The new office manager really runs a tight ship.* □ *Captain Jones is known for running a taut ship.*

run afoul of someone or something See *fall afoul of someone or something.*

run after someone to chase someone of the opposite sex hoping for a date or some attention. (Also literal.) □ *Is John still running after Ann?* □ *No, Ann is running after John.*

run an errand AND **go on an errand** to take a short trip to do a specific thing. □ *I've got to run an errand. I'll be back in a minute.* □ *John has gone on an errand. He'll be back shortly.*

run (around) in circles See the following entry.

run around like a chicken with its head cut off AND **run (around) in circles** to run around frantically and aimlessly; to be in a state of chaos. (See also *go (a)round in circles.*) □ *I spent all afternoon running around like a chicken with its head cut off.* □ *If you run around in circles, you'll never get anything done.* □ *Get organized and stop running in circles.*

run around with someone AND **go around with someone** to be friends with someone; to go places with regular friends. □ *John and I were great friends. We used to run around with each other all the time.* □ *Mary went around with Jane for about a year.*

run circles around someone AND **run rings around someone** to outrun or outdo someone. (Informal.) □ *John is a much better racer than Mary. He can run circles around her.* □ *Mary can run rings around Sally.*

run counter to something to be in opposition to something; to run against something. (This has nothing to do with running.) □ *Your proposal runs counter to what is required by the manager.* □ *His idea runs counter to good sense.*

run for it to try to escape by running. (Informal.) □ *The guard's not looking. Let's run for it!* □ *The convict tried to run for it, but the guard caught him.*

run for one's life to run away to save one's life. □ *The dam has burst! Run for your life!* □ *The captain told us all to run for our lives.*

run in the family for a characteristic to appear in all (or most) members of a family. □ *My grandparents lived well into their nineties, and it runs in the family.* □ *My brothers and I have red hair. It runs in the family.*

run into a stone wall to come to a barrier against further progress. (Informal. Also literal.) □ *We've run into a stone wall in our investigation.* □ *Algebra was hard for Tom, but he really ran into a stone wall with geometry.*

run into someone See *bump into someone.*

run like clockwork to run very well; to progress very well. □ *I want this office to run like clockwork — with everything on time and everything done right.* □ *The plans for the party were made and we knew that we could depend on Alice to make sure that everything ran like clockwork.*

run-of-the-mill common or average; typical. □ *The restaurant we went to was nothing special — just run-of-the-mill.* □ *The service was good, but the food was run-of-the-mill or worse.*

run off See under *run off with someone or something.*

run off at the mouth to talk excessively. (Slang.) □ *Shut up, John. You're always running off at the mouth.* □ *There is no need to run off at the mouth. Stop talking so much for so long.*

308

run off with someone or something 1. to take something or someone away; to steal something or kidnap someone. □ *The thief ran off with the lady's purse.* □ *The kidnapper ran off with the baby.* **2.** [with *someone*] AND **run off** to run away with someone, as in an elopement. □ *Tom ran off with Ann.* □ *Tom and Ann ran off and got married.*

run out of gas to use up all the gasoline available. □ *I hope we don't run out of gas.* □ *I am sorry I am late. I ran out of gas.*

run out of time to use up all the available time. □ *I ran out of time and couldn't finish.* □ *I hope she answers the question before she runs out of time.*

run rings around someone See *run circles around someone.*

run riot AND **run wild** to get out of control. □ *The dandelions have run riot in our lawn.* □ *The children ran wild at the birthday party and had to be taken home.*

run scared to behave as if one were going to fail. (Informal. Typically said of someone running for election.) □ *The mayor was running scared, but won anyway.* □ *When we lost that big contract, everyone in the office was running scared. We thought we'd be fired.*

run short (of something) to use up almost all of something; to have too little or few of something left. □ *We are running short of milk. Please buy some on the way home.* □ *When it comes to money, we are always running short.*

run someone in to take someone to the police station and make an arrest. □ *"Don't run me in," cried the driver. "I'm innocent."* T *The police officer was angry and ran in the motorist.*

run someone or something down 1. to degrade physically or put wear on someone or something. □ *All these years of hard work have run Mrs. Brown down severely.* T *Our neighbors ran down their house before they sold it.* **2.**

to say bad things about someone or something. □ *Why are you always running your friends down?* T *Don't run down my paintings! You just don't understand art!* **3.** to look for and finally find someone or something. □ *I finally ran John Smith down. He had moved to another town.* T *I will see if I can run down the book that you want.*

run someone ragged to run someone hard and fast; to keep someone very busy. (Informal.) □ *This busy season is running us all ragged at the store.* □ *What a busy day. I ran myself ragged.*

run something into the ground AND **drive something into the ground** to carry something too far. (Informal.) □ *It was a good joke at first, Tom, but you've run it into the ground.* □ *Just because everyone laughed once, you don't have to drive it into the ground.*

run something up 1. to raise a flag. □ *I run it up every day except when it's raining.* T *We run up the flag every day.* **2.** to add to a bill; to add many charges to one's account. □ *He ran the bill up until they asked him to pay part of it.* T *Tom ran up a big bill at the hotel.*

run that by (someone) again say that again. (Slang.) □ *I didn't hear you. Could you run that by me again?* □ *Run that by again. I don't believe my ears.*

run the good race to do the best that one could; to live life as well and as fully as possible. (Also literal.) □ *He didn't get what he wanted, but he ran the good race.* □ *Joan ran the good race, and she will be remembered by all of us.*

run the risk (of something) See *run a risk (of something).*

run through something 1. to waste something; to use up something rapidly. (Also literal.) □ *Have you run through all those eggs already?* □ *I ran through my allowance in one day.* **2.** to read through something rapidly. □ *I ran through your report, and it looks okay.* □ *I didn't read the novel, I only ran through it.*

run to seed AND **go to seed** to become worn-out and uncared for. (Said especially of a lawn that needs care.) □ *Look at that lawn. The whole thing has run to seed.* □ *Pick things up around here. This place is going to seed. What a mess!*

run to something to amount to a certain amount of money. □ *In the end, the bill ran to thousands of dollars.* □ *His account ran to more than I expected.*

run wild See *run riot.*

rustle something up to find and prepare some food. (Folksy.) □ *I'm sure he can rustle something up.* ⊤ *Just go out into the kitchen and ask Bill to rustle up some food.*

S

sack out to go to bed; to go to sleep. (Slang. Compare with *hit the sack* at *hit the hay.*) □ *Look at the clock. It's time to sack out.* □ *John sacks out at about nine o'clock.*

sacred cow something that is regarded by some people with such respect and veneration that they do not like it being criticized by anyone in any way. (From the fact that the cow is regarded as sacred in India and is not eaten or mistreated.) □ *A university education is a sacred cow in the Smith family. Fred is regarded as a failure because he quit school at 16.* □ *Don't talk about eating meat to Pam. Vegetarianism is one of her sacred cows.*

sadder but wiser unhappy but educated [about someone or something—after an unpleasant event]. (Fixed order.) □ *After the accident, I was sadder but wiser, and would never make the same mistake again.* □ *We left the meeting sadder but wiser, knowing that we could not ever come to an agreement with Becky's aunt.*

saddle someone with something to give someone something undesirable, annoying, or difficult to deal with. (Informal.) □ *Mary says she doesn't want to be saddled with a baby, but her husband would just love one.* □ *Jim saddled Eddie with the most boring jobs so that he would leave.*

safe and sound safe and whole or healthy. (Fixed order.) □ *It was a rough trip, but we got there safe and sound.* □ *I'm glad to see you here safe and sound.*

safety in numbers safety through concealment in large numbers of people or other creatures. □ *We stayed close together, thinking that there was safety in numbers.* □ *The elderly people went out together for a walk, knowing that there was safety in numbers.*

sail (right) through something to finish something quickly and easily. (Informal. Also literal.) □ *The test was not difficult. I sailed right through it.* □ *Bob sailed through his homework in a short amount of time.*

sail under false colors to pretend to be something that one is not. (Originally nautical, referring to a pirate ship disguised as an innocent merchant ship.) □ *John has been sailing under false colors. He's really a spy.* □ *I thought you were wearing that uniform because you worked here. You are sailing under false colors.*

salt of the earth the most worthy of people; a very good or worthy person. (A biblical reference, *Matthew, 5:13.*) □ *Mrs. Jones is the salt of the earth. She is the first to help anyone in trouble.* □ *Frank's mother is the salt of the earth. She has five children of her own and yet fosters three others.*

salt something away to store or save something. (Originally referred to preserving food and storing it.) □ *Mary salted some extra candy away for use during the holidays.* Ⓣ *I salted away about $1,000 when I worked as a clerk in the grocery store.*

same here Me too!; I agree! (Informal.) □ BOB: *I'll have chocolate ice cream!* BILL: *Same here.* □ MARY: *I'll* vote for the best candidate. TOM: *Same here!*

same old story something that occurs or has occurred in the same way often. □ *Jim's got no money. It's the same old story. He's spent it all on clothing.* □ *The company is getting rid of workers. It's the same old story — a shortage of orders.*

save one's breath to refrain from talking, explaining, or arguing. □ *There is no sense in trying to convince her. Save your breath.* □ *Tell her to save her breath. He won't listen to her.*

save (one's) face to preserve one's good standing or high position (after a failure). □ *The ambassador was more interested in saving his face than winning the argument.* □ *Most diplomats are concerned with saving face.*

save someone's neck See the following entry.

save someone's skin AND **save someone's neck** to save someone from injury, embarrassment, or punishment. (Informal.) □ *I saved my skin by getting the job done on time.* □ *Thanks for saving my neck! I would have fallen down the stairs if you hadn't held my arm.*

save something for a rainy day to reserve something — usually money — for some future need. (Also literal. *Save something* can be replaced with *put something aside, hold something back, keep something,* etc.) □ *I've saved a little money for a rainy day.* □ *Keep some extra candy for a rainy day.*

save the day to produce a good result when a bad result was expected. □ *The team was expected to lose, but Sally made many points and saved the day.* □ *Your excellent speech saved the day.*

save up (for something) to save money for something. □ *I'm saving up for a bicycle.* □ *I'll have to save up for a long time. It costs a lot of money.*

saved by the bell rescued from a difficult or dangerous situation just in time by something that brings the situation to a sudden end. (From the sounding of a bell marking the end of a round in a boxing match.) □ *James didn't know the answer to the question but he was saved by the bell when the teacher was called away from the room.* □ *I couldn't think of anything to say to the woman at the bus stop, but I was saved by the bell when my bus arrived.*

saving grace the one thing that saves or redeems someone or something that would otherwise be a total disaster. □ *Her saving grace is that she has a lot of money.* □ *The saving grace for the whole evening was the good music played by the band.*

say a mouthful to say a lot; to say something very important or meaningful. (Folksy.) □ *When you said things were busy around here, you said a mouthful. It is terribly busy.* □ *You sure said a mouthful, Bob. Things are really busy.*

say something in a roundabout way to imply something without saying it; to say something indirectly; to speak using circumlocution. □ *Why don't you say what you mean? Why do you always say something in a roundabout way?* □ *What did she mean? Why did she say it in a roundabout way?*

say something (right) to someone's face to say something (unpleasant) directly to someone. □ *She knew I thought she was rude because I said it right to her face.* □ *I thought she felt that way about me, but I never thought she'd say it to my face.*

say something under one's breath to say something so softly that almost no one can hear it. □ *John was saying something under his breath, and I don't think it was very pleasant.* □ *I'm glad he said it under his breath. If he had said it out loud, it would have caused an argument.*

say the word to give a signal to begin; to say yes or okay. □ *I'm ready to start any time you say the word.* □ *We'll all shout "Happy Birthday!" when I say the word.*

say uncle to surrender; to give in. (Informal.) □ *Ann held Bobby down on the ground until he said uncle.* □ *Why isn't it enough to win the argument? Why do you demand that I say uncle?*

scarcer than hens' teeth See *(as) scarce as hens' teeth.*

scare one out of one's wits See *frighten one out of one's wits.*

scare someone or something up to search for and find someone or something. (Slang.) □ *Go out in the kitchen and scare some food up.* Ⓣ *I'll see if I can scare up somebody to fix the broken chair.*

scare someone stiff to scare someone severely; to *frighten someone to death.* (*Stiff* means dead.) □ *That loud noise scared me stiff.* □ *The robber jumped out and scared us stiff.*

scare someone to death See *frighten someone to death.*

scare the living daylights out of someone See *frighten the wits out of someone.*

scare the wits out of someone See *frighten the wits out of someone.*

scared stiff badly frightened. □ *We were scared stiff by the robber.* □ *I was scared stiff when the dog growled at me.*

scared to death See *frightened to death.*

scrape something together to assemble something quickly, usually from a small supply of components. □ *I'll try to scrape something together for dinner.* Ⓣ *We really should try to have a party to celebrate the boss's birthday. Let's try to scrape together a little something.*

scrape the bottom of the barrel to select from among the worst; to choose from what is left over. □ *You've bought a bad-looking car. You really scraped the bottom of the barrel to get that one.* □ *The worker you sent over was the worst I've ever seen. Send me another—and don't scrape the bottom of the barrel.*

scratch around (for something) to look here and there for something. (Infor-

mal.) □ *Let me scratch around for a better bargain. Maybe I can come up with something you like.* □ *I'll scratch around for a week or two and see what I come up with.*

scratch someone's back to do a favor for someone in return for a favor done for you. (Informal. Also literal.) □ *You scratch my back, and I'll scratch yours.* □ *We believe that the mayor has been scratching the treasurer's back.*

scratch the surface to just begin to find out about something; to examine only the superficial aspects of something. □ *The investigation of the governor's staff revealed some suspicious dealing. It is thought that the investigators have just scratched the surface.* □ *We don't know how bad the problem is. We've only scratched the surface.*

scream bloody murder to complain bitterly; to complain unduly. (Slang. See also *cry bloody murder.*) □ *When we put him in an office without a window, he screamed bloody murder.* □ *There is something wrong next door. Everyone is screaming bloody murder.*

screw around (with someone or something) See *mess around (with someone or something).*

screw someone or something up to cause trouble for someone or something. (Slang.) □ *Your advice about making a lot of money really screwed me up. Now I'm broke.* Ⓣ *Your efforts screwed up the entire project.*

screw up one's courage to build up one's courage. □ *I guess I have to screw up my courage and go to the dentist.* □ *I spent all morning screwing up my courage to take my driver's test.*

scrimp and save to be very thrifty; to live on very little money, often in order to save up for something. □ *We had to scrimp and save in order to send the children to college.* □ *The Smiths scrimp and save all year in order to go on a Caribbean cruise.*

seamy side of life the most unpleasant or roughest aspect of life. (Informal. A reference to the inside of a garment where the seams show.) ☐ *Doctors in that area really see the seamy side of life.* ☐ *Mary saw the seamy side of life when she worked as a volunteer in the shelter.*

search high and low (for someone or something) See *hunt high and low (for someone or something).*

search something with a fine-tooth comb See *go over something with a fine-tooth comb.*

second nature to someone easy and natural for someone. ☐ *Swimming is second nature to Jane.* ☐ *Driving is no problem for Bob. It's second nature to him.*

second to none better than everything. ☐ *This is an excellent car—second to none.* ☐ *Her suggestion was second to none, and the manager accepted it eagerly.*

see a man about a dog to leave for some unmentioned purpose. (Informal. Often refers to going to the rest room.) ☐ *I don't know where Tom went. He said he had to see a man about a dog.* ☐ *When John said he was going to see a man about a dog, I thought he would be gone for only a minute.*

see about something to ask about something; to check on something. ☐ *I'll have to see about your request to leave early.* ☐ *I must see about the cake I have in the oven.*

see double to see two of everything instead of one. ☐ *When I was driving, I saw two people on the road instead of one. I'm seeing double. There's something wrong with my eyes.* ☐ *Mike thought he was seeing double when he saw Mary. He didn't know she had a twin.*

see eye to eye (with someone) (about something) AND **see eye to eye (with someone) (on something)** to view something in the same way (as someone else). ☐ *John and Ann see eye to eye about the new law. Neither of them likes it.* ☐ *John sees eye to eye with*

Ann *about it.* ☐ *That's interesting because they rarely see eye to eye.*

see eye to eye (with someone) (on something) See the previous entry.

see fit (to do something) to decide to do something. ☐ *If I see fit to return, I'll bring Bill with me.* ☐ *She'll do it if she sees fit.*

see into something See *look into something.*

see no objection (to something) AND **not see any objection (to something)** not to think of any objection to something. ☐ *I see no objection to your idea.* ☐ *Do you see any objection?* ☐ *I do not see any objection to anything you have done.*

see one's way clear (to do something) to find it possible to do something. ☐ *I'd be happy if you could see your way clear to attend our meeting.* ☐ *I wanted to be there, but I couldn't see my way clear.*

see red to be angry. (Informal.) ☐ *Whenever I think of the needless destruction of trees, I see red.* ☐ *Bill really saw red when the tax bill arrived.*

see someone home to accompany someone home. ☐ *Bill agreed to see his aunt home after the movie.* ☐ *You don't need to see me home. It's perfectly safe, and I can get there on my own.*

see someone to the door See *show someone (to) the door.*

see something through to follow through on something until it is completed. (Compare with *see through someone or something.*) ☐ *Mary is prepared to see the project through.* ☐ *It's going to be an unpleasant experience, but I hope you'll see it through.*

see stars to see flashing lights after receiving a blow to the head. ☐ *I saw stars when I bumped my head on the attic ceiling.* ☐ *The little boy saw stars when he fell headfirst onto the concrete.*

see the color of someone's money to verify that someone has money or has enough money. (Slang.) ☐ *So, you* want to make a bet? *Not until I see the color of your money.* □ *I want to see the color of your money before we go any further with this business deal.*

see the (hand)writing on the wall to know that something is certain to happen. □ *If you don't improve your performance, they'll fire you. Can't you see the writing on the wall?* □ *I know I'll get fired. I can see the handwriting on the wall.*

see the last of someone or something to see someone or something for the last time. □ *I'm glad to see the last of that old car. It has a lot of problems.* □ *The people at my office were happy to see the last of John. He caused a lot of trouble before he left.*

see the light to understand something clearly at last. (See also the following two entries.) □ *After a lot of studying and asking many questions, I finally saw the light.* □ *I know that geometry is difficult. Keep working at it. You'll see the light pretty soon.*

see the light (at the end of the tunnel) to foresee an end to something, such as a problem or a task, after a long period of time. □ *I had been horribly ill for two months before I began to see the light at the end of the tunnel.* □ *I began to see the light one day in early spring. At that moment, I knew I'd get well.* □ *When I got to the last chapter, I could see the light at the end of the tunnel.*

see the light (of day) to come to the end of a very busy time. □ *Finally, when the holiday season was over, we could see the light of day. We had been so busy!* □ *When business lets up for a while, we'll be able to see the light.*

see the sights to see the important things in a place; to see what tourists usually see. □ *We plan to visit Paris and see the sights.* □ *Everyone left the hotel early in the morning to see the sights.*

see things to imagine one sees someone or something that is not there. □ *Jean says that she saw a ghost, but she*

was just seeing things. □ *I thought I was seeing things when Bill walked into the room. Someone had told me he was dead.*

see through someone or something to understand or detect the true nature of someone or something. (Compare with *see something through.*) □ *You can't fool me anymore. I can see through you and all your tricks.* □ *This plan is designed to make money for you, not to help people. I can see through it! I'm not a fool!*

see to someone or something to take care of someone or something. □ *Tom will see to the horses. Come to the house and freshen up.* □ *I hear the doorbell. Will someone please see to the door?* □ *This paper needs filling out. Will you please see to it?*

see which way the wind is blowing to determine what is the most expedient thing to do. □ *We studied the whole situation to see which way the wind was blowing and decided to avoid any conflict at that time.* □ *Sam failed to see which way the wind was blowing and got himself caught up in an argument.*

seeing is believing one must believe something that one sees. □ *I never would have thought that a cow could swim, but seeing is believing.* □ *I can hardly believe we are in Paris, but there's the Eiffel Tower, and seeing is believing.*

seize the bull by the horns See *take the bull by the horns.*

seize the opportunity to take advantage of an opportunity. □ *My uncle offered me a trip to Europe, so I seized the opportunity.* □ *Whenever you have a chance, you should seize the opportunity.*

seize (up)on something to (figuratively) take hold of something and make an issue of it. (Also literal.) □ *Whenever I mention money, you seize on it and turn it into an argument!* □ *The lawyer seized upon one point and asked many questions about it.*

sell like hotcakes [for something] to be sold very fast. □ *The delicious candy sold like hotcakes.* □ *The fancy new cars were selling like hotcakes.*

sell someone a bill of goods to get someone to believe something that isn't true; to deceive someone. (Informal.) □ *Don't pay any attention to what John says. He's just trying to sell you a bill of goods.* □ *I'm not selling you a bill of goods. What I say is true.*

sell someone down the river See under *sell (someone or something) out.*

sell someone on something to convince someone of something. (Informal.) □ *You don't have to sell me on the value of an education.* □ *Try to sell John on going to Mexico for a vacation.*

sell (someone or something) out **1.** [with *someone*] AND **sell someone down the river** to betray someone; to reveal damaging information about someone. (Slang, especially criminal slang.) □ *Bill told everything he knew about Bob, and that sold Bob down the river.* □ *You'll be sorry if you sell me out.* T *Lefty sold out, and we'll all soon be arrested.* **2.** [with *something*] to sell all of something. □ *You've sold them all out?* T *We sold out all our red ones yesterday.*

sell someone or something short to underestimate someone or something; to fail to see the good qualities of someone or something. □ *This is a very good restaurant. Don't sell it short.* □ *When you say that John isn't interested in music, you're selling him short. Did you know he plays the violin quite well?*

sell something for a song to sell something for very little money. (As in trading something of value for the singing of a song.) □ *I had to sell my car for a song because I needed the money in a hurry.* □ *I have two geometry books and I would sell one of them for a song.*

sell something off to sell much or all of something. □ *Please try to sell these*

items off. We have too many of them. T *I sold off all my books.*

sell something on credit to sell something now and let the purchase pay for it later. (Compare with *buy something on credit.*) □ *I'm sorry, we don't sell groceries on credit. It's strictly cash-and-carry.* □ *There is a shop around the corner that sells clothing on credit.*

send one about one's business to send someone away, usually in an unfriendly way. □ *Is that annoying man on the telephone again? Please send him about his business.* □ *Ann, I can't clean up the house with you running around. I'm going to have to send you about your business.*

send someone or something up to ridicule or make fun of someone or something; to satirize someone or something. (Informal.) □ *John is always sending Jane up by mocking the way she walks.* □ *The drama group sent their leaders up.*

send someone (out) on an errand to send someone out to do a specific task. □ *Mother sent Billy out on an errand.* □ *I'm late because Bill sent me on an errand.*

send someone packing to send someone away; to dismiss someone, possibly rudely. □ *I couldn't stand him anymore, so I sent him packing.* □ *The maid proved to be so incompetent that I had to send her packing.*

send someone to the showers to send a player out of the game and off the field, court, etc. (From sports.) □ *John played so badly that the coach sent him to the showers after the third quarter.* □ *After the fistfight, the coaches sent both players to the showers.*

send someone up the river to send someone to prison. (Slang.) □ *The judge sent Bill up the river for ten years.* □ *The same judge sent him up the river the last time.*

send something C.O.D. to send merchandise to someone who will pay for it when it is delivered. (*C.O.D.* means "cash on delivery" or "collect on delivery.") □ *I sent away for a record album and asked them to send it C.O.D.* □ *This person has ordered a copy of our record. Send the record C.O.D.*

send up a trial balloon to suggest something and see how people respond to it; to test public opinion. (Slang.) □ *Mary had an excellent idea, but when we sent up a trial balloon, the response was very negative.* □ *Don't start the whole project without sending up a trial balloon.*

separate but equal segregated but of equal value or quality. (A doctrine once sanctioned by the U.S. Supreme Court regarding racial segregation. Fixed order.) □ *The separate but equal doctrine was abandoned years ago.* □ *They were provided with facilities that were said to be separate but equal—but were really of a lower standard.*

separate the men from the boys to separate the competent from those who are less competent. □ *This is the kind of task that separates the men from the boys.* □ *This project requires a lot of thinking. It'll separate the men from the boys.*

separate the sheep from the goats to divide people into two groups. □ *Working in a place like this really separates the sheep from the goats.* □ *We can't go on with the game until we separate the sheep from the goats. Let's see who can jump the farthest.*

serve as a guinea pig [for someone] to be experimented on; to allow some sort of test to be performed on someone. □ *Try it on someone else! I don't want to serve as a guinea pig!* □ *Jane agreed to serve as a guinea pig. She'll be the one to try out the new flavor of ice cream.*

serve notice to announce (something). □ *John served notice that he wouldn't prepare the coffee anymore.* □ *I'm serving notice that I'll resign as secretary next month.*

serve someone right [for an act or event] to punish someone fairly [for doing something]. □ *John copied off my test paper. It would serve him right if he fails the test.* □ *It'd serve John right if he got arrested.*

serve someone's purpose See *answer someone's purpose.*

set a precedent to establish a pattern; to set a policy that must be followed in future cases. □ *I'll do what you ask this time, but it doesn't set a precedent.* □ *We've already set a precedent in matters such as these.*

set eyes on someone or something AND **lay eyes on someone or something** to see someone or something for the first time. □ *I knew when I set eyes on that car that it was the car for me.* □ *Have you ever laid eyes on such a beautiful flower?*

set fire to someone or something AND **set someone or something on fire** to ignite someone or something; to put someone or something to flames. □ *The thief set fire to the building.* □ *The poor man accidentally set himself on fire.*

set foot somewhere to go or enter somewhere. (Often in the negative.) □ *If I were you, I wouldn't set foot in that town.* □ *I wouldn't set foot in her house! Not after the way she spoke to me.*

set forth (on something) AND **launch forth (on something)** **1.** to start out on something. (See also *take off (on something).*) □ *We intend to set forth on our journey very early in the morning.* □ *What time will you launch forth?* **2.** to begin presenting a speech or an explanation. □ *As soon as John set forth on his speech, three people walked out.* □ *Every time he launches forth, somebody walks out.*

set great store by someone or something to have positive expectations for someone or something; to have high hopes for someone or something. □ *I set great store by my computer and its ability to help me in my work.* □ *We set* *great store by John because of his quick mind.*

set in to begin. (Often said of weather or climatic conditions.) □ *Winter set in very early this year.* □ *We got the windows closed before the storm set in.*

set in one's ways leading a fixed life-style; living according to one's own established patterns. □ *At her age, she's getting sort of set in her ways.* □ *If you weren't so set in your ways, you'd be able to understand young people better.*

set one back on one's heels to surprise, shock, or overwhelm someone. □ *Her sudden announcement set us all back on our heels.* □ *The manager scolded me, and that really set me back on my heels.*

set one's heart against something to turn against something; to become totally against something. (See also *have one's heart set against something.*) □ *Jane set her heart against going to Australia.* □ *I set my heart against her departure.*

set one's heart on something to become determined about something. □ *Jane set her heart on going to London.* □ *Todd had set his heart on returning.*

set one's sights on something to select something as one's goal. □ *I set my sights on a master's degree from the state university.* □ *Don't set your sights on something you cannot possibly do.*

set sail (for somewhere) to depart in a boat for somewhere. (In a sailboat or powerboat.) □ *This ship sets sail for Japan in two days.* □ *When do you set sail?*

set someone back (some amount of money) to cost someone (an amount of money). (Informal.) □ *This coat set me back about $250.* □ *That dinner at the restaurant last night really set us back.*

set someone or something off 1. [with *someone*] to get someone very excited and angry. □ *Whenever I see someone mistreating an animal, it really sets me off.* ⊤ *The tax bill set off Bob. He raved for an hour!* **2.** [with *something*] to start something. □ *Don't set another discussion off, please!* ⊤ *The question of taxes set off an argument.*

set someone or something on fire See *set fire to someone or something.*

set someone or something straight (See also *put something straight.*) **1.** [with *someone*] to explain (something) to someone. □ *I don't think you understand about taxation. Let me set you straight.* □ *Ann was confused, so I set her straight.* **2.** [with *something*] to explain something (to someone). □ *This is very confusing, but with a little explaining I can set it straight.* □ *We'll set this matter straight in a short time.*

set someone or something up 1. [with *someone*] to lead—by deception—a person to play a particular role in an event; to arrange an event—usually by deception—so that a specific person takes the consequences for the event; to frame someone. (Informal or slang. Also literal.) □ *I had nothing to do with the robbery! I was just standing there. Somebody must have set me up!* ⊤ *John isn't the one who started the fight. Somebody set up the poor guy.* **2.** [with *something*] to put something together; to erect something. □ *My parents bought me a dollhouse, but I had to set it up myself.* ⊤ *It took nearly an hour to set up the tent.* **3.** [with *something*] to establish or found something. □ *We set up a fund to buy food for the needy.* □ *The business owners set a bank up in the small town.* **4.** [with *something*] to make plans for something. □ *John and Mary are hard at work setting something up for the meeting.* ⊤ *Sally and Tom set up a party for Saturday night.*

set someone up (as something) to establish someone as something. (Compare with *set someone up (in business).*) □ *Bill set himself up as boss.* □ *When Mary got her degree, she set herself up as a consultant.* ⊤ *My father* *set up my sisters as co-owners of the family business.* □ *He set them up with the help of a lawyer.*

set someone up (in business) to help establish someone in business; to provide the money someone needs to start a business. □ *My father set my sisters up in business.* □ *He helped set them up so he could keep the business in the family.*

set someone's teeth on edge 1. [for a sour or bitter taste] to irritate one's mouth and make it feel funny. □ *Have you ever eaten a lemon? It'll set your teeth on edge.* □ *I can't stand food that sets my teeth on edge.* **2.** [for a person or a noise] to be irritating or get on one's nerves. □ *Please don't scrape your fingernails on the blackboard! It sets my teeth on edge!* □ *Here comes Bob. He's so annoying. He really sets my teeth on edge.*

set something down to something See *put something down to something.*

set something right AND **put something right** to correct something; to alter a situation to make it more fair. (See also *make something good.*) □ *This is a very unfortunate situation. I'll ask the people responsible to set this matter right.* □ *I'm sorry that we overcharged you. We'll try to put it right.*

set something straight See *put something straight.*

set the ball rolling See *get the ball rolling.*

set the stage for something to prepare for something; to get all of the appropriate things in place for something. (Also literal, as in the theater.) □ *The events of the past week have set the stage for further negotiation with the other side.* □ *Your comments set the stage for the next step — which is the hard one.*

set the table to place plates, glasses, napkins, etc., on the table before a meal. (The opposite of *clear the table.*) □ *Jane, would you please set the table?* □ *I'm tired of setting the table. Ask someone else to do it.*

set the world on fire to do exciting things that bring fame and glory. (Frequently negative.) □ *I'm not very ambitious. I don't want to set the world on fire.* □ *You don't have to set the world on fire. Just do a good job.*

set tongues (a)wagging to cause people to start gossiping. □ *The affair between the boss and her accountant set tongues awagging.* □ *If you don't get the lawn mowed soon, you will set tongues wagging in the neighborhood.*

set up shop somewhere to establish one's place of work somewhere. (Informal.) □ *Mary set up shop in a small office building on Oak Street.* □ *The police officer said, "You can't set up shop right here on the sidewalk!"*

set upon someone or something to attack someone or something violently. □ *The dogs set upon the bear and chased it up a tree.* □ *Bill set upon Tom and struck him hard in the face.*

settle a score with someone AND **settle the score (with someone)** to clear up a problem with someone; to get even with someone. (Slang. See also *have a score to settle (with someone).*) □ *John wants to settle a score with his neighbor.* □ *Tom, it's time you and I settled the score.*

settle down 1. to calm down. □ *Now, children, it's time to settle down and start class.* □ *If you don't settle down, I'll send you all home.* **2.** to settle into a stable way of life; to get married and settle into a stable way of life. □ *Tom, don't you think it's about time you settled down and stopped all of this running around?* □ *Bill and Ann decided to settle down and raise some children.*

settle for something to agree to accept something (even though something else would be better). □ *We wanted a red one, but settled for a blue one.* □

Ask your grocer for Wilson's canned corn — the best corn in cans. Don't settle for less.

settle on something to decide on something. □ *We've discussed the merits of all of them, and we've settled on this one.* □ *I can't settle on one or the other, so I'll buy both.*

settle someone's affairs to deal with one's business matters; to manage the business affairs of someone who can't. □ *When my uncle died, I had to settle his affairs.* □ *I have to settle my affairs before going to Mexico for a year.*

settle the score (with someone) See *settle a score with someone.*

settle up with someone to pay someone what one owes; to pay someone one's share of something. □ *I must settle up with Jim for the bike I bought for him.* □ *Fred paid the whole restaurant bill and we all settled up with him later.*

sew something up to complete something; to secure something. (Informal. Also literal.) □ *The manager told me to sew the contract up, or else.* Ⓣ *Let's sew up this contract today.*

shack up (with someone) See *sleep with someone.*

shades of someone or something reminders of someone or something; reminiscent of someone or something. □ *When I met Jim's mother, I thought "shades of Aunt Mary."* □ *"Shades of grade school," said Jack as the university lecturer rebuked him for being late.*

shake (hands) on something to clasp and shake the hand of someone as a sign of agreement about something. □ *The two people didn't sign a contract; they just shook hands on the terms of the agreement.* □ *I think it would be better to sign an agreement and shake on it.*

shake hands (with someone) to clasp and shake the hand of someone as a greeting. □ *His hands were full, and I didn't know whether to try to shake hands with him or not.* □ *He put down his packages, and we shook hands.*

shake in one's boots AND **quake in one's boots** to be afraid; to shake from fear. □ *I was shaking in my boots because I had to go see the manager.* □ *Stop quaking in your boots, Bob. I'm not going to fire you.*

shake someone or something down 1. [with *someone*] to extort money from someone; to blackmail someone. (Slang, especially criminal slang.) □ *The gang of criminals made a living from shaking people down.* Ⓣ *Lefty was trying to shake down the storekeeper.* **2.** [with *something*] to try something out; to test something and give the flaws a chance to appear. (Informal.) □ *We took the new car out for a trip to shake it down.* Ⓣ *You need to shake down a complicated piece of machinery when you first get it. Then any problems will show up while the guarantee is still in effect.*

shake someone or something off 1. [with *someone*] to get rid of someone; to get free of someone who is bothering you. (Slang.) □ *Stop bothering me! What do I have to do to shake you off?* Ⓣ *I wish I could shake off John. He's such a pest!* **2.** [with *something*] to avoid getting a disease, such as a cold; to fight something off. (Informal.) □ *I thought I was catching a cold, but I guess I shook it off.* Ⓣ *I hope I can shake off this cold pretty soon.*

shake someone or something up 1. [with *someone*] to shock or upset someone. (Slang. See also *shook up.*) □ *The sight of the injured man shook me up.* Ⓣ *Your rude remark really shook up Tom.* **2.** to jostle or knock someone or something around; to toss someone or something back and forth. □ *We rode over a rough road, and that shook us up.* Ⓣ *The accident shook up John quite a bit.* **3.** to reorganize something or a group of people. □ *The new manager shook the office up and made things run a lot better.* Ⓣ *The coach shook the team up before the last game and made them better organized.*

shake something off See *toss something off.*

shake the lead out See *get the lead out.*

Shame on someone. What a shameful thing!; someone should be ashamed. □ *You've torn your shirt again, Billy! Shame on you!* □ *When Billy tore his shirt, his mother said, "Shame on you!"*

shape someone up to get someone into good physical shape; to make someone behave or perform better. (See also *shape up.*) □ *I've got to shape myself up to improve my health.* ⊤ *The trainer was told that he'd have to shape up the boxer before the fight.*

shape up to improve one's behavior or performance; to improve one's physical shape. □ *Look at this, John! What a poor job you've done! It's time you shaped up!* □ *If I'm going to run in the marathon, I'm going to have to shape up.*

Shape up or ship out. either to improve one's performance (or behavior) or leave or quit. (Fixed order.) □ *Okay, Tom. That's the end. Shape up or ship out!* □ *John was late again, so I told him to shape up or ship out.*

share and share alike with equal shares. □ *I kept five and gave the other five to Mary—share and share alike.* □ *The two roommates agreed that they would divide expenses—share and share alike.*

sharp as a razor See *(as) sharp as a razor.*

shed crocodile tears AND **cry crocodile tears** to shed false tears; to pretend that one is weeping. □ *The child wasn't hurt, but she shed crocodile tears anyway.* □ *He thought he could get his way if he cried crocodile tears.*

shed (some) light on something AND **throw (some) light on something** to reveal something about something; to clarify something. (Also with *any.*) □ *This discussion has shed some light on the problem.* □ *Let's see if Ann can throw any light on this question.*

shell something out to pay money (out). (Slang.) □ *You'll have to shell plenty out to settle this bill.* ⊤ *The*

traffic ticket turned out to be very expensive. I had to shell out $150.

shift for oneself AND **fend for oneself** to get along by oneself; to support oneself. □ *I'm sorry, I can't pay your rent anymore. You'll just have to shift for yourself.* □ *When I became twenty years old, I left home and began to fend for myself.*

shine up to someone to try to gain someone's favor by being extra nice. □ *John is a nice guy, except that he's always trying to shine up to the professor.* □ *Mary never tries to shine up to the manager.*

shipping and handling the costs of handling a product and transporting it. (See also *postage and handling.* Fixed order.) □ *Shipping and handling charges were included in the price.* □ *The cost of the goods is low and shipping and handling added only a few cents.*

ships that pass in the night people who meet each other briefly by chance and who are unlikely to meet again. □ *Mary wanted to see Jim again, but to him, they were ships that passed in the night.* □ *When you travel a lot on business, you meet many ships that pass in the night.*

shirk one's duty to neglect one's job or task. □ *The guard was fired for shirking his duty.* □ *You cannot expect to continue shirking your duty without someone noticing.*

shook up upset; shocked. (Slang. See also *shake someone or something up.*) □ *Relax, man! Don't get shook up!* □ *I always get shook up when I see something like that.*

shoot from the hip 1. to fire a gun that is held at one's side, against one's hip. (This increases one's speed in firing a gun.) □ *When I lived at home on the farm, my father taught me to shoot from the hip.* □ *I quickly shot the snake before it bit my horse. I'm glad I learned to shoot from the hip.* **2.** to speak directly and frankly. (Informal.) □ *John has a tendency to shoot from the hip, but he* *generally speaks the truth.* □ *Don't pay any attention to John. He means no harm. It's just his nature to shoot from the hip.*

shoot one's mouth off to boast or talk too much; to tell someone's secrets. (Slang.) □ *Don't pay any attention to Bob. He's always shooting his mouth off.* ⊤ *Oh, Sally! Stop shooting off your mouth! You don't know what you're talking about.*

shoot something out 1. to stick, throw, or thrust something outward. □ *The diamond shot bright shafts of light out when the sun fell on it.* ⊤ *The little girl shot out her tongue at the teacher.* **2.** to settle a matter by the use of guns. (Slang. Typical of gangster or western movies.) □ *Bill and the cowboy — with whom he had been arguing — went out in the street and shot it out.* ⊤ *Don't they know they can settle a problem by talking? They don't need to shoot out the problem when they can talk it over.*

shoot the breeze to spend time chatting. (Slang. See also the following entry.) □ *I went over to Bob's place and shot the breeze for about an hour.* □ *Don't spend so much time shooting the breeze. Get to work!*

shoot the bull to spend time chatting about one's accomplishments, especially with others who are doing the same. (Slang. See also the previous entry.) □ *Those guys out in the backyard are just sitting around shooting the bull.* □ *It was raining, so everybody spent the day indoors drinking beer and shooting the bull.*

shoot the works to do everything; to use up everything; to bet everything. (Slang.) □ *Shall I bet half our money, or shall I shoot the works?* □ *We shot the works at the carnival — spent every cent we brought with us.*

shop around (for something) to shop at different stores to find what you want at the best price. □ *I've been shopping around for a new car, but they are all priced too high.* □ *You can find a bargain, but you'll have to shop around.*

short and sweet brief (and pleasant because of briefness). (Fixed order.) □ *That was a good sermon — short and sweet.* □ *I don't care what you say, as long as you make it short and sweet.*

short of something not having enough of something. □ *I wanted to bake a cake, but I was short of eggs.* □ *Usually at the end of the month, I'm short of money.*

shot in the arm a boost; something that gives someone energy. (Informal.) □ *Thank you for cheering me up. It was a real shot in the arm.* □ *Your friendly greeting card was just what I needed — a real shot in the arm.*

shot in the dark a random or wild guess or try. (Slang.) □ *I don't know how I guessed the right answer. It was just a shot in the dark.* □ *I was lucky to hire such a good worker as Sally. When I hired her, it was just a shot in the dark.*

shot through with something containing something; interwoven, intermixed, or filled with something. □ *The rose was a lovely pink shot through with streaks of white.* □ *John's comments are often shot through with sarcasm.* □ *I want a well-marbled steak — one shot through with fat.*

shot to hell See *(all) shot to hell.*

shotgun wedding a forced wedding. (Informal. From imagery of the bride's father having threatened the bridegroom with a shotgun to force him to marry.) □ *Mary was six months pregnant when she married Bill. It was a real shotgun wedding.* □ *Bob would never have married Jane if she hadn't been pregnant. Jane's father saw to it that it was a shotgun wedding.*

should have stood in bed should have stayed in bed. □ *What a horrible day! I should have stood in bed.* □ *The minute I got up and heard the news this morning, I knew I should have stood in bed.*

shoulder to shoulder side by side; with a shared purpose. □ *The two armies fought shoulder to shoulder against the* *joint enemy.* □ *The strikers said they would stand shoulder to shoulder against the management.*

shove someone or something down someone's throat AND **ram someone or something down someone's throat; force someone or something down someone's throat** to force someone or something on someone. (Slang and a little rude.) □ *I don't want any more insurance, and I don't want anyone to shove any insurance down my throat.* □ *Mary isn't invited to my party, and I don't wish for anyone to ram her down my throat!* □ *Someone is always trying to force some stupid propaganda down my throat.*

show-and-tell a trivial presentation of something of little interest. (From the name of a classroom period in the lower grades where children bring something interesting into the classroom and show it to the rest of the class. Also literal. Fixed order.) □ *I wouldn't call that meeting useful. It was sort of a grown-up show-and-tell.* □ *After the show-and-tell session where the author talked about his book, we all went into the hall and had refreshments.*

show good faith to demonstrate good intentions or good will. □ *I'm certain that you showed good faith when you signed the contract.* □ *Do you doubt that she is showing good faith?*

show of hands a vote expressed by people raising their hands. □ *We were asked to vote for the candidates for captain by a show of hands.* □ *Jack wanted us to vote on paper, not by a show of hands, so that we could have a secret ballot.*

show one's hand to reveal one's intentions to someone. (From card games.) □ *I don't know whether Jim is intending to marry Jane or not. He's not one to show his hand.* □ *If you want to get a raise, don't show the boss your hand too soon.*

show one's (true) colors to show what one is really like or what one is really thinking. □ *Whose side are you on, John? Come on. Show your colors.* □

It's hard to tell what Mary is thinking. She never shows her true colors.

show signs of something to show hints or indications of something. □ *I let the horse run at full speed until it began to show signs of tiring.* □ *Sally is showing signs of going to sleep.*

show someone or something off to display someone or something so that the best features are apparent. Ⓣ *Mrs. Williams was showing off her baby to the neighbors.* □ *Bill drove around all afternoon showing his new car off.*

show someone the ropes to tell or show someone how something is to be done. □ *Since this was my first day on the job, the manager spent a lot of time showing me the ropes.* □ *Take some time and show the new boy the ropes.*

show someone (to) the door AND **see someone to the door** to lead or take someone to the door or exit. □ *After we finished our talk, she showed me to the door.* □ *Bill and I finished our chat as he saw me to the door.*

show someone up to make someone's faults or shortcomings apparent. Ⓣ *John's excellent effort really showed up Bill, who didn't try very hard at all.* □ *John is always trying to show someone up to make himself look better.*

show someone up as something to reveal that someone is really something (else). □ *The investigation showed her up as a fraud.* □ *The test showed the banker up as unqualified.*

show something to good advantage to display the best features of something; to display something so that its best features are apparent. □ *Put the vase in the center of the table and show it to good advantage.* □ *Having and using a large vocabulary shows your intelligence to good advantage.*

shuffle off this mortal coil to die. (Often jocular or formal euphemism. Not often used in consoling someone.) □ *Cousin Fred shuffled off this mortal coil after drinking a jug full of rat poison.* □ *When I shuffle off this mortal* coil, I want to go out in style — bells, flowers, and a long, boring funeral.

shut someone up to silence someone. □ Oh, shut yourself up! ⊤ Will you please shut up that crying baby!

shut something down See close something down.

shut the door on someone or something AND **close the door on someone or something 1.** to close the door in order to keep someone or something out. □ Bob opened the door, and when he saw it was Mary, he closed the door on her. □ "Don't shut the door on me!" screamed Mary. **2.** [with something] to terminate, exclude, or obstruct something. □ Your bad attitude shuts the door on any future cooperation from me. □ The bad service at that store closes the door on any more business from my company.

shy away (from someone or something) to avoid someone or something. □ The dog shies away from John since he kicked it. □ I can understand why the dog would shy away. □ I shy away from eating onions. I think I'm allergic to them.

sick and tired of someone or something disgusted and annoyed with someone or something. (Fixed order.) □ I'm sick and tired of Ann and her whistling. □ We are all sick and tired of this old car.

sick as a dog See (as) sick as a dog.

sick in bed remaining in bed while (one is) ill. □ Tom is sick in bed with the flu. □ He's been sick in bed for nearly a week.

side against someone to be against someone; to take sides against someone. □ I thought you were my friend! I never thought you would side against me! □ The two brothers were always siding against their sister.

side with someone to join with someone; to take someone else's part; to be on someone's side. □ Why is it that you always side with him when he and I

argue? □ I never side with anybody. I form my own opinions.

sight for sore eyes a welcome sight. (Folksy.) □ Oh, am I glad to see you here! You're a sight for sore eyes. □ I'm sure hungry. This meal is a sight for sore eyes.

sign on the dotted line to place one's signature on a contract or other important paper. □ This agreement isn't properly concluded until we both sign on the dotted line. □ Here are the papers for the purchase of your car. As soon as you sign on the dotted line, that beautiful, shiny automobile will be all yours!

sign on (with someone) to sign an agreement to work with or for someone, especially on a ship. □ The sailor signed on with Captain Smith. □ Hardly any other sailor was willing to sign on.

sign one's own death warrant to (figuratively) sign a paper that calls for one's death. □ I wouldn't ever gamble a large sum of money. That would be signing my own death warrant. □ The killer signed his own death warrant when he walked into the police station and gave himself up.

signed, sealed, and delivered formally and officially signed; [for a formal document to be] executed. (Fixed order.) □ Here is the deed to the property — signed, sealed, and delivered. □ I can't begin work on this project until I have the contract signed, sealed, and delivered.

silly season the time of year, usually late in the summer, when there is a lack of important news and newspapers contain articles about unimportant or trivial things instead. □ It must be the silly season. There's a story here about peculiarly shaped potatoes. □ There's a piece on the front page about people with big feet. Talk about the silly season!

simmer down to get quiet or calm. (Informal.) □ Hey, you guys! Simmer down! Stop all the noise and go to sleep!

sit on someone or something

□ *I'm very busy now. Please come back in a few hours when things have simmered down a bit.*

sing a different tune AND **sing another tune** to change one's manner, usually from bad to good. (Almost the same as *dance to another tune.*) □ *When she learned that I was a bank director, she began to sing a different tune.* □ *You will sing a different tune as soon as you find out how right I am!*

sing another tune See the previous entry.

sing someone's praises to praise someone highly and enthusiastically. □ *The boss is singing the praises of his new secretary.* □ *The theater critics are singing the praises of the young actor.*

single file See *(in) single file.*

sink in [for knowledge] to be understood. (Informal. Also literal.) □ *I heard what you said, but it took a while for it to sink in.* □ *I pay careful attention to everything I hear in class, but it usually doesn't sink in.*

sink into despair [for someone] to grieve or become depressed. □ *After losing all my money, I sank into despair.* □ *There is no need to sink into despair. Everything is going to be all right.*

sink one's teeth into something 1. to take a bite of some kind of food, usually a special kind of food. □ *I can't wait to sink my teeth into a nice juicy steak.* □ *Look at that chocolate cake! Don't you want to sink your teeth into that?* **2.** to get a chance to do, learn, or control something. □ *That appears to be a very challenging assignment. I can't wait to sink my teeth into it.* □ *Being the manager of this department is a big task. I'm very eager to sink my teeth into it.*

sink or swim to fail or succeed. (Fixed order.) □ *After I've studied and learned all I can, I have to take the test and sink or swim.* □ *It's too late to help John now. It's sink or swim for him.*

sit at someone's feet to admire someone greatly; to be influenced by some-

one's teaching; to be taught by someone. □ *Jack sat at the feet of Picasso when he was studying in Europe.* □ *Tom would love to sit at the feet of the musician Yehudi Menuhin.*

sit back and let something happen to relax and not interfere with something; to let something happen without playing a part in it. □ *I can't just sit back and let you waste all our money!* □ *Don't worry. Just sit back and let things take care of themselves.*

sit bolt upright to sit up straight. □ *Tony sat bolt upright and listened to what the teacher was saying to him.* □ *After sitting bolt upright for almost an hour in that crowded airplane, I swore I would never travel again.*

sit (idly) by to remain inactive when other people are doing something; to ignore a situation that calls for help. □ *Bob sat idly by even though everyone else was hard at work.* □ *I can't sit by while all those people need food.*

sit in for someone to take someone else's place in a specific activity. (The activity usually involves being seated.) □ *I can't be at the meeting Thursday. Will you sit in for me?* □ *Sorry, I can't sit in for you. John is also going to be absent, and I am sitting in for him.*

sit in (on something) to witness or observe something without participating. (Usually involves being seated.) □ *I can't sign up for the history class, but I have permission to sit in on it.* □ *I asked the professor if I could sit in.*

sit on its hands [for an audience] to refuse to applaud. □ *We saw a very poor performance of the play. The audience sat on its hands for the entire play.* □ *The audience just sat on its hands.*

sit on one's hands to do nothing; to fail to help. □ *When we needed help from Mary, she just sat on her hands.* □ *We need the cooperation of everyone. You can't sit on your hands!*

sit on someone or something to hold someone or something back; to delay someone or something. (Informal. Also literal.) □ *The project cannot be* *finished because the city council is sitting on the final approval.* □ *Ann deserves to be promoted, but the manager is sitting on her because of a disagreement.*

sit on the fence not to take sides in a dispute; not to make a clear choice between two possibilities. (Also literal.) □ *When Jane and Tom argue, it is well to sit on the fence and then you won't make either of them angry.* □ *No one knows which of the candidates Joan will vote for. She's sitting on the fence.*

sit something out not to participate in something; to wait until something is over before participating. □ *Oh, please play with us. Don't sit it out.* Ⓣ *I'm tired of playing cards, so I think I'll sit out this game.*

sit through something to witness or endure all of something. □ *The performance was so bad that I could hardly sit through it.* □ *You can't expect small children to sit through a long movie.*

sit tight to wait; to wait patiently. (Informal. This does not necessarily refer to sitting.) □ *Just relax and sit tight. I'll be right with you.* □ *We were waiting in line for the gates to open when someone came out and told us to sit tight because it wouldn't be much longer before we could go in.*

sit up and take notice to become alert and pay attention. □ *A loud noise from the front of the room caused everyone to sit up and take notice.* □ *The company wouldn't pay any attention to my complaints. When I had my lawyer write them a letter, they sat up and took notice.*

sit up with someone to stay with someone through the night, especially with a sick or troubled person or with someone who is waiting for something. □ *I had to sit up with my younger sister when she was ill.* □ *I sat up with Bill while he waited for an overseas telephone call.*

sit with someone 1. to stay with someone; to *sit up with someone.* □ *Sally was upset, so I sat with her for a while.*

□ *My uncle sat with me my first day in the hospital.* 2. to stay with and care for one or more children; to baby-sit for someone. □ *I hired Mrs. Wilson to sit with the children.* □ *We couldn't go out for dinner because we couldn't find anyone to sit with the kids.*

sitting on a powder keg in a risky or explosive situation; in a situation where something serious or dangerous may happen at any time. (Informal. A powder keg is a keg of gunpowder.) □ *Things are very tense at work. The whole office is sitting on a powder keg.* □ *The fire at the oil field seems to be under control for now, but all the workers there are sitting on a powder keg.*

(sitting) on top of the world feeling wonderful; glorious; ecstatic. □ *Wow, I feel on top of the world.* □ *Since he got a new job, he's on top of the world.*

sitting pretty living in comfort or luxury; in a good situation. (Informal.) □ *My uncle died and left enough money for me to be sitting pretty for the rest of my life.* □ *Now that I have a good-paying job, I'm sitting pretty.*

sitting target someone or something that is in a position that is easily attacked. □ *The old man was a sitting target for the burglars. He lived alone and did not have a telephone.* □ *People recently hired will be sitting targets if the company needs to cut back.*

six of one and half a dozen of the other about the same one way or another. (Fixed order.) □ *It doesn't matter to me which way you do it. It's six of one and half a dozen of the other.* □ *What difference does it make? They're both the same — six of one and half a dozen of the other.*

size someone or something up to observe someone or something to get information; to *check someone or something out.* □ *The comedian sized the audience up and decided not to use his new material.* Ⓣ *I like to size up a situation before I act.*

skate on thin ice to be in a risky situation. (See also *on thin ice*. Also literal.) □ *I try to stay well informed so I don't end up skating on thin ice when the teacher asks me a question.* □ *You are skating on thin ice when you ask me that!*

skeleton in the closet a hidden and shocking secret. (Often in the plural.) □ *You can ask anyone about how reliable I am. I don't mind. I don't have any skeletons in the closet.* □ *My uncle was in jail for a day once. That's our family's skeleton in the closet.*

skin someone alive to be very angry with someone; to scold someone severely. (Folksy.) □ *I was so mad at Jane that I could have skinned her alive.* □ *If I don't get home on time, my parents will skin me alive.*

skip bail See *jump bail*.

skip out (on someone or something) to sneak away from someone; to leave someone in secret. (Slang.) □ *I heard that Bill skipped out on his wife.* □ *I'm not surprised. I thought he should have skipped out long ago.*

slack off **1.** to taper off; to reduce gradually. □ *Business tends to slack off during the winter months.* □ *The storms begin to slack off in April.* **2.** to become less active; to become lazy or inefficient. □ *Near the end of the school year, Sally began to slack off, and her grades showed it.* □ *John got fired for slacking off during the busy season.*

slap in the face an insult; an act that causes disappointment or discouragement. □ *Losing the election was a slap in the face for the club president.* □ *Failing to get into a good college was a slap in the face to Tim after his years of study.*

slap someone down to rebuke or rebuff someone. (Also literal.) □ *You may disagree with her, but you needn't slap her down like that.* □ *I only asked you what time it was! There's no need to slap me down! What a rotten humor you're in!*

slap someone on the wrist See *give someone a slap on the wrist*.

slap someone's wrist See *give someone a slap on the wrist*.

slap something together See *throw something together*.

slated for something scheduled for something. (As if a schedule had been written on a slate.) □ *John was slated for Friday's game, but he couldn't play with the team.* □ *Ann is slated for promotion next year.*

slated to do something scheduled to do something. □ *John was slated to play ball Friday.* □ *Who is slated to work this weekend?*

sleep in to oversleep; to sleep late in the morning. □ *If you sleep in again, you'll get fired.* □ *I really felt like sleeping in this morning.*

sleep like a log to sleep very soundly. □ *Nothing can wake me up. I usually sleep like a log.* □ *Everyone in our family sleeps like a log, so no one heard the fire engines in the middle of the night.*

sleep on something to think about something overnight; to weigh a decision overnight. □ *I don't know whether I agree to do it. Let me sleep on it.* □ *I slept on it, and I've decided to accept your offer.*

sleep something off to sleep while the effects of liquor or drugs pass away. □ *John drank too much and went home to sleep it off.* ⊤ *Bill is at home sleeping off the effects of the drug they gave him.*

sleep with someone AND **shack up (with someone)** to have sex with someone; to copulate with someone. (Euphemistic. This may not involve sleep. The expressions with *shack* are slang, and they are not used to refer to marital sex.) □ *Everyone assumes that Mr. Franklin doesn't sleep with Mrs. Franklin.* □ *Somebody said he shacks up with a girlfriend downtown.* □ *They've been shacking up for years now.*

slice of the cake a share of something. □ *There's not much work around and* *so everyone must get a slice of the cake.* □ *The company makes huge profits and the workers want a slice of the cake.*

slick as a whistle See *(as) slick as a whistle.*

slip away AND **slip off; slip out** to go away or escape quietly or in secret. □ *I slipped away when no one was looking.* □ *Let's slip off somewhere and have a little talk.* □ *I'll try to slip out for an hour or two when Tom is asleep.*

slip of the tongue an error in speaking where a word is pronounced incorrectly, or where something that the speaker did not mean to say is said. □ *I didn't mean to tell her that. It was a slip of the tongue.* □ *I failed to understand the instructions because the speaker made a slip of the tongue at an important point.*

slip off See *slip away.*

slip one's mind [for something that was to be remembered] to be forgotten. □ *I meant to go to the grocery store on the way home, but it slipped my mind.* □ *My birthday slipped my mind. I guess I wanted to forget it.*

slip out **1.** [for secret information] to be revealed. □ *I asked her to keep our engagement secret, but she let it slip out.* □ *I didn't mean to tell. It just slipped out.* **2.** See *slip away.*

slip through someone's fingers to get away from someone; for someone to lose track (of something or someone). □ *I had a copy of the book you want, but somehow it slipped through my fingers.* □ *There was a detective following me, but I managed to slip through his fingers.*

slip up to make an error. (Informal. Also without *up.*) □ *Try as hard as you can to do it right and not slip up.* □ *Everything was going fine until the last minute when I slipped up.*

slippery as an eel See *(as) slippery as an eel.*

Slow and steady wins the race. a proverb meaning that deliberateness and determination will lead to success, or (literally) a reasonable pace will win a race. □ *I worked my way through college in six years. Now I know what they mean when they say, "Slow and steady wins the race."* □ *Ann won the race because she started off slowly and established a good pace. The other runners tried to sprint the whole distance, and they tired out before the final lap. Ann's trainer said, "You see! I told you! Slow and steady wins the race."*

slow on the draw (Slang. Compare with *quick on the draw.*) **1.** slow in drawing a gun. (Cowboy and gangster talk.) □ *Bill got shot because he's so slow on the draw.* □ *The gunslinger said, "I have to be fast. If I'm slow on the draw, I'm dead."* **2.** AND **slow on the uptake** slow to figure something out; slow-thinking. □ *Sally didn't get the joke because she's sort of slow on the draw.* □ *Bill— who's slow on the uptake—didn't get the joke until it was explained to him.*

slow on the uptake See under *slow on the draw.*

slow someone or something down See the following entry.

slow someone or something up AND **slow someone or something down** to cause someone or something to reduce speed. (The phrases with *up* are informal.) □ *I'm in a hurry. Don't try to slow me down.* Ⓣ *Please slow up the train. There are sheep near the track.* Ⓣ *Slow up! I can't keep up with you.* Ⓣ *Okay, I'll slow down.* □ *Did I slow myself down enough?*

slow(ly) but sure(ly) slowly but with a purpose; slowly and deliberately. (The expression without the *-ly* is informal. Fixed order.) □ *Slowly but surely, the little train reached the top of the mountain.* □ *Progress was slow but sure. Someday we would be finished.*

sly as a fox See *(as) sly as a fox.*

smack-dab in the middle right in the middle. (Informal.) □ *I want a big helping of mashed potatoes with a glob* *of butter smack-dab in the middle.* □ *Tom and Sally were having a terrible argument, and I was trapped — smack-dab in the middle.*

small fry 1. unimportant people. □ *The police have only caught the small fry. The leader of the gang is still free.* □ *You people are just small fry! I want to talk to the boss.* **2.** children. □ *Peter's taking the small fry to the zoo.* □ *We should take the small fry to the pantomime.*

small hours (of the night) AND **wee hours (of the night)** the hours immediately after midnight. □ *The dance went on into the small hours of the night.* □ *Jim goes to bed in the wee hours and gets up at lunchtime.*

small print the part of a document that is not easily noticed, often because of the smallness of the print, and that often contains important information. □ *You should have read the small print before signing the contract.* □ *You should always read the small print in an insurance policy.*

small-time small; on a small scale. (Informal.) □ *Our business is small-time just now, but it's growing.* □ *He's a small-time crook.*

smell a rat to suspect that something is wrong; to sense that someone has caused something wrong. (Slang.) □ *I don't think this was an accident. I smell a rat. Bob had something to do with this.* □ *The minute I came in, I smelled a rat. Sure enough, I had been robbed.*

smile on someone or something to be favorable to someone or something. □ *Fate smiled on me and I got the job.* □ *Lady luck smiled on our venture and we made a profit.*

smoke and mirrors deception and confusion. (Said of statements or more complicated rhetoric used to mislead people rather than inform. Refers to the way a magician uses optical illusion to create believability while performing a trick. Fixed order.) □ *Most people know that the politician was just using smoke and mirrors to*

make things look better than they really were. □ *Her report was little more than smoke and mirrors. No one will believe any of it.*

smoke someone or something out to force someone or something out (of something), perhaps with smoke. (In cowboy or gangster talk this refers to the smoke from gunfire.) □ *There was a mouse in the attic, but I smoked it out.* ⊤ *The sheriff and the deputies smoked out the bank robbers.*

smooth something out See the following entry.

smooth something over AND **smooth something out** to reduce the intensity of an argument or a misunderstanding; to try to make people feel better about something that has happened. (Also literal.) □ *Mary and John had a terrible argument, and they are both trying to smooth it over.* □ *Let's get everyone together and try to smooth things out. We can't keep on arguing with one another.* ⊤ *We can smooth over the whole affair.*

snake in the grass a low and deceitful person. □ *Sally said that Bob couldn't be trusted because he was a snake in the grass.* □ *"You snake in the grass!" cried Sally. "You cheated me."*

snap out of something to become suddenly freed from a state. (Informal. The state can be a depression, an illness, unconsciousness, etc.) □ *I was very depressed for a week, but this morning I snapped out of it.* □ *It isn't often that a cold gets me down. Usually I can snap out of it quickly.*

snap something up 1. to grab and buy something. □ *I always snap bargains up whenever I go shopping.* ⊤ *I went to the store, and they had soup on sale, so I snapped up plenty.* **2.** to make something go faster. □ *You're playing this music too slowly. Snap it up!* ⊤ *This performance is getting slow and dull. Let's snap up the whole thing!*

sniff someone or something out to locate someone or something. (Also literal.) ⊤ *I'll see if I can sniff out the* *correct stylus for your stereo.* □ *Billy was lost, but by looking around, we were able to sniff him out.*

snug as a bug in a rug See *(as) snug as a bug in a rug.*

so-and-so a despised person. (Informal. This expression is used in place of other very insulting terms. Often modified, as in the examples.) □ *You dirty so-and-so! I can't stand you!* □ *Don't you call me a so-and-so, you creep!*

so be it this is the way it will be. □ *If you insist on running off and marrying her, so be it. Only don't say I didn't warn you!* □ *Mary has decided that this is what she wants. So be it.*

so far as anyone knows See *(as) far as anyone knows.*

so far as I'm concerned See *(as) far as I'm concerned.*

so far as possible See *as far as possible.*

So far, so good. All is going well so far. (Fixed order.) □ *We are half finished with our project. So far, so good.* □ *The operation is proceeding quite nicely — so far, so good.*

So it goes. That is the kind of thing that happens.; That is life. □ *Too bad about John and his problems. So it goes.* □ *I just lost a twenty-dollar bill, and I can't find it anywhere. So it goes.*

so long good-bye. (Informal.) □ *So long, see you later.* □ *As John got out of the car, he said, "Thanks for the ride. So long."*

so long as See under *as long as.*

so much for someone or something that is the last of someone or something; there is no need to consider someone or something anymore. □ *It just started raining. So much for our picnic this afternoon.* □ *So much for John. He just called in sick and can't come to work today.*

so much the better even better; all to the better. (Informal.) □ *Please come to the picnic. If you can bring a salad,* so much the better. □ *The flowers look lovely on the shelf. It would be so much the better if you put them on the table.*

so quiet you could hear a pin drop See *so still you could hear a pin drop.*

so-so not good and not bad; mediocre. (Informal.) □ *I didn't have a bad day. It was just so-so.* □ *The players put on a so-so performance.*

so still you could hear a pin drop AND **so quiet you could hear a pin drop** very quiet. (Also with *can.*) □ *When I came into the room, it was so still you could hear a pin drop. Then everyone shouted, "Happy birthday!"* □ *Please be quiet. Be so quiet you can hear a pin drop.*

so to speak as one might say; said a certain way, even though the words are not exactly accurate. □ *John helps me with my taxes. He's my accountant, so to speak.* □ *I just love my little poodle. She's my baby, so to speak.*

soaked to the skin with one's clothing wet clear through to the skin. □ *I was caught in the rain and got soaked to the skin.* □ *Oh, come in and dry off! You must be soaked to the skin.*

sober as a judge See *(as) sober as a judge.*

sock something away to store something in a safe place. (Informal.) □ *While I worked in the city, I was able to sock $100 away every month.* Ⓣ *At the present time, I can't sock away that much.*

soft as a baby's bottom See *(as) soft as a baby's bottom.*

soil one's hands See *get one's hands dirty.*

(some) new blood new personnel; new members brought into a group to revive it. □ *This company needs some new blood on its board to bring in new ideas.* □ *We're trying to get some new blood in the club. Our membership is falling.* □ *Our club needs new blood. It has become boring.* □ *The firm's man-*

agement has at last got a little new blood. Things should improve now.

someone or something checks out someone or something is verified or authenticated. (Informal.) ☐ *I spent all afternoon working with my checkbook, trying to get the figures to check out.* ☐ *The police wouldn't believe that I am who I say I am until they made a few telephone calls to see if my story checked out.*

someone's bread and butter someone's income; someone's livelihood — the source of one's food. (Also literal.) ☐ *I can't miss another day of work. That's my bread and butter.* ☐ *I like to go to business conferences. That's good because that's my bread and butter.*

something about someone or something something strange or curious about someone or something. ☐ *There is something about Jane. I just can't figure her out.* ☐ *I love Mexican food. There's just something about it.*

something else something wonderful; something extra special. (Informal. Also literal.) ☐ *Did you see her new car? That's really something else!* ☐ *John hit a ball yesterday that went out of the stadium and kept on going. He's something else!*

something else (again) something entirely different. (Informal.) ☐ *Borrowing is one thing, but stealing is something else.* ☐ *Skindiving is easy and fun, but scuba diving is something else again.*

something of the sort something of the kind just mentioned. ☐ *The tree isn't exactly a spruce tree, just something of the sort.* ☐ *Jane has a cold or something of the sort.*

something or other something; one thing or another. (Informal.) ☐ *I can't remember what Ann said — something or other.* ☐ *A messenger came by and dropped off something or other at the front desk.*

something to that effect meaning something like that. (Informal.) ☐ *She said she wouldn't be available until after three, or something to that effect.* ☐ *I was told to keep out of the house — or something to that effect.*

something's up something is going to happen; something is going on. (Slang.) ☐ *Everybody looks very nervous. I think something's up.* ☐ *From the looks of all the activity around here, I think something's up.*

somewhere to hang (up) one's hat a place to live; a place to call one's home. ☐ *What I need is somewhere to hang up my hat. I just can't stand all this traveling.* ☐ *A home is a lot more than a place to hang your hat.*

son of a bitch (Informal. Use with caution.) **1.** a very horrible person. (Usually intended as a strong insult. Never used casually.) ☐ *Bill called Bob a son of a bitch, and Bob punched Bill in the face.* ☐ *This guy's a son of a bitch. He treats everybody rotten.* **2.** a useless thing. ☐ *This car is a son of a bitch. It won't ever start when it's cold.* ☐ *This bumpy old road needs paving. It's a real son of a bitch.* **3.** a difficult task. (Informal.) ☐ *This job is a son of a bitch.* ☐ *I can't do this kind of thing. It's too hard — a real son of a bitch.*

son of a gun (Informal.) **1.** a horrible person. (A euphemism for *son of a bitch*. Use with caution.) ☐ *When is that plumber going to show up and fix this leak? The stupid son of a gun!* ☐ *Bob is a rotten son of a gun if he thinks he can get away with that.* **2.** old (male) friend. (A friendly — male to male — way of referring to a friend. Use with caution.) ☐ *Why Bill, you old son of a gun, I haven't seen you in three or four years.* ☐ *When is that son of a gun John going to come visit us? He's neglecting his friends.*

soon as possible See *(as) soon as possible.*

sooner or later eventually; in the short term or in the long term. (Fixed order.) ☐ *He'll have to pay the bill sooner or later.* ☐ *She'll get what she deserves sooner or later.*

sort of something AND **kind of something** almost something; somewhat; somehow. (Informal.) □ *Isn't it sort of cold out?* □ *That was kind of a stupid thing to do, wasn't it?*

sort something out to clear up confusion; to straighten out something disorderly. (Also literal.) T *Now that things are settled down, I can sort out my life.* □ *This place is a mess. Let's sort things out before we do anything else.*

sound as a dollar See *(as) sound as a dollar.*

sound off (about something) to speak loudly and freely about something, especially when complaining. (Informal.) □ *The people at the bus stop were sounding off about the poor transportation services.* □ *Bob was sounding off about the government's economic policies.* □ *Sam sounds off every chance he gets.*

sound someone out to try to find out what someone thinks (about something). □ *I don't know what Jane thinks about your suggestion, but I'll sound her out.* T *Please sound out everyone in your department.*

soup something up to make something (especially a car) more powerful. (Slang.) □ *I wish someone would soup my car up. It'll hardly run.* T *Bill spent all summer souping up that old car he bought.*

sow one's wild oats to do wild and foolish things in one's youth. (Often assumed to have some sort of sexual meaning.) □ *Dale was out sowing his wild oats last night, and he's in jail this morning.* □ *Mrs. Smith told Mr. Smith that he was too old to be sowing his wild oats.*

spaced-out dopey; giddy. (Slang.) □ *I don't see how Sally can accomplish anything. She's so spaced-out!* □ *She's not really spaced-out. She acts that way on purpose.*

speak for itself AND **speak for themselves** not to need explaining; to have an obvious meaning. □ *The evidence*

speaks for itself. □ *The facts speak for themselves. Tom is guilty.* □ *Your results speak for themselves. You need to work harder.*

speak for themselves See the previous entry.

speak highly of someone or something to say good things about someone or something. (Note the variations in the examples. See also *think a lot of someone or something.*) □ *Ann speaks quite highly of Jane's work.* □ *Everyone speaks very highly of Jane.*

speak of the devil said when someone whose name has just been mentioned appears or is heard from. □ *Well, speak of the devil! Hello, Tom. We were just talking about you.* □ *I had just mentioned Sally when—speak of the devil—she walked in the door.*

speak off the cuff to speak in public without preparation. □ *I'm not too good at speaking off the cuff.* □ *I need to prepare a speech for Friday, although I speak off the cuff quite well.*

speak one's mind to say frankly what one thinks (about something). (Compare with *speak out (on something).*) □ *Please let me speak my mind, and then you can do whatever you wish.* □ *You can always depend on John to speak his mind. He'll let you know what he really thinks.*

speak out of turn to say something unwise or imprudent; to say the right thing at the wrong time. □ *Excuse me if I'm speaking out of turn, but what you are proposing is quite wrong.* □ *Bob was quite honest, even if he was speaking out of turn.*

speak out (on something) to say something frankly and directly; to *speak one's mind.* (See also *speak up.*) □ *This law is wrong, and I intend to speak out on it until it is repealed.* □ *You must speak out. People need to know what you think.*

speak the same language [for people] to have similar ideas, tastes, etc. (Also literal.) □ *Jane and Jack get along very well. They really speak the same* *language about almost everything.* □ *Bob and his father didn't speak the same language when it comes to politics.*

speak up 1. to speak more loudly. □ *They can't hear you in the back of the room. Please speak up.* □ *What? Speak up, please. I'm hard of hearing.* **2.** to *speak out (on something).* □ *If you think that this is wrong, you must speak up and say so.* □ *I'm too shy to speak up.*

speak up for someone or something to speak in favor of someone or something. □ *If anybody says bad things about me, I hope you speak up for me.* □ *I want to speak up for the rights of students.*

speak with a forked tongue to tell lies; to try to deceive someone. □ *Jean's mother sounds very charming, but she speaks with a forked tongue.* □ *People tend to believe Fred because he seems plausible, but we know he speaks with a forked tongue.*

spell something out 1. to spell something (in letters). (Also without *out*.) □ *I can't understand your name. Can you spell it out?* Ⓣ *Please spell out all the strange words so I can write them down correctly.* **2.** to give all the details of something. □ *I want you to understand this completely, so I'm going to spell it out very carefully.* Ⓣ *The instruction book for my computer spells out everything very carefully.*

spell trouble to signify future trouble; to mean trouble. (Informal.) □ *This letter that came today spells trouble.* □ *The sky looks angry and dark. That spells trouble.*

spick-and-span very clean. (Informal. Fixed order.) □ *I have to clean up the house and get it spick-and-span for the party Friday night.* □ *I love to have everything around me spick-and-span.*

spill the beans See *let the cat out of the bag.*

spin one's wheels to be in motion, but get nowhere. (Slang.) □ *This is a terrible job. I'm just spinning my wheels and not getting anywhere.* □ *Get*

organized and try to accomplish something. Stop spinning your wheels!

spin something off to create something as a by-product of something else. □ *When the company reorganized, it spun its banking division off.* Ⓣ *By spinning off part of its assets, a company gets needed capital.*

spit (something) up to throw something up; to vomit something. (A little gentler than *throw (something) up*.) □ *I guess that the food didn't agree with the dog, because he spit it up.* Ⓣ *The baby has been spitting up all morning.* Ⓣ *Bob spit up his whole dinner.*

split hairs to quibble; to try to make petty distinctions. □ *They don't have any serious differences. They are just splitting hairs.* □ *Don't waste time splitting hairs. Accept it the way it is.*

split one's sides (with laughter) to laugh so hard that one's sides almost split. (Always an exaggeration.) □ *The members of the audience almost split their sides with laughter.* □ *When I heard what happened to Patricia, I almost split my sides.*

split people up to separate two or more people (from one another). □ *If you two don't stop chattering, I'll have to split you up.* □ *The group of people grew too large, so we had to split them up.* Ⓣ *I will have to split up that twosome in the corner.*

split something fifty-fifty See *divide something fifty-fifty.*

split the difference to divide the difference (with someone else). □ *You want to sell for $120, and I want to buy for $100. Let's split the difference and close the deal at $110.* □ *I don't want to split the difference. I want $120.*

split up [for people] to separate or leave one another. (Informal. This can refer to divorce or separation.) □ *I heard that Mr. and Mrs. Brown have split up.* □ *Our little club had to split up because everyone was too busy.*

spoken for taken; reserved (for someone). □ *I'm sorry, but this one is* *already spoken for.* □ *Pardon me. Can I sit here, or is this seat spoken for?*

spook someone or something to startle or disorient someone or something. (Folksy.) □ *A snake spooked my horse, and I nearly fell off.* □ *Your warning spooked me, and I was upset for the rest of the day.*

spoon-feed someone to treat someone with too much care or help; to teach someone with methods that are too easy and do not stimulate the learner to independent thinking. (Also literal.) □ *The teacher spoon-feeds the students by dictating notes on the novel instead of getting the children to read the books.* □ *You mustn't spoon-feed the new recruits by telling them what to do all the time. They must use their initiative.*

sporting chance a reasonably good chance. (See also *fighting chance*.) □ *If you hurry, you have a sporting chance of catching the bus.* □ *The small company has only a sporting chance of getting the export order.*

spout off (about someone or something) to talk too much about someone or something. (Informal.) □ *Why do you always have to spout off about things that don't concern you?* □ *Everyone in our office spouts off about the boss.* □ *There is no need to spout off like that. Calm down and think about what you're saying.*

spread it on thick See *lay it on thick.*

spread like wildfire to spread rapidly and without control. □ *The epidemic is spreading like wildfire. Everyone is getting sick.* □ *John told a joke that was so funny it spread like wildfire.*

spread oneself too thin to do so many things that you can do none of them well. □ *It's a good idea to get involved in a lot of activities, but don't spread yourself too thin.* □ *I'm too busy these days. I'm afraid I've spread myself too thin.*

spring for something to treat (someone) to something. (Slang.) □ *John and I went out last night, and he sprang*

for dinner. □ *At the park Bill usually springs for ice cream.*

spring something on someone to surprise someone with something. (Informal.) □ *I'm glad you told me now, rather than springing it on me at the last minute.* □ *I sprang the news on my parents last night. They were not glad to hear it.*

spruce someone or something up to make someone or something clean and orderly. □ *I'll be ready to go as soon as I spruce myself up a bit.* ⊤ *I have to spruce up the house for the party.*

square accounts (with someone) 1. to settle one's financial accounts with someone. □ *I have to square accounts with the bank this week, or it'll take back my car.* □ *I called the bank and said I needed to come in and square accounts.* **2.** to get even with someone; to straighten out a misunderstanding with someone. (Informal.) □ *I'm going to square accounts with Tom. He insulted me in public, and he owes me an apology.* □ *Tom, you and I are going to have to square accounts.*

square deal a fair and honest transaction; fair treatment. (Informal.) □ *All the workers want is a square deal, but their boss underpays them.* □ *You always get a square deal with that travel company.*

square meal a nourishing, filling meal. □ *All you've eaten today is junk food. You should sit down to a square meal.* □ *The poor old man hadn't had a square meal in weeks.*

square off (for something) to get ready for an argument or a fight. □ *John was angry and appeared to be squaring off for a fight.* □ *When those two square off, everyone gets out of the way.*

square peg in a round hole a misfit. □ *John can't seem to get along with the people he works with. He's just a square peg in a round hole.* □ *I'm not a square peg in a round hole. It's just that no one understands me.*

square someone or something away to get someone or something arranged or properly taken care of. □ *See if you can square Bob away in his new office.* T *Please square away the problems we discussed earlier.*

square up to someone or something to face someone or something bravely; to tackle someone or something. □ *You'll have to square up to the bully or he'll make your life miserable.* □ *It's time to square up to your financial problems. You can't just ignore them.*

square up with someone to pay someone what one owes; to pay one's share of something to someone. (Informal.) □ *I'll square up with you later if you pay the whole bill now.* □ *Bob said he would square up with Tom for his share of the gas.*

squared away arranged or properly taken care of. □ *Is Ann squared away yet?* □ *I will talk to you when I am squared away.*

squeak by (someone or something) just to get by someone or something. (Informal.) □ *The guard was almost asleep, so I squeaked by him.* □ *I wasn't very well prepared for the test, and I just squeaked by.*

squirrel something away to hide or store something. (Folksy.) □ *Billy has been squirreling candy away in his top drawer.* T *I've been squirreling away a little money each week for years.*

stab someone in the back to betray someone. (Informal. Also literal.) □ *I thought we were friends! Why did you stab me in the back?* □ *You don't expect a person whom you trust to stab you in the back.*

stack something up to make a stack of things. (Also without the *up*.) □ *Where should I stack them up?* T *Please stack up these boxes.*

stack the cards (against someone or something) See the following entry.

stack the deck (against someone or something) AND **stack the cards (against someone or something)** to arrange things against someone or something. (Slang. Originally from card playing.) □ *I can't get ahead at my office. Someone has stacked the cards against me.* □ *Do you really think that someone has stacked the deck? Isn't it just fate?*

stake a claim (to something) to lay or make a claim for something. (Informal.) □ *I want to stake a claim to that last piece of pie.* □ *You don't need to stake a claim. Just ask politely.*

stall someone or something off to put off or delay someone or something. □ *The sheriff is at the door. I'll stall him off while you get out the back door.* T *You can stall off the sheriff, but you can't stall off justice.*

stamp someone or something out 1. [with *someone*] to get rid of or kill someone. (Slang.) □ *You just can't stamp somebody out on your own!* T *The victim wanted to stamp out the robbers without a trial.* **2.** [with *something*] to extinguish something. □ *Quick, stamp that fire out before it spreads.* T *Tom stamped out the sparks before they started a fire.* **3.** [with *something*] to eliminate something. □ *The doctors hope they can stamp cancer out.* T *Many people think that they can stamp out evil.*

stand a chance to have a chance. □ *Do you think I stand a chance of winning first place?* □ *Everyone stands a chance of catching the disease.*

stand and deliver to give up something to someone who demands it. (Originally used by highway robbers asking for passengers' valuables. Now used figuratively. Fixed order.) □ *And when the tax agent says "Stand and deliver" you have to be prepared to pay what is demanded.* □ *The robber stopped the coach and demanded of Lady Ellen, "Stand and deliver!"*

stand behind someone or something AND **stand (in) back of someone or something** to endorse or guarantee something or the actions of a person. (Also literal.) □ *Our company stands behind this product 100 percent.* □ *I* *stand behind Bill and everything he does.*

stand by to wait and remain ready. (Generally heard in communication, such as broadcasting, telephones, etc.) □ *Your transatlantic telephone call is almost ready. Please stand by.* □ *Is everyone ready for the telecast? Only ten seconds — stand by.*

stand by someone to support someone; to continue supporting someone even when things are bad. (Compare with *stick by someone or something.* Also literal.) □ *Don't worry. I'll stand by you no matter what.* □ *I feel as though I have to stand by my brother even if he goes to jail.*

stand corrected to admit that one has been wrong. □ *I realize that I accused him wrongly. I stand corrected.* □ *We appreciate now that our conclusions were wrong. We stand corrected.*

stand for something 1. to endure something. □ *The teacher won't stand for any whispering in class.* □ *We just can't stand for that kind of behavior.* **2.** to signify something. □ *In a traffic signal, the red light stands for "stop."* □ *The abbreviation* Dr. *stands for "doctor."* **3.** to endorse or support an ideal. □ *The mayor claims to stand for honesty in government and jobs for everyone.* □ *Every candidate for public office stands for all the good things in life.*

stand in awe (of someone or something) to be overwhelmed with respect for someone or something. □ *Many people stand in awe of the president.* □ *Bob says he stands in awe of a big juicy steak. I think he's exaggerating.* □ *When it comes to food, you can say that it's delicious, but one hardly stands in awe.*

stand (in) back of someone or something See *stand behind someone or something.*

stand in (for someone) to substitute for someone; to serve in someone's place. □ *The famous opera singer was ill, and an inexperienced singer had to stand in*

for her. □ *The new singer was grateful for the opportunity to stand in.*

stand in someone's way to be a barrier to someone's desires or intentions. (Also literal.) □ *I know you want a divorce so you can marry Ann. Well, I won't stand in your way. You can have the divorce.* □ *I know you want to leave home, and I don't want to stand in your way. You're free to go.*

stand on ceremony to hold rigidly to protocol or formal manners. (Often in the negative.) □ *Please help yourself to more. Don't stand on ceremony.* □ *We are very informal around here. Hardly anyone stands on ceremony.*

stand on one's own two feet to be independent and self-sufficient. (Informal. Compare with *get back on one's feet.*) □ *I'll be glad when I have a good job and can stand on my own two feet.* □ *When Jane gets out of debt, she'll be able to stand on her own two feet again.*

stand one's ground AND **hold one's ground** to stand up for one's rights; to resist an attack. □ *The lawyer tried to confuse me when I was giving testimony, but I managed to stand my ground.* □ *Some people were trying to crowd us off the beach, but we held our ground.*

stand out to be uniquely visible or conspicuous. □ *This computer stands out as one of the best available.* □ *Because John is so tall, he really stands out in a crowd.*

stand over someone to monitor or watch over someone. □ *You don't have to stand over me. I can do it by myself.* □ *I know from previous experience that if I don't stand over you, you'll never finish.*

stand pat to remain as is; to preserve the status quo. (Informal.) □ *We can't just stand pat! We have to keep making progress!* □ *This company isn't increasing sales. It's just standing pat.*

stand someone in good stead to be useful or beneficial to someone. □ *This is a fine overcoat. I'm sure it'll stand you in good stead for many years.* □ *I* *did the mayor a favor that I'm sure will stand me in good stead.*

stand someone to a treat to pay for food or drink for someone as a special favor. □ *We went to the zoo, and my father stood us all to a treat. We had ice cream and soft drinks.* □ *We went to a nice restaurant and had a fine meal. It was even better when Mr. Williams told us he'd stand us to a treat, and he picked up the bill.*

stand someone up to fail to meet someone for a date or an appointment. □ *John and Jane were supposed to go out last night, but she stood him up.* ⊤ *If you stand up people very often, you'll find that you have no friends at all.*

stand still for something AND **hold still for something** to tolerate or endure something. (Often in the negative.) □ *I won't stand still for that kind of behavior!* □ *She won't hold still for that kind of talk.*

stand to reason to seem reasonable; [for a fact or conclusion] to survive careful or logical evaluation. □ *It stands to reason that it'll be colder in January than it is in November.* □ *It stands to reason that Bill left in a hurry, although no one saw him go.*

stand up and be counted to state one's support (for someone or something); to *come out for* someone or something. □ *If you believe in more government help for farmers, write your representative — stand up and be counted.* □ *I'm generally in favor of what you propose, but not enough to stand up and be counted.*

stare someone in the face See *look someone in the face.*

stark raving mad totally insane; completely crazy; out of control. (Often an exaggeration.) □ *When she heard about what happened at the office, she went stark raving mad.* □ *You must be stark raving mad if you think I would trust you with my car!*

start from scratch to start from the beginning; to start from nothing. (Informal. Compare with *make something*

from scratch.) □ *Whenever I bake a cake, I start from scratch. I never use a cake mix in a box.* □ *I built every bit of my own house. I started from scratch and did everything with my own hands.*

start off on the wrong foot to begin [something] by doing something wrong. (See also *be off on the wrong foot; get off on the wrong foot.*) □ *I don't want to start off on the wrong foot by saying something stupid. What should I say?* □ *Poor Donna started off on the wrong foot when she arrived forty minutes late.*

start (off) with a clean slate AND **start (over) with a clean slate** to start out again afresh; to ignore the past and start over again. □ *I plowed under all last year's flowers so I could start with a clean slate next spring.* □ *If I start off with a clean slate, then I'll know exactly what each plant is.* □ *When Bob got out of jail, he started over with a clean slate.*

start (over) with a clean slate See the previous entry.

start someone in (as something) AND **start someone out (as something)** to start someone on a job as a certain kind of worker. □ *I got a job in a restaurant today. They started me in as a dishwasher.* □ *I now work for the telephone company. They started me out as a local operator.*

start someone out (as something) See the previous entry.

start something to start a fight or an argument. (Also literal. *Something* is *anything* or *nothing* in the negative.) □ *Hey, you! Better be careful unless you want to start something.* □ *I don't want to start anything. I'm just leaving.*

start something up to start something, such as a car or some procedure. (Also without *up.*) ⊤ *It was cold, but I managed to start up the car without any difficulty.* □ *We can't start the project up until we have more money.*

start the ball rolling See *get the ball rolling.*

stay after someone See *keep after someone.*

stay in touch (with someone) See *keep in touch (with someone).*

stay put not to move; to stay where one is. (Informal.) □ *We've decided to stay put and not to move to Florida.* □ *If the children just stay put, their parents will come for them soon.*

steady as a rock See *(as) steady as a rock.*

steal a base to sneak from one base to another in baseball. □ *The runner stole second base, but he nearly got put out on the way.* □ *Tom runs so slowly that he never tries to steal a base.*

steal a march (on someone) to get some sort of an advantage over someone without being noticed. □ *I got the contract because I was able to steal a march on my competitor.* □ *You have to be clever and fast — not dishonest — to steal a march.*

steal someone's thunder to lessen someone's force or authority. □ *What do you mean by coming in here and stealing my thunder? I'm in charge here!* □ *Someone stole my thunder by leaking my announcement to the press.*

steal the show See the following entry.

steal the spotlight AND **steal the show** to give the best performance in a show, play, or some other event; to get attention for oneself. □ *The lead in the play was very good, but the butler stole the show.* □ *Ann always tries to steal the spotlight when she and I make a presentation.*

steamed up angry. (Informal.) □ *What Bob said really got me steamed up.* □ *Why do you get so steamed up about nothing?*

steer clear (of someone or something) to avoid someone or something. □ *John is mad at me, so I've been steering clear of him.* □ *Steer clear of that book. It has many errors in it.* □ *Good advice. I'll steer clear.*

step-by-step little by little, one step at a time. (Refers both to walking and fol-

lowing instructions.) □ *Just follow the instructions step-by-step, and everything will be fine.* □ *The old man slowly moved across the lawn step-by-step.*

step down (from something) to resign a job or a responsibility. (Also literal.) □ *The mayor stepped down from office last week.* □ *It's unusual for a mayor to step down.*

step into someone's shoes to take over a job or some role from someone. □ *I was prepared to step into the boss's shoes, so there was no disruption when he left for another job.* □ *There was no one who could step into Alice's shoes when she left, so everything came to a stop.*

step into (the breach) to move into a space or vacancy. □ *When Ann resigned as president, I stepped into the breach.* □ *A number of people asked me to step in and take her place.*

step on it See *step on the gas.*

step on someone's toes to interfere with or offend someone. (Also literal. Note the example with *anyone.*) □ *When you're in public office, you have to avoid stepping on anyone's toes.* □ *Ann stepped on someone's toes during the last campaign and lost the election.*

step on the gas AND **step on it** hurry up. (Informal.) □ *I'm in a hurry, driver. Step on it!* □ *I can't step on the gas, mister. There's too much traffic.*

step out of line to misbehave; to do something offensive. (Also literal.) □ *I'm terribly sorry. I hope I didn't step out of line.* □ *John is a lot of fun to go out with, but he has a tendency to step out of line.*

step (right) up to move forward, toward someone. □ *Step up and get your mail when I call your name.* □ *Come on, everybody. Step right up and help yourself to supper.*

step something up to cause something to go faster. Ⓣ *The factory was not making enough cars, so they stepped up production.* □ *The music was not fast enough, so the conductor told everyone to step it up.*

stew in one's own juice to be left alone to suffer one's anger or disappointment. (Informal.) □ *John has such a terrible temper. When he got mad at us, we just let him go away and stew in his own juice.* □ *After John stewed in his own juice for a while, he decided to come back and apologize to us.*

stick around [for a person] to remain in a place. (Informal.) □ *The kids stuck around for a time after the party was over.* □ *Oh, Ann. Please stick around for a while. I want to talk to you later.*

stick by someone or something AND **stick with someone or something** to support someone or something; to continue supporting someone or something when things are bad. (Informal. Compare with *stand by someone.*) □ *Don't worry. I'll stick by you no matter what.* □ *I feel as if I have to stick by my brother even if he goes to jail.* □ *I'll stick by my ideas whether you like them or not.*

Stick 'em up! See *Hands up!*

stick-in-the-mud someone who is stubbornly old-fashioned. □ *Come on to the party with us and have some fun. Don't be an old stick-in-the-mud!* □ *Tom is no stick-in-the-mud. He's really up-to-date.*

stick one's foot in one's mouth See *put one's foot in one's mouth.*

stick one's neck out (for someone or something) to take a risk. (Informal.) □ *Why should I stick my neck out to do something for her? What's she ever done for me?* □ *He made a risky investment. He stuck his neck out for the deal because he thought he could make some money.*

stick one's nose in(to something) See *poke one's nose in(to something).*

stick out like a sore thumb to be very prominent or unsightly; to be obvious and visible. (Informal.) □ *Bob is so tall that he sticks out like a sore thumb in a crowd.* □ *The house next door needs painting. It sticks out like a sore thumb.*

stick someone or something up 1. [with *something*] to affix or attach something onto a wall, post, etc. □ *This notice ought to be on the bulletin board. Please stick it up.* Ⓣ *I'm going to stick up this poster near the entrance.* **2.** to rob someone or something. □ *One robber stuck the cashier up first, but someone sounded the alarm before any money was taken.* Ⓣ *The robbers came in and tried to stick up the bank, but they got caught first.*

stick someone with someone or something to burden someone with someone or something. (Informal.) □ *The dishonest merchant stuck me with a faulty television set.* □ *John stuck me with his talkative uncle and went off with his friends.*

stick something out to endure something. (Also literal.) □ *The play was terribly boring, but I managed to stick it out.* □ *College was very difficult for Bill, but he decided to stick it out.*

stick to one's guns to remain firm in one's convictions; to stand up for one's rights. (Informal. Compare with *stand one's ground.*) □ *I'll stick to my guns on this matter. I'm sure I'm right.* □ *Bob can be persuaded to do it our way. He probably won't stick to his guns on this point.*

stick to one's ribs [for food] to last long and fortify one well; [for food] to sustain one even in the coldest weather. □ *This oatmeal ought to stick to your ribs. You need something hearty on a cold day like this.* □ *I don't want soup! I want something that will stick to my ribs.*

stick together to remain together as a group. (Informal. Also literal.) □ *Come on, you guys. Let's stick together. Otherwise somebody will get lost.* □ *Our group of friends has managed to stick together for almost twenty years.*

stick up for someone or something to support someone or something; to speak in favor of someone or something. □ *Everyone was making unpleasant remarks about John, but I* *stuck up for him.* □ *Our team was losing, but I stuck up for it anyway.*

stick with someone or something See *stick by someone or something.*

sticks and stones elements of harm [directed at someone]. (Part of a rhyme, "Sticks and stone may break my bones, but words will never hurt me." Also literal. Fixed order.) □ *I have had enough of your sticks and stones. I have enough trouble without your adding to it.* □ *After the opposing candidate had used sticks and stones for a month, suddenly there were kind words heard.*

stir someone or something up 1. [with *someone*] to make someone angry or excited; to make someone get active. □ *I need a cup of hot coffee to stir me up in the morning.* Ⓣ *Reading the newspaper always stirs up my father.* **2.** [with *something*] to cause trouble; to foment disagreement and difficulty. Ⓣ *They stirred up quite a commotion.* Ⓣ *Who stirred up this matter?*

stir up a hornet's nest to create trouble or difficulties. (Informal.) □ *What a mess you have made of things. You've really stirred up a hornet's nest.* □ *Bill stirred up a hornet's nest when he discovered the theft.*

stock up (on something) to build up a supply of something. □ *Before the first snow, we always stock up on firewood.* □ *John drinks a lot of milk, so we stock up when we know he's coming.*

stoop to doing something to degrade oneself or condescend to doing something; to do something that is beneath one. □ *Whoever thought that the manager of the department would stoop to typing?* □ *I never dreamed that Bill would stoop to stealing.*

stop-and-go halting repeatedly; stopping and continuing repeatedly. (Fixed order.) □ *This project has been stop-and-go since we began. Problems keep appearing.* □ *The traffic was stop-and-go for miles. I thought I would never get here!*

stop at nothing to do everything possible (to accomplish something); to be unscrupulous. □ *Bill would stop at nothing to get his way.* □ *Bob is completely determined to get promoted. He'll stop at nothing.*

stop by (some place) AND **stop in (some place)** to visit some place, usually briefly. □ *I was coming home, but I decided to stop by my aunt's on the way.* □ *She was very glad that I stopped in.*

stop in (some place) See the previous entry.

stop, look, and listen to exercise caution, especially at street corners and railroad crossings, by stopping, looking to the left and to the right, and listening for approaching vehicles or a train. (Also used figuratively for exercising extreme caution in general. Fixed order.) □ *Sally's mother trained her to stop, look, and listen at every street corner.* □ *It is a good practice to stop, look, and listen at a railroad crossing.* □ *You really should stop, look, and listen before you take any risks with your hard-earned money.*

stop off (some place) to stop somewhere on the way to some other place. □ *I stopped off at the store to buy milk on the way home.* □ *We stopped off for a few minutes and chatted with my uncle.*

stop over (some place) to break one's journey, usually overnight or even longer. (Compare to *lay over (somewhere).*) □ *On our way to New York, we stopped over in Philadelphia for the night.* □ *That's a good place to stop over. There are some nice hotels in Philadelphia.*

stop short of (doing) something not to go as far as doing something; not to go as far as something. □ *Fortunately Bob stopped short of hitting Tom.* □ *The boss criticized Jane's work, but stopped short of reprimanding her.* □ *Jack was furious but stopped short of hitting Tom.* □ *Jane wouldn't stop short of telling lies in order to get a job.*

straight and narrow a straight and law-abiding route through life. (Informal. From *straight and narrow pathway*. Fixed order.) □ *You should have no trouble with the police if you stick to the straight and narrow.* □ *Roger was the kind who followed the straight and narrow every day of his life.*

(straight) from the horse's mouth from an authoritative or dependable source. □ *I know it's true! I heard it straight from the horse's mouth!* □ *This comes straight from the horse's mouth, so it has to be believed.*

straight from the shoulder sincerely; frankly; holding nothing back. □ *Sally always speaks straight from the shoulder. You never have to guess what she really means.* □ *Bill gave a good presentation — straight from the shoulder and brief.*

straighten someone or something out 1. [with *someone*] to make someone understand something. (Also literal.) □ *Jane was confused about the date, so I straightened her out.* ⊤ *I took a few minutes and straightened out everyone.* **2.** [with *someone*] to reform someone. □ *Most people think that jail never straightens anybody out.* ⊤ *The judge felt that a few years at hard labor would straighten out the thief.* **3.** [with *something*] to make a situation less confused. □ *John made a mess of the contract, so I helped him straighten it out.* ⊤ *Please straighten out your checking account. It's all messed up.*

straighten someone or something up 1. to put someone or something into an upright position. □ *The fence is tilted. Please straighten up that post when you get a chance.* □ *Bill, you're slouching again. Straighten yourself up.* **2.** to tidy up someone or something. □ *John straightened himself up a little before going on stage.* ⊤ *This room is a mess. Let's straighten up this place, right now!*

straighten up 1. to sit or stand more straight. □ *Billy's mother told him to straighten up or he'd fall out of his chair.* □ *John straightened up so he'd look taller.* **2.** to behave better. □ *Bill*

was acting badly for a while; then he straightened up. □ *Sally, straighten up, or I will punish you!*

strapped (for something) (Informal.) very much in need of money. □ *I'm strapped for a few bucks. Can you loan me five dollars?* □ *Sorry, I'm strapped, too.*

stretch a point AND **stretch the point** to interpret a point flexibly and with great latitude. □ *Would it be stretching a point to suggest that everyone is invited to your picnic?* □ *To say that everyone is invited is stretching the point.*

stretch one's legs to walk around after sitting down or lying down for a time. □ *We wanted to stretch our legs during the theater interval.* □ *After sitting in the car all day, the travelers decided to stretch their legs.*

stretch the point See *stretch a point*.

stretch the truth to exaggerate; to misrepresent the truth just a little bit. □ *She was stretching the truth when she said everything was ready for the party.* □ *I don't want to stretch the truth. Our town is probably the wealthiest around here.*

(strictly) on the up-and-up honest; fair and straight. (Slang. Compare with *on the level*.) □ *Do you think that the mayor is on the up-and-up?* □ *Yes, the mayor is strictly on the up-and-up.*

strike a balance (between two things) to find a satisfactory compromise between two extremes. □ *The political party must strike a balance between the right wing and the left wing.* □ *Jane is overdressed for the party and Sally is underdressed. What a pity they didn't strike a balance.*

strike a bargain to reach an agreement on a price (for something). □ *They argued for a while and finally struck a bargain.* □ *They were unable to strike a bargain, so they left.*

strike a chord (with someone) to cause someone to remember something; to remind someone or something; to be familiar. □ *The woman in the portrait struck a chord and I realized that it was my grandmother.* □ *His name strikes a chord with me, but I don't know why.*

strike a happy medium AND **hit a happy medium** to find a compromise position; to arrive at a position halfway between two unacceptable extremes. □ *Ann likes very spicy food, but Bob doesn't care for spicy food at all. We are trying to find a restaurant that strikes a happy medium.* □ *Tom is either very happy or very sad. He can't seem to hit a happy medium.*

strike a match to light a match. □ *Mary struck a match and lit a candle.* □ *When Sally struck a match to light a cigarette, Jane said quickly, "No smoking, please."*

strike a sour note AND **hit a sour note** to signify something unpleasant. (Informal.) □ *Jane's sad announcement struck a sour note at the annual banquet.* □ *News of the crime hit a sour note in our holiday celebration.*

strike it rich to acquire wealth suddenly. (Informal.) □ *If I could strike it rich, I wouldn't have to work anymore.* □ *Sally ordered a dozen oysters and found a huge pearl in one of them. She struck it rich!*

strike out 1. [for a baseball batter] to be declared "out" after three strikes. (See also *strike someone out*.) □ *Bill almost never strikes out.* □ *John struck out at least once in every game this season.* **2.** to fail. (Slang.) □ *Ann did her best, but she struck out anyway.* □ *Give it another try. Just because you struck out once doesn't mean you can't do better now.*

strike out at someone or something to (figuratively or literally) hit at or attack someone or something. □ *She was so angry she struck out at the person she was arguing with.* □ *I was frantic. I wanted to strike out at everything and everybody.*

strike someone funny to seem funny to someone. □ *Sally has a great sense of humor. Everything she says strikes me*

funny. □ *Why are you laughing? Did something I said strike you funny?*

strike someone out [for a baseball pitcher] to get a batter declared "out" after three strikes. □ *I never thought he'd strike Tom out.* Ⓣ *Bill struck out all our best players.*

strike someone's fancy to appeal to someone. (See also *tickle someone's fancy*.) □ *I'll have some ice cream, please. Chocolate strikes my fancy right now.* □ *Why don't you go to the store and buy a record album that strikes your fancy?*

strike the right note to achieve the desired effect; to do something suitable or pleasing. (A musical reference.) □ *Meg struck the right note when she wore a dark suit to the interview.* □ *The politician's speech failed to strike the right note with the crowd.*

strike up a conversation to start a conversation (with someone). □ *I struck up an interesting conversation with someone on the bus yesterday.* □ *It's easy to strike up a conversation with someone when you're traveling.*

strike up a friendship to become friends (with someone). □ *I struck up a friendship with John while we were on a business trip together.* □ *If you're lonely, you should go out and try to strike up a friendship with someone you like.*

strike while the iron is hot to do something at the best possible time; to do something when the time is ripe. □ *He was in a good mood, so I asked for a loan of $200. I thought I'd better strike while the iron was hot.* □ *Please go to the bank and settle this matter now! They are willing to be reasonable. You've got to strike while the iron is hot.*

string along (with someone) to accompany someone; to *run around with someone*. □ *Sally seemed to know where she was going, so I decided to string along with her.* □ *She said it was okay if I strung along.*

string something out to draw something out (in time); to make something last a long time. (Also literal.) □ *The meeting was long enough. There was no need to string it out further with all those speeches.* ⊤ *They tried to string out the meeting to make things seem more important.*

stroke of luck a bit of luck; a lucky happening. □ *I had a stroke of luck and found Tom at home when I called. He's not usually there.* □ *Unless I have a stroke of luck, I'm not going to finish this report by tomorrow.*

strong as an ox See *(as) strong as an ox.*

struggle to the death a bitter struggle to the end. (Literal and figurative uses.) □ *The wolf and the elk fought in a struggle to the death.* □ *I had a terrible time getting my car started. It was a struggle to the death, but it finally started.*

strung out 1. extended in time; overly long. □ *Why was that lecture so strung out? She talked and talked.* □ *It was strung out because there was very little to be said.* 2. doped or drugged. (Slang.) □ *Bob acted very strangely—as if he were strung out or something.* □ *I've never seen Bob or any of his friends strung out.*

stubborn as a mule See *(as) stubborn as a mule.*

stuck on someone or something 1. [with *someone*] to be fond of or in love with someone. □ *John was stuck on Sally, but she didn't know it.* □ *He always is stuck on the wrong person.* 2. [with *something*] to be locked into an idea, cause, or purpose. □ *Mary is really stuck on the idea of going to France this spring.* □ *You've proposed a good plan, Jane, but you're stuck on it. We may have to make some changes.*

stuck with someone or something burdened with someone or something; left having to care for someone or something. (Informal.) □ *Please don't leave me stuck with your aunt. She talks too much.* □ *My roommate quit school and left me stuck with the telephone bill.*

stuff and nonsense nonsense. (Informal. Fixed order.) □ *Come on! Don't give me all that stuff and nonsense!* □ *I don't understand this book. It's all stuff and nonsense as far as I am concerned.*

stuff the ballot box to put fraudulent ballots into a ballot box; to cheat in counting the votes in an election. □ *The election judge was caught stuffing the ballot box in the election yesterday.* □ *Election officials are supposed to guard against stuffing the ballot box.*

stumble across someone or something AND **stumble into someone or something; stumble on someone or something** to find someone or something, usually by accident. □ *I stumbled across an interesting book yesterday when I was shopping.* □ *Guess who I stumbled into at the library yesterday?* □ *I stumbled on a real bargain at the bookstore last week.*

stumble into someone or something 1. to bump into someone or something accidentally. □ *I stumbled into John, and I apologized. It was my fault.* □ *I stumbled into a post and hurt my arm.* 2. See the previous entry. 3. [with *something*] to enter something or a place by stumbling. □ *I tripped on the curb and stumbled into the car.* □ *I stumbled into the house, exhausted and in need of a cool drink.*

stumble on someone or something 1. See *stumble across someone or something.* 2. to trip over someone or something. □ *There were three of us sleeping in the small tent. Each of us would stumble on the others whenever we went out or came in.* □ *I stumbled on the curb and twisted my ankle.*

stumbling block something that prevents or obstructs progress. □ *We'd like to buy that house, but the high price is the stumbling block.* □ *Jim's age is a stumbling block to getting another job. He's over 60.*

subject to something likely to have or get something, usually a disease or ailment. □ *Bill is subject to fainting spells.* □ *Bob says he's subject to colds and the flu.*

subscribe to something to have a standing order for a magazine or something similar. □ *I usually buy my monthly magazines at the newsstand. I don't subscribe to them.* □ *I subscribe to all the magazines I read because it's nice to have them delivered by mail.*

such and such someone or something whose name has been forgotten or should not be said. (Informal.) □ *Mary said that such and such was coming to her party, but I forgot their names.* □ *If you walk into a store and ask for such and such and they don't have it, you go to a different store.*

such as it is in the imperfect state that one sees it; in the less-than-perfect condition in which one sees it. □ *This is where I live. This is my glorious home — such as it is.* □ *I've worked for days on this report, and I've done the best that I can do. It's my supreme effort — such as it is.*

Such is life! that is the way things happen. □ *Oh, well. Everything can't be perfect. Such is life!* □ *So I failed my test. Such is life! I can take it again some time.*

suck someone in AND **take someone in** to deceive someone. (The expression with *suck* is slang.) □ *I try to shop carefully so that no one can take me in.* ⊤ *I think that someone sucked in both of them. I don't know why they bought this car.*

suit someone to a T AND **fit someone to a T** to be very appropriate for someone. □ *This kind of job suits me to a T.* □ *This is Sally's kind of house. It fits her to a T.*

suit yourself to do something one's own way; to do something to please oneself. □ *Okay, if you don't want to do it my way, suit yourself.* □ *Take either of the books that you like. Suit yourself. I'll read the other one.*

sum and substance a summary; the gist. (Fixed order. See also *form and substance*.) □ *Can you quickly tell me the sum and substance of your proposal?* □ *In trying to explain the sum and substance of the essay, Thomas failed to mention the middle name of the hero.*

sum something up to summarize something. (Also literal, to figure out the total.) □ *At the end of the lecture, Dr. Williams summed the important points up.* □ *He said when he finished, "Well, that about sums it up."*

Sunday-go-to-meeting clothes one's best clothes. (Folksy. See also *in one's Sunday best*.) □ *John was all dressed up in his Sunday-go-to-meeting clothes.* □ *I hate to be wearing my Sunday-go-to-meeting clothes when everyone else is casually dressed.*

supply and demand the availability of things or people as compared to the need to utilize the things or people; the availability of goods compared to the number of willing customers for the goods. (Fixed order.) □ *Sometimes you can find what you want by shopping around and other times almost no store carries the items you are looking for. It depends entirely on supply and demand.* □ *Sometimes customers ask for things we do not carry in stock and other times we have things in abundance that no one wants to buy. Whether or not we can make money off of a product depends entirely on supply and demand.*

surf and turf fish and beef; lobster and beef. (A type of meal incorporating both expensive seafood and an expensive cut of beef. Refers to the sea and to the pasture. Fixed order.) □ *Walter ordered the surf and turf, but Alice ordered only a tiny salad.* □ *No surf and turf for me. I want fish and fish alone.*

survival of the fittest the idea that the most able or fit will survive (while the less able and less fit will perish). (This is used literally as a part of the theory of evolution.) □ *In college, it's the survival of the fittest. You have to keep working in order to survive and graduate.* □ *I don't give my houseplants very good care, but the ones I have are really* *flourishing. It's the survival of the fittest, I guess.*

swallow one's pride to forget one's pride and accept something humiliating. □ *I had to swallow my pride and admit that I was wrong.* □ *When you're a student, you find yourself swallowing your pride quite often.*

swallow something, hook, line, and sinker to believe something completely. (Slang. These terms refer to fishing and fooling a fish into being caught. Fixed order.) □ *I made up a story about why I was so late. The boss swallowed it, hook, line, and sinker.* □ *I feel like a fool. I swallowed it, hook, line, and sinker.*

swan song the last work or performance of a playwright, musician, actor, etc., before death or retirement. □ *His portrayal of Lear was the actor's swan song.* □ *We didn't know that her performance last night was the singer's swan song.*

swear by someone or something 1. to take an oath on someone or something. □ *My uncle is sort of old-fashioned. He makes promises by swearing by his "sainted mother."* □ *He sometimes swears by his foot!* **2.** to have complete faith and confidence in someone or something. □ *I'm willing to swear by John. He's completely dependable.* □ *This is an excellent brand of detergent. My sister swears by it.*

sweat blood to be very anxious and tense. (Slang.) □ *What a terrible test! I was really sweating blood at the last.* □ *Bob is such a bad driver. I sweat blood every time I ride with him.*

sweat something out to endure or wait for something that causes tension or boredom. (Informal.) □ *I had to wait for her in the reception area. It was a long wait, but I managed to sweat it out.* T *I took the test and then spent a week sweating out the results.*

sweep one off one's feet AND **knock one off one's feet 1.** to knock someone down. □ *The wind swept me off my feet.* □ *Bill punched Bob playfully, and*

knocked him off his feet. **2.** to overwhelm someone (figuratively). (Informal.) □ *Mary is madly in love with Bill. He swept her off her feet.* □ *The news was so exciting that it knocked me off my feet.*

sweep something under the carpet AND **sweep something under the rug** to try to hide something unpleasant, shameful, etc., from the attention of others. □ *The boss said he couldn't sweep the theft under the carpet, that he'd have to call in the police.* □ *Roger had a tendency to sweep all the problems under the rug.*

sweep something under the rug See the previous entry.

sweet and low pleasing and quiet. (Referring to music. Fixed order.) □ *Play me something that is sweet and low.* □ *I like dance music that is sweet and low — not any of this rowdy, violent stuff.*

sweet and sour a combination of fruity sweet and sour, but not necessarily salty, flavors. (Typically referring to certain Chinese-American foods. Fixed order.) □ *I prefer sweet and sour pork to anything else on the menu.* □ *Alice does not care for sweet and sour dishes, but she will usually eat whatever we serve her.*

sweet nothings affectionate but unimportant or meaningless words spoken to a loved one. □ *Jack was whispering sweet nothings in Joan's ear when they were dancing.* □ *The two lovers sat in the cinema exchanging sweet nothings.*

sweet on someone fond of someone. (Folksy.) □ *Tom is sweet on Mary. He may ask her to marry him.* □ *Mary's sweet on him, too.*

sweet-talk someone to talk convincingly to someone with much flattery. (Folksy.) □ *I didn't want to help her, but she sweet-talked me into it.* □ *He sweet-talked her for a while, and she finally agreed to go to the dance with him.*

swift and sure fast and certain. (As with the flight of a well-aimed arrow. Fixed order.) □ *The response of the* *governor to the criticism by the opposing party was swift and sure.* □ *The boxer's punch was swift and sure and resulted in a quick knockout and a very short match.*

swim against the current See the following entry.

swim against the tide AND **swim against the current** to do the opposite of everyone else; to go against the trend.

□ *Bob tends to do what everybody else does. He isn't likely to swim against the tide.* □ *Mary always swims against the current. She's a very contrary person.*

swing into action See *go into action.*

swing something to make something happen. (Slang.) □ *I hope I can swing a deal that will make us all a lot of money.* □ *We all hope you can swing it.*

T

tail wagging the dog a situation where a small part is controlling the whole thing. □ *John was just hired yesterday, and today he's bossing everyone around. It's a case of the tail wagging the dog.* □ *Why is this small matter so important? Now the tail is wagging the dog!*

take a backseat (to someone) to defer to someone; to give control to someone. □ *I decided to take a backseat to Mary and let her manage the project.* □ *I had done the best I could, but it was time to take a backseat and let someone else run things.*

take a bath (on something) to have large financial losses on an investment. (Slang.) □ *I took a bath on all my oil stock. I should have sold it sooner.* □ *I don't mind losing a little money now and then, but I really took a bath this time.*

take a bow to bow and receive credit for a good performance. □ *At the end of the concerto, the pianist rose and took a bow.* □ *The audience applauded wildly and demanded that the conductor come out and take a bow again.*

take a break AND **take one's break** to have a short rest period in one's work. □ *It's ten o'clock—time to take a break.* □ *I don't usually take my break until 10:30.*

take a chance AND **take a risk** to try something where failure or bad fortune is likely. □ *Come on, take a chance. You may lose, but it's worth trying.* □ *I'm not reckless, but I don't mind taking a risk now and then.*

take a crack at something to *have a try at something;* to give something a try. (Informal.) □ *I don't think I can convince her to leave, but I'll take a crack at it.* □ *Someone had to try to rescue the child. Bill said he'd take a crack at it.*

take a dig at someone AND **take digs at someone** to insult someone; to say something that will irritate a person. (Slang.) □ *Jane took a dig at Bob for being late all the time.* □ *Jane is always taking digs at Bob, but she never really means any harm.*

take a dim view of something to regard something skeptically or pessimistically. □ *My aunt takes a dim view of most things that young people do.* □ *The manager took a dim view of my efforts on the project. I guess I didn't try hard enough.*

take a fancy to someone or something AND **take a liking to someone or something; take a shine to someone or something** to develop a fondness or a preference for someone or something. (Folksy.) □ *John began to take a fancy to Sally late last August at the picnic.* □ *I've never taken a liking to cooked carrots.* □ *I think my teacher has taken a shine to me.*

take a gander (at someone or something) to examine someone or something; to *take a look (at someone or something).* (Slang.) □ *Hey, will you take a gander at that fancy car!* □ *Drive it over here so I can take a gander.*

take a hand in something to help plan or do something. □ *I was glad to take* *a hand in planning the picnic.* □ *Jane refused to take a hand in any of the work.*

take a hard line (with someone) to be firm with someone; to have a firm policy for dealing with someone. □ *The manager takes a hard line with people who show up late.* □ *This is a serious matter. The police are likely to take a hard line.*

take a hike See *take a walk.*

take a hint to understand a hint and behave accordingly. □ *I said I didn't want to see you anymore. Can't you take a hint? I don't like you.* □ *Sure I can take a hint, but I'd rather be told directly.*

take a leaf out of someone's book to behave or to do something in the way that someone else would. □ *When you act like that, you're taking a leaf out of your sister's book, and I don't like it!* □ *You had better do it your way. Don't take a leaf out of my book. I don't do it well.*

take a licking See *get a licking.*

take a liking to someone or something See *take a fancy to someone or something.*

take a load off one's feet See *get a load off one's feet.*

take a look (at someone or something) to examine (briefly) someone or something. (Also with *have,* as in the examples.) □ *I asked the doctor to take a look at my ankle that has been hurting.* □ *"So your ankle's hurting,"* said the doctor. *"Let's take a look."* □ *Please have a look at my car. It's not running well.*

take a new turn [for something] to begin a new course or direction. □ *When I received the telegram with the exciting news, my life took a new turn.* □ *I began taking the medicine at noon, and by evening the disease had begun to take a new turn. I was getting better!*

take a nosedive See *go into a nosedive.*

take a powder to leave (a place); to sneak out or run out (of a place).

(Slang.) □ *When the police came to the door, Tom decided it was time to take a powder. He left by the back door.* □ *When the party got a little dull, Bill and his friend took a powder.*

take a punch at someone to strike or strike at someone. (Informal.) □ *Mary got so angry at Bob that she took a punch at him.* □ *She took a punch at him, but she missed.*

take a rain check (on something) See *get a rain check (on something).*

take a risk See *take a chance.*

take a shellacking See *get a shellacking.*

take a shine to someone or something See *take a fancy to someone or something.*

take a shot at something See *take a try at something.*

take a spill to have a fall; to tip over. (Also with *bad, nasty, quite,* etc. Also with *have.*) □ *Ann tripped on the curb and took a nasty spill.* □ *John had quite a spill when he fell off his bicycle.*

take a stab at something See *take a try at something.*

take a stand (against someone or something) to take a position in opposition to someone or something; to oppose or resist someone or something. □ *The treasurer was forced to take a stand against the board because of its wasteful spending.* □ *The treasurer took a stand, and others agreed.*

take a try at something AND **take a shot at something; take a stab at something; take a whack at something** to give something a try. (The expression with *shot* is informal. Also with *have;* see the variants at *have a try at something.* The second, third, and fourth entries are also literal.) □ *I don't know if I can eat a whole pizza, but I'll be happy to take a shot at it.* □ *I can't seem to get this computer to work right. Would you like to take a try at it?* □ *Sure. Take a stab at it.* □ *I don't know if I can do it or not, but I'll take a whack at it.*

take a turn for the better to start to improve; to start to get well. (The opposite of the following entry.) □ *She was very sick for a month; then suddenly she took a turn for the better.* □ *Things are taking a turn for the better at my store. I may make a profit this year.*

take a turn for the worse to start to get worse. (The opposite of the previous entry.) □ *It appeared that she was going to get well; then, unfortunately, she took a turn for the worse.* □ *My job was going quite well; then last week things took a turn for the worse.*

take a walk AND **take a hike** to leave somewhere. (Slang. Also literal.) □ *He was rude to me, so I just took a walk and left him standing there.* □ *He was getting on my nerves, so I told him to take a hike.*

take a whack at someone or something (Slang. *Whack* is sometimes spelled *wack.* Also with *have,* as in the examples.) **1.** [with *someone*] to hit at someone; to hit someone. □ *He took a whack at me, so I punched him.* □ *Don't try to take a whack at me again!* □ *I'll have a wack at you!* **2.** [with *something*] See *take a try at something.*

take advantage of someone or something 1. [with *someone*] to cheat or deceive someone. □ *The store owner took advantage of me, and I'm angry.* □ *You must be alert when you shop to make sure that someone doesn't take advantage of you.* **2.** to utilize someone or something to one's own benefit. □ *Jane can be of great help to me, and I intend to take advantage of her.* □ *Try to take advantage of every opportunity that comes your way.*

take after someone to resemble a close, older relative. □ *Don't you think that Sally takes after her mother?* □ *No, Sally takes after her Aunt Ann.*

take (a)hold of someone or something AND **get (a)hold of someone or something** to get in control of someone or something. (Also literal.) □ *Take hold of yourself! Calm down and relax.*

□ *She took a few minutes to get ahold of herself, and then she spoke.*

take aim (at someone or something) 1. to aim (something) at someone or something. □ *The hunter took aim at the deer and pulled the trigger.* □ *You must take aim carefully before you shoot.* **2.** to prepare to deal with someone or something. □ *Now we have to take aim at the problem and try to get it solved.* □ *He turned to me and took aim. I knew he was going to scold me severely.*

take an interest (in something) to develop an interest in something. □ *I wish John would take an interest in his schoolwork.* □ *We hoped you'd take an interest and join our club.*

take care of someone to beat or kill someone. (Slang, especially criminal slang. Also literal.) □ *The crook threatened to take care of the witness.* □ *"If you breathe a word of what you saw, my gang will take care of you," said the thief.*

take charge (of someone or something) to take (over) control of someone or something. □ *The president came in late and took charge of the meeting.* □ *When the new manager took charge, things really began to happen.*

take cold See *catch cold.*

take digs at someone See *take a dig at someone.*

take effect See *go into effect.*

take exception (to something) to disagree with something (that someone has said). □ *I take exception to your remarks, and I would like to discuss them with you.* □ *I'm sorry you take exception. Let's discuss the matter.*

take five to take a five-minute rest period. (Slang.) □ *Okay, everybody. Take five!* □ *Hey, Bob. I'm tired. Can we take five?*

take forty winks See *catch forty winks.*

take (great) pains (to do something) to make a great effort to do something. □ *Tom took pains to decorate the* room exactly right. □ We took pains to get there on time.

take heart to be brave; to have courage. □ *Take heart, John. Things could be worse!* □ *I told her to take heart and try again next time.*

take heed to be cautious. □ *Take heed, and don't get involved with the wrong kind of people.* □ *Just take heed, and you'll be safe.*

take ill See *take sick.*

take issue (with someone) to argue with someone; to dispute a point with someone. □ *I hate to take issue with you on such a minor point, but I'm quite sure you're wrong.* □ *I don't mind if you take issue, but I'm sure I'm right.*

take it away to start up a performance. (Slang. Typically a public announcement of the beginning of a musical performance. Also literal.) □ *And now, here is the band playing "Song of Songs." Take it away!* □ *Sally will now sing us a song. Take it away, Sally!*

Take it easy. Good-bye and take care of yourself. (Informal.) □ *Bye, Tom. Take it easy.* □ *Take it easy. I'll see you later.*

take it easy (on someone or something) **1.** to be gentle (with someone or something). (See also *go easy (on someone or something).*) □ *Take it easy on Mary. She's been sick.* □ *Please take it easy on the furniture. It has to last us many years.* □ *Take it easy! You will break the chair!* **2.** [with *something*] to use less of something (rather than more). (Informal.) □ *Take it easy on the soup. There's just enough for one serving for each person.* □ *Please take it easy! There are hardly any left.*

take it or leave it to accept something (the way it is) or forget it. (Informal. Fixed order.) □ *This is my last offer. Take it or leave it.* □ *It's not much, but it's the only food we have. You can take it or leave it.*

take it slow to move or go slowly. (Informal.) □ *The road is rough, so take it slow.* □ *This book is very hard to read, and I have to take it slow.*

take it upon oneself to do something See *make it one's business to do something.*

take kindly to something to be agreeable to something. □ *My father doesn't take kindly to anyone using his tools.* □ *I hope they'll take kindly to our request.*

take leave of one's senses to become irrational. (Often verbatim with *one's*.) □ *What are you doing? Have you taken leave of your senses?* □ *What a terrible situation! It's enough to make one take leave of one's senses.*

take liberties with someone or something AND **make free with someone or something** to use or abuse someone or something. □ *You are overly familiar with me, Mr. Jones. One might think you were taking liberties with me.* □ *I don't like it when you make free with my lawn mower. You should at least ask when you want to borrow it.*

take no stock in something AND **not take stock in something** to pay no attention to someone; not to believe or accept something. □ *I take no stock in anything John has to say.* □ *He doesn't take stock in your opinions either.*

take note (of something) to observe and remember something. □ *Please take note of the point I'm about to make.* □ *Here is something else of which you should take note.*

take notice (of something) to observe something. □ *I didn't take notice of when he came in.* □ *They say he came in late, but I didn't take notice.*

take off **1.** to leave the ground and begin to fly. (As with a bird or an airplane.) □ *When do we take off?* □ *The eagle took off and headed toward the mountains.* **2.** to become popular and successful. □ *Her book really took off after her television appearance.* □ *The idea took off, and soon everyone was talking about it.*

take off (after someone or something) AND **take out (after someone or some-**

thing) to begin to chase someone or something. □ *The bank guard took off after the robber.* □ *Did you see that police car take off?* □ *It took out after the bank robber's car.*

take off (from work) not to go to work (for a period of time). □ *I had to take off from work in order to renew my driver's license.* □ *I hate to take off for something like that.*

take off (on something) AND **launch forth (on something)** to start out a lecture on something; to begin a discussion of something. (See also *set forth (on something).*) □ *My father took off on the subject of taxes and talked for an hour.* □ *My uncle is always launching forth on the state of the economy.* □ *When he launches forth, I leave the room.*

take off one's hat (to someone) to offer praise for someone's good accomplishments. □ *I have to take off my hat to Mayor Johnson. She has done an excellent job.* □ *Yes, we all ought to take off our hats. She is our best mayor ever.*

take offense (at someone or something) to become resentful of someone or something. □ *Bill took offense at Mary for her thoughtless remarks.* □ *Almost everyone took offense at Bill's new book.* □ *I'm sorry you took offense. I meant no harm.*

take office to begin serving as an elected or appointed official. □ *When did the mayor take office?* □ *All the elected officials took office just after the election.*

take one at one's word to believe what someone says and act accordingly. □ *She told me to go jump in the lake, and I took her at her word.* □ *You shouldn't take her at her word. She frequently says things she doesn't really mean.*

take one's break See *take a break.*

take one's cue from someone to use someone else's behavior or reactions as a guide to one's own. (From the theatrical cue as a signal to speak, etc.) □ *If you don't know which*

spoons to use at the dinner, just take your cue from John.* □ *The other children took their cue from Tommy and ignored the new boy.*

take one's death of cold See *catch one's death (of cold).*

take (one's) leave (of someone) to say good-bye to someone and leave. □ *I took leave of the hostess at an early hour.* □ *One by one, the guests took their leave.*

take one's medicine to accept the punishment or the bad fortune that one deserves. (Informal. Also literal.) □ *I know I did wrong, and I know I have to take my medicine.* □ *Billy knew he was going to get spanked, and he didn't want to take his medicine.*

take one's own life to kill oneself; to commit suicide. □ *Bob tried to take his own life, but he was stopped in time.* □ *Later, he was sorry that he had tried to take his own life.*

take one's time to use as much time (to do something) as one wants. □ *There is no hurry. Please take your time.* □ *If you take your time, you'll be late.*

take out (after someone or something) See *take off (after someone or something).*

take part (in something) to participate in something. □ *They invited me to take part in their celebration.* □ *I was quite pleased to take part.*

take pity (on someone or something) to feel sorry for someone or something. □ *We took pity on the hungry people and gave them some warm food.* □ *She took pity on the little dog and brought it in to get warm.* □ *Please take pity! Please help us!*

take place to happen. □ *When will this party take place?* □ *It's taking place right now.*

take root to begin to take hold or have effect. (Also literal, referring to plants.) □ *Things will begin to change when my new policies take root.* □ *My ideas began to take root and influence other people.*

take sick AND **take ill** to become ill. (Folksy.) □ *I took sick with a bad cold last week.* □ *I hope I don't take ill before final exams.*

take sides to choose one side of an argument. □ *They were arguing, but I didn't want to take sides, so I left.* □ *I don't mind taking sides on important issues.*

take someone apart to beat someone up. (Slang.) □ *Don't talk to me that way, or I'll take you apart.* T *He was so mad that I thought he was going to take apart all of us.*

take someone down a notch (or two) See the following entry.

take someone down a peg (or two) AND **take someone down a notch (or two)** to reprimand someone who is acting too arrogant. □ *The teacher's scolding took Bob down a notch or two.* □ *He was so rude that someone was bound to take him down a peg or two.*

take someone down (to size) See *cut someone down (to size).*

take someone for a fool See *take someone for an idiot.*

take someone for a ride to trick or deceive someone. (Informal.) □ *Old people are being taken for a ride by bogus workmen.* □ *Whoever sold Tom that car took him for a ride. It needs a new engine.*

take someone for an idiot AND **take someone for a fool** to assume that someone is stupid. □ *I wouldn't do anything like that! Do you take me for an idiot?* □ *I don't take you for a fool. I think you're very clever.*

take someone for someone or something to mistake someone for someone or something. □ *I took Bill for his brother, Bob. They look so much alike!* □ *I took Mr. Brown for the gardener, and he was a little bit insulted.*

take someone in See *suck someone in.*

take someone into one's confidence to trust someone with confidential information; to tell a secret to someone and trust the person to keep the secret. □ *We are good friends, but I didn't feel I could take her into my confidence.* □ *I know something very important about Jean. Can I take you into my confidence?*

take someone or something away to remove someone or something. □ *I don't want any more soup. Please take it away.* T *Take away Bill and John. They are bothering me.*

take someone or something by storm to overwhelm someone or something; to attract a great deal of attention from someone or something. □ *Jane is madly in love with Tom. He took her by storm at the office party, and they've been together ever since.* □ *The singer took the world of opera by storm with her performance in* La Boheme.

take someone or something by surprise to startle or surprise someone or something. □ *She came into the room and took them by surprise.* □ *I took the little bird by surprise, and it flew away.*

take someone or something for granted to accept someone or something — without gratitude — as a matter of course. □ *We tend to take a lot of things for granted.* □ *Mrs. Franklin complained that Mr. Franklin takes her for granted.*

take someone or something in 1. to observe someone or something. (See also *suck someone in.*) □ *The zoo is too big to take in the whole thing in one day.* T *It takes two days to take in the museum.* **2.** to provide shelter for someone or something. □ *When I needed a place to live, my uncle took me in.* T *Mrs. Wilson took in the lonely little dog and gave it a warm home.* **3.** [with *something*] to inhale, drink, or eat something. T *I think I'll go for a walk and take in some fresh air.* T *Jane was very ill, but she managed to take in a little broth.*

take someone or something into account to remember to consider someone or something. □ *I hope you'll take Bill and Bob into account when you plan the party.* T *I'll try to take into ac-*

count all the things that are important in a situation like this.

take someone or something on to undertake to deal with someone or something. □ *Mrs. Smith is such a problem. I don't feel like taking her on just now.* ⊤ *I'm too busy to take on any new problems.*

take someone or something out 1. [with *someone*] to take someone out on the town on a date. (Also literal.) □ *I hear that Tom has been taking Ann out.* ⊤ *No, Tom has been taking out Mary.* **2.** [with *someone*] to remove someone who is acting as a barrier, especially in football. (Informal.) □ *Okay, Bill. Get in there and take the quarterback out.* ⊤ *Our player ran fast and took out the player of the opposing team before he could tackle our runner.* **3.** [with *someone*] to kill someone. (Criminal slang.) □ *The thief who drove the car was afraid that the other thieves were going to take him out, too.* ⊤ *The crooks took out the witness to the crime.*

take someone or something over to take charge (of someone or something); to assume control of someone or something. □ *The new manager will take the office over next week.* ⊤ *Will you please take over your children? I can't seem to control them.*

take someone or something wrong to misunderstand someone or something. □ *Please don't take me wrong, but I believe that your socks don't match.* □ *You'll probably take this wrong, but I have to say that I've never seen you looking better.*

take someone to task to scold or reprimand someone. □ *The teacher took John to task for his bad behavior.* □ *I lost a big contract, and the boss took me to task in front of everyone.*

take someone to the cleaners to abuse or damage someone. (Slang.) □ *There was a real rough guy there who threatened to take me to the cleaners if I didn't cooperate.* □ *The crook said he'd take anybody who interfered to the cleaners.*

take someone under one's wing(s) to take over and care for a person. □ *John wasn't doing well in geometry until the teacher took him under her wing.* □ *I took the new workers under my wings, and they learned the job in no time.*

take someone up on something to take advantage of someone's offer of something. (Informal.) □ *I'd like to take you up on your offer to help.* ⊤ *We took up the Browns on their invitation to come to dinner.*

take someone's breath away 1. to cause someone to be out of breath due to a shock or hard exercise. □ *Walking this fast takes my breath away.* □ *Mary frightened me and took my breath away.* **2.** to overwhelm someone with beauty or grandeur. □ *The magnificent painting took my breath away.* □ *Ann looked so beautiful that she took my breath away.*

take something to endure something; to survive something. (Also literal.) □ *I don't think I can take any more scolding today. I've been in trouble since I got up this morning.* □ *Mary was very insulting to Tom, but he can take it.*

take something amiss AND **take something the wrong way** to understand something as wrong or insulting. (Compare with *take someone or something wrong.*) □ *Would you take it amiss if I told you I thought you look lovely?* □ *Why would anyone take such a nice compliment amiss?* □ *I was afraid you'd take it the wrong way.*

take something at face value to accept something exactly the way it appears to be. □ *I don't know whether I can take her story at face value, but I will assume that she is not lying.* □ *The committee took the report at face value and approved the suggested changes.*

take something back to withdraw or cancel one's statement. (Also literal.) □ *I heard what you said, and I'm very insulted. Please take it back.* ⊤ *Take back your words, or I'll never speak to you again!*

take something in stride to accept something as natural or expected. □

The argument surprised him, but he took it in stride. □ *It was a very rude remark, but Mary took it in stride.*

take something lying down to endure something unpleasant without fighting back. □ *He insulted me publicly. You don't expect me to take that lying down, do you?* □ *I'm not the kind of person who'll take something like that lying down.*

take something on faith to accept or believe something on the basis of little or no evidence. □ *Please try to believe what I'm telling you. Just take it on faith.* □ *Surely you can't expect me to take a story like that on faith.*

take something on the chin to experience and endure a direct (figurative or literal) blow or assault. □ *The bad news was a real shock, but John took it on the chin.* □ *The worst luck comes my way, and I always end up taking it on the chin.*

take something out on someone or something to direct (or redirect) one's anger or fear onto someone or something. □ *I don't care if you're mad at your brother. Don't take it out on me!* □ *John took his anger out on the wall by kicking it.*

take something the wrong way See *take something amiss.*

take something to heart to take something very seriously. □ *John took the criticism to heart and made an honest effort to improve.* □ *I know Bob said a lot of cruel things to you, but he was angry. You shouldn't take those things to heart.*

take something up 1. to begin to deal with an issue. (See also the following entry.) □ *That's too big a job for today. I'll take it up tomorrow.* T *Now we'll take up the task of the election of officers.* **2.** to make the bottom of a skirt or pants cuffs higher off the floor. □ *I'll have to take this skirt up. It's too long for me.* T *Please take up my pants cuffs. They are an inch too long.*

take something up (with someone) to raise and discuss a matter with someone. □ *This is a very complicated problem. I'll have to take it up with the office manager.* T *She'll take up this problem with the owner in the morning.*

take something (up)on oneself to make something one's responsibility. □ *I took it upon myself to order more pencils since we were running out of them.* □ *I'm glad that you took it on yourself to do that.*

take something with a grain of salt See the following entry.

take something with a pinch of salt AND **take something with a grain of salt** to listen to a story or an explanation with considerable doubt. □ *You must take anything she says with a grain of salt. She doesn't always tell the truth.* □ *They took my explanation with a pinch of salt. I was sure they didn't believe me.*

take steps (to prevent something) to do what is necessary to prevent something. □ *I took steps to prevent John from learning what we were talking about.* □ *I have to keep John from knowing what I've been doing. I can prevent it if I take steps.*

take stock (of something) to make an appraisal of resources and potentialities. □ *I spent some time yesterday taking stock of my good and bad qualities.* □ *We all need to take stock now and then.*

take the bit between the teeth See the following entry.

take the bit in one's teeth AND **take the bit between the teeth** to put oneself in charge. □ *Someone needed to direct the project, so I took the bit in my teeth.* □ *If you want to get something done, you've got to take the bit between your teeth and get to work.*

take the bitter with the sweet to accept the bad things along with the good things. □ *We all have disappointments. You have to learn to take the bitter with the sweet.* □ *There are good days and bad days, but every day you take the bitter with the sweet. That's life.*

take the bull by the horns AND **seize the bull by the horns** to meet a challenge directly. □ *If we are going to solve this problem, someone is going to have to take the bull by the horns.* □ *This threat isn't going to go away by itself. We are going to seize the bull by the horns and settle this matter once and for all.*

take the cake to win the prize; to be the best or the worse. (Folksy.) □ *Look at those fireworks. If they don't take the cake, I don't know what does.* □ *Well, Jane, this dinner really takes the cake! It's delicious.* □ *Tom really messed it up. What he did really takes the cake.*

take the day off to choose not to go to work for one day. (Compare with *get the day off.*) □ *The sun was shining, and it was warm, so I took the day off and went fishing.* □ *Jane wasn't feeling well, so she took the day off.*

take the edge off (something) to remove the essence, power, or "bite" of something. □ *I had to tell her some very sad things, so I spoke slowly and softly to take the edge off the news.* □ *I put sugar in my coffee to take the edge off.*

take the initiative (to do something) to activate oneself to do something even if one has not been asked to do it. (See also *make it one's business to do something.*) □ *The door hinges squeak because no one will take the initiative to oil them.* □ *Sometimes, in order to get things done, you have to take the initiative.*

take the law into one's own hands to attempt to administer the law; to act as a judge and jury for someone who has done something wrong. □ *Citizens don't have the right to take the law into their own hands.* □ *The shopkeeper took the law into his own hands when he tried to arrest the thief.*

take the liberty of doing something to assume the right to do something. □ *Since I knew you were arriving late, I took the liberty of securing a hotel room for you.* □ *May I take the liberty of addressing you by your first name?*

take the lid off something to begin to deal with a problem. (Informal. Also literal.) □ *Now that you've taken the lid off that problem, we'll have to deal with it.* □ *I have this matter settled for now. Please don't take the lid off it again.*

take the rap (for someone or something) (Slang, especially criminal slang.) **1.** [with *someone*] to take the blame (for something) for someone else. □ *I don't want to take the rap for you.* □ *John robbed the bank, but Tom took the rap for him.* **2.** [with *something*] to take the blame for (doing) something. □ *I won't take the rap for the crime. I wasn't even in town.* □ *Who'll take the rap for it? Who did it?*

take the stand to go to and sit in the witness chair in a courtroom. □ *I was in court all day, waiting to take the stand.* □ *The lawyer asked the witness to take the stand.*

take the starch out of someone (Informal.) **1.** to make someone less arrogant or stiff. □ *I told a joke that made Mr. Jones laugh very hard. It really took the starch out of him.* □ *John is so arrogant. I'd really like to take the starch out of him!* **2.** to make someone tired and weak. □ *This hot weather really takes the starch out of me.* □ *What a long day! It sure took the starch out of me.*

take the trouble (to do something) to make an effort to do something (that one might not otherwise do). □ *I wish I had taken the trouble to study this matter more carefully.* □ *I just didn't have enough time to take the trouble.*

take the wind out of someone's sails to challenge someone's boasting or arrogance. (Informal.) □ *John was bragging about how much money he earned until he learned that most of us make more. That took the wind out of his sails.* □ *Learning that one has been totally wrong about something can really take the wind out of one's sails.*

take the words out of one's mouth [for someone else] to say what you were going to say. (Informal. Also with *right,* as in the example.) □ *John said exactly what I was going to say. He took the words out of my mouth.* □ *I agree with you, and I wanted to say the same thing. You took the words right out of my mouth.*

take time off not to work for a period of time—a few minutes or a longer period. (Compare with *get time off.*) □ *I had to take time off to go to the dentist.* □ *Mary took time off to have a cup of coffee.*

take to one's heels to run away. □ *The little boy said hello and then took to his heels.* □ *The man took to his heels to try to get to the bus stop before the bus left.*

take to someone or something to become fond of or attracted to someone or something. (Informal.) □ *Mary didn't take to her new job, and she quit after two weeks.* □ *Mary seemed to take to John right away.*

take too much on to undertake to do too much work or too many tasks. □ *Don't take too much on, or you won't be able to do any of it well.* Ⓣ *Ann tends to take on too much and get exhausted.*

take turns ((at) doing something) to do something, one (person) at a time (rather than everyone all at once). □ *Please take turns at reading the book.* □ *Everyone is taking turns looking at the picture.* □ *It's more orderly when everyone takes turns.*

take up a collection to collect money for a specific project. □ *We wanted to send Bill some flowers, so we took up a collection.* □ *The office staff took up a collection to pay for the office party.*

take up arms (against someone or something) to prepare to fight against someone or something. □ *Everyone in the town took up arms against the enemy.* □ *They were all so angry that the leader convinced them to take up arms.*

take up one's abode somewhere to settle down and live somewhere. (Formal.) □ *I took up my abode downtown*

near my office. □ *We decided to take up our abode in a warmer climate.*

take up room See *take up space.*

take up someone's time to require too much of someone else's time; to waste someone's time. (Also with *so much of* or *too much of,* as in the examples.) □ *You're taking up my time. Please go away.* □ *I'm sorry. I didn't mean to take up so much of your time.* □ *This problem is taking up too much of my time.*

take up space AND **take up room** to fill or occupy space. (Note the variations in the examples.) □ *The piano is taking up too much room in our living room.* □ *John, you're not being any help at all. You're just taking up space.*

take up time to require or fill time. (Note the variations in the examples. Also without *up.*) □ *This project is taking up too much time.* □ *This kind of thing always takes up time.*

take up where one left off to start up again in the very place that one left off. □ *I had to leave the room for a minute, but when I got back, I took up where I left off.* □ *It's time to stop for lunch. After lunch, we will take up where we left off.*

take up with someone to become a friend or companion to someone. □ *Billy's mother was afraid that he was taking up with the wrong kind of people.* □ *John and Bob took up with each other and became close friends.*

taken aback surprised and confused. □ *When Mary told me the news, I was taken aback for a moment.* □ *When I told my parents I was married, they were completely taken aback.*

taken for dead appearing to be dead; assumed to be dead. □ *I was so ill with the flu that I was almost taken for dead.* □ *The accident victims were so seriously injured that they were taken for dead at first.*

talk a blue streak to talk very much and very rapidly. (Informal.) □ *Billy didn't talk until he was six, and then he started talking a blue streak.* □ *I can't* *understand anything Bob says. He talks a blue streak, and I can't follow his thinking.*

talk back (to someone) to respond (to a rebuke) rudely or impertinently. □ *John got in trouble for talking back to the teacher.* □ *A student never gains anything by talking back.*

talk big to brag or boast; to talk in an intimidating manner. (Slang.) □ *John is always talking big, but he hasn't really accomplished a lot in life.* □ *She talks big, but she's harmless.*

talk down to someone to speak to someone in a patronizing manner; to speak to someone in the simplest way. □ *The manager insulted everyone in the office by talking down to them.* □ *Please don't talk down to me. I can understand almost anything you have to say.*

talk in circles to talk in a confusing or roundabout manner. □ *I couldn't understand a thing he said. All he did was talk in circles.* □ *We argued for a long time and finally decided that we were talking in circles.*

talk of the town the subject of gossip; someone or something that everyone is talking about. □ *Joan's argument with city hall is the talk of the town.* □ *Fred's father is the talk of the town since the police arrested him.*

talk oneself out to talk until one can talk no more. □ *After nearly an hour, he had talked himself out. Then we began to ask questions.* □ *I talked myself out in the meeting, but no one would support my position.*

talk shop to talk about business matters at a social event (where business talk is out of place). (Informal.) □ *All right, everyone, we're not here to talk shop. Let's have a good time.* □ *Mary and Jane stood by the punch bowl, talking shop.*

talk someone down 1. to win out over someone in an argument; to convince someone by arguing. □ *She loves to argue. She takes pleasure in talking someone down.* □ *She tried to talk me down, but I held my ground.* **2.** to convince someone to lower the price. □ *She wanted $2,000 for the car, but I talked her down.* □ *This is my final offer. Don't try to talk me down.*

talk someone into (doing) something to overcome someone's objections to doing something; to convince someone to do something. □ *They talked me into going to the meeting, even though I didn't really have the time.* □ *No one can talk me into doing something illegal.*

talk someone or something up to promote or speak in support of someone or something. (Informal.) □ *I've been talking up the party all day, trying to get people to come.* □ *The mayor is running for reelection, and everyone at city hall is talking her up.*

talk someone out of (doing) something to convince someone not to do something. □ *I tried to talk her out of going, but she insisted.* □ *Don't try to talk me out of quitting school. My mind is made up.*

talk someone out of something to convince someone to give something up. □ *This is my candy, and you can't talk me out of it.* □ *I tried to talk her out of her property, but she didn't want to sell.*

talk someone's ear off See under *talk someone's head off.*

talk someone's head off (Slang.) **1.** [for someone] to speak too much. □ *Why does John always talk his head off? Doesn't he know he bores people?* □ *She talks her head off and doesn't seem to know what she's saying.* **2.** AND **talk someone's ear off** to talk to and bore someone. □ *John is very friendly, but watch out or he'll talk your head off.* □ *My uncle always talked my ear off whenever I went to visit him.*

talk something out to talk about all aspects of a problem or disagreement. □ *Ann and Sally had a problem, so they agreed to talk it out.* Ⓣ *It's better to talk out a disagreement than to stay mad.*

talk something over to discuss something. □ *Come into my office so we can talk this over.* ⊤ *We talked over the plans for nearly an hour.*

talk through one's hat to talk nonsense; to brag and boast. (Informal.) □ *John isn't really as good as he says. He's just talking through his hat.* □ *Stop talking through your hat and start being sincere!*

talk turkey to talk business; to talk frankly. (Slang.) □ *Okay, Bob, we have business to discuss. Let's talk turkey.* □ *John wanted to talk turkey, but Jane just wanted to joke around.*

talk until one is blue in the face to talk until one is exhausted. (Informal.) □ *I talked until I was blue in the face, but I couldn't change her mind.* □ *She had to talk until she was blue in the face in order to convince him.*

talked out tired of talking; unable to talk more. (Folksy. See also *talk oneself out*.) □ *I can't go on. I'm all talked out.* □ *She was talked out in the first hour of discussion.*

tamper with something to attempt to alter or change something; to meddle with or damage something. □ *Someone has tampered with my door lock.* □ *Please don't tamper with my stereo.*

tan someone's hide to spank someone. (Folksy.) □ *Billy's mother said she'd tan Billy's hide if he ever did that again.* □ *"I'll tan your hide if you're late!" said Tom's father.*

taper off (doing something) to stop doing something gradually. □ *My doctor told me to taper off smoking cigarettes.* □ *I have to taper off because I can't stop all at once.*

tar and feather someone to chastise someone severely. (Also literal. Fixed order.) □ *They threatened to tar and feather me if I ever came back into their town.* □ *I don't believe that they'd really tar and feather me, but they could be very unpleasant.*

tarred with the same brush sharing the same characteristic(s); having the same good or bad points as someone else. □ *Jack and his brother are tarred with the same brush. They're both crooks.* □ *The Smith children are tarred with the same brush. They're all lazy.*

tax-and-spend spending freely and taxing heavily. (Referring to a legislative body that repeatedly passes expensive new laws and keeps raising taxes to pay for the cost. Fixed order.) □ *I hope that people do not elect another tax-and-spend Congress this time.* □ *The only thing worse than a tax-and-spend legislature is one that spends and runs up a worsening deficit.*

tea and crumpets a fancy or fussy meeting or reception where refreshments, especially sweet and insubstantial refreshments are served. (Also literal, referring to a genteel appointment where tea and some light pastries are served. Fixed order.) □ *I don't have time to spend the afternoon having tea and crumpets with the office staff. I have work to do!* □ *Almost every one of my Sunday afternoons is taken up with tea and crumpets for this cause and tea and crumpets for that cause! My rest and relaxation is the only cause I am interested in this Sunday!*

teach someone a lesson to get even with someone for bad behavior. (Also literal.) □ *John tripped me, so I punched him. That ought to teach him a lesson.* □ *That taught me a lesson. I won't do it again.*

team up with someone to join with someone. □ *I teamed up with Jane to write the report.* □ *I had never teamed up with anyone else before. I had always worked alone.*

tear into someone or something 1. [with *someone*] to criticize and scold someone. □ *Tom tore into John and yelled at him for an hour.* □ *Don't tear into me like that. You have no right to speak to me that way.* 2. to attack or fight with someone or something. □ *The boxer tore into his opponent.* □ *The lion tore into the herd of zebras.*

tear off to leave or depart in a great hurry. (Informal.) □ *Well, excuse me. I have to tear off.* □ *Bob tore off down the street, chasing the fire engine.*

tear one's hair (out) to be anxious, frustrated, or angry. (Not literal.) □ *I was so nervous, I was about to tear my hair.* □ *I had better get home. My parents will be tearing their hair out.*

tear someone or something down 1. to criticize or degrade someone or something. □ *Tom is always tearing Jane down. I guess he doesn't like her.* Ⓣ *It's not nice to tear down the people who work in your office.* □ *Why are you always tearing my projects down?* **2.** [with *something*] to dismantle or destroy something. □ *They plan to tear the old building down and build a new one there.* Ⓣ *They'll tear down the building in about two weeks.*

tear someone up to cause someone much grief. (Slang. Also literal.) □ *The news of Tom's death really tore Bill up.* Ⓣ *Bad news tears up some people. Other people can take it calmly.*

tee someone off to make someone angry. (Slang.) □ *That kind of talk really tees me off!* □ *Don't let him tee you off. He doesn't mean any harm.*

tell it to the marines I do not believe you (maybe the marines will). (Informal.) □ *That's silly. Tell it to the marines.* □ *I don't care how good you think your reason is. Tell it to the marines!*

tell its own story AND **tell its own tale** [for the state of something] to indicate clearly what has happened. □ *The upturned boat told its own tale. The fisherman had drowned.* □ *The girl's tear-stained face told its own story.*

tell its own tale See the previous entry.

tell on someone to report someone's bad behavior; to tattle on someone. □ *If you do that again, I'll tell on you!* □ *Please don't tell on me. I'm in enough trouble as it is.*

tell one to one's face to tell (something) to someone directly. □ *I'm sorry that Sally feels that way about me. I wish she had told me to my face.* □ *I won't tell Tom that you're mad at him. You should tell him to his face.*

tell people apart to distinguish one person or a group of people from another person or group of people. □ *Tom and John are brothers, and you can hardly tell them apart.* □ *Our team is wearing red, and the other team is wearing orange. I can't tell them apart.*

tell someone a thing or two AND **tell someone where to get off** to scold someone; to express one's anger to someone; to *tell someone off.* (Informal.) □ *Wait till I see Sally. I'll tell her a thing or two!* □ *She told me where to get off and then started in scolding Tom.*

tell someone off to scold someone; to attack someone verbally. (This has a sense of finality about it.) □ *I was so mad at Bob that I told him off.* Ⓣ *By the end of the day, I had told off everyone else, too.*

tell someone where to get off See *tell someone a thing or two.*

tell tales out of school to tell secrets or spread rumors. □ *I wish that John would keep quiet. He's telling tales out of school again.* □ *If you tell tales out of school a lot, people won't know when to believe you.*

tell things apart to distinguish one thing or a group of things from another thing or group of things. □ *This one is gold, and the others are brass. Can you tell them apart?* □ *Without their labels, I can't tell them apart.*

tell time 1. to keep or report the correct time. □ *This clock doesn't tell time very accurately.* □ *My watch stopped telling time, so I had to have it repaired.* **2.** to be able to read time from a clock or watch. □ *Billy is only four. He can't tell time yet.* □ *They are teaching the children to tell time at school.*

tell which is which See *know which is which.*

tempest in a teapot an uproar about practically nothing. □ *This isn't a serious problem—just a tempest in a teapot.* □ *Even a tempest in a teapot can take a lot of time to get settled.*

thank one's lucky stars to be thankful for one's luck. □ *You can thank your lucky stars that I was there to help you.* □ *I thank my lucky stars that I studied the right things for the test.*

thanks to someone or something due to someone or something; because of someone or something. (This does not refer to gratitude.) □ *Thanks to the storm, we have no electricity.* □ *Thanks to Mary, we have tickets to the game. She bought them early before they were sold out.*

That ain't hay. That is not a small amount of money. (Folksy.) □ *I paid forty dollars for it, and that ain't hay!* □ *Bob lost his wallet with $200 in it—and that ain't hay.*

That makes two of us. The same is true for me. □ *So you're going to the football game? That makes two of us.* □ BILL: *I just passed my biology test.* BOB: *That makes two of us!*

That takes care of that. That is settled. □ *That takes care of that, and I'm glad it's over.* □ *I spent all morning dealing with this matter, and that takes care of that.*

That'll be the day. I don't believe that the day will ever come (when something will happen). □ *Do you really think that John will pass geometry? That'll be the day.* □ *John graduate? That'll be the day!*

That's about the size of it. It is final and correct. (Slang.) □ MARY: *Do you mean that you aren't going?* TOM: *That's about the size of it.* □ *At the end of his speech Bob said, "That's about the size of it."*

That's all for someone. Someone will get no more chances to do things correctly. □ *That's all for you, Tom. I've had all I can take from you. One disappointment after another.* □ *You've*

gone too far, Mary. That's all for you. Good-bye!

That's all she wrote. That is all. (Slang.) □ *At the end of his informal talk, Tom said, "That's all she wrote."* □ *Sally looked at the empty catsup bottle and said, "That's all she wrote."*

That's that. It is permanently settled and need not be dealt with again. □ *I said no, and that's that.* □ *You can't come back. I told you to leave, and that's that.*

That's the last straw. AND **That's the straw that broke the camel's back.** the final thing; the last little burden or problem that causes everything to collapse. (From the image of a camel being loaded down with much weight, one straw at a time. Finally, at some point, when one is adding straw after straw, one straw will finally be too much and the camel's back will break.) □ *When Sally came down sick, that was the straw that broke the camel's back.* □ *When she showed up late, that was the straw that broke the camel's back.* □ *Your last word was the straw that broke the camel's back. Why did you have to say that?*

That's the straw that broke the camel's back. See the previous entry.

That's the ticket. That is exactly what is needed. □ *That's the ticket, John. You're doing it just the way it should be done.* □ *That's the ticket! I knew you could do it.*

That's the way the ball bounces. AND **That's the way the cookie crumbles.** That is too bad.; Those things happen. (Slang.) □ *Sorry to hear about your problems. That's the way the ball bounces.* □ *John wrecked his car and then lost his job. That's the way the cookie crumbles.*

That's the way the cookie crumbles. See the previous entry.

(the) be-all and (the) end-all something that is the very best or most important; something so good that it will end the search for something better.

☐ *Finishing the building of his boat became the be-all and end-all of Roger's existence.* ☐ *Sally is the be-all and the end-all of Don's life.*

the bottom line (Slang.) **1.** the last figure on a financial balance sheet. ☐ *What's the bottom line? How much do I owe you?* ☐ *Don't tell me all those figures! Just tell me the bottom line.* **2.** the result; the final outcome. ☐ *I know about all the problems, but what is the bottom line? What will happen?* ☐ *The bottom line is that you have to go to the meeting because no one else can.*

the cards are stacked against one luck is against one. (Informal. See also *have the cards stacked against one; stack the cards (against someone or something).*) ☐ *I have the worst luck. The cards are stacked against me all the time.* ☐ *How can I accomplish anything when the cards are stacked against me?*

The coast is clear. There is no visible danger. ☐ *I'm going to stay hidden here until the coast is clear.* ☐ *You can come out of your hiding place now. The coast is clear.*

the daily grind [someone's] everyday work routine. (Informal.) ☐ *I'm getting very tired of the daily grind.* ☐ *When my vacation was over, I had to go back to the daily grind.*

the devil's own job See *devil of a job.*

The early bird gets the worm. a proverb meaning that the early person will get the reward. ☐ *Don't be late again! Don't you know that the early bird gets the worm?* ☐ *I'll be there before the sun is up. After all, the early bird gets the worm.*

The game is up. AND **The jig is up.** The deception is over.; The illegal activity has come to an end. ☐ *When the police were waiting for them inside the bank vault, the would-be robbers knew that the game was up.* ☐ *"The jig is up!" said the cop as he grabbed the shoulder of the pickpocket.*

the here and now the present, as opposed to the past or the future. ☐ *I don't care what's happening tomorrow or next week! I care about the here and now.* ☐ *The past is dead. Let's worry about the here and now.*

The honeymoon is over. The early pleasant beginning has ended. ☐ *Okay, the honeymoon is over. It's time to settle down and do some hard work.* ☐ *I knew the honeymoon was over when they started yelling at me to work faster.*

the in thing (to do) the fashionable thing to do. ☐ *Eating low-fat food is the in thing to do.* ☐ *Bob is very old-fashioned. He never does the in thing.*

The jig is up. See *The game is up.*

The jury is still out (on someone or something). a decision has not been reached on someone or something; the people making the decision on someone or something have not yet decided. (Also literal.) ☐ *The jury is still out on Jane. We don't know what we are going to do about her.* ☐ *The jury is still out on the question of building a new parking lot.*

the likes of someone someone; anyone like someone. (Informal. Almost always in a negative sense.) ☐ *I don't like Bob. I wouldn't do anything for the likes of him.* ☐ *Nobody wants the likes of him around.*

the more the merrier the more people there are, the happier they will be. ☐ *Of course you can have a ride with us! The more the merrier.* ☐ *The manager hired a new employee even though there's not enough work for all of us now. Oh, well, the more the merrier.*

the opposite sex (from the point of view of a female) males; (from the point of view of a male) females. (Also with *member of,* as in the example.) ☐ *Ann is crazy about the opposite sex.* ☐ *Bill is very shy when he's introduced to the opposite sex.* ☐ *Do members of the opposite sex make you nervous?*

the other side of the tracks the poorer section of town or the richer section of town, depending on perspective. (Usually refers to *the wrong side of the tracks*.) □ *He is from a wealthy family and I am from a very humble background, but he is the first boy I have met from the other side of the tracks, and I want to marry him.* □ *I hear he is dating someone from the other side of the tracks.*

the other way round the reverse; the opposite. □ *No, it won't fit that way. Try it the other way round.* □ *It doesn't make any sense like that. It belongs the other way round.*

The party's over. A happy or fortunate time has come to an end. (Informal.) □ *We go back to school tomorrow. The party's over.* □ *The staff hardly worked at all under the old management, but they'll find the party's over now.*

the pits the worst possible. (Slang.) □ *John is such a boring person. He's the pits.* □ *This restaurant isn't the best, but it's not the pits either.*

The plot thickens. Things are becoming more complicated or interesting. □ *The police assumed that the woman was murdered by her ex-husband, but he has an alibi. The plot thickens.* □ *John is supposed to be going out with Mary, but I saw him last night with Sally. The plot thickens.*

the point of no return the halfway point; the point at which it is too late to turn back. (Often with *past*.) □ *The flight was past the point of no return, so we had to continue to our destination.* □ *The entire project is past the point of no return; we will have to continue with it.*

the pot calling the kettle black [an instance of] someone with a fault accusing someone else of having the same fault. □ *Ann is always late, but she was rude enough to tell everyone when I was late. Now that's the pot calling the kettle black!* □ *You're calling me thoughtless? That's really a case of the pot calling the kettle black.*

the same to you the same comment applies to you. (Informal. This can be a polite or a rude comment.) □ BILL: *Have a pleasant evening.* BOB: *Thank you. The same to you.* □ MARY: *You're the most horrible person I've ever met!* JOHN: *The same to you!*

The shoe is on the other foot. a proverb meaning that one is experiencing the same things that one caused another person to experience. (Note the variations in the examples. See also *have the shoe on the other foot*.) □ *The teacher is taking a course in summer school and is finding out what it's like when the shoe is on the other foot.* □ *When the policeman was arrested, he learned what it was like to have the shoe on the other foot.*

The sky's the limit. There is no limit to the success that can be achieved or the money that can be gained or spent. □ *If you take a job with us, you'll find the promotion prospects very good. The sky's the limit, in fact.* □ *The insurance salesmen were told that the sky was the limit when it came to potential earnings.*

the upshot of something the result or outcome of something. □ *The upshot of my criticism was a change in policy.* □ *The upshot of the argument was an agreement to hire a new secretary.*

The worm (has) turned. Someone who is usually patient and humble has decided to stop being so. □ *Jane used to be treated badly by her husband and she just accepted it, but one day she hit him. The worm turned all right.* □ *Tom used to let the other boys bully him on the playground, but one day the worm turned and he's now leader of their gang.*

the wrong side of the tracks the poor part of a town. (Often with *come from, be from,* or *live on,* as in the examples. Compare with *the other side of the tracks*.) □ *They said that Bob was from the wrong side of the tracks, but that it didn't matter.* □ *We went to a school that was on the wrong side of the tracks, and we all got a fine education.*

Them's fighting words. Those are words that will start a fight. (Folksy. Note that *them is* is permissible in this expression.) □ *Better not talk like that around here. Them's fighting words.* □ *Them's fighting words, and you'd better be quiet unless you want trouble.*

then and there right then. (Fixed order.) □ *I asked him right then and there exactly what he meant.* □ *I decided to settle the matter then and there and not wait until Monday.*

There are plenty of other fish in the sea. There are other choices. (Used to refer to persons.) □ *When John broke up with Ann, I told her not to worry. There are plenty of other fish in the sea.* □ *It's too bad that your secretary quit, but there are plenty of other fish in the sea.*

there is no doing something one is not permitted to do something. (Informal.) □ *There is no arguing with Bill.* □ *There is no cigarette smoking here.*

There is trouble brewing. See *Trouble is brewing.*

There will be the devil to pay. There will be lots of trouble. (Informal. See *have the devil to pay.*) □ *If you damage my car, there will be the devil to pay.* □ *Bill broke a window, and now there will be the devil to pay.*

There's more than one way to skin a cat. a proverb meaning that there is more than one way to do something. □ *If that way won't work, try another way. There's more than one way to skin a cat.* □ *Don't worry, I'll figure out a way to get it done. There's more than one way to skin a cat.*

There's no accounting for taste. a proverb meaning that there is no explanation for people's preferences. □ *Look at that purple and orange car! There's no accounting for taste.* □ *Some people seemed to like the music, although I thought it was worse than noise. There's no accounting for taste.*

thick and fast in large numbers or amounts and at a rapid rate. □ *The enemy soldiers came thick and fast.* □

New problems seem to come thick and fast.

thick as pea soup See *(as) thick as pea soup.*

thick as thieves See *(as) thick as thieves.*

thick-skinned not easily upset or hurt; insensitive. (The opposite of *thin-skinned.*) □ *Tom won't worry about your insults. He's completely thick-skinned.* □ *Jane's so thick-skinned she didn't realize Fred was being rude to her.*

thin on top balding. (Informal.) □ *James is wearing a hat because he's getting thin on top.* □ *Father got a little thin on top as he got older.*

thin-skinned easily upset or hurt; sensitive. (The opposite of *thick-skinned.*) □ *You'll have to handle Mary's mother carefully. She's very thin-skinned.* □ *Jane weeps easily when people tease her. She's too thin-skinned.*

Things are looking up. Conditions are looking better. □ *Since I got a salary increase, things are looking up.* □ *Things are looking up at school. I'm doing better in all my classes.*

think a great deal of someone or something See the following entry.

think a lot of someone or something AND **think a great deal of someone or something; think highly of someone or something; think much of someone or something** to think well of someone or something. (See also *speak highly of someone or something.*) □ *The teacher thinks a lot of Mary and her talents.* □ *No one really thinks a great deal of the new policies.* □ *I think highly of John.* □ *The manager doesn't think much of John and says so to everyone.*

think back (on someone or something) to remember and think about someone or something. □ *When I think back on Sally and the good times we had together, I get very sad.* □ *I like to think back on my childhood and try to remember what it was like.*

think better of something to reconsider something; to think again and decide not to do something. □ *Jack was going to escape, but he thought better of it.* □ *Jill had planned to resign, but thought better of it.*

think highly of someone or something See *think a lot of someone or something.*

think little of someone or something AND **think nothing of someone or something** to have a low opinion of someone or something. □ *Most experts think little of Jane's theory.* □ *People may think nothing of it now, but in a few years everyone will praise it.* □ *The critics thought little of her latest book.*

think much of someone or something See *think a lot of someone or something.*

think nothing of someone or something See *think little of someone or something.*

think on one's feet to think while one is talking. □ *If you want to be a successful teacher, you must be able to think on your feet.* □ *I have to write out everything I'm going to say, because I can't think on my feet too well.*

think out loud to say one's thoughts aloud. □ *Excuse me. I didn't really mean to say that. I was just thinking out loud.* □ *Mr. Johnson didn't prepare a speech. He just stood there and thought out loud. It was a terrible presentation.*

think someone or something fit for something to believe that someone or something is suitable for something. □ *I don't think John fit for the job.* □ *Do you think this car fit for a long trip?*

think something out to think through something; to prepare a plan or scheme. □ *This is an interesting problem. I'll have to take some time and think it out.* Ⓣ *We spent all morning thinking out our plan.*

think something over to consider something; to think about something (before giving a decision). □ *Please think it over and give me your decision in the morning.* Ⓣ *I need more time to think over your offer.*

think something up to contrive or invent something. □ *Don't worry. I'll find a way to do it. I can think something up in time to get it done.* Ⓣ *John thought up a way to solve our problem.*

think the world of someone or something to be very fond of someone or something. □ *Mary thinks the world of her little sister.* □ *The old lady thinks the world of her cats.*

think twice (before doing something) to consider carefully whether one should do something; to be cautious about doing something. □ *You should think twice before quitting your job.* □ *That's a serious decision, and you should certainly think twice.*

thither and yon there and everywhere. (Archaic. See also *hither, thither, and yon.* Fixed order.) □ *I sent my résumé thither and yon, but no one responded.* □ *The children are all scattered thither and yon, and it is difficult for them to get home for the holidays.*

thrash something out to discuss something thoroughly and solve any problems. □ *The committee took hours to thrash the whole matter out.* Ⓣ *Fred and Anne thrashed out the reasons for their constant disagreements.*

thrill someone to death See the following entry.

thrill someone to pieces AND **thrill someone to death** to please or excite someone very much. (Informal. Not literal.) □ *John sent flowers to Ann and thrilled her to pieces.* □ *Your wonderful comments thrilled me to death.*

thrilled to death AND **thrilled to pieces** very excited; very pleased. □ *She was thrilled to death to get the flowers.* □ *I'm just thrilled to pieces to have you visit me.*

thrilled to pieces See the previous entry.

through and through thoroughly; completely. □ *I've studied this report* *through and through trying to find the facts you've mentioned.* □ *I was angry through and through, and I had to sit and recover before I could talk to anyone.*

through hell and high water through all sorts of severe difficulties. (Use *hell* with caution.) □ *I came through hell and high water to get to this meeting on time. Why don't you start on time?* □ *You'll have to go through hell and high water to accomplish your goal, but it'll be worth it.*

through thick and thin through good times and bad times. (Fixed order.) □ *We've been together through thick and thin and we won't desert each other now.* □ *Over the years, we went through thick and thin and enjoyed every minute of it.*

throw a fit to become very angry; to put on a display of anger. (Folksy.) □ *Sally threw a fit when I showed up without the things she asked me to buy.* □ *My dad threw a fit when I got home three hours late.*

throw a monkey wrench into the works to cause problems for someone's plans. (Informal.) □ *I don't want to throw a monkey wrench into the works, but have you checked your plans with a lawyer?* □ *When John refused to help us, he really threw a monkey wrench into the works.*

throw a party (for someone) to give or hold a party (for someone). □ *Mary was leaving town, so we threw a party for her.* □ *Fred is having a birthday. Do you know a place where we could throw a party?*

throw caution to the wind to become very careless. □ *Jane, who is usually cautious, threw caution to the wind and went windsurfing.* □ *I don't mind taking a little chance now and then, but I'm not the type of person who throws caution to the wind.*

throw cold water on something See *pour cold water on something.*

throw down the gauntlet to challenge (someone) to an argument or (figurat-

ive) to combat. □ *When Bob challenged my conclusions, he threw down the gauntlet. I was ready for an argument.* □ *Frowning at Bob is the same as throwing down the gauntlet. He loves to get into a fight about something.*

throw good money after bad to waste additional money after wasting money once. □ *I bought a used car and then had to spend $300 on repairs. That was throwing good money after bad.* □ *The Browns are always throwing good money after bad. They bought an acre of land that turned out to be swamp, and then had to pay to have it filled in.*

throw in the sponge See the following entry.

throw in the towel AND **throw in the sponge** to quit (doing something). (Informal.) □ *When John could stand no more of Mary's bad temper, he threw in the towel and left.* □ *Don't give up now! It's too soon to throw in the sponge.*

throw one's hands up in despair to give up; to raise one's hands making a sign of giving up. □ *John threw his hands up in despair because they wouldn't let him see his brother in the hospital.* Ⓣ *There was nothing I could do to help. I threw up my hands in despair and left.*

throw one's hands up in horror to be shocked; to raise one's hands as if one had been frightened. □ *When Bill heard the bad news, he threw his hands up in horror.* Ⓣ *I could do no more. I had seen more than I could stand. I just threw up my hands in horror and screamed.*

throw one's weight around to attempt to boss people around; to give orders. (Informal.) □ *The district manager came to our office and tried to throw his weight around, but no one paid any attention to him.* □ *Don't try to throw your weight around in this office. We know who our boss is.*

throw oneself at someone AND **fling oneself at someone** to give oneself willingly to someone else for romance. □ *I guess that Mary really likes John.*

She practically threw herself at him when he came into the room. □ *Everyone could see by the way Tom flung himself at Jane that he was going to ask her for a date.*

throw oneself at someone's feet to bow down humbly at someone's feet. (Both figurative and literal.) □ *Do I have to throw myself at your feet in order to convince you that I'm sorry?* □ *I love you sincerely, Jane. I'll throw myself at your feet and await your command. I'm your slave!*

throw oneself at the mercy of the court See the following entry.

throw oneself on the mercy of the court AND **throw oneself at the mercy of the court** to plead for mercy from a judge in a courtroom. □ *Your honor, please believe me, I didn't do it on purpose. I throw myself on the mercy of the court and beg for a light sentence.* □ *Jane threw herself at the mercy of the court and hoped for the best.*

throw (some) light on something See *shed (some) light on something.*

throw someone to confuse someone. □ *You threw me for a minute when you asked for my identification. I thought you recognized me.* □ *The question the teacher asked was so hard that it threw me, and I became very nervous.*

throw someone a curve 1. to pitch a curve ball to someone in baseball. □ *The pitcher threw John a curve, and John swung wildly against thin air.* □ *During that game, the pitcher threw everyone a curve at least once.* 2. to confuse someone by doing something unexpected. □ *When you said "house" you threw me a curve. The password was supposed to be "home."* □ *John threw me a curve when we were making our presentation, and I forgot my speech.*

throw someone for a loop AND **knock someone for a loop** to confuse or shock someone. (Informal. This is more severe and upsetting than *throw someone a curve.*) □ *When Bill heard the news, it threw him for a loop.* □

The manager knocked Bob for a loop by firing him on the spot.

throw someone for a loss to cause someone to be uncertain or confused. (Often passive.) □ *The stress of being in front of so many people threw Ann for a loss. She forgot her speech.* □ *It was a difficult problem. I was thrown for a loss for an answer.*

throw someone off the track 1. to cause one to lose one's place in the sequence of things. □ *The interruption threw me off the track for a moment, but I soon got started again with my presentation.* □ *Don't let little things throw you off the track. Concentrate on what you're doing.* 2. AND **throw someone off the trail** to cause someone to lose the trail (when following someone or something). □ *The raccoon threw us off the track by running through the creek.* □ *The robber threw the police off the trail by leaving town.*

throw someone off the trail See under *throw someone off the track.*

throw someone or something off 1. [with *someone*] to confuse someone; to mislead someone. □ *The interruption threw me off, and I lost my place in the speech.* □ *Little noises throw me off. Please try to be quiet.* □ *Your comment threw me off.* 2. [with *something*] to resist or recover from a disease. □ *It was a bad cold, but I managed to throw it off in a few days.* Ⓣ *I can't seem to throw off my cold. I've had it for weeks.* 3. [with *something*] to emit or give off an odor. □ *The small animal threw a strong odor off.* Ⓣ *The flowers threw off a heavy perfume.*

throw someone out (of something) to force a person to leave a place or an organization. (Also literal.) □ *John behaved so badly that they threw him out of the party.* □ *I was very loud, but they didn't throw me out.* □ *They threw Toni out of the club because she was so unpleasant.*

throw someone over to end a romance with someone. □ *Jane threw Bill over. I think she met someone she likes better.*

□ *Bill was about ready to throw her over, so it's just as well.*

throw someone to the wolves to (figuratively) sacrifice someone. (Not literal.) □ *The press was demanding an explanation, so the mayor blamed the mess on John and threw him to the wolves.* □ *I wouldn't let them throw me to the wolves! I did nothing wrong, and I won't take the blame for their errors.*

throw someone's name around to impress people by saying you know a famous or influential person. (Informal.) □ *You won't get anywhere around here by throwing the mayor's name around.* □ *When you get to the meeting, just throw my name around a bit, and people will pay attention to you.*

throw something into the bargain to include something in a deal. □ *To encourage me to buy a new car, the car dealer threw a free radio into the bargain.* □ *If you purchase three pounds of chocolates, I'll throw one pound of salted nuts into the bargain.*

throw something together AND **slap something together** to assemble or arrange something in haste. □ *Don't just slap something together! Use care and do it right.* □ *You assembled this device very badly. It seems that you just slapped it together.* ⊤ *John went into the kitchen to throw something together for dinner.*

throw (something) up to vomit something. (Compare with *spit (something) up*.) □ *The meat was bad, and I threw it up.* ⊤ *I hate to throw up.* ⊤ *Billy threw up his dinner.*

throw something up to someone to mention a shortcoming to someone repeatedly. □ *I know I'm thoughtless. Why do you keep throwing it up to me?* □ *Bill was always throwing Jane's faults up to her.*

throw the baby out with the bath(water) to dispose of the good while trying to get rid of the bad. □ *In her haste to talk down the idea containing a few disagreeable points, she has thrown the baby out with the bathwater.* ⊤ *Hasty*

action will result in throwing out the baby with the bath.

throw the book at someone to charge or convict someone with as many crimes as is possible. (Slang.) □ *I made the police officer angry, so he took me to the station and threw the book at me.* □ *The judge threatened to throw the book at me if I didn't stop insulting the police officer.*

thrust and parry to enter into verbal combat [with someone]; to compete actively [with someone]. (From the sport of fencing. Also literal. Fixed order.) □ *I spent the entire afternoon thrusting and parrying with a committee of so-called experts in the field of insurance.* □ *I do not intend to stand here and thrust and parry with you over a simple matter like this. Let's get someone else's opinion.*

thumb a ride AND **hitch a ride** to get a ride from a passing motorist; to make a sign with one's thumb that indicates to passing drivers that one is begging for a ride. □ *My car broke down on the highway, and I had to thumb a ride to get back to town.* □ *Sometimes it's dangerous to hitch a ride with a stranger.*

thumb one's nose at someone or something to (figuratively or literally) make a rude gesture of disgust with one's thumb and nose at someone or something. □ *The tramp thumbed his nose at the lady and walked away.* □ *You can't just thumb your nose at people who give you trouble. You've got to learn to get along.*

thumb through something AND **leaf through something** to look through a book, magazine, or newspaper, without reading it carefully. □ *I've only thumbed through this book, but it looks very interesting.* □ *I leafed through a magazine while waiting to see the doctor.*

thumbs down on someone or something opposed to someone or something. (See also *turn thumbs down (on someone or something)*.) □ *Bob is thumbs down on hiring anyone else.* □ *I had* *hoped that she'd agree with our plan, but she's thumbs down on it.*

thumbs up on someone or something in favor of someone or something. (See also *turn thumbs up (on someone or something).*) □ *Bob is thumbs up on hiring Claude.* □ *I never hoped she'd agree with our plan, but she's totally thumbs up on it.*

tickle someone pink AND **tickle someone to death** to please or entertain someone very much. (Informal. Never literal.) □ *Bill told a joke that really tickled us all pink.* □ *I know that these flowers will tickle her to death.*

tickle someone to death See the previous entry.

tickle someone's fancy to interest someone; to make someone curious. (See also *strike someone's fancy.*) □ *I have an interesting problem here that I think will tickle your fancy.* □ *This doesn't tickle my fancy at all. This is dull and boring.*

tickled pink AND **tickled to death** very much pleased or entertained. (Informal.) □ *I was tickled to death to have you visit us.* □ *We were tickled pink when your flowers arrived.*

tickled to death See the previous entry.

tide someone over [for a portion of something] to last until someone can get some more. □ *I don't get paid until next Wednesday. Could you lend me thirty dollars to tide me over?* □ *Could I borrow some coffee to tide me over until I can get to the store tomorrow?*

tie into something to connect to something. □ *I'm trying to get my home computer to tie in with the big one at the university.* □ *Could I tie into your water line while I'm waiting for mine to be repaired?* □ *What you just told me ties into John's version of the event.*

tie someone down to restrict or encumber someone. (Also literal.) □ *I'd like to go fishing every weekend, but my family ties me down.* □ *I don't want to tie you down, but you do have responsibilities here at home.*

tie someone or something up 1. [with *someone*] to keep someone busy or occupied. (Also literal.) □ *Sorry, this matter will tie me up for about an hour.* Ⓣ *The same matter will tie up almost everyone in the office.* **2.** [with *something*] to conclude and finalize something. (Informal. Also literal.) Ⓣ *Let's try to tie up this deal by Thursday.* □ *We'll manage to tie our business up by Wednesday at the latest.*

tie someone (up) in knots to become anxious or upset. (Informal.) □ *John tied himself in knots worrying about his wife during the operation.* □ *This waiting and worrying really ties me up in knots.*

tie someone's hands to prevent someone from doing something. (See also *have one's hands tied.* Also literal.) □ *I'd like to help you, but my boss has tied my hands.* □ *Please don't tie my hands with unnecessary restrictions. I'd like the freedom to do whatever is necessary.*

tie the knot to get married. (Informal.) □ *Well, I hear that you and John are going to tie the knot.* □ *My parents tied the knot almost forty years ago.*

tie traffic up to cause road traffic to stop. □ *If you tie traffic up for too long, you'll get a traffic ticket.* Ⓣ *Please don't stop on the roadway. It'll tie up traffic.*

tied down restricted by responsibilities. (Also literal.) □ *I love my home, but sometimes I don't like being tied down.* □ *I don't feel tied down, even though I have a lot of responsibility.*

tied to one's mother's apron strings dominated by one's mother; dependent on one's mother. □ *Tom is still tied to his mother's apron strings.* □ *Isn't he a little old to be tied to his mother's apron strings?*

tied up busy. (Also literal.) □ *How long will you be tied up?* □ *I will be tied up in a meeting for an hour.*

tight as a tick See *(as) tight as a tick.*

tight as Dick's hatband See *(as) tight as Dick's hatband.*

tighten one's belt to manage to spend less money. □ *Things are beginning to cost more and more. It looks as if we'll all have to tighten our belts.* □ *Times are hard, and prices are high. I can tighten my belt for only so long.*

tightfisted (with money) AND **closefisted (with money)** very stingy with money. □ *The manager is very closefisted with expenditures.* □ *My parents are very tightfisted with money.*

till the cows come home See *(un)til the cows come home*

tilt at windmills to fight battles with imaginary enemies; to fight against unimportant enemies or issues. (As with the fictional character, Don Quixote, who attacked windmills.) □ *Aren't you too smart to go around tilting at windmills?* □ *I'm not going to fight this issue. I've wasted too much of my life tilting at windmills.*

time after time AND **time and (time) again** repeatedly; *over and over (again).* □ *You've made the same error time after time! Please try to be more careful!* □ *I've told you time and again not to do that.* □ *You keep saying the same thing over and over, time and time again. Stop it!* □ *I have told you time and again: don't put wet garbage in the trash can!*

time and (time) again See the previous entry.

time flies time passes very quickly. (From the Latin *tempus fugit*.) □ *I didn't really think it was so late when the party ended. Doesn't time fly?* □ *Time simply flew while the old friends exchanged news.*

Time is money. (My) time is valuable, so don't waste it. □ *I can't afford to spend a lot of time standing here talking. Time is money, you know!* □ *People who keep saying time is money may be working too hard.*

Time is up. The allotted time has run out. □ *You must stop now. Your time is up.* □ *Time's up! Turn in your tests whether you're finished or not.*

time out [a call to] stop the clock (in a sporting event that is played in a fixed time period). □ *The coach made a sign for time out, and the clock stopped and a buzzer sounded.* □ *After someone called time out, the players gathered around the coach.*

time was (when) there was a time when; at a time in the past. □ *Time was when old people were taken care of at home.* □ *Time was when people didn't travel around so much.*

Time will tell. a proverb meaning that something will become known in the course of time. □ *I don't know if things will improve. Time will tell.* □ *Who knows what the future will bring? Only time will tell.*

tip someone off to give someone a hint; to warn someone. (Slang.) □ *I tipped John off that there would be a test in his algebra class.* ⊤ *I didn't want to tip off everyone, so I only told John.*

tip the scales at something to weigh some amount. □ *Tom tips the scales at nearly 200 pounds.* □ *I'll be glad when I tip the scales at a few pounds less.*

tits and ass a public display of [the human female] breasts and buttocks. (Referring to television, film, and stage performances in which women exhibit prominent and well-formed breasts and buttocks or in which these body parts are emphasized or made prominent. Use caution with the expression. Fixed order.) □ *We have a really fine choice on television tonight. There is brutal violence on channel 2, bloody horror on channel 5, and tits and ass on channel 10.* □ *Without tits and ass, many Broadway musicals would flop.*

to a great extent mainly; largely. □ *To a great extent, Mary is the cause of her own problems.* □ *I've finished my work to a great extent. There is nothing important left to do.*

to and fro toward and away from (something). (Compare with *back and forth*. Fixed order.) □ *The puppy* was very active—running to and fro—wagging its tail. □ The lion in the cage moved to and fro, watching the people in front of the cage.

to boot in addition; besides. (Informal.) □ For breakfast I had my usual two eggs and a slice of ham to boot. □ When I left for school, my parents gave me an airplane ticket and fifty dollars to boot.

to date up to the present time. □ How much have you accomplished to date? □ I've done everything I'm supposed to have done to date.

to hell and gone very much gone; has gone to hell. (Use hell with caution.) □ All my hard work is to hell and gone. □ When you see everything you've planned to hell and gone, you get kind of angry.

to no avail AND **of no avail** with no effect; unsuccessful. □ All of my efforts were to no avail. □ Everything I did to help was of no avail. Nothing worked.

to one's heart's content as much as one wants. □ John wanted a week's vacation so he could go to the lake and fish to his heart's content. □ I just sat there, eating chocolate to my heart's content.

to put it mildly to understate something; to say something politely. (Note the variation in the examples.) □ She was angry at almost everyone—to put it mildly. □ To say she was angry is putting it mildly. □ To put it mildly, she was enraged.

to say nothing of someone or something not to even mention the importance of someone or something. □ John and Mary had to be taken care of, to say nothing of Bill, who would require even more attention. □ I'm having enough difficulty painting the house, to say nothing of the garage that is very much in need of paint.

to say the least at the very least; without dwelling on the subject; to put it mildly. □ We were not at all pleased with her work—to say the least. □

When they had an accident, they were upset to say the least.

to some extent to some degree; in some amount; partly. □ I've solved this problem to some extent. □ I can help you understand this to some extent.

to someone's liking in a way that pleases someone. □ I hope I've done the work to your liking. □ Sally didn't find the meal to her liking and didn't eat any of it.

to someone's way of thinking in someone's opinion. □ This isn't satisfactory to my way of thinking. □ To my way of thinking, this is the perfect kind of vacation.

to the best of one's ability as well as one is able. □ I did the work to the best of my ability. □ You should always work to the best of your ability.

to the best of one's knowledge as far as one knows; from one's knowledge. □ This is the true story to the best of my knowledge. □ To the best of my knowledge, John is the only person who can answer that question.

to the bitter end to the very end. (Originally nautical. This originally had nothing to do with bitterness.) □ I kept trying to the bitter end. □ It took me a long time to get through school, but I worked hard at it all the way to the bitter end.

to the contrary as the opposite of what has been stated; contrary to what has been stated. (Compare with on the contrary.) □ The brown horse didn't beat the black horse. To the contrary, the black one won. □ Among spiders, the male is not the larger one. To the contrary, the female is larger.

to the core all the way through; basically and essentially. (Usually with some negative sense, such as evil, rotten, etc.) □ Bill said that John is evil to the core. □ This organization is rotten to the core.

to the ends of the earth to the remotest and most inaccessible points on the earth. □ I'll pursue him to the ends of *the earth.* □ *We've explored almost the whole world. We've traveled to the ends of the earth trying to learn about our world.*

to the last to the end; to the conclusion. □ *All of us kept trying to the last.* □ *It was a very boring play, but I sat through it to the last.*

to the letter exactly as instructed; exactly as written. □ *I didn't make an error. I followed your instruction to the letter.* □ *We didn't prepare the recipe to the letter, but the cake still turned out very well.*

to the nth degree to the maximum amount. (Informal.) □ *Jane is a perfectionist and tries to be careful to the nth degree.* □ *This scientific instrument is accurate to the nth degree.*

to the tune of some amount of money a certain amount of money. (Informal.) □ *My checking account is overdrawn to the tune of $340.* □ *My wallet was stolen, and I'm short of money to the tune of seventy dollars.*

To the victors belong the spoils. a proverb meaning that the winners achieve power over people and property. □ *The mayor took office and immediately fired many workers and hired new ones. Everyone said, "To the victors belong the spoils."* □ *The office of president includes the right to live in the White House and at Camp David. To the victors belong the spoils.*

to whom it may concern to the person to whom this applies. (A form of address used when you do not know the name of the person who handles the kind of business you are writing about.) □ *The letter started out, "To whom it may concern."* □ *When you don't know who to write to, just say, "To whom it may concern."*

toe the line See the following entry.

toe the mark AND **toe the line** to do what one is expected to do; to follow the rules. □ *You'll get ahead, Sally. Don't worry. Just toe the mark, and everything will be okay.* □ *John finally*

got fired. He just couldn't learn to toe the line.

toing and froing (on something) moving back and forth on an issue, first deciding one way and then changing to another. □ *The boss spent most of the afternoon toing and froing on the question of who was to handle the Wilson account.* □ *I wish you would stop toing and froing and make up your mind.*

Tom, Dick, and Harry See *(every) Tom, Dick, and Harry.*

tone something down to make something less extreme. □ *That yellow is too bright. Please try to tone it down.* Ⓣ *Can you tone down your remarks? They seem quite strong for this situation.*

tongue-in-cheek insincere; joking. □ *Ann made a tongue-in-cheek remark to John, and he got mad because he thought she was serious.* □ *The play seemed very serious at first, but then everyone saw that it was tongue-in-cheek, and they began laughing.*

too big for one's britches too haughty for one's status or age. (Folksy or informal.) □ *Bill's getting a little too big for his britches, and somebody's going to straighten him out.* □ *You're too big for your britches, young man! You had better be more respectful.*

too close for comfort [for a misfortune or a threat] to be dangerously close. (See also *close to home.*) □ *That car nearly hit me! That was too close for comfort.* □ *When I was in the hospital, I nearly died from pneumonia. Believe me, that was too close for comfort.*

too good to be true almost unbelievable; so good as to be unbelievable. □ *The news was too good to be true.* □ *When I finally got a big raise, it was too good to be true.*

Too many cooks spoil the broth. See the following entry.

Too many cooks spoil the stew. AND **Too many cooks spoil the broth.** a proverb meaning that too many people trying to manage something simply spoil it.

□ *Let's decide who is in charge around here. Too many cooks spoil the stew.* □ *Everyone is giving orders, but no one is following them! Too many cooks spoil the broth.*

too much of a good thing more of a thing than is good or useful. □ *I usually take short vacations. I can't stand too much of a good thing.* □ *Too much of a good thing can make you sick, especially if the good thing is chocolate.*

toot one's own horn AND **blow one's own horn** to boast or praise oneself. □ *Tom is always tooting his own horn. Is he really as good as he says he is?* □ *I find it hard to blow my own horn, but I manage.*

top someone or something to do or be better than someone or something. (Informal.) □ *Ann has done very well, but I don't think she can top Jane.* □ *Do you think your car tops mine when it comes to gas mileage?*

top something off to add to the difficulty of something. □ *Jane lost her job, and to top that off, she caught the flu.* □ *I had a bad day, and to top it off, I have to go to a meeting tonight.*

top something off (with something) to end or terminate something with something; to put something on the top of something. □ *They topped the building off with a tall flagpole.* ⊤ *He topped off each piece of pie with a heap of whipped cream.* ⊤ *That's the way to top off a piece of pie!*

toss one's cookies to vomit. (Slang.) □ *Don't run too fast after you eat or you'll toss your cookies.* □ *Oh, I feel terrible. I think I'm going to toss my cookies.*

toss one's hat into the ring to state that one is running for an elective office. (Informal.) □ *Jane wanted to run for treasurer, so she tossed her hat into the ring.* □ *The mayor never tossed his hat into the ring. Instead he announced his retirement.*

toss something off AND **shake something off 1.** to throw something off (of oneself). □ *Bob coughed so hard he* shook his blanket off. ⊤ *Tom tossed off his jacket and sat down to watch television.* **2.** to ignore or resist the bad effects of something. □ *John insulted Bob, but Bob just tossed it off.* ⊤ *If I couldn't shake off insults, I'd be miserable.*

touch a sore point See the following entry.

touch a sore spot AND **touch a sore point** to refer to a sensitive matter that will upset someone. (Also literal.) □ *I seem to have touched a sore spot. I'm sorry. I didn't mean to upset you.* □ *When you talk to him, avoid talking about money. It's best not to touch a sore point if possible.*

touch and go very uncertain or critical. (Fixed order.) □ *Things were touch and go at the office until a new manager was hired.* □ *Jane had a serious operation, and everything was touch and go for two days after her surgery.*

touch base (with someone) to talk to someone; to confer with someone. (Slang.) □ *I need to touch base with John on this matter.* □ *John and I touched base on this question yesterday, and we are in agreement.*

touch on something to mention something; to talk about something briefly. □ *In tomorrow's lecture I'd like to touch on the matter of taxation.* □ *The teacher only touched on the subject. There wasn't time to do more than that.*

touch someone for something to ask someone for a loan of something, usually a sum of money. (Informal.) □ *Fred's always trying to touch people for money.* □ *Jack touched John for ten dollars.*

touch someone or something off 1. [with *someone*] to make someone very angry. □ *Your rude comments touched Mary off. She's very angry at you.* ⊤ *I didn't mean to touch off anyone. I was only being honest.* **2.** [with *something*] to ignite something; to start something. □ *A few sparks touched all the fireworks off at once.* ⊤ *The argument touched off a serious fight.*

touch something up to repair a paint job on something. □ *We don't need to paint the whole room. We can just touch the walls up.* Ⓣ *You should touch up scratches on your car as soon as they occur.*

touched by someone or something emotionally affected or moved by someone or something. □ *Sally was very nice to me. I was very touched by her.* □ *I was really touched by your kind letter.*

touched (in the head) crazy. (Folksy or slang.) □ *Sometimes Bob acts like he's touched in the head.* □ *In fact, I thought he was touched.*

tough act to follow a difficult presentation or performance to follow with one's own performance. □ *Bill's speech was excellent. It was a tough act to follow, but my speech was good also.* □ *In spite of the fact that I had a tough act to follow, I did my best.*

tough as old boots See *(as) tough as old boots.*

tough break a bit of bad fortune. (Slang.) □ *I'm sorry to hear about your accident. Tough break.* □ *John had a lot of tough breaks when he was a kid, but he's doing okay now.*

tough it out to endure a difficult situation. (Slang.) □ *Geometry is very hard for John, but he managed to tough it out until the end of the year.* □ *This was a very bad day at the office. A few times, I was afraid I wouldn't be able to tough it out.*

tough nut to crack See *hard nut to crack.*

tough row to hoe a difficult task to undertake. □ *It was a tough row to hoe, but I finally got a college degree.* □ *Getting the contract signed is going to be a tough row to hoe, but I'm sure I can do it.*

tower of strength a person who can always be depended on to provide support and encouragement, especially in times of trouble. □ *Mary was a tower of strength when Jean was* in the hospital. She looked after her whole family. □ *Jack was a tower of strength during the time that his father was unemployed.*

town-and-gown the relations between a town and the university located within the town; the relations between university students and the nonstudents who live in a university town. (Usually in reference to a disagreement. Fixed order.) □ *There is another town-and-gown dispute in Adamsville over the amount the university costs the city for police services.* □ *There was more town-and-gown strife reported at Larry's Bar and Grill last Saturday night.*

toy with someone or something 1. [with *someone*] to tease someone; to deal lightly with someone's emotions. □ *Ann broke up with Tom because he was just toying with her. He was not serious at all.* □ *Don't toy with me! I won't have it!* **2.** [with *something*] to play or fiddle with something. □ *Stop toying with the radio, or you'll break it.* □ *John sat there toying with a pencil all through the meeting.*

trade on something to use a fact or a situation to one's advantage. □ *Tom was able to trade on the fact that he had once been in the Army.* □ *John traded on his poor eyesight to get a seat closer to the stage.*

train of thought pattern of thinking; sequence of ideas; what one was just thinking about. (See *lose one's train of thought.*) □ *My train of thought is probably not as clear as it should be.* □ *I cannot seem to follow your train of thought on this matter. Will you explain it a little more carefully, please?*

trial and error trying repeatedly for success. (Fixed order.) □ *I finally found the right key after lots of trial and error.* □ *Sometimes trial and error is the only way to get something done.*

trials and tribulations problems and tests of one's courage or perseverance. (Fixed order.) □ *I suppose I have the normal trials and tribulations for a person of my background, but some days are just a little too much for me.* □ *I* *promise not to tell you of the trials and tribulations of my day if you promise not to tell me yours!*

Trick or treat! Give me a treat of some kind or I will play a trick on you! (The formulaic expression said by children after they ring someone's doorbell and the door is answered on Halloween. It is now understood to mean simply that the child is requesting a treat of some kind — candy, fruit, popcorn, etc. Fixed order.) □ *"Trick or treat!" cried Jimmy when the door opened.* □ *Mr. Franklin opened the door to find four very small children dressed like flowers standing silently on his doorstep. After a moment, he said, "Isn't anyone going to say 'Trick or treat'?"*

tried-and-true tested by time and proven to be sound. (Fixed order.) □ *I have a tried-and-true remedy for poison ivy.* □ *All of her investment ideas are tried-and-true and you ought to be able to make money if you follow them.*

trip someone up 1. to trip someone. □ *Bob tripped himself up on his own feet.* ⊺ *The loose gravel beside the track tripped up Bob, and he fell.* **2.** to cause difficulty for someone; to cause someone to fail. □ *Bill tripped Tom up during the spelling contest, and Tom lost.* ⊺ *I didn't mean to trip up anyone. I'm sorry I caused trouble.*

trot something out to mention something regularly or habitually, without giving it much thought. (Informal.) □ *Jack always trots the same excuses out for being late.* ⊺ *When James disagreed with Mary, she simply trotted out her same old political arguments.*

Trouble is brewing. AND **There is trouble brewing.** Trouble is developing. □ *Trouble's brewing at the office. I have to get there early tomorrow.* □ *There is trouble brewing in the government. The prime minister may resign.*

trouble one's head about someone or something to worry about someone or something; to *trouble oneself about someone or something* that is none of one's business. (Folksy. Usually in the

negative. Also with *pretty,* as in the example. Usually in the negative, meaning to mind one's own business.) □ *Now, now, don't trouble your pretty head about all these things.* □ *You needn't trouble your head about Sally.*

trouble oneself about someone or something to worry oneself about someone or something. (Usually in the negative.) □ *Please don't trouble yourself about me. I'm doing fine.* □ *I can't take time to trouble myself about this matter. Do it yourself.*

trouble oneself (to do something) to bother oneself to do something. □ *He didn't even trouble himself to turn off the light when he left.* □ *No, thank you. I don't need any help. Please don't trouble yourself.*

trouble someone for something to ask someone to pass something or give something. (Usually a question.) □ *Could I trouble you for the salt?* □ *Could I trouble you for some advice?*

trouble someone to do something to ask someone to do something. (Usually a question.) □ *Could I trouble you to pass the salt?* □ *Could I trouble you to give me some advice?*

true to form exactly as expected; following the usual pattern. (Often with *running,* as in the example.) □ *As usual, John is late. At least he's true to form.* □ *And true to form, Mary left before the meeting was adjourned.* □ *This winter season is running true to form — miserable!*

true to one's word keeping one's promise. □ *True to his word, Tom showed up at exactly eight o'clock.* □ *We'll soon know if Jane is true to her word. We'll see if she does what she promised.*

trumped-up false; fraudulently devised. □ *They tried to have Tom arrested on a trumped-up charge.* □ *Bob gave some trumped-up excuse for not being at the meeting.*

truth will out eventually, the truth will become known; truth tends to become known, even when it is being concealed. □ *The truth will out! Some* *day my name will be cleared.* □ *We just found out about corruption in the mayor's office. Like they say, "The truth will out."*

try one's hand (at something) to take a try at something. □ *Someday I'd like to try my hand at flying a plane.* □ *Give me a chance. Let me try my hand!*

try one's luck (at something) to attempt to do something (where success requires luck). □ *My great-grandfather came to California to try his luck at finding gold.* □ *I went into a gambling casino to try my luck.*

try out (for something) to test one's fitness for a role in a play, a position on a sports team, etc. □ *I sing pretty well, so I thought I'd try out for the chorus.* □ *Hardly anyone else showed up to try out.*

try (out) one's wings to try to do something one has recently become qualified to do. (Like a young bird uses its wings to try to fly.) □ *John just got his driver's license and wants to borrow the car to try out his wings.* □ *I learned to skin-dive, and I want to go to the seaside to try my wings.* Ⓣ *She was eager to try out her wings.*

try someone's patience to do something annoying that may cause someone to lose patience; to cause someone to be annoyed. □ *Stop whistling. You're trying my patience. Very soon I'm going to lose my temper.* □ *Some students think it's fun to try the teacher's patience.*

try something out on someone to test something on someone (to see how it works or if it is liked). □ *I found a recipe for oyster stew and tried it out on my roommate.* Ⓣ *I'm glad you didn't try out that stuff on me!* □ *I have a tremendous idea! Let me try it out on you.* Ⓣ *I want to try out my plan on you. Please give me your honest opinion.*

tuck into something to eat something with hunger and enjoyment. (Informal.) □ *The children really tucked into the ice cream.* □ *Jean would like to*

have tucked into the chocolate cake, but she's on a strict diet.

tuckered out See *(all) tuckered out.*

tune someone or something out to ignore someone or something; to become unaware of someone or something. □ *Sally annoys me sometimes, so I just tune her out.* Ⓣ *Your radio doesn't bother me. I just tune out the noise.*

tune (something) in to set a radio or television control so as to receive something. □ *Why don't you try to tune the ball game in?* Ⓣ *This is a cheap radio, and I can't tune in distant stations.* □ *Please try to tune in.*

turn a blind eye to someone or something to ignore something and pretend you do not see it. □ *The usher turned a blind eye to the little boy who sneaked into the theater.* □ *How can you turn a blind eye to all those starving children?*

turn a deaf ear (to someone or something) to ignore what someone says; to ignore a cry for help. □ *How can you just turn a deaf ear to their cries for food and shelter?* □ *The government has turned a deaf ear.*

turn in to go to bed. □ *It's late. I think I'll turn in.* □ *We usually turn in at about midnight.*

turn of the century the end of one century and the beginning of another. □ *It's just a few years until the turn of the century.* □ *People like to celebrate the turn of the century.*

turn on a dime to turn in a very tight turn. (Informal.) □ *This car handles very well. It can turn on a dime.* □ *The speeding car turned on a dime and headed in the other direction.*

turn on the waterworks to begin to cry. (Slang.) □ *Every time Billy got homesick, he turned on the waterworks.* □ *Sally hurt her knee and turned on the waterworks for about twenty minutes.*

turn one's back (on someone or something) to abandon or ignore someone or something. (Also literal.) □ *Don't* *turn your back on your old friends.* □ *Bob has a tendency to turn his back on serious problems.* □ *This matter needs your attention. Please don't just turn your back.*

turn one's nose up at someone or something to sneer at someone or something; to reject someone or something. □ *John turned his nose up at Ann, and that hurt her feelings.* ⊤ *I never turn up my nose at dessert, no matter what it is.*

turn out (all right) AND **pan out; work out (all right)** to end satisfactorily. (Compare with *work out for the best.*) □ *I hope everything turns out all right.* □ *Oh, yes. It'll all pan out.* □ *Things usually work out, no matter how bad they seem.*

turn over AND **kick over** [for an engine] to start or to rotate. □ *My car engine was so cold that it wouldn't even turn over.* □ *The engine turned over a few times and then stopped for good.*

turn over a new leaf to start again with the intention of doing better; to begin again, ignoring past errors. □ *Tom promised to turn over a new leaf and do better from now on.* □ *After a minor accident, Sally decided to turn over a new leaf and drive more carefully.*

turn (over) in one's grave [for a dead person] to be shocked or horrified. (Refers to something that would be so shocking to a person who is actually dead, that the dead person would quicken enough to turn over. Never literal.) □ *If Beethoven heard Mary play one of his sonatas, he'd turn over in his grave.* □ *If Aunt Jane knew what you were doing with her favorite chair, she would turn over in her grave.*

turn someone off to discourage or disgust someone. (Informal.) □ *His manner really turns me off.* ⊤ *That man has a way of turning off everyone he comes in contact with.*

turn someone on to excite someone; to excite someone sexually. (Informal.) □ *Sally said she preferred not to watch movies that attempted to turn people on.*

⊤ *The lecture was very good. It turned on the whole class.*

turn someone or something down **1.** [with *someone*] to refuse or deny someone. □ *I applied for a job with the city, but they turned me down.* ⊤ *They turned down Mary who also applied.* **2.** to deny someone's request. □ *I offered her some help, but she turned it down.* ⊤ *She had turned down John's offer of help, too.* **3.** [with *something*] to fold part of something downward. □ *The hotel maid turned the bed down while I was at dinner.* ⊤ *In the mail-order catalog, I always turn down a page that interests me.* **4.** [with *something*] to lower the volume or amount of something, such as heat, sound, water, air pressure, etc. □ *It's hot in here. Please turn down the heat.* □ *Turn the stereo down. It's too loud.*

turn someone or something out **1.** [with *someone*] to send someone out of somewhere. □ *I didn't pay my rent, so the manager turned me out.* ⊤ *I'm glad it's not winter. I'd hate to turn out someone in the snow.* **2.** [with *something*] to manufacture something; to produce something. □ *John wasn't turning enough work out, so the manager had a talk with him.* ⊤ *This machine can turn out two thousand items a day.*

turn someone or something up to search for and find someone or something. □ *Let me try to see if I can turn someone up who knows how to do the job.* ⊤ *I turned up a number of interesting items when I went through Aunt Jane's attic.*

turn someone's head [for flattery or success] to distract someone; to cause someone not to be sensible. (Also literal.) □ *Don't let our praise turn your head. You're not perfect!* □ *Her successes had turned her head. She was now quite arrogant.*

turn someone's stomach to make someone (figuratively or literally) ill. □ *This milk is spoiled. The smell of it turns my stomach.* □ *The play was so bad that it turned my stomach.*

turn something to good account to use something in such a way that it is to one's advantage; to make good use of a situation, experience, etc. □ *Pam turned her illness to good account and did a lot of reading.* □ *Many people turn their retirement time to good account and take up interesting hobbies.*

turn something to one's advantage to make an advantage for oneself out of something (which might otherwise be a disadvantage). □ *Sally found a way to turn the problem to her advantage.* □ *The ice cream store manager was able to turn the hot weather to her advantage.*

turn the clock back to try to return to the past. (Also literal.) □ *You are not facing up to the future. You are trying to turn the clock back to a time when you were more comfortable.* □ *Let us turn the clock back and pretend we are living at the turn of the century — the time that our story takes place.* ⊤ *No, you can't turn back the clock.*

turn the heat up (on someone) to use force to persuade someone to do something; to increase the pressure on someone to do something. (Informal.) □ *Management is turning the heat up to increase production.* ⊤ *The teacher really turned up the heat on the students by saying that everyone would be punished if the real culprit was not found.*

turn the other cheek to ignore abuse or an insult. □ *When Bob got mad at Mary and yelled at her, she just turned the other cheek.* □ *Usually I turn the other cheek when someone is rude to me.*

turn the tables (on someone) to cause a reversal in someone's plans; to make one's plans turn back on one. □ *I went to Jane's house to help get ready for a surprise party for Bob. It turned out that the surprise party was for me! Jane really turned the tables on me!* □ *Turning the tables like that requires a lot of planning and a lot of secrecy.*

turn the tide to cause a reversal in the direction of events; to cause a reversal in public opinion. □ *It looked as if the team was going to lose, but near the end of the game, our star player turned the tide.* □ *At first, people were opposed to our plan. After a lot of discussion, we were able to turn the tide.*

turn thumbs down (on someone or something) to veto someone or something; to reject someone or something. (See also *thumbs down on someone or something.*) □ *The board of directors turned thumbs down on my proposal.* □ *The turned thumbs down without even hearing my explanation.* □ *The committee turned thumbs down on Carl and we did not hire him after all.*

turn thumbs up (on someone or something) to accept someone or something; to approve someone or something. (See also *thumbs up on someone or something.*) □ *The board of directors turned thumbs up on my proposal and voted to fund the project.* □ *The committee turned thumbs up on Carl as the new manager.* □ *When the boss turned thumbs up, I knew everything was okay.*

turn to to begin to get busy. □ *Come on, you guys! Turn to! Let's get to work.* □ *If you people will turn to, we can finish this work in no time at all.*

turn to someone or something (for something) to seek something from someone or something. □ *I turned to Ann for help.* □ *Bill turned to aspirin for relief from his headache.*

turn turtle to turn upside down. (Slang.) □ *The sailboat turned turtle, but the sailors only got wet.* □ *The car ran off the road and turned turtle in the ditch.*

turn up to appear. □ *We'll send out invitations and see who turns up.* □ *Guess who turned up at my door last night?*

turn up one's toes to die. (Slang.) □ *When I turn up my toes, I want a big funeral with lots of flowers.* □ *Our cat turned up his toes during the night. He was nearly ten years old.*

twiddle one's thumbs to fill up time by playing with one's fingers. □ *What am I supposed to do while waiting for you? Sit here and twiddle my thumbs?* □ *Don't sit around twiddling your thumbs. Get busy!*

twist someone around one's little finger to manipulate and control someone. □ *Bob really fell for Jane. She can twist him around her little finger.* □ *Billy's mother has twisted him around her little finger. He's very dependent on her.*

twist someone's arm to force or persuade someone. (Also literal.) □ *At first she refused, but after I twisted her arm a little, she agreed to help.* □ *I didn't want to run for mayor, but everyone twisted my arm.*

two of a kind people or things of the same type or that are similar in character, attitude, etc. □ *Jack and Tom are two of a kind. They're both ambitious.* □ *The companies are two of a kind. They both pay their employees badly.*

two-time someone to cheat on or betray one's spouse or lover by dating or seeing someone else. (Slang.) □ *When Mrs. Franklin learned that Mr. Franklin was two-timing her, she left him.* □ *Ann told Bob that if he ever two-timed her, she would cause him a lot of trouble.*

two's company(, three's a crowd) a saying meaning that often two people would want to be alone and a third person would be in the way. (Fixed order.) □ *Two's company. I'm sure Tom and Jill won't want his sister to go to the movies with them.* □ *John has been invited to join Jane and Peter on their picnic, but he says "Two's company, three's a crowd."*

U

ugly as sin See *(as) ugly as sin.*

under a cloud (of suspicion) to be suspected of (doing) something. □ *Someone stole some money at work, and now everyone is under a cloud of suspicion.* □ *Even the manager is under a cloud.*

under construction being built or repaired. □ *We cannot travel on this road because it's under construction.* □ *Our new home has been under construction all summer. We hope to move in next month.*

under fire during an attack. □ *There was a scandal in city hall, and the mayor was forced to resign under fire.* □ *John is a good lawyer because he can think under fire.*

under one's own steam by one's own power or effort. (Informal.) □ *I missed my ride to class, so I had to get there under my own steam.* □ *John will need some help with this project. He can't do it under his own steam.*

under someone's (very) nose See *(right) under someone's (very) nose.*

under the aegis of someone AND **under the auspices of someone** under the sponsorship of someone or some group; under the control or monitoring of someone or some group. □ *The entire project fell under the aegis of Thomas.* □ *The entire program is under the auspices of Acme-Global Paper Co., Inc.*

under the auspices of someone See the previous entry.

under the circumstances in a particular situation; because of the circumstances. □ *I'm sorry to hear that you're ill. Under the circumstances, you may take the day off.* □ *We won't expect you to come to work for a few days, under the circumstances.*

under the counter [bought or sold] in secret or illegally. (Also literal.) □ *The drugstore owner was arrested for selling liquor under the counter.* □ *The clerk sold dirty books under the counter.*

under the influence (of alcohol) drunk; nearly drunk; affected by alcohol. □ *She behaves quite rudely when under the influence of alcohol.* □ *Ed was stopped by a police officer for driving while under the influence.*

under the sun anywhere at all. □ *This is the largest cattle ranch under the sun.* □ *Isn't there anyone under the sun who can help me with this problem?*

under the table in secret, as with the giving of a bribe. (Informal. Also literal.) □ *The mayor had been paying money to the construction company under the table.* □ *Tom transferred the deed to the property to his wife under the table.*

under the weather ill. □ *I'm a bit under the weather today, so I can't go to the office.* □ *My head is aching, and I feel a little under the weather.*

under the wire just barely in time or on time. (Informal.) □ *I turned in my report just under the wire.* □ *Bill was the last person to get in the door. He got in under the wire.*

until all hours until very late. □ *Mary is out until all hours, night after night.*

□ *If I'm up until all hours two nights in a row, I'm just exhausted.*

(un)til the cows come home until the last; until very late. (Folksy or informal. Referring to the end of the day, when the cows come home to be fed and milked.) □ *We were having so much fun that we decided to stay at school until the cows came home.* □ *Where've you been? Who said you could stay out till the cows come home?*

up a blind alley at a dead end; on a route that leads nowhere. (Informal.) □ *I have been trying to find out something about my ancestors, but I'm up a blind alley. I can't find anything.* □ *The police are up a blind alley in their investigation of the crime.*

up a tree in a difficult situation and unable to get out; stymied and confused. (Slang.) □ *I'm really up a tree on this problem.* □ *Geometry is too hard for me. It's got me up a tree.*

up against something having trouble with something. (The *something* is often *it*, meaning facing trouble in general.) □ *Jane is up against a serious problem.* □ *Yes, she really looks as if she's up against it.*

up and about healthy and moving about — not sick in bed. □ *Mary is getting better. She should be up and about in a few days.* □ *She can't wait until she's up and about. She's tired of being in bed.*

up and around out of bed and moving about or able to move about. (Refers to a person who has just arisen for the day or to someone who has been sick in bed. Fixed order.) □ *When Tom is up and around, ask him to call me.* □ *The flu put Alice into bed for three days, but she was up and around on the fourth.*

up and at them to get up and go at people or things; to get active and get busy. (Informal. Usually *them* is *'em.* Fixed order.) □ *Come on, Bob — up and at 'em!* □ *There is a lot of work to be done around here. Up and at 'em, everybody!*

up and away up into the air and into flight. (Said of a bird or an airplane. Fixed order.) □ *After a few seconds of speeding down the runway, our flight to Tucson was up and away.* □ *Just before the cat pounced on the sparrows, they were up and away and the cat was left with empty paws and jaws.*

up-and-coming enterprising and alert. (Fixed order.) □ *Jane is a hard worker — really up-and-coming.* □ *Bob is also an up-and-coming youngster who is going to become well known.*

up for grabs available to anyone. (Slang.) □ *Mary quit yesterday, and her job is up for grabs.* □ *Who's in charge around here? This whole organization is up for grabs.*

up-front (Slang.) **1.** sincere and open. □ *Ann is a very up-front kind of person. Everyone feels easy around her.* □ *It's hard to tell what Tom is really thinking. He's not very up-front.* **2.** in advance. □ *I ordered a new car, and they wanted 20 percent up-front.* □ *I couldn't afford to pay that much up-front. I'd have to make a smaller deposit.*

up in arms rising up in anger; (figuratively or literally) armed with weapons. □ *My father was really up in arms when he got his tax bill this year.* □ *The citizens were up in arms, pounding on the gates of the palace, demanding justice.*

up in the air (about someone or something) undecided about someone or something; uncertain about someone or something. □ *I don't know what Sally plans to do. Things were sort of up in the air the last time we talked.* □ *Let's leave this question up in the air until next week.*

up in years AND **advanced in years; along in years; on in years** old; elderly. □ *My uncle is up in years and can't hear too well.* □ *Many people lose their hearing somewhat when they are along in years.*

up North to or at the northern part of the country or the world. (See also back *East,* down *South,* and *out West.*) □ *I don't like living up North. I want to move down South where it's warm.* □ *When you say "up North," do you mean where the polar bears live, or just in the northern states?*

up the creek (without a paddle) in a bad situation. (Slang. Use with caution. There is a taboo version of this phrase.) □ *What a mess I'm in. I'm really up the creek without a paddle.* □ *I tried to prevent it, but I seem to be up the creek, too.*

up-to-date modern; contemporary; up to the current standards of fashion. □ *I'd like to see a more up-to-date report on Mr. Smith.* □ *This is not an up-to-date record of the construction project.* □ *I'm having my living room redecorated to bring it up-to-date.* □ *I don't care if my rooms are up-to-date. I just want them to be comfortable.*

up to no good doing something bad. (Informal.) □ *I could tell from the look on Tom's face that he was up to no good.* □ *There are three boys in the front yard. I don't know what they are doing, but I think they are up to no good.*

up to one's ears (in something) See *up to one's neck (in something).*

up to one's eyeballs (in something) See the following entry.

up to one's neck (in something) AND **up to one's ears (in something); up to one's eyeballs (in something)** having a lot of something; very much involved in something. (Informal.) □ *I can't come to the meeting. I'm up to my neck in these reports.* □ *Mary is up to her ears in her work.* □ *I am up to my eyeballs in things to do! I can't do any more!*

up to par as good as the standard or average; up to standard. □ *I'm just not feeling up to par today. I must be coming down with something.* □ *The manager said that the report was not up to par and gave it back to Mary to do over again.*

up to scratch See the following entry.

up to snuff AND **up to scratch** as good as is required; meeting the minimum requirements. (Slang. Compare with *up to par.*) □ *Sorry, Tom. Your performance isn't up to snuff. You'll have to improve or find another job.* □ *My paper wasn't up to scratch, so I got an F.*

up to someone to be someone's own choice. □ *She said I didn't have to go if I didn't want to. It's entirely up to me.* □ *It's up to Mary whether she takes the job or tries to find another one.*

up to something 1. occupied in some activity, often something secret or wrong. □ *Those kids are up to something. They're too quiet.* □ *Goodness knows what that child will be up to next.* **2.** capable of something; fit enough for something. □ *John's not up to doing a job of that kind.* □ *Mary's mother's been ill and is not up to traveling yet.* **3.** to be as good as something; to be good enough for something. □ *This work's not up to the standard of the class.* □ *Your last essay was not up to your best.*

up-to-the-minute the very latest or most recent. □ *I want to hear some up-to-the-minute news on the hostage situation.* □ *I just got an up-to-the-minute report on Tom's health.*

upper crust the higher levels of society; the upper class. (Informal. From the top, as opposed to the bottom, crust of a pie.) □ *Jane speaks like that because she pretends to be from the upper crust, but her father was a miner.* □ *James is from the upper crust, but he is penniless.*

ups and downs good fortune and bad fortune. (Fixed order.) □ *I've had my ups and downs, but in general life has been good to me.* □ *All people have their ups and downs.*

upset the apple cart to mess up or ruin something. □ *Tom really upset the apple cart by telling Mary the truth about Jane.* □ *I always knew he'd upset the apple cart.*

use every trick in the book to use every method possible. (Informal.) □ *I used every trick in the book, but I still* couldn't manage to get a ticket to the game Saturday. □ *Bob tried to use every trick in the book, but he still failed.*

use one's head AND **use one's noggin; use one's noodle** to use one's own intelligence. (The words *noggin* and *noodle* are slang terms for "head.") □ *You can do better in math if you'll just use your head.* □ *Jane uses her noggin and gets things done correctly and on time.* □ *Yes, she sure knows how to use her noodle.*

use one's noggin See the previous entry.

use one's noodle See *use one's head.*

use some elbow grease use some effort. (Slang. As if lubricating one's elbow would make one more efficient. Note the variations in the examples.) □ *Come on, Bill. You can do it. Just use some elbow grease.* □ *I tried elbow grease, but it doesn't help get the job done.*

use someone or something as an excuse to blame someone or something (for a failure). □ *John used his old car as an excuse for not going to the meeting.* □ *My husband was sick in bed, and I used him as an excuse.*

use strong language to swear, threaten, or use abusive language. □ *I wish you wouldn't use strong language in front of the children.* □ *If you feel that you have to use strong language with the manager, perhaps you had better let me do the talking.*

used to someone or something accustomed to someone or something. □ *I'm not used to Jane yet. She's a bit hard to get along with.* □ *How long does it take to get used to this weather?*

V

vale of tears the earth; mortal life on earth. (A "valley" of tears.) □ *When it comes time for me to leave this vale of tears, I hope I can leave some worthwhile memories behind.* □ *Uncle Fred left this vale of tears early this morning.*

vanish into thin air to disappear without leaving a trace. □ *My money gets spent so fast. It seems to vanish into thin air.* □ *When I came back, my car was gone. I had locked it, and it couldn't have vanished into thin air!*

Variety is the spice of life. a proverb meaning that differences and changes make life interesting. □ *Mary reads all kinds of books. She says variety is the spice of life.* □ *The Franklins travel all over the world so they can learn how different people live. After all, variety is the spice of life.*

vent one's spleen to get rid of one's feelings of anger caused by someone or something by attacking someone or something else. □ *Jack vented his spleen at his wife whenever things went badly at work.* □ *Peter vented his spleen on his car by kicking it when he lost the race.*

verge on something to be almost something. □ *Your blouse is a lovely color. It seems to be blue verging on purple.* □ *Sally has a terrible case of the flu, and they are afraid it's verging on pneumonia.*

very thing the exact thing that is required. □ *The vacuum cleaner is the very thing for cleaning the stairs.* □ *I have the very thing to remove that stain.*

villain of the piece someone or something that is responsible for something bad or wrong. □ *I wondered who told the newspapers about the local scandal. I discovered that Joan was the villain of the piece.* □ *We couldn't think who had stolen the meat. The dog next door turned out to be the villain of the piece.*

vim and vigor energy and enthusiasm. (Fixed order.) □ *I just don't seem to have the vim and vigor that I had a few years ago.* □ *Alice appeared with all the vim and vigor of youth, and began to help carry in the packages.*

vote a straight ticket to cast a ballot with all the votes for members of the same political party. □ *I'm not a member of any political party, so I never vote a straight ticket.* □ *I usually vote a straight ticket because I believe in the principles of one party and not in the other's.*

vote with one's feet to express one's dissatisfaction with something by leaving, especially by walking away. □ *I think that the play is a total flop. Most of the audience voted with its feet during the second act.* □ *I am prepared to vote with my feet if the meeting appears to be a waste of time.*

W

wade in(to something) to start in (doing) something immediately. (Also literal.) □ *I need some preparation. I can't just wade into the job and start doing things correctly.* □ *We don't expect you to wade in. We'll tell you what to do.*

wag one's chin to chatter or chat with someone. (Slang.) □ *We stood around and wagged our chins for almost an hour.* □ *Don't just wag your chin. Stop talking and get to work!*

wait-and-see attitude a skeptical attitude; an uncertain attitude where someone will just wait and see what happens. (Fixed order.) □ *John thought that Mary couldn't do it, but he took a wait-and-see attitude.* □ *His wait-and-see attitude didn't influence me at all.*

wait on someone hand and foot to serve someone very well, attending to all personal needs. □ *I don't mind bringing you your coffee, but I don't intend to wait on you hand and foot.* □ *I don't want anyone to wait on me hand and foot. I can take care of myself.*

wait up (for someone or something) 1. to stay up late waiting for someone to arrive or something to happen. □ *I'll be home late. Don't wait up for me.* □ *We waited up for the coming of the new year, and then we went to bed.* **2.** AND **hold up (for someone or something)** to wait for someone or something to catch up. □ *Hey! Don't go so fast. Wait up for me.* □ *Hold up! You're going too fast.*

waiting in the wings ready or prepared to do something, especially to take over someone else's job or position. (From waiting at the side of the stage to go on.) □ *Mr. Smith retires as manager next year, and Mr. Jones is just waiting in the wings.* □ *Jane was waiting in the wings, hoping that a member of the hockey team would drop out and she would get a place on the team.*

walk a tightrope to be in a situation where one must be very cautious. (Also literal.) □ *I've been walking a tightrope all day. I need to relax.* □ *Our business is about to fail. We've been walking a tightrope for three months.*

walk all over someone to treat someone badly. (Also literal.) □ *She's so mean to her children. She walks all over them.* □ *The manager had walked all over Ann for months. Finally she quit.*

walk away with something AND **walk off with something 1.** to win something easily. (Informal.) □ *John won the tennis match with no difficulty. He walked away with it.* □ *Our team walked away with first place.* **2.** to take or steal something. □ *I think somebody just walked off with my purse!* □ *Somebody walked off with my daughter's bicycle.*

walk off with something See the previous entry.

walk on air to be very happy; to be euphoric. (Never literal.) □ *Ann was walking on air when she got the job.* □ *On the last day of school, all the children are walking on air.*

walk on eggs to be very cautious. (Informal. Never literal.) □ *The manager is very hard to deal with. You really have* *to walk on eggs.* □ *I've been walking on eggs ever since I started working here.*

walk out (on someone or something) 1. [with *someone*] to abandon someone; to leave one's spouse. □ *Mr. Franklin walked out on Mrs. Franklin last week.* □ *Bob walked out on Jane without saying good-bye.* **2.** to leave a performance (of something by someone). □ *We didn't like the play at all, so we walked out.* □ *John was giving a very dull speech, and a few people even walked out on him.*

walk the floor to pace nervously while waiting. □ *While Bill waited for news of the operation, he walked the floor for hours on end.* □ *Walking the floor won't help. You might as well sit down and relax.*

walk the plank to suffer punishment at the hand of someone. (From the image of pirates making their blindfolded captives commit suicide by walking off the end of a plank jutting out over the open sea.) □ *Fred may think he can make the members of my department walk the plank, but we will fight back.* □ *Tom thought he could make John walk the plank, but John fought back.*

Walls have ears. We may be overheard. □ *Let's not discuss this matter here. Walls have ears, you know.* □ *Shhh. Walls have ears. Someone may be listening.*

want for nothing to lack nothing; to have everything one needs or wishes. □ *The Smiths don't have much money, but their children seem to want for nothing.* □ *Jean's husband spoils her. She wants for nothing.*

warm as toast See *(as) warm as toast.*

warm the bench [for a player] to remain out of play during a game — seated on a bench. □ *John spent the whole game warming the bench.* □ *Mary never warms the bench. She plays from the beginning to the end.*

warm the cockles of someone's heart to make someone warm and happy. □ *It warms the cockles of my heart to hear*

you say that. □ *Hearing that old song again warmed the cockles of her heart.*

warm up to someone to become friendly with someone; to get used to a person and become friends. □ *It took a while before John warmed up to me, but then we became good friends.* □ *It's hard to warm up to Sally. She's very quiet and shy.*

warts and all including all the faults and disadvantages. □ *Jim has many faults, but Jean loves him, warts and all.* □ *The place where we went on vacation had some dismal aspects, but we liked it, warts and all.*

wash a few things out to do a little bit of laundry, such as socks and underclothing. □ *I'm sorry I can't go out tonight. I've got to wash a few things out.* T *I'll be ready to leave in just a minute. I've just got to wash out a few things.*

wash-and-wear referring to clothing made out of a kind of cloth that looks presentable after washing without ironing. (Fixed order.) □ *I always travel with wash-and-wear clothing.* □ *All his shirts are wash-and-wear, and this makes his life much easier since he used to burn them when he ironed them.*

wash one's dirty linen in public See *air one's dirty linen in public.*

wash one's hands of someone or something to end one's association with someone or something. □ *I washed my hands of Tom. I wanted no more to do with him.* □ *That car was a real headache. I washed my hands of it long ago.*

washed-out exhausted; lacking energy. (Informal.) □ *Pam was completely washed-out after the birth of the baby.* □ *I feel washed-out. I need a vacation.*

washed-up finished. (Informal.) □ *"You're through, Tom," said the manager, "fired — washed-up!"* □ *Max is washed-up as a bank teller.*

waste one's breath to waste one's time talking; to talk in vain. (Informal.) □ *Don't waste your breath talking to her.*

She won't listen. □ *You can't persuade me. You're just wasting your breath.*

waste someone to kill someone. (Slang, especially criminal slang.) □ *The thief tried to waste the bank guard after the bank robbery.* □ *The crook said, "Try that again, and I'll waste you!"*

watch one's step to act with care and caution so as not to make a mistake or offend someone. (Also literal.) □ *John had better watch his step with the new boss. He won't put up with his lateness.* □ *Mary was told by the lecturer to watch her step and stop missing classes.*

watch out See under *watch out for someone or something.*

watch out for someone or something AND **look out for someone or something 1.** [with *someone*] to watch over and care for someone. □ *When I was a kid, my older brother always watched out for me.* □ *I really needed someone to look out for me then.* **2.** to be on guard for someone or something; to be on watch for the arrival or approach of someone or something. □ *Watch out for someone wearing a white carnation.* □ *Look out for John and his friends. They'll be coming this way very soon.* **3.** AND **look out; watch out** to try to avoid a confrontation with someone or something. □ *Watch out! That car nearly hit you!* □ *Look out for John. He's looking for you, and he's really mad.* □ *Thanks. I'd better look out.*

watch someone like a hawk to watch someone very carefully. □ *The teacher watched the students like a hawk to make sure they did not cheat on the quiz.* □ *We have to watch Jim like a hawk in case he runs away.*

water something down to dilute something; to thin something out and make it lighter. (Figuratively or literal.) □ *The punch was good until someone watered it down.* ⊤ *Professor Jones sometimes waters down his lectures so people can understand them better.*

water under the bridge [something] past and forgotten. □ *Please don't*

worry about it anymore. It's all water under the bridge. □ *I can't change the past. It's water under the bridge.*

wax and wane to increase and then decrease, especially with reference to the phases of the moon. □ *As the moon waxes and wanes, so does the height of the tide change.* □ *Voter sentiment about the tax proposal waxes and wanes with each passing day.*

ways and means referring to the raising of money to pay for something. (Typically refers to a government committee or a committee of some organization charged with raising money. Fixed order.) □ *The suggestion was referred to the ways and means committee for discussion at the next meeting.* □ *The proposed legislation is stalled in ways and means.*

weak as a kitten See *(as) weak as a kitten.*

wear and tear (on something) the process of wearing down or breaking down something. (Fixed order.) □ *Driving in freezing weather means lots of wear and tear on your car.* □ *I drive carefully and sensibly to avoid wear and tear.*

wear more than one hat to have more than one set of responsibilities; to hold more than one office. □ *The mayor is also the police chief. She wears more than one hat.* □ *I have too much to do to wear more than one hat.*

wear off to become less; to stop gradually. □ *The effects of the painkiller wore off and my tooth began to hurt.* □ *I was annoyed at first, but my anger wore off.*

wear on someone to bother or annoy someone. □ *We stayed with them only a short time because my children seemed to wear on them.* □ *Always being short of money wears on a person after a while.*

wear one's heart on one's sleeve AND **have one's heart on one's sleeve** to display one's feelings openly and habitually, rather than keep them private. □ *John always has his heart on* *his sleeve so that everyone knows how he feels.* □ *Because she wears her heart on her sleeve, it's easy to hurt her feelings.*

wear out one's welcome to stay too long (at an event to which one has been invited); to visit somewhere too often. □ *Tom visited the Smiths so often that he wore out his welcome.* □ *At about midnight, I decided that I had worn out my welcome, so I went home.*

wear someone down to overcome someone's objections; to persist until someone has been persuaded. □ *John didn't want to go, but we finally wore him down.* ⊤ *We were unable to wear down John, and when we left, he was still insisting on running away from home.*

wear someone out to exhaust someone; to make someone tired. □ *The coach made the team practice until he wore them out.* ⊤ *If he wears out everybody on the team, nobody will be left to play in the game.*

weasel out (of something) to (figuratively or literally) get out or sneak out of something. (Informal.) □ *I don't want to go to the meeting. I think I'll try to weasel out of it.* □ *You had better be there! Don't try to weasel out!*

weave in and out (of something) to move, drive, or walk in and out of something, such as traffic, a line, etc. □ *The car was weaving in and out of traffic dangerously.* □ *The deer ran rapidly through the forest, weaving in and out of the trees.*

wee hours (of the night) See *small hours (of the night).*

weed someone or something out to remove someone or something unwanted or undesirable from a group or collection. □ *We had to weed them out one by one.* ⊤ *The auditions were held to weed out the actors with the least ability.* ⊤ *I'm going through my books to weed out those that I don't need anymore.*

week in, week out every week, week after week. (Informal. Fixed order.) □ *We have the same old food, week in,*

week out. □ *I'm tired of this job. I've done the same thing—week in, week out—for three years.*

weigh on someone's mind [for something] to be in a person's thoughts; [for something] to be bothering someone's thinking. □ *This problem has been weighing on my mind for many days now.* □ *I hate to have things weighing on my mind. I can't sleep when I'm worried.*

weigh someone down [for a thought] to worry or depress someone. (Also literal.) □ *All these problems really weigh me down.* ⊤ *Financial problems have been weighing down our entire family.*

weigh someone's words 1. to consider carefully what someone says. □ *I listened to what he said, and I weighed his words very carefully.* □ *Everyone was weighing his words. None of us knew exactly what he meant.* 2. to consider one's own words carefully when speaking. □ *I always weigh my words when I speak in public.* □ *John was weighing his words carefully because he didn't want to be misunderstood.*

welcome someone with open arms See *receive someone with open arms.*

welcome to do something to be free to do something. □ *You're welcome to leave whenever you wish.* □ *He's welcome to join the club whenever he feels he's ready.*

well and good See *(all) well and good.*

well-fixed See the following entry.

well-heeled AND **well-fixed; well-off** wealthy; with sufficient money. □ *My uncle can afford a new car. He's well-heeled.* □ *Everyone in his family is well-off.*

well-off See the previous entry.

well-to-do wealthy and of good social position. (Often with *quite,* as in the examples.) □ *The Jones family is quite well-to-do.* □ *There is a gentleman waiting for you at the door. He appears quite well-to-do.*

well up in years aged; old. □ *Jane's husband is well up in years. He is nearly 75.* □ *Joan's well up in years but healthy.*

wet behind the ears AND **not dry behind the ears** young and inexperienced. □ *John's too young to take on a job like this! He's still wet behind the ears!* □ *He may be wet behind the ears, but he's well trained and totally competent.* □ *Tom is going into business by himself? Why, he's hardly dry behind the ears.* □ *That kid isn't dry behind the ears. He'll go broke in a month.*

wet blanket a dull or depressing person who spoils other people's enjoyment. □ *Jack's fun at parties, but his brother's a wet blanket.* □ *I was with Anne and she was being a real wet blanket.*

wet someone's whistle to take a drink of something. (Folksy.) □ *Wow, am I thirsty. I need something to wet my whistle.* □ *Hey, Sally! Give her something to wet her whistle.*

whale the tar out of someone See *beat the living daylights out of someone.*

What are you driving at? What are you implying?; What do you mean? (Informal.) □ *What are you driving at? What are you trying to say?* □ *Why are you asking me all these questions? What are you driving at?*

what makes someone tick something that motivates someone; something that makes someone behave in a certain way. (Informal.) □ *William is sort of strange. I don't know what makes him tick.* □ *When you get to know people, you find out what makes them tick.*

What's done is done. It is final and in the past. □ *It's too late to change it now. What's done is done.* □ *What's done is done. The past cannot be altered.*

What's keeping you? What is taking you so long?; Why are you still there and not here? □ *Dinner is ready, and you are still at work. I telephoned to ask what's keeping you.* □ *What's keeping you? I am ready to go and you are still in there dressing.*

What's the good of something? What is the point of something?; Why bother with something? □ *What's the good of my going at all if I'll be late?* □ *There is no need to get there early. What's the good of that?*

What's with someone? What is bothering or affecting someone? (Slang.) □ *John seems upset. What's with him?* □ *There's nothing wrong with me. What's with you?*

wheel and deal to take part in clever but sometimes dishonest or immoral business deals. □ *John loves to wheel and deal in the money markets.* □ *Jack got tired of all the wheeling and dealing of big business and retired to run a pub in the country.*

when all is said and done when everything is finished and settled; when everything is considered. (See also *after all is said and done.*) □ *When all is said and done, this isn't such a bad part of the country to live in after all.* □ *When all is said and done, I believe I had a very enjoyable time on my vacation.*

When in Rome, do as the Romans do. a proverb meaning that one should behave in the same way that the local people behave. □ *I don't usually eat lamb, but I did when I went to Australia. When in Rome, do as the Romans do.* □ *I always carry an umbrella when I visit London. When in Rome, do as the Romans do.*

when it comes right down to it all things considered; when one really thinks about something. □ *When it comes right down to it, I'd like to find a new job.* □ *When it comes right down to it, he can't really afford a new car.*

when it comes to something as for something; speaking about something. (Informal.) □ *When it comes to fishing, John is an expert.* □ *When it comes to trouble, Mary really knows how to cause it.*

when least expected when one does not expect (something). □ *An old car is likely to give you trouble when least expected.* □ *My pencil usually breaks when least expected.*

when one is good and ready when one is completely ready. (Informal. Fixed order.) □ *I'll be there when I'm good and ready.* □ *Ann will finish the job when she's good and ready and not a minute sooner.*

when push comes to shove when the situation becomes more difficult; when matters escalate. (See also *if push comes to shove.*) □ *When push comes to shove, I will take a stronger position.* □ *When push comes to shove, I will come up with the money you need.*

When the cat's away, the mice will play. Some people will get into mischief when they are not being watched. □ *The students behaved very badly for the substitute teacher. When the cat's away, the mice will play.* □ *John had a wild party at his house when his parents were out of town. When the cat's away, the mice will play.*

when the chips are down at the final, critical moment; when things really get difficult. □ *When the chips are down, I know that I can depend on Jean to help out.* □ *I knew you would come and help when the chips were down.*

when the going gets rough See the following entry.

when the going gets tough AND **when the going gets rough** when things get extremely difficult; when it becomes difficult to proceed. (Also literal when referring to travel. A second line is sometimes added to the main entry phrase: *When the going gets tough, the tough get going.* This means that when things become difficult, strong people began to work or move faster and harder.) □ *When the going gets tough, I will be there to help you.* □ *I appreciate the kind words you sent to us when the going got a little rough last month.*

when the time is ripe at exactly the right time. □ *I'll tell her the good news when the time is ripe.* □ *When the time is ripe, I'll bring up the subject again.*

where one is coming from one's point of view. (Slang.) □ *I think I know what you mean. I know where you're coming from.* □ *Man, you don't know where I'm coming from! You don't understand a single word I say.*

where one lives See *close to home.*

Where there's a will there's a way. a proverb meaning that one can do something if one really wants to. □ *Don't give up, Ann. You can do it. Where there's a will there's a way.* □ *They told John he'd never walk again after his accident. He worked at it, and he was able to walk again! Where there's a will there's a way.*

Where there's smoke there's fire. a proverb meaning that some evidence of a problem probably indicates that there really is a problem. □ *There is a lot of noise coming from the classroom. There is probably something wrong. Where there's smoke there's fire.* □ *I think there is something wrong at the old house on the corner. The police are there again. Where there's smoke there's fire.*

whet someone's appetite to cause someone to be interested in something and to be eager to have, know, learn, etc., more about it. □ *Seeing that film really whetted my sister's appetite for horror films. She now sees as many as possible.* □ *My appetite for theater was whetted when I was very young.*

while away the time to spend or waste time. □ *I like to read to while away the time.* Ⓣ *Jane whiles the time away by daydreaming.*

whip something into shape See *lick something into shape.*

whip something up to prepare, create, or put something together. (Informal.) □ *I haven't written my report yet, but I'll whip one up before the deadline.* Ⓣ *Come in and sit down. I'll go whip up something to eat.*

white as a sheet See *(as) white as a sheet.*

white as the driven snow See *(as) white as the driven snow.*

white elephant something that is useless and which is either a nuisance or is expensive to keep up. (From the gift of a white elephant by the Kings of Siam [Thailand] to courtiers who displeased them, knowing the cost of the upkeep would ruin them.) □ *Bob's father-in-law has given him an old Rolls-Royce, but it's a real white elephant. He has no place to park it and can't afford the maintenance on it.* □ *Those antique vases Aunt Mary gave me are white elephants. They're ugly and take ages to clean.*

whole ball of wax AND **whole shooting match** the whole thing; the whole matter or affair; the entire affair or organization. □ *John is not a good manager. Instead of delegating jobs to others, he runs the whole shooting match himself.* □ *There's not a hard worker in that whole shooting match.* □ *I will be glad to be finished with this project. I want to be done with the whole ball of wax.* □ *I am tired of this job. I am fed up with the whole ball of wax.*

whole shooting match See the previous entry.

whoop it up to enjoy oneself in a lively and noisy manner. (Informal.) □ *John's friends really whooped it up at his bachelor party.* □ *Jean wants to have a party and whoop it up to celebrate her promotion.*

whys and wherefores of something the reason or causes relating to something. □ *I refuse to discuss the whys and wherefores of my decision. It's final.* □ *Bob doesn't know the whys and wherefores of his contract. He just knows that it means he will get a lot of money when he finishes the work.*

wide-awake completely awake. □ *After the telephone rang, I was wide-awake for an hour.* □ *I'm not very wide-awake at six o'clock in the morning.*

wide of the mark **1.** far from the target. □ *Tom's shot was wide of the mark.* □ *The pitch was quite fast, but wide of the mark.* **2.** inadequate; far from what is required or expected. □ *Jane's efforts were sincere, but wide of the mark.* □ *He failed the course because everything he did was wide of the mark.*

wild about someone or something enthusiastic about someone or something. □ *Bill is wild about chocolate ice cream.* □ *Sally is wild about Tom and his new car.*

wild-goose chase a worthless hunt or chase; a futile pursuit. □ *I wasted all afternoon on a wild-goose chase.* □ *John was angry because he was sent out on a wild-goose chase.*

Wild horses couldn't drag someone. nothing could force someone (to go somewhere). (Informal.) □ *I refuse to go to that meeting! Wild horses couldn't drag me.* □ *Wild horses couldn't drag her to that game.*

will not hear of something to refuse to tolerate or permit something. □ *You mustn't drive home alone. I won't hear of it.* □ *My parents won't hear of my staying out that late.*

win by a nose to win by the slightest amount of difference. (Informal. As in a horse race where one horse wins with only its nose ahead of the horse that comes in second.) □ *I ran the fastest race I could, but I only won by a nose.* □ *Sally won the race, but she only won by a nose.*

win out (over someone or something) to beat someone or something in a race or a contest. □ *My horse won out over yours, so you lose your bet.* □ *I knew I could win out if I just kept trying.*

win someone over to succeed in gaining the support and sympathy of someone. □ *Jane's parents disapproved of her engagement at first, but she won them over.* □ *I'm trying to win the boss over and get him to give us the day off.*

win the day See *carry the day.*

wind down to decrease or diminish. □ *Things are very busy now, but they'll wind down in about an hour.* □ *I hope business winds down soon. I'm exhausted.*

wind something up to conclude something. (Also literal.) □ *Today we'll wind that deal up with the bank.* ⊤ *I have a few items of business to wind up; then I'll be with you.*

wind up doing something See *end up doing something.*

wind up somewhere See *end up somewhere.*

wine and dine someone to treat someone to an expensive meal of the type that includes fine wines; to entertain someone lavishly. (Fixed order.) □ *The lobbyists wined and dined the senators one by one in order to influence them.* □ *We were wined and dined every night and given the best hotel accommodations in town.*

wing it to do the best that one can in a situation, especially when one is not prepared. (Compare with *play something by ear.*) □ *I lost my notes before my speech, and I had to wing it.* □ *The professor, it turned out, was winging it in every single lecture.*

wink at something to ignore something. (Informal.) □ *Billy caused me a little trouble, but I just winked at it.* □ *This is a serious matter, and you can't expect me just to wink at it.*

wipe someone or something out (Slang.) **1.** to cause someone to be broke. □ *They wiped me out in the poker game.* ⊤ *The crop failure wiped out all the farmers.* **2.** to exterminate someone or something. □ *The hunters came and wiped all the deer out.* ⊤ *The crooks wiped out the two witnesses.*

wipe someone's slate clean to (figuratively) erase someone's (bad) record. □ *I'd like to wipe my slate clean and start all over again.* □ *Bob did badly in high school, but he wiped his slate clean and did a good job in college.*

wipe something off 1. to remove something (from something else) by wiping

or rubbing. □ *There is mud on your shirt. Please wipe it off.* ⊤ *My shirt has catsup on it. I must wipe off the catsup.* **2.** to tidy or clean something by wiping (something else) off. □ *Please wipe the table off. There's water on it.* ⊤ *Wipe off your shirt. There's catsup on it.*

wipe the floor up with someone to beat or physically abuse someone. (Slang. Usually said as a threat.) □ *You say that to me one more time, and I'll wipe the floor up with you.* ⊤ *Oh, yeah! You're not big enough to wipe up the floor with anybody!*

wise as an owl See *(as) wise as an owl.*

wise up (to someone or something) to begin to understand the truth about someone or something. (Slang.) □ *It was almost a week before I began to wise up to John. He's a total phony.* □ *You had better stay hidden for a while. The police are beginning to wise up.*

wish something off on someone to pass something off onto someone else. (Informal.) □ *I don't want to have to deal with your problems. Don't wish them off on me.* ⊤ *The storekeeper wished off the defective watch on the very next customer who came in.*

wishful thinking believing that something is true or that something will happen just because one wishes that it were true or would happen. □ *Hoping for a car as a birthday present is just wishful thinking. Your parents can't afford it.* □ *Mary thinks that she is going to get a big rise, but that's wishful thinking. Her boss is so mean.*

with a heavy heart sadly. □ *With a heavy heart, she said good-bye.* □ *We left school on the last day with a heavy heart.*

with a view to doing something AND **with an eye to doing something** with the intention of doing something. □ *I came to this school with a view to getting a degree.* □ *The mayor took office with an eye to improving the town.*

with a will with determination and enthusiasm. □ *The children worked with a will to finish the project on time.* □

The workers set about manufacturing the new products with a will.

with all one's heart and soul very sincerely. □ *Oh, Bill, I love you with all my heart and soul, and I always will!* □ *She thanked us with all her heart and soul for the gift.*

with an eye to doing something See *with a view to doing something.*

with bells on (one's toes) eagerly, willingly, and on time. □ *Oh, yes! I'll meet you at the restaurant. I'll be there with bells on.* □ *All the smiling children were there waiting for me with bells on their toes.*

with both hands tied behind one's back See *with one hand tied behind one's back.*

with each passing day as days pass, one by one; day by day. □ *Things grow more expensive with each passing day.* □ *We are all growing older with each passing day.*

with every (other) breath [saying something] repeatedly or continually. □ *Bob was out in the yard, raking leaves and cursing with every other breath.* □ *The child was so grateful that she was thanking me with every breath.*

with flying colors easily and excellently. □ *John passed his geometry test with flying colors.* □ *Sally qualified for the race with flying colors.*

(with) hat in hand with humility. (Also literal.) □ *She stormed off but came back with hat in hand when she ran out of money.* □ *We had to go hat in hand to the committee to get a grant for our proposal.*

with it (Slang.) **1.** alert and knowledgeable. □ *Jane isn't making any sense. She's not really with it tonight.* □ *Jean's mother is not really with it anymore. She's going senile.* □ *Peter's not with it yet. He's only just come round from the anesthetic.* **2.** up-to-date. □ *My parents are so old-fashioned. I'm sure they were never with it.* □ *Why do you wear those baggy old clothes? Why aren't you with it?*

with no strings attached AND **without any strings attached** unconditionally; with no obligations attached. □ *My parents gave me a computer without any strings attached.* □ *I want this only if there are no strings attached.*

with one hand tied behind one's back AND **with both hands tied behind one's back** under a handicap; easily. □ *I could put an end to this argument with one hand tied behind my back.* □ *John could do this job with both hands tied behind his back.*

with something to spare See *and something to spare.*

with the best will in the world however much one wishes to do something or however hard one tries to do something. □ *With the best will in the world, Jack won't be able to help Mary get the job.* □ *With the best will in the world, they won't finish the job in time.*

wither on the vine AND **die on the vine** [for something] to decline or fade away at an early stage of development. (Also literal, in reference to grapes or other fruit.) □ *You have a great plan, Tom. Let's keep it alive. Don't let it wither on the vine.* □ *The whole project died on the vine when the contract was canceled.*

within a stone's throw (of something) AND **(just) a stone's throw away (from something); (just) a stone's throw (from something)** very close (to something). (Possibly as close as the distance one could throw a stone. It usually refers to a distance much greater than one could throw a stone.) □ *The police department was located within a stone's throw of our house.* □ *We live in Carbondale, and that's just a stone's throw away from the Mississippi River.* □ *Come visit. We live just a stone's throw away.* □ *John saw Mary across the street, just a stone's throw away.* □ *Philadelphia is a stone's throw from New York City.*

within an inch of one's life very close to taking one's life; almost to death. □ *The accident frightened me within an inch of my life.* □ *When Mary was* *seriously ill in the hospital, she came within an inch of her life.*

within bounds See *within limits.*

within calling distance See the following entry.

within hailing distance AND **within calling distance** close enough to hear someone call out. □ *When the boat came within hailing distance, I asked if I could borrow some gasoline.* □ *We weren't within calling distance, so I couldn't hear what you said to me.*

within limits AND **within bounds** up to a certain point; with certain restrictions. □ *You're free to do what you want — within limits, of course.* □ *You must try to keep behavior at the party within bounds.*

within reason reasonable; reasonably. □ *You can do anything you want within reason.* □ *I'll pay any sum you ask — within reason.*

within someone's grasp See the following entry.

within someone's reach AND **within someone's grasp** almost in the possession of someone. □ *My goals are almost within my reach, so I know I'll succeed.* □ *We almost had the contract within our grasp, but the deal fell through at the last minute.*

without any strings attached See *with no strings attached.*

without batting an eye without showing alarm or response; without blinking an eye. □ *I knew I had insulted her, but she turned to me and asked me to leave without batting an eye.* □ *Right in the middle of the speech — without batting an eye — the speaker walked off the stage.*

without fail for certain; absolutely. □ *I'll be there at noon without fail.* □ *The plane leaves on time every day without fail.*

without further ado without further talk. (An overworked phrase usually heard in public announcements.) □ *And without further ado, I would like to introduce Mr. Bill Franklin!* □ *The*

time has come to leave, so without further ado, good evening and good-bye.

without question absolutely; certainly. □ *She agreed to help without question.* □ *She said, "I stand ready to support you without question."*

without rhyme or reason without purpose, order, or reason. (See variations in the examples. Fixed order.) □ *The teacher said my report was disorganized. My paragraphs seemed to be without rhyme or reason.* □ *Everything you do seems to be without rhyme or reason.* □ *This procedure is without rhyme or reason.*

without so much as doing something without even doing something. □ *Jane borrowed Bob's car without so much as asking his permission.* □ *Mary's husband walked out without so much as saying good-bye.*

Woe is me! I am unfortunate.; I am unhappy. (Usually humorous.) □ *Woe is me! I have to work when the rest of the office staff is off.* □ *Woe is me. I have the flu and my friends have gone to a party.*

wolf in sheep's clothing someone or something threatening that is disguised as someone or something kind. □ *Beware of the police chief. He seems polite, but he's a wolf in sheep's clothing.* □ *This proposal seems harmless enough, but I think it's a wolf in sheep's clothing.*

woman to woman See *man to man.*

won't hold water to be inadequate, insubstantial, or ill-conceived. (Informal. See also *not hold water.*) □ *Sorry, your ideas won't hold water. Nice try, though.* □ *The lawyer's case wouldn't hold water, so the defendant was released.*

woolgathering daydreaming. (From the practice of wandering along collecting tufts of sheep's wool from hedges.) □ *John never listens to the teacher. He's always woolgathering.* □ *I wish my new secretary would get on with the work and stop woolgathering.*

word by word one word at a time. □ *We examined the contract word by word to make sure everything was the way we wanted.* □ *We compared the stories word by word to see what made them different.*

word for word in the exact words; verbatim. □ *I memorized the speech, word for word.* □ *I can't recall word for word what she told us.*

word to the wise a good piece of advice; a word of wisdom. □ *If I can give you a word to the wise, I would suggest going to the courthouse about an hour before your trial.* □ *Here is a word to the wise. Keep your eyes open and your mouth shut.*

words to that effect other words that have about the same meaning. □ *She told me I ought to read more carefully — or words to that effect.* □ *I was instructed to go to the devil, or words to that effect.*

work like a horse to work very hard. □ *I've been working like a horse all day, and I'm tired.* □ *I'm too old to work like a horse. I'd prefer to relax more.*

work on someone or something 1. [with *someone*] to try to convince someone about something. (Informal.) □ *We worked on Tom for nearly an hour, but we couldn't get him to change his mind.* □ *I'll work on him for a while, and I'll change his mind.* **2.** [with *someone*] to give medical treatment to someone. □ *The dentist was working on Mary while I waited for her in the other room.* □ *The surgeon worked on the patient, trying to stop the bleeding.* **3.** [with *something*] to repair, build, or adjust something. □ *The carpenter worked on the fence for three hours.* □ *Bill is out working on his car engine.*

work one's fingers to the bone to work very hard. □ *I worked my fingers to the bone so you children could have everything you needed. Now look at the way you treat me!* □ *I spent the day working my fingers to the bone, and now I want to relax.*

work (one's way) into something to (literally or figuratively) squeeze into something. □ *Ann worked her way into the club, and now she's a member in good standing.* □ *The skunk worked its way into the hollow log.*

work one's way through college to hold a job that pays part of one's college expenses. □ *Tom couldn't get a loan, so he had to work his way through college.* □ *I worked my way through college, and that made college seem more valuable to me.*

work one's way up to advance in one's job or position, from the beginning level to a higher level. □ *I haven't always been president of this bank. I started as a teller and worked my way up.* □ *If I work my way up, can I be president of the bank?*

work out to exercise. □ *I have to work out every day in order to keep healthy.* □ *Working out a lot gives me a big appetite.*

work out (all right) See *turn out (all right).*

work out for the best to end up in the best possible way. □ *Don't worry. Things will work out for the best.* □ *It seems bad now, but it'll work out for the best.*

work someone or something in to insert someone or something (into a schedule or a line). □ *The doctor's schedule was very busy, but the nurse agreed to try to work me in.* □ *The mechanic had many cars to fix, but he said he'd work my car in.* ⊤ *I'm glad he could work in my car.*

work someone or something up 1. [with *someone*] to get someone ready for something, especially medical treatment. ⊤ *The coach worked up the whole team before the game.* □ *The doctor told the nurse to work Mr. Franklin up for surgery.* **2.** [with *something*] to create, cook, or arrange something. ⊤ *Bob is in the kitchen working up dinner.* □ *Is there something planned for Friday night, or should we work something up?*

work someone over to threaten, intimidate, or beat someone. (Slang, especially criminal slang.) □ *I thought they were really going to work me over, but they only asked a few questions.* ⊤ *The police worked over Bill until he told where the money was hidden.*

work something into something to rob or knead something into something else. □ *You should work more butter into the dough before baking the bread.* □ *Work this lotion into your skin to make your sunburn stop hurting.*

work something off to get rid of something, such as fat, by doing physical exercise. □ *Bob put on weight on his vacation and is trying to work it off by swimming regularly.* □ *Jane tried to work off her depression by playing a game of tennis.*

work something out to settle a problem. (Also literal.) □ *It was a serious problem, but we managed to work it out.* ⊤ *I'm glad we can work out our problems without fighting.*

work through channels to try to get something done by going through the proper procedures and persons. (See also *go through channels*.) □ *You can't accomplish anything around here if you don't work through channels.* □ *I tried working through channels, but it takes too long. This is an emergency.*

work wonders (with someone or something) to be surprisingly beneficial to someone or something; to be very helpful with someone or something. □ *This new medicine works wonders with my headaches.* □ *Jean was able to work wonders with the office staff. They improved their efficiency as soon as she took over.*

worm one's way out of something to squeeze or wiggle out of a problem or a responsibility. (Informal.) □ *This is your job, and you can't worm your way out of it!* □ *I'm not trying to worm my way out of anything!*

worm something out of someone to get some kind of information out of someone. (Informal.) □ *He didn't want to tell me the truth, but I finally wormed it out of him.* □ *She succeeded in worming the secret out of me. I didn't mean to tell it.*

worth its weight in gold very valuable. □ *This book is worth its weight in gold.* □ *Oh, Bill. You're wonderful. You're worth your weight in gold.*

worth one's salt worth one's salary. □ *Tom doesn't work very hard, and he's just barely worth his salt, but he's very easy to get along with.* □ *I think he's more than worth his salt. He's a good worker.*

worth someone's while worth one's time and trouble. (See also *make it worth someone's while*.) □ *The job pays so badly it's not worth your while even going for an interview.* □ *It's not worth Mary's while going all that way just for a one-hour meeting.*

worthy of the name deserving to be so called; good enough to enjoy a specific name. □ *There was not an actor worthy of the name in that play.* □ *Any art critic worthy of the name would know that painting to be a fake.*

would as soon do something See *had as soon do something*.

wouldn't dream of doing something would not even consider doing something. (Informal.) □ *I wouldn't dream of taking your money!* □ *I'm sure that John wouldn't dream of complaining to the manager.*

wouldn't touch something with a ten-foot pole would not be involved with something under any circumstances. □ *I know about the piece of vacant land for sale on Maple Street. I wouldn't touch it with a ten-foot pole because there used to be a gas station there and the soil is polluted.* □ *I wouldn't touch that book with a ten-foot pole. It is nothing but gossip and scandal.*

wrap something up to terminate something. (Informal. Also literal. See also *get something sewed up*.) □ *It's time to wrap this project up and move on to something else.* ⊤ *Let's wrap up this discussion. It's time to go home.*

wrapped up in someone or something concerned and involved with someone or something. □ *Sally is wrapped up in her work.* □ *Ann is all wrapped up in her children and their activities.*

wreak havoc with something to cause a lot of trouble with something; to ruin or damage something. □ *Your attitude will wreak havoc with my project.* □ *The weather wreaked havoc with our picnic plans.*

write someone or something off 1. [with *something*] to absorb a debt or a loss in accounting. □ *The bill couldn't be collected, so we had to write it off.* ⊤ *The bill was too large, and we couldn't write off the amount. We decided to sue.* **2.** to drop someone or something from consideration. □ *The manager wrote Tom off for a promotion.* ⊤ *I wrote off that piece of land as worthless. It can't be used for anything.*

write someone or something up 1. [with *something*] to prepare a bill, order, or statement. □ *Please write the order up and send me a copy.* ⊤ *As soon as I finish writing up your check, I'll bring you some more coffee.* **2.** to write an article about someone or something. □ *A reporter wrote me up for the Sunday paper.* □ *I wrote up a local factory and sent the story to a magazine, but they didn't buy the story.*

write something down to write something; to make a note of something. (Also without *down*.) □ *If I write it down, I won't forget it.* ⊤ *I wrote down everything she said.*

write something out to spell or write a number or an abbreviation. □ *Don't just write "7," write it out.* ⊤ *Please write out all abbreviations, such as* Doctor *for* Dr.

wrote the book on something to be very authoritative about something; to know enough about something to write the definitive book on it. (Always in past tense. Also literal.) □ *Ted wrote the book on unemployment. He's been looking for work in three states for two years.* □ *Do I know about misery? I wrote the book on misery!*

X

X marks the spot this is the exact spot. (Can be used literally when someone draws an X to mark an exact spot.) □ *This is where the rock struck my car—X marks the spot.* □ *Now, please move that table over here. Yes, right here—X marks the spot.*

Y

year in, year out year after year, all year long. (Fixed order.) □ *I seem to have hay fever year in, year out. I never get over it.* □ *John wears the same old suit, year in, year out.*

yield the right-of-way to give the right to turn or move forward to another person or vehicle. (See also *have the right-of-way.*) □ *When you're driving, it's better to yield the right-of-way than to have a wreck.* □ *You must always yield the right-of-way when you're making a left turn.*

You bet (your boots)! AND **You can bet on it!** surely; absolutely. (Informal.) □ BILL: *Coming to the meeting next Saturday?* BOB: *You bet!* □ *You bet your boots I'll be there!*

You can bet on it! See the previous entry.

You can say that again! AND **You said it!** That is true.; You are correct. (Informal. The word *that* is emphasized.) □ MARY: *It sure is hot today.* JANE: *You can say that again!* □ BILL: *This cake is yummy!* BOB: *You said it!*

You can't please everyone. It is not possible to make everyone happy. (Said when someone has made a complaint or when someone has pointed out a flaw that cannot be fixed.) □ *When Jean complained about the choices on the dinner menu, the waiter said, "Sorry. You can't please everyone."* □ *Jerry reported that many of his friends had noticed that the colors of the walls in the living room clashed. His mother said, "Oh, well. You can't please everyone."*

You can't take it with you. You should enjoy your money now, because it is no good when you're dead. □ *My uncle is a wealthy miser. I keep telling him, "You can't take it with you."* □ *If you have money, you should make out a will. You can't take it with you, you know!*

You can't teach an old dog new tricks. a proverb meaning that old people cannot learn anything new. (Also used literally of dogs.) □ *"Of course I can learn," bellowed Uncle John. "Who says you can't teach an old dog new tricks?"* □ *I'm sorry. I can't seem to learn to do it right. Oh, well. You can't teach an old dog new tricks.*

you know as you are aware, or should be aware. (Informal. This should not be overused.) □ *This is a very valuable book, you know.* □ *Goldfish can be overfed, you know.*

You said it! See *You can say that again!*

You scratch my back and I'll scratch yours. You do a favor for me and I'll do a favor for you.; If you do something for me that I cannot do for myself, I will do something for you that you cannot do for yourself. (Could also be literal.) □ *I'll grab the box on the top shelf if you will creep under the table and pick up my pen. You scratch my back, and I'll scratch yours.* □ *Politicians are always saying to one another, "You scratch my back and I'll scratch yours."*

Your guess is as good as mine. Your answer is likely to be as correct as mine. (Informal.) □ *I don't know* *where the scissors are. Your guess is as good as mine.* □ *Your guess is as good as mine as to when the train will arrive.*

yours truly 1. a closing phrase at the end of a letter, just before the signature. □ *Yours truly, Tom Jones* □ *Best wishes from yours truly, Bill Smith* **2.** oneself; I; me. (Informal.) □ *There's nobody here right now but yours truly.* □ *Everyone else got up and left the table leaving yours truly to pay the bill.*

Z

zero in on something to aim or focus directly on something. (Informal.) □ *"Now," said Mr. Smith, "I would like to zero in on another important point."* □ *Mary is very good about zeroing in on the most important and helpful ideas.*

zonk out to pass out; to fall asleep. (Slang.) □ *I was so tired after playing football that I almost zonked out on the floor.* □ *I had a cup of coffee before the test to keep from zonking out in the middle of it.*

zoom in (on someone or something) 1. to fly or move rapidly at someone or something. (Slang.) □ *The hawk zoomed in on the sparrow.* □ *The angry bees zoomed in on Jane and stung her.* □ *When the door opened, the cat zoomed in.* **2.** [for a photographer] to use a zoom lens to get a closer view of someone or something. □ *Bill zoomed in on Sally's face just as she grinned.* □ *On the next shot I'll zoom in for a close-up.*

PHRASE-FINDER INDEX

Use this index to find the form of a phrase that you want to look up in the dictionary. First, pick out any major word in the phrase you are seeking. Second, look that word up in this index to find the form of the phrase used in this dictionary. Third, look up the phrase in the dictionary. See **Hints** below.

Some of the words occurring in the dictionary entries are not listed as entries in this index. Some words are omitted because they occur so frequently that their lists would cover many pages. In these instances, you should look up the phrase under some other word. Most of the grammar or function words are not indexed. In addition, the most numerous verbs, *be, get, go, have, make,* and *take,* are not indexed.

Uses

This index provides a convenient way to find the complete form of an entry from only a single major word in the entry phrase.

Hints

1. When you are trying to find a phrase in this index, look up the noun first, if there is one.

2. When you are looking for a noun, try first to find the singular form or the simplest form of the noun.

3. When you are looking for a verb, try first to find the present tense form or the simplest form of the verb.

4. In most phrases where a noun or pronoun is a variable part of a phrase, it will be represented by the words "someone" or "something" in the form of the phrase used in the dictionary. If you do not find the noun you want in the index, it may, in fact, be a variable word.

5. This is an index of forms, not meanings. The phrases in an index entry may not have any meaning in common — they share only some form of the word they are listed under. Consult the dictionary for information about meaning.

ABACK
taken aback

ABET
aid and abet someone

ABIDE
abide by something

ABILITY
to the best of one's ability

ABLE
able to breathe (easily) again □ able to breathe (freely) again □ able to do something blindfolded □ able to do something standing on one's head □ able to make something □ able to take a joke □ able to take just so much □ able to take something □ not able □ not able to call one's time one's own □ not able to go on □ not able to help something □ not able to make anything out of someone or something □ not able to see the forest for the trees □ not able to wait □ ready, willing, and able

ABODE
take up one's abode somewhere

ABOVE
above and beyond (something) □ (above and) beyond the call of duty □ above suspicion □ cut above someone or something □ get one's head above water □ head and shoulders above someone or something □ keep one's head above water □ over and above something

ABOVEBOARD
honest and aboveboard □ open and aboveboard

ABREAST
keep abreast (of something)

ABSENCE
conspicuous by one's absence □ in the absence of someone or something

ABSENT
absent without leave

ACCIDENT
have an accident

ACCORD
of one's own accord

ACCORDING
according to all accounts □ according to Hoyle □ according to one's own lights □ according to someone or something

ACCOUNT
according to all accounts □ balance the accounts □ blow-by-blow account □ by all accounts □ cook the accounts □ give a good account of oneself □ not on any account □ on account □ on any account □ on no account □ on someone's account □ square accounts (with someone) □ take someone or something into account □ There's no accounting for taste. □ turn something to good account

ACCUSTOMED
accustomed to someone or something

ACE
ace in the hole □ come within an ace of doing something □ have an ace up one's sleeve □ hold all the aces

ACID
acid test

ACKNOWLEDGE
acknowledge receipt (of something) □ acknowledge someone to be right

ACQUIRE
acquire a taste for something

ACROSS
across the board □ cut across something □ get someone or something across □ get something across (to someone) □ put someone or something across □ stumble across someone or something

ACT
act as someone □ act high-and-mighty □ act of faith □ act of God □ act of war □ act one's age □ act something out □ act up □ catch someone in the act (of doing something) □ caught in the act □ clean up one's act □ get into the act □ get one's act together □ in the act (of doing something) □ keep up an act □ keep up one's act □ put on an act □ read someone the riot act □ tough act to follow

ACTION

Actions speak louder than words. □ all talk (and no action) □ go into action □ piece of the action □ swing into action

ACTIVE

on active duty

ADAM

not know someone from Adam

ADD

add fuel to the fire □ add fuel to the flame □ add insult to injury □ add up (to something)

ADDRESS

address someone as something

ADIEU

bid adieu to someone or something □ bid someone or something adieu

ADO

much ado about nothing □ without further ado

ADVANCE

advanced in years □ pay in advance

ADVANTAGE

get the advantage of someone □ get the advantage over someone □ show something to good advantage □ take advantage of someone or something □ turn something to one's advantage

ADVOCATE

play (the) devil's advocate

AEGIS

under the aegis of someone

AFFAIRS

fine state of affairs □ pretty state of affairs □ settle someone's affairs

AFIRE

like a house afire

AFOUL

fall afoul of someone or something □ run afoul of someone or something

AFRAID

afraid of one's own shadow

AFT

fore and aft

AFTER

after a fashion □ after all □ after all is said and done □ after hours □

after the fact □ after the fashion of someone or something □ day after day □ get after someone □ keep after someone □ live happily ever after □ morning after (the night before) □ much sought after □ name someone after someone else □ run after someone □ stay after someone □ take after someone □ take off (after someone or something) □ take out (after someone or something) □ throw good money after bad □ time after time

AGAIN

able to breathe (easily) again □ able to breathe (freely) again □ at it again □ be oneself again □ Come again? □ do something over (again) □ (every) now and again □ now and again □ off again, on again □ on again, off again □ over and over (again) □ run that by (someone) again □ something else (again) □ time and (time) again □ You can say that again!

AGAINST

against someone's will □ against the clock □ bang one's head against a brick wall □ bear a grudge (against someone) □ beat one's head against the wall □ dead set against someone or something □ fight against time □ for the odds to be against one □ get two strikes against one □ go against the grain □ guard against someone or something □ have a case (against someone) □ have a grudge against someone □ have one's heart set against something □ have something against someone or something □ have the cards stacked against one □ hold a grudge against someone □ hold something against someone □ hope against (all) hope □ lift a hand (against someone or something) □ nurse a grudge (against someone) □ one's heart is set against something □ pit someone or something against someone or something □ play both ends (against the middle) □ play someone off against someone else □ race against time □ raise a hand (against someone or something) □ set one's heart against something □ side against someone □ stack the cards (against someone or something) □ stack the deck (against someone or something) □ swim against the current □ swim against the tide □ take a stand (against someone or something) □ take up arms (against someone or something) □ the cards are stacked against one □ up against something

AGE
act one's age □ be of age □ come of age □ in a coon's age □ in this day and age □ ripe old age

AGREE
not agree with someone

AHEAD
ahead of one's time □ ahead of the game □ ahead of time □ come out ahead □ dead ahead □ full steam ahead □ get the go-ahead □ give someone the go-ahead □ one jump ahead (of someone or something) □ one move ahead (of someone or something)

AHOLD
get (a)hold of someone or something □ take (a)hold of someone or something

AID
aid and abet someone

AIM
aim to do something □ take aim (at someone or something)

AIN'T
That ain't hay.

AIR
air one's dirty linen in public □ air one's grievances □ air something out □ breath of fresh air □ build castles in the air □ clear the air □ full of hot air □ get the air □ give someone the air □ have one's nose in the air □ in the air □ off the air □ on the air □ one's nose is in the air □ out of thin air □ pull something out of thin air □ put on airs □ up in the air (about someone or something) □ vanish into thin air □ walk on air

AISLE
have them rolling in the aisles

ALCOHOL
under the influence (of alcohol)

ALERT
on the alert (for someone or something)

ALIKE
share and share alike

ALIVE
alive and kicking □ alive and well □ alive with someone or something □ more dead than alive □ skin someone alive

ALLEY
right down someone's alley □ right up someone's alley □ up a blind alley

ALLOW
allow for someone or something

ALLOWANCE
make allowance(s) (for someone or something)

ALONE
go it alone □ leave well enough alone □ let alone someone or something □ let well enough alone

ALONG
along in years □ get along (in years) □ get along (on a shoestring) □ get along (with someone) □ get along (with someone or something) □ get along (without (someone or something)) □ go along for the ride □ go along (with someone or something) □ inch along (something) □ play along with someone or something □ string along (with someone)

ALONGSIDE
alongside (of) someone or something

ALPHA
alpha and omega

ALTOGETHER
in the altogether

AMISS
take something amiss

AMOUNT
amount to something □ amount to the same thing □ set someone back (some amount of money) □ to the tune of some amount of money

ANALYSIS
in the final analysis □ in the last analysis

ANDS
no ifs, ands, or buts about it

ANGEL
fools rush in (where angels fear to tread)

ANON
ever and anon

ANOTHER
another country heard from □ (another) nail in someone's or something's coffin □ dance to another tune □ get another guess coming □ get another think coming □ horse of another color □ keep something for another occasion □ leave something for another occasion □ One good turn deserves another. □ One man's meat is another man's poison. □ one way or another □ sing another tune

ANSWER
answer for someone or something □ answer someone's purpose □ answer to someone □ not take no for an answer

ANT
get ants in one's pants

ANY
any number of someone or something □ any port in a storm □ at any cost □ at any rate □ by any means □ go to any length □ in any case □ in any event □ not on any account □ not see any objection (to something) □ on any account □ without any strings attached

ANYONE
as far as anyone knows □ not give anyone the time of day □ so far as anyone knows

ANYTHING
can't do anything with someone or something □ not able to make anything out of someone or something □ not for (anything in) the world

APART
be poles apart □ come apart at the seams □ fall apart at the seams □

take someone apart □ tell people apart □ tell things apart

APE
go ape (over someone or something)

APPEAR
appear as something □ appear out of nowhere

APPEARANCE
by all appearances □ keep up appearances □ make an appearance □ put in an appearance

APPETITE
whet someone's appetite

APPLE
apple of someone's eye □ apples and oranges □ as easy as (apple) pie □ easy as (apple) pie □ in apple-pie order □ upset the apple cart

APPOINT
at the appointed time

APPOINTMENT
make an appointment (with someone)

APPROVAL
on approval

APRON
tied to one's mother's apron strings

AREA
gray area

ARGUMENT
get into an argument (with someone)

ARM
arm in arm □ cost an arm and a leg □ give one's right arm (for someone or something) □ pay an arm and a leg (for something) □ put the arm on someone □ receive someone with open arms □ shot in the arm □ take up arms (against someone or something) □ twist someone's arm □ up in arms □ welcome someone with open arms

ARMED
armed and dangerous □ armed to the teeth

ARMOUR
chink in one's armour

AROUND
all around Robin Hood's barn □

(a)round the clock □ (a)round-the-clock □ beat around the bush □ blue around the gills □ boss someone around □ bring someone around □ bring something crashing down (around one) □ cast around for someone or something □ come (a)round □ drop around (sometime) □ enough to go (a)round □ every time one turns around □ fiddle around (with someone or something) □ find one's way (around) □ fool around (with someone or something) □ get around □ get around to doing something □ get (around) to something □ go (a)round in circles □ go (a)round the bend □ go around with someone □ green around the gills □ hang around (with someone) □ have been around □ hem and haw (around) □ horse around □ kick someone or something around □ kid around (with someone) □ knock someone or something around □ know one's way around □ mess around (with someone or something) □ monkey around (with someone or something) □ mope around □ nose around □ order someone around □ pal around (with someone) □ pale around the gills □ play around (with someone or something) □ poke around □ rally (a)round someone or something □ run (around) in circles □ run around like a chicken with its head cut off □ run around with someone □ run circles around someone □ run rings around someone □ scratch around (for something) □ screw around (with someone or something) □ shop around (for something) □ stick around □ throw one's weight around □ throw someone's name around □ twist someone around one's little finger □ up and around

ARRANGE
arrange something with someone □ arrange to do something with someone

ARRANGEMENT
make arrangements (for someone or something)

ARREAR
in arrears

ARRIVE
arrive in a body □ arrive on the scene

ASIDE
(all) joking aside □ (all) kidding aside □ as an aside □ aside from someone or something □ kidding aside

ASK
ask for something □ ask for the moon □ ask for trouble □ ask someone out □ for the asking □ one's for the asking

ASLEEP
asleep at the switch □ fall asleep

ASS
tits and ass

ASSAULT
assault and battery

ASSURED
rest assured

ASTRAY
go astray

ATTACH
with no strings attached □ without any strings attached

ATTENTION
attract someone's attention □ pay attention (to someone or something)

ATTITUDE
devil-may-care attitude □ wait-and-see attitude

ATTRACT
attract someone's attention

AUCTION
Dutch auction

AUGUR
augur well for someone or something

AUSPICE
under the auspices of someone

AVAIL
of no avail □ to no avail

AVAILABLE
make someone or something available to someone

AVERAGE
on the average

AVOID
avoid someone or something like the plague

AWAGGING
set tongues (a)wagging

AWAKE
wide-awake

AWAY
away from one's desk □ blow someone or something away □ carried away □ come away empty-handed □ do away with someone or something □ draw (someone's) fire (away from someone or something) □ eat away at someone or something □ explain something away □ far and away the best □ fire away at someone or something □ fritter something away □ get away (from it all) □ get away with something □ get carried away □ give the bride away □ give the game away □ go away empty-handed □ hammer away (at someone or something) □ (just) a stone's throw away □ lay someone or something away □ make away with someone or something □ pass away □ peg away (at something) □ plug away (at something) □ put someone away □ right away □ salt something away □ shy away (from someone or something) □ slip away □ sock something away □ square someone or something away □ squared away □ squirrel something away □ take it away □ take someone or something away □ take someone's breath away □ up and away □ walk away with something □ When the cat's away, the mice will play. □ while away the time

AWE
in awe (of someone or something) □ stand in awe (of someone or something)

AWKWARDNESS
main strength and awkwardness

AWOL
go AWOL

AX
get the ax □ give someone the ax □ have an ax to grind (with someone)

BABE
babe in the woods

BABY
as soft as a baby's bottom □ soft as a baby's bottom □ throw the baby out with the bath(water)

BACK
back and fill □ back and forth □ back down (from someone or something) □ back East □ back in circulation □ back of the beyond □ back off (from someone or something) □ back order something □ back out (of something) □ back someone or something up □ back the wrong horse □ back-to-back □ back to square one □ back to the drawing board □ back to the salt mines □ behind someone's back □ break one's back (to do something) □ break the back of something □ cut back (on something) □ date back (to sometime) □ double back (on someone or something) □ fall back on someone or something □ from way back □ get back (at someone) □ get back into circulation □ get back into harness □ get back on one's feet □ get back (to someone) □ Get off someone's back! □ get someone's back up □ give someone a pat on the back □ give someone the shirt off one's back □ go back on one's word □ hang back □ hark(en) back to something □ have back at someone □ have eyes in the back of one's head □ have one's back to the wall □ knock something back □ know someone or something like the back of one's hand □ laid-back □ like water off a duck's back □ on someone's back □ pat someone on the back □ pay someone a back-handed compliment □ pin someone's ears back □ put one's back (in)to something □ put something on the back burner □ roll something back □ scratch someone's back □ set one back on one's heels □ set someone back (some amount of money) □ sit back and let something happen □ stab someone in the back □ stand (in) back of someone or something □ take something back □ talk back (to someone) □ That's the

straw that broke the camel's back. □ think back (on someone or something) □ turn one's back (on someone or something) □ turn the clock back □ with both hands tied behind one's back □ with one hand tied behind one's back □ You scratch my back and I'll scratch yours.

BACKSEAT
take a backseat (to someone)

BACKWARDS
bend over backwards (to do something) □ fall over backwards (to do something) □ know something backwards and forwards □ know something forwards and backwards □ lean over backwards (to do something)

BACKYARD
in one's (own) backyard

BACON
bring home the bacon

BAD
as bad as all that □ bad blood (between people) □ bad-mouth someone or something □ be off to a bad start □ come to a bad end □ get off to a bad start □ go bad □ go from bad to worse □ good riddance (to bad rubbish) □ have a bad effect (on someone or something) □ have a run of bad luck □ in a bad mood □ in a bad way □ in bad faith □ in bad sorts □ in bad taste □ in bad (with someone) □ leave a bad taste in someone's mouth □ not half bad □ throw good money after bad

BAG
bag and baggage □ bag of tricks □ leave someone holding the bag □ let the cat out of the bag □ mixed bag □ put on the feed bag

BAGGAGE
bag and baggage

BAIL
bail out (of something) □ bail someone or something out □ jump bail □ out on bail □ skip bail

BAIT
bait and switch □ fish or cut bait □ rise to the bait

BALANCE
balance the accounts □ balance the books □ catch someone off-balance □ checks and balances □ hang in the balance □ in the balance □ strike a balance (between two things)

BALL
(all) balled up □ ball and chain □ ball of fire □ balled up □ behind the eight ball □ carry the ball □ drop the ball □ get the ball rolling □ have a ball □ have something on the ball □ have the ball in one's court □ keep one's eye on the ball □ keep the ball rolling □ new ball game □ on the ball □ pitch someone a curve (ball) □ play ball (with someone) □ set the ball rolling □ start the ball rolling □ That's the way the ball bounces. □ whole ball of wax

BALLOON
go over like a lead balloon □ send up a trial balloon

BALLOT
stuff the ballot box

BANANA
go bananas

BAND
beat the band

BANDWAGON
climb on the bandwagon □ get on the bandwagon □ jump on the bandwagon

BANG
bang one's head against a brick wall □ get a bang out of someone or something □ give someone a bang □ go over with a bang

BANK
bank on something □ break the bank

BAPTISM
baptism of fire

BAR
no holds barred

BARGAIN
bargain for something □ bargain on something □ drive a hard bargain □ hold one's end (of the bargain) up □ in the bargain □ more than someone

bargained for □ strike a bargain □ throw something into the bargain

BARGE
barge in (on someone or something)

BARK
bark up the wrong tree □ One's bark is worse than one's bite.

BARN
all around Robin Hood's barn

BARRED
no holds barred

BARREL
as funny as a barrel of monkeys □ as much fun as a barrel of monkeys □ get someone over a barrel □ let someone have it (with both barrels) □ lock, stock, and barrel □ more fun than a barrel of monkeys □ scrape the bottom of the barrel

BARRELHEAD
cash on the barrelhead

BASE
base one's opinion on something □ get to first base (with someone or something) □ off base □ reach first base (with someone or something) □ steal a base □ touch base (wiith someone)

BASIS
on a first-name basis (with someone)

BASKET
put all one's eggs in one basket

BAT
as blind as a bat □ blind as a bat □ go to bat for someone □ have bats in one's belfry □ like a bat out of hell □ not bat an eyelid □ right off the bat □ without batting an eye

BATH
take a bath (on something) □ throw the baby out with the bath(water)

BATHROOM
go to the bathroom

BATHWATER
throw the baby out with the bath-(water)

BATTEN
batten down the hatches

BATTERY
assault and battery

BATTLE
battle something out

BAWL
bawl someone out

BEAD
draw a bead on someone or something

BEAM
broad in the beam □ on the beam

BEAN
full of beans □ not know beans (about someone or something) □ not worth a hill of beans □ spill the beans

BEAR
as hungry as a bear □ bear a grudge (against someone) □ bear fruit □ bear one's cross □ bear someone or something in mind □ bear something out □ bear the brunt (of something) □ bear watching □ bear with someone or something □ get one's bearings □ grin and bear it □ hungry as a bear □ loaded for bear

BEARD
beard the lion in his den

BEAT
beat a dead horse □ beat a (hasty) retreat □ beat a path to someone's door □ beat about the bush □ beat around the bush □ beat one's brains out (to do something) □ beat one's head against the wall □ beat someone down (to size) □ beat someone to the draw □ beat someone to the punch □ beat someone up □ beat something into someone's head □ beat the band □ beat the clock □ beat the gun □ beat the living daylights out of someone □ beat the pants off someone □ beat the rap □ beat the stuffing out of someone □ beat the tar out of someone □ off the (beaten) track □ one's heart misses a beat □ one's heart skips a beat □ pound a beat

BEAUTY
Beauty is only skin-deep.

BEAVER
as busy as a beaver □ eager beaver

BECK
at someone's beck and call

BECOMING
becoming to someone

BED
bed-and-breakfast □ bed of roses □ Early to bed, early to rise(, makes a man healthy, wealthy, and wise.) □ get out of the wrong side of the bed □ get up on the wrong side of the bed □ go to bed (with someone) □ go to bed with the chickens □ make someone's bed □ make the bed □ put someone or something to bed □ put to bed with a shovel □ should have stood in bed □ sick in bed

BEE
as busy as a bee □ birds and the bees □ busy as a bee □ get a bee in one's bonnet □ make a beeline for someone or something □ none of someone's beeswax □ put a bee in someone's bonnet

BEEF
beef something up

BEELINE
make a beeline for someone or something

BEER
(all) beer and skittles □ beer and skittles

BEESWAX
none of someone's beeswax

BEFORE
before long □ before you can say Jack Robinson □ before you know it □ cast (one's) pearls before swine □ count one's chickens before they hatch □ cross a bridge before one comes to it □ cry before one is hurt □ morning after (the night before) □ Pride goes before a fall. □ put the cart before the horse □ think twice (before doing something)

BEG
beg off (on something) □ beg the question □ beg to differ (with someone) □ go begging

BEGGAR
beggar description □ Beggars can't be choosers.

BEGIN
begin to see daylight □ begin to see the light □ beginning of the end

BEHALF
in behalf of someone □ in someone's behalf □ on behalf of someone □ on someone's behalf

BEHAVIOR
get time off for good behavior □ on one's best behavior

BEHIND
be behind in something □ be behind on something □ behind closed doors □ behind someone's back □ behind the eight ball □ behind the scenes □ behind the times □ burn one's bridges (behind one) □ close ranks (behind someone or something) □ driving force (behind someone or something) □ not dry behind the ears □ power behind the throne □ stand behind someone or something □ wet behind the ears □ with both hands tied behind one's back □ with one hand tied behind one's back

BEHOOVE
it behooves one to do something

BELABOR
belabor the point

BELFRY
have bats in one's belfry

BELIEVE
believe it or not □ lead someone to believe something □ not believe one's eyes □ seeing is believing

BELL
bell, book, and candle □ ring a bell □ saved by the bell □ with bells on (one's toes)

BELONG
To the victors belong the spoils.

BELOW
hit (someone) below the belt

BELT
belt something out □ get something

under one's belt □ hit (someone) below the belt □ tighten one's belt

BENCH
on the bench □ warm the bench

BEND
bend over backwards (to do something) □ bend someone's ear □ go (a)round the bend □ on bended knee

BENEATH
feel it beneath one (to do something)

BENEFIT
get the benefit of the doubt □ give someone the benefit of the doubt □ of benefit (to someone)

BENT
bent on doing something □ hell-bent for leather

BERTH
give someone or something a wide berth

BESIDE
be beside oneself (with something) □ beside oneself (with something) □ beside the point □ beside the question

BEST
(all) for the best □ at best □ at one's best □ best bib and tucker □ best-laid plans of mice and men □ best-laid schemes of mice and men □ best part of something □ come off second-best □ do one's (level) best □ even in the best of times □ far and away the best □ for the best □ get the best of someone □ give something one's best shot □ had best do something □ have the best of both worlds □ He laughs best who laughs last. □ in one's (own) (best) interest(s) □ in one's Sunday best □ in the best of health □ make the best of something □ on one's best behavior □ put one's best foot forward □ to the best of one's ability □ to the best of one's knowledge □ with the best will in the world □ work out for the best

BET
bet one's bottom dollar □ bet one's life □ hedge one's bets □ You bet (your boots)! □ You can bet on it!

BETTER
all better now □ better late than never □ better off (doing something) □ better off (if one were somewhere else) □ better off (if something were done) □ better off (somewhere) □ do someone one better □ for better or for worse □ for the better □ get better □ get the better of someone □ go someone one better □ had better do something □ Half a loaf is better than none. □ have seen better days □ know better □ one's better half □ so much the better □ take a turn for the better □ think better of something

BETWEEN
bad blood (between people) □ between a rock and a hard place □ between life and death □ between the devil and the deep blue sea □ between you, me, and the lamppost □ betwixt and between □ draw a line between something and something else □ fall between two stools □ few and far between □ hit someone (right) between the eyes □ no love lost (between someone and someone else) □ read between the lines □ strike a balance (between two things) □ take the bit between the teeth

BETWIXT
betwixt and between

BEYOND
above and beyond (something) □ (above and) beyond the call of duty □ back of the beyond □ beyond a reasonable doubt □ beyond measure □ beyond one's depth □ beyond one's means □ beyond the call of duty □ beyond the pale □ beyond the shadow of a doubt □ beyond words □ can't see beyond the end of one's nose □ live beyond one's means

BIB
best bib and tucker

BID
bid adieu to someone or something □ bid someone or something adieu

BIDE
bide one's time

BIG

as big as all outdoors □ as big as life □ as big as life and twice as ugly □ big and bold □ big as all outdoors □ big as life and twice as ugly □ big frog in a small pond □ big of someone □ cut a big swath □ get a big send-off □ give someone a big send-off □ go over big with someone □ have a big mouth □ make a big deal about something □ talk big □ too big for one's britches

BIGGER

have eyes bigger than one's stomach □ one's eyes are bigger than one's stomach

BILL

fill the bill □ foot the bill □ get a clean bill of health □ give someone a clean bill of health □ pad the bill □ sell someone a bill of goods

BIND

in a bind

BINGE

binge and purge □ go on a binge

BIRD

A bird in the hand is worth two in the bush. □ A little bird told me. □ as free as a bird □ birds and the bees □ bird's-eye view □ Birds of a feather flock together. □ early bird □ eat like a bird □ for the birds □ free as a bird □ kill two birds with one stone □ The early bird gets the worm.

BIRTH

give birth to something

BIRTHDAY

in one's birthday suit

BIT

champ at the bit □ do one's bit □ hair of the dog that bit one □ not a bit □ one little bit □ quite a bit □ take the bit between the teeth □ take the bit in one's teeth

BITCH

son of a bitch

BITE

bite off more than one can chew □ bite one's nails □ bite one's tongue □ bite someone's head off □ bite the bullet □ bite the dust □ bite the hand that feeds one □ One's bark is worse than one's bite. □ put the bite on someone

BITTER

bitter pill to swallow □ take the bitter with the sweet □ to the bitter end

BLACK

as black as one is painted □ as black as pitch □ black-and-blue □ black as one is painted □ black as pitch □ black out □ black sheep of the family □ get a black eye □ give someone a black eye □ in black and white □ in the black □ put something down in black and white □ the pot calling the kettle black

BLAME

lay the blame on someone or something □ place the blame on someone or something □ put the blame on someone or something

BLANCHE

give carte blanche to someone □ give someone carte blanche

BLANK

draw a blank □ give a blank check to someone □ give someone a blank check

BLANKET

wet blanket

BLAST

(at) full blast □ blast off □ full blast

BLAZE

blaze a trail

BLEEP

bleep something out

BLESSING

blessing in disguise

BLIND

as blind as a bat □ blind as a bat □ blind leading the blind □ turn a blind eye to someone or something □ up a blind alley

BLINDFOLD

able to do something blindfolded

BLINK

on the blink

BLOCK
chip off the old block □ knock someone's block off □ on the block □ put one's head on the block (for someone or something) □ stumbling block

BLOOD
bad blood (between people) □ blood, sweat, and tears □ bloody but unbowed □ cry bloody murder □ draw blood □ flesh and blood □ in cold blood □ in one's blood □ in the blood □ make someone's blood boil □ make someone's blood run cold □ new blood □ scream bloody murder □ (some) new blood □ sweat blood

BLOW
blow a fuse □ blow a gasket □ blow-by-blow account □ blow-by-blow description □ blow hot and cold □ blow off steam □ blow one's cookies □ blow one's cool □ blow one's cork □ blow one's lines □ blow one's lunch □ blow one's own horn □ blow one's stack □ blow one's top □ blow over □ blow someone or something away □ blow someone or something off □ blow someone or something to smithereens □ blow someone's cover □ blow someone's mind □ blow something □ blow something out of all proportion □ blow the lid off (something) □ blow the whistle (on someone) □ blow up □ blow up (at someone) □ blow up in someone's face □ come to blows (over something) □ see which way the wind is blowing

BLOWOUT
have a blowout

BLUE
between the devil and the deep blue sea □ black-and-blue □ blue around the gills □ burn with a low blue flame □ come out of the blue □ get the blues □ like a bolt out of the blue □ once in a blue moon □ out of a clear blue sky □ out of the blue □ talk a blue streak □ talk until one is blue in the face

BLUFF
call someone's bluff

BLUSH
at first blush

BOARD
across the board □ back to the drawing board □ go by the board □ go overboard □ on board □ room and board

BOAT
in the same boat (as someone) □ miss the boat □ rock the boat

BODY
arrive in a body □ come in a body □ go in a body □ keep body and soul together □ over my dead body

BOG
bog down

BOGGLE
boggle someone's mind

BOIL
boil down to something □ boil something down □ have a low boiling point □ make someone's blood boil

BOLD
big and bold

BOLT
like a bolt out of the blue □ nuts and bolts (of something) □ sit bolt upright

BOMBSHELL
drop a bomb(shell) □ explode a bombshell

BONE
(all) skin and bones □ bone of contention □ bone up (on something) □ chilled to the bone □ cut someone or something to the bone □ feel something in one's bones □ have a bone to pick (with someone) □ know something in one's bones □ make no bones about it □ nothing but skin and bones □ work one's fingers to the bone

BONER
pull a boner

BONNET
get a bee in one's bonnet □ put a bee in someone's bonnet

BOOK
balance the books □ be (like) an open book □ bell, book, and candle □ by the book □ close the books (on

someone or something) □ coffee-table book □ crack a book □ go by the book □ have one's nose in a book □ hit the books □ in one's book □ know someone or something like a book □ make book on something □ one for the (record) books □ read someone like a(n open) book □ take a leaf out of someone's book □ throw the book at someone □ use every trick in the book □ wrote the book on something

BOOM
lower the boom on someone

BOOT
as tough as old boots □ boot someone or something out □ die in one's boots □ die with one's boots on □ get the boot □ give someone the boot □ quake in one's boots □ shake in one's boots □ to boot □ tough as old boots □ You bet (your boots)!

BOOTSTRAPS
pull oneself up (by one's own boot-straps)

BORE
bore someone stiff □ bore someone to death □ bored stiff □ bored to death

BOREDOM
die of boredom

BORN
born and bred □ born and raised □ born out of wedlock □ born with a silver spoon in one's mouth □ in all one's born days □ not born yesterday

BORROW
borrow trouble □ live on borrowed time

BOSS
boss someone around

BOTH
burn the candle at both ends □ cut both ways □ have a foot in both camps □ have it both ways □ have the best of both worlds □ land on both feet □ let someone have it (with both barrels) □ make (both) ends meet □ play both ends (against the middle) □ with both hands tied behind one's back

BOTHER
hot and bothered

BOTTLE
bottle something up □ crack open a bottle □ hit the bottle

BOTTOM
as soft as a baby's bottom □ at the bottom of the hour □ at the bottom of the ladder □ bet one's bottom dollar □ bottom out □ from the bottom of one's heart □ from top to bottom □ get to the bottom of something □ hit bottom □ learn something from the bottom up □ scrape the bottom of the barrel □ soft as a baby's bottom □ the bottom line

BOUNCE
That's the way the ball bounces.

BOUND
bound and determined □ bound for somewhere □ bound hand and foot □ bound to (do something) □ by leaps and bounds □ duty bound (to do something) □ out of bounds □ within bounds

BOW
bow and scrape □ bow out □ take a bow

BOWL
bowl someone over

BOX
open Pandora's box □ stuff the ballot box

BOY
All work and no play makes Jack a dull boy. □ separate the men from the boys

BRAIN
beat one's brains out (to do something) □ brain someone □ have something on the brain □ pick someone's brain(s) □ rack one's brain(s)

BRANCH
hold out the olive branch

BRASS
double in brass □ get down to brass tacks

BRAVE

put on a brave face □ put on a (brave) front □ put up a (brave) front

BREACH

step into (the breach)

BREAD

bread and butter □ bread-and-butter letter □ bread and water □ greatest thing since sliced bread □ know which side one's bread is buttered on □ someone's bread and butter

BREADTH

by a hair('s breadth)

BREAK

at the break of dawn □ Break a leg! □ break camp □ break down □ break even □ break ground (for something) □ Break it up! □ break loose (from someone or something) □ break new ground □ break off (with someone) □ break one's back (to do something) □ break one's neck (to do something) □ break one's word □ break out □ break out (in something) □ break (out) in(to) tears □ break out (of something) □ break someone or something down □ break someone or something in □ break someone or something up □ break someone's fall □ break someone's heart □ break something down (for someone) □ break something down (into something) □ break something to pieces □ break the back of something □ break the bank □ break the ice □ break the news (to someone) □ break through (something) □ break up (with someone) □ breaking and entering □ die of a broken heart □ get a break □ give someone a break □ make a break for something or somewhere □ make or break someone □ take a break □ take one's break □ That's the straw that broke the camel's back. □ tough break

BREAKFAST

bed-and-breakfast

BREAST

make a clean breast of something

BREATH

(all) in one breath □ breath of fresh air □ catch one's breath □ Don't hold your breath. □ get time to catch one's breath □ hold one's breath □ in one breath □ in the same breath □ out of breath □ save one's breath □ say something under one's breath □ take someone's breath away □ waste one's breath □ with every (other) breath

BREATHE

able to breathe (easily) again □ able to breathe (freely) again □ breathe down someone's neck □ breathe easy □ breathe one's last □ hardly have time to breathe □ not breathe a word (about someone or something) □ not breathe a word of (something)

BRED

born and bred

BREED

Familiarity breeds contempt.

BREEZE

shoot the breeze

BREW

There is trouble brewing. □ Trouble is brewing.

BRICK

bang one's head against a brick wall □ bricks and mortar □ drop a brick □ hit (someone) like a ton of bricks □ hit the bricks

BRIDE

give the bride away

BRIDGE

burn one's bridges (behind one) □ burn one's bridges in front of one □ cross a bridge before one comes to it □ cross a bridge when one comes to it □ water under the bridge

BRIEF

hold no brief for someone or something □ in brief

BRIGHT

bright and early □ bright-eyed and bushy-tailed □ get a bright idea □ give someone a bright idea

BRIM

filled to the brim

BRING
bring down the curtain (on something) □ bring home the bacon □ bring someone around □ bring someone or something out in droves □ bring someone or something up □ bring someone or something up to date □ bring someone to □ bring someone up to date (on someone or something) □ bring something about □ bring something crashing down (around one) □ bring something home to someone □ bring something into question □ bring something off □ bring something to a head □ bring something to light □ bring the house down □ bring up the rear

BRITCHES
too big for one's britches

BROAD
broad in the beam □ have broad shoulders □ in broad daylight

BROKE
die of a broken heart □ flat broke □ go broke □ go for broke □ That's the straw that broke the camel's back.

BROTH
Too many cooks spoil the broth.

BROTHER
be one's brother's keeper

BROW
by the sweat of one's brow □ knit one's brow

BROWN
do something up brown

BRUNT
bear the brunt (of something)

BRUSH
brush up (on something) □ get the brush-off □ give someone the brush-off □ have a brush with something □ tarred with the same brush

BUCK
buck for something □ buck up □ make a fast buck □ make a quick buck □ pass the buck

BUCKET
drop in the bucket □ kick the bucket

BUCKLE
buckle down (to something)

BUD
nip something in the bud

BUFF
in the buff

BUG
as snug as a bug in a rug □ bug out □ bug someone □ snug as a bug in a rug

BUGGY
horse and buggy

BUILD
build a fire under someone □ build castles in Spain □ build castles in the air □ build (someone or something) up □ build something to order □ build up to something

BUILT
Rome wasn't built in a day.

BULL
bull in a china shop □ cock-and-bull story □ full of bull □ hit the bull's-eye □ seize the bull by the horns □ shoot the bull □ take the bull by the horns

BULLET
bite the bullet

BULLPEN
in the bullpen

BUM
give someone a bum steer □ give someone the bum's rush

BUMP
bump into someone □ bump someone off □ get goose bumps □ like a bump on a log

BUNDLE
bundle of nerves □ make a bundle

BURN
burn one's bridges (behind one) □ burn one's bridges in front of one □ burn (oneself) out □ burn out □ burn someone at the stake □ burn someone in effigy □ burn someone or something to a crisp □ burn someone up □ burn the candle at both ends □ burn the midnight oil □ burn with a low blue flame □ burned to a cinder □ burned up □ crash and burn □

fiddle while Rome burns □ get one's fingers burned □ have money to burn □ keep the home fires burning □ Money burns a hole in someone's pocket. □ put something on the back burner

BURST
burst at the seams □ burst in on someone or something □ burst into flames □ burst into tears □ burst out crying □ burst out laughing □ burst with joy □ burst with pride

BURY
bury one's head in the sand □ bury the hatchet □ dead and buried

BUSH
A bird in the hand is worth two in the bush. □ beat about the bush □ beat around the bush

BUSHEL
hide one's light under a bushel

BUSHY
bright-eyed and bushy-tailed

BUSINESS
business as usual □ business end of something □ do a land-office business □ drum some business up □ get down to business □ get one's nose out of someone's business □ give someone the business □ go about one's business □ have no business doing something □ keep one's nose out of someone's business □ make it one's business to do something □ mind one's own business □ monkey business □ one means business □ send one about one's business □ set someone up (in business)

BUSMAN
busman's holiday

BUST
bust a gut (to do something)

BUSTLE
hustle and bustle

BUSY
as busy as a beaver □ as busy as a bee □ as busy as Grand Central Station □ busy as a bee □ busy as Grand Central Station □ get busy

BUT
all over but the shouting □ bloody but unbowed □ but for someone or something □ can't help but do something □ everything but the kitchen sink □ gone but not forgotten □ It never rains but it pours. □ last but not least □ no buts about it □ no ifs, ands, or buts about it □ nothing but skin and bones □ nothing but something □ poor but clean □ sadder but wiser □ separate but equal □ slow(ly) but sure(ly)

BUTT
butt in (on someone or something)

BUTTER
bread and butter □ bread-and-butter letter □ butter someone up □ know which side one's bread is buttered on □ look as if butter wouldn't melt in one's mouth □ someone's bread and butter

BUTTERFLY
get butterflies in one's stomach □ give one butterflies in one's stomach

BUTTON
button one's lip □ on the button □ press the panic button □ push the panic button

BUY
buy a pig in a poke □ buy someone off □ buy something □ buy something for a song □ buy something on credit □ buy something sight unseen □ buy something to go □ not buy something

BUZZ
give someone a buzz

BYE
kiss something good-bye

BYGONES
Let bygones be bygones.

BYWAYS
highways and byways

CABOODLE
kit and caboodle

CAHOOTS
in cahoots (with someone)

CAIN
raise cain (with someone or something)

CAKE
as flat as a pancake □ as nutty as a fruitcake □ eat one's cake and have it too □ flat as a pancake □ have one's cake and eat it too □ nutty as a fruitcake □ piece of cake □ sell like hotcakes □ slice of the cake □ take the cake

CALF
kill the fatted calf

CALL
(above and) beyond the call of duty □ at someone's beck and call □ beyond the call of duty □ call a meeting □ call a spade a spade □ call for someone or something □ call it a day □ call it a night □ call it quits □ call of nature □ call someone down □ call someone names □ call someone on the carpet □ call someone or something in □ call someone or something into question □ call someone or something off □ call someone or something up □ call someone's bluff □ call the dogs off □ call the meeting to order □ call the shots □ call the tune □ have a close call □ He who pays the piper calls the tune. □ not able to call one's time one's own □ on call □ the pot calling the kettle black □ within calling distance

CAMEL
That's the straw that broke the camel's back.

CAMP
break camp □ have a foot in both camps

CAN
before you can say Jack Robinson □ bite off more than one can chew □ catch-as-catch-can □ game that two can play □ more someone or something than one can shake a stick at □ no can do □ open a can of worms □ You can bet on it! □ You can say that again!

CANARY
look like the cat that swallowed the canary

CANCEL
cancel something out

CANDLE
bell, book, and candle □ burn the candle at both ends □ can't hold a candle to someone □ not hold a candle to someone or something

CANOE
paddle one's own canoe

CAN'T
Beggars can't be choosers. □ can't □ can't carry a tune □ can't do anything with someone or something □ can't help but do something □ can't hold a candle to someone □ can't make heads or tails (out) of someone or something □ can't see beyond the end of one's nose □ can't see one's hand in front of one's face □ can't stand (the sight of) someone or something □ can't stomach someone or something □ You can't please everyone. □ You can't take it with you. □ You can't teach an old dog new tricks.

CAP
cap and gown □ feather in one's cap □ put one's thinking cap on

CARD
have the cards stacked against one □ in the cards □ lay one's cards on the table □ play one's cards close to one's vest □ play one's cards close to the chest □ play one's cards right □ play one's cards well □ play one's trump card □ put one's cards on the table □ stack the cards (against someone or something) □ the cards are stacked against one

CARE
could(n't) care less □ devil-may-care attitude □ devil-may-care manner □ for all I care □ in care of someone □ in the care of someone □ not care two hoots about someone or something □ not have a care in the world □ take care of someone □ That takes care of that.

CARPET
call someone on the carpet □ get the red-carpet treatment □ give someone the red-carpet treatment □ roll out

the red carpet for someone □ sweep something under the carpet

CARRIAGE
horse and carriage

CARRY
can't carry a tune □ carried away □ carry (a lot of) weight (with someone or something) □ carry a torch (for someone) □ carry coals to Newcastle □ carry on (about someone or something) □ carry on somehow □ carry on (with someone or something) □ carry on without someone or something □ carry one's cross □ carry one's (own) weight □ carry over □ carry something off □ carry something out □ carry something over □ carry the ball □ carry the day □ carry the torch □ carry the torch (for someone) □ carry the weight of the world on one's shoulders □ carry through (on something) □ cash-and-carry □ get carried away

CART
put the cart before the horse □ upset the apple cart

CARTE
give carte blanche to someone □ give someone carte blanche

CASE
case in point □ get down to cases □ Get off someone's case! □ have a case (against someone) □ in any case □ in case of something □ in case something happens □ in the case of someone or something □ just in case □ make a federal case out of something □ on someone's case □ open-and-shut case

CASH
cash-and-carry □ cash in (on something) □ cash in one's chips □ cash on the barrelhead □ cash or credit □ cash something in □ cold, hard cash

CAST
cast about for someone or something □ cast around for someone or something □ cast doubt(s) (on someone or something) □ cast in the same mold □ cast one's lot in with someone □

cast (one's) pearls before swine □ cast the first stone □ die is cast

CASTLE
build castles in Spain □ build castles in the air

CAT
Cat got your tongue? □ Curiosity killed the cat. □ let the cat out of the bag □ look like something the cat dragged in □ look like the cat that swallowed the canary □ not enough room to swing a cat □ play cat and mouse (with someone) □ rain cats and dogs □ There's more than one way to skin a cat. □ When the cat's away, the mice will play.

CATCH
catch-as-catch-can □ catch cold □ catch forty winks □ catch hell □ catch it □ catch (on) fire □ catch on (to someone or something) □ catch one off one's guard □ catch one with one's pants down □ catch one's breath □ catch one's death (of cold) □ catch sight of someone or something □ catch some Zs □ catch someone in the act (of doing something) □ catch someone napping □ catch someone off-balance □ catch someone off guard □ catch someone red-handed □ catch someone's eye □ catch the devil □ catch up (to someone or something) □ catch up (with someone or something) □ caught in the act □ caught in the cross fire □ caught in the middle □ caught red-handed □ caught short □ get time to catch one's breath □ not let someone catch someone doing something □ not want to catch someone doing something

CAUGHT
caught in the act □ caught in the cross fire □ caught in the middle □ caught red-handed □ caught short

CAUSE
cause a commotion □ cause a stir □ cause (some) eyebrows to raise □ cause (some) tongues to wag □ lost cause

CAUTION
throw caution to the wind

CAVE
cave in (to someone or something)

CEASE
cease and desist

CEILING
hit the ceiling

CENT
not worth a red cent □ put one's two cents (worth) in

CENTER
off-center □ on dead center

CENTRAL
as busy as Grand Central Station □ busy as Grand Central Station

CENTURY
turn of the century

CEREMONY
stand on ceremony

CHAIN
ball and chain

CHAIR
play first chair

CHALK
chalk something up to something

CHAMP
champ at the bit

CHANCE
by chance □ chance something □ chance (up)on someone or something □ fat chance □ fighting chance □ ghost of a chance □ have a snowball's chance in hell □ jump at the chance □ let the chance slip by □ on the off-chance □ once-in-a-lifetime chance □ sporting chance □ stand a chance □ take a chance

CHANGE
and change □ change hands □ change horses in the middle of the stream □ change someone's mind □ change someone's tune □ change the subject □ go through the changes □ have a change of heart

CHANNELS
go through channels □ work through channels

CHAPTER
chapter and verse

CHARACTER
in character □ out of character

CHARGE
charge someone or something up □ charged up □ get a charge out of someone or something □ give someone a charge □ in the charge of someone □ take charge (of someone or something)

CHARLEY
get a charley horse

CHARM
charm the pants off (of) someone

CHASE
give chase (to someone or something) □ go chase oneself □ lead someone on a merry chase □ wild-goose chase

CHEAP
dirt cheap

CHEAT
cheat on someone

CHECK
check in (on someone or something) □ check into something □ checks and balances □ cut (someone) a check □ get a checkup □ get a rain check (on something) □ give a blank check to someone □ give someone a blank check □ give someone a rain check (on something) □ hold someone or something in check □ honor someone's check □ keep someone or something in check □ make a check out (to someone) □ pick up the check □ someone or something checks out □ take a rain check (on something)

CHECKUP
get a checkup

CHEEK
cheek by jowl □ tongue-in-cheek □ turn the other cheek

CHEER
cheer someone on □ cheer someone up □ cheer up

CHEESE
cheesed off

CHEST
get something off one's chest □ play one's cards close to the chest

CHEW
bite off more than one can chew □ chew someone out □ chew the fat □ chew the rag

CHICKEN
chicken out (of something) □ count one's chickens before they hatch □ for chicken feed □ go to bed with the chickens □ no spring chicken □ run around like a chicken with its head cut off

CHILD
child's play □ expecting (a child)

CHILDHOOD
in one's second childhood

CHILL
chilled to the bone

CHIME
chime in (with something)

CHIN
keep one's chin up □ make chin music □ take something on the chin □ wag one's chin

CHINA
bull in a china shop

CHINK
chink in one's armour

CHIP
cash in one's chips □ chip in (on something) □ chip in something on something □ chip off the old block □ chip something in (on something) □ chips and dip □ have a chip on one's shoulder □ in the chips □ when the chips are down

CHOICE
by choice □ Hobson's choice

CHOKE
choke someone up □ choke something off

CHOOSE
Beggars can't be choosers. □ choose up sides □ nothing to choose from □ pick and choose

CHOOSER
Beggars can't be choosers.

CHOP
lick one's chops

CHORD
strike a chord (with someone)

CHURCH
as poor as a church mouse □ church and state □ poor as a church mouse

CINDER
burned to a cinder

CIRCLE
come full circle □ go (a)round in circles □ in a vicious circle □ run (around) in circles □ run circles around someone □ talk in circles

CIRCULATION
back in circulation □ get back into circulation □ out of circulation

CIRCUMSTANCE
extenuating circumstances □ under the circumstances

CIRCUS
like a three-ring circus

CIVIL
keep a civil tongue (in one's head)

CLAIM
stake a claim (to something)

CLAM
as happy as a clam □ clam up □ happy as a clam

CLAMP
clamp down (on someone or something) □ put the clamps on (someone)

CLAP
clap eyes on someone or something

CLASS
cut class

CLAY
have feet of clay

CLEAN
as clean as a whistle □ clean as a whistle □ clean out (of something) □ clean up □ clean up one's act □ come clean (with someone) □ get a clean bill of health □ give someone a clean bill of health □ have a clean conscience (about someone or something) □ have clean hands □ keep one's nose clean □ make a clean breast of something □ make a clean sweep □ poor but clean □ start (off) with a

clean slate ☐ start (over) with a clean slate ☐ wipe someone's slate clean

CLEANERS
take someone to the cleaners

CLEAR
as clear as crystal ☐ as clear as mud ☐ clear as crystal ☐ clear as mud ☐ clear out ☐ clear sailing ☐ clear someone's name ☐ clear something up ☐ clear the air ☐ clear the decks ☐ clear the table ☐ clear up ☐ free and clear ☐ have a clear conscience (about someone or something) ☐ in the clear ☐ loud and clear ☐ make someone's position clear ☐ out of a clear blue sky ☐ see one's way clear (to do something) ☐ steer clear (of someone or something) ☐ The coast is clear.

CLIMB
climb on the bandwagon ☐ climb the wall(s)

CLIP
clip someone's wings

CLOAK
cloak-and-dagger

CLOCK
against the clock ☐ (a)round the clock ☐ (a)round-the-clock ☐ beat the clock ☐ round the clock ☐ round-the-clock ☐ turn the clock back

CLOCKWORK
as regular as clockwork ☐ go like clockwork ☐ regular as clockwork ☐ run like clockwork

CLOSE
at close range ☐ behind closed doors ☐ close at hand ☐ close in (on someone or something) ☐ close one's eyes to something ☐ close ranks ☐ close ranks (behind someone or something) ☐ close ranks (with someone) ☐ close something down ☐ close the books (on someone or something) ☐ close the door on someone or something ☐ close to home ☐ close to someone ☐ close up shop ☐ draw something to a close ☐ draw to a close ☐ get close (to someone or something) ☐ have a close call ☐ have a close shave ☐ hit one close to

home ☐ keep (close) watch (on someone or something) ☐ keep (close) watch (over someone or something) ☐ play one's cards close to one's vest ☐ play one's cards close to the chest ☐ too close for comfort

CLOSEFISTED
closefisted (with money)

CLOSET
come out of the closet ☐ skeleton in the closet

CLOTH
make something up out of whole cloth

CLOTHES
Sunday-go-to-meeting clothes

CLOTHING
wolf in sheep's clothing

CLOUD
cloud up ☐ Every cloud has a silver lining. ☐ have one's head in the clouds ☐ on cloud nine ☐ under a cloud (of suspicion)

CLOVER
in clover

CLUB
Join the club!

CLUE
clue someone in (on something) ☐ have a clue (about something)

CLUTCH
clutch at straws

COAL
carry coals to Newcastle ☐ haul someone over the coals ☐ rake someone over the coals

COAST
coast-to-coast ☐ The coast is clear.

COAT
coat and tie

COATTAILS
hang on someone's coattails ☐ ride on someone's coattails

COCK
cock-and-bull story ☐ cock of the walk ☐ go off half-cocked

COCKLES
warm the cockles of someone's heart

COD
send something C.O.D.

COFFEE
coffee and Danish □ coffee-table book □ coffee, tea, or milk

COFFIN
(another) nail in someone's or something's coffin □ nail in someone's or something's coffin

COIL
shuffle off this mortal coil

COINCIDENCE
by coincidence

COLD
be a cold fish □ blow hot and cold □ catch cold □ catch one's death (of cold) □ cold comfort □ cold, hard cash □ dash cold water on something □ get cold feet □ get the cold shoulder □ give someone the cold shoulder □ go cold turkey □ in cold blood □ in cold storage □ keep someone out in the cold □ knock someone out (cold) □ leave someone out in the cold □ make someone's blood run cold □ out cold □ pour cold water on something □ take cold □ take one's death of cold □ throw cold water on something

COLLAR
hot under the collar

COLLECTION
take up a collection

COLLEGE
work one's way through college

COLOR
come through something with flying colors □ horse of a different color □ horse of another color □ lend color to something □ off-color □ sail under false colors □ see the color of someone's money □ show one's (true) colors □ with flying colors

COMB
go over something with a fine-tooth comb □ search something with a fine-tooth comb

COME
come a cropper □ come about □ Come again? □ Come and get it! □ come and gone □ come apart at the seams □ come (a)round □ come away empty-handed □ come by something □ come by something honestly □ come clean (with someone) □ come down □ come down hard on someone or something □ come down in the world □ come down to earth □ come down to something □ come down with something □ come from far and wide □ come full circle □ come hell or high water □ come home (to roost) □ come home to someone □ come in a body □ come in for something □ come in handy □ come in out of the rain □ come into its own □ come into one's own □ come into something □ come of age □ come off □ Come off it! □ come off second-best □ come on □ come on like gangbusters □ come on somehow □ come on the scene □ come out □ come out ahead □ come out for someone or something □ come out in the wash □ come out of nowhere □ come out of one's shell □ come out of the blue □ come out of the closet □ come out with something □ come over □ come someone's way □ come through □ come through something with flying colors □ come to □ come to a bad end □ come to a dead end □ come to a head □ come to a pretty pass □ come to a standstill □ come to an end □ come to an untimely end □ come to blows (over something) □ come to grief □ come to grips with something □ come to life □ come to light □ come to mind □ come to naught □ come to nothing □ come to one's senses □ come to pass □ come to rest □ come to terms (with someone or something) □ come to the fore □ come to the point □ come to the same thing □ come to think of it □ come true □ come unglued □ come up □ come up in the world □ come up smelling like roses □ come up with someone or something □ come what may □ come with the territory □ come within an ace of doing something □ come within an inch of doing something □ cross a bridge before one comes to it □ cross

a bridge when one comes to it □ dream come true □ easy come, easy go □ easy to come by □ First come, first served. □ get another guess coming □ get another think coming □ get what's coming to one □ give one what's coming to one □ have come a long way □ have something coming (to one) □ if push comes to shove □ if worst comes to worst □ Johnny-come-lately □ not know enough to come in out of the rain □ not know if one is coming or going □ not know whether one is coming or going □ till the cows come home □ (un)til the cows come home □ up-and-coming □ when it comes right down to it □ when it comes to something □ when push comes to shove □ where one is coming from

COMEBACK
make a comeback

COMEUPPANCE
get one's comeuppance

COMFORT
cold comfort □ creature comforts □ too close for comfort

COMFORTABLE
as comfortable as an old shoe □ comfortable as an old shoe

COMMAND
have a good command of something

COMMISSION
out of commission

COMMIT
commit something to memory

COMMON
have something in common (with someone or something)

COMMOTION
cause a commotion

COMPANY
keep company (with someone) □ keep someone company □ part company (with someone) □ two's company(, three's a crowd)

COMPLAIN
nothing to complain about

COMPLIMENT
fish for a compliment □ pay someone a back-handed compliment □ pay someone a compliment □ pay someone a left-handed compliment □ return someone's compliment □ return the compliment

COMPOSURE
regain one's composure

CONCERN
as far as someone or something is concerned □ so far as I'm concerned □ to whom it may concern

CONCERT
in concert (with someone)

CONCLUSION
jump to conclusions □ leap to conclusions

CONDITION
in condition □ in good condition □ in mint condition □ in the pink (of condition) □ out of condition

CONFIDE
confide in someone

CONFIDENCE
take someone into one's confidence

CONK
conk out

CONNIPTION
have a conniption (fit)

CONQUER
divide and conquer

CONSCIENCE
have a clean conscience (about someone or something) □ have a clear conscience (about someone or something) □ in (all) good conscience

CONSEQUENCE
in consequence (of something)

CONSIDERATION
in consideration of something □ out of consideration (for someone or something)

CONSPICUOUS
conspicuous by one's absence □ make oneself conspicuous

CONSTRUCTION
under construction

CONTEMPT
Familiarity breeds contempt.

CONTENT
to one's heart's content

CONTENTION
bone of contention

CONTRADICTION
contradiction in terms

CONTRARY
on the contrary □ to the contrary

CONTROL
control the purse strings □ out of control

CONVENIENCE
at someone's earliest convenience

CONVERSATION
strike up a conversation

CONVERT
preach to the converted

CONVICTION
have the courage of one's convictions

COOK
cook someone's goose □ cook something up □ cook the accounts □ cooking with gas □ Too many cooks spoil the broth. □ Too many cooks spoil the stew.

COOKIE
blow one's cookies □ juice and cookies □ That's the way the cookie crumbles. □ toss one's cookies

COOL
as cool as a cucumber □ blow one's cool □ cool as a cucumber □ cool down □ Cool it! □ cool off □ cool one's heels □ cool someone down □ cool someone off □ keep cool □ keep one's cool □ lose one's cool □ play it cool

COON
in a coon's age

COOP
fly the coop

COP
cop a plea □ cop out

COPYCAT
be a copycat

CORE
rotten to the core □ to the core

CORK
blow one's cork □ pop one's cork

CORNER
cut corners □ have turned the corner □ out of the corner of one's eye

CORRECT
stand corrected

COST
at all costs □ at any cost □ cost a pretty penny □ cost an arm and a leg

COUGH
cough something up

COULD
could do with someone or something □ could(n't) care less □ so quiet you could hear a pin drop □ so still you could hear a pin drop

COULDN'T
could(n't) care less □ Wild horses couldn't drag someone.

COUNSEL
keep one's own counsel

COUNT
count noses □ count on someone or something □ count one's chickens before they hatch □ count someone in (on something) □ count someone out (for something) □ down for the count □ every minute counts □ every moment counts □ stand up and be counted

COUNTER
run counter to something □ under the counter

COUNTRY
another country heard from

COURAGE
Dutch courage □ have the courage of one's convictions □ pluck up one's courage □ screw up one's courage

COURSE
as a matter of course □ in due course □ in the course of time □ par for the course

COURT
have the ball in one's court □ throw

oneself at the mercy of the court □ throw oneself on the mercy of the court

COURTESY
out of courtesy (to someone)

COVER
blow someone's cover □ cover a lot of ground □ cover for someone □ cover someone's tracks (up) □ cover something up □ cover the territory □ cover the waterfront □ duck and cover

COW
sacred cow □ till the cows come home □ (un)til the cows come home

COZY
cozy up (to someone)

CRACK
at the crack of dawn □ crack a book □ crack a joke □ crack a smile □ crack down (on someone or something) □ crack open a bottle □ crack someone or something up □ crack something wide open □ crack up □ get cracking □ hard nut to crack □ have a crack at something □ make cracks (about someone or something) □ not all something is cracked up to be □ not what something is cracked up to be □ paper over the cracks (in something) □ take a crack at something □ tough nut to crack

CRACKING
get cracking

CRADLE
from the cradle to the grave □ rob the cradle

CRAMP
cramp someone's style

CRANK
crank something out

CRANNY
nook and cranny

CRASH
bring something crashing down (around one) □ crash and burn

CRAW
have something stick in one's craw

CRAZY
as crazy as a loon □ crazy about someone or something □ crazy as a loon □ drive someone crazy □ go stir-crazy □ like crazy

CREAM
cream of the crop

CREATE
create a scene □ create a stink (about something) □ create an uproar

CREATION
in creation

CREATURE
creature comforts

CREDENCE
give credence to something

CREDIT
be a credit to someone or something □ buy something on credit □ cash or credit □ do credit to someone □ do someone credit □ extend credit (to someone) □ extend someone credit □ get credit (for something) □ give credit where credit is due □ give someone credit (for something) □ sell something on credit

CREEK
up the creek (without a paddle)

CREEP
get the creeps □ give someone the creeps

CRISP
burn someone or something to a crisp

CROCODILE
cry crocodile tears □ shed crocodile tears

CROOK
by hook or (by) crook

CROP
cream of the crop

CROPPER
come a cropper

CROSS
at cross-purposes □ bear one's cross □ carry one's cross □ caught in the cross fire □ cross a bridge before one comes to it □ cross a bridge when one comes to it □ cross-examine someone □ cross one's fingers □ cross one's

heart (and hope to die) □ cross someone up □ cross someone's mind □ cross someone's palm with silver □ cross swords (with someone) (on something) □ cross the Rubicon □ double-cross someone □ get one's wires crossed □ keep one's fingers crossed (for someone or something) □ look at someone cross-eyed

CROW
as the crow flies □ make someone eat crow

CROWD
follow the crowd □ two's company(, three's a crowd)

CRUMBLE
That's the way the cookie crumbles.

CRUMPET
tea and crumpets

CRUSH
crushed by something □ get a crush on someone

CRUST
upper crust

CRUTCH
as funny as a crutch □ funny as a crutch

CRUX
crux of the matter

CRY
burst out crying □ cry before one is hurt □ cry bloody murder □ cry crocodile tears □ cry one's eyes out □ cry over spilled milk □ cry wolf □ crying need for someone or something □ crying shame □ far cry from something □ For crying out loud! □ hue and cry

CRYSTAL
as clear as crystal □ clear as crystal

CUCUMBER
as cool as a cucumber □ cool as a cucumber

CUE
cue someone in □ take one's cue from someone

CUFF
off-the-cuff □ put something on the cuff □ speak off the cuff

CUP
in one's cups □ not one's cup of tea □ not someone's cup of tea

CURE
An ounce of prevention is worth a pound of cure.

CURIOSITY
Curiosity killed the cat.

CURL
curl someone's hair □ curl up and die □ make someone's hair curl

CURRENT
swim against the current

CURRY
curry favor (with someone)

CURTAIN
be curtains for someone or something □ bring down the curtain (on something) □ ring down the curtain (on something)

CURVE
pitch someone a curve (ball) □ throw someone a curve

CUSTOMER
one to a customer

CUT
cut a big swath □ cut a fine figure □ cut a wide swath □ cut above someone or something □ cut across something □ cut-and-dried □ cut and paste □ cut and run □ cut back (on something) □ cut both ways □ cut class □ cut corners □ cut loose (from someone or something) □ cut loose (with something) □ cut no ice (with someone) □ cut off □ cut off one's nose to spite one's face □ cut one's eyeteeth on something □ cut one's losses □ cut one's (own) throat □ cut out for something □ cut out the deadwood □ cut out to be something □ cut (someone) a check □ cut someone dead □ cut someone down (to size) □ cut someone in □ cut someone off without a penny □ cut someone or something to the bone □ cut someone or something up □ cut someone to the quick □ cut teeth □ cut the ground out from under someone □ cut up □ fish or cut bait □ have one's

work cut out for one □ one's work is cut out for one □ run around like a chicken with its head cut off

CYLINDER
firing on all cylinders □ hitting on all cylinders

DAB
smack-dab in the middle

DAGGER
cloak-and-dagger □ look daggers at someone

DAILY
daily dozen □ the daily grind

DAISY
as fresh as a daisy □ fresh as a daisy □ pushing up daisies

DAMAGE
do someone damage

DAMN
damn someone or something with faint praise

DANCE
dance to another tune □ dance with death □ go into one's song and dance (about something)

DANDER
get someone's dander up

DANDY
fine and dandy

DANGER
fly into the face of danger

DANGEROUS
A little knowledge is a dangerous thing. □ armed and dangerous

DANISH
coffee and Danish

DARE
dare someone (to do something)

DARK
dark horse □ in the dark (about someone or something) □ shot in the dark

DARKEN
darken someone's door

DASH
dash cold water on something □ dash something off

DATE
at an early date □ bring someone or something up to date □ bring someone up to date (on someone or something) □ date back (to sometime) □ out-of-date □ to date □ up-to-date

DAVY
Davy Jones's locker □ go to Davy Jones's locker

DAWN
at the break of dawn □ at the crack of dawn □ dawn on someone

DAY
all day long □ all hours (of the day and night) □ all in a day's work □ all the livelong day □ as different as night and day □ as plain as day □ at the end of the day □ by the day □ call it a day □ carry the day □ day after day □ day and night □ day in and day out □ day in, day out □ day-to-day □ different as night and day □ Every dog has his day. □ Every dog has its day. □ for days on end □ forever and a day □ from day to day □ from this day forward □ from this day on □ get the day off □ have a field day □ have had its day □ have seen better days □ in all one's born days □ in one's salad days □ in this day and age □ late in the day □ make a day of doing something □ make a day of it □ night and day □ nine days' wonder □ not give anyone the time of day □ one of these days □ one's days are numbered □ order of the day □ pass the time of day (with someone) □ plain as day □ Rome wasn't built in a day. □ save something for a rainy day □ save the day □ see the light (of day) □ take the day off □ That'll be the day. □ win the day □ with each passing day

DAYLIGHT
beat the living daylights out of someone □ begin to see daylight □ daylight robbery □ frighten the living daylights out of someone □ in broad daylight □ scare the living daylights out of someone

DEAD
as dead as a dodo □ as dead as a

doornail □ beat a dead horse □ come to a dead end □ cut someone dead □ dead ahead □ dead and buried □ dead and gone □ dead as a dodo □ dead as a doornail □ dead duck □ dead in someone's or something's tracks □ dead letter □ dead loss □ dead on one's or its feet □ dead set against someone or something □ dead to the world □ drop dead □ have someone dead to rights □ in a dead heat □ knock someone dead □ leave someone for dead □ more dead than alive □ on dead center □ over my dead body □ taken for dead

DEADWOOD
cut out the deadwood

DEAF
deaf and dumb □ fall on deaf ears □ turn a deaf ear (to someone or something)

DEAL
deal in something □ get a raw deal □ give someone a raw deal □ make a big deal about something □ square deal □ think a great deal of someone or something □ wheel and deal

DEATH
at death's door □ be death on something □ between life and death □ bore someone to death □ bored to death □ catch one's death (of cold) □ dance with death □ death and taxes □ death on someone or something □ die a natural death □ frighten someone to death □ frightened to death □ kiss of death □ look like death warmed over □ matter of life and death □ scare someone to death □ scared to death □ sign one's own death warrant □ struggle to the death □ take one's death of cold □ thrill someone to death □ thrilled to death □ tickle someone to death □ tickled to death

DEBT
head over heels in debt □ pay one's debt (to society)

DECIDE
decide in favor of someone or something

DECISION
eleventh-hour decision

DECK
clear the decks □ on deck □ stack the deck (against someone or something)

DEEP
Beauty is only skin-deep. □ between the devil and the deep blue sea □ deep-six someone or something □ go off the deep end □ in deep □ in deep water □ jump off the deep end

DEFIANCE
in defiance (of someone or something)

DEGREE
get the third degree □ give someone the third degree □ to the nth degree

DELIVER
signed, sealed, and delivered □ stand and deliver

DEMAND
in great demand □ supply and demand

DEN
beard the lion in his den

DENT
make a dent in something

DEPOSIT
on deposit

DEPTH
beyond one's depth

DESCRIPTION
beggar description □ blow-by-blow description □ play-by-play description

DESERT
desert a sinking ship □ get one's just deserts

DESERVE
One good turn deserves another.

DESIGN
have designs on someone or something

DESIRE
leave a lot to be desired

DESIST
cease and desist

DESK
away from one's desk

DESPAIR
sink into despair □ throw one's hands up in despair

DETAIL
down to the last detail

DETERMINED
bound and determined

DEVIL
between the devil and the deep blue sea □ catch the devil □ devil-may-care attitude □ devil-may-care manner □ devil of a job □ for the devil of it □ full of the devil □ get the devil □ give someone the devil □ give the devil her due □ give the devil his due □ go to (the devil) □ have the devil to pay □ play (the) devil's advocate □ raise the devil (with someone or something) □ speak of the devil □ the devil's own job □ There will be the devil to pay.

DIAMOND
diamond in the rough

DIBS
have dibs on something □ put (one's) dibs on something

DICK
as tight as Dick's hatband □ (every) Tom, Dick, and Harry □ tight as Dick's hatband □ Tom, Dick, and Harry

DICKENS
raise the dickens (with someone or something)

DIE
cross one's heart (and hope to die) □ curl up and die □ die a natural death □ die in one's boots □ die is cast □ die laughing □ die of a broken heart □ die of boredom □ die on the vine □ die with one's boots on □ do or die □ dying to do something

DIET
on a diet

DIFFER
beg to differ (with someone)

DIFFERENCE
make no difference (to someone) □ split the difference

DIFFERENT
as different as night and day □ different as night and day □ horse of a different color □ march to a different drummer □ sing a different tune

DIG
dig in □ dig one's heels in □ dig one's own grave □ dig some dirt up on someone □ dig someone or something □ dig someone or something up □ dig something out □ take a dig at someone □ take digs at someone

DILEMMA
on the horns of a dilemma

DIM
take a dim view of something

DIME
dime a dozen □ nickel and dime someone □ not worth a dime □ turn on a dime

DINE
dine out □ wine and dine someone

DINT
by dint of something

DIP
chips and dip □ dip in(to something)

DIRECTIONS
ride off in all directions

DIRT
dig some dirt up on someone □ dirt cheap □ hit pay dirt

DIRTY
air one's dirty linen in public □ dirty old man □ dirty one's hands □ dirty work □ down-and-dirty □ get a dirty look from someone □ get one's hands dirty □ give someone a dirty look □ quick and dirty □ wash one's dirty linen in public

DISEASE
down with a disease □ have foot-in-mouth disease

DISGUISE
blessing in disguise

DISH
do the dishes

DISHWATER
as dull as dishwater

DISORDERLY
drunk and disorderly

DISPOSAL
put someone or something at someone's disposal

DISPOSED
be well-disposed toward someone or something

DISTANCE
go the distance □ keep one's distance (from someone or something) □ within calling distance □ within hailing distance

DITCH
last-ditch effort

DITCHWATER
as dull as ditchwater □ dull as ditchwater

DIVE
go into a nosedive □ take a nosedive

DIVIDE
divide and conquer □ divide something fifty-fifty

DOCTOR
just what the doctor ordered

DODO
as dead as a dodo □ dead as a dodo

DOG
as sick as a dog □ call the dogs off □ dog and pony show □ dog-eat-dog □ dog in the manger □ Every dog has his day. □ Every dog has its day. □ go to the dogs □ hair of the dog that bit one □ lead a dog's life □ Let sleeping dogs lie. □ live a dog's life □ put on the dog □ rain cats and dogs □ see a man about a dog □ sick as a dog □ tail wagging the dog □ You can't teach an old dog new tricks.

DOGHOUSE
in the doghouse

DOLDRUMS
in the doldrums

DOLL
get (all) dolled up

DOLLAR
as sound as a dollar □ bet one's bottom dollar □ dollar for dollar □ feel

like a million (dollars) □ look like a million dollars □ sound as a dollar

DOOM
doomed to failure

DOOR
as big as all outdoors □ at death's door □ beat a path to someone's door □ behind closed doors □ close the door on someone or something □ darken someone's door □ door-to-door □ from door to door □ get one's foot in the door □ keep the wolf from the door □ open the door to something □ see someone to the door □ show someone (to) the door □ shut the door on someone or something

DOORNAIL
as dead as a doornail □ dead as a doornail

DOORSTEP
at someone's doorstep □ on someone's doorstep

DOSE
dose of one's own medicine

DOT
on the dot □ sign on the dotted line

DOUBLE
do a double take □ double back (on someone or something) □ double-cross someone □ double in brass □ double up (with someone) □ on the double □ see double

DOUBT
beyond a reasonable doubt □ beyond the shadow of a doubt □ cast doubt(s) (on someone or something) □ doubting Thomas □ get the benefit of the doubt □ give someone the benefit of the doubt □ no doubt

DOWNHILL
downhill all the way □ downhill from here on □ go downhill

DOWNS
ups and downs

DOZEN
by the dozen □ by the dozens □ daily dozen □ dime a dozen □ six of one and half a dozen of the other

DRABS
dribs and drabs

DRAG
be a drag (on someone) □ drag one's feet □ feel dragged out □ knock-down-drag-out fight □ look like something the cat dragged in □ Wild horses couldn't drag someone.

DRAIN
down the drain □ pour money down the drain

DRAW
beat someone to the draw □ draw a bead on someone or something □ draw a blank □ draw a line between something and something else □ draw blood □ draw interest □ draw someone or something out □ draw (someone's) fire (away from someone or something) □ draw something to a close □ draw something up □ draw the line (at something) □ draw to a close □ quick on the draw □ slow on the draw

DRAWING
back to the drawing board

DRAWN
drawn and quartered

DREAM
dream come true □ pipe dream □ wouldn't dream of doing something

DRESS
(all) dressed up □ dress someone down □ dressed to kill □ dressed to the nines □ dressed up □ give someone a (good) dressing-down

DRIBS
dribs and drabs

DRIED
cut-and-dried

DRINK
drink to excess □ drunk and disorderly

DRIVE
as white as the driven snow □ drive a hard bargain □ drive at something □ drive someone crazy □ drive someone mad □ drive someone out (of office) □ drive someone to the wall □ drive someone up the wall □ drive some-thing home □ drive something into the ground □ driving force (behind someone or something) □ What are you driving at? □ white as the driven snow

DRIVER
in the driver's seat

DROP
at the drop of a hat □ drop a bomb-(shell) □ drop a brick □ drop around (sometime) □ drop by (sometime) □ drop by the wayside □ drop dead □ drop in (on someone) □ drop in one's tracks □ drop in the bucket □ drop in the ocean □ drop in (to say hello) □ drop off (to sleep) □ drop out (of something) □ drop someone □ drop someone a few lines □ drop someone a line □ drop someone's name □ drop the ball □ drop the other shoe □ so quiet you could hear a pin drop □ so still you could hear a pin drop

DROVES
bring someone or something out in droves

DROWN
drown one's sorrows □ drown one's troubles □ drown someone or some-thing out

DRUG
drug on the market

DRUM
drum some business up □ drum someone out of something □ drum something into someone('s head)

DRUMMER
march to a different drummer

DRUNK
drunk and disorderly

DRUTHERS
have one's druthers

DRY
as dry as dust □ cut-and-dried □ dry as dust □ dry run □ dry someone out □ dry up □ high and dry □ leave someone high and dry □ not dry be-hind the ears

DUCK
as a duck takes to water □ as easy as duck soup □ be a sitting duck □ dead

duck □ duck and cover □ easy as duck soup □ get one's ducks in a row □ like a sitting duck □ like sitting ducks □ like water off a duck's back □ lovely weather for ducks

DUDGEON
in high dudgeon

DUE
give credit where credit is due □ give the devil her due □ give the devil his due □ in due course □ in due time □ pay one's dues

DULL
All work and no play makes Jack a dull boy. □ as dull as dishwater □ as dull as ditchwater □ dull as ditchwater

DUMB
deaf and dumb

DUMP
down in the dumps

DUST
as dry as dust □ bite the dust □ dry as dust

DUTCH
Dutch auction □ Dutch courage □ Dutch treat □ Dutch uncle □ go Dutch □ in Dutch (with someone)

DUTY
(above and) beyond the call of duty □ beyond the call of duty □ do one's duty □ duty bound (to do something) □ in the line of duty □ off duty □ on active duty □ on duty □ shirk one's duty

DYED
dyed-in-the-wool

DYING
dying to do something

EACH
made for each other □ with each passing day

EAGER
eager beaver

EAGLE
eagle eye

EAR
be all ears □ be all eyes (and ears) □ bend someone's ear □ fall on deaf ears □ get someone's ear □ give (an) ear to someone or something □ give one's ear to someone or something □ go in one ear and out the other □ have one's ear to the ground □ in one ear and out (of) the other □ keep one's ear to the ground □ lend an ear (to someone) □ make a silk purse out of a sow's ear □ not dry behind the ears □ pin someone's ears back □ play by ear □ play something by ear □ prick up one's ears □ talk someone's ear off □ turn a deaf ear (to someone or something) □ up to one's ears (in something) □ Walls have ears. □ wet behind the ears

EARLY
at an early date □ at someone's earliest convenience □ bright and early □ early bird □ early on □ Early to bed, early to rise(, makes a man healthy, wealthy, and wise.) □ The early bird gets the worm.

EARN
A penny saved is a penny earned. □ earn one's keep

EARNEST
in earnest

EARTH
all over the earth □ come down to earth □ down-to-earth □ like nothing on earth □ move heaven and earth to do something □ on earth □ salt of the earth □ to the ends of the earth

EASE
at ease □ ease off (on someone or something) □ ease up (on someone or something) □ ill at ease

EAST
back East

EASY
able to breathe (easily) again □ as easy as (apple) pie □ as easy as duck soup □ as easy as rolling off a log □ breathe easy □ easier said than done □ easy as (apple) pie □ easy as duck soup □ easy as rolling off a log □ easy come, easy go □ Easy does it. □ easy to come by □ free and easy □ get off easy □ go easy (on someone or

EAT

something) □ on easy street □ Take it easy. □ take it easy (on someone or something)

EAT

dog-eat-dog □ eat (a meal) out □ eat and run □ eat away at someone or something □ eat high on the hog □ eat humble pie □ eat like a bird □ eat like a horse □ eat one's cake and have it too □ eat one's hat □ eat one's heart out □ eat one's words □ eat out of someone's hands □ eat someone out □ eat someone out of house and home □ eat something up □ have one's cake and eat it too □ make someone eat crow

EBB

ebb and flow

EDGE

edge someone out □ get the edge on someone □ get the edge over someone □ on edge □ set someone's teeth on edge □ take the edge off (something)

EDGEWAYS

get a word in edgeways

EDGEWISE

get a word in edgewise

EEL

as slippery as an eel □ slippery as an eel

EFFECT

go into effect □ have a bad effect (on someone or something) □ something to that effect □ take effect □ words to that effect

EFFIGY

burn someone in effigy □ hang someone in effigy

EFFORT

all-out effort □ last-ditch effort □ make an all-out effort

EGG

egg someone on □ have egg on one's face □ lay an egg □ put all one's eggs in one basket □ walk on eggs

EIGHT

behind the eight ball

EITHER

either feast or famine

ELBOW

elbow someone out (of something) □ rub elbows (with someone) □ use some elbow grease

ELEMENT

in one's element □ out of one's element

ELEPHANT

white elephant

ELEVENTH

at the eleventh hour □ eleventh-hour decision

ELSE

better off (if one were somewhere else) □ draw a line between something and something else □ in someone else's place □ in someone else's shoes □ mistake someone for someone else □ mix someone up with someone else □ name someone after someone else □ name someone for someone else □ no love lost (between someone and someone else) □ play someone off against someone else □ put oneself in someone else's place □ put oneself in someone else's shoes □ something else □ something else (again)

EMPTY

come away empty-handed □ go away empty-handed

END

All's well that ends well. □ at loose ends □ at one's wit's end □ at the end of nowhere □ at the end of one's rope □ at the end of one's tether □ at the end of the day □ be-all and (the) end-all □ beginning of the end □ burn the candle at both ends □ business end of something □ can't see beyond the end of one's nose □ come to a bad end □ come to a dead end □ come to an end □ come to an untimely end □ end in itself □ end of the line □ end of the road □ end something up □ end up by doing something □ end up doing something □ end up (somehow) □ end up somewhere □ end up with the short end of the stick □ for days on end □ for hours on end □ get the short end of the stick □ go off the deep end □ hold one's end (of the bargain) up □ jump off the deep end □ make (both) ends meet □ make someone's hair stand on end □ meet one's end □ no end of something □ not see farther than the end of one's nose □ not see past the end of one's nose □ odds and ends □ play both ends (against the middle) □ put an end to something □ see the light (at the end of the tunnel) □ (the) be-all and (the) end-all □ to the bitter end □ to the ends of the earth

ENGAGE
engage in small talk

ENGLISH
in plain English

ENOUGH
Enough is enough. □ enough to go (a)round □ get up enough nerve (to do something) □ good enough for someone or something □ have had enough □ leave well enough alone □ let well enough alone □ not enough room to swing a cat □ not know enough to come in out of the rain □ old enough to be someone's father □ old enough to be someone's mother

ENTER
breaking and entering □ enter one's mind

ENVY
green with envy

EQUAL
equal to someone or something □ other things being equal □ separate but equal

ERRAND
go on an errand □ on a fool's errand □ run an errand □ send someone (out) on an errand

ERROR
trial and error

ESCAPE
escape someone's notice

EVE
on the eve of something

EVEN
be even steven □ break even □ even in the best of times □ get even (with someone) □ keep on an even keel □ keep something on an even keel

EVENT
in any event □ in the event of something □ in the unlikely event of something

EVER
ever and anon □ forever and ever □ live happily ever after

EVERY
at every turn □ Every cloud has a silver lining. □ Every dog has his day. □ Every dog has its day. □ every inch a something □ every inch the something □ every last one □ every living soul □ every minute counts □ every moment counts □ (every) now and again □ (every) now and then □ (every) once in a while □ every time one turns around □ (every) Tom, Dick, and Harry □ every which way □ hang on someone's every word □ use every trick in the book □ with every (other) breath

EVERYONE
You can't please everyone.

EVERYTHING
everything but the kitchen sink □ everything from A to Z □ everything from soup to nuts

EVERYWHERE
here, there, and everywhere

EVIDENCE
much in evidence

EVIL
Money is the root of all evil.

EXAMINE
cross-examine someone

EXAMPLE
hold someone or something up (as an example) □ make an example of someone

EXCEPTION
exception that proves the rule □ make an exception (for someone) □ take exception (to something)

EXCESS
drink to excess

EXCHANGE
exchange more than ___ words with someone □ in exchange (for someone or something)

EXCUSE
excuse someone □ use someone or something as an excuse

EXHIBITION
make an exhibition of oneself

EXPECT
expecting (a child) □ when least expected

EXPECTATION
measure up (to someone's expectations)

EXPEDITION
go on a fishing expedition

EXPENSE
at the expense of someone or something □ expense is no object □ go to the expense (of doing something) □ out-of-pocket expenses

EXPLAIN
explain oneself □ explain something away

EXPLODE
explode a bombshell

EXTEND
extend credit (to someone) □ extend one's sympathy (to someone) □ extend someone credit

EXTENT
to a great extent □ to some extent

EXTENUATING
extenuating circumstances

EYE
apple of someone's eye □ be all eyes (and ears) □ bird's-eye view □ bright-eyed and bushy-tailed □ catch someone's eye □ cause (some) eyebrows to raise □ clap eyes on someone or something □ close one's eyes to something □ cry one's eyes out □ cut one's eyeteeth on something □ eagle eye □ eyeball-to-eyeball □ feast one's eyes (on someone or something) □ get a black eye □ get someone's eye □ get stars in one's eyes □ give someone a black eye □ give someone the eye □ have an eye for someone or something □ have an eye on someone or something □ have an eye out (for someone or something) □ have eyes bigger than one's stomach □ have eyes in the back of one's head □ hit someone (right) between the eyes □ hit the bull's-eye □ in one's mind's eye □ in the public eye □ in the twinkling of an eye □ keep an eye on someone or something □ keep an eye out (for someone or something) □ keep one's eye on the ball □ keep one's eyes open (for someone or something) □ keep one's eyes peeled (for someone or something) □ keep one's weather eye open □ lay eyes on someone or something □ look at someone cross-eyed □ look someone in the eye □ make eyes (at someone) □ more (to something) than meets the eye □ naked eye □ not bat an eyelid □ not believe one's eyes □ one's eyes are bigger than one's stomach □ only have eyes for someone □ open someone's eyes (to something) □ out of the corner of one's eye □ pull the wool over someone's eyes □ raise some eyebrows □ see eye to eye (with someone) (about something) □ see eye to eye (with someone) (on something) □ set eyes on someone or something □ sight for sore eyes □ turn a blind eye to someone or something □ up to one's eyeballs (in something) □ with an eye to doing something □ without batting an eye

EYEBALL
eyeball-to-eyeball □ up to one's eyeballs (in something)

EYEBROWS
cause (some) eyebrows to raise □ raise some eyebrows

EYELID
not bat an eyelid

EYETEETH
cut one's eyeteeth on something

FACE
as plain as the nose on one's face □ at

face value □ blow up in someone's face □ can't see one's hand in front of one's face □ cut off one's nose to spite one's face □ do an about-face □ face someone down □ face the music □ face-to-face □ fall flat (on its face) □ fall flat (on one's face) □ feed one's face □ fly in the face of someone or something □ fly into the face of danger □ have egg on one's face □ hide one's face in shame □ keep a straight face □ look someone in the face □ lose face □ make a face (at someone) □ not show one's face □ on the face of it □ plain as the nose on one's face. □ put on a brave face □ red in the face □ save (one's) face □ say something (right) to someone's face □ slap in the face □ take something at face value □ talk until one is blue in the face □ tell one to one's face

FACT
after the fact □ as a matter of fact □ facts of life □ get down to the facts □ in fact □ matter-of-fact

FAIL
doomed to failure □ without fail

FAILURE
doomed to failure

FAINT
damn someone or something with faint praise

FAIR
do something fair and square □ fair and impartial □ fair and square □ fair game □ fair to middling □ fair-weather friend □ give someone a fair shake □ play fair

FAITH
act of faith □ in bad faith □ in good faith □ pin one's faith on someone or something □ show good faith □ take something on faith

FALL
as easy as falling off a log □ break someone's fall □ fall afoul of someone or something □ fall (all) over oneself □ fall all over someone □ fall apart at the seams □ fall asleep □ fall back on someone or something □ fall

between two stools □ fall by the wayside □ fall down on the job □ fall flat (on its face) □ fall flat (on one's face) □ fall for someone or something □ fall from grace □ fall head over heels □ fall head over heels in love (with someone) □ fall in □ fall in for something □ fall in love (with someone) □ fall in with someone or something □ fall into a trap □ fall in(to) line □ fall in(to) place □ fall into someone's trap □ fall into the trap □ fall off □ fall on deaf ears □ fall out □ fall out (with someone about something) □ fall out (with someone over something) □ fall over backwards (to do something) □ fall short (of something) □ fall through □ fall to □ fall (up)on someone or something □ Pride goes before a fall. □ riding for a fall □ See also *fell*.

FALSE
lull someone into a false sense of security □ sail under false colors

FAMILIAR
have a familiar ring

FAMILIARITY
Familiarity breeds contempt.

FAMILY
(all) in the family □ black sheep of the family □ in a family way □ in the family □ in the family way □ like one of the family □ run in the family

FAMINE
either feast or famine

FAN
be a fan of someone □ fan the flames (of something)

FANCY
flight of fancy □ footloose and fancy-free □ strike someone's fancy □ take a fancy to someone or something □ tickle someone's fancy

FAR
as far as anyone knows □ as far as it goes □ as far as possible □ as far as someone or something is concerned □ come from far and wide □ far and away the best □ far be it from me to do something □ far cry from something □ far from it □ far into the

night ☐ far out ☐ few and far between ☐ from far and near ☐ go so far as to say something ☐ go too far ☐ so far as anyone knows ☐ so far as I'm concerned ☐ so far as possible ☐ So far, so good.

FARM
farm someone or something out

FARTHER
not see farther than the end of one's nose

FASHION
after a fashion ☐ after the fashion of someone or something ☐ go out of fashion ☐ out of fashion

FAST
fast and furious ☐ get nowhere fast ☐ hard-and-fast ☐ make a fast buck ☐ make fast work of someone or something ☐ play fast and loose (with someone or something) ☐ pull a fast one ☐ thick and fast

FAT
chew the fat ☐ fat and happy ☐ fat chance ☐ kill the fatted calf ☐ live off the fat of the land

FATE
leave one to one's fate

FATHER
old enough to be someone's father

FAULT
find fault (with someone or something) ☐ generous to a fault

FAUNA
flora and fauna

FAVOR
curry favor (with someone) ☐ decide in favor of someone or something ☐ in favor of someone ☐ in favor (of someone or something) ☐ in someone's favor ☐ out of favor (with someone) ☐ return the favor

FEAR
fools rush in (where angels fear to tread) ☐ for fear of something ☐ in fear and trembling ☐ never fear

FEAST
either feast or famine ☐ feast one's eyes (on someone or something)

FEATHER
as light as a feather ☐ Birds of a feather flock together. ☐ feather in one's cap ☐ feather one's (own) nest ☐ in fine feather ☐ knock someone over with a feather ☐ light as a feather ☐ make the feathers fly ☐ ruffle someone's feathers ☐ tar and feather someone

FED
fed up (to some place) (with someone or something)

FEDERAL
make a federal case out of something

FEED
bite the hand that feeds one ☐ fed up (to some place) (with someone or something) ☐ feed one's face ☐ feed someone a line ☐ feed the kitty ☐ for chicken feed ☐ put on the feed bag ☐ spoon-feed someone

FEEL
feel at home ☐ feel dragged out ☐ feel fit ☐ feel free (to do something) ☐ feel it beneath one (to do something) ☐ feel like a million (dollars) ☐ feel like a new person ☐ feel like something ☐ feel on top of the world ☐ feel out of place ☐ feel put-upon ☐ feel someone out ☐ feel something in one's bones ☐ feel up to something ☐ get the feel of something ☐ have mixed feelings (about someone or something) ☐ have the feel of something ☐ no hard feelings ☐ put out (some) feelers

FEELER
put out (some) feelers

FEELINGS
have mixed feelings (about someone or something) ☐ no hard feelings

FEET
dead on one's or its feet ☐ drag one's feet ☐ get a load off one's feet ☐ get back on one's feet ☐ get cold feet ☐ get one's feet on the ground ☐ get one's feet wet ☐ get to one's feet ☐ have feet of clay ☐ keep one's feet on the ground ☐ knock one off one's feet ☐ land on both feet ☐ land on one's feet ☐ let grass grow under one's feet

□ on one's feet □ regain one's feet □ sit at someone's feet □ stand on one's own two feet □ sweep one off one's feet □ take a load off one's feet □ think on one's feet □ throw oneself at someone's feet □ vote with one's feet

FELL
at one fell swoop □ in one fell swoop

FELLOW
hail-fellow-well-met

FENCE
fence someone in □ mend (one's) fences □ on the fence (about something) □ sit on the fence

FEND
fend for oneself

FERRET
ferret something out of someone or something

FEVER
run a fever

FEW
drop someone a few lines □ few and far between □ precious few □ quite a few □ wash a few things out

FIDDLE
as fit as a fiddle □ fiddle about (with someone or something) □ fiddle around (with someone or something) □ fiddle while Rome burns □ fit as a fiddle □ play second fiddle (to someone)

FIELD
have a field day □ out in left field □ play the field

FIFTY
divide something fifty-fifty □ go fifty-fifty (on something) □ split something fifty-fifty

FIGHT
fight against time □ fight someone or something hammer and tongs □ fight someone or something tooth and nail □ fighting chance □ go down fighting □ knock-down-drag-out fight □ Them's fighting words.

FIGURE
cut a fine figure □ figure in something □ figure on something □ figure someone or something out □ in round figures

FILE
have something on file □ (in) single file □ rank and file □ single file

FILL
back and fill □ fill someone in (on someone or something) □ fill someone's shoes □ fill the bill □ filled to the brim □ get one's fill of someone or something

FINAL
final fling □ get the final word □ in the final analysis

FIND
find fault (with someone or something) □ find it in one's heart (to do something) □ find one's or something's way somewhere □ find one's own level □ find one's tongue □ find one's way (around) □ find oneself □ find someone or something out □ find (something) out the hard way □ Finders keepers(, losers weepers.) □ lost-and-found

FINDERS
Finders keepers(, losers weepers.)

FINE
cut a fine figure □ fine and dandy □ fine kettle of fish □ fine state of affairs □ go over something with a fine-tooth comb □ in fine feather □ search something with a fine-tooth comb

FINGER
cross one's fingers □ get one's fingers burned □ have a finger in the pie □ have one's finger in the pie □ have something at one's fingertips □ have sticky fingers □ keep one's fingers crossed (for someone or something) □ lay a finger on someone or something □ lay the finger on someone □ not lift a finger (to help someone) □ point the finger at someone □ put one's finger on something □ put the finger on someone □ slip through someone's fingers □ twist someone around one's little finger □ work one's fingers to the bone

FINGERTIP
have something at one's fingertips

FINISH
from start to finish

FIRE
add fuel to the fire □ ball of fire □ baptism of fire □ build a fire under someone □ catch (on) fire □ caught in the cross fire □ draw (someone's) fire (away from someone or something) □ fire away at someone or something □ firing on all cylinders □ hang fire □ have too many irons in the fire □ hold one's fire □ keep the home fires burning □ like a house on fire □ open fire (on someone) □ out of the frying pan into the fire □ play with fire □ set fire to someone or something □ set someone or something on fire □ set the world on fire □ under fire □ Where there's smoke there's fire.

FIRST
at first □ at first blush □ at first glance □ cast the first stone □ first and foremost □ first and ten □ First come, first served. □ first of all □ first off □ first thing (in the morning) □ first things first □ get to first base (with someone or something) □ in the first instance □ in the first place □ love at first sight □ not know the first thing about someone or something □ of the first water □ on a first-name basis (with someone) □ play first chair □ reach first base (with someone or something)

FISH
be a cold fish □ fine kettle of fish □ fish for a compliment □ fish for something □ fish in troubled waters □ fish or cut bait □ go on a fishing expedition □ have other fish to fry □ like a fish out of water □ neither fish nor fowl □ There are plenty of other fish in the sea.

FIST
closefisted (with money) □ hand over fist □ tightfisted (with money)

FIT
as fit as a fiddle □ by fits and starts □

feel fit □ fit and trim □ fit as a fiddle □ fit for a king □ fit in someone □ fit in (with someone or something) □ fit like a glove □ fit someone in(to something) □ fit someone or something out (with something) □ fit someone to a T □ fit to be tied □ fit to kill □ have a conniption (fit) □ have a fit □ If the shoe fits, wear it. □ see fit (to do something) □ survival of the fittest □ think someone or something fit for something □ throw a fit

FIVE
nine-to-five job □ take five

FIX
fix someone up (with someone or something) □ fix someone's wagon □ get a fix on something □ give someone a fix on something □ in a fix □ well-fixed

FIZZLE
fizzle out

FLAME
add fuel to the flame □ burn with a low blue flame □ burst into flames □ fan the flames (of something) □ go up in flames

FLARE
flare up

FLASH
as quick as a flash □ flash in the pan □ in a flash □ quick as a flash

FLAT
as flat as a pancake □ fall flat (on its face) □ fall flat (on one's face) □ flat as a pancake □ flat broke □ flat out □ in nothing flat □ leave someone flat

FLEA
not hurt a flea

FLESH
flesh and blood □ flesh something out □ in the flesh

FLIES
as the crow flies □ no flies on someone □ time flies

FLIGHT
flight of fancy

FLING
final fling □ fling oneself at someone

FLIP
do a flip-flop (on something) □ flip one's lid □ flip one's wig

FLOAT
float a loan

FLOCK
Birds of a feather flock together.

FLOOR
get in (on the ground floor) □ get the floor □ mop the floor up with someone □ walk the floor □ wipe the floor up with someone

FLOP
do a flip-flop (on something)

FLORA
flora and fauna

FLOTSAM
flotsam and jetsam

FLOW
ebb and flow

FLUFF
fluff one's lines

FLUNK
flunk out □ flunk someone out

FLY
as the crow flies □ be flying high □ come through something with flying colors □ do something on the fly □ fly-by-night □ fly in the face of someone or something □ fly in the ointment □ fly in the teeth of someone or something □ fly into the face of danger □ fly off the handle □ fly the coop □ get off to a flying start □ Go fly a kite! □ It'll never fly. □ make the feathers fly □ make the fur fly □ no flies on someone □ time flies □ with flying colors

FOAM
foam at the mouth

FOB
fob something off (on someone)

FOE
friend or foe

FOG
in a fog

FOLD
fold something up □ fold, spindle, or mutilate □ fold up

FOLLOW
follow in someone's footsteps □ follow in someone's tracks □ follow one's heart □ follow one's nose □ follow someone or something up □ follow suit □ follow the crowd □ follow through (on something) □ follow up (on someone or something) □ tough act to follow

FOND
fond of someone or something

FOOD
food for thought

FOOL
A fool and his money are soon parted. □ fool around (with someone or something) □ fool's paradise □ fools rush in (where angels fear to tread) □ make a fool out of someone □ nobody's fool □ on a fool's errand □ penny-wise and pound-foolish □ play the fool □ take someone for a fool

FOOLISH
penny-wise and pound-foolish

FOOT
be off on the wrong foot □ bound hand and foot □ dead on one's or its feet □ drag one's feet □ foot the bill □ footloose and fancy-free □ get a load off one's feet □ get back on one's feet □ get cold feet □ get off on the wrong foot □ get one's feet on the ground □ get one's feet wet □ get one's foot in the door □ get to one's feet □ have a foot in both camps □ have feet of clay □ have foot-in-mouth disease □ have one foot in the grave □ have the shoe on the other foot □ hotfoot it out of somewhere □ keep one's feet on the ground □ knock one off one's feet □ land on both feet □ land on one's feet □ let grass grow under one's feet □ not set foot somewhere □ on foot □ on one's feet □ play footsie (with someone) □ put one's best foot forward □ put one's foot down (about something) □ put one's foot in it □ put one's foot in one's mouth □ regain one's feet □

set foot somewhere ☐ sit at someone's feet ☐ stand on one's own two feet ☐ start off on the wrong foot ☐ stick one's foot in one's mouth ☐ sweep one off one's feet ☐ take a load off one's feet ☐ The shoe is on the other foot. ☐ think on one's feet ☐ throw oneself at someone's feet ☐ vote with one's feet ☐ wait on someone hand and foot ☐ wouldn't touch something with a ten-foot pole

FOOTLOOSE
footloose and fancy-free

FOOTSIE
play footsie (with someone)

FOOTSTEP
follow in someone's footsteps

FORBIDDEN
forbidden fruit

FORCE
driving force (behind someone or something) ☐ force someone or something down someone's throat ☐ force someone out (of office) ☐ force someone to the wall ☐ force someone's hand ☐ force to be reckoned with ☐ in force ☐ join forces (with someone) ☐ out in force

FORE
come to the fore ☐ fore and aft

FOREMOST
first and foremost

FOREST
not able to see the forest for the trees

FOREVER
forever and a day ☐ forever and ever ☐ lost and gone forever

FORGET
forget oneself ☐ forgive and forget ☐ gone but not forgotten

FORGIVE
forgive and forget

FORGOTTEN
gone but not forgotten

FORK
fork money out (for something) ☐ fork something over

FORKED
speak with a forked tongue

FORM
form an opinion ☐ form and substance ☐ true to form

FORT
hold the fort

FORTH
back and forth ☐ hold forth ☐ launch forth (on something) ☐ set forth (on something)

FORTY
catch forty winks ☐ forty winks ☐ take forty winks

FORWARD
from this day forward ☐ look forward to something ☐ put one's best foot forward ☐ put something forward

FORWARDS
know something backwards and forwards ☐ know something forwards and backwards

FOUL
foul one's own nest ☐ foul play ☐ foul someone or something up ☐ foul up ☐ fouled up

FOUND
lost-and-found

FOURS
on all fours

FOWL
neither fish nor fowl

FOX
as sly as a fox ☐ sly as a fox

FREE
able to breathe (freely) again ☐ as free as a bird ☐ feel free (to do something) ☐ footloose and fancy-free ☐ free and clear ☐ free and easy ☐ free as a bird ☐ free-for-all ☐ get a free hand (with someone or something) ☐ get off scot-free ☐ give free rein to someone ☐ give someone a free hand (with something) ☐ give someone free rein ☐ go scot-free ☐ make free with someone or something ☐ of one's own free will

FREEDOM
give one one's freedom

FRESH
as fresh as a daisy □ breath of fresh air □ fresh as a daisy □ fresh out (of something) □ get fresh (with someone)

FRIEND
A friend in need is a friend indeed. □ be friends with someone □ fair-weather friend □ friend or foe

FRIENDSHIP
strike up a friendship

FRIGHTEN
frighten one out of one's wits □ frighten someone to death □ frighten the living daylights out of someone □ frighten the wits out of someone

FRIGHTENED
frightened to death

FRITTER
fritter something away

FRITZ
on the fritz

FRO
to and fro

FROG
big frog in a small pond □ get a frog in one's throat

FROING
toing and froing (on something)

FROM
another country heard from □ aside from someone or something □ away from one's desk □ back down (from someone or something) □ back off (from someone or something) □ be from Missouri □ break loose (from someone or something) □ come from far and wide □ cut loose (from someone or something) □ cut the ground out from under someone □ downhill from here on □ draw (someone's) fire (away from someone or something) □ everything from A to Z □ everything from soup to nuts □ fall from grace □ far be it from me to do something □ far cry from something □ far from it □ from day to day □ from door to door □ from far and near □ from hand to hand □ from head to toe □ from pillar to post □ from rags to

riches □ from start to finish □ from stem to stern □ from the bottom of one's heart □ from the cradle to the grave □ from the ground up □ from the heart □ from the horse's mouth □ from the outset □ from the word go □ from this day forward □ from this day on □ from time to time □ from tip to toe □ from top to bottom □ from way back □ get a dirty look from someone □ get away (from it all) □ get out from under someone or something □ go from bad to worse □ hail from somewhere □ keep one's distance (from someone or something) □ keep the wolf from the door □ knock the props out from under someone □ know something from memory □ learn something from the bottom up □ live from hand to mouth □ make something from scratch □ not know from nothing □ not know someone from Adam □ nothing to choose from □ out from under (something) □ pull the rug out (from under someone) □ separate the men from the boys □ separate the sheep from the goats □ shoot from the hip □ shy away (from someone or something) □ start from scratch □ step down (from something) □ (straight) from the horse's mouth □ straight from the shoulder □ take off (from work) □ take one's cue from someone □ where one is coming from

FRONT
burn one's bridges in front of one □ can't see one's hand in front of one's face □ cover the waterfront □ out front □ put on a (brave) front □ put up a (brave) front □ up-front

FRUIT
bear fruit □ forbidden fruit

FRUITCAKE
as nutty as a fruitcake □ nutty as a fruitcake

FRY
have other fish to fry □ out of the frying pan into the fire □ small fry

FUEL
add fuel to the fire □ add fuel to the flame

FULL
as full as a tick □ (at) full blast □ at full speed □ at full tilt □ come full circle □ full blast □ full of beans □ full of bull □ full of hot air □ full of it □ full of Old Nick □ full of oneself □ full of prunes □ full of the devil □ full steam ahead □ get into full swing □ have one's hands full (with someone or something) □ in full swing

FUN
as much fun as a barrel of monkeys □ fun and games □ make fun (of someone or something) □ more fun than a barrel of monkeys □ poke fun (at someone)

FUNNY
as funny as a barrel of monkeys □ as funny as a crutch □ funny as a crutch □ funny ha-ha □ funny peculiar □ strike someone funny

FUR
make the fur fly □ rub someone('s fur) the wrong way

FURIOUS
fast and furious

FURTHER
without further ado

FUSE
blow a fuse

FUSS
kick up a fuss □ make a fuss (over someone or something)

FUTURE
in the near future

GAB
have the gift of gab

GAIN
gain ground □ ill-gotten gains □ Nothing ventured, nothing gained.

GALLERY
play to the gallery

GAME
ahead of the game □ at this stage of the game □ fair game □ fun and games □ game that two can play □ give the game away □ name of the game □ new ball game □ The game is up.

GANDER
take a gander (at someone or something)

GANG
gang up (on someone)

GANGBUSTERS
come on like gangbusters

GARDEN
lead someone down the garden path

GAS
cooking with gas □ gas up □ out of gas □ run out of gas □ step on the gas

GASKET
blow a gasket

GASP
at the last gasp

GATE
get the gate □ give someone the gate

GATHER
A rolling stone gathers no moss.

GAUNTLET
throw down the gauntlet

GEAR
gear (oneself) up (for something) □ get into high gear □ in high gear

GENERAL
as a (general) rule

GENEROUS
generous to a fault

GHOST
ghost of a chance □ give up the ghost

GIFT
have the gift of gab

GILD
gild the lily

GILLS
blue around the gills □ green around the gills □ pale around the gills

GIRD
gird (up) one's loins

GIVE
give a blank check to someone □ give a good account of oneself □ give (an) ear to someone or something □ give-and-take □ give as good as one

gets ☐ give birth to something ☐ give carte blanche to someone ☐ give chase (to someone or something) ☐ give credence to something ☐ give credit where credit is due ☐ give free rein to someone ☐ give ground ☐ give her the gun ☐ give in (to someone or something) ☐ give it the gun ☐ give it to someone (straight) ☐ give of oneself ☐ give one a run for one's money ☐ Give one an inch, and one will take a mile. ☐ give one butterflies in one's stomach ☐ give one one's freedom ☐ give one one's walking papers ☐ give one what's coming to one ☐ give one's ear to someone or something ☐ give one's right arm (for someone or something) ☐ give out ☐ give out with something ☐ give rise to something ☐ give someone a bang ☐ give someone a big send-off ☐ give someone a black eye ☐ give someone a blank check ☐ give someone a break ☐ give someone a bright idea ☐ give someone a bum steer ☐ give someone a buzz ☐ give someone a charge ☐ give someone a clean bill of health ☐ give someone a dirty look ☐ give someone a fair shake ☐ give someone a fix on something ☐ give someone a free hand (with something) ☐ give someone a (good) dressing-down ☐ give someone a hand (for something) ☐ give someone a hand (with someone or something) ☐ give someone a hard time ☐ give someone a head start (on someone or something) ☐ give someone a kick ☐ give someone a licking ☐ give someone a line ☐ give someone a pain ☐ give someone a pat on the back ☐ give someone a piece of one's mind ☐ give someone a rain check (on something) ☐ give someone a raw deal ☐ give someone a reputation (as a something) ☐ give someone a reputation (for doing something) ☐ give someone a ring ☐ give someone a rough idea (about something) ☐ give someone a rough idea (of something) ☐ give someone a shellacking ☐ give someone a slap on the wrist ☐ give someone a start ☐ give someone a swelled head ☐ give someone a

tongue-lashing ☐ give someone carte blanche ☐ give someone credit (for something) ☐ give someone free rein ☐ give someone gray hair(s) ☐ give someone hell ☐ give someone or something a wide berth ☐ give someone or something the (old) heave-ho ☐ give someone pause ☐ give someone some skin ☐ give someone the air ☐ give someone the ax ☐ give someone the benefit of the doubt ☐ give someone the boot ☐ give someone the brush-off ☐ give someone the bum's rush ☐ give someone the business ☐ give someone the cold shoulder ☐ give someone the creeps ☐ give someone the devil ☐ give someone the eye ☐ give someone the gate ☐ give someone the glad hand ☐ give someone the go-ahead ☐ give someone the go-by ☐ give someone the green light ☐ give someone the hard sell ☐ give someone the high sign ☐ give someone the low-down (on someone or something) ☐ give someone the once-over ☐ give someone the red-carpet treatment ☐ give someone the runaround ☐ give someone the sack ☐ give someone the shirt off one's back ☐ give someone the slip ☐ give someone the third degree ☐ give someone the willies ☐ give someone the works ☐ give someone tit for tat ☐ give someone to understand something ☐ give someone what for ☐ give something a lick and a promise ☐ give something one's best shot ☐ give the bride away ☐ give the devil her due ☐ give the devil his due ☐ give the game away ☐ give up the ghost ☐ give vent to something ☐ give voice to something ☐ given to understand ☐ not give a hang about someone or something ☐ not give a hoot about someone or something ☐ not give anyone the time of day ☐ not give two hoots about someone or something

GLAD
get the glad hand ☐ give someone the glad hand

GLANCE
at first glance

GLASS
have a glass jaw

GLITTER
All that glitters is not gold.

GLORY
in one's glory

GLOSS
gloss something over

GLOVE
fit like a glove □ hand in glove (with someone) □ handle someone with kid gloves

GLUTTON
glutton for punishment

GOAT
get someone's goat □ make someone the scapegoat for something □ separate the sheep from the goats

GOD
act of God □ Honest to God. □ honest-to-God

GOLD
All that glitters is not gold. □ as good as gold □ gold mine of information □ good as gold □ have a heart of gold □ worth its weight in gold

GOLLY
by guess and by golly

GONER
be a goner

GOOD
all in good time □ all to the good □ (all) well and good □ as good as done □ as good as gold □ as good as one's word □ do someone a good turn □ do someone good □ do someone's heart good □ for good □ for good measure □ get on the good side of someone □ get out while the getting is good □ get the goods on someone □ get time off for good behavior □ give a good account of oneself □ give as good as one gets □ give someone a (good) dressing-down □ good and something □ good as done □ good as gold □ good enough for someone or something □ good-for-nothing □ good riddance (to bad rubbish) □ have a good command of something

□ have a good head on one's shoulders □ have a (good) mind to do something □ have a good thing going □ (have) never had it so good □ in (all) good conscience □ in good condition □ in good faith □ in good hands □ in good repair □ in good shape □ in good spirits □ in good time □ in good (with someone) □ keep good time □ kiss something good-bye □ make good as something □ make good (at something) □ make good money □ make good on something □ make good time □ make someone look good □ make something good □ never had it so good □ No news is good news. □ on good terms (with someone) □ One good turn deserves another. □ put in a good word (for someone) □ put something to (good) use □ run the good race □ sell someone a bill of goods □ show good faith □ show something to good advantage □ So far, so good. □ stand someone in good stead □ throw good money after bad □ too good to be true □ too much of a good thing □ turn something to good account □ up to no good □ well and good □ What's the good of something? □ when one is good and ready □ Your guess is as good as mine.

GOODNESS
Honest to goodness. □ honest-to-goodness

GOOF
goof off

GOOSE
cook someone's goose □ get goose bumps □ get goose pimples □ gone goose □ wild-goose chase

GOT
Cat got your tongue? □ ill-gotten gains

GOWN
cap and gown □ town-and-gown

GRABS
up for grabs

GRACE
fall from grace □ saving grace

GRADE
make the grade

GRAIN
go against the grain □ take something with a grain of salt

GRAND
as busy as Grand Central Station □ busy as Grand Central Station

GRANT
take someone or something for granted

GRASP
get a grasp of something □ grasp at straws □ within someone's grasp

GRASS
let grass grow under one's feet □ snake in the grass

GRASSHOPPER
knee-high to a grasshopper

GRAVE
as quiet as the grave □ dig one's own grave □ from the cradle to the grave □ have one foot in the grave □ quiet as the grave □ turn (over) in one's grave

GRAVY
ride the gravy train

GRAY
get gray hair(s) □ give someone gray hair(s) □ gray area □ gray matter

GREASE
as quick as greased lightning □ grease someone's palm □ like greased lightning □ quick as greased lightning □ use some elbow grease

GREAT
go great guns □ greatest thing since sliced bread □ in great demand □ in great haste □ make a great show of something □ no great shakes □ set great store by someone or something □ take (great) pains (to do something) □ think a great deal of someone or something □ to a great extent

GREEK
(all) Greek to me □ Greek to me

GREEN
get the green light □ give someone the green light □ green around the gills □ green with envy □ have a green thumb

GRIEF
come to grief

GRIEVANCE
air one's grievances

GRIN
grin and bear it

GRIND
grind to a halt □ have an ax to grind (with someone) □ the daily grind

GRINDSTONE
keep one's nose to the grindstone □ put one's nose to the grindstone

GRIP
come to grips with something □ lose one's grip

GRIST
grist for someone's mill

GRIT
grit one's teeth

GRITTY
get down to the nitty-gritty

GROSS
gross someone out

GROUND
break ground (for something) □ break new ground □ cover a lot of ground □ cut the ground out from under someone □ drive something into the ground □ from the ground up □ gain ground □ get in (on the ground floor) □ get one's feet on the ground □ get something off (the ground) □ give ground □ ground someone □ have one's ear to the ground □ hold one's ground □ keep one's ear to the ground □ keep one's feet on the ground □ lose ground □ one's old stamping ground □ run something into the ground □ stand one's ground

GROW
grow on someone □ grow out of something □ have growing pains □ let grass grow under one's feet □ outgrow something

GRUDGE
bear a grudge (against someone) □

have a grudge against someone ☐
hold a grudge against someone ☐
nurse a grudge (against someone)

GUARD
catch one off one's guard ☐ catch
someone off guard ☐ guard against
someone or something ☐ on (one's)
guard

GUESS
by guess and by golly ☐ get another
guess coming ☐ outguess someone ☐
Your guess is as good as mine.

GUINEA
serve as a guinea pig

GUM
gum something up ☐ gum up the
works

GUN
beat the gun ☐ give her the gun ☐
give it the gun ☐ go great guns ☐ gun
for someone ☐ jump the gun ☐ shotgun wedding ☐ son of a gun ☐ stick
to one's guns

GUT
bust a gut (to do something) ☐ hate
someone's guts

GUTTER
in the gutter

HA
funny ha-ha

HABIT
kick a habit ☐ kick the habit

HACK
hack something

HACKLES
get someone's hackles up

HAIL
hail-fellow-well-met ☐ hail from somewhere ☐ within hailing distance

HAIR
by a hair('s breadth) ☐ curl someone's
hair ☐ get gray hair(s) ☐ get in someone's hair ☐ give someone gray
hair(s) ☐ hair of the dog that bit one
☐ hang by a hair ☐ let one's hair
down ☐ make someone's hair curl ☐
make someone's hair stand on end ☐
neither hide nor hair ☐ part some-

one's hair ☐ split hairs ☐ tear one's
hair (out)

HALE
hale and hearty

HALF
at half-mast ☐ go off half-cocked ☐
Half a loaf is better than none. ☐
half-and-half ☐ have half a mind to
do something ☐ have half a notion to
do something ☐ not half bad ☐ one's
better half ☐ six of one and half a
dozen of the other

HALFHEARTED
halfhearted (about someone or something)

HALFWAY
meet someone halfway

HALT
grind to a halt

HAM
ham something up

HAMBURGER
make hamburger out of someone or
something

HAMMER
fight someone or something hammer
and tongs ☐ go at it hammer and
tongs ☐ hammer away (at someone or
something) ☐ hammer something
home ☐ hammer something out

HAND
A bird in the hand is worth two in the
bush. ☐ at hand ☐ bite the hand that
feeds one ☐ bound hand and foot ☐
can't see one's hand in front of one's
face ☐ catch someone red-handed ☐
caught red-handed ☐ change hands
☐ close at hand ☐ come away
empty-handed ☐ dirty one's hands ☐
do something by hand ☐ do something hands down ☐ eat out of someone's hands ☐ force someone's hand
☐ from hand to hand ☐ get a free
hand (with someone or something) ☐
get a hand with something ☐ get one's
hands dirty ☐ get one's hands on
someone or something ☐ get the glad
hand ☐ get the upper hand (on someone) ☐ give someone a free hand

(with something) □ give someone a hand (for something) □ give someone a hand (with someone or something) □ give someone the glad hand □ go away empty-handed □ hand in glove (with someone) □ hand in hand □ hand it to someone □ hand-me-down □ hand over fist □ hand over hand □ hand something down (to someone) □ hands down □ Hands off! □ Hands up! □ hat in hand □ have a hand in something □ have clean hands □ have one's hand in the till □ have one's hands full (with someone or something) □ have one's hands tied □ have someone or something in one's hands □ have someone or something on one's hands □ have something at hand □ have something in hand □ in good hands □ keep one's hand in (something) □ keep one's hands off (someone or something) □ know someone or something like the back of one's hand □ know someone or something like the palm of one's hand □ lay one's hands on someone or something □ lend a hand (to someone) □ lend (someone) a hand □ lift a hand (against someone or something) □ live from hand to mouth □ near at hand □ old hand at doing something □ on (the) one hand □ on the other hand □ out of hand □ pay someone a back-handed compliment □ pay someone a left-handed compliment □ put one's hand to the plow □ put one's hand(s) on something □ putty in someone's hands □ raise a hand (against someone or something) □ shake (hands) on something □ shake hands (with someone) □ show of hands □ show one's hand □ sit on its hands □ sit on one's hands □ soil one's hands □ take a hand in something □ take the law into one's own hands □ throw one's hands up in despair □ throw one's hands up in horror □ tie someone's hands □ try one's hand (at something) □ wait on someone hand and foot □ wash one's hands of someone or something □ with both hands tied behind one's back □ (with) hat in hand □ with one hand tied behind one's back

HANDBASKET
go to hell in a handbasket

HANDFUL
by the handful

HANDLE
fly off the handle □ get a handle on something □ handle someone with kid gloves □ postage and handling □ shipping and handling

HANDWRITING
read the handwriting on the wall □ see the (hand)writing on the wall

HANDY
come in handy

HANG
get the hang of something □ hang a left □ hang a right □ hang around (with someone) □ hang back □ hang by a hair □ hang by a thread □ hang fire □ hang in the balance □ hang in there □ hang loose □ hang on someone's coattails □ hang on someone's every word □ hang on (to someone or something) □ hang out (somewhere) □ hang out (with someone) □ hang someone in effigy □ hang tough □ hang up □ have something hanging over one's head □ hung up (on someone or something) □ keep someone or something hanging in midair □ leave someone or something hanging in midair □ let it all hang out □ not give a hang about someone or something □ somewhere to hang (up) one's hat

HAPPEN
happen (up)on someone or something □ in case something happens □ no matter what happens □ sit back and let something happen

HAPPILY
live happily ever after

HAPPY
as happy as a clam □ as happy as a lark □ fat and happy □ happy as a clam □ happy as a lark □ hit a happy medium □ live happily ever after □ strike a happy medium

HARD
as hard as nails □ between a rock and

a hard place □ cold, hard cash □ come down hard on someone or something □ do something the hard way □ drive a hard bargain □ find (something) out the hard way □ get the hard sell □ give someone a hard time □ give someone the hard sell □ hard-and-fast □ hard as nails □ hard nut to crack □ hard on someone's heels □ hard pressed (to do something) □ hard put (to do something) □ hard up (for something) □ have a hard time □ learn (something) the hard way □ no hard feelings □ play hard to get □ take a hard line (with someone)

HARDLY
hardly have time to breathe

HARE
as mad as a March hare □ mad as a March hare

HARKEN
hark(en) back to something

HARNESS
get back into harness

HARP
harp on something

HARRY
(every) Tom, Dick, and Harry

HASH
hash something over

HASTE
beat a (hasty) retreat □ Haste makes waste. □ in great haste

HASTY
beat a (hasty) retreat

HAT
as mad as a hatter □ at the drop of a hat □ be old hat □ eat one's hat □ hat in hand □ keep something under one's hat □ mad as a hatter □ pass the hat □ pull something out of a hat □ somewhere to hang (up) one's hat □ take off one's hat (to someone) □ talk through one's hat □ toss one's hat into the ring □ wear more than one hat □ (with) hat in hand

HATBAND
as tight as Dick's hatband □ tight as Dick's hatband

HATCH
batten down the hatches □ count one's chickens before they hatch □ down the hatch

HATCHET
bury the hatchet

HATE
hate someone's guts

HATTER
as mad as a hatter □ mad as a hatter

HAUL
haul someone in □ haul someone over the coals □ haul up (somewhere) □ over the long haul □ over the short haul

HAVOC
play havoc with someone or something □ raise havoc with someone or something □ wreak havoc with something

HAW
hem and haw (around)

HAWK
watch someone like a hawk

HAY
hit the hay □ That ain't hay.

HAYSTACK
like looking for a needle in a haystack

HAYWIRE
go haywire

HEAD
able to do something standing on one's head □ bang one's head against a brick wall □ beat one's head against the wall □ beat something into someone's head □ bite someone's head off □ bring something to a head □ bury one's head in the sand □ can't make heads or tails (out) of someone or something □ come to a head □ drum something into someone('s head) □ fall head over heels □ fall head over heels in love (with someone) □ from head to toe □ get a head start (on someone or something) □ get one's head above water □ get someone or something out of one's head □ get

something into someone's thick head □ give someone a head start (on someone or something) □ give someone a swelled head □ go over someone's head □ go to someone's head □ have a good head on one's shoulders □ have a price on one's head □ have eyes in the back of one's head □ have one's head in the clouds □ have rocks in one's head □ have something hanging over one's head □ head and shoulders above someone or something □ head for someone or something □ head for the last round-up □ head over heels in debt □ head over heels in love (with someone) □ head someone or something off □ head something up □ heads or tails □ heads will roll □ hide one's head in the sand □ hit the nail on the head □ hold one's head up □ in over one's head □ keep a civil tongue (in one's head) □ keep one's head □ keep one's head above water □ knock some heads together □ lose one's head (over someone or something) □ make someone's head spin □ make someone's head swim □ off the top of one's head □ on someone's head □ out of one's head □ over someone's head □ put ideas into someone's head □ put one's head on the block (for someone or something) □ rear its ugly head □ run around like a chicken with its head cut off □ talk someone's head off □ touched (in the head) □ trouble one's head about someone or something □ turn someone's head □ use one's head

HEALTH
Early to bed, early to rise(, makes a man healthy, wealthy, and wise.) □ get a clean bill of health □ give someone a clean bill of health □ in the best of health

HEAR
hear a peep out of someone □ hear of something □ so quiet you could hear a pin drop □ so still you could hear a pin drop □ will not hear of something

HEARD
another country heard from

HEART
break someone's heart □ cross one's heart (and hope to die) □ die of a broken heart □ do someone's heart good □ eat one's heart out □ find it in one's heart (to do something) □ follow one's heart □ from the bottom of one's heart □ from the heart □ get at the heart of the matter □ get to the heart of the matter □ halfhearted (about someone or something) □ have a change of heart □ have a heart □ have a heart of gold □ have a heart of stone □ have a heart-to-heart (talk) □ have a soft spot in one's heart for someone or something □ have one's heart go out to someone □ have one's heart in the right place □ have one's heart on one's sleeve □ have one's heart set against something □ have one's heart set on something □ have one's heart stand still □ heart and soul □ know something by heart □ learn something by heart □ lose heart □ one's heart goes out to someone □ one's heart is in one's mouth □ one's heart is in the right place □ one's heart is set against something □ one's heart is set on something □ one's heart misses a beat □ one's heart skips a beat □ one's heart stands still □ open one's heart (to someone) □ pour one's heart (out to someone) □ set one's heart against something □ set one's heart on something □ take heart □ take something to heart □ to one's heart's content □ warm the cockles of someone's heart □ wear one's heart on one's sleeve □ with a heavy heart

HEARTY
hale and hearty

HEAT
in a dead heat □ in heat □ put the heat on (someone) □ turn the heat up (on someone)

HEAVE
get the (old) heave-ho □ give someone or something the (old) heave-ho

HEAVEN
in seventh heaven □ move heaven and earth to do something

HEAVY
heavy going □ hot and heavy □ with a heavy heart

HECK
for the heck of it

HEDGE
hedge one's bets

HEED
take heed

HEEL
cool one's heels □ dig one's heels in □ down-at-the-heels □ fall head over heels □ fall head over heels in love (with someone) □ hard on someone's heels □ head over heels in debt □ head over heels in love (with someone) □ kick up one's heels □ on the heels of something □ set one back on one's heels □ take to one's heels □ well-heeled

HEELED
well-heeled

HELL
(all) shot to hell □ as hot as hell □ as mad as hell □ catch hell □ come hell or high water □ for the hell of it □ get hell □ give someone hell □ go to (hell) □ go to hell in a handbasket □ have a snowball's chance in hell □ have hell to pay □ hell-bent for leather □ hot as hell □ like a bat out of hell □ mad as hell □ raise hell (with someone or something) □ shot to hell □ through hell and high water □ to hell and gone

HELLO
drop in (to say hello)

HELP
can't help but do something □ help oneself □ help someone or something out (with someone or something) □ not able to help something □ not lift a finger (to help someone) □ pitch in (and help)

HEM
hem and haw (around) □ hem someone or something in

HEN
as mad as a wet hen □ as scarce as hens' teeth □ mad as a wet hen □ scarcer than hens' teeth

HERD
ride herd on someone or something

HERRING
red herring

HIDE
have someone's hide □ hide-and-seek □ hide one's face in shame □ hide one's head in the sand □ hide one's light under a bushel □ neither hide nor hair □ tan someone's hide

HIGH
act high-and-mighty □ as high as a kite □ as high as the sky □ be flying high □ come hell or high water □ eat high on the hog □ get into high gear □ get the high sign □ give someone the high sign □ go sky-high □ high and dry □ high-and-mighty □ high as the sky □ high man on the totem pole □ high on something □ hit the high spots □ hunt high and low (for someone or something) □ in high dudgeon □ in high gear □ It's high time! □ knee-high to a grasshopper □ leave someone high and dry □ live high off the hog □ live high on the hog □ look high and low (for someone or something) □ search high and low (for someone or something) □ through hell and high water

HIGHFLIER
highflier

HIGHLY
speak highly of someone or something □ think highly of someone or something

HIGHTAIL
hightail it out of somewhere

HIGHWAYS
highways and byways

HIKE
take a hike

HILL
as old as the hills □ make a mountain out of a molehill □ not worth a hill of beans □ old as the hills □ over the hill

HINGE

hinge on something

HINT

take a hint

HIP

shoot from the hip

HISTORY

go down in history

HIT

hit a happy medium □ hit a snag □
hit a sour note □ hit-and-miss □
hit-and-run □ hit bottom □ hit it off
(with someone) □ hit one close to
home □ hit one where one lives □ hit
one's stride □ hit-or-miss □ hit pay
dirt □ hit (someone) below the belt
□ hit (someone) like a ton of bricks
□ hit someone (right) between the
eyes □ hit someone up (for something) □ hit the books □ hit the
bottle □ hit the bricks □ hit the
bull's-eye □ hit the ceiling □ hit the
hay □ hit the high spots □ hit the
jackpot □ hit the nail on the head □
hit the road □ hit the sack □ hit the
skids □ hit the spot □ hit (up)on
something □ hitting on all cylinders
□ make a hit (with someone or something) □ pinch-hit (for someone)

HITCH

hitch a ride

HITHER

hither and thither □ hither, thither,
and yon

HO

get the (old) heave-ho □ give someone or something the (old) heave-ho

HOB

play hob with someone or something
□ raise hob with someone or something

HOBSON

Hobson's choice

HOE

tough row to hoe

HOG

eat high on the hog □ go hog-wild □
go whole hog □ live high off the hog
□ live high on the hog

HOIST

hoist with one's own petard

HOLD

can't hold a candle to someone □
Don't hold your breath. □ get (a)hold
of someone or something □ get hold
of someone or something □ hold a
grudge against someone □ hold a
meeting □ hold all the aces □ hold
forth □ hold no brief for someone or
something □ hold on (to someone or
something) □ hold one's breath □
hold one's end (of the bargain) up □
hold one's fire □ hold one's ground
□ hold one's head up □ hold one's
own □ hold one's peace □ hold one's
temper □ hold one's tongue □ hold
out (for someone or something) □
hold out the olive branch □ hold
someone down □ hold someone or
something in check □ hold someone
or something over □ hold someone or
something still □ hold someone or
something up □ hold someone or
something up (as an example) □ hold
something against someone □ hold
still □ hold still for something □ hold
the fort □ hold the line (at someone
or something) □ hold true □ hold up
□ hold up (for someone or something) □ hold up on something □
hold water □ hold with something □
Hold your horses! □ Hold your
tongue! □ lay hold of someone or
something □ leave someone holding
the bag □ no holds barred □ not hold
a candle to someone or something □
not hold a stick to someone or something □ not hold water □ on hold □
put someone or something on hold □
take (a)hold of someone or something
□ won't hold water

HOLE

ace in the hole □ hole in one □ hole
up (somewhere) □ in the hole □
Money burns a hole in someone's
pocket. □ out of the hole □ pick
holes in something □ square peg in a
round hole

HOLIDAY

busman's holiday

HOLLER

hoot and holler

HOLY
holier-than-thou

HOME
at home □ at home with someone or something □ bring home the bacon □ bring something home to someone □ close to home □ come home (to roost) □ come home to someone □ drive something home □ eat someone out of house and home □ feel at home □ hammer something home □ hit one close to home □ home in (on someone or something) □ keep the home fires burning □ make oneself at home □ nothing to write home about □ see someone home □ till the cows come home □ (un)til the cows come home

HONEST
honest and aboveboard □ Honest to God. □ honest-to-God □ Honest to goodness. □ honest-to-goodness □ Honest to Pete. □ honest-to-Pete

HONESTLY
come by something honestly

HONEYMOON
The honeymoon is over.

HONOR
do the honors □ honor someone's check □ in honor of someone or something □ on one's honor

HOOD
all around Robin Hood's barn

HOOK
by hook or (by) crook □ get one's hooks into someone or something □ get (someone) off the hook □ hooked (on something) □ let someone off (the hook) □ swallow something, hook, line, and sinker

HOOKY
play hooky

HOOP
jump through a hoop □ jump through hoops

HOOT
hoot and holler □ not care two hoots about someone or something □ not give a hoot about someone or some-thing □ not give two hoots about someone or something

HOP
hop, skip, and a jump □ Hop to it! □ hopped up

HOPE
cross one's heart (and hope to die) □ hope against (all) hope □ in hopes of something

HOPELESS
hopeless at doing something

HOPPED
hopped up

HORIZON
loom large (on the horizon) □ on the horizon

HORN
blow one's own horn □ horn in (on someone or something) □ lock horns (with someone) □ on the horns of a dilemma □ seize the bull by the horns □ take the bull by the horns □ toot one's own horn

HORNET
as mad as a hornet □ mad as a hornet □ stir up a hornet's nest

HORROR
throw one's hands up in horror

HORSE
back the wrong horse □ beat a dead horse □ change horses in the middle of the stream □ dark horse □ eat like a horse □ from the horse's mouth □ get a charley horse □ Hold your horses! □ horse and buggy □ horse and carriage □ horse around □ horse of a different color □ horse of another color □ horse sense □ put the cart before the horse □ (straight) from the horse's mouth □ Wild horses couldn't drag someone. □ work like a horse

HORSEPLAY
horseplay

HOT
as hot as hell □ blow hot and cold □ full of hot air □ get in(to) hot water □ hot and bothered □ hot and heavy □ hot as hell □ hot on something □

hot under the collar □ in hot water □ in the hot seat □ make it hot for someone □ on the hot seat □ strike while the iron is hot

HOTCAKES
sell like hotcakes

HOTFOOT
hotfoot it out of somewhere

HOUR
after hours □ all hours (of the day and night) □ at the bottom of the hour □ at the eleventh hour □ at the top of the hour □ by the hour □ eleventh-hour decision □ for hours on end □ keep late hours □ on the hour □ small hours (of the night) □ until all hours □ wee hours (of the night)

HOUSE
bring the house down □ eat someone out of house and home □ keep house □ like a house afire □ like a house on fire □ on the house □ put one's house in order

HOW
know-how

HOYLE
according to Hoyle

HUE
hue and cry

HUFF
in a huff

HUMAN
milk of human kindness

HUMBLE
eat humble pie

HUMP
over the hump

HUNDRED
one in a hundred

HUNG
hung up (on someone or something)

HUNGRY
as hungry as a bear □ hungry as a bear

HUNT
hunt-and-peck □ hunt high and low

(for someone or something) □ hunt someone or something up

HURRY
get a hurry on

HURT
cry before one is hurt □ not hurt a flea

HUSH
hush money

HUSTLE
hustle and bustle

HYDE
Jekyll and Hyde

ICE
break the ice □ cut no ice (with someone) □ on thin ice □ put something on ice □ skate on thin ice

IDEA
get a bright idea □ get a rough idea (about something) □ get a rough idea (of something) □ give someone a bright idea □ give someone a rough idea (about something) □ give someone a rough idea (of something) □ put ideas into someone's head

IDIOT
take someone for an idiot

IDLY
sit (idly) by

IF
better off (if one were somewhere else) □ better off (if something were done) □ if push comes to shove □ If the shoe fits, wear it. □ if worst comes to worst □ look as if butter wouldn't melt in one's mouth □ make as if to do something □ no ifs, ands, or buts about it □ not know if one is coming or going

IFS
no ifs, ands, or buts about it

ILL
ill at ease □ ill-gotten gains □ take ill

IMAGE
be the spit and image of someone □ be the spitting image of someone

IMPARTIAL
fair and impartial

IMPRESSION
make an impression (on someone)

INCH
come within an inch of doing something □ every inch a something □ every inch the something □ Give one an inch, and one will take a mile. □ inch along (something) □ inch by inch □ within an inch of one's life

INCUMBENT
incumbent upon someone to do something

INDEED
A friend in need is a friend indeed.

INFLUENCE
under the influence (of alcohol)

INFORMATION
gold mine of information

INITIATIVE
take the initiative (to do something)

INJURY
add insult to injury

INNOCENT
as innocent as a lamb □ innocent as a lamb

INS
ins and outs of something

INSIDE
get the inside track □ know something inside out

INSTANCE
in the first instance

INSTRUMENTAL
instrumental in doing something

INSULT
add insult to injury

INTENTS
for all intents and purposes

INTEREST
draw interest □ have a vested interest in something □ in one's (own) (best) interest(s) □ in the interest of someone or something □ take an interest (in something)

INVOLVE
get involved (with someone)

IOTA
not one iota

IRISH
get someone's Irish up

IRON
have too many irons in the fire □ iron something out □ strike while the iron is hot

ITCH
have an itching palm □ have an itchy palm

IVORY
live in an ivory tower

JACK
All work and no play makes Jack a dull boy. □ before you can say Jack Robinson □ jack-of-all-trades □ jack someone or something up

JACKPOT
hit the jackpot

JAM
get into a jam □ get out of a jam □ get someone out of a jam □ in a jam

JAW
have a glass jaw

JAYBIRD
as naked as a jaybird □ naked as a jaybird

JAZZ
jazz something up

JEKYLL
Jekyll and Hyde

JETSAM
flotsam and jetsam

JIFFY
in a jiffy

JIG
The jig is up.

JOB
devil of a job □ do a job on someone or something □ do a snow job on someone □ fall down on the job □ lay down on the job □ lie down on the job □ nine-to-five job □ on the job □ the devil's own job

JOCKEY
jockey for position

JOHNNY
Johnny-come-lately □ Johnny-on-the-spot

JOIN
join forces (with someone) □ Join the club!

JOINT
put someone's nose out of joint

JOKE
able to take a joke □ (all) joking aside □ crack a joke □ no joke

JONES
Davy Jones's locker □ go to Davy Jones's locker □ keep up (with the Joneses)

JOWL
cheek by jowl

JOY
burst with joy □ pride and joy

JUDGE
as sober as a judge □ judge one on one's own merit(s) □ judge something on its own merit(s) □ judging by something □ sober as a judge

JUICE
juice and cookies □ stew in one's own juice

JUMP
get the jump on someone □ hop, skip, and a jump □ jump all over someone □ jump at something □ jump at the chance □ jump at the opportunity □ jump bail □ jump down someone's throat □ jump off the deep end □ jump on someone □ jump on the bandwagon □ jump out of one's skin □ jump the gun □ jump the track □ jump through a hoop □ jump through hoops □ jump to conclusions □ jumping-off place □ jumping-off point □ one jump ahead (of someone or something)

JUMPSTART
get a jump(start)

JUNCTURE
at this juncture

JURY
The jury is still out (on someone or something).

JUST
able to take just so much □ get one's just deserts □ in (just) a second □ (just) a stone's throw away □ just in case □ just one of those things □ just so □ just the same □ just the same (to someone) □ just what the doctor ordered

JUSTICE
do justice to something □ miscarriage of justice □ poetic justice

KEEL
keel over □ keep on an even keel □ keep something on an even keel

KEEN
keen about someone or something □ keen on someone or something

KEEP
be one's brother's keeper □ earn one's keep □ Finders keepers(, losers weepers.) □ for keeps □ in keeping (with something) □ keep a civil tongue (in one's head) □ keep a stiff upper lip □ keep a straight face □ keep abreast (of something) □ keep after someone □ keep an eye on someone or something □ keep an eye out (for someone or something) □ Keep at it! □ keep at someone □ keep at someone or something □ keep body and soul together □ keep (close) watch (on someone or something) □ keep (close) watch (over someone or something) □ keep company (with someone) □ keep cool □ keep good time □ keep house □ keep in touch (with someone) □ keep late hours □ keep off (something) □ keep on an even keel □ keep on one's toes □ keep on someone □ keep one's chin up □ keep one's cool □ keep one's distance (from someone or something) □ keep one's ear to the ground □ keep one's eye on the ball □ keep one's eyes open (for someone or something) □ keep one's eyes peeled (for someone or something) □ keep one's feet on the ground □ keep one's fingers crossed (for someone or something) □ keep one's hand in (something) □ keep one's hands off (someone or something) □ keep one's

head □ keep one's head above water □ keep one's mouth shut (about someone or something) □ keep one's nose clean □ keep one's nose out of someone's business □ keep one's nose to the grindstone □ keep one's own counsel □ keep one's place □ keep one's temper □ keep one's weather eye open □ keep one's wits about one □ keep one's word □ keep pace (with someone or something) □ keep quiet (about someone or something) □ keep someone company □ keep someone in line □ keep someone in stitches □ keep someone on tenterhooks □ keep someone or something hanging in midair □ keep someone or something in check □ keep someone or something in mind □ keep someone or something quiet □ keep someone or something still □ keep someone or something up □ keep someone out in the cold □ keep someone posted □ keep something down □ keep something for another occasion □ keep something on an even keel □ keep something quiet □ keep something to oneself □ keep something under one's hat □ keep something under wraps □ keep still □ keep still (about someone or something) □ keep tabs (on someone or something) □ keep the ball rolling □ keep the home fires burning □ keep the lid on something □ keep the wolf from the door □ keep time □ keep to oneself □ keep track (of someone or something) □ keep up an act □ keep up appearances □ keep up one's act □ keep up (with someone or something) □ keep up (with the Joneses) □ keep up (with the times) □ Keep your shirt on! □ out of keeping (with something) □ play for keeps □ What's keeping you?

KEG
sitting on a powder keg

KETTLE
fine kettle of fish □ the pot calling the kettle black

KEY
keyed up

KIBOSH
put the kibosh on something

KICK
alive and kicking □ for kicks □ get a kick out of someone or something □ give someone a kick □ kick a habit □ kick off □ kick oneself (for doing something) □ kick over □ kick someone or something around □ kick someone or something out □ kick something in □ kick something off □ kick the bucket □ kick the habit □ kick up □ kick up a fuss □ kick up a row □ kick up a storm □ kick up one's heels

KID
(all) kidding aside □ handle someone with kid gloves □ kid around (with someone) □ kid stuff □ kidding aside □ no kidding

KILL
Curiosity killed the cat. □ dressed to kill □ fit to kill □ in at the kill □ in on the kill □ kill the fatted calf □ kill time □ kill two birds with one stone □ make a killing

KILTER
out of kilter

KIN
kith and kin

KIND
all kinds of someone or something □ in kind □ kind of something □ milk of human kindness □ nothing of the kind □ take kindly to something □ two of a kind

KINDNESS
milk of human kindness

KING
fit for a king □ pay a king's ransom (for something)

KISS
kiss and make up □ kiss and tell □ kiss of death □ kiss something goodbye

KIT
kit and caboodle

KITCHEN
everything but the kitchen sink

KITE
as high as a kite □ Go fly a kite!

KITH
kith and kin

KITTEN
as weak as a kitten □ weak as a kitten

KITTY
feed the kitty

KNEE
knee-high to a grasshopper □ on bended knee

KNIFE
go under the knife

KNIT
knit one's brow

KNOCK
knock about (somewhere) □ knock-down-drag-out fight □ knock it off □ knock off work □ knock on wood □ knock one off one's feet □ knock oneself out (to do something) □ knock some heads together □ knock someone dead □ knock someone down (to size) □ knock someone for a loop □ knock someone off □ knock someone or something about □ knock someone or something around □ knock someone out (cold) □ knock someone over with a feather □ knock someone's block off □ knock something back □ knock something down □ knock something off □ knock the props out from under someone

KNOT
tie someone (up) in knots □ tie the knot

KNOW
as far as anyone knows □ be an unknown quantity □ before you know it □ for all I know □ in the know □ know a thing or two (about someone or something) □ know a trick or two □ know (all) the tricks of the trade □ know better □ know-how □ know one's ABCs □ know one's onions □ know one's place □ know one's stuff □ know one's way about □ know one's way around □ know someone by sight □ know someone or something like a book □ know someone or something like the back of one's hand □ know someone or something like the palm of one's hand □ know something backwards and forwards □ know something by heart □ know something forwards and backwards □ know something from memory □ know something in one's bones □ know something inside out □ know something only too well □ know the ropes □ know the score □ know what's what □ know where someone stands (on someone or something) □ know which is which □ know which side one's bread is buttered on □ not know beans (about someone or something) □ not know enough to come in out of the rain □ not know from nothing □ not know if one is coming or going □ not know someone from Adam □ not know the first thing about someone or something □ not know where to turn □ not know whether one is coming or going □ not know which way to turn □ so far as anyone knows □ you know

KNOWLEDGE
A little knowledge is a dangerous thing. □ to the best of one's knowledge

KNUCKLE
get one's knuckles rapped □ knuckle down (to something) □ knuckle under (to someone or something) □ rap someone's knuckles

LABOR
labor of love

LACE
lace into someone or something

LADDER
at the bottom of the ladder

LAID
best-laid plans of mice and men □ best-laid schemes of mice and men □ laid-back □ laid up

LAMB
as innocent as a lamb □ in two shakes of a lamb's tail □ innocent as a lamb □ like lambs to the slaughter

LAMPPOST
between you, me, and the lamppost

LAND

do a land-office business □ land of Nod □ land on both feet □ land on one's feet □ land up somehow or somewhere □ live off the fat of the land

LANGUAGE

in plain language □ speak the same language □ use strong language

LAP

in the lap of luxury □ lap something up

LARGE

as large as life □ at large □ by and large □ large as life □ loom large (on the horizon)

LARK

as happy as a lark □ happy as a lark

LASH

get a tongue-lashing □ give someone a tongue-lashing

LAST

as a last resort □ at (long) last □ at the last gasp □ at the last minute □ be the last person □ breathe one's last □ down to the last detail □ every last one □ get the last laugh □ get the last word □ He laughs best who laughs last. □ He who laughs last, laughs longest. □ head for the last roundup □ in the last analysis □ last but not least □ last-ditch effort □ last will and testament □ on someone's or something's last legs □ see the last of someone or something □ That's the last straw. □ to the last

LATE

at the latest □ better late than never □ Johnny-come-lately □ keep late hours □ late in life □ late in the day □ of late □ sooner or later

LATHER

in a lather

LAUGH

burst out laughing □ die laughing □ get the last laugh □ He laughs best who laughs last. □ He who laughs last, laughs longest. □ laugh out of the other side of one's mouth □ laugh something off □ laugh up one's sleeve

□ no laughing matter □ split one's sides (with laughter)

LAUGHINGSTOCK

make a laughingstock of oneself or something □ make oneself or something a laughingstock

LAUGHTER

split one's sides (with laughter)

LAUNCH

launch forth (on something)

LAURELS

look to one's laurels □ rest on one's laurels

LAW

law unto oneself □ lay down the law □ take the law into one's own hands

LAY

best-laid plans of mice and men □ best-laid schemes of mice and men □ laid-back □ laid up □ lay a finger on someone or something □ lay an egg □ lay down on the job □ lay down one's life (for someone or something) □ lay down the law □ lay eyes on someone or something □ lay hold of someone or something □ lay into someone or something □ lay it on thick □ lay it on with a trowel □ lay low □ lay off (someone or something) □ lay one's cards on the table □ lay one's hands on someone or something □ lay over (somewhere) □ lay someone off □ lay someone or something away □ lay someone up □ lay something by □ lay something in □ lay something on someone □ lay something on the line □ lay something to rest □ lay something to waste □ lay the blame on someone or something □ lay the finger on someone □ lay waste to something

LEAD

blind leading the blind □ get the lead out □ go over like a lead balloon □ lead a dog's life □ lead off □ lead someone by the nose □ lead someone down the garden path □ lead someone on a merry chase □ lead someone to believe something □ lead someone to do something □ lead the life of

Riley □ lead up to something □ shake the lead out

LEAF
leaf through something □ take a leaf out of someone's book □ turn over a new leaf

LEAGUE
in league (with someone) □ not in the same league with someone or something

LEAK
leak something (out)

LEAN
lean on someone □ lean over backwards (to do something)

LEAP
by leaps and bounds □ leap at the opportunity □ leap to conclusions

LEARN
learn something by heart □ learn something by rote □ learn something from the bottom up □ learn something the hard way □ learn the ropes □ learn to live with something □ live and learn

LEASE
new lease on life

LEAST
at least □ last but not least □ least of all □ line of least resistance □ path of least resistance □ to say the least □ when least expected

LEATHER
hell-bent for leather

LEAVE
absent without leave □ leave a bad taste in someone's mouth □ leave a lot to be desired □ leave a sinking ship □ leave no stone unturned □ leave one to one's fate □ leave oneself wide open for something □ leave oneself wide open to something □ leave someone flat □ leave someone for dead □ leave someone high and dry □ leave someone holding the bag □ leave someone in peace □ leave someone in the lurch □ leave someone or something hanging in midair □ leave someone out in the cold □ leave something for another occasion □

leave something on □ leave something open □ leave well enough alone □ leave word (with someone) □ take it or leave it □ take leave of one's senses □ take (one's) leave (of someone) □ take up where one left off

LEFT
hang a left □ left and right □ out in left field □ pay someone a left-handed compliment □ right and left □ take up where one left off

LEG
Break a leg! □ cost an arm and a leg □ get one's sea legs □ not have a leg to stand on □ on someone's or something's last legs □ pay an arm and a leg (for something) □ pull someone's leg □ stretch one's legs

LEISURE
at leisure □ at one's leisure

LEND
lend a hand (to someone) □ lend an ear (to someone) □ lend color to something □ lend oneself or itself to something □ lend (someone) a hand

LENGTH
at length □ at some length □ go to any length

LESS
could(n't) care less □ in less than no time □ less than pleased □ more or less □ See also *least*.

LESSON
teach someone a lesson

LET
Don't let someone or something get you down. □ let alone someone or something □ Let bygones be bygones. □ let go (with something) □ let grass grow under one's feet □ let her rip □ let it all hang out □ let it roll □ let loose (with something) □ let off steam □ let one's hair down □ let oneself go □ Let sleeping dogs lie. □ let someone down □ let someone go □ let someone have it (with both barrels) □ let someone in on something □ let someone off (the hook) □ let someone or something off □ let something (get) out □ let something out □ let something ride □ let

something slide □ let something slide by □ let something slip by □ let something slip (out) □ let the cat out of the bag □ let the chance slip by □ let things slide □ let up (on someone or something) □ let well enough alone □ live and let live □ not let someone catch someone doing something □ sit back and let something happen

LETTER
bread-and-butter letter □ dead letter □ to the letter

LEVEL
do one's (level) best □ find one's own level □ level with someone □ on the level

LIBERTY
at liberty □ take liberties with someone or something □ take the liberty of doing something

LICK
get a licking □ give someone a licking □ give something a lick and a promise □ lick one's chops □ lick one's lips □ lick something into shape □ take a licking

LID
blow the lid off (something) □ flip one's lid □ keep the lid on something □ take the lid off something

LIE
Let sleeping dogs lie. □ lie down on the job □ lie in state □ lie in wait for someone or something □ lie low □ lie through one's teeth □ take something lying down

LIEU
in lieu of something

LIFE
all walks of life □ as big as life □ as big as life and twice as ugly □ as large as life □ bet one's life □ between life and death □ big as life and twice as ugly □ come to life □ facts of life □ for the life of one □ Get a life! □ get the shock of one's life □ have the time of one's life □ in the prime of life □ large as life □ late in life □ lay down one's life (for someone or something) □ lead a dog's life □ lead the life of Riley □ life is too short □ life

of the party □ live a dog's life □ make life miserable for someone □ matter of life and death □ milestone in someone's life □ never in one's life □ new lease on life □ not on your life □ one's way of life □ run for one's life □ seamy side of life □ Such is life! □ take one's own life □ Variety is the spice of life. □ within an inch of one's life

LIFETIME
once-in-a-lifetime chance

LIFT
lift a hand (against someone or something) □ not lift a finger (to help someone)

LIGHT
according to one's own lights □ all sweetness and light □ as light as a feather □ begin to see the light □ bring something to light □ come to light □ get off lightly □ get the green light □ give someone the green light □ hide one's light under a bushel □ in light of something □ in the spotlight □ light as a feather □ light into someone or something □ light out (for somewhere) □ light out (of somewhere) □ make light of something □ once-over-lightly □ out like a light □ see the light □ see the light (at the end of the tunnel) □ see the light (of day) □ shed (some) light on something □ steal the spotlight □ throw (some) light on something

LIGHTLY
get off lightly □ once-over-lightly

LIGHTNING
as quick as greased lightning □ Lightning never strikes twice (in the same place). □ like greased lightning □ quick as greased lightning

LIKE
and the like □ avoid someone or something like the plague □ be (like) an open book □ come on like gangbusters □ come up smelling like roses □ eat like a bird □ eat like a horse □ feel like a million (dollars) □ feel like a new person □ feel like something □ fit like a glove □ go like clockwork □ go over like a lead balloon □ have a

mind like a steel trap □ hit (someone) like a ton of bricks □ know someone or something like a book □ know someone or something like the back of one's hand □ know someone or something like the palm of one's hand □ like a bat out of hell □ like a bolt out of the blue □ like a bump on a log □ like a fish out of water □ like a house afire □ like a house on fire □ like a sitting duck □ like a three-ring circus □ like crazy □ like greased lightning □ like it or lump it □ like lambs to the slaughter □ like looking for a needle in a haystack □ like mad □ like nothing on earth □ like one of the family □ like sitting ducks □ like water off a duck's back □ look like a million dollars □ look like death warmed over □ look like something □ look like something the cat dragged in □ look like the cat that swallowed the canary □ off like a shot □ out like a light □ packed (in) like sardines □ read someone like a(n open) book □ run around like a chicken with its head cut off □ run like clockwork □ sell like hotcakes □ sleep like a log □ spread like wildfire □ stick out like a sore thumb □ take a liking to someone or something □ the likes of someone □ to someone's liking □ watch someone like a hawk □ work like a horse

LIKELY
as likely as not □ in the unlikely event of something □ likely as not

LILY
gild the lily

LIMB
out on a limb

LIMBO
in limbo

LIMELIGHT
in the limelight

LIMIT
go the limit □ go to the limit □ off limits □ The sky's the limit. □ within limits

LINE
blow one's lines □ draw a line be-
tween something and something else □ draw the line (at something) □ drop someone a few lines □ drop someone a line □ end of the line □ Every cloud has a silver lining. □ fall in(to) line □ feed someone a line □ fluff one's lines □ get a line on someone or something □ give someone a line □ hold the line (at someone or something) □ in line □ in line with something □ in the line of duty □ keep someone in line □ lay something on the line □ line of least resistance □ line one's own pockets □ line someone or something up with something □ line someone up (for something) □ muff one's lines □ on line □ out of line □ out of line (with something) □ party line □ put something on the line □ read between the lines □ sign on the dotted line □ step out of line □ swallow something, hook, line, and sinker □ take a hard line (with someone) □ the bottom line □ toe the line

LINEN
air one's dirty linen in public □ wash one's dirty linen in public

LION
beard the lion in his den □ lion's share (of something)

LIP
button one's lip □ keep a stiff upper lip □ lick one's lips □ pay lip service (to something)

LIST
on a waiting list

LISTEN
listen to reason □ stop, look, and listen

LARGE
as large as life □ at large □ by and large □ large as life □ loom large (on the horizon)

LARK
as happy as a lark □ happy as a lark

LASH
get a tongue-lashing □ give someone a tongue-lashing

LAST

as a last resort □ at (long) last □ at the last gasp □ at the last minute □ be the last person □ breathe one's last □ down to the last detail □ every last one □ get the last laugh □ get the last word □ He laughs best who laughs last. □ He who laughs last, laughs longest. □ head for the last roundup □ in the last analysis □ last but not least □ last-ditch effort □ last will and testament □ on someone's or something's last legs □ see the last of someone or something □ That's the last straw. □ to the last

LATE

at the latest □ better late than never □ Johnny-come-lately □ keep late hours □ late in life □ late in the day □ of late □ sooner or later

LATHER

in a lather

LAUGH

burst out laughing □ die laughing □ get the last laugh □ He laughs best who laughs last. □ He who laughs last, laughs longest. □ laugh out of the other side of one's mouth □ laugh something off □ laugh up one's sleeve □ no laughing matter □ split one's sides (with laughter)

LAUGHINGSTOCK

make a laughingstock of oneself or something □ make oneself or something a laughingstock

LAUGHTER

split one's sides (with laughter)

LAUNCH

launch forth (on something)

LAURELS

look to one's laurels □ rest on one's laurels

LAW

law unto oneself □ lay down the law □ take the law into one's own hands

LAY

best-laid plans of mice and men □ best-laid schemes of mice and men □ laid-back □ laid up □ lay a finger on someone or something □ lay an egg

□ lay down on the job □ lay down one's life (for someone or something) □ lay down the law □ lay eyes on someone or something □ lay hold of someone or something □ lay into someone or something □ lay it on thick □ lay it on with a trowel □ lay low □ lay off (someone or something) □ lay one's cards on the table □ lay one's hands on someone or something □ lay over (somewhere) □ lay someone off □ lay someone or something away □ lay someone up □ lay something by □ lay something in □ lay something on someone □ lay something on the line □ lay something to rest □ lay something to waste □ lay the blame on someone or something □ lay the finger on someone □ lay waste to something

LEAD

blind leading the blind □ get the lead out □ go over like a lead balloon □ lead a dog's life □ lead off □ lead someone by the nose □ lead someone down the garden path □ lead someone on a merry chase □ lead someone to believe something □ lead someone to do something □ lead the life of Riley □ lead up to something □ shake the lead out

LEAF

leaf through something □ take a leaf out of someone's book □ turn over a new leaf

LEAGUE

in league (with someone) □ not in the same league with someone or something

LEAK

leak something (out)

LEAN

lean on someone □ lean over backwards (to do something)

LEAP

by leaps and bounds □ leap at the opportunity □ leap to conclusions

LEARN

learn something by heart □ learn something by rote □ learn something from the bottom up □ learn (something) the hard way □ learn the ropes □ learn to live with something □ live and learn

LEASE

new lease on life

LEAST

at least □ last but not least □ least of all □ line of least resistance □ path of least resistance □ to say the least □ when least expected

LEATHER

hell-bent for leather

LEAVE

absent without leave □ leave a bad taste in someone's mouth □ leave a lot to be desired □ leave a sinking ship □ leave no stone unturned □ leave one to one's fate □ leave oneself wide open for something □ leave oneself wide open to something □ leave someone flat □ leave someone for dead □ leave someone high and dry □ leave someone holding the bag □ leave someone in peace □ leave someone in the lurch □ leave someone or something hanging in midair □ leave someone out in the cold □ leave something for another occasion □ leave something on □ leave something open □ leave well enough alone □ leave word (with someone) □ take it or leave it □ take leave of one's senses □ take (one's) leave (of someone) □ take up where one left off

LEFT

hang a left □ left and right □ out in left field □ pay someone a left-handed compliment □ right and left □ take up where one left off

LEG

Break a leg! □ cost an arm and a leg □ get one's sea legs □ not have a leg to stand on □ on someone's or something's last legs □ pay an arm and a leg (for something) □ pull someone's leg □ stretch one's legs

LEISURE

at leisure □ at one's leisure

LEND

lend a hand (to someone) □ lend an ear (to someone) □ lend color to

something □ lend oneself or itself to something □ lend (someone) a hand

LENGTH

at length □ at some length □ go to any length

LESS

could(n't) care less □ in less than no time □ less than pleased □ more or less

LESSON

teach someone a lesson

LET

Don't let someone or something get you down. □ let alone someone or something □ Let bygones be bygones. □ let go (with something) □ let grass grow under one's feet □ let her rip □ let it all hang out □ let it roll □ let loose (with something) □ let off steam □ let one's hair down □ let oneself go □ Let sleeping dogs lie. □ let someone down □ let someone go □ let someone have it (with both barrels) □ let someone in on something □ let someone off (the hook) □ let someone or something off □ let something (get) out □ let something out □ let something ride □ let something slide □ let something slide by □ let something slip by □ let something slip (out) □ let the cat out of the bag □ let the chance slip by □ let things slide □ let up (on someone or something) □ let well enough alone □ live and let live □ not let someone catch someone doing something □ sit back and let something happen

LETTER

bread-and-butter letter □ dead letter □ to the letter

LEVEL

do one's (level) best □ find one's own level □ level with someone □ on the level

LIBERTY

at liberty □ take liberties with someone or something □ take the liberty of doing something

LICK

get a licking □ give someone a licking □ give something a lick and a promise

□ lick one's chops □ lick one's lips □ lick something into shape □ take a licking

LID

blow the lid off (something) □ flip one's lid □ keep the lid on something □ take the lid off something

LIE

Let sleeping dogs lie. □ lie down on the job □ lie in state □ lie in wait for someone or something □ lie low □ lie through one's teeth □ take something lying down

LIEU

in lieu of something

LIFE

all walks of life □ as big as life □ as big as life and twice as ugly □ as large as life □ bet one's life □ between life and death □ big as life and twice as ugly □ come to life □ facts of life □ for the life of one □ Get a life! □ get the shock of one's life □ have the time of one's life □ in the prime of life □ large as life □ late in life □ lay down one's life (for someone or something) □ lead a dog's life □ lead the life of Riley □ life is too short □ life of the party □ live a dog's life □ make life miserable for someone □ matter of life and death □ milestone in someone's life □ never in one's life □ new lease on life □ not on your life □ one's way of life □ run for one's life □ seamy side of life □ Such is life! □ take one's own life □ Variety is the spice of life. □ within an inch of one's life

LIFETIME

once-in-a-lifetime chance

LIFT

lift a hand (against someone or something) □ not lift a finger (to help someone)

LIGHT

according to one's own lights □ all sweetness and light □ as light as a feather □ begin to see the light □ bring something to light □ come to light □ get off lightly □ get the green light □ give someone the green light

□ hide one's light under a bushel □ in light of something □ in the spotlight □ light as a feather □ light into someone or something □ light out (for somewhere) □ light out (of somewhere) □ make light of something □ once-over-lightly □ out like a light □ see the light □ see the light (at the end of the tunnel) □ see the light (of day) □ shed (some) light on something □ steal the spotlight □ throw (some) light on something

LIGHTLY

get off lightly □ once-over-lightly

LIGHTNING

as quick as greased lightning □ Lightning never strikes twice (in the same place). □ like greased lightning □ quick as greased lightning

LIKE

and the like □ avoid someone or something like the plague □ be (like) an open book □ come on like gangbusters □ come up smelling like roses □ eat like a bird □ eat like a horse □ feel like a million (dollars) □ feel like a new person □ feel like something □ fit like a glove □ go like clockwork □ go over like a lead balloon □ have a mind like a steel trap □ hit (someone) like a ton of bricks □ know someone or something like a book □ know someone or something like the back of one's hand □ know someone or something like the palm of one's hand □ like a bat out of hell □ like a bolt out of the blue □ like a bump on a log □ like a fish out of water □ like a house afire □ like a house on fire □ like a sitting duck □ like a three-ring circus □ like crazy □ like greased lightning □ like it or lump it □ like lambs to the slaughter □ like looking for a needle in a haystack □ like mad □ like nothing on earth □ like one of the family □ like sitting ducks □ like water off a duck's back □ look like a million dollars □ look like death warmed over □ look like something □ look like something the cat dragged in □ look like the cat that swallowed the canary □ off like a shot □ out like a light □ packed (in) like sardines □

read someone like a(n open) book □ run around like a chicken with its head cut off □ run like clockwork □ sell like hotcakes □ sleep like a log □ spread like wildfire □ stick out like a sore thumb □ take a liking to someone or something □ the likes of someone □ to someone's liking □ watch someone like a hawk □ work like a horse

LIKELY
as likely as not □ in the unlikely event of something □ likely as not

LILY
gild the lily

LIMB
out on a limb

LIMBO
in limbo

LIMELIGHT
in the limelight

LIMIT
go the limit □ go to the limit □ off limits □ The sky's the limit. □ within limits

LINE
blow one's lines □ draw a line between something and something else □ draw the line (at something) □ drop someone a few lines □ drop someone a line □ end of the line □ Every cloud has a silver lining. □ fall in(to) line □ feed someone a line □ fluff one's lines □ get a line on someone or something □ give someone a line □ hold the line (at someone or something) □ in line □ in line with something □ in the line of duty □ keep someone in line □ lay something on the line □ line of least resistance □ line one's own pockets □ line someone or something up with something □ line someone up (for something) □ muff one's lines □ on line □ out of line □ out of line (with something) □ party line □ put something on the line □ read between the lines □ sign on the dotted line □ step out of line □ swallow something, hook, line, and sinker □ take a hard

line (with someone) □ the bottom line □ toe the line

LINEN
air one's dirty linen in public □ wash one's dirty linen in public

LION
beard the lion in his den □ lion's share (of something)

LIP
button one's lip □ keep a stiff upper lip □ lick one's lips □ pay lip service (to something)

LIST
on a waiting list

LISTEN
listen to reason □ stop, look, and listen

LITTLE
A little bird told me. □ A little knowledge is a dangerous thing. □ little by little □ make little of someone or something □ one little bit □ precious little □ quite a little □ think little of someone or something □ twist someone around one's little finger

LIVE
beat the living daylights out of someone □ every living soul □ frighten the living daylights out of someone □ have to live with something □ hit one where one lives □ learn to live with something □ live a dog's life □ live and learn □ live and let live □ live beyond one's means □ live by one's wits □ live for the moment □ live from hand to mouth □ live happily ever after □ live high off the hog □ live high on the hog □ live in □ live in an ivory tower □ live it up □ live off the fat of the land □ live on borrowed time □ live out of a suitcase □ live something down □ live through something □ live up to something □ live within one's means □ make a living □ not a living soul □ scare the living daylights out of someone □ where one lives

LIVELONG
all the livelong day

LOAD

get a load of someone or something ☐ get a load off one's feet ☐ get a load off one's mind ☐ loaded for bear ☐ take a load off one's feet

LOAF

Half a loaf is better than none.

LOAN

float a loan

LOCK

lock horns (with someone) ☐ lock something in ☐ lock, stock, and barrel

LOCKER

Davy Jones's locker ☐ go to Davy Jones's locker

LOG

as easy as falling off a log ☐ as easy as rolling off a log ☐ easy as rolling off a log ☐ like a bump on a log ☐ sleep like a log

LOGGERHEADS

at loggerheads (with someone)

LOINS

gird (up) one's loins

LONG

all day long ☐ all night long ☐ as long as ☐ at (long) last ☐ before long ☐ go a long way in doing something ☐ go a long way toward doing something ☐ have come a long way ☐ He who laughs last, laughs longest. ☐ in the long run ☐ long and (the) short of it ☐ Long time no see. ☐ make a long story short ☐ not by a long shot ☐ not long for this world ☐ over the long haul ☐ so long ☐ so long as

LOOK

get a dirty look from someone ☐ give someone a dirty look ☐ like looking for a needle in a haystack ☐ look as if butter wouldn't melt in one's mouth ☐ look at someone cross-eyed ☐ look daggers at someone ☐ look down on someone or something ☐ look down one's nose at someone or something ☐ look for trouble ☐ look forward to something ☐ look high and low (for someone or something) ☐ look in (on someone or something) ☐ look into

something ☐ look like a million dollars ☐ look like death warmed over ☐ look like something ☐ look like something the cat dragged in ☐ look like the cat that swallowed the canary ☐ look on someone as something ☐ look out ☐ look out for someone or something ☐ look someone in the eye ☐ look someone in the face ☐ look someone or something over ☐ look someone or something up ☐ look the other way ☐ look to one's laurels ☐ look to someone or something (for something) ☐ look up to someone ☐ make someone look good ☐ make someone look ridiculous ☐ stop, look, and listen ☐ take a look (at someone or something) ☐ Things are looking up.

LOOKOUT

on the lookout (for someone or something)

LOOM

loom large (on the horizon)

LOON

as crazy as a loon ☐ crazy as a loon

LOOP

knock someone for a loop ☐ throw someone for a loop

LOOSE

at loose ends ☐ break loose (from someone or something) ☐ cut loose (from someone or something) ☐ cut loose (with something) ☐ hang loose ☐ have a screw loose ☐ let loose (with something) ☐ on the loose ☐ play fast and loose (with someone or something)

LORD

lord it over someone

LOSE

Finders keepers(, losers weepers.) ☐ get lost ☐ lose face ☐ lose ground ☐ lose heart ☐ lose one's cool ☐ lose one's grip ☐ lose one's head (over someone or something) ☐ lose one's marbles ☐ lose one's mind ☐ lose one's reason ☐ lose one's shirt ☐ lose one's temper ☐ lose one's touch (with someone or something) ☐ lose one's train of thought ☐ lose oneself (in something) □ lose out (on something) □ lose out to someone or something □ lose sleep (over someone or something) □ lost-and-found □ lost and gone forever □ lost cause □ lost in thought □ lost on someone □ make up for lost time □ no love lost (between someone and someone else)

LOSERS
Finders keepers(, losers weepers.)

LOSS
at a loss (for words) □ cut one's losses □ dead loss □ throw someone for a loss

LOST
get lost □ lost-and-found □ lost and gone forever □ lost cause □ lost in thought □ lost on someone □ make up for lost time □ no love lost (between someone and someone else)

LOT
carry (a lot of) weight (with someone or something) □ cast one's lot in with someone □ cover a lot of ground □ have a lot going (for one) □ have a lot of promise □ have a lot on one's mind □ leave a lot to be desired □ quite a lot □ think a lot of someone or something

LOUD
Actions speak louder than words. □ For crying out loud! □ loud and clear □ think out loud

LOUSE
louse something up

LOUSY
lousy with something

LOVE
fall head over heels in love (with someone) □ fall in love (with someone) □ head over heels in love (with someone) □ in love (with someone or something) □ labor of love □ love at first sight □ lovely weather for ducks □ make love (to someone) □ no love lost (between someone and someone else) □ not for love nor money

LOVELY
lovely weather for ducks

LOW
burn with a low blue flame □ get the low-down (on someone or something) □ give someone the low-down (on someone or something) □ have a low boiling point □ hunt high and low (for someone or something) □ lay low □ lie low □ look high and low (for someone or something) □ low man on the totem pole □ lower one's sights □ lower one's voice □ lower the boom on someone □ search high and low (for someone or something) □ sweet and low

LOWER
lower one's sights □ lower one's voice □ lower the boom on someone

LUCK
as luck would have it □ down on one's luck □ have a run of bad luck □ have one's luck run out □ in luck □ luck out □ one's luck runs out □ out of luck □ press one's luck □ push one's luck □ stroke of luck □ thank one's lucky stars □ try one's luck (at something)

LUCKY
thank one's lucky stars

LULL
lull someone into a false sense of security

LUMP
get a lump in one's throat □ like it or lump it

LUNCH
blow one's lunch □ out to lunch

LUNG
at the top of one's lungs

LURCH
leave someone in the lurch

LUXURY
in the lap of luxury

LYING
take something lying down

MAD
as mad as a hatter □ as mad as a hornet □ as mad as a March hare □ as mad as a wet hen □ as mad as hell □ drive someone mad □ get mad (at someone or something) □ in a mad

rush ☐ like mad ☐ mad about someone or something ☐ mad as a hatter
☐ mad as a hornet ☐ mad as a March
hare ☐ mad as a wet hen ☐ mad as
hell ☐ stark raving mad

MADE
have something made ☐ made for
each other ☐ made to measure ☐
made to order

MADNESS
have method in one's madness

MAIDEN
maiden voyage

MAIL
by return mail

MAIN
main strength and awkwardness ☐
might and main

MAN
be all things to all men ☐ best-laid
plans of mice and men ☐ best-laid
schemes of mice and men ☐ dirty old
man ☐ Early to bed, early to rise(,
makes a man healthy, wealthy, and
wise.) ☐ high man on the totem pole
☐ low man on the totem pole ☐
man-about-town ☐ man in the street
☐ man to man ☐ odd man out ☐
One man's meat is another man's
poison. ☐ see a man about a dog ☐
separate the men from the boys

MANGER
dog in the manger

MANNER
all manner of someone or something
☐ devil-may-care manner

MANY
have too many irons in the fire ☐ in
so many words ☐ many is the time ☐
Too many cooks spoil the broth. ☐
Too many cooks spoil the stew.

MARBLE
lose one's marbles ☐ not have all
one's marbles

MARCH
as mad as a March hare ☐ mad as a
March hare ☐ march to a different
drummer ☐ steal a march (on someone)

MARE
by shank's mare ☐ go (somewhere) by
shank's mare

MARINES
tell it to the marines

MARK
mark my word(s) ☐ mark someone or
something down ☐ mark something
up ☐ off the mark ☐ toe the mark ☐
wide of the mark ☐ X marks the spot

MARKET
drug on the market ☐ in the market
(for something) ☐ on the market ☐
play the market

MAST
at half-mast

MASTER
be a past master at something

MATCH
meet one's match ☐ mix and match ☐
strike a match ☐ whole shooting
match

MATTER
as a matter of course ☐ as a matter of
fact ☐ crux of the matter ☐ for that
matter ☐ get at the heart of the matter ☐ get to the heart of the matter ☐
gray matter ☐ matter-of-fact ☐ matter of life and death ☐ matter of
opinion ☐ no laughing matter ☐ no
matter what happens

MAY
be that as it may ☐ come what may ☐
devil-may-care attitude ☐ devil-may-
care manner ☐ to whom it may concern

MEAL
eat (a meal) out ☐ make a meal of
something ☐ square meal

MEALYMOUTHED
mealymouthed

MEAN
beyond one's means ☐ by all means
☐ by all means of something ☐ by
any means ☐ by means of something
☐ by no means ☐ live beyond one's
means ☐ live within one's means ☐

mean nothing (to someone) □ mean something (to someone) □ mean to (do something) □ one means business □ ways and means

MEASURE
beyond measure □ for good measure □ made to measure □ measure up (to someone or something) □ measure up (to someone's expectations)

MEAT
make mincemeat out of someone or something □ meat-and-potatoes □ One man's meat is another man's poison.

MECCA
Mecca for someone

MEDICINE
dose of one's own medicine □ get a taste of one's own medicine □ take one's medicine

MEDIUM
hit a happy medium □ strike a happy medium

MEET
call a meeting □ call the meeting to order □ hail-fellow-well-met □ hold a meeting □ make (both) ends meet □ meet one's end □ meet one's match □ meet one's Waterloo □ meet someone halfway □ meet the requirements (for something) □ more (to something) than meets the eye □ Sunday-go-to-meeting clothes

MELT
look as if butter wouldn't melt in one's mouth □ melt in one's mouth

MEMORY
commit something to memory □ know something from memory

MEN
be all things to all men □ best-laid plans of mice and men □ best-laid schemes of mice and men □ separate the men from the boys

MEND
mend (one's) fences □ mend one's ways □ on the mend

MENTION
mention someone or something in passing

MERCY
at someone's mercy □ at the mercy of someone □ throw oneself at the mercy of the court □ throw oneself on the mercy of the court

MERIT
judge one on one's own merit(s) □ judge something on its own merit(s)

MERRY
lead someone on a merry chase □ make merry □ the more the merrier

MESS
get into a mess □ get out of a mess □ mess about (with someone or something) □ mess around (with someone or something) □ mess someone or something up

MESSAGE
get the message

MET
hail-fellow-well-met

METHOD
have method in one's madness

MICE
best-laid plans of mice and men □ best-laid schemes of mice and men □ When the cat's away, the mice will play.

MIDAIR
keep someone or something hanging in midair □ leave someone or something hanging in midair

MIDAS
have the Midas touch

MIDDLE
caught in the middle □ change horses in the middle of the stream □ in the middle of nowhere □ middle-of-the-road □ play both ends (against the middle) □ smack-dab in the middle

MIDDLING
fair to middling

MIDNIGHT
burn the midnight oil

moment □ live for the moment □ moment of truth □ not for a moment □ on the spur of the moment

MONEY

A fool and his money are soon parted. □ closefisted (with money) □ fork money out (for something) □ get a run for one's money □ get one's money's worth □ give one a run for one's money □ have money to burn □ hush money □ in the money □ make good money □ Money burns a hole in someone's pocket. □ money is no object □ Money is the root of all evil. □ money talks □ not for love nor money □ on the money □ pour money down the drain □ Put your money where your mouth is! □ see the color of someone's money □ set someone back (some amount of money) □ throw good money after bad □ tightfisted (with money) □ Time is money. □ to the tune of some amount of money

MONKEY

as funny as a barrel of monkeys □ as much fun as a barrel of monkeys □ make a monkey out of someone □ monkey around (with someone or something) □ monkey business □ more fun than a barrel of monkeys □ throw a monkey wrench into the works

MONTH

by the month □ in a month of Sundays

MOOD

in a bad mood □ in no mood to do something

MOON

ask for the moon □ once in a blue moon □ promise someone the moon □ promise the moon (to someone)

MOP

mop the floor up with someone

MOPE

mope around

MORE

bite off more than one can chew □ exchange more than ___ words with someone □ more dead than alive □ more fun than a barrel of monkeys □

more often than not □ more or less □ more someone or something than one can shake a stick at □ more than someone bargained for □ more (to something) than meets the eye □ the more the merrier □ There's more than one way to skin a cat. □ wear more than one hat

MORNING

first thing (in the morning) □ morning after (the night before)

MORTAL

shuffle off this mortal coil

MORTAR

bricks and mortar

MOSS

A rolling stone gathers no moss.

MOST

at most □ for the most part □ make the most of something

MOTHBALLS

put something in mothballs

MOTHER

old enough to be someone's mother □ tied to one's mother's apron strings

MOTION

go through the motions

MOUNTAIN

make a mountain out of a molehill

MOUSE

as poor as a church mouse □ as quiet as a mouse □ play cat and mouse (with someone) □ poor as a church mouse □ quiet as a mouse

MOUTH

bad-mouth someone or something □ born with a silver spoon in one's mouth □ by word of mouth □ down in the mouth □ foam at the mouth □ from the horse's mouth □ have a big mouth □ have foot-in-mouth disease □ keep one's mouth shut (about someone or something) □ laugh out of the other side of one's mouth □ leave a bad taste in someone's mouth □ live from hand to mouth □ look as if butter wouldn't melt in one's mouth □ make someone's mouth water □ melt in one's mouth □ not open one's mouth □ one's heart is in one's mouth

□ put one's foot in one's mouth □ put words into someone's mouth □ Put your money where your mouth is! □ run off at the mouth □ say a mouthful □ shoot one's mouth off □ stick one's foot in one's mouth □ (straight) from the horse's mouth □ take the words out of one's mouth

MOUTHFUL
say a mouthful

MOVE
get a move on □ move heaven and earth to do something □ move in □ move in (on someone or something) □ move into something □ move up (in the world) □ movers and shakers□ not move a muscle □ on the move □ one move ahead (of someone or something) □ prime mover

MOVER
movers and shakers □ prime mover

MUCH
able to take just so much □ as much fun as a barrel of monkeys □ much ado about nothing □ much in evidence □ much sought after □ not miss much □ so much for someone or something □ so much the better □ take too much on □ think much of someone or something □ too much of a good thing □ without so much as doing something

MUD
as clear as mud □ clear as mud □ muddy the water □ one's name is mud □ stick-in-the-mud

MUDDY
muddy the water

MUFF
muff one's lines

MULE
as stubborn as a mule □ stubborn as a mule

MULL
mull something over

MUM
mum's the word

MURDER
cry bloody murder □ scream bloody murder

MUSCLE
muscle in (on something) □ not move a muscle

MUSIC
face the music □ make chin music

MUST
be a must

MUSTER
pass muster

MUTILATE
fold, spindle, or mutilate

NAIL
(another) nail in someone's or something's coffin □ as hard as nails □ bite one's nails □ fight someone or something tooth and nail □ go at it tooth and nail □ hard as nails □ hit the nail on the head □ nail in someone's or something's coffin □ nail someone or something down

NAKED
as naked as a jaybird □ naked as a jaybird □ naked eye

NAME
call someone names □ clear someone's name □ drop someone's name □ in name only □ in someone's name □ make a name (for oneself) □ name of the game □ name someone after someone else □ name someone for someone else □ on a first-name basis (with someone) □ one's name is mud □ throw someone's name around □ worthy of the name

NAP
catch someone napping

NAPE
by the nape of the neck

NARROW
straight and narrow

NATURAL
die a natural death

NATURE
call of nature □ second nature to someone

NAUGHT
come to naught

NEAR
from far and near □ have a near miss

□ in the near future □ near at hand □ nowhere near

NECESSITY
out of necessity

NECK
break one's neck (to do something) □ breathe down someone's neck □ by the nape of the neck □ get it in the neck □ in some neck of the woods □ millstone about one's neck □ neck and neck □ pain in the neck □ risk one's neck (to do something) □ save someone's neck □ stick one's neck out (for someone or something) □ up to one's neck (in something)

NEED
A friend in need is a friend indeed. □ crying need for someone or something

NEEDLE
like looking for a needle in a haystack □ on pins and needles

NEITHER
neither fish nor fowl □ neither here nor there □ neither hide nor hair

NERVE
bundle of nerves □ get on someone's nerves □ get up enough nerve (to do something) □ of all the nerve

NEST
feather one's (own) nest □ foul one's own nest □ stir up a hornet's nest

NEVER
better late than never □ (have) never had it so good □ It never rains but it pours. □ It'll never fly. □ Lightning never strikes twice (in the same place). □ never fear □ never had it so good □ never in one's life □ never mind □ now or never

NEW
break new ground □ break the news (to someone) □ feel like a new person □ new ball game □ new blood □ new lease on life □ new one on someone □ No news is good news. □ ring in the new year □ (some) new blood □ take a new turn □ turn over a new leaf □ You can't teach an old dog new tricks.

NEWCASTLE
carry coals to Newcastle

NEXT
next to nothing

NICK
full of Old Nick □ in the (very) nick of time

NICKEL
nickel and dime someone □ not worth a plugged nickel

NIGHT
all hours (of the day and night) □ all night long □ as different as night and day □ burn the midnight oil □ call it a night □ day and night □ different as night and day □ far into the night □ fly-by-night □ make a night of doing something □ morning after (the night before) □ night and day □ night on the town □ night owl □ one-night stand □ ships that pass in the night □ small hours (of the night) □ wee hours (of the night)

NINE
dressed to the nines □ nine days' wonder □ nine-to-five job □ on cloud nine

NIP
nip and tuck □ nip something in the bud

NITTY
get down to the nitty-gritty

NO
A rolling stone gathers no moss. □ all talk (and no action) □ All work and no play makes Jack a dull boy. □ by no means □ cut no ice (with someone) □ expense is no object □ have no business doing something □ have no staying power □ hold no brief for someone or something □ in less than no time □ in no mood to do something □ in no time (at all) □ in no uncertain terms □ it's no use (doing something) □ leave no stone unturned □ Long time no see. □ make no bones about it □ make no difference (to someone) □ make no mistake (about it) □ money is no object □ no buts about it □ no can do □ no doubt □ no end of something □ no

flies on someone □ no great shakes □ no hard feelings □ no holds barred □ no ifs, ands, or buts about it □ no joke □ no kidding □ no laughing matter □ no love lost (between someone and someone else) □ no matter what happens □ No news is good news. □ no problem □ no skin off someone's nose □ no skin off someone's teeth □ no sooner said than done □ no spring chicken □ no sweat □ no trespassing □ no two ways about it □ no way □ no-win situation □ no wonder □ not take no for an answer □ of no avail □ on no account □ see no objection (to something) □ take no stock in something □ the point of no return □ there is no doing something □ There's no accounting for taste. □ to no avail □ up to no good □ with no strings attached

NOBODY
nobody's fool

NOD
get the nod □ land of Nod □ nod off

NOGGIN
use one's noggin

NONE
Half a loaf is better than none. □ have none of something □ none of someone's beeswax □ none other than someone □ none the wiser □ none the worse for wear □ none too something □ second to none

NONSENSE
stuff and nonsense

NOODLE
use one's noodle

NOOK
nook and cranny

NOR
neither fish nor fowl □ neither here nor there □ neither hide nor hair □ not for love nor money

NORTH
up North

NOSE
as plain as the nose on one's face □ can't see beyond the end of one's nose □ count noses □ cut off one's nose to

spite one's face □ follow one's nose □ get one's nose out of someone's business □ have one's nose in a book □ have one's nose in the air □ keep one's nose clean □ keep one's nose out of someone's business □ keep one's nose to the grindstone □ lead someone by the nose □ look down one's nose at someone or something □ no skin off someone's nose □ nose about □ nose around □ nose in(to something) □ nose someone out □ not see farther than the end of one's nose □ not see past the end of one's nose □ on the nose □ one's nose is in the air □ pay through the nose (for something) □ plain as the nose on one's face □ poke one's nose in(to something) □ put one's nose to the grindstone □ put someone's nose out of joint □ (right) under someone's (very) nose □ rub someone's nose in it □ stick one's nose in(to something) □ thumb one's nose at someone or something □ turn one's nose up at someone or something □ under someone's (very) nose □ win by a nose

NOSEDIVE
go into a nosedive □ take a nosedive

NOT
All that glitters is not gold. □ as likely as not □ believe it or not □ gone but not forgotten □ last but not least □ likely as not □ more often than not □ not a bit □ not a living soul □ not able □ not able to call one's time one's own □ not able to go on □ not able to help something □ not able to make anything out of someone or something □ not able to see the forest for the trees □ not able to wait □ not agree with someone □ not all something is cracked up to be □ not all there □ not at all □ not bat an eyelid □ not believe one's eyes □ not born yesterday □ not breathe a word (about someone or something) □ not breathe a word of (something) □ not buy something □ not by a long shot □ not care two hoots about someone or something □ not dry behind the ears □ not enough room to swing a

cat □ not for a moment □ not for (anything in) the world □ not for love nor money □ not give a hang about someone or something □ not give a hoot about someone or something □ not give anyone the time of day □ not give two hoots about someone or something □ not half bad □ not have a care in the world □ not have a leg to stand on □ not have all one's marbles □ not hold a candle to someone or something □ not hold a stick to someone or something □ not hold water □ not hurt a flea □ not in the same league with someone or something □ not know beans (about someone or something) □ not know enough to come in out of the rain □ not know from nothing □ not know if one is coming or going □ not know someone from Adam □ not know the first thing about someone or something □ not know where to turn □ not know whether one is coming or going □ not know which way to turn □ not let someone catch someone doing something □ not lift a finger (to help someone) □ not long for this world □ not miss much □ not move a muscle □ not on any account □ not on your life □ not one iota □ not one's cup of tea □ not open one's mouth □ not see any objection (to something) □ not see farther than the end of one's nose □ not see past the end of one's nose □ not set foot somewhere □ not show one's face □ not sleep a wink □ not someone's cup of tea □ not take no for an answer □ not take stock in something □ not up to scratch □ not up to snuff □ not utter a word □ not want to catch someone doing something □ not what something is cracked up to be □ not worth a dime □ not worth a hill of beans □ not worth a plugged nickel □ not worth a red cent □ will not hear of something

NOTCH
take someone down a notch (or two)

NOTE
hit a sour note □ make a note of something □ strike a sour note □ strike the right note □ take note (of something)

NOTHING
all or nothing □ come to nothing □ good-for-nothing □ have nothing on someone or something □ have nothing to do with someone or something □ Here goes nothing. □ in nothing flat □ like nothing on earth □ make nothing of something □ make something out of nothing □ mean nothing (to someone) □ much ado about nothing □ next to nothing □ not know from nothing □ nothing but skin and bones □ nothing but something □ nothing doing □ nothing down □ nothing of the kind □ nothing short of something □ nothing to choose from □ nothing to complain about □ nothing to it □ nothing to sneeze at □ nothing to speak of □ nothing to write home about □ Nothing ventured, nothing gained. □ stop at nothing □ sweet nothings □ think nothing of someone or something □ to say nothing of someone or something □ want for nothing

NOTICE
escape someone's notice □ serve notice □ sit up and take notice □ take notice (of something)

NOTION
have half a notion to do something

NOW
all better now □ (every) now and again □ (every) now and then □ now and again □ now and then □ now or never □ the here and now

NOWHERE
appear out of nowhere □ at the end of nowhere □ come out of nowhere □ get nowhere fast □ in the middle of nowhere □ nowhere near

NTH
to the nth degree

NUISANCE
make a nuisance of oneself

NULL
null and void

NUMBER
any number of someone or something □ by the numbers □ do a number on someone or something □ get someone's number □ in round numbers □ one's days are numbered □ one's number is up □ quite a number □ safety in numbers

NURSE
nurse a grudge (against someone)

NUT
everything from soup to nuts □ hard nut to crack □ nuts about someone or something □ nuts and bolts (of something) □ off one's nut □ tough nut to crack

NUTSHELL
in a nutshell

NUTTY
as nutty as a fruitcake □ nutty as a fruitcake

OAR
put one's oar in

OAT
sow one's wild oats

OBJECT
expense is no object □ money is no object

OBJECTION
not see any objection (to something) □ raise an objection (to someone or something) □ see no objection (to something)

OCCASION
keep something for another occasion □ leave something for another occasion □ on occasion □ rise to the occasion

OCCUR
occur to someone

OCEAN
drop in the ocean

ODD
at odds (with someone) □ for the odds to be against one □ odd man out □ odds and ends

ODOR
odor of sanctity

OFFENSE
take offense (at someone or something)

OFFICE
do a land-office business □ drive someone out (of office) □ force someone out (of office) □ take office

OFFING
in the offing

OFTEN
more often than not

OIL
burn the midnight oil □ oil someone's palm □ pour oil on troubled water(s)

OINTMENT
fly in the ointment

OLD
as comfortable as an old shoe □ as old as the hills □ as tough as old boots □ be old hat □ chip off the old block □ comfortable as an old shoe □ dirty old man □ full of Old Nick □ get the (old) heave-ho □ give someone or something the (old) heave-ho □ of the old school □ old as the hills □ old enough to be someone's father □ old enough to be someone's mother □ old hand at doing something □ one's old stamping ground □ ripe old age □ same old story □ tough as old boots □ You can't teach an old dog new tricks.

OLIVE
hold out the olive branch

OMEGA
alpha and omega

ONCE
all at once □ at once □ (every) once in a while □ get the once-over □ give someone the once-over □ once and for all □ once in a blue moon □ once-in-a-lifetime chance □ once in a while □ once-over-lightly □ once upon a time

ONE
(all) in one breath □ all in one piece □ as black as one is painted □ as one □ at one fell swoop □ back to square one □ better off (if one were somewhere else) □ bite off more than one

can chew □ bite the hand that feeds one □ black as one is painted □ bring something crashing down (around one) □ burn one's bridges (behind one) □ burn one's bridges in front of one □ catch one off one's guard □ catch one with one's pants down □ cross a bridge before one comes to it □ cross a bridge when one comes to it □ cry before one is hurt □ do someone one better □ every last one □ every time one turns around □ feel it beneath one (to do something) □ for the life of one □ for the odds to be against one □ frighten one out of one's wits □ get one's wits about one □ get two strikes against one □ get what's coming to one □ give as good as one gets □ give one a run for one's money □ Give one an inch, and one will take a mile. □ give one butterflies in one's stomach □ give one one's freedom □ give one one's walking papers □ give one what's coming to one □ go in one ear and out the other □ go someone one better □ hair of the dog that bit one □ have a lot going (for one) □ have one foot in the grave □ have one's work cut out for one □ have something coming (to one) □ have the cards stacked against one □ hit one close to home □ hit one where one lives □ hole in one □ in one breath □ in one ear and out (of) the other □ in one fell swoop □ it behooves one to do something □ judge one on one's own merit(s) □ just one of those things □ keep one's wits about one □ kill two birds with one stone □ knock one off one's feet □ leave one to one's fate □ like one of the family □ more someone or something than one can shake a stick at □ new one on someone □ not know if one is coming or going □ not know whether one is coming or going □ not one iota □ off to one side □ on (the) one hand □ one and all □ one and only □ one and the same □ one at a time □ one by one □ one for the (record) books □ One good turn deserves another. □ one in a hundred □ one in a million □ one in a thousand □ one jump ahead (of someone

or something) □ one little bit □ One man's meat is another man's poison. □ one means business □ one move ahead (of someone or something) □ one-night stand □ one of these days □ one to a customer □ one-track mind □ one up (on someone) □ one way or another □ one's work is cut out for one □ pull a fast one □ put all one's eggs in one basket □ put one in one's place □ put one through one's paces □ read one one's rights □ scare one out of one's wits □ send one about one's business □ set one back on one's heels □ six of one and half a dozen of the other □ sweep one off one's feet □ take one at one's word □ take up where one left off □ talk until one is blue in the face □ tell one to one's face □ the cards are stacked against one □ There's more than one way to skin a cat. □ wear more than one hat □ when one is good and ready □ where one is coming from □ where one lives □ with one hand tied behind one's back

ONION
know one's onions

ONLY
Beauty is only skin-deep. □ in name only □ It (only) stands to reason. □ know something only too well □ one and only □ only have eyes for someone

ONTO
onto someone or something

OPEN
be (like) an open book □ crack open a bottle □ crack something wide open □ for openers □ get something out in the open □ keep one's eyes open (for someone or something) □ keep one's weather eye open □ leave oneself wide open for something □ leave oneself wide open to something □ leave something open □ not open one's mouth □ open a can of worms □ open and aboveboard □ open-and-shut case □ open fire (on someone) □ open one's heart (to someone) □ open Pandora's box □ open season (on someone or something) □ open

someone's eyes (to something) □ open something up □ open the door to something □ open up □ open up (on someone or something) □ open up (to someone) □ open up (with someone) □ open with something □ read someone like a(n open) book □ receive someone with open arms □ welcome someone with open arms

OPENERS
for openers

OPINION
base one's opinion on something □ form an opinion □ in one's opinion □ matter of opinion

OPPORTUNITY
jump at the opportunity □ leap at the opportunity □ seize the opportunity

OPPOSITE
the opposite sex

ORANGE
apples and oranges

ORBIT
go into orbit □ in orbit

ORDER
back order something □ build something to order □ call the meeting to order □ in apple-pie order □ in order to do something □ in short order □ just what the doctor ordered □ made to order □ make something to order □ on order □ order of the day □ order someone about □ order someone around □ order something to go □ out of order □ put one's house in order

ORDINARY
out of the ordinary

OTHER
drop the other shoe □ go in one ear and out the other □ have other fish to fry □ have the shoe on the other foot □ in one ear and out (of) the other □ in other words □ laugh out of the other side of one's mouth □ look the other way □ made for each other □ none other than someone □ on the other hand □ other things being equal □ six of one and half a dozen of the other □ something or other □ the

other side of the tracks □ the other way round □ The shoe is on the other foot. □ There are plenty of other fish in the sea. □ turn the other cheek □ with every (other) breath

OUNCE
An ounce of prevention is worth a pound of cure.

OUTDOORS
as big as all outdoors □ big as all outdoors

OUTGROW
outgrow something

OUTGUESS
outguess someone

OUTS
ins and outs of something

OUTSET
at the outset □ from the outset

OUTSIDE
at the (very) outside □ outside of something

OVERBOARD
go overboard

OWL
as wise as an owl □ night owl □ wise as an owl

OWN
according to one's own lights □ afraid of one's own shadow □ blow one's own horn □ carry one's (own) weight □ come into its own □ come into one's own □ cut one's (own) throat □ dig one's own grave □ do one's (own) thing □ dose of one's own medicine □ feather one's (own) nest □ find one's own level □ for one's (own) part □ for one's (own) sake □ foul one's own nest □ get a taste of one's own medicine □ get one's (own) way (with someone or something) □ hoist with one's own petard □ hold one's own □ in a world of one's own □ in one's (own) backyard □ in one's (own) (best) interest(s) □ judge one on one's own merit(s) □ judge something on its own merit(s) □ keep one's own counsel □ line one's own pockets □ mind one's own business □ not able to call one's time one's own

□ of one's own accord □ of one's own free will □ on one's own □ on one's own time □ own up (to something) □ paddle one's own canoe □ pay someone's (own) way □ pick on someone your own size □ pull one's (own) weight □ pull oneself up (by one's own bootstraps) □ sign one's own death warrant □ stand on one's own two feet □ stew in one's own juice □ take one's own life □ take the law into one's own hands □ tell its own story □ tell its own tale □ the devil's own job □ toot one's own horn □ under one's own steam

OX
as strong as an ox □ strong as an ox

PACE
at a snail's pace □ keep pace (with someone or something) □ put one through one's paces □ put something through its paces

PACK
pack a punch □ pack a wallop □ pack them in □ packed (in) like sardines □ send someone packing

PAD
pad the bill

PADDLE
paddle one's own canoe □ up the creek (without a paddle)

PAIN
give someone a pain □ have growing pains □ pain in the neck □ take (great) pains (to do something)

PAINT
as black as one is painted □ black as one is painted □ paint the town red

PAL
pal around (with someone)

PALE
beyond the pale □ pale around the gills

PALM
cross someone's palm with silver □ grease someone's palm □ have an itching palm □ have an itchy palm □ know someone or something like the palm of one's hand □ oil someone's palm

PAN
flash in the pan □ out of the frying pan into the fire □ pan out

PANCAKE
as flat as a pancake □ flat as a pancake

PANDORA
open Pandora's box

PANIC
press the panic button □ push the panic button

PANTS
beat the pants off someone □ by the seat of one's pants □ catch one with one's pants down □ charm the pants off (of) someone □ get ants in one's pants

PAPER
get one's walking papers □ give one one's walking papers □ paper over the cracks (in something) □ put something on paper

PAR
on par (with someone or something) □ par for the course □ up to par

PARADISE
fool's paradise

PARCEL
part and parcel (of something)

PAROLE
out on parole

PARRY
thrust and parry

PART
A fool and his money are soon parted. □ best part of something □ do one's part □ for one's (own) part □ for the most part □ in part □ part and parcel (of something) □ part company (with someone) □ part someone's hair □ parting of the ways □ take part (in something)

PARTAKE
partake of something

PARTICULAR
in particular

PARTY
life of the party □ party line □ The

party's over. □ throw a party (for someone)

PASS
come to a pretty pass □ come to pass □ in passing □ make a pass at someone □ mention someone or something in passing □ pass as someone or something □ pass away □ pass muster □ pass on □ pass out □ pass the buck □ pass the hat □ pass the time □ pass the time of day (with someone) □ pass through someone's mind □ ships that pass in the night □ with each passing day

PAST
be a past master at something □ not see past the end of one's nose □ past someone's or something's prime

PASTE
cut and paste

PASTURE
put someone or something out to pasture

PAT
give someone a pat on the back □ pat someone on the back □ stand pat

PATCH
patch someone or something up

PATH
beat a path to someone's door □ lead someone down the garden path □ path of least resistance

PATIENCE
try someone's patience

PAUL
rob Peter to pay Paul

PAUSE
give someone pause

PAVE
pave the way (for someone or something)

PAVEMENT
pound the pavement

PAY
have hell to pay □ have the devil to pay □ He who pays the piper calls the tune. □ hit pay dirt □ pay a king's ransom (for something) □ pay an arm and a leg (for something) □ pay as

you go □ pay-as-you-go □ pay attention (to someone or something) □ pay for something □ pay in advance □ pay lip service (to something) □ pay one's debt (to society) □ pay one's dues □ pay someone a back-handed compliment □ pay someone a compliment □ pay someone a left-handed compliment □ pay (someone) a visit □ pay someone or something off □ pay someone's (own) way □ pay the piper □ pay through the nose (for something) □ pay up □ rob Peter to pay Paul □ There will be the devil to pay.

PEA
as thick as pea soup □ thick as pea soup

PEACE
hold one's peace □ leave someone in peace □ make peace (with someone)

PEACOCK
as proud as a peacock □ proud as a peacock

PEANUT
for peanuts

PEARL
cast (one's) pearls before swine

PECK
hunt-and-peck

PECULIAR
funny peculiar

PEDESTAL
put someone on a pedestal

PEEL
keep one's eyes peeled (for someone or something)

PEEP
hear a peep out of someone

PEG
peg away (at something) □ square peg in a round hole □ take someone down a peg (or two)

PENCHANT
have a penchant for doing something

PENNY
A penny saved is a penny earned. □ cost a pretty penny □ cut someone off

without a penny □ penny-wise and pound-foolish

PEOPLE
bad blood (between people) □ be all things to all people □ split people up □ tell people apart

PEP
pep someone or something up

PERISH
Perish the thought. □ publish or perish

PERK
perk someone or something up

PERSON
be the last person □ do something in person □ feel like a new person

PET
be the teacher's pet

PETARD
hoist with one's own petard

PETE
Honest to Pete. □ honest-to-Pete

PETER
peter out □ rob Peter to pay Paul

PHYSICAL
get physical (with someone)

PICK
have a bone to pick (with someone) □ have a pick-me-up □ pick a quarrel (with someone) □ pick and choose □ pick at someone or something □ pick holes in something □ pick on someone or something □ pick on someone your own size □ pick one's way through something □ pick someone or something off □ pick someone or something up □ pick someone's brain(s) □ pick something over □ pick something to pieces □ pick up □ pick up the check □ pick up the tab □ picked over

PICKLE
in a (pretty) pickle

PICTURE
as pretty as a picture □ get the picture □ pretty as a picture □ put someone in the picture

PIE
as easy as (apple) pie □ easy as (apple) pie □ eat humble pie □ have a finger in the pie □ have one's finger in the pie □ in apple-pie order □ pie in the sky

PIECE
all in one piece □ break something to pieces □ give someone a piece of one's mind □ go to pieces □ pick something to pieces □ piece of cake □ piece of the action □ thrill someone to pieces □ thrilled to pieces □ villain of the piece

PIG
buy a pig in a poke □ serve as a guinea pig

PILE
make a pile □ pile in(to something) □ pile out (of something) □ pile something up □ pile up

PILL
bitter pill to swallow

PILLAR
from pillar to post

PIMPLE
get goose pimples

PIN
on pins and needles □ pin one's faith on someone or something □ pin someone down (on something) □ pin someone's ears back □ pin something on someone □ so quiet you could hear a pin drop □ so still you could hear a pin drop

PINCH
in a pinch □ pinch-hit (for someone) □ take something with a pinch of salt

PINK
in the pink (of condition) □ tickle someone pink □ tickled pink

PIPE
pipe down □ pipe dream □ pipe up with something □ Put that in your pipe and smoke it!

PIPER
He who pays the piper calls the tune. □ pay the piper

PIT

pit someone or something against someone or something □ the pits

PITCH

as black as pitch □ black as pitch □ in there pitching □ make a pitch (for someone or something) □ pitch in (and help) □ pitch someone a curve (ball)

PITY

take pity (on someone or something)

PLACE

all over the place □ between a rock and a hard place □ fall in(to) place □ fed up (to some place) (with someone or something) □ feel out of place □ go places □ have one's heart in the right place □ in place □ in place of someone or something □ in someone else's place □ in the first place □ in the second place □ jumping-off place □ keep one's place □ know one's place □ Lightning never strikes twice (in the same place). □ one's heart is in the right place □ out of place □ place someone □ place the blame on someone or something □ put one in one's place □ put oneself in someone else's place □ stop by (some place) □ stop in (some place) □ stop off (some place) □ stop over (some place) □ take place

PLAGUE

avoid someone or something like the plague

PLAIN

as plain as day □ as plain as the nose on one's face □ in plain English □ in plain language □ plain and simple □ plain as day □ plain as the nose on one's face □ put something plainly

PLAN

best-laid plans of mice and men

PLANK

walk the plank

PLAY

All work and no play makes Jack a dull boy. □ child's play □ foul play □ game that two can play □ make a play (for someone) □ play about (with someone or something) □ play along with someone or something □ play around (with someone or something) □ play ball (with someone) □ play both ends (against the middle) □ play by ear □ play-by-play description □ play cat and mouse (with someone) □ play fair □ play fast and loose (with someone or something) □ play first chair □ play footsie (with someone) □ play for keeps □ play hard to get □ play havoc with someone or something □ play hob with someone or something □ play hooky □ play it safe □ play on something □ play one's cards close to one's vest □ play one's cards close to the chest □ play one's cards right □ play one's cards well □ play one's trump card □ play politics □ play possum □ play second fiddle (to someone) □ play someone for something □ play someone off against someone else □ play someone or something down □ play someone or something up □ play something by ear □ play (the) devil's advocate □ play the field □ play the fool □ play the market □ play to the gallery □ play tricks (on someone) □ play up to someone □ play with fire □ played out □ When the cat's away, the mice will play.

PLEA

cop a plea

PLEASE

as pleased as punch □ less than pleased □ pleased as punch □ You can't please everyone.

PLENTY

There are plenty of other fish in the sea.

PLOT

The plot thickens.

PLOW

plow into someone or something □ put one's hand to the plow

PLUCK

pluck up one's courage

PLUG

not worth a plugged nickel □ plug away (at something) □ plug something in □ plug something up □ pull the plug (on someone or something)

POCKET
have someone in one's pocket □ line one's own pockets □ Money burns a hole in someone's pocket. □ out-of-pocket expenses

POETIC
poetic justice

POINT
at the point of doing something □ at this point (in time) □ belabor the point □ beside the point □ case in point □ come to the point □ get to the point □ have a low boiling point □ jumping-off point □ make a point □ make a point of doing something □ make a point of someone or something □ make points (with someone) □ miss the point □ on the point of doing something □ point someone or something out □ point something up □ point the finger at someone □ stretch a point □ stretch the point □ the point of no return □ touch a sore point

POISON
One man's meat is another man's poison.

POKE
buy a pig in a poke □ poke about □ poke around □ poke fun (at someone) □ poke one's nose in(to something)

POLE
be poles apart □ high man on the totem pole □ low man on the totem pole □ wouldn't touch something with a ten-foot pole

POLISH
polish something off

POLITICS
play politics

POND
big frog in a small pond

PONY
dog and pony show

POOP
poop out □ pooped out

POOR
as poor as a church mouse □ in poor taste □ poor as a church mouse □ poor but clean

POP
pop off □ pop one's cork □ pop the question □ pop up

PORT
any port in a storm

POSITION
jockey for position □ make someone's position clear

POSSESS
possessed by something □ possessed of something

POSSIBLE
as far as possible □ as soon as possible □ so far as possible □ soon as possible

POSSUM
play possum

POST
between you, me, and the lamppost □ from pillar to post □ keep someone posted

POSTAGE
postage and handling

POT
go to pot □ hit the jackpot □ tempest in a teapot □ the pot calling the kettle black

POTATO
meat-and-potatoes

POUND
An ounce of prevention is worth a pound of cure. □ penny-wise and pound-foolish □ pound a beat □ pound something out □ pound the pavement

POUR
It never rains but it pours. □ pour cold water on something □ pour it on thick □ pour money down the drain □ pour oil on troubled water(s) □ pour one's heart (out to someone)

POWDER
sitting on a powder keg □ take a powder

POWER
have no staying power □ power behind the throne □ powers that be

PRACTICAL
for all practical purposes

PRACTICE
in practice □ make a practice of something □ make something a practice □ out of practice □ put something into practice

PRAISE
damn someone or something with faint praise □ praise someone or something to the skies □ sing someone's praises

PREACH
preach to the converted

PRECEDENT
set a precedent

PRECIOUS
precious few □ precious little

PREMIUM
at a premium

PRESENCE
presence of mind

PRESENT
at present □ at the present time

PRESS
hard pressed (to do something) □ press one's luck □ press someone to the wall □ press the panic button □ pressed for time

PRETTY
as pretty as a picture □ come to a pretty pass □ cost a pretty penny □ in a (pretty) pickle □ pretty as a picture □ Pretty is as pretty does. □ pretty state of affairs □ sitting pretty

PREVAIL
prevail (up)on someone

PREVENT
take steps (to prevent something)

PREVENTION
An ounce of prevention is worth a pound of cure.

PRICE
have a price on one's head

PRICK
prick up one's ears

PRIDE
burst with pride □ pride and joy □ Pride goes before a fall. □ pride oneself in something □ pride oneself on something □ swallow one's pride

PRIME
in its prime □ in one's prime □ in the prime of life □ past someone's or something's prime □ prime mover

PRINT
in print □ out of print □ put something into print □ small print

PRIVATE
in private

PROBABILITY
in all probability

PROBLEM
no problem

PROGRESS
in progress

PROMISE
give something a lick and a promise □ have a lot of promise □ promise someone the moon □ promise the moon (to someone)

PROP
knock the props out from under someone

PROPORTION
blow something out of all proportion □ out of all proportion

PROUD
as proud as a peacock □ do someone proud □ proud as a peacock

PROVE
exception that proves the rule

PRUNE
full of prunes

PSYCHE
psyche out □ psyche someone out □ psyche someone up □ psyched out □ psyched up (for something)

PUBLIC
air one's dirty linen in public □ do something in public □ in the public eye □ wash one's dirty linen in public

PUBLISH
publish or perish

PULL
have pull with someone □ pull a boner □ pull a fast one □ pull a stunt (on someone) □ pull a trick (on someone) □ pull one's (own) weight □ pull one's punches □ pull oneself together □ pull oneself up (by one's own bootstraps) □ pull out all the stops □ pull rank (on someone) □ pull someone or something down □ pull someone through (something) □ pull someone's leg □ pull someone's or something's teeth □ pull something off □ pull something on someone □ pull something out of a hat □ pull something out of thin air □ pull something together □ pull strings □ pull the plug (on someone or something) □ pull the rug out (from under someone) □ pull the wool over someone's eyes □ pull through □ pull up (somewhere) □ pull up stakes

PUNCH
as pleased as punch □ beat someone to the punch □ pack a punch □ pleased as punch □ pull one's punches □ take a punch at someone

PUNISHMENT
glutton for punishment

PURE
pure and simple

PURGE
binge and purge

PURPOSE
answer someone's purpose □ at cross-purposes □ for all intents and purposes □ for all practical purposes □ serve someone's purpose

PURSE
control the purse strings □ make a silk purse out of a sow's ear

PURSUIT
in pursuit of something

PUSH
if push comes to shove □ push off □ push one's luck □ push someone to the wall □ push the panic button □ pushing up daisies □ when push comes to shove

PUT
feel put-upon □ hard put (to do something) □ put a bee in someone's bonnet □ put a stop to something □ put all one's eggs in one basket □ put an end to something □ put ideas into someone's head □ put in a good word (for someone) □ put in an appearance □ put off by someone or something □ put on □ put on a brave face □ put on a (brave) front □ put on airs □ put on an act □ put on the dog □ put on the feed bag □ put one in one's place □ put one through one's paces □ put one's back (in)to something □ put one's best foot forward □ put one's cards on the table □ put (one's) dibs on something □ put one's finger on something □ put one's foot down (about something) □ put one's foot in it □ put one's foot in one's mouth □ put one's hand to the plow □ put one's hand(s) on something □ put one's head on the block (for someone or something) □ put one's house in order □ put one's nose to the grindstone □ put one's oar in □ put one's shoulder to the wheel □ put one's thinking cap on □ put one's two cents (worth) in □ put oneself in someone else's place □ put oneself in someone else's shoes □ put out (about someone or something) □ put out (some) feelers □ put someone away □ put someone down as something □ put someone down (for something) □ put someone in the picture □ put someone on □ put someone on a pedestal □ put someone on the spot □ put someone or something across □ put someone or something at someone's disposal □ put someone or something down □ put someone or something off □ put someone or something on hold □ put someone or something out □ put someone or something out of one's mind □ put someone or something out to pasture □ put someone or something to bed □ put someone or something to sleep □ put someone or something up □ put someone through the wringer □

put someone to shame □ put someone to the test □ put someone up to something □ put someone wise to someone or something □ put someone's nose out of joint □ put something by □ put something down in black and white □ put something down to something □ put something forward □ put something in □ put something in mothballs □ put something into practice □ put something into print □ put something into words □ put something on ice □ put something on paper □ put something on the back burner □ put something on the cuff □ put something on the line □ put something over □ put something over (on someone) □ put something plainly □ put something right □ put something straight □ put something through its paces □ put something to (good) use □ put something to rest □ put something together □ Put that in your pipe and smoke it! □ put the arm on someone □ put the bite on someone □ put the blame on someone or something □ put the cart before the horse □ put the clamps on (someone) □ put the finger on someone □ put the heat on (someone) □ put the kibosh on something □ put the screws on (someone) □ put the skids on (something) □ put the squeeze (on someone) □ put the touch on someone □ put to bed with a shovel □ put to it □ put two and two together □ put up a (brave) front □ Put up or shut up! □ put up with someone or something □ put upon by someone □ put weight on □ put words into someone's mouth □ Put your money where your mouth is! □ stay put □ to put it mildly

PUTTY
putty in someone's hands

PUZZLE
puzzle something out

QT
on the QT

QUAKE
quake in one's boots

QUANDARY
in a quandary

QUANTITY
be an unknown quantity

QUARREL
pick a quarrel (with someone)

QUARTER
drawn and quartered

QUEST
in quest of someone or something

QUESTION
beg the question □ beside the question □ bring something into question □ call someone or something into question □ out of the question □ pop the question □ without question

QUICK
as quick as a flash □ as quick as a wink □ as quick as greased lightning □ cut someone to the quick □ make a quick buck □ quick and dirty □ quick as a flash □ quick as greased lightning □ quick on the draw □ quick on the trigger □ quick on the uptake

QUIET
as quiet as a mouse □ as quiet as the grave □ keep quiet (about someone or something) □ keep someone or something quiet □ keep something quiet □ quiet as a mouse □ quiet as the grave □ so quiet you could hear a pin drop

QUIT
call it quits

QUITE
quite a bit □ quite a few □ quite a little □ quite a lot □ quite a number

RACE
race against time □ rat race □ run the good race □ Slow and steady wins the race.

RACK
go to rack and ruin □ rack one's brain(s)

RAG
chew the rag □ from rags to riches □ in rags □ run someone ragged

RAGE
all the rage

RAIN
as right as rain □ come in out of the rain □ get a rain check (on something) □ give someone a rain check (on something) □ It never rains but it pours. □ not know enough to come in out of the rain □ rain cats and dogs □ rain or shine □ rain something out □ right as rain □ save something for a rainy day □ take a rain check (on something)

RAISE
born and raised □ cause (some) eyebrows to raise □ raise a hand (against someone or something) □ raise a stink (about something) □ raise an objection (to someone or something) □ raise cain (with someone or something) □ raise havoc (with someone or something) □ raise hell (with someone or something) □ raise hob with someone or something □ raise one's sights □ raise one's voice (to someone) □ raise some eyebrows □ raise the devil (with someone or something) □ raise the dickens (with someone or something)

RAKE
rake someone over the coals □ rake something off □ rake up something

RALLY
rally (a)round someone or something

RAM
ram someone or something down someone's throat

RAMBLE
ramble on (about someone or something)

RANDOM
at random

RANGE
at close range

RANK
close ranks □ close ranks (behind someone or something) □ close ranks (with someone) □ pull rank (on someone) □ rank and file

RANSOM
pay a king's ransom (for something)

RANT
rant and rave (about someone or something)

RAP
beat the rap □ get one's knuckles rapped □ rap someone's knuckles □ take the rap (for someone or something)

RARING
rarin' to go

RAT
rat on someone □ rat race □ smell a rat

RATE
at any rate □ at that rate □ at this rate □ rate with someone

RATHER
had rather do something

RATTLE
rattle something off

RAVE
rant and rave (about someone or something) □ stark raving mad

RAW
get a raw deal □ give someone a raw deal □ in the raw

RAZOR
as sharp as a razor □ sharp as a razor

REACH
out of reach □ reach first base (with someone or something) □ reach for the sky □ reach one's stride □ within someone's reach

READ
Do you read me? □ read between the lines □ read one one's rights □ read someone like a(n open) book □ read someone out of something □ read someone the riot act □ read someone's mind □ read something into something □ read something over □ read something through □ read the handwriting on the wall □ read up (on someone or something)

READY
get ready (to do something) □ ready,

willing, and able □ rough-and-ready
□ when one is good and ready

REAL
for real

REAR
bring up the rear □ rear its ugly head

REASON
It (only) stands to reason. □ listen to
reason □ lose one's reason □ stand
to reason □ within reason □ without
rhyme or reason

REASONABLE
beyond a reasonable doubt

RECEIPT
acknowledge receipt (of something)

RECEIVE
receive someone with open arms

RECKON
force to be reckoned with □ reckon
with someone or something

RECORD
for the record □ off the record □ one
for the (record) books

RED
catch someone red-handed □ caught
red-handed □ get the red-carpet
treatment □ give someone the
red-carpet treatment □ in the red □
not worth a red cent □ out of the red
□ paint the town red □ red herring
□ red in the face □ red tape □ roll
out the red carpet for someone □ see
red

REEL
reel something off

REGAIN
regain one's composure □ regain
one's feet

REGULAR
as regular as clockwork □ regular as
clockwork

REIN
give free rein to someone □ give
someone free rein

RELATIVE
relative to someone or something

RELIGION
get religion

REPAIR
in good repair

REPUTATION
get a reputation (as a something) □
get a reputation (for doing something)
□ give someone a reputation (as a
something) □ give someone a reputation (for doing something)

REQUEST
at someone's request

REQUIRE
meet the requirements (for something)

REQUIREMENT
meet the requirements (for something)

RESIGN
resign oneself to something

RESISTANCE
line of least resistance □ path of least
resistance

RESORT
as a last resort

REST
come to rest □ lay something to rest
□ put something to rest □ rest assured □ rest on one's laurels

RESULT
as a result of something □ result in
something

RETREAT
beat a (hasty) retreat

RETURN
by return mail □ return someone's
compliment □ return the compliment
□ return the favor □ the point of no
return

REV
rev something up

RHYME
without rhyme or reason

RIB
stick to one's ribs

RICH
from rags to riches □ strike it rich

RID
get rid of someone or something

RIDDANCE
good riddance (to bad rubbish)

RIDE
go along for the ride □ hitch a ride □ let something ride □ ride herd on someone or something □ ride off in all directions □ ride on someone's coattails □ ride roughshod over someone or something □ ride something out □ ride the gravy train □ riding for a fall □ take someone for a ride □ thumb a ride

RIDICULOUS
make someone look ridiculous

RIGHT
acknowledge someone to be right □ all right □ All right for you! □ all right with someone □ as right as rain □ give one's right arm (for someone or something) □ go right through someone □ hang a right □ have a right to do something □ have one's heart in the right place □ have someone dead to rights □ have the right to do something □ hit someone (right) between the eyes □ in one's right mind □ in the right □ left and right □ make something right □ one's heart is in the right place □ play one's cards right □ put something right □ read one one's rights □ right and left □ right as rain □ right away □ right down someone's alley □ right off the bat □ right on time □ right side up □ (right) under someone's (very) nose □ right up someone's alley □ sail (right) through something □ say something (right) to someone's face □ serve someone right □ set something right □ step (right) up □ strike the right note □ turn out (all right) □ when it comes right down to it □ work out (all right) □ yield the right-of-way

RILEY
lead the life of Riley

RING
give someone a ring □ have a familiar ring □ like a three-ring circus □ ring a bell □ ring down the curtain (on something) □ ring in the new year □ ring something up □ ring true □ run

rings around someone □ toss one's hat into the ring

RIOT
read someone the riot act □ run riot

RIP
let her rip □ rip into someone or something □ rip someone or something off

RIPE
ripe old age □ when the time is ripe

RISE
Early to bed, early to rise(, makes a man healthy, wealthy, and wise.) □ get a rise out of someone □ give rise to something □ Rise and shine! □ rise to the bait □ rise to the occasion

RISK
risk one's neck (to do something) □ run a risk (of something) □ run the risk (of something) □ take a risk

RIVER
sell someone down the river □ send someone up the river

ROAD
end of the road □ get the show on the road □ hit the road □ middle-of-the-road

ROB
rob Peter to pay Paul □ rob the cradle

ROBBERY
daylight robbery

ROBIN
all around Robin Hood's barn

ROBINSON
before you can say Jack Robinson

ROCK
as steady as a rock □ between a rock and a hard place □ have rocks in one's head □ on the rocks □ rock the boat □ steady as a rock

ROCKER
off one's rocker

ROLL
A rolling stone gathers no moss. □ as easy as rolling off a log □ easy as rolling off a log □ get rolling □ get the ball rolling □ have them rolling in

the aisles □ heads will roll □ keep the ball rolling □ let it roll □ roll in □ roll one's sleeves up □ roll out the red carpet for someone □ roll something back □ rolling in something □ set the ball rolling □ start the ball rolling

ROMANS
When in Rome, do as the Romans do.

ROME
fiddle while Rome burns □ Rome wasn't built in a day. □ When in Rome, do as the Romans do.

ROOF
go through the roof

ROOM
not enough room to swing a cat □ room and board □ take up room

ROOST
come home (to roost) □ rule the roost

ROOT
Money is the root of all evil. □ root for someone or something □ rooted to the spot □ take root

ROPE
at the end of one's rope □ know the ropes □ learn the ropes □ rope someone into doing something □ show someone the ropes

ROSE
bed of roses □ come up smelling like roses

ROTE
learn something by rote

ROTTEN
rotten to the core

ROUGH
diamond in the rough □ get a rough idea (about something) □ get a rough idea (of something) □ give someone a rough idea (about something) □ give someone a rough idea (of something) □ have a rough time (of it) □ rough-and-ready □ rough-and-tumble □ rough it □ rough someone up □ when the going gets rough

ROUGHSHOD
ride roughshod over someone or something

ROUND
all year round □ in round figures □ in round numbers □ round out something □ round something off □ round the clock □ round-the-clock □ round-trip ticket □ square peg in a round hole □ the other way round

ROUNDABOUT
say something in a roundabout way

ROUNDUP
head for the last roundup

ROW
get one's ducks in a row □ kick up a row □ tough row to hoe

RUB
rub elbows (with someone) □ rub off (on someone) □ rub salt in the wound □ rub shoulders with someone □ rub someone out □ rub someone('s fur) the wrong way □ rub someone's nose in it □ rub something in

RUBBISH
good riddance (to bad rubbish)

RUBICON
cross the Rubicon

RUFFLE
ruffle someone's feathers

RUG
as snug as a bug in a rug □ pull the rug out (from under someone) □ snug as a bug in a rug □ sweep something under the rug

RUIN
go to rack and ruin □ go to wrack and ruin

RULE
as a (general) rule □ exception that proves the rule □ rule of thumb □ rule someone or something out □ rule the roost

RUN
cut and run □ do something on the run □ dry run □ eat and run □ get a run for one's money □ give one a run for one's money □ have a run of bad luck □ have one's luck run out □

hit-and-run □ in the long run □ in the running □ in the short run □ make a run for it □ make someone's blood run cold □ off and running □ off to a running start □ one's luck runs out □ out of the running □ run a fever □ run a risk (of something) □ run a taut ship □ run a temperature □ run a tight ship □ run afoul of someone or something □ run after someone □ run an errand □ run (around) in circles □ run around like a chicken with its head cut off □ run around with someone □ run circles around someone □ run counter to something □ run for it □ run for one's life □ run in the family □ run into a stone wall □ run into someone □ run like clockwork □ run-of-the-mill □ run off □ run off at the mouth □ run off with someone or something □ run out of gas □ run out of time □ run rings around someone □ run riot □ run scared □ run short (of something) □ run someone in □ run someone or something down □ run someone ragged □ run something into the ground □ run something up □ run that by (someone) again □ run the good race □ run the risk (of something) □ run through something □ run to seed □ run to something □ run wild

RUNAROUND
get the runaround □ give someone the runaround

RUNNING
in the running □ off and running □ off to a running start □ out of the running

RUSH
fools rush in (where angels fear to tread) □ give someone the bum's rush □ in a mad rush

RUSTLE
rustle something up

SACK
get the sack □ give someone the sack □ hit the sack □ sack out

SACRED
sacred cow

SAD
sadder but wiser

SADDLE
saddle someone with something

SAFE
play it safe □ safe and sound □ safety in numbers

SAFETY
safety in numbers

SAID
after all is said and done □ easier said than done □ no sooner said than done □ when all is said and done □ You said it!

SAIL
clear sailing □ sail (right) through something □ sail under false colors □ set sail (for somewhere) □ take the wind out of someone's sails

SAKE
for one's (own) sake □ for the sake of someone or something

SALAD
in one's salad days

SALE
for sale □ on sale

SALT
back to the salt mines □ rub salt in the wound □ salt of the earth □ salt something away □ take something with a grain of salt □ take something with a pinch of salt □ worth one's salt

SAME
all the same □ all the same (to someone) □ amount to the same thing □ at the same time □ by the same token □ cast in the same mold □ come to the same thing □ in the same boat (as someone) □ in the same breath □ just the same □ just the same (to someone) □ Lightning never strikes twice (in the same place). □ not in the same league with someone or something □ one and the same □ same here □ same old story □ speak the same language □ tarred with the same brush □ the same to you

SANCTITY
odor of sanctity

SAND
bury one's head in the sand ☐ hide one's head in the sand

SARDINE
packed (in) like sardines

SAVE
A penny saved is a penny earned. ☐ save one's breath ☐ save (one's) face ☐ save someone's neck ☐ save someone's skin ☐ save something for a rainy day ☐ save the day ☐ save up (for something) ☐ saved by the bell ☐ saving grace ☐ scrimp and save

SAY
after all is said and done ☐ before you can say Jack Robinson ☐ drop in (to say hello) ☐ easier said than done ☐ get one's say ☐ go so far as to say something ☐ goes without saying ☐ have a say (in something) ☐ no sooner said than done ☐ on someone's say-so ☐ say a mouthful ☐ say something in a roundabout way ☐ say something (right) to someone's face ☐ say something under one's breath ☐ say the word ☐ say uncle ☐ to say nothing of someone or something ☐ to say the least ☐ when all is said and done ☐ You can say that again! ☐ You said it!

SCALE
tip the scales at something

SCAPEGOAT
make someone the scapegoat for something

SCARCE
as scarce as hens' teeth ☐ make oneself scarce ☐ scarcer than hens' teeth

SCARE
run scared ☐ scare one out of one's wits ☐ scare someone or something up ☐ scare someone stiff ☐ scare someone to death ☐ scare the living daylights out of someone ☐ scare the wits out of someone ☐ scared stiff ☐ scared to death

SCENE
arrive on the scene ☐ behind the scenes ☐ come on the scene ☐ create a scene ☐ make a scene ☐ make the scene

SCHEDULE
on schedule

SCHEME
best-laid schemes of mice and men

SCHOOL
of the old school ☐ tell tales out of school

SCORE
have a score to settle (with someone) ☐ know the score ☐ settle a score with someone ☐ settle the score (with someone)

SCOT
get off scot-free ☐ go scot-free

SCRAPE
bow and scrape ☐ have a scrape (with someone or something) ☐ scrape something together ☐ scrape the bottom of the barrel

SCRATCH
make something from scratch ☐ not up to scratch ☐ scratch around (for something) ☐ scratch someone's back ☐ scratch the surface ☐ start from scratch ☐ up to scratch ☐ You scratch my back and I'll scratch yours.

SCREAM
scream bloody murder

SCREW
have a screw loose ☐ put the screws on (someone) ☐ screw around (with someone or something) ☐ screw someone or something up ☐ screw up one's courage

SCRIMP
scrimp and save

SEA
(all) at sea (about something) ☐ at sea (about something) ☐ between the devil and the deep blue sea ☐ get one's sea legs ☐ There are plenty of other fish in the sea.

SEAL
signed, sealed, and delivered

SEAM
burst at the seams ☐ come apart at the seams ☐ fall apart at the seams

SEAMY
seamy side of life

SEARCH

in search of someone or something □ search high and low (for someone or something) □ search something with a fine-tooth comb

SEASON

in season □ off season □ open season (on someone or something) □ out of season □ silly season

SEAT

by the seat of one's pants □ in the driver's seat □ in the hot seat □ on the hot seat

SECOND

come off second-best □ get one's second wind □ get second thoughts about someone or something □ in a split second □ in (just) a second □ in one's second childhood □ in the second place □ on second thought □ play second fiddle (to someone) □ second nature to someone □ second to none

SECRET

do something in secret

SECURITY

lull someone into a false sense of security

SEE

begin to see daylight □ begin to see the light □ buy something sight unseen □ can't see beyond the end of one's nose □ can't see one's hand in front of one's face □ have seen better days □ Long time no see. □ not able to see the forest for the trees □ not see any objection (to something) □ not see farther than the end of one's nose □ not see past the end of one's nose □ see a man about a dog □ see about something □ see double □ see eye to eye (with someone) (about something) □ see eye to eye (with someone) (on something) □ see fit (to do something) □ see into something □ see no objection (to something) □ see one's way clear (to do something) □ see red □ see someone home □ see someone to the door □ see something through □ see stars □ see the color of someone's money □ see the (hand)writing on the wall □

see the last of someone or something □ see the light □ see the light (at the end of the tunnel) □ see the light (of day) □ see the sights □ see things □ see through someone or something □ see to someone or something □ see which way the wind is blowing □ seeing is believing □ wait-and-see attitude

SEED

go to seed □ run to seed

SEEK

hide-and-seek □ much sought after

SEIZE

seize the bull by the horns □ seize the opportunity □ seize (up)on something

SELL

get the hard sell □ give someone the hard sell □ sell like hotcakes □ sell someone a bill of goods □ sell someone down the river □ sell someone on something □ sell (someone or something) out □ sell someone or something short □ sell something for a song □ sell something off □ sell something on credit

SEND

get a big send-off □ give someone a big send-off □ send one about one's business □ send someone or something up □ send someone (out) on an errand □ send someone packing □ send someone to the showers □ send someone up the river □ send something C.O.D. □ send up a trial balloon

SENSE

come to one's senses □ horse sense □ in a sense □ lull someone into a false sense of security □ make sense □ make sense out of someone or something □ out of one's senses □ take leave of one's senses

SEPARATE

separate but equal □ separate the men from the boys □ separate the sheep from the goats

SERVE

First come, first served. □ serve as a guinea pig □ serve notice □ serve someone right □ serve someone's purpose

SERVICE
be at someone's service □ be of service (to someone) □ out of service □ pay lip service (to something)

SET
all set □ (all) set to do something □ at a set time □ dead set against someone or something □ get set □ have one's heart set against something □ have one's heart set on something □ not set foot somewhere □ one's heart is set against something □ one's heart is set on something □ set a precedent □ set eyes on someone or something □ set fire to someone or something □ set foot somewhere □ set forth (on something) □ set great store by someone or something □ set in □ set in one's ways □ set one back on one's heels □ set one's heart against something □ set one's heart on something □ set one's sights on something □ set sail (for somewhere) □ set someone back (some amount of money) □ set someone or something off □ set someone or something on fire □ set someone or something straight □ set someone or something up □ set someone up (as something) □ set someone up (in business) □ set someone's teeth on edge □ set something down to something □ set something right □ set something straight □ set the ball rolling □ set the stage for something □ set the table □ set the world on fire □ set tongues (a)wagging □ set up shop somewhere □ set upon someone or something

SETTLE
have a score to settle (with someone) □ settle a score with someone □ settle down □ settle for something □ settle on something □ settle someone's affairs □ settle the score (with someone) □ settle up with someone

SEVEN
at sixes and sevens

SEVENTH
in seventh heaven

SEW
get something sewed up □ sew something up

SEX
the opposite sex

SHACK
shack up (with someone)

SHADE
shades of someone or something

SHADOW
afraid of one's own shadow □ beyond the shadow of a doubt

SHAKE
give someone a fair shake □ in two shakes of a lamb's tail □ more someone or something than one can shake a stick at □ movers and shakers □ no great shakes □ shake (hands) on something □ shake hands (with someone) □ shake in one's boots □ shake someone or something down □ shake someone or something off □ shake someone or something up □ shake something off □ shake the lead out □ shook up

SHAKER
movers and shakers

SHAME
crying shame □ hide one's face in shame □ put someone to shame □ Shame on someone.

SHANK
by shank's mare □ go (somewhere) by shank's mare

SHAPE
in good shape □ in shape □ lick something into shape □ out of shape □ shape someone up □ shape up □ Shape up or ship out. □ whip something into shape

SHARE
lion's share (of something) □ share and share alike

SHARP
as sharp as a razor □ at sometime sharp □ sharp as a razor

SHAVE
have a close shave

SHED
shed crocodile tears □ shed (some) light on something

SHEEP
black sheep of the family □ separate the sheep from the goats □ wolf in sheep's clothing

SHEET
as white as a sheet □ white as a sheet

SHELL
come out of one's shell □ shell something out

SHELLACKING
get a shellacking □ give someone a shellacking □ take a shellacking

SHIFT
shift for oneself

SHINE
rain or shine □ Rise and shine! □ shine up to someone □ take a shine to someone or something

SHIP
desert a sinking ship □ leave a sinking ship □ run a taut ship □ run a tight ship □ Shape up or ship out. □ shipping and handling □ ships that pass in the night

SHIRK
shirk one's duty

SHIRT
give someone the shirt off one's back □ Keep your shirt on! □ lose one's shirt

SHOCK
get the shock of one's life

SHOE
as comfortable as an old shoe □ comfortable as an old shoe □ drop the other shoe □ fill someone's shoes □ have the shoe on the other foot □ If the shoe fits, wear it. □ in someone else's shoes □ put oneself in someone else's shoes □ step into someone's shoes □ The shoe is on the other foot.

SHOESTRING
get along (on a shoestring)

SHOOK
shook up

SHOOT
shoot from the hip □ shoot one's mouth off □ shoot something out □ shoot the breeze □ shoot the bull □ shoot the works □ whole shooting match

SHOP
bull in a china shop □ close up shop □ go window-shopping □ set up shop somewhere □ shop around (for something) □ talk shop

SHORT
caught short □ end up with the short end of the stick □ fall short (of something) □ for short □ get the short end of the stick □ in short □ in short order □ in short supply □ in the short run □ life is too short □ long and (the) short of it □ make a long story short □ make short work of someone or something □ nothing short of something □ over the short haul □ run short (of something) □ sell someone or something short □ short and sweet □ short of something □ stop short of (doing) something

SHOT
(all) shot to hell □ call the shots □ give something one's best shot □ have a shot at something □ not by a long shot □ off like a shot □ shot in the arm □ shot in the dark □ shot through with something □ shot to hell □ take a shot at something

SHOTGUN
shotgun wedding

SHOULD
should have stood in bed

SHOULDER
carry the weight of the world on one's shoulders □ get the cold shoulder □ give someone the cold shoulder □ have a chip on one's shoulder □ have a good head on one's shoulders □ have broad shoulders □ head and shoulders above someone or something □ on someone's shoulders □ put one's shoulder to the wheel □ rub shoulders with someone □ shoulder to shoulder □ straight from the shoulder

SHOUT
all over but the shouting

SHOVE
if push comes to shove □ shove someone or something down someone's throat □ when push comes to shove

SHOVEL
put to bed with a shovel

SHOW
dog and pony show □ get the show on the road □ goes to show you □ make a great show of something □ not show one's face □ show-and-tell □ show good faith □ show of hands □ show one's hand □ show one's (true) colors □ show signs of something □ show someone or something off □ show someone the ropes □ show someone (to) the door □ show someone up □ show someone up as something □ show something to good advantage □ steal the show

SHOWER
send someone to the showers

SHUFFLE
shuffle off this mortal coil

SHUT
keep one's mouth shut (about someone or something) □ open-and-shut case □ Put up or shut up! □ shut someone up □ shut something down □ shut the door on someone or something

SHY
shy away (from someone or something)

SICK
as sick as a dog □ be sick □ get sick □ sick and tired of someone or something □ sick as a dog □ sick in bed □ take sick

SIDE
be a thorn in someone's side □ choose up sides □ drop by the wayside □ fall by the wayside □ get on the good side of someone □ get out of the wrong side of the bed □ get up on the wrong side of the bed □ know which side one's bread is buttered on □ laugh out of the other side of one's mouth □ off to one side □ right side up □ seamy side of life □ side against someone □ side with someone □ split one's sides (with laughter) □ take sides □ the other side of the tracks □ the wrong side of the tracks

SIGHT
buy something sight unseen □ can't stand (the sight of) someone or something □ catch sight of someone or something □ know someone by sight □ love at first sight □ lower one's sights □ out of sight □ Out of sight, out of mind. □ raise one's sights □ see the sights □ set one's sights on something □ sight for sore eyes

SIGN
get the high sign □ give someone the high sign □ show signs of something □ sign on the dotted line □ sign on (with someone) □ sign one's own death warrant □ signed, sealed, and delivered

SILK
make a silk purse out of a sow's ear

SILLY
silly season

SILVER
born with a silver spoon in one's mouth □ cross someone's palm with silver □ Every cloud has a silver lining.

SIMMER
simmer down

SIMPLE
plain and simple □ pure and simple

SIN
as ugly as sin □ ugly as sin

SINCE
greatest thing since sliced bread

SING
sing a different tune □ sing another tune □ sing someone's praises

SINGLE
(in) single file □ single file

SINK
desert a sinking ship □ everything but the kitchen sink □ leave a sinking ship □ sink in □ sink into despair □ sink

one's teeth into something □ sink or swim □ swallow something, hook, line, and sinker

SINKER
swallow something, hook, line, and sinker

SIT
at a sitting □ be a sitting duck □ like a sitting duck □ like sitting ducks □ sit at someone's feet □ sit back and let something happen □ sit bolt upright □ sit (idly) by □ sit in for someone □ sit in (on something) □ sit on its hands □ sit on one's hands □ sit on someone or something □ sit on the fence □ sit something out □ sit through something □ sit tight □ sit up and take notice □ sit up with someone □ sit with someone □ sitting on a powder keg □ (sitting) on top of the world □ sitting pretty □ sitting target

SITUATION
no-win situation

SIX
at sixes and sevens □ deep-six someone or something □ six of one and half a dozen of the other

SIZE
beat someone down (to size) □ cut someone down (to size) □ knock someone down (to size) □ pick on someone your own size □ size someone or something up □ take someone down (to size) □ That's about the size of it.

SKATE
skate on thin ice

SKELETON
skeleton in the closet

SKID
hit the skids □ put the skids on (something)

SKIN
(all) skin and bones □ Beauty is only skin-deep. □ by the skin of one's teeth □ get under someone's skin □ give someone some skin □ jump out of one's skin □ no skin off someone's nose □ no skin off someone's teeth □

nothing but skin and bones □ save someone's skin □ skin someone alive □ soaked to the skin □ There's more than one way to skin a cat. □ thick-skinned □ thin-skinned

SKIP
hop, skip, and a jump □ one's heart skips a beat □ skip bail □ skip out (on someone or something)

SKITTLES
(all) beer and skittles □ beer and skittles

SKULL
get something through someone's thick skull

SKY
as high as the sky □ go sky-high □ high as the sky □ out of a clear blue sky □ pie in the sky □ praise someone or something to the skies □ reach for the sky □ The sky's the limit.

SLACK
slack off

SLAP
get a slap on the wrist □ give someone a slap on the wrist □ slap in the face □ slap someone down □ slap someone on the wrist □ slap someone's wrist □ slap something together

SLATE
slated for something □ slated to do something □ start (off) with a clean slate □ start (over) with a clean slate □ wipe someone's slate clean

SLAUGHTER
like lambs to the slaughter

SLEEP
drop off (to sleep) □ Let sleeping dogs lie. □ lose sleep (over someone or something) □ not sleep a wink □ put someone or something to sleep □ sleep in □ sleep like a log □ sleep on something □ sleep something off □ sleep with someone

SLEEVE
have an ace up one's sleeve □ have one's heart on one's sleeve □ have something up one's sleeve □ laugh up one's sleeve □ roll one's sleeves up □ wear one's heart on one's sleeve

SLICE
greatest thing since sliced bread □ slice of the cake

SLICK
as slick as a whistle □ slick as a whistle

SLIDE
let something slide □ let something slide by □ let things slide

SLIP
as slippery as an eel □ get the slip □ give someone the slip □ let something slip by □ let something slip (out) □ let the chance slip by □ slip away □ slip of the tongue □ slip off □ slip one's mind □ slip out □ slip through someone's fingers □ slip up □ slippery as an eel

SLIPPERY
as slippery as an eel □ slippery as an eel

SLOW
Slow and steady wins the race. □ slow on the draw □ slow on the uptake □ slow someone or something down □ slow someone or something up □ slow(ly) but sure(ly) □ take it slow

SLOWLY
slow(ly) but sure(ly)

SLY
as sly as a fox □ do something on the sly □ sly as a fox

SMACK
smack-dab in the middle

SMALL
big frog in a small pond □ engage in small talk □ small fry □ small hours (of the night) □ small print □ small-time

SMELL
come up smelling like roses □ smell a rat

SMILE
crack a smile □ smile on someone or something

SMITHEREENS
blow someone or something to smithereens

SMOKE
go up in smoke □ have a smoke □ Put that in your pipe and smoke it! □ smoke and mirrors □ smoke someone or something out □ Where there's smoke there's fire.

SMOOTH
smooth something out □ smooth something over

SNAG
hit a snag

SNAIL
at a snail's pace

SNAKE
snake in the grass

SNAP
snap out of something □ snap something up

SNEEZE
nothing to sneeze at

SNIFF
sniff someone or something out

SNIT
in a snit

SNOW
as white as the driven snow □ do a snow job on someone □ white as the driven snow

SNOWBALL
have a snowball's chance in hell

SNUFF
not up to snuff □ up to snuff

SNUG
as snug as a bug in a rug □ snug as a bug in a rug

SO
able to take just so much □ be so □ do so □ go so far as to say something □ (have) never had it so good □ have so □ in so many words □ just so □ never had it so good □ on someone's say-so □ so-and-so □ so be it □ so far as anyone knows □ so far as I'm concerned □ so far as possible □ So far, so good. □ So it goes. □ so long □ so long as □ so much for someone or something □ so much the better □ so quiet you could hear a pin drop □

so-so □ so still you could hear a pin drop □ so to speak □ without so much as doing something

SOAK
soaked to the skin

SOBER
as sober as a judge □ sober as a judge

SOCIETY
pay one's debt (to society)

SOCK
sock something away

SOFT
as soft as a baby's bottom □ have a soft spot in one's heart for someone or something □ soft as a baby's bottom

SOIL
soil one's hands

SOME
and then some □ at some length □ catch some Zs □ cause (some) eyebrows to raise □ cause (some) tongues to wag □ dig some dirt up on someone □ drum some business up □ fed up (to some place) (with someone or something) □ give someone some skin □ in some neck of the woods □ It takes (some) getting used to. □ knock some heads together □ put out (some) feelers □ raise some eyebrows □ set someone back (some amount of money) □ shed (some) light on something □ (some) new blood □ stop by (some place) □ stop in (some place) □ stop off (some place) □ stop over (some place) □ throw (some) light on something □ to some extent □ to the tune of some amount of money □ use some elbow grease

SOMEHOW
carry on somehow □ come on somehow □ do somehow by someone □ end up (somehow) □ land up somehow or somewhere

SOMETIME
at sometime sharp □ date back (to sometime) □ drop around (sometime) □ drop by (sometime)

SOMEWHERE
better off (if one were somewhere else) □ better off (somewhere) □ bound for somewhere □ end up somewhere □ find one's or something's way somewhere □ go (somewhere) by shank's mare □ hail from somewhere □ hang out (somewhere) □ haul up (somewhere) □ hightail it out of somewhere □ hole up (somewhere) □ hotfoot it out of somewhere □ knock about (somewhere) □ land up somehow or somewhere □ lay over (somewhere) □ light out (for somewhere) □ light out (of somewhere) □ make a break for something or somewhere □ make for somewhere □ not set foot somewhere □ on one's way (somewhere) □ on the way (somewhere) □ pull up (somewhere) □ set foot somewhere □ set sail (for somewhere) □ set up shop somewhere □ somewhere to hang (up) one's hat □ take up one's abode somewhere □ wind up somewhere

SON
son of a bitch □ son of a gun

SONG
buy something for a song □ go into one's song and dance (about something) □ sell something for a song □ swan song

SOON
A fool and his money are soon parted. □ as soon as possible □ had as soon do something □ had sooner do something □ no sooner said than done □ soon as possible □ sooner or later □ would as soon do something

SORE
sight for sore eyes □ stick out like a sore thumb □ touch a sore point □ touch a sore spot

SORROW
drown one's sorrows

SORT
in bad sorts □ out of sorts □ something of the sort □ sort of something □ sort something out

SOUGHT
much sought after

SOUL
every living soul □ heart and soul □

keep body and soul together □ not a living soul

SOUND
as sound as a dollar □ safe and sound □ sound as a dollar □ sound off (about something) □ sound someone out

SOUP
as easy as duck soup □ as thick as pea soup □ easy as duck soup □ everything from soup to nuts □ in the soup □ soup something up □ thick as pea soup

SOUR
hit a sour note □ strike a sour note □ sweet and sour

SOUTH
down South

SOW
make a silk purse out of a sow's ear □ sow one's wild oats

SPACE
spaced-out □ take up space

SPADE
call a spade a spade

SPAIN
build castles in Spain

SPAN
spick-and-span

SPARE
and something to spare □ have something to spare □ in one's spare time □ with something to spare

SPAZ
have a spaz

SPEAK
Actions speak louder than words. □ nothing to speak of □ on speaking terms (with someone) □ so to speak □ speak for itself □ speak for themselves □ speak highly of someone or something □ speak of the devil □ speak off the cuff □ speak one's mind □ speak out of turn □ speak out (on something) □ speak the same language □ speak up □ speak up for someone or something □ speak with a forked tongue □ spoken for

SPEED
at full speed

SPELL
spell something out □ spell trouble

SPEND
tax-and-spend

SPICE
Variety is the spice of life.

SPICK
spick-and-span

SPILL
cry over spilled milk □ spill the beans □ take a spill

SPIN
go into a tailspin □ make someone's head spin □ spin one's wheels □ spin something off

SPINDLE
fold, spindle, or mutilate

SPIRIT
in good spirits

SPIT
be the spit and image of someone □ be the spitting image of someone □ spit (something) up

SPITE
cut off one's nose to spite one's face □ in spite of someone or something

SPLEEN
vent one's spleen

SPLIT
in a split second □ split hairs □ split one's sides (with laughter) □ split people up □ split something fifty-fifty □ split the difference □ split up

SPOIL
To the victors belong the spoils. □ Too many cooks spoil the broth. □ Too many cooks spoil the stew.

SPOKEN
spoken for

SPONGE
throw in the sponge

SPOOK
spook someone or something

SPOON
born with a silver spoon in one's mouth □ spoon-feed someone

SPORT
sporting chance

SPOT
have a soft spot in one's heart for someone or something □ hit the high spots □ hit the spot □ in a (tight) spot □ Johnny-on-the-spot □ on the spot □ put someone on the spot □ rooted to the spot □ touch a sore spot □ X marks the spot

SPOTLIGHT
in the spotlight □ steal the spotlight

SPOUT
spout off (about someone or something)

SPREAD
spread it on thick □ spread like wildfire □ spread oneself too thin

SPRING
no spring chicken □ spring for something □ spring something on someone

SPRUCE
spruce someone or something up

SPUR
on the spur of the moment

SQUARE
back to square one □ do something fair and square □ fair and square □ square accounts (with someone) □ square deal □ square meal □ square off (for something) □ square peg in a round hole □ square someone or something away □ square up to someone or something □ square up with someone □ squared away

SQUEAK
squeak by (someone or something)

SQUEEZE
put the squeeze (on someone)

SQUIRREL
squirrel something away

STAB
stab someone in the back □ take a stab at something

STACK
blow one's stack □ have the cards stacked against one □ stack something up □ stack the cards (against someone or something) □ stack the deck (against someone or something) □ the cards are stacked against one

STAG
go stag

STAGE
at this stage □ at this stage of the game □ in a stage whisper □ set the stage for something

STAKE
at stake □ burn someone at the stake □ pull up stakes □ stake a claim (to something)

STALL
stall someone or something off

STAMP
one's old stamping ground □ stamp someone or something out

STAND
able to do something standing on one's head □ can't stand (the sight of) someone or something □ have one's heart stand still □ It (only) stands to reason. □ know where someone stands (on someone or something) □ make someone's hair stand on end □ not have a leg to stand on □ one-night stand □ one's heart stands still □ should have stood in bed □ stand a chance □ stand and deliver □ stand behind someone or something □ stand by □ stand by someone □ stand corrected □ stand for something □ stand in awe (of someone or something) □ stand (in) back of someone or something □ stand in (for someone) □ stand in someone's way □ stand on ceremony □ stand on one's own two feet □ stand one's ground □ stand out □ stand over someone □ stand pat □ stand someone in good stead □ stand someone to a treat □ stand someone up □ stand still for something □ stand to reason □ stand up and be counted □ take a stand (against someone or something) □ take the stand

STANDSTILL
come to a standstill

STAR
get stars in one's eyes □ see stars □ thank one's lucky stars

STARCH
take the starch out of someone

START
be off to a bad start □ by fits and starts □ for starters □ from start to finish □ get a head start (on someone or something) □ get a jump(start) □ get a start □ get off to a bad start □ get off to a flying start □ get one's start □ give someone a head start (on someone or something) □ give someone a start □ off to a running start □ start from scratch □ start off on the wrong foot □ start (off) with a clean slate □ start (over) with a clean slate □ start someone in (as something) □ start someone out (as something) □ start something □ start something up □ start the ball rolling

STARTERS
for starters

STATE
church and state □ fine state of affairs □ lie in state □ pretty state of affairs

STATION
as busy as Grand Central Station □ busy as Grand Central Station

STAY
have no staying power □ stay after someone □ stay in touch (with someone) □ stay put

STEAD
stand someone in good stead

STEADY
as steady as a rock □ go steady (with someone) □ Slow and steady wins the race. □ steady as a rock

STEAL
steal a base □ steal a march (on someone) □ steal someone's thunder □ steal the show □ steal the spotlight

STEAM
blow off steam □ full steam ahead □ let off steam □ steamed up □ under one's own steam

STEEL
have a mind like a steel trap

STEER
give someone a bum steer □ steer clear (of someone or something)

STEM
from stem to stern

STEP
in step (with someone or something) □ out of step (with someone or something) □ step-by-step □ step down (from something) □ step into someone's shoes □ step into (the breach) □ step on it □ step on someone's toes □ step on the gas □ step out of line □ step (right) up □ step something up □ take steps (to prevent something) □ watch one's step

STERN
from stem to stern

STEVEN
be even steven

STEW
get (oneself) into a stew (over someone or something) □ in a stew (about someone or something) □ stew in one's own juice □ Too many cooks spoil the stew.

STICK
end up with the short end of the stick □ get the short end of the stick □ have one's words stick in one's throat □ have something stick in one's craw □ have sticky fingers □ more someone or something than one can shake a stick at □ not hold a stick to someone or something □ stick around □ stick by someone or something □ Stick 'em up! □ stick-in-the-mud □ stick one's foot in one's mouth □ stick one's neck out (for someone or something) □ stick one's nose in(to something) □ stick out like a sore thumb □ stick someone or something up □ stick someone with someone or something □ stick something out □ stick to one's guns □ stick to one's ribs □ stick together □ stick up for someone or something □ stick with someone or something □ sticks and stones

STIFF

bore someone stiff □ bored stiff □ keep a stiff upper lip □ scare someone stiff □ scared stiff

STILL

have one's heart stand still □ hold someone or something still □ hold still □ hold still for something □ keep someone or something still □ keep still □ keep still (about someone or something) □ one's heart stands still □ so still you could hear a pin drop □ stand still for something □ The jury is still out (on someone or something).

STINK

create a stink (about something) □ make a stink (about something) □ raise a stink (about something)

STIR

cause a stir □ go stir-crazy □ stir someone or something up □ stir up a hornet's nest

STITCH

keep someone in stitches

STOCK

have something in stock □ in stock □ lock, stock, and barrel □ make a laughingstock of oneself or something □ make oneself or something a laughingstock □ not take stock in something □ out of stock □ stock up (on something) □ take no stock in something □ take stock (of something)

STOMACH

can't stomach someone or something □ get butterflies in one's stomach □ give one butterflies in one's stomach □ have eyes bigger than one's stomach □ one's eyes are bigger than one's stomach □ turn someone's stomach

STONE

A rolling stone gathers no moss. □ cast the first stone □ have a heart of stone □ (just) a stone's throw away □ keep one's nose to the grindstone □ kill two birds with one stone □ leave no stone unturned □ millstone about one's neck □ put one's nose to the grindstone □ run into a stone wall □

sticks and stones □ within a stone's throw (of something)

STOOD

should have stood in bed

STOOL

fall between two stools

STOOP

stoop to doing something

STOP

pull out all the stops □ put a stop to something □ stop-and-go □ stop at nothing □ stop by (some place) □ stop in (some place) □ stop, look, and listen □ stop off (some place) □ stop over (some place) □ stop short of (doing) something

STORAGE

in cold storage

STORE

have something in store (for someone) □ mind the store □ set great store by someone or something

STORM

any port in a storm □ kick up a storm □ take someone or something by storm

STORY

cock-and-bull story □ make a long story short □ same old story □ tell its own story

STRAIGHT

get something straight □ give it to someone (straight) □ go straight □ keep a straight face □ put something straight □ set someone or something straight □ set something straight □ straight and narrow □ (straight) from the horse's mouth □ straight from the shoulder □ vote a straight ticket

STRAIGHTEN

straighten someone or something out □ straighten someone or something up □ straighten up

STRAP

strapped (for something)

STRAW

clutch at straws □ grasp at straws □ That's the last straw. □ That's the straw that broke the camel's back.

STREAK
talk a blue streak

STREAM
change horses in the middle of the stream

STREET
down the street □ man in the street □ on easy street

STRENGTH
main strength and awkwardness □ on the strength of something □ tower of strength

STRETCH
at a stretch □ stretch a point □ stretch one's legs □ stretch the point □ stretch the truth

STRICTLY
(strictly) on the up-and-up

STRIDE
hit one's stride □ reach one's stride □ take something in stride

STRIKE
get two strikes against one □ go (out) on strike □ Lightning never strikes twice (in the same place). □ strike a balance (between two things) □ strike a bargain □ strike a chord (with someone) □ strike a happy medium □ strike a match □ strike a sour note □ strike it rich □ strike out □ strike out at someone or something □ strike someone funny □ strike someone out □ strike someone's fancy □ strike the right note □ strike up a conversation □ strike up a friendship □ strike while the iron is hot

STRING
control the purse strings □ get along (on a shoestring) □ have someone on the string □ pull strings □ string along (with someone) □ string something out □ tied to one's mother's apron strings □ with no strings attached □ without any strings attached

STROKE
have a stroke □ stroke of luck

STRONG
as strong as an ox □ strong as an ox □ use strong language

STRUGGLE
struggle to the death

STRUNG
strung out

STUBBORN
as stubborn as a mule □ stubborn as a mule

STUCK
stuck on someone or something □ stuck with someone or something

STUFF
beat the stuffing out of someone □ kid stuff □ know one's stuff □ stuff and nonsense □ stuff the ballot box

STUMBLE
stumble across someone or something □ stumble into someone or something □ stumble on someone or something

STUMBLING
stumbling block

STUNT
pull a stunt (on someone)

STYLE
cramp someone's style □ go out of style □ in style □ out of style

SUBJECT
change the subject □ subject to something

SUBSCRIBE
subscribe to something

SUBSTANCE
form and substance □ sum and substance

SUCH
such and such □ such as it is □ Such is life!

SUCK
suck someone in

SUDDEN
all of a sudden

SUIT
follow suit □ in one's birthday suit □ suit someone to a T □ suit yourself

SUITCASE
live out of a suitcase

SUM
sum and substance □ sum something up

SUN
under the sun

SUNDAY
in a month of Sundays □ in one's Sunday best □ Sunday-go-to-meeting clothes

SUNDRY
all and sundry

SUPPLY
in short supply □ supply and demand

SURE
for sure □ slow(ly) but sure(ly) □ swift and sure

SURELY
slow(ly) but sure(ly)

SURF
surf and turf

SURFACE
scratch the surface

SURPRISE
take someone or something by surprise

SURVIVAL
survival of the fittest

SUSPICION
above suspicion □ under a cloud (of suspicion)

SWALLOW
bitter pill to swallow □ look like the cat that swallowed the canary □ swallow one's pride □ swallow something, hook, line, and sinker

SWAN
swan song

SWATH
cut a big swath □ cut a wide swath

SWEAR
swear by someone or something.

SWEAT
blood, sweat, and tears □ by the sweat of one's brow □ no sweat □ sweat blood □ sweat something out

SWEEP
make a clean sweep □ sweep one off one's feet □ sweep something under the carpet □ sweep something under the rug

SWEET
all sweetness and light □ have a sweet tooth □ short and sweet □ sweet and low □ sweet and sour □ sweet nothings □ sweet on someone □ sweet-talk someone □ take the bitter with the sweet

SWELL
give someone a swelled head

SWIFT
swift and sure

SWIM
in the swim of things □ make someone's head swim □ out of the swim of things □ sink or swim □ swim against the current □ swim against the tide

SWINE
cast (one's) pearls before swine

SWING
get into full swing □ get into the swing of things □ in full swing □ not enough room to swing a cat □ swing into action □ swing something

SWITCH
asleep at the switch □ bait and switch

SWOOP
at one fell swoop □ in one fell swoop

SWORD
cross swords (with someone) (on something)

SYMPATHY
extend one's sympathy (to someone)

SYSTEM
all systems (are) go □ get something out of one's system

T
done to a T □ fit someone to a T □ suit someone to a T

TAB
keep tabs (on someone or something) □ pick up the tab

TABLE
clear the table □ coffee-table book □ lay one's cards on the table □ put one's cards on the table □ set the table □ turn the tables (on someone) □ under the table

TACK
get down to brass tacks

TAIL
bright-eyed and bushy-tailed □ can't make heads or tails (out) of someone or something □ Get off someone's tail! □ heads or tails □ in two shakes of a lamb's tail □ tail wagging the dog

TAILSPIN
go into a tailspin

TALE
tell its own tale □ tell tales out of school

TALK
all talk (and no action) □ engage in small talk □ have a heart-to-heart (talk) □ money talks □ sweet-talk someone □ talk a blue streak □ talk back (to someone) □ talk big □ talk down to someone □ talk in circles □ talk of the town □ talk oneself out □ talk shop □ talk someone down □ talk someone into (doing) something □ talk someone or something up □ talk someone out of (doing) something □ talk someone out of something □ talk someone's ear off □ talk someone's head off □ talk something out □ talk something over □ talk through one's hat □ talk turkey □ talk until one is blue in the face □ talked out

TAMPER
tamper with something

TAN
tan someone's hide

TANGENT
go off on a tangent

TAPE
red tape

TAPER
taper off (doing something)

TAR
beat the tar out of someone □ tar and feather someone □ tarred with the same brush □ whale the tar out of someone

TARGET
on target □ sitting target

TASK
take someone to task

TASTE
acquire a taste for something □ get a taste of one's own medicine □ in bad taste □ in poor taste □ leave a bad taste in someone's mouth □ There's no accounting for taste.

TAT
give someone tit for tat

TAUT
run a taut ship

TAX
death and taxes □ tax-and-spend

TEA
coffee, tea, or milk □ not one's cup of tea □ not someone's cup of tea □ tea and crumpets

TEACH
teach someone a lesson □ You can't teach an old dog new tricks.

TEACHER
be the teacher's pet

TEAM
team up with someone

TEAPOT
tempest in a teapot

TEAR
blood, sweat, and tears □ break (out) in(to) tears □ burst into tears □ cry crocodile tears □ shed crocodile tears □ tear into someone or something □ tear off □ tear one's hair (out) □ tear someone or something down □ tear someone up □ vale of tears □ wear and tear (on something)

TEE
tee someone off

TEETH
armed to the teeth □ as scarce as hens' teeth □ by the skin of one's teeth □ cut teeth □ fly in the teeth of someone or something □ get one's teeth into something □ grit one's teeth □ lie through one's teeth □ no skin off someone's teeth □ pull someone's or something's teeth □ scarcer than hens' teeth □ set someone's teeth on edge □ sink one's teeth into

something □ take the bit between the teeth □ take the bit in one's teeth

TELL
A little bird told me. □ kiss and tell □ show-and-tell □ tell it to the marines □ tell its own story □ tell its own tale □ tell on someone □ tell one to one's face □ tell people apart □ tell someone a thing or two □ tell someone off □ tell someone where to get off □ tell tales out of school □ tell things apart □ tell time □ tell which is which □ Time will tell.

TEMPER
hold one's temper □ keep one's temper □ lose one's temper

TEMPERATURE
run a temperature

TEMPEST
tempest in a teapot

TEN
first and ten □ wouldn't touch something with a ten-foot pole

TENTERHOOKS
keep someone on tenterhooks

TERM
come to terms (with someone or something) □ contradiction in terms □ in no uncertain terms □ in terms of something □ on good terms (with someone) □ on speaking terms (with someone)

TERRITORY
come with the territory □ cover the territory

TEST
acid test □ put someone to the test

TESTAMENT
last will and testament

TETHER
at the end of one's tether

THAN
Actions speak louder than words. □ better late than never □ bite off more than one can chew □ easier said than done □ exchange more than ___ words with someone □ Half a loaf is better than none. □ have eyes bigger than one's stomach □ holier-than-

thou □ in less than no time □ less than pleased □ more dead than alive □ more fun than a barrel of monkeys □ more often than not □ more someone or something than one can shake a stick at □ more than someone bargained for □ more (to something) than meets the eye □ no sooner said than done □ none other than someone □ not see farther than the end of one's nose □ One's bark is worse than one's bite. □ one's eyes are bigger than one's stomach □ scarcer than hens' teeth □ There's more than one way to skin a cat. □ wear more than one hat

THANK
thank one's lucky stars □ thanks to someone or something

THEN
and then some □ (every) now and then □ now and then □ then and there

THICK
as thick as pea soup □ as thick as thieves □ get something into someone's thick head □ get something through someone's thick skull □ lay it on thick □ pour it on thick □ spread it on thick □ The plot thickens. □ thick and fast □ thick as pea soup □ thick as thieves □ thick-skinned □ through thick and thin

THICKENS
The plot thickens.

THIEVE
as thick as thieves □ thick as thieves

THIN
on thin ice □ out of thin air □ pull something out of thin air □ skate on thin ice □ spread oneself too thin □ thin on top □ thin-skinned □ through thick and thin □ vanish into thin air

THING
A little knowledge is a dangerous thing. □ amount to the same thing □ be all things to all men □ be all things to all people □ come to the same thing □ do one's (own) thing □ first thing (in the morning) □ first things first □ get a thing about someone or

something □ get into the swing of things □ greatest thing since sliced bread □ have a good thing going □ have a thing going (with someone) □ in the swim of things □ just one of those things □ know a thing or two (about someone or something) □ let things slide □ not know the first thing about someone or something □ of all things □ other things being equal □ out of the swim of things □ see things □ strike a balance (between two things) □ tell someone a thing or two □ tell things apart □ the in thing (to do) □ Things are looking up. □ too much of a good thing □ very thing □ wash a few things out

THINK
come to think of it □ get another think coming □ put one's thinking cap on □ think a great deal of someone or something □ think a lot of someone or something □ think back (on someone or something) □ think better of something □ think highly of someone or something □ think little of someone or something □ think much of someone or something □ think nothing of someone or something □ think on one's feet □ think out loud □ think someone or something fit for something □ think something out □ think something over □ think something up □ think the world of someone or something □ think twice (before doing something) □ to someone's way of thinking □ wishful thinking

THIRD
get the third degree □ give someone the third degree

THITHER
hither and thither □ hither, thither, and yon □ thither and yon

THOMAS
doubting Thomas

THORN
be a thorn in someone's side

THOSE
just one of those things

THOU
holier-than-thou

THOUGHT
food for thought □ get second thoughts about someone or something □ lose one's train of thought □ lost in thought □ on second thought □ Perish the thought. □ train of thought

THOUSAND
one in a thousand

THRASH
thrash something out

THREAD
hang by a thread

THREE
like a three-ring circus □ two's company(, three's a crowd)

THRILL
thrill someone to death □ thrill someone to pieces □ thrilled to death □ thrilled to pieces

THROAT
cut one's (own) throat □ force someone or something down someone's throat □ get a frog in one's throat □ get a lump in one's throat □ have one's words stick in one's throat □ jump down someone's throat □ ram someone or something down someone's throat □ shove someone or something down someone's throat

THRONE
power behind the throne

THROUGH
been through the mill □ break through (something) □ carry through (on something) □ come through □ come through something with flying colors □ fall through □ follow through (on something) □ get something through someone's thick skull □ get through something □ get through (to someone) □ get through with something □ go right through someone □ go through □ go through channels □ go through something □ go through the changes □ go through the motions □ go through the roof □ go through with something □ jump through a hoop □ jump through

hoops □ leaf through something □ lie through one's teeth □ live through something □ make one's way through something □ pass through someone's mind □ pay through the nose (for something) □ pick one's way through something □ pull someone through (something) □ pull through □ put one through one's paces □ put someone through the wringer □ put something through its paces □ read something through □ run through something □ sail (right) through something □ see something through □ see through someone or something □ shot through with something □ sit through something □ slip through someone's fingers □ talk through one's hat □ through and through □ through hell and high water □ through thick and thin □ thumb through something □ work one's way through college □ work through channels

THROW
(just) a stone's throw away □ throw a fit □ throw a monkey wrench into the works □ throw a party (for someone) □ throw caution to the wind □ throw cold water on something □ throw down the gauntlet □ throw good money after bad □ throw in the sponge □ throw in the towel □ throw one's hands up in despair □ throw one's hands up in horror □ throw one's weight around □ throw oneself at someone □ throw oneself at someone's feet □ throw oneself at the mercy of the court □ throw oneself on the mercy of the court □ throw (some) light on something □ throw someone □ throw someone a curve □ throw someone for a loop □ throw someone for a loss □ throw someone off the track □ throw someone off the trail □ throw someone or something off □ throw someone out (of something) □ throw someone over □ throw someone to the wolves □ throw someone's name around □ throw something into the bargain □ throw something together □ throw (something) up □ throw something up to someone □ throw the baby out with

the bath(water) □ throw the book at someone □ within a stone's throw (of something)

THRUST
thrust and parry

THUMB
all thumbs □ get someone under one's thumb □ have a green thumb □ rule of thumb □ stick out like a sore thumb □ thumb a ride □ thumb one's nose at someone or something □ thumb through something □ thumbs down on someone or something □ thumbs up on someone or something □ turn thumbs down (on someone or something) □ turn thumbs up (on someone or something) □ twiddle one's thumbs

THUNDER
steal someone's thunder

TICK
as full as a tick □ as tight as a tick □ make someone or something tick □ tight as a tick □ what makes someone tick

TICKET
round-trip ticket □ That's the ticket. □ vote a straight ticket

TICKLE
tickle someone pink □ tickle someone to death □ tickle someone's fancy □ tickled pink □ tickled to death

TIDE
swim against the tide □ tide someone over □ turn the tide

TIE
coat and tie □ fit to be tied □ have one's hands tied □ tie into something □ tie someone down □ tie someone or something up □ tie someone (up) in knots □ tie someone's hands □ tie the knot □ tie traffic up □ tied down □ tied to one's mother's apron strings □ tied up □ with both hands tied behind one's back □ with one hand tied behind one's back

TIGHT
as tight as a tick □ as tight as Dick's hatband □ in a (tight) spot □ run a tight ship □ sit tight □ tight as a tick

☐ tight as Dick's hatband ☐ tighten one's belt

TIGHTFISTED
tightfisted (with money)

TIGHTROPE
walk a tightrope

TILL
have one's hand in the till ☐ till the cows come home

TILT
at full tilt ☐ tilt at windmills

TIME
ahead of one's time ☐ ahead of time ☐ all in good time ☐ all the time ☐ at a set time ☐ at all times ☐ at the appointed time ☐ at the present time ☐ at the same time ☐ at this point (in time) ☐ at times ☐ behind the times ☐ bide one's time ☐ even in the best of times ☐ every time one turns around ☐ fight against time ☐ for the time being ☐ from time to time ☐ get time off ☐ get time off for good behavior ☐ get time to catch one's breath ☐ give someone a hard time ☐ hardly have time to breathe ☐ have a hard time ☐ have a rough time (of it) ☐ have a whale of a time ☐ have the time of one's life ☐ in due time ☐ in good time ☐ in less than no time ☐ in no time (at all) ☐ in one's spare time ☐ in the course of time ☐ in the (very) nick of time ☐ in time ☐ It's about time! ☐ It's high time! ☐ keep good time ☐ keep time ☐ keep up (with the times) ☐ kill time ☐ live on borrowed time ☐ Long time no see. ☐ make good time ☐ make time (for someone or something) ☐ make time (with someone) ☐ make up for lost time ☐ many is the time ☐ not able to call one's time one's own ☐ not give anyone the time of day ☐ on one's own time ☐ on time ☐ once-in-a-lifetime chance ☐ once upon a time ☐ one at a time ☐ out of time (with someone or something) ☐ pass the time ☐ pass the time of day (with someone) ☐ pressed for time ☐ race against time ☐ right on time ☐ run out of time ☐ small-time ☐ take one's time ☐ take time off ☐ take up

someone's time ☐ take up time ☐ tell time ☐ time after time ☐ time and (time) again ☐ time flies ☐ Time is money. ☐ Time is up. ☐ time out ☐ time was (when) ☐ Time will tell. ☐ two-time someone ☐ when the time is ripe ☐ while away the time

TIMELY
come to an untimely end

TIP
from tip to toe ☐ have something on the tip of one's tongue ☐ on the tip of one's tongue ☐ tip someone off ☐ tip the scales at something

TIPTOE
on tiptoe

TIRED
sick and tired of someone or something

TIT
give someone tit for tat ☐ tits and ass

TOAST
as warm as toast ☐ warm as toast

TOE
from head to toe ☐ from tip to toe ☐ keep on one's toes ☐ on one's toes ☐ step on someone's toes ☐ toe the line ☐ toe the mark ☐ turn up one's toes ☐ with bells on (one's toes)

TOGETHER
Birds of a feather flock together. ☐ get it (all) together ☐ get one's act together ☐ go together ☐ keep body and soul together ☐ knock some heads together ☐ pull oneself together ☐ pull something together ☐ put something together ☐ put two and two together ☐ scrape something together ☐ slap something together ☐ stick together ☐ throw something together

TOING
toing and froing (on something)

TOKEN
as a token (of something) ☐ by the same token

TOLD
A little bird told me. ☐ all told

TOM

(every) Tom, Dick, and Harry ☐ Tom, Dick, and Harry

TON

hit (someone) like a ton of bricks

TONE

tone something down

TONG

fight someone or something hammer and tongs ☐ go at it hammer and tongs

TONGUE

bite one's tongue ☐ Cat got your tongue? ☐ cause (some) tongues to wag ☐ find one's tongue ☐ get a tongue-lashing ☐ give someone a tongue-lashing ☐ have something on the tip of one's tongue ☐ hold one's tongue ☐ Hold your tongue! ☐ keep a civil tongue (in one's head) ☐ on the tip of one's tongue ☐ set tongues (a)wagging ☐ slip of the tongue ☐ speak with a forked tongue ☐ tongue-in-cheek

TOO

be too ☐ do too ☐ eat one's cake and have it too ☐ go too far ☐ have one's cake and eat it too ☐ have too ☐ have too many irons in the fire ☐ know something only too well ☐ life is too short ☐ none too something ☐ spread oneself too thin ☐ take too much on ☐ too big for one's britches ☐ too close for comfort ☐ too good to be true ☐ Too many cooks spoil the broth. ☐ Too many cooks spoil the stew. ☐ too much of a good thing

TOOT

toot one's own horn

TOOTH

armed to the teeth ☐ as scarce as hens' teeth ☐ by the skin of one's teeth ☐ cut teeth ☐ fight someone or something tooth and nail ☐ fly in the teeth of someone or something ☐ get one's teeth into something ☐ go at it tooth and nail ☐ go over something with a fine-tooth comb ☐ grit one's teeth ☐ have a sweet tooth ☐ lie through one's teeth ☐ no skin off someone's teeth ☐ pull someone's or

something's teeth ☐ scarcer than hens' teeth ☐ search something with a fine-tooth comb ☐ set someone's teeth on edge ☐ sink one's teeth into something ☐ take the bit between the teeth ☐ take the bit in one's teeth

TOP

at the top of one's lungs ☐ at the top of one's voice ☐ at the top of the hour ☐ blow one's top ☐ feel on top of the world ☐ from top to bottom ☐ off the top of one's head ☐ on top ☐ on top of something ☐ on top of the world ☐ over the top ☐ (sitting) on top of the world ☐ thin on top ☐ top someone or something ☐ top something off ☐ top something off (with something)

TORCH

carry a torch (for someone) ☐ carry the torch ☐ carry the torch (for someone)

TOSS

toss one's cookies ☐ toss one's hat into the ring ☐ toss something off

TOTEM

high man on the totem pole ☐ low man on the totem pole

TOUCH

get in touch (with someone) ☐ have the Midas touch ☐ keep in touch (with someone) ☐ lose one's touch (with someone or something) ☐ out of touch (with someone or something) ☐ put the touch on someone ☐ stay in touch (with someone) ☐ touch a sore point ☐ touch a sore spot ☐ touch and go ☐ touch base (with someone) ☐ touch on something ☐ touch someone for something ☐ touch someone or something off ☐ touch something up ☐ touched by someone or something ☐ touched (in the head) ☐ wouldn't touch something with a ten-foot pole

TOUGH

as tough as old boots ☐ get tough (with someone) ☐ hang tough ☐ tough act to follow ☐ tough as old boots ☐ tough break ☐ tough it out ☐ tough nut to crack ☐ tough row to hoe ☐ when the going gets tough

TOW
have someone or something in tow

TOWARD
be well-disposed toward someone or something ☐ go a long way toward doing something

TOWEL
throw in the towel

TOWER
live in an ivory tower ☐ tower of strength

TOWN
all over town ☐ go to town ☐ man-about-town ☐ night on the town ☐ out of town ☐ out on the town ☐ paint the town red ☐ talk of the town ☐ town-and-gown

TOY
toy with someone or something

TRACK
cover someone's tracks (up) ☐ dead in someone's or something's tracks ☐ drop in one's tracks ☐ follow in some-one's tracks ☐ get the inside track ☐ jump the track ☐ keep track (of someone or something) ☐ lose track (of someone or something) ☐ off the (beaten) track ☐ off the track ☐ on the track of someone or something ☐ on the wrong track ☐ one-track mind ☐ the other side of the tracks ☐ the wrong side of the tracks ☐ throw someone off the track

TRADE
jack-of-all-trades ☐ know (all) the tricks of the trade ☐ trade on some-thing

TRAFFIC
tie traffic up

TRAIL
blaze a trail ☐ on the trail of someone or something ☐ throw someone off the trail

TRAIN
lose one's train of thought ☐ ride the gravy train ☐ train of thought

TRAP
fall into a trap ☐ fall into someone's trap ☐ fall into the trap ☐ have a mind like a steel trap

TREAD
fools rush in (where angels fear to tread)

TREAT
Dutch treat ☐ stand someone to a treat ☐ Trick or treat!

TREATMENT
get the red-carpet treatment ☐ give someone the red-carpet treatment

TREE
bark up the wrong tree ☐ not able to see the forest for the trees ☐ up a tree

TREMBLE
in fear and trembling

TRESPASS
no trespassing

TRIAL
on trial ☐ send up a trial balloon ☐ trial and error ☐ trials and tribulations

TRIBULATION
trials and tribulations

TRICK
bag of tricks ☐ do the trick ☐ know a trick or two ☐ know (all) the tricks of the trade ☐ play tricks (on someone) ☐ pull a trick (on someone) ☐ Trick or treat! ☐ use every trick in the book ☐ You can't teach an old dog new tricks.

TRIED
tried-and-true

TRIGGER
quick on the trigger

TRIM
fit and trim

TRIP
round-trip ticket ☐ trip someone up

TROLLEY
off one's trolley

TROT
trot something out

TROUBLE
ask for trouble ☐ borrow trouble ☐ drown one's troubles ☐ fish in troubled waters ☐ go to the trouble (of doing something) ☐ go to the

trouble (to do something) □ look for trouble □ pour oil on troubled water(s) □ spell trouble □ take the trouble (to do something) □ There is trouble brewing. □ Trouble is brewing. □ trouble one's head about someone or something □ trouble oneself about someone or something □ trouble oneself (to do something) □ trouble someone for something □ trouble someone to do something

TROWEL
lay it on with a trowel

TRUE
come true □ dream come true □ hold true □ ring true □ show one's (true) colors □ too good to be true □ tried-and-true □ true to form □ true to one's word

TRULY
yours truly

TRUMP
play one's trump card

TRUMPED
trumped-up

TRUTH
moment of truth □ stretch the truth □ truth will out

TRY
have a try at something □ take a try at something □ tried-and-true □ try one's hand (at something) □ try one's luck (at something) □ try (out) one's wings □ try out (for something) □ try someone's patience □ try something out on someone

TUBE
down the tubes

TUCK
nip and tuck □ tuck into something

TUCKER
best bib and tucker

TUCKERED
(all) tuckered out □ tuckered out

TUMBLE
rough-and-tumble

TUNE
call the tune □ can't carry a tune □ change someone's tune □ dance to another tune □ He who pays the piper calls the tune. □ in tune with someone or something □ out of tune (with someone or something) □ sing a different tune □ sing another tune □ to the tune of some amount of money □ tune someone or something out □ tune (something) in

TUNNEL
see the light (at the end of the tunnel)

TURF
surf and turf

TURKEY
go cold turkey □ talk turkey

TURN
at every turn □ do someone a good turn □ done to a turn □ every time one turns around □ have turned the corner □ in turn □ leave no stone unturned □ not know where to turn □ not know which way to turn □ One good turn deserves another. □ out of turn □ speak out of turn □ take a new turn □ take a turn for the better □ take a turn for the worse □ take turns ((at) doing something) □ The worm (has) turned. □ turn a blind eye to someone or something □ turn a deaf ear (to someone or something) □ turn in □ turn of the century □ turn on a dime □ turn on the waterworks □ turn one's back (on someone or something) □ turn one's nose up at someone or something □ turn out (all right) □ turn over □ turn over a new leaf □ turn (over) in one's grave □ turn someone off □ turn someone on □ turn someone or something down □ turn someone or something out □ turn someone or something up □ turn someone's head □ turn someone's stomach □ turn something to good account □ turn something to one's advantage □ turn the clock back □ turn the heat up (on someone) □ turn the other cheek □ turn the tables (on someone) □ turn the tide □ turn thumbs down (on someone or something) □ turn thumbs up (on someone or something) □ turn to □ turn to someone or something (for something) □ turn turtle □ turn up □ turn up one's toes

TURTLE
turn turtle

TWICE
as big as life and twice as ugly ☐ big as life and twice as ugly ☐ Lightning never strikes twice (in the same place). ☐ think twice (before doing something)

TWIDDLE
twiddle one's thumbs

TWINKLE
in the twinkling of an eye

TWIST
twist someone around one's little finger ☐ twist someone's arm

TWO
A bird in the hand is worth two in the bush. ☐ fall between two stools ☐ game that two can play ☐ get two strikes against one ☐ in two shakes of a lamb's tail ☐ kill two birds with one stone ☐ know a thing or two (about someone or something) ☐ know a trick or two ☐ no two ways about it ☐ not care two hoots about someone or something ☐ not give two hoots about someone or something ☐ put one's two cents (worth) in ☐ put two and two together ☐ stand on one's own two feet ☐ strike a balance (between two things) ☐ take someone down a notch (or two) ☐ take someone down a peg (or two) ☐ tell someone a thing or two ☐ That makes two of us. ☐ two of a kind ☐ two-time someone ☐ two's company(, three's a crowd)

UGLY
as big as life and twice as ugly ☐ as ugly as sin ☐ big as life and twice as ugly ☐ rear its ugly head ☐ ugly as sin

UNBOWED
bloody but unbowed

UNCERTAIN
in no uncertain terms

UNCLE
Dutch uncle ☐ say uncle

UNDER
build a fire under someone ☐ cut the ground out from under someone ☐ get out from under someone or some-thing ☐ get someone under one's thumb ☐ get something under one's belt ☐ get something under way ☐ get under someone's skin ☐ get under way ☐ go under ☐ go under the knife ☐ hide one's light under a bushel ☐ hot under the collar ☐ keep something under one's hat ☐ keep something under wraps ☐ knock the props out from under someone ☐ knuckle under (to someone or something) ☐ let grass grow under one's feet ☐ out from under (something) ☐ pull the rug out (from under someone) ☐ (right) under someone's (very) nose ☐ sail under false colors ☐ say something under one's breath ☐ sweep something under the carpet ☐ sweep something under the rug ☐ take someone under one's wing(s) ☐ under a cloud (of suspicion) ☐ under construction ☐ under fire ☐ under one's own steam ☐ under someone's (very) nose ☐ under the aegis of someone ☐ under the auspices of someone ☐ under the circumstances ☐ under the counter ☐ under the influence (of alcohol) ☐ under the sun ☐ under the table ☐ under the weather ☐ under the wire ☐ water under the bridge

UNDERSTAND
give someone to understand something ☐ given to understand

UNGLUED
come unglued

UNKNOWN
be an unknown quantity

UNLIKELY
in the unlikely event of something

UNSEEN
buy something sight unseen

UNTIL
make it (until something) ☐ talk until one is blue in the face ☐ until all hours ☐ (un)til the cows come home

UNTIMELY
come to an untimely end

UNTO
law unto oneself

UNTURNED
leave no stone unturned

UPON
chance (up)on someone or something □ fall (up)on someone or something □ feel put-upon □ happen (up)on someone or something □ hit (up)on something □ incumbent upon someone to do something □ once upon a time □ prevail (up)on someone □ put upon by someone □ seize (up)on something □ set upon someone or something □ take it upon oneself to do something □ take something (up) on oneself

UPPER
get the upper hand (on someone) □ keep a stiff upper lip □ upper crust

UPRIGHT
sit bolt upright

UPROAR
create an uproar □ make an uproar

UPS
ups and downs

UPSET
upset the apple cart

UPSHOT
the upshot of something

UPTAKE
quick on the uptake □ slow on the uptake

USE
get used to someone or something □ It takes (some) getting used to. □ it's no use (doing something) □ put something to (good) use □ use every trick in the book □ use one's head □ use one's noggin □ use one's noodle □ use some elbow grease □ use someone or something as an excuse □ use strong language □ used to someone or something

USED
get used to someone or something □ It takes (some) getting used to. □ used to someone or something

USUAL
business as usual

UTTER
not utter a word

VACATION
on vacation

VAIN
do something in vain

VALE
vale of tears

VALUE
at face value □ take something at face value

VANISH
vanish into thin air

VARIETY
Variety is the spice of life.

VENGEANCE
do something with a vengeance

VENT
give vent to something □ vent one's spleen

VENTURE
Nothing ventured, nothing gained.

VERGE
on the verge (of doing something) □ verge on something

VERSE
chapter and verse

VERY
at the (very) outside □ in the (very) nick of time □ (right) under someone's (very) nose □ under someone's (very) nose □ very thing

VEST
have a vested interest in something □ play one's cards close to one's vest

VICIOUS
in a vicious circle

VICTOR
To the victors belong the spoils.

VIEW
bird's-eye view □ in view of something □ on view □ take a dim view of something □ with a view to doing something

VIGOR
vim and vigor

VILLAIN
villain of the piece

VIM
vim and vigor

VINE
die on the vine □ wither on the vine

VIRTUE
by virtue of something

VISIT
pay (someone) a visit

VOICE
at the top of one's voice □ give voice to something □ have a voice (in something) □ lower one's voice □ raise one's voice (to someone)

VOID
null and void

VOTE
vote a straight ticket □ vote with one's feet

VOYAGE
maiden voyage

WADE
wade in(to something)

WAG
cause (some) tongues to wag □ tail wagging the dog □ wag one's chin

WAGON
fix someone's wagon □ on the wagon

WAIT
lie in wait for someone or something □ not able to wait □ on a waiting list □ wait-and-see attitude □ wait on someone hand and foot □ wait up (for someone or something) □ waiting in the wings

WAKE
in the wake of something

WALK
all walks of life □ cock of the walk □ get one's walking papers □ give one one's walking papers □ take a walk □ walk a tightrope □ walk all over someone □ walk away with something □ walk off with something □ walk on air □ walk on eggs □ walk out (on someone or something) □ walk the floor □ walk the plank

WALL
bang one's head against a brick wall □ beat one's head against the wall □ climb the wall(s) □ drive someone to the wall □ drive someone up the wall □ force someone to the wall □ go to the wall □ have one's back to the wall □ off-the-wall □ press some ne to the wall □ push someone to the wall □ read the handwriting on the wall □ run into a stone wall □ see the (hand)-writing on the wall □ Walls have ears.

WALLOP
pack a wallop

WANE
wax and wane

WANT
not want to catch someone doing something □ want for nothing

WAR
act of war □ all-out war

WARM
as warm as toast □ look like death warmed over □ warm as toast □ warm the bench □ warm the cockles of someone's heart □ warm up to someone

WARPATH
on the warpath

WARRANT
sign one's own death warrant

WART
warts and all

WASH
come out in the wash □ wash a few things out □ wash-and-wear □ wash one's dirty linen in public □ wash one's hands of someone or something □ washed-out □ washed-up

WASTE
go to waste □ Haste makes waste. □ lay something to waste □ lay waste to something □ waste one's breath □ waste someone

WATCH
bear watching □ keep (close) watch (on someone or something) □ keep (close) watch (over someone or something) □ watch one's step □ watch

out □ watch out for someone or something □ watch someone like a hawk

WATER
as a duck takes to water □ bread and water □ come hell or high water □ dash cold water on something □ fish in troubled waters □ get in(to) hot water □ get one's head above water □ hold water □ in deep water □ in hot water □ keep one's head above water □ like a fish out of water □ like water off a duck's back □ make someone's mouth water □ muddy the water □ not hold water □ of the first water □ pour cold water on something □ pour oil on troubled water(s) □ through hell and high water □ throw cold water on something □ water something down □ water under the bridge □ won't hold water

WATERFRONT
cover the waterfront

WATERLOO
meet one's Waterloo

WATERWORKS
turn on the waterworks

WAVE
make waves

WAX
none of someone's beeswax □ wax and wane □ whole ball of wax

WAY
all the way □ by the way □ by way of something □ come someone's way □ cut both ways □ do something the hard way □ downhill all the way □ every which way □ find one's or something's way somewhere □ find one's way (around) □ find (something) out the hard way □ from way back □ get one's (own) way (with someone or something) □ get something under way □ get under way □ go a long way in doing something □ go a long way toward doing something □ go all the way (with someone) □ go out of one's way (to do something) □ have a way with someone or something □ have come a long way □ have it both ways □ in a bad way □ in a

family way □ in the family way □ in the way of something □ in the worst way □ know one's way about □ know one's way around □ learn (something) the hard way □ look the other way □ make one's way through something □ make way □ make way (for someone or something) □ mend one's ways □ no two ways about it □ no way □ not know which way to turn □ on one's way (somewhere) □ on one's way to doing something □ on the way (somewhere) □ on the way to doing something □ one way or another □ one's way of life □ out of one's way □ out of the way □ out-of-the-way □ parting of the ways □ pave the way (for someone or something) □ pay someone's (own) way □ pick one's way through something □ rub someone ('s fur) the wrong way □ say something in a roundabout way □ see one's way clear (to do something) □ see which way the wind is blowing □ set in one's ways □ stand in someone's way □ take something the wrong way □ That's the way the ball bounces. □ That's the way the cookie crumbles. □ the other way round □ There's more than one way to skin a cat. □ to someone's way of thinking □ ways and means □ Where there's a will there's a way. □ work (one's way) into something □ work one's way through college □ work one's way up □ worm one's way out of something □ yield the right-of-way

WAYSIDE
drop by the wayside □ fall by the wayside

WEAK
as weak as a kitten □ have a weakness for someone or something □ weak as a kitten

WEAKNESS
have a weakness for someone or something

WEALTHY
Early to bed, early to rise(, makes a man healthy, wealthy, and wise.)

WEAR
If the shoe fits, wear it. □ none the

worse for wear □ wash-and-wear □ wear and tear (on something) □ wear more than one hat □ wear off □ wear on someone □ wear one's heart on one's sleeve □ wear out one's welcome □ wear someone down □ wear someone out

WEASEL
weasel out (of something)

WEATHER
fair-weather friend □ keep one's weather eye open □ lovely weather for ducks □ under the weather

WEAVE
weave in and out (of something)

WEDDING
shotgun wedding

WEDLOCK
born out of wedlock

WEE
wee hours (of the night)

WEED
weed someone or something out

WEEK
by the week □ week in, week out

WEEPERS
Finders keepers(, losers weepers.)

WEIGH
weigh on someone's mind □ weigh someone down □ weigh someone's words

WEIGHT
carry (a lot of) weight (with someone or something) □ carry one's (own) weight □ carry the weight of the world on one's shoulders □ pull one's (own) weight □ put weight on □ throw one's weight around □ worth its weight in gold

WELCOME
wear out one's welcome □ welcome someone with open arms □ welcome to do something

WELL
alive and well □ (all) well and good □ All's well that ends well. □ augur well for someone or something □ be well-disposed toward someone or something □ get well □ hail-fellow-well-met □ know something only too well □ leave well enough alone □ let well enough alone □ play one's cards well □ well and good □ well-fixed □ well-heeled □ well-off □ well-to-do □ well up in years

WEST
out West

WET
all wet □ as mad as a wet hen □ get one's feet wet □ get wet □ mad as a wet hen □ wet behind the ears □ wet blanket □ wet someone's whistle

WHACK
out of w(h)ack □ take a whack at someone or something

WHALE
have a whale of a time □ whale the tar out of someone

WHATEVER
for what(ever) it's worth

WHEEL
put one's shoulder to the wheel □ spin one's wheels □ wheel and deal

WHEN
cross a bridge when one comes to it □ time was (when) □ when all is said and done □ When in Rome, do as the Romans do. □ when it comes right down to it □ when it comes to something □ when least expected □ when one is good and ready □ when push comes to shove □ When the cat's away, the mice will play. □ when the chips are down □ when the going gets rough □ when the going gets tough □ when the time is ripe

WHERE
fools rush in (where angels fear to tread) □ give credit where credit is due □ hit one where one lives □ know where someone stands (on someone or something) □ not know where to turn □ Put your money where your mouth is! □ take up where one left off □ tell someone where to get off □ where one is coming from □ where one lives □ Where there's a will there's a way. □ Where there's smoke there's fire.

WHEREFORES
whys and wherefores of something

WHEREWITHAL
have the wherewithal (to do something)

WHET
whet someone's appetite

WHETHER
not know whether one is coming or going

WHICH
every which way □ know which is which □ know which side one's bread is buttered on □ not know which way to turn □ see which way the wind is blowing □ tell which is which

WHILE
(every) once in a while □ fiddle while Rome burns □ get out while the getting is good □ make it worth someone's while □ once in a while □ strike while the iron is hot □ while away the time □ worth someone's while

WHIP
whip something into shape □ whip something up

WHISKER
by a whisker

WHISPER
in a stage whisper

WHISTLE
as clean as a whistle □ as slick as a whistle □ blow the whistle (on someone) □ clean as a whistle □ slick as a whistle □ wet someone's whistle

WHITE
as white as a sheet □ as white as the driven snow □ in black and white □ put something down in black and white □ white as a sheet □ white as the driven snow □ white elephant

WHOLE
go whole hog □ make something up out of whole cloth □ on the whole □ whole ball of wax □ whole shooting match

WHOOP
whoop it up

WHYS
whys and wherefores of something

WIDE
all wool and a yard wide □ come from far and wide □ crack something wide open □ cut a wide swath □ give someone or something a wide berth □ leave oneself wide open for something □ leave oneself wide open to something □ wide-awake □ wide of the mark

WIG
flip one's wig

WILD
go hog-wild □ run wild □ sow one's wild oats □ wild about someone or something □ wild-goose chase □ Wild horses couldn't drag someone.

WILDFIRE
spread like wildfire

WILL
against someone's will □ at will □ last will and testament □ of one's own free will □ Where there's a will there's a way. □ with a will □ with the best will in the world

WILLIES
get the willies □ give someone the willies

WILLING
ready, willing, and able

WIN
no-win situation □ Slow and steady wins the race. □ win by a nose □ win out (over someone or something) □ win someone over □ win the day

WIND
get one's second wind □ get wind of something □ gone with the wind □ in the wind □ see which way the wind is blowing □ take the wind out of someone's sails □ throw caution to the wind □ wind down □ wind something up □ wind up doing something □ wind up somewhere

WINDMILLS
tilt at windmills

WINDOW
go window-shopping

WINE
wine and dine someone

WING
clip someone's wings □ on the wing □ take someone under one's wing(s) □ try (out) one's wings □ waiting in the wings □ wing it

WINK
as quick as a wink □ catch forty winks □ forty winks □ not sleep a wink □ take forty winks □ wink at something

WIPE
wipe someone or something out □ wipe someone's slate clean □ wipe something off □ wipe the floor up with someone

WIRE
down to the wire □ get one's wires crossed □ under the wire

WISE
as wise as an owl □ Early to bed, early to rise(, makes a man healthy, wealthy, and wise.) □ get wise (to someone or something) □ none the wiser □ penny-wise and pound-foolish □ put someone wise to someone or something □ sadder but wiser □ wise as an owl □ wise up (to someone or something) □ word to the wise

WISH
wish something off on someone

WISHFUL
wishful thinking

WIT
at one's wit's end □ frighten one out of one's wits □ frighten the wits out of someone □ get one's wits about one □ keep one's wits about one □ live by one's wits □ scare one out of one's wits □ scare the wits out of someone

WITHER
wither on the vine

WITHIN
come within an ace of doing something □ come within an inch of doing something □ live within one's means □ within a stone's throw (of something) □ within an inch of one's life □ within bounds □ within calling distance □ within hailing distance □ within limits □ within reason □ within someone's grasp □ within someone's reach

WITHOUT
absent without leave □ carry on without someone or something □ cut someone off without a penny □ do without (someone or something) □ get along (without (someone or something)) □ go without (something) □ goes without saying □ up the creek (without a paddle) □ without any strings attached □ without batting an eye □ without fail □ without further ado □ without question □ without rhyme or reason □ without so much as doing something

WOE
Woe is me!

WOLF
cry wolf □ keep the wolf from the door □ throw someone to the wolves □ wolf in sheep's clothing

WOMAN
woman to woman

WONDER
nine days' wonder □ no wonder □ work wonders (with someone or something)

WOOD
babe in the woods □ in some neck of the woods □ knock on wood □ out of the woods

WOOL
all wool and a yard wide □ dyed-in-the-wool □ pull the wool over someone's eyes □ woolgathering

WORD
Actions speak louder than words. □ as good as one's word □ at a loss (for words) □ beyond words □ break one's word □ by word of mouth □ eat one's words □ exchange more than ___ words with someone □ from the word go □ get a word in edgeways □ get a word in edgewise □ get the final word □ get the last word □ get the word □ go back on one's word □ hang on someone's every word □ have a word with someone □ have one's words stick in one's throat □ in

a word □ in other words □ in so many words □ keep one's word □ leave word (with someone) □ mark my word(s) □ mince (one's) words □ mum's the word □ not breathe a word (about someone or something) □ not breathe a word of (something) □ not utter a word □ put in a good word (for someone) □ put something into words □ put words into someone's mouth □ say the word □ take one at one's word □ take the words out of one's mouth □ Them's fighting words. □ true to one's word □ weigh someone's words □ word by word □ word for word □ word to the wise □ words to that effect

WORK
all in a day's work □ All work and no play makes Jack a dull boy. □ all worked up (about something) □ all worked up (over something) □ at work □ dirty work □ get down to work □ get the works □ get worked up (about something) □ get worked up (over something) □ give someone the works □ gum up the works □ have one's work cut out for one □ in the works □ knock off work □ make fast work of someone or something □ make short work of someone or something □ one's work is cut out for one □ out of work □ shoot the works □ take off (from work) □ throw a monkey wrench into the works □ work like a horse □ work on someone or something □ work one's fingers to the bone □ work (one's way) into something □ work one's way through college □ work one's way up □ work out □ work out (all right) □ work out for the best □ work someone or something in □ work someone or something up □ work someone over □ work something into something □ work something off □ work something out □ work through channels □ work wonders (with someone or something)

WORLD
all over the world □ carry the weight of the world on one's shoulders □ come down in the world □ come up in the world □ dead to the world □ feel on top of the world □ for all the world □ have the best of both worlds □ in a world of one's own □ in the world □ move up (in the world) □ not for (anything in) the world □ not have a care in the world □ not long for this world □ on top of the world □ out of this world □ set the world on fire □ (sitting) on top of the world □ think the world of someone or something □ with the best will in the world

WORM
open a can of worms □ The early bird gets the worm. □ The worm (has) turned. □ worm one's way out of something □ worm something out of someone

WORSE
for better or for worse □ go from bad to worse □ none the worse for wear □ One's bark is worse than one's bite. □ take a turn for the worse

WORST
at (the) worst □ get the worst of something □ if worst comes to worst □ in the worst way

WORTH
A bird in the hand is worth two in the bush. □ An ounce of prevention is worth a pound of cure. □ for all it's worth □ for what(ever) it's worth □ get one's money's worth □ make it worth someone's while □ not worth a dime □ not worth a hill of beans □ not worth a plugged nickel □ not worth a red cent □ put one's two cents (worth) in □ worth its weight in gold □ worth one's salt □ worth someone's while

WORTHY
worthy of the name

WOULD
as luck would have it □ look as if butter wouldn't melt in one's mouth □ would as soon do something □ wouldn't dream of doing something □ wouldn't touch something with a ten-foot pole

WOUND
rub salt in the wound

WRACK
go to wrack and ruin

WRAP
get something wrapped up □ keep something under wraps □ wrap something up □ wrapped up in someone or something

WREAK
wreak havoc with something

WRENCH
throw a monkey wrench into the works

WRINGER
put someone through the wringer

WRIST
get a slap on the wrist □ give someone a slap on the wrist □ slap someone on the wrist □ slap someone's wrist

WRITE
nothing to write home about □ That's all she wrote. □ write someone or something off □ write someone or something up □ write something down □ write something out □ wrote the book on something

WRONG
back the wrong horse □ bark up the wrong tree □ be off on the wrong foot □ get off on the wrong foot □ get out of the wrong side of the bed □ get up on the wrong side of the bed □ go wrong □ in the wrong □ on the wrong track □ rub someone('s fur) the wrong way □ start off on the wrong foot □ take someone or something wrong □ take something the wrong way □ the wrong side of the tracks

WROTE
That's all she wrote. □ wrote the book on something

YARD
all wool and a yard wide

YEAR
advanced in years □ all year round □ along in years □ by the year □ get along (in years) □ on in years □ ring in the new year □ up in years □ well up in years □ year in, year out

YESTERDAY
not born yesterday

YIELD
yield the right-of-way

YON
hither, thither, and yon □ thither and yon

Z
catch some Zs □ everything from A to Z

ZERO
zero in on something

ZONK
zonk out

ZOOM
zoom in (on someone or something)

Appendix

Irreversible Binomials and Trinomials

The following sequences of words are joined by *and, or, but* or some type of implied conjunction. The words are found only in the sequences shown here and are not reversible. Those marked with an asterisk are entries in this dictionary.

above and beyond* See *above and beyond something.*

Adam and Eve

alive and kicking*

again and again

aid and abet* See *aid and abet someone.*

alive and well*

all and sundry*

all or nothing*

all work and no play* See *All work and no play makes a Jack a dull boy.*

alpha and omega*

apples and oranges*

arm and a leg* See *cost and arm and a leg.*

armed and dangerous*

arts and letters (a division of a university)

arts and sciences (a division of a university)

assault and battery*

back and fill*

back and forth*

backwards and forwards* See *know something backwards and forwards.*

bacon and eggs

bacon, lettuce, and tomato [sandwich]

bag and baggage*

bait and switch*

ball and chain*

bar and grill

beck and call* See *at someone's beck and call.*

bed-and-breakfast*

beer and pretzels

beer and skittles* See *(all) beer and skittles.*

before and after

bell, book, and candle*

between you, me, and the lamppost*

betwixt and between*

bib and tucker* See *best bib and tucker.*

big and bold*

binge and purge*

birds and the bees*

biscuits and gravy

black and blue

black and white* See *in black and white.*

blood and gore

blood and guts

blood, sweat, and tears*

bloody but unbowed*

body and soul* See *keep body and soul together.*

born and bred*

born and raised*

bound and determined*

bound and gagged

bourbon and water

bow and scrape*

bread and butter*

bread and water

breaking and entering*

bricks and mortar*

bride and groom

bright and early*

bright-eyed and bushy-tailed

business or pleasure

by and by*

by and large*

by guess and by golly*

cap and gown*

cash-and-carry*

cash or credit*

cat and mouse* See *play cat and mouse (with someone).*

cats and dogs* See *rain cats and dogs.*

cause and effect

cease and desist*

chapter and verse*

checks and balances*

cheese and crackers

chips and dip*

church and state*

clip and save

cloak-and-dagger*

coat and tie*

cock and bull* See *cock-and-bull story.*

coffee and danish*

coffee and doughnuts

coffee, tea, or milk*

come and gone*

coming or going* See *not know if one is coming or going.*

cookies and milk

country and western [music]

crash and burn*

cream and sugar

crime and punishment

cup and saucer

curds and whey

cut-and-dried*

cut and paste*

cut and run

cute and cuddly

dark and stormy

day and age* See *in this day and age.*

day in and day out*

dead and buried*

dead and gone*

dead or alive

deaf and dumb*

death and destruction

death and taxes*

decline and fall

dilation and curettage

divide and conquer*

do or die*

dog and pony show*

doom and gloom

down-and-dirty*

down-and-out*

drawn and quartered*

dribs and drabs*

drum and bugle

drunk and disorderly*

duck and cover*

duck and drake

easy come, easy go*

eat and run*

ebb and flow*

ever and anon*

fad and fashion

fair and impartial*

fair and square*

faith, hope, and charity

far and away* See *far and away the best.*

far and wide* See *come from far and wide.*

fast and furious*

fast and loose* See *play fast and loose (with someone or something).*

fat and happy*

Father, Son, and Holy ghost

fear and loathing

fear and trembling* See *in fear and trembling.*

feast or famine* See *either feast or famine.*

fin and feather

few and far between*

field and stream

fight or flight

Finders keepers(, losers weepers).*

fine and dandy*

first and foremost*

first and last

first and ten*

first come, first served*

first, last, and always

fish and chips

neither fish nor fowl*

fish or cut bait*

fit and trim*

fits and starts* See *by fits and starts.*

flesh and blood*

flora and fauna*

flotsam and jetsam*

fold, spindle, or mutilate*

food and drink

food and water

footloose and fancy-free*

for better or for worse*

fore and aft*

forever and a day*

forever and always

forgive and forget*

form and substance*

franks and beans (frankfurters and beans)

free and clear*

free and easy*

friend or foe*

fries and a shake (French fries and a milkshake)

front and center

fun and games

give-and-take*

God and country

gone but not forgotten*

good and ready* See *when one is good and ready.*

goose and gander

grin and bear it*

hale and hearty*

half-and-half*

ham and eggs

hammer and nails

hammer and sickle

hammer and tongs* See *go at it hammer and tongs.*

hand and foot* See *bound hand and foot.*

hard-and-fast*

hat and gloves

have and to hold

head and shoulders* See *head and shoulders above someone or something.*

head over heels* See *head over heels in debt; head over heels in love (with someone).*

head to toe* See *from head to toe.*

heads or tails*

health and welfare

heart and soul*

heating and air-conditioning

heaven and earth* See *move heaven and earth to do something.*

hell and damnation

hell or high water* See *come hell or high water.*

hem and haw* See *hem and haw (around).*

hen and chicken

here and there*

here, there, and everywhere

hide-and-seek*

hide nor hair* See *neither hide nor hair.*

high and dry* See *leave someone high and dry.*

high-and-mighty*

highways and byways*

hill and dale

hit-and-miss*

hit-and-run*

hit-or-miss*

hither and thither*

hither, thither, and yon*

honest and aboveboard*

hook, line, and sinker* See *swallow something hook, line, and sinker.*

hook or crook* See *by hook or (by) crook.*

hoot and holler*

hop, skip, and a jump*

horse and buggy*

horse and carriage*

hot and bothered*

hot and cold* See *blow hot and cold.*

hot and heavy*

hot and humid

house and home* See *eat someone out of house and home.*

hue and cry*

hunt-and-peck*

husband and wife

hustle and bustle*

ice-cream and cake

in and of itself*

in and out

in sickness and in health

ins and outs* See *ins and outs of something.*

intents and purposes* See *for all intents and purposes.*

jack and jill

Jekyll and Hyde*

Jesus, Mary, and Joseph

joint and several

jot and tittle

juice and cookies*

king and queen

kiss and tell*

kit and caboodle*

kith and kin*

knife and fork

knife, fork, and spoon

ladies and gentlemen

last but not least*

last will and testament*

law and order

leaps and bounds* See *by leaps and bounds.*

lick and a promise* See *give something a lick and a promise.*

lie, cheat, and steal

life and death* See *matter of life and death.*

life or death

like it or lump it*

live and learn*

live and let live*

liver and onions

lock and key

lock, stock, and barrel*

long and (the) short it*

lost-and-found*

lost and gone forever*

loud and clear*

love and marriage

love nor money* See *not for love nor money*.

make or break* See *make or break someone*.

main strength and awkwardness*

man and wife

master and servant

meat and drink

meat-and-potatoes*

meek and mild

mergers and acquisitions

mice and men* See *best-laid plans of mice and men*.

might and main*

miles and miles

milk and cookies

milk and honey

mind and body

mix and match*

more or less*

mortar and pestle

mother and child

motherhood and apple pie

movers and shakers*

Mr. and Mrs.

name and address

needle and thread

new and improved

nice and easy

nickel and dime someone*

nip and tuck*

nook and cranny*

nothing ventured, nothing gained*

now and again*

now and then*

now or never*

null and void*

nuts and bolts* See *nuts and bolts (of something)*.

odds and ends*

off and running*

old and gray

once and for all*

one and all*

one and only*

one and the same*

open-and-shut case*

out and about*

Out of sight, out of mind.*

over and above* See *over and above something*.

over and done with*

over and over* See *over and over (again)*.

over and under

pain and suffering

part and parcel* See *part and parcel (of something)*.

past and present

peaches and cream

peanut butter and jelly

pen and ink

pen and pencil

pencil and paper

penny-wise and pound-foolish*

pick and choose*

pickles and onions

pins and needles* See *on pins and needles*.

plain and simple*

pomp and circumstance

poor but clean*

pork and beans

postage and handling*

potatoes and gravy

pots and pans

power and might

pride and joy*

pride and prejudice

principal and interest

profit and loss

pros and cons

p's and q's* See *mind one's p's and q's.*

publish or perish*

pure and simple*

Put up or shut up!*

question and answer

quick and dirty*

rack and pinion

rain or shine*

rank and file*

rant and rave* See *rant and rave (about someone or something).*

rape and pillage

read and write

reading and writing

ready and able

ready and willing

ready, willing, and able*

red, white, and blue

research and development

rest and recreation

rest and relaxation

rhyme or reason* See *without rhyme or reason.*

rice and beans

rice and peas

right and wrong

right or wrong

rise and fall

Rise and shine!*

rock and a hard place* See *between a rock and a hard place.*

rock and roll

rocks and rills

rod and reel

rod and staff

room and board*

root and branch

rough-and-ready*

rough-and-tumble*

rum and coke

rythym and blues

sackcloth and ashes

sadder but wiser*

sadism and masochism

safe and sound*

said and done* See *after all is said and done.*

salt and pepper

sand and sea

sane and sober

sausage and eggs

savings and loan

scotch and soda

scotch and water

search and destroy

seek and destroy

separate but equal*

sex and violence

Shape up or ship out.*

shave and shower

shipping and handling*

shirt and tie

shoes and socks

short and fat

short and sassy

short and stout

short and sweet

show-and-tell*

sick and tired* See *sick and tired of someone or something.*

signed, sealed, and delivered*

sink or swim*

sir or madam

six of one and half a dozen of another*

sixes and sevens* See *at sixes and sevens.*

skin and bones* See *(all) skin and bones.*

skull and crossbones

slim and trim

slings and arrows "... of outrageous fortune" Shakespeare.

slip and slide

slow and sure

slow(ly) but sure(ly)*

smoke and mirrors

So far, so good.*

soap and water

Sodom and Gomorrah

song and dance* See *go into one's song and dance (about something).*

sooner or later*

sound and fury

soup and salad

soup and sandwich

spick-and-span*

spit and image* See *be the spit and image of someone.*

stand and deliver*

stars and stripes

start and stop

stem to stern* See *from stem to stern.*

sticks and stones*

stop-and-go*

stop, look, and listen

straight and narrow*

strawberries and cream

stuff and nonsense*

sugar and spice

suit and tie

sum and substance*

supply and demand*

surf and turf*

sweet and low*

sweet and sour*

sweetness and light* See *all sweetness and light.*

swift and sure*

take it or leave it*

tall and thin

tar and feather* See *tar and feather someone.*

tax-and-spend*

tea and crumpets*

then and there*

thick and thin* See *through thick and thin.*

thither and yon*

thrust and parry*

thunder and lightning

time and (time) again*

time and space

tip to toe* See *from tip to toe.*

tits and ass*

to and fro*

toing and froing* See *toing and froing (on something).*

Tom, Dick, and Harry* See *(every) Tom, Dick, and Harry.*

tool and die

tooth and nail* See *fight someone or something tooth and nail.*

touch and go*

town-and-gown*

town and country

trial and error*

trials and tribulations*

Trick or treat!*

tried-and-true*

twist and shout

two's company(, three's a crowd)*

up and around*

up-and-coming*

up and at them*

up and away*

up and down

ups and downs*

vim and vigor*

vinegar and oil

waifs and strays

wait and see*   See *wait-and-see atti-tude.*

war and peace

wash-and-wear*

wax and wane*

ways and means*

weak and weary

wear and tear*   See *wear and tear (on something).*

week in, week out*

weights and measures

well and good*   See *(all) well and good.*

wiggle and squirm

wine and cheese

wine and dine*   See *wine and dine someone.*

wit and wisdom

wrack and ruin*   See *go to wrack and ruin.*

year in, year out*